TO DARE AND TO CONQUER

Also by Derek Leebaert

The Fifty-Year Wound

TO DARE AND TO CONQUER

Special Operations and the Destiny of Nations, from Achilles to Al Qaeda

Derek Leebaert

LITTLE, BROWN AND COMPANY
New York Boston

Little, Brown and Company
Time Warner Book Group
1271 Avenue of the Americas, New York, NY 10020
Visit our Web site at www.twbookmark.com

Maps by Jeffrey L. Ward

First Edition: March 2006

The image on page 414 was taken from *Military Atlas of World War One* by Arthur Banks, published by Pen & Sword Books Ltd.

Library of Congress Cataloging-in-Publication Data

Leebaert, Derek.
    To dare and to conquer : special operations and the destiny of nations, from Achilles to Al Qaeda / Derek Leebaert. — 1st ed.
        p. cm.
    Includes bibliographical references and index.
    ISBN 0-316-14384-7
    1. Special forces (Military science)   I. Title.
U262.L44   2006
356'.16'09 — dc22   2005012414

10 9 8 7 6 5 4 3 2 1

Q-FF

Book design by Bernard Klein

Printed in the United States of America

For Jeanne Christgau Leebaert,
Information Service of Free France, 1942–44,
and for Corporal Onno Leebaert, USMC, 2006

CONTENTS

TO DARE AND TO CONQUER

INTRODUCTION

———————

CONSIDER TIGER hunting. To understand the nature of the hunt, we must, of course, grasp the nature of the beast, but also of the hunter and the terrain, the weapons and techniques of pursuit, possibly the reasons for the chase. Is the beast being hunted across thinly covered hills, or through dark jungle? Will villagers pass on word of the tiger's whereabouts, and supply the hunter with shelter and porters? Is he to deploy lines of beaters, or will he crouch high in a *machan* over tethered bait? Is the tiger a healthy predator, content to feed on deer and buffalo, or a cunning man-eater who will circle back, or perhaps lie in ambush?

The greatest of tiger hunters was Jim Corbett, for whom India has named one of its largest national parks. For more than thirty years, as the British Raj faded in the first half of the last century, he hunted tigers no one else had been able to destroy: always with rubber-soled shoes and exquisitely selected rifles, always by stalking, always alone, his only companion for many of those years a faithful spaniel. As he listened to and imitated the cries of the creatures around him (including the tiger's full-throated roar), Corbett brought stealth and surprise to a level that could turn his quarry's natural advantages to his own deadly favor.

These were not sporting expeditions, nor was it by any means clear that the odds lay with Corbett. The assignments were undertaken for district governments seeking to protect their people, scores of whom had already been devoured. Corbett knew these villagers, their languages and folkways, knew also that he must weave into his skills the ways of the killer he pursued. Otherwise he would meet not only a particularly nasty end, but terror would still oppress the people of a country he had quietly made his own.

War has been intertwined with hunting for millennia. The word *venison,* originally "hunted meat," comes from the same Indo-European root as the Russian *voina,* meaning war. Certain French armored units still dignify themselves as *chasseurs,* huntsmen, while several elite German and Austrian formations are styled *Jaeger,* or hunters, a reminder that they were first recruited from the gamekeepers of central European forests. A guest of the more established officers' messes in Italy or Spain is likely to dine beneath stag or boar heads glaring from the walls, the high-toned British regiments preferring paintings, of distinctly mixed quality, celebrating the fox hunt. In the United States, which finds its romance on the frontier, the comparable designation for light, fast-moving outfits is Rangers, harking back to the days when woodsmen passed almost overnight from hunters into warriors who contested mastery of the forests with Mohawks and Hurons on the edge of an unknown world.

At the start of the twenty-first century, one of the most evocative words of war is *commando.* A Portuguese colonial term, it rubbed off from that most ancient of white empires in tropical Africa onto the tough militias of Dutch settlers and French Protestant refugees which struck at native marauders operating across the South African tableland. These Boer commandos went on to prove extraordinarily difficult for the imperially confident British in a war over the gold and diamonds of the veldt. Remarkable was the impression they made, not least upon their one-time prisoner, the young Winston Churchill.

Forty-one years later, in the first full year of World War II, Churchill found himself roughly in the position the Boers had faced: on the receiving end of a formidable and hungry world power. His thoughts returning to his old enemies, he created a superelite of commandos, men who would band together as "specially trained troops of the hunter class who can develop a reign of terror down these coasts [of occupied Europe] . . . leaving a trail of German corpses behind them."

Today, in a world so different, certain destructive tasks must still be assigned to extraordinary teams acting intensely and often alone, whether as a handful of seekers to snatch and "render" a suspected terrorist (as the abduction of such people is called by the profession) or in detachments of hundreds or more to overthrow a criminal state. As the essential arm of special warfare, commandos are now superbly trained and disciplined warriors whose missions are compact, highly focused, usually swift, often secret, inescapably perilous, and — if successful — likely to pay off in big ways. Commandos confront objectives that cannot be expected to yield before sheer numbers of troops or weight of firepower. Indeed, their missions are intended precisely to get around such familiar calculations of advantage, whether out of necessity or an instinct for the main chance. Such a fine-honed way of war, we argue, has been able repeatedly to redirect history.

For at least three thousand years, the special operation has shaped and reshaped itself on land, on sea, on coast and river, now in the air and beneath the waves. The men who accomplish such missions have not only exploited short-term opportunities — as did pirates (experts in naval special warfare) on the Spanish Main — but by imaginative daring have actually gone on to conquer and to hold, bringing down entire political systems by unstringing the defenses of great powers in ways not before attempted. In gaining victory, commandos succeed by being able to detect the hairline cracks in the forbidding wall of enemy might.

To be sure, commandos (or special operators, the cooler Pentagon synonym by which they may more generally be called) need not always go about their enterprise alone. They often work in combination with armies and navies, and most of their assaults focus on limited objectives — taking a mountain pass, cutting out a galleon, night raiding an enemy camp. But time and again the special operation (and the larger mode of special warfare that can grow out of it) introduces immensely enduring consequences: undoing some small but vibrant Greek city-state before it could reach the heights of an Athens or Corinth; allowing Alexander to pounce on places one final step beyond the hardest fighting and longest marching of armies; demoralizing Rome from pressing beyond the Elbe; taking gruesomely well-defended Antioch, which lay across the Crusaders' path to Jerusalem; cracking open great Constantinople (twice) as massive sieges faltered; making possible the defeat of two of the world's most militarily successful states by penny-packets of Conquistadors (conquerors); all the way through to today, when a raid may not deliver merely a wasplike sting but, properly equipped, perhaps the first and final serpent's bite.

Special operations can be thought of in dynamic terms, like a single plank atop a fulcrum. Consider a heavily muscled man in full combat gear and cradling a Squad Automatic Weapon who squats on one side of a seesaw. There are two ways to catapult him from his seat: place even heavier bruisers with even more equipment on the other end, or deftly move the fulcrum, thereby enabling one light, casually dressed fellow with a K-bar knife to launch him skyward. The analogy is not exact: it neglects the element of surprise, since that clever little fellow would hardly want to position himself so obviously across from the beefy machine gunner. But in its demonstration of leverage — one of the two key ingredients of special operations, along with tremendous risk — this example shows how seemingly insignificant capacities and feather-light moves can make a decisive difference. If looked at another way, with an actual man-eater in mind, we might remember that when colonial officials dispatched hordes of shooters against the tiger, the beast was simply given time to lose itself in home ground. When Corbett, with a rifle and a little dog, went after it, the outcome was rather different.

While examining the history-changing rewards of special warfare, we also explain how this method of conflict came into being and how it has evolved; how its practitioners have reasoned; what prowess, arms, and doctrine they have resorted to from the days of spears and bows to nuclear weapons; and what may now be lurking in the anteroom. When we compare these warriors and their ventures, it becomes obvious that — over a very long time and very wide spaces, as well as across vast variations in technology, culture, and human organization — intriguing similarities throw a new perspective on the past. And on the future. It is no coincidence that a silver Trojan Horse has been featured on the badge of the 10th Special Forces Group ever since the Green Berets were created some three millennia after the city fell.

We offer a way of regarding special operations and their unusual players that is intended to be both deeper and wider than even these polymaths of violence have taken into account. The special operation, as absorbing as it is in itself, is yet more telling as a still-unexamined instrument of historical change. We believe that this argument has not previously been made. In part, that is because so many of today's foreign- and defense-policy commentators rarely look systematically at history, or at least down its longer vistas. And when they do, it is often to extract soundbite "lessons" that do not always hold up under detailed scrutiny.

Such polemical uses are apparent in the dubious comparisons so common in talk of special operations. For instance, we hear that Xenophon's hideously bloody extraction of a failed army of Greek mercenaries playing at dynastic politics in fifth-century B.C. Persia offers a model for special forces mobility; or that America's early-twentieth-century counterguerrilla entanglements in the Philippines and the Caribbean somehow contain insights for twenty-first-century "small wars" (ignoring differences in the reach, intermingling, and hitting power of today's troublemakers); or that the sustained terror supposed to have been inflicted on Allied occupiers by the Nazi Werwolf guerrilla movement (which robotically closed down with Germany's surrender before it got into gear) compares to what America has encountered in Iraq. Confusions of culture, geography, and combat experiences are why so many discussions of special operations, and the framing of defense policies of which these are increasingly a part, have proved far less helpful than they could have been.

Historians, in turn, have done much to illuminate "the face of battle." The best writings of recent years have enormously enlarged the thoughtful civil population's understanding of the realities of war. Yet battle remains the centerpiece of such studies: the surrounded Roman army foundering at Cannae, the slope of slaughtered knights at Agincourt, the Turkish fleet at Navarino blown up like a range of volcanoes, the stalemated killing fields of the Somme. The story of special warfare, however, is to be found among the interstices of day-to-day frictions and counterblows of tribes rising into city-states, into robust nations, and then perhaps into empires and superpowers. Even the most deftly realized portraits of war have usually given the commando short shrift. Furthermore, those historians who best comprehend strategy and combat often pass over the armed malice of the vicious sect, cell, and alienated clique touting itself as a political movement.

Discussion of conflict, whether by military historians or in the flood of books and articles that debate defense and world order, has generally drawn too little on the tales and contemporary fiction that surround the events being addressed. Such an approach neglects not only one of the most revealing means of understanding times and places but often the most entertaining. The poetry of ancient Ireland, the doom-laden epic *Beowulf,* medieval outlaw legends, the pioneering historical novels of Defoe, the narratives of Fenimore Cooper and of Dumas, of Balzac, Tolstoy, Chesterton, John Buchan, and Faulkner offer insight not only into the possibilities of their eras but, as we will see, into aspects of special warfare that might well concern us. World War I tankers knew H. G. Wells's "The Land Ironclads" (1903) virtually by heart. And for more than one hundred years, writers of science fiction have often been far ahead of the planning of general staffs.

Engaging with those imaginative writers who have put ideas into practitioners' heads — or at least cleverly interpreted new possibilities — plays another vital part in keying the ear to the strange music of the jungle. To recognize the connections among extreme missions, the often aberrant people who conceive and conduct them, and what these ventures go up against, we must lay out the full makeup of the nations involved. Like Corbett, our book examines the colors, sounds, and movements of the surroundings, the better to give life and vitality to the deadly beings who most concern our story.

‡

AN OPPONENT'S strength does not consist of numbers only or plain superiority of weapons, important as they are. Strength may lie in his being thousands of miles away, deeply entrenched or concealed, or in some intimidating renown of plain unchallenged invincibility, like the Red Army as it entered Afghanistan. The stronger one is, however, perhaps the weaker, too. And the weaker an opponent seems, the stronger he may well be. This book is an attempt to show why each of those two confounding sentences makes perfect sense. Those who can jolt the fulcrum by some fairly tiny, utterly unanticipated move can shift the whole weight of conflict and, often with it, the events that have come to shape our lives.

To find one's way to the heart of overwhelming power has often called forth the highest — and most chilling — ingenuity. Missions not only may be silent but so focused and fast that they can only succeed by exploiting the adversary's most vulnerable spot. The special operation must keep being reinvented against endlessly self-reinventing societies, while remaining one pace ahead. For better or worse, the discipline exists at the forefront of all sorts of innovation.

Yet in every new strength lies a weakness. As the workings of steadily richer, technically profounder nations become more sophisticated by such very achievements, they are likely to expose themselves to unexpected strokes of violence that are the markers of special warfare.

In 1862, for instance, the Confederacy was given to naming battles after railheads (Manassas, Sharpsburg, Murfreesboro) and was mighty pleased that secession had not come before its component states had been connected east to west by railroads. But over one astonishing morning nineteen random recruits had been able to infiltrate its battle lines with the purpose of hijacking a passenger train necessary to be an instrument of ruination. As shaken observers concluded, the spine of the Confederacy had nearly been severed in a few hours' frenzied chase. There is a parallel to 9/11 when nineteen far more vicious hijackers used such easily assembled means to collapse one of the largest structures ever built, and to torpedo the nerve center of our nation's defense.

Of course, contests of this kind, once begun, are by no means necessarily one-sided; there is no need to romanticize the thrusts of the few, and the assuredly strong in terms of efficient, big armies and state-of-the-art weaponry can certainly respond in kind. But unlike the dispersed, the rather small, or the apparently weak, the strong have a range of choices — perhaps, indeed, believe they have more than is the case. Under lesser pressure, the strong have often failed to imagine their vulnerabilities until dangerously late in the game.

The vocabulary is barely a century old, but the activities of special warfare are as old as civilization. The reflections on crossing rivers by Clausewitz, the greatest intellectual inheritor of Napoleonic warfare, offer little of value today, but Gideon's destruction of a great army with the aid of three hundred carefully selected fighters is as valuable to consider as it was when the scribes first recorded how he shattered a nation before Rome was built. Indeed, within the lifetimes of many among us, there existed no special operations forces in the form we now think of them, no sharply honed warriors trained for pinpointed missions — undetectable until the blow falls — against mountain citadels or urban labyrinths. But since earliest times, there have been raiders, then bands of heroes that grew together in the turbulence of city-states, and "picked men" taken from increasingly professionalized armies to face the most demanding battlefield obstacles. Eventually arrived the so-often-improvised outfits of World War II, such as the U.S. Army muleskinners turned terrifying "ghost soldiers" in the Philippines.

Exceptional temperament and endurance have always been required. No matter that, for the outside world, these distinguishing traits only became visible after a guileful strike or astounding abduction, rather than as a way of life chosen by men who worked in ceaseless preparation at Fort Bragg or at Coronado. In our time, eminent classicists comfortably discern "commandos" and "commando operations" in the most startling features of even Alexander's unsurpassed conquests; distinguished scholars of Renaissance warfare acclaim "commando tactics" in the strife of Italy, densely sown with strongholds against which only little armies could usually be brought. Here, too, in a proper continuity, we apply these modern terms to past struggles.

Our story concentrates on the Western experience, because what has materialized in that tradition of warfare has had a uniquely worldwide impact. The record of deadly enterprise in the Americas, for instance, whether in conquest or rebellion, is huge and instructive. The doings of pre-Columbian peoples, however, are for the most part lost to us. Likewise, though the Asian experience is fascinating, notably the contrasts between East and West, to explore this in detail would require much more space than we have available. What we present here is a breadth of practice that is itself enormous, a story of combat ranging from the days of swords and haywagons to those of airborne descents and microelectronics. The great issues go so deep as to display a historic tie as well as curious meshings of shape and vision.

To take in so broad a span of centuries, and to extend it into tomorrow, we have organized our argument accordingly. In the first chapter, we start by shedding new light on recent events, and then define special operations and special units, as well as their characteristics under the long test of time. The story thereafter unfolds chronologically, each chapter examining the warring societies of a given era, their means of defense and organization, the different strengths of attackers and attacked, and the profound changes these operations introduced or catalyzed. The move against a highly sophisticated tribal confederation like the Aztecs, the challenge posed by tiny naval units against the land supremacy of Bonaparte, or the parachuting in of two Czech patriots to kill the monstrous Reinhard Heydrich — each entailed the pursuit of a very different objective. But all required that dreadful odds be faced by brave men with particularly clear minds.

Special operations, like all great enterprises, appear in forms as wide as the world. But their stories and their lessons come down to a few incandescent principles: act undismayed, strike hard, move fast, think daringly, reason deeply, draw rapid but rational conclusions. Such modes of war, as so often, pioneer the ways of peace. The assault commander of Alexander's day succeeded by applying unexpected strengths to previously unnoticed weakness. He could find critical paths in featureless rockfaces. Looking at that type of problem in light of experience, his achievements were not too different from those of an entrepreneur in a hyperinnovative industry of the twenty-first century, or an administrator maximizing services in the teeth of special interests, or a technologist getting a complex software program online without delay.

Anyone not a narcissist is eager to find a model for learning more without postponing decision making, adapting shrewdly without losing focus, understanding the opposition as clearly as he knows his own task. How to assemble not just a team but a band of brothers, sharpen one's instincts without feeding one's fantasies, discern in an adversary's strength a lever reversible to victory? Without such skills, the Midianites would have picked clean the bones of Israel, Alexander's army would have withered in the cold beneath the Sogdian Rock, Spain would have ruled the warm seas — but also IBM would have been a monopoly and American towns a vista of one-branch stores.

Enterprise and leadership find their opportunities in intellectual as well as physical courage, in mutual loyalty and authority won by common effort quite as much as by command. Businesses are ever more charged with the creative destruction that lies at the core of high-technological, relentlessly innovative economies. As they fight their way through the storm of information and projections of the future, they find themselves joined not just in spirit but in thought and operational approach with probably the oldest of those disciplines which have had to substitute quality and nerve for numbers and time. They too are engaged in unforgiving conflicts of the sort that quantity alone can never settle. To this end, the special operation and the commando may have much to tell us about top performance in our daily lives.

‡

SHORTLY AFTER Soviet power dissolved, I found myself working as a management consultant on a Pentagon study aiming to establish new roles for America's special operations forces in the surely more peaceful years to come. It overlapped with a commitment to coauthoring an MIT trilogy during the 1990s in which several of us examined the accelerating effects of the information technology revolution, with all its fascinating complexities and startling vulnerabilities. Thus intrigued, I began to explore the consequences to America of the country's long exposure to an ongoing planetary ordeal of "neither war nor peace." A book resulted about the successes, failures, and price of U.S. foreign policy from 1945 to 2002, as America led its allies to bring down the most dangerous empire of all, only to find itself immediately beset by a different kind of evildoer. The point was to determine how the world had been arranged over these decades and to offer some guidance for meeting challenges to come.

Continuously in the background were the possibilities of special warfare, the means to act tellingly far below the threshold of nuclear threat — whether it was parachuting heroic but doomed Ukrainian operators to give some touch of hope to resistance in Stalin's Soviet Union, or President Kennedy's excitements over men "trained to live off nature's land, trained in combat, hand to hand"; the humiliating fiasco at Desert One as America first grappled with Islamic fundamentalism in 1980; eventually, U.S. secret strategy of undercutting ruthlessly proficient KGB special operators and the Red Army itself in Afghanistan; and finally, the emergence of the highly adept U.S. Special Operations Command, which circles the globe today.

As we enter another era neither fully at war nor, to say the least, at peace, who knows whether the world is a more uniformly dangerous place than that endured by the past two generations? But we can conclude that we are trekking through something more like a beast-ridden jungle than the relatively clear uplands of conventional, "soldierly" confrontation. Unfixed terrain is particularly the special warrior's province. Let us now follow him to see how the destiny of nations has passed through his hands.

Part I

1

Who Dares Wins*
Special Operations, Special Forces, Special Targets

* Motto of Britain's Special Air Service (SAS)

LESS THAN six weeks after a band of kamikaze air pirates destroyed the World Trade Center towers and blasted in the Pentagon's northeast face, 199 U.S. Army Rangers parachuted into the night upon an isolated landing strip sixty miles from Kandahar deep in the southern Afghan desert. A still undisclosed but truly small number of "black" special operators (who serve in units unacknowledged by the Pentagon but going by such names as Delta Force and Gray Fox) landed by silenced helicopter to hit the compound of the head of the regime at the edge of the city itself, while SAS elements struck buildings believed to house other Al Qaeda and Taliban leaders. A key purpose was to demonstrate to the enemy and to the world that soldiers of the democracies could reach at will deep inside the most forbidding of enemy territory. It was akin to Lieutenant Colonel Jimmy Doolittle's squadron raining few but utterly unanticipated bombs on Tokyo just months after Pearl Harbor. All were out by dawn from a land for centuries a byword for consuming its invaders, and whose intransigent resistance had done so much to ruin the Soviet colossus just ten years earlier.

"When can we get our teams in?" the secretary of defense had demanded in a September 25 strategy meeting. "When CIA tells us they are ready," unhelpfully replied the air force general at the head of U.S. Special Operations Command — not until, that is to say, the agency had some notion of what was going on inside Afghanistan. "I want targets worldwide," continued the secretary. "But we don't have actionable intelligence," the general countered.[1] There might have been much to discuss, but not enough to jump on.

The very day following, the first seven-man CIA insertion of paramilitary experts, as well as a former station chief in Pakistan, were flown by agency pilots over the Hindu Kush from Uzbekistan into the Afghan northeast. They had been gathered swiftly at Langley headquarters and dispatched to convince the Northern Alliance, a loose confederation of mutually predatory warlords aligned against the Taliban, to cooperate with America's imminent retaliation. They were also to lay the groundwork for the arrival of twelve-man Green Beret teams, or operational detachments.

Those Special Forces soldiers, as the Green Berets prefer to be called, were not intended to execute a decisive move, let alone to slice through northern Afghanistan under close air support to overthrow the Taliban. They were to follow their calling of living and working with all sorts of fighting men whose countries (or in this case, factions) enjoy more or less friendly ties to the United States. In their current mission, they were to join with the Northern Alliance in a holding action until U.S. divisions could be prepped and lifted to embark on a campaign that the military chiefs expected to take at least two years.

In none of the record of sporadic outrage during the preceding decade had U.S. commandos been deployed against terrorists, let alone to unravel a terrorist state. Nor had the obscure workings of CIA specialists, responsible under law for covert action, drawn any visible blood from an increasingly aggressive enemy. As the defense secretary impatiently judged, the agency had devoted the two weeks since the atrocity to pleading with the military for medics, more pilots, and logistical capacities to get a handful of its own people on the ground merely to discover what might ultimately be possible. "They've neglected to do what they should have been doing all along," he snapped, taking in the enormous gap in the "sensor-to-shooter loop," the time required between identifying and bringing down these menacing objectives.

The former agency station chief who had gone in on the twenty-sixth with what the Operations Directorate unadmiringly calls its "knuckle draggers" would soon make his own complaints public at the "delays in getting army Special Forces teams into Afghanistan," and "infighting among the various Special Operations components." To him, plans put forward by Delta operators were "impossible and lame," and "the U.S. military community" would not permit its commandos to accompany him because his fly-in was said to be "too dangerous." "We have begged and pleaded," he exclaimed, but the nation's special operations forces were reluctant to cooperate. "This situation is broken!"[2] On all counts, there would be much to answer for in the arrangement of U.S. commando and intelligence operations, certainly by an intelligence service whose parking lot at Langley had been merely half full on 9/12, when the federal workforce in Washington was told that only essential employees need show up at the office.[3]

In time, the 9/11 commission would commend the use of joint CIA-military teams in Afghanistan. But without even knowing decades of well-concealed CIA paramilitary blunders, it came to conclude that responsibility for covert commando actions should henceforth shift to the Pentagon, a recommendation that cut to the core of the agency's storied Directorate of Operations, renamed the National Clandestine Service. The quarrel distills thirty centuries' failure to come fully to terms with this deadly arm of war — its possibilities, its moral standing, its effects on the larger sphere of violence. Is it dirty work, or the apotheosis of the warrior's craft? (It has been both.) With whom to trust it? Where to apply it next?

Nonetheless, within weeks of the Rangers' descent, U.S. improvisation combined with the Special Forces' speed and agility to marshal the tribes and impart the momentum for the drive on Kabul, center of Taliban authority. That capital fell on November 13 to a mode of war that had taken form overnight largely under Green Beret sergeants and air force Special Tactics combat controllers. Commandos urged horses through hostile valleys to pinpoint air strikes with satellite-linked laser markers — a step back into Kipling's day to recoil in a blow out of science fiction. Though it was only one move in crushing a preindustrial foe, it was a crucial one, accomplished on the ground by just 315 special operators.

By this time, the Joint Chiefs of Staff's original concept, showing its claws as Operation Enduring Freedom, was being pared way back. The brass's initial reaction to press photos of the Green Berets who surfaced among the warlords was to order that the soldiers' beards come off, right now, an order wisely rescinded. Instead, the Green Berets' finest hour was welcomed as reason not to plunk down big conventional forces, as had the Russians. The number of armed Americans in the country would thereby essentially be capped.

A problem lay in ignoring the fact that the first thing one needs to know about a weapon is what cannot be done with it. Should it be perfect for this or that tight spot, one may fatally be tempted to bring it into a different type of fight. The next move against the Taliban and Al Qaeda showed that there was little understanding among the war planners about what special operations forces could *not* do, as an irresistible entity seemed suddenly to be at hand.

In December, the same formula used to take Kabul was applied against bin Laden himself and fifteen hundred to two thousand well-armed fighters holed up in the miles of reinforced granite caves and deeply dug tunnels of Tora Bora, a fortress complex buried amid the thirteen thousand-foot peaks along the Pakistani border. During the 1980s, the CIA-financed *mujahideen* (Children of God) had constructed the nearly impenetrable labyrinth as a refuge from Red Army tanks and helicopter gun ships. Now the agency discovered that the maps it had received from the mujahideen were missing in its files at Langley.[4] Despite such inconvenience, some three dozen U.S. special operators were ordered to choreograph an assault against this bastion by roughly twenty-five hundred motley Afghan allies, backed by ground-busting saturation airstrikes. At Tora Bora, senior commanders decided not to commit more American ground forces, not even any of the two thousand Marines who were ready at their just-built Camp Rhino to patrol the border crossings through which bin Laden and perhaps eight hundred of his followers would slip away.

Nor did the Pentagon's civilian leadership know much about the use of special operations forces. Before 9/11, the eight-month-old administration had no serious interest in the subject. The White House had not even gotten around by late summer to appointing a credible person to fill the office of assistant secretary for special operations and low intensity conflict.[5] Besides offering guidance about the limits of the discipline, true experts on special warfare would spend months acquainting the secretary and his deputy with the facts of how much deeper and more devastatingly than commonly believed U.S. commandos could go in the first war of the twenty-first century.

✝

WHEN DOES an operation break out of the pack, pass from remarkable conventional performance to the truly special? When must such an undertaking be singled out as uniquely the province of special forces?[6] What are they anyhow, and who are these people?

The special operation keeps testing the limits of familiar procedure — its own side's and the other's. That is why it is called "special." It is not only distinct from the standard military practices of its times but runs contrary to many of the principles on which commanders — especially field commanders properly concerned with mass, administration, unit cooperation — place prime importance. "Conventional" wars between armies, navies, and air forces must rely on a body of tried-and-true approaches. Those approaches steadily change, but at any given time generals and admirals are able to draw on a repertoire of carefully tested formulas for dispensing firepower, deploying fighting men, mobilizing reinforcements, managing supply lines (the true mark of the strategist), and for pulling back to regroup. Commanders apply sound practical principles to the terrifying irrationalities of violence, attempting to establish some degree of predictability amid the chaos of the battlefield. All these measures draw on experience, hard-earned wisdom, and sternly refined techniques.

The special operation, however, embraces an utterly different arithmetic as well as ethos. There may be no battlefield, no supply lines. What a special operation sets out to achieve is often said to be impossible. So its warriors repeatedly find themselves improvising. Their stealth cannot be matched by a division or fleet, and the operators rely on a continuously renewed novelty to attain the absurdly high leverage that characterizes such ventures.

In conventional combat, the main offensive is likely to be directed, where possible, against the enemy's weaker points, such as thinly held terrain or an exposed flank. The special operation often finds its peculiar advantage in targeting the enemy's most heavily defended positions — striking directly at his confident strength and dignity. It is more like a needle that pierces to vital organs through chinks in the armor than an axe blade hacking at metal-plated torsos. It eschews the bulkier goals of taking ground, killing as many enemy soldiers as possible, asserting mastery of the seas. Since a special operation is likely to be reaching deeper and faster into hostile environments, whether by infiltrating a citadel, "clearing a room" in a hostage rescue, or appearing suddenly on the other side of the world, there may be no possibility of retreat or even of assistance. Extreme missions, like extreme sports, rarely offer second chances.[7]

The special operation is not defined by its size. To achieve as much as possible with as little as possible (or at least with the little that may be available) pretty much dictates that it be conducted by fewer warriors than are mustered in its main forces, let alone than in those of the enemy. However, that does not restrict the special operation to inserting tiny parties of grease-faced men onto rocky coasts. What prevails is the "Commando idea," as Churchill called it — of guile unified with fortitude and imagination.[8] In the deadliest of all wars, he backed every initiative, from a two-man team parachuting into occupied Europe to hunt down a single Nazi beast to the nine thousand men of the only outfit in that war known as the "Special Force," whose wholesaling of top-end guerrilla techniques disordered an entire Japanese army in Burma. But at their best, all such operations are masterpieces of economy and of a level of performance that cannot be expected from the steadiest of regular fighting men and women.

As with Churchill's hit teams and the Special Force, these undertakings can be carried out either independently or in tandem with one's own big guns. They can be tactical (say, far-in reconnaissance of an enemy missile site) or they can upend a country, as the world saw in Afghanistan. The spectrum of special operations extends from rather rare army-sized ventures of supreme risk to a haze of minute, but often decisive, killer-bee actions. Mystique has conditioned us to think of the special operation as a single dramatic blow, assuming that if it is special, it is brilliant, and if brilliant, accomplished in the twinkling of an eye. But the methods of the hunter can be applied unrelentingly for months, or indeed years. Over this longer duration, the term *special warfare* can mean full-scale campaigns of unconventional combat that entail astounding arrays of startling little commando assaults on the way to final victory.

The damage that the special operation can inflict is much greater than the hurt to be endured by the attackers' side should the effort fail and its warriors perish short of their target. When successful, the payoffs can be huge compared to the lives, money, and matériel committed. Because a special operation is undertaken by the comparatively few in an unusually constricted period of time, it is also more subject to chance, or to the Law of Small Numbers, best summarized in the baseball wisdom that "anything can happen in a short series." Time and again a single detail — a helicopter's hydraulic system failing in the desert, the Gestapo picking out the way an American rather than a Frenchman holds a cigarette — has brought disaster on excellent planning.

To better its chances, the special operation may have to work extremely fast, lunging straight at the heart of power; or it may require mind-numbing patience as its warriors embed themselves in a hostile city for months. Deception and disguise offer it further dimensions of leverage. Unable to employ supply lines, it may have to rely on newfound local allies for transport, food, even weapons — or take them from the enemy dead. Initial success must serve as the finest of recruiting offices in the field, as was the case in Afghanistan and for Hannibal as well as the Conquistadors. Success requires more than ruse or trickery. Cleverness alone can only go so far; eventually the successful special operation must call on a bank of hard-tested skills. The access and confusion that tricks can provide are inevitably eclipsed by the need for consistently effective follow-through. Twenty-three men descending a rope ladder at night from the belly of a wooden horse must then be tough and smart enough to make their way through the city, signal the awaiting fleet from its walls, and very silently (a skill in itself) open the gates.

Surprise is one of the central ingredients of all warfare, but a special operation is all surprise in its explosive combination of ingenuity and economy. The commandos then swell the impact of that initial shock. Their attack magnifies itself in the enemy's mind: terror soaks through a battle line or through an entire nation stampeded into a quest for perfect, and therefore exhausting and paralyzing, security. A sharp, focused strike can consume the energies of millions of people who never witnessed the act: if it is televised, all the better for the attackers.

The most promising special operation at any given moment is likely to be that which moves the frontier of surprise the next bound forward. (If a special operation's form could be entirely anticipated, its relatively modest size would make it easy to smash.) To that end, the modes of special warfare keep changing, only to become familiar as time passes. Combat within buildings, for instance, is reborn with each iteration of urban civilization; amphibious techniques change with the materials of ships and forts; jungle fighting moves from reliance on machetes to "smart-dust" sensors scattered among the tendrils. The uniqueness of the most original missions — such as gliders descending on a fortress roof — burns down with the speed of a fuse as the enemy comes up with simple but reliable responses.

Emphasis on technical ingenuity is one of the several differences between special operations and guerrilla warfare, which throughout history has been the sole recourse of the weak and so often the backward against the strong. The special operator and the guerrilla share common approaches, such as the bomb on the rail line, the back-alley ambush, and fighters often dressed to be indistinguishable from the wider population. Yet the guerrilla is unlikely to have any technological edge — and when he does, it is often supplied from outside his borders, he and his friends becoming proxies for wider interests. He also needs leadership more than do regular soldiers, let alone commandos. The guerrilla just about always expects the enemy to come to him and bitterly defends his own turf, where his greatest advantage is an intimate command of his land and people, often preferring to pounce only after he has been able to muster a numerical advantage. He opportunistically hits the enemy where it is weak — killing couriers, obliterating an unwary patrol, perhaps setting bombs off in the street. He avoids decisive confrontation and works with a different sense of time as he compels the enemy to spindle out its resources and patience. In contrast, the purpose of a special operation can be consciously to match itself against immensely superior numbers as it exploits enemy illusions of safety, targeting one thunderbolt blow against his daunting strengths.

To be sure, guerrillas can pull off spectacular feats, as when half-naked Viet Cong sappers crawled at night through the concertina wire of a Green Beret camp with satchels of explosives strapped to their backs, or Palestinian shooters knocked off an Israeli cabinet member amid his Shin Bet bodyguards in a Jerusalem hallway to then fade safely into Ramallah. However, such skilled undertakings are not the main reason for guerrilla success. Instead, guerrillas count more on the leverage brought by wrecking softer targets like police stations, train trestles, convoys, hotels, and restaurants — killing by paper cut as opposed to by lance.

That said, the special operation melds into guerrilla warfare when expert cadres arrive as a vanguard outfit in what has up till then been a localized conflict. They may serve as advisers or combat leaders as they mobilize indigenous people against a common enemy. And as guerrillas are becoming increasingly professional, more professional soldiers are fighting with guerrilla techniques, with no one side having a monopoly on reaching out across oceans into the heartland of the other.

To the Duke of Marlborough (great soldier-statesman of the late seventeenth and early eighteenth centuries), long-range penetration was thirty miles — and the horses might break down on the way back. Today, it can be thousands of miles, at the endpoint of a technological chain of C-130J transport aircraft and armed dune buggies. At one end of this way of war may be the skill and knowledge to destroy an easily camouflaged germ laboratory without releasing its ghastly pathogens; at the other, having to know which kind of disgusting fungus to force down as one lives off the land on the long but invisible approach.

Unlike regular warfare, a special operation may be covert or clandestine, either kept secret both before and after, or merely secret while it is under way. Always deniable are the energetic transactions known as "special activities," which include abduction and assassination. Even in our era, when the most focused and personalized of killing is just as likely to be inflicted by a cruise missile as by a single operator or a tiny hit team, the chances of success are boosted by reconnaissance that puts understanding eyes on the target. Like the mission itself, the leverage is extreme, offering potentially immense political consequences. It is the work not of a John Hinckley but, perhaps, of a John Wilkes Booth.

To lay down a complete definition of what special operations can and must be, and who is licensed to conduct them, is to expose oneself to truly regrettable ripostes. Nonetheless, committees work hard to hammer out definitions, which end up being more successful at shedding light on the institutional system that is creating them than in clarifying the details.

In the United States, each of the three armed services tweaks its definition toward an emphasis on the particular skills of its own special branch: the Army Special Operations Command, rightly proud of its Green Berets, light-infantry Rangers, secret Delta Force, and Special Operations Aviation Regiment, as well as Civil Affairs and Psychological Operations units; the Naval Special Warfare Command deploying its SEALs and boat teams; the Air Force Special Operations Command dispatching pilots, pararescuers, and Special Tactics combat (air) controllers "any time, any place," according to its motto. The Marines, who believe with reason that everything they do is extraordinary, do not fall under the umbrella of the overarching U.S. Special Operations Command, simply designating select units as "special operations capable."[9] Only a happy fortune has created this formidable overlap of missions and capabilities, as in the days when America confronted the Soviet Union with a nuclear "triad" of air force ICBMs and B-52s, army shorter-range missiles, and the navy's warhead-delivering submarines — the three steel legs that slammed creatively into place entirely by happenstance, each coming to exercise a particular role.

To grasp what really constitutes a special operation as high authority envisions it, one must extrapolate. Pentagon manuals, of course, offer one numbing definition: "Operations conducted by specially organized, trained, and equipped military and paramilitary forces to achieve military, political, economic, and information objectives by unconventional military means in hostile, denied, or politically sensitive regions." They go on to note that such an undertaking may be shaped by political as well as entirely military considerations, that it may weave vitally into operational intelligence, and that its practitioners are subject to an exceptional level of danger. This leaves a lot of room between the dots.

"Paramilitary" here may obscurely embrace foreign state police forces or the CIA's beleaguered Special Operations group. It does not include the most vicious enemies (so far) of our interests or those of our allies. And therein lies a mistake. By stating that special operations fit into boxes solely "military" and "paramilitary," we leave ourselves open to exceedingly effective people from entire categories that do not fall into this list. It is as dangerous to diminish one's enemies by supposing that they cannot pull off attacks every bit as impressively special as those of oneself, as it is to dismiss them because their strategically planned savageries do not fit the pattern of regular warfare. (Like the jihadists, men and women who are undeniably terrorists but often anything but cowardly, the Viet Cong — equally despicable in bombing and torturing civilians — were also repeatedly condemned as cowards.) Such sweeping opinions may be comforting, but they are denial rather than judgment, a standard rationalization of fear and anger that works only to the advantage of the attacker.

Today's enemies and tomorrow's are not about to match the rigor, training, and matériel of the Green Berets, SEALs, or SAS who oppose them. Instead, theirs are the ancient resources of sacrificial passion and stealth as they look with appraising eyes at our cities, businesses, and government departments. As the past repeatedly shows, handfuls of improbable, on the face of it ill-suited people have time and again suddenly materialized to deploy focused, equally leveraged, and intricate procedures that have put fortresses, treasure houses, capitals, bridges, and defiles into other hands and, with them, the direction of history.

‡

IT HAS BECOME doctrine that an operation can only be special if accomplished by a recognizably special force, composed of warriors like those embraced by the U.S. Special Operations Command, masters of parachuting, mountaineering, amphibious insertion, and close-quarters battle. Forces charged with special warfare have become unusually sharp instruments in the arsenals of every state that relies on more than the goodwill and forbearance of its neighbors: Russia's *spetsnaz,* France's 1er RPIMa, Israel's Sayeret Mat'Kal, Norway's FSK and excellent Kystjegere ("coastal hunters"), among others known and unknown. Only since World War II, however, have senior officers or intelligence-service mandarins most anywhere been able to turn to such a standing force of warriors already so completely and expensively prepared.

For most of time, a legate of the Roman state, a margrave on the barbarian frontier, or a cocked-hatted eighteenth-century general running his spyglass over a citadel could only call for volunteers or simply draft likely looking fellows. The "picked men" we read about in history books may have had some unusual talent, such as crag-scaling after errant sheep, perhaps a previous calling like gamekeeping — or, yet better, poaching. Often they brought nothing to the challenge but pluck and muscle. What the commander called on was not a special force in the form that comes to mind today. Instead, he might have been lucky enough to have at hand some rather superior types of warriors who would frequently pay in blood for a lack of twenty-first-century commando selection and schooling. Those who survived were rewarded and usually returned to the ranks from which they so briefly emerged.

For instance, Alexander's commando operations stand out even amid his unmatched feats of conquest because they consistently accomplished the unprecedented in surprisingly deft new ways: steady in conjunction with an unstoppable army, taking impregnable passes, scaling the impossible peak, helping subdue never-taken cities. But the particular Macedonians and Greeks who drove home such victories were not brigaded as an ongoing special force that would hold together for much more than a campaign or at most a generation. That such cadres should be maintained permanently to face challenges similarly hair-raising next time, let alone kept up during peace, is a practice just about unknown until the 1950s, the commando outfits of World War II having been disbanded by the democracies as well as by the Soviet Union with the defeat of the original axis of evil.

Whether by some serendipitous personal experience or simply inherent daring, all these men were exceptional *before* they took up their missions; they were not honed in commandolike techniques, nor could they build on carefully studied criteria. There was no more need to be certified as a special warrior than, say, as a poet. Today there is an entire discipline of special operations, offering a large literature, carefully argued doctrine, and career paths that can take an officer of promise to the center chair of the Joint Chiefs of Staff. Extreme missions of a kind previously organized the day before the event are now embarked on with a spirit much closer to the maxim of the U.S. Navy when refueling huge ships in a storm: "not easy, just routine."

The special operation and the special force run parallel through time but by no means fully interlock. What remains the same are the distinct qualities of those who embark on these ventures, perhaps only as part of an impromptu team accomplishing some extreme mission that historians might now identify as those of commandos. Just as an objective is unlikely to be achieved by familiar methods, so it is unlikely to be attained by the regular soldier or sailor of the era, no matter how many brave souls may boldly step forward to seek a place among "the picked." Of course, from the beginning of organized, more than tribal warfare, some formations have been honed to be more "elite" than the rest.[10] A corps d'élite can be counted on to be able to hold a line longer than any other unit, to take an apparently impregnable hill, to cover a retreat, to set new standards in such fundamental virtues of the soldier as endurance, patience, and disciplined execution in horrific circumstances. Its victories and defeats offer riveting examples of courage and sacrifice: at Blenheim in 1704, the crack French regiments covering the disintegrating center died in their infantry squares, as was terribly clear the next day from where the bodies lay.

In all fighting forces it makes sense to concentrate the unusually strong, brave, and resilient into elite formations of the line — the Sacred Band of Thebes, Caesar's Tenth Legion, Bonaparte's Imperial Guard. However, there is more than bravery and brawn to mark members of a special force. They are distinguished "Not by Strength, by Guile," as the motto of Britain's Special Boat Service goes, and they are able to pick those so often fleeting opportunities where guile just may work. Once a special force is launched on its mission, it can seldom be guided from above; and even if radios and satellite links should permit commanders to put in their two cents along the way, it is rarely a good idea that they should. The special force must direct itself along the lines it alone can assess, performing as a self-contained act of war mounted by self-sufficient people.

Only as special forces became established during our own era did they begin to acquire traditions, and occasionally a distinct appearance, the combination of green beret and jump (or mountain) boots itself being an example. Through most of history, special warriors have had no traditions at all — and such a force (where it exists for more than a moment) contains people of the sort who do not need to be bucked up by regimental songs and battle flags. Notions of chivalry or gentlemanly warfare are also going to be in short supply. The special force may not be in existence long enough to cultivate them, and, should it endure, these traditions tend to be at odds with its ways of destruction.

Unlike regular formations and corps d'élite, the special force stands little chance of any corresponding courtesy when cornered or captured. If it is effective, it will be dreaded; and fear and kindness do not travel well together. The special force may not only be well beyond rescue deep in enemy terrain, but its warriors may not be in uniform and able to invoke even the slightest protection of what laws of war may exist. One of Hitler's top generals was hanged at Nuremberg in no small part for carrying out his führer's Commando Order (*Kommandobefehl*) decreeing the execution of all Allied prisoners from such units. Today, commandos run to ground in North Korea or Iran are not about to be the subjects of prisoner-exchange negotiations; and our opponents who are caught in Seattle, Lyon, or Tokyo indeed may be allowed to live, but still pass forever into the darkness where state power entombs its enemies in steel and concrete.

The warriors who embark on special operations know both the risks they shoulder and the whole picture of each highly focused undertaking. Even with the best of intentions of speaking truth to his men (and now women) and counting on them for the maximum of personal initiative, the commander of a conventional line unit cannot share the entire perspective of an operation with each lieutenant or supply sergeant, nor would it be useful to specify the frightening dangers ahead. But to be effective, each member of the special force needs to understand completely what he or she is getting into. All forces function on discipline, to be sure. The special ones operate more on prowess — preparing, when they can, far more by rehearsal than by drill.

Across all the years where we can document them, the warriors who compose a special force are likely to be those most deemed capable of independent initiative without orders. Grave decisions must be left to the discretion of remarkably junior people on the spot. This enlightened concession to the abilities of ordinary folk has by now seeped into all worthwhile conventional units as well. But even today the special force is characterized by far more responsibility handled by, say, sergeants. There is also more give-and-take between ranks than is otherwise to be found — a spirit akin to the original riflemen Rangers of the frontier, or the two hundred or so cavalry raiders who enabled John Mosby, the "Grey Ghost," to make the hand of the Confederacy felt throughout hundreds of miles of nominally occupied Virginia countryside. Subordinates may even veto the conclusions of their leaders, and are poised to replace them should they fall.

Commandos frequently select their own weapons, for instance, the type of noise-suppressed machine gun deemed most suitable. The Green Berets may have their own serial-numbered twelve-inch knife, which no one outside the fraternity is permitted to buy or own.

But that is more a nod to a common spirit than necessity; no one is required to carry it. Indeed, the point is that for the special operator, little is standard issue — and so it was for Henry Morgan's buccaneers ravaging the Spanish Main, or Francis Marion's men slipping out of the Carolina swamps. While it is the task of senior commanders or, today, perhaps even a president, to assign the mission, it is the special force — and each individual within — that must figure out how best to accomplish it and what to take along.

Conscript armies can certainly fight impressively in the worst of surroundings against terrifying odds. We only have to think of raw American draftees who stood alongside the Marines at the "frozen Chosin" Reservoir against Chinese human-wave attacks during the Korean War. Conventional forces will also contain men and women capable of pulling off the most audacious commandolike feats. Simply read the back-page obituaries of long-ago World War II heroes, such as an Indiana farmboy forming a squad of privates to wipe out from behind an entrenched position of Waffen-SS. What distinguishes today's special force from such hypercharged, spur-of-the-moment volunteers is the combination of experience and pooled, refined knowledge. Yet the vital talents of the commando may not be fully trainable. It takes imagination to conceive of a truly special operation: it requires character of an unusual sort to execute it in the face of all the obstacles indifferent chance will raise.

One of the best descriptions of the qualities of the modern special operator comes from a legendary entrepreneur of havoc whom we will meet when discussing World War II. With rare meticulousness, Major Vladimir Peniakoff — a Belgian-born White Russian who led the smallest independent unit of the British Army, some two dozen men raiding through North Africa in jeeps — had no tolerance of commando spirit (or the "dash" of the Guardsmen he abhorred) if it was not married to a scientific exactness. "Successful adventures in our line of business," he recalled, "depended on a rigorous attention to detail." The men whom he brought across sand seas the enemy thought impassable "had to have minds like ants, stamp collectors, watchmakers, and accountants" — orderly, precise, matter of fact, inured to tedium. No matter how extreme, the missions had to be "tidy and thrifty."[11] There could be no working off of adrenaline. There is good reason why the Green Berets call themselves "the quiet professionals"; why it is the wiles of Odysseus rather than the wrath of Achilles that brings down the proud city.

The qualities of self-command — discipline from within, a sense of proportion, respect for the rest of the world even when one seeks to do it harm — are to be found among all superior fighting men, just as they are among good people in general, perhaps especially in the demanding professions. One still insufficiently noted characteristic that stands out among those undertaking extreme missions, however, is the ability to contend with loneliness. Loyalty to a little group of one's fellows ("small-unit cohesion") has been known for centuries to be the essential element in all combat. So, too, among special warriors, except that they have to be able to excel amid an isolation and often solitude rarely demanded of the conventional soldier or sailor.

It is a state of experience akin to being on twenty-four-hour-a-day sentry duty in Indian country. There are so many of the enemy, and so few of those going in. It is a capacity that can apply equally to the Conquistadors (three or four hundred of whom faced millions on what might as well have been another planet) as much as to the underwater demolition team (three or four men just as thoroughly cut off by the unforgiving sea) or to a Crusader strike squad throwing its ropes over the walls of Antioch, perhaps only a hundred yards away from thousands of friends but in an environment so ferocious that the distance might as well be reckoned in light-years; surely like Corbett's solitary stalking of man-eaters, a quality shared most obviously by snipers and assassins — ultimate warriors working alone.

Through much of our story, and especially as this "line of business" has evolved over the past five centuries from gunpowder to insertions by submarine, there has been a deep vein of eccentricity winding among the leaders of special forces and often among those who follow them. The story of special warfare is one of unusual styles of leadership and of a higher proportion of unconventional people (to put it mildly) than among regular military formations, let alone than in civil life: Sir Francis Drake walking a fine line between piracy and public war; Robert Rogers of the Rangers in and out of jail much of his adult life; Benedict Arnold, supreme operator of the Revolution; the Earl of Dundonald, the only Royal Navy captain to have been stripped of his knighthood for a characteristically heroic-scale fraud; Orde Wingate, the one English-speaking general of World War II to openly attempt suicide; "Mad Mike" Calvert of the SAS and "Mr. Nichols" of Korea cashiered for vice — and this is just for starters. That so many wild outliers have made their ways by a kind of homing instinct onto the landscape of special warfare should not overshadow the prevailing qualities of leadership that underpin their achievements, gifts so evident today among their heirs.

Many of the people who gave rise to the legends are like renowned builders of private fortunes — curious combinations of cantankerousness, apparently irrational determination, uncanny insight, a sense of the big picture, and self-confidence only distinguishable from egomania by its real-world results. Churchill made it explicit that the type of men he wanted in the original giant-killer commandos were to be those capable of success in any walk of life they chose, not by-the-book people, however brave and intelligent, but warriors who saw things new in a world already terribly recast by Nazi triumph.

‡

To DO the rare or unprecedented, new voices must be listened to as well as new approaches taken. Skills that may never before have had decisive military effect come to be channeled and put to use. Time and again, special warfare has served both to dynamize new technology and to enable the achievements on a larger scale of previously marginalized people: miners bring their molelike methods and particular cold courage; frontiersmen carrying personally crafted rifles offset their inherent insubordination with shadowlike penetration; the rabble of manic inventors and scientists who would bankrupt any normal business find extraordinary ways of doing (for once) intended harm. Because such ways of war must resort to any means available to even the odds, the people who plan and lead them are more open than the rest of us to embracing most any novelty that offers a seriously better chance of success.

The mind wide open to new approaches — so essential to special operations, as to most enterprising developments — can trace in the solution of one problem the solving of another. We see this repeatedly in the use of innocent tools and devices, such as tent pegs for a crag-scaler's piton, or sport gliders for silent insertion, or passenger trains (or airliners) for destruction. Instruments that had evolved for one purpose are examined for what they can undo, rather than do.[12]

The special warrior may not only be bringing new technologies of his own to the mission but may have to grapple in the frame of his opponent's. For instance, in World War II, it could not be taken for granted that German and British commandos pouncing upon the enemy would be able to commandeer his trucks: driving, let alone driving a foreign-made vehicle, was still an unusual skill, requiring one more sieving even among people who had already proven themselves so versatile.

In special operations, the finely tuned intelligence gathering required from the outset can be more essential than to the most well-planned of conventional attacks. When select forces are employed to make and seize astonishing opportunities — to open a citadel's gates from inside, to trample an empire, to shatter some high-tech plexus — there is a premium on knowledge. What does an opponent rely on that can unexpectedly be turned against him? What can be accomplished that he thinks impossible? Where can his pride in achievement most readily be twisted into confusion and fear? Can a happy confidence in the underpinnings of his day-to-day world — its transportation or financial systems, say — be broken before the eyes of millions? The most effective means of assault are not necessarily the most ruinous but rather those which infect the enemy with a sense of being unfit for the challenge.

For a special operator to have a thorough grasp of "the map" does not mean that he has mastered topography only, but the microenvironment in which his enemy lives. "We were never on the defensive except by accident and in error," recalled T. E. Lawrence, one of the more eccentric and least modest of the mode's practitioners, in his memoir of desert warfare, *Seven Pillars of Wisdom*. "The corollary of such a rule was perfect 'intelligence,' so that we could plan in certainty. . . . Understanding must be faultless, leaving no room for chance." Knowledge is power and, here, a dark and crimson one.

Such meticulous intelligence work enforces itself today. For example, it is one thing to understand Arab history, but to know the record of Christian-Druze conflict in Lebanon is quite another, and the various shifting places of specific families and family members another level of complexity yet. When the United States entered Somalia in December 1992, the CIA had a one-line database, such as it was, on the various armed groups, militias, and warlord factions.[13] Americans confronting the clan-based Somali forces first tried to apply the same techniques just used successfully to display Iraqi order of battle (so-called bubble charts) in the 1991 Gulf War — an unhelpful measure against opponents who were far closer to the Hatfields and McCoys than to Saddam's Republican Guards. Rangers, Green Berets, and Delta Force commandos were at least able to locate and count from the ground the patched-up trucks, the few decrepit tanks, and the jeeps mounted with crew-served twin .50-caliber machine guns or cannon that comprised the hostile militia. But the overall lack of feel for the enemy in Mogadishu amid his tangled streets compounded the confusion of a brave, well-meaning venture that ended in the nineteen dead of *Black Hawk Down*.

Not only do extreme missions keep intersecting with the similarly shadowy trails of the intelligence services, but long before special forces were maintained on a standing basis characters kept slipping onstage who bridged the worlds of spy, special operator, and mainline military or naval commander. A direct link extends, for instance, between the combination of intelligence and special operations that the British ran against Bonaparte's occupied continent and those conducted against western Europe's next greatest massacre-maker, Hitler, a century and a quarter later. This intertwining of the commando and the intelligence officer not only distinguishes special warriors and their tasks from the world of conventional forces; it arouses one more pattern of resentment among the brass. It also moves the special force closer to the policy makers.

Since at least World War I, democratic political leaders who send huge numbers of citizen-soldiers to their deaths have been preoccupied with finding "ways around" carnage at the front. To such perspectives, special forces are alluring not just for their economy of lives and money, but for their morale-boosting drama, and often for their distance from the nation's military hierarchies. Special operations can also be pursued as short and sharp responses to intractable international problems way below the need to plunge the nation into all-out war — or so it is hoped. Many political leaders are drawn to these peculiar elites and take a certain defiant pride in serving as patrons of warrior cultures which annoy the high command for having made a virtue of not doing things the usual army or navy (or air force) way.

More happily for the politician (and painfully for the brass), a special mode of war can thrill a public desperate for conclusive action. The enormous London headlines won by the initial commando assaults that Churchill ordered into France during summer 1940 came in happy contrast to history's largest evacuation, at Dunkirk, which seemed to be all that the generals could offer. Today, newspapers and TV shows clamor with breathless recountings of tiny yet dazzling successes (such as the commando rescue of Private Jessica Lynch in Iraq), which can eclipse in the public mind much larger, less dramatic achievements (or stalemates). A 150-man raid on an island becomes big news; moving 60,000 men forward, without a casualty, for the decisive push, looks to be mundane bureaucracy, not that Generals Grant or Eisenhower would have thought so.

Other unusual taps into civil society make their curious contributions and are worth noting as we seek to expand our understanding of the many forms and appearances of the commando and his art. How are special operation techniques applied when the struggle for power at home descends into violence?

By definition, a coup d'état entails the illegitimate seizure of the machinery of government. It resembles, as the foremost student of the phenomenon reminds us, "a military operation," although, it might be noted, usually with a lot more concern to avoid collateral damage by those who seek to hold ongoing political power over their own people.[14] Except for when the coup is staged by the military en masse, as in some Peruvian or Pakistani takeover, such operations are, in their own way, special indeed. A daring few strike suddenly and precisely against numbers that would be overwhelming — if alertly deployed — and then turn their abruptly seized power outward. They leverage themselves by zeroing in with the speed of raiders on the strong points (overconfident citadels, routine-bound ministries). They exploit inside information, such as official schedules, as well as their opponents' blasé standard operating procedures. They exaggerate their presence by bluff and deception. The dying Corsican, having nothing else to provide, gave his loyal retainer advice beyond treasure in such situations: "Put your thumb on the blade and strike upwards" — a lesson for all who hope to overthrow a civil order from within.

Since a special operation need by no means spring from a strictly military outfit, it is worth recognizing it as well in the more elaborate forms of crime. A daring few can also pull off meticulous bank robberies or ambush armored cars in crowded downtowns. Such supremely coordinated exploits (crowned by equally astute escapes) also rivet public attention and are the stuff of the best crime fiction. Michael Connelly's *The Black Echo,* for instance, describes a Vietnam "tunnel rat" veteran's part in a team that burrows into Los Angeles banks and how a former tunnel-rat brother warrior tracks down and ambushes the venturers in their turn. It is a tale evoking special technique and character against the backdrop of an all-too-conventional large force, in this case the LAPD, the narrative needing only a few changes of place and time to be describing authentic commando feats.

The extreme operation as a means of crime has unusual salience in the early twenty-first century and for reasons beyond alerting us to new procedures, any of which may be aimed at our country, not just our savings. A nation's enemies draw richly on lawbreakers who could care less about the aims of an attacker. Drug lords move their poisons using pilots trained under very different auspices; smugglers pass their human cargo over continents and oceans. Assailants with agendas other than the merely criminal find the means to slip along these obscure paths and to exploit an underworld of hideouts and tailor-crafted false identities. In trying to determine the principles of commitment to any high cause, W. H. Auden quotes a Hassidic rabbi who bids those interested in service to take stock of a thief: "He does his service by night. If he does not finish what he sets out to do in one night, he devotes the next night to it. He and all those who work for him, love one another. . . . He endures blows and hardships and it matters nothing to him. He likes his trade and would not exchange it for any other."[15] If we throw in some penchant for imaginative violence, we could as well be explaining the commando.

In an era in which awareness of the possibilities of terror has become part of daily life, it is worth considering the multitude of ways by which any society is exposed to those of its dissidents or to malevolent outsiders able to harness these skills. The means keep changing, and now are changing faster than ever before, often by hands barely noticed. There is always an interplay of new ways of doing harm, new ways of anticipating and countering them, and always new opportunities for the special few to apply to the utmost their sharp-edged warrior talents.

2

Even Troy Must Fall

Hidden Ways, from the Wooden Horse to the Rise of Macedon, ca. 1200 to ca. 400 B.C.

*"For where the lion's skin will not reach, you must patch it
with the fox's."*
LYSANDER, SPARTAN GENERAL AND NAVAL SUPREMO

MUCH THAT is known about what can be described as special operations before credible military history emerges, around the later fifth century B.C., lies in the twilight between reality and myth. The story of the Trojan Horse, or accounts of border warfare in the Book of Judges, with its curiously named heroes — Shamsun (Samson), Shamgan, Shammash — strange figures all, but not necessarily imaginary ones, are what anthropologists call "trickster stories," though the Horse offers a tang of authentic danger and achievement. Yet not all is limited to conjecture.

Around the Mediterranean of Homeric and biblical times, an increasing number of people were living more intensely, lifting their eyes above the plough and anvil, beginning to record the verses of the traveling singer, the strange words of the priest. Whatever disasters might have befallen, such as the Greek Dark Age and the Babylonian Captivity of the Jews, each couple of centuries following showed higher achievement than the ones before. A growing division of labor began to yield not only literacy, civil technology, and trade from afar but — as the melancholy results of increased wealth and range of knowledge — also subtler means of violence, greater hostages to fortune, as well as deadlier specializations of arms. There was no obvious body of precedent from which to learn, just heroic tales recounted at the fireside, curious reports brought by merchants whose voyages happened on a burned-out city, or the sobbing memories of a slave girl in the evening, recalling how she had met her fate and how her family had died.

To be sure, from earliest recorded times, kings have raised crack regiments, notably of household troops: the Ten Thousand Immortals of the Great King of Persia; Alexander's Companion cavalry; the Sacred Band of Thebes (the ultimate select infantry regiment, a tight-knit force of 150 homosexual couples). But "commando operations" and "commandos," as they can be identified in the classical world, are something different, even though they draw on these star formations. Assaults became special in these centuries — and over most of history thereafter — when bold dreams were turned into fact practically overnight against an enemy just a bit less aware.

Each mode of civilization has its means of offense and types of vulnerability. A strongly positioned city might keep an army at bay, if not starve the attackers away. Yet given sufficient skill and guile, its fissures were there to be found by the stealthy few, just as a small desert nation hammered by a more numerous enemy might destroy its tormentors once it turned to an innovative band of its best men plunging out of the night. Many are the ancient stories of deception and chicanery. Hundreds of times the knife in the night, the tiny party that knew its task, destroyed a dynasty, a culture, a state. Homeric literature, biblical tales, and the Great War of the Greeks offer a vision of conflict where it is recognized that more than courage and endurance alone are needed to win.

‡

OF ALL these stories, the most famous is that of the Trojan Horse. The war itself begins with a Trojan prince running away with the beautiful queen of Sparta, though the control of a crucial trade route may have been the real reason for what historic war there actually was. Had the Trojans been allowed to get away with lifting Helen, the Spartans believed, then they might have no qualms about stealing yet another queen or committing some additional outrage. They had to be stopped, perhaps before they grew stronger — reasoning still heard today. The war also possessed elements of a hostage rescue, except that Helen's husband was ready to slit her throat for her infidelity.[1]

So the Greeks sailed from Nauplia on the southeast of the Peloponnese (the "Island of Pelops," the great southern figleaf peninsula of Greece), perhaps around 1250 B.C. Once they had fought the winds to reach Troy, a delegation was sent to negotiate. It got nowhere: dignity and security combined to dictate war. The first nine years of conflict entailed not only besieging Troy itself but also wrecking the neighboring kingdoms that were provisioning the enemy: they were either with the Greeks or against them.

What is usually deemed the greatest of verse epics, Homer's *Iliad,* finally compiled around 700 B.C., narrates the events of the last months of this very first world war between Europe and Asia on one of time's earliest battlegrounds. The characters are not just warriors, but exalted princely figures, for whom greatness in battle is the highest virtue. Homer offers what may be the best description of conventional combat, distinct from the entirely different final assault that will doom the proud city:

> *At last the armies clashed in one strategic point,*
> *they slammed their shields together, pike scraped pike*
> *with the grappling strength of fighters armed in*
> *bronze*
> *and their round shields pounded, boss on welded*
> *boss,*
> *and the sound of struggle roared and rocked the earth.*
> *Screams of men and cries of triumph breaking in one*
> *breath,*
> *fighters killing, fighters killed, and the ground*
> *streamed blood.*
> *. . . .*
> *and miles away in the hills a shepherd hears the*
> *thunder —*
> *so from the grinding armies broke the cries and crash*
> *of war.*

This is as close to a straight-out crunching of flesh and metal as war can get. Absent some convulsion, they will all go on killing each other until no one is left.

Homer ends the *Iliad* with the funeral of the Trojan hero Hector amid a grief that weighs on both weary hosts. (All Greeks knew how the city fell.) Apparently, the city could maintain itself indefinitely against the greatest armies and, despite the Trojans being heavily outnumbered, leave their opponents wasting away on the plain. Then in one night of carnage and rape, Troy was burned to ruins, the king's daughter ritually slain, the baby son of its great paladin hurled to his death. The means by which this came about have been the fountainhead for all special operations ever since.

It was Sinon, the planted defector, who provided the concealing "legend" that the Greeks had lost heart and sailed home. The Horse, he explained, had been left as a conciliatory offering to the gods for a safe journey back. The Greeks' simulation of demoralized flight tempted the Trojans to bear the gift off as their own prize, thereby admitting the hidden foe. The resort to cunning brought to the Greeks what had not been achieved by a decade of bloody frontal assault. Of course, it would have been less risky and probably just as effective had Troy been penetrated through its drainage tunnel, which Odysseus, already known as a deadly night raider, had used a few months earlier to devastate enemy morale by carrying off the Palladium (perhaps a meteorite), the talismanic luck of Troy. But the glorious, seductive Horse makes for a better story, as imagination thrusts mindless persistence aside. And it is heroic Odysseus — Homer's "man of wiles," "of twists and turns," having at first shammed madness to avoid having to fight a whole war to retrieve one errant wife — who conceives of the Horse.[2]

The sheer size of the Horse dictated tearing down part of the city wall to haul it triumphantly in, warnings to other Trojans from skeptics against "Greeks bearing gifts" being dismissed as windy nonsense. That night, amid the stupor that followed victorious feasting, Sinon unsealed the Horse's belly, and Odysseus and twenty-two raiders clambered down their rope ladder out into a relaxing city.[3] Signals flickered to the silently returning fleet. Technical guile and shrewd anticipation of enemy behavior united: the brilliant idea would have been nothing without actually building something so splendid that it had to be seized, and without putting the right men in place within.

It is such forethought and novelty, as well as the picked nature of the two dozen infiltrators, that make this truly a "special operation": the coordination, the timing, the subtlety of false context — the cover story that tricks the enemy to compromise his greatest strength. Yet in this war of brutal chieftains, such a resort to intellect is a last throw, not an early move. It took ten years of pointless attrition before matters were resolved in hours by substituting the silent access of a handful within for the noisy confrontation of multitudes without. Hector and Achilles, Sarpedon and Paris, Aias and Machaon, all are unforgotten after thirty centuries. Yet as we think today of how to meet our own far-flung military objectives, it is wise to remember cunning fellows who used subtler, stealthier ways, like Odysseus.

Perhaps somewhat less than a century later, we detect in the story of Gideon, as much as in that of Troy, an increasing sense of the rewards of quality and thought over heavy mass action. The disorganized Hebrew pastoralists in the Valley of Jezreel were tormented by predatory raids by the Midianites, nomadic tribesmen coming in from the east, numberless "as grasshoppers" says the scribe. In response, Gideon distilled an elite strike force from a rabble of thirty-two thousand angry victims, probably most of the able-bodied men in the nation. He first weeded out the faint of heart — twenty-two thousand out of the original mass. Then, by a test of drinking alertly from a stream, he sieved out those who were bravely determined but lacked the warrior's instinct of constant vigilance. Only three hundred passed the selection.

Gideon's dismissal of the frightened and the inept underscores a rule of special operations: the more extreme the mission, the more important it is to know one's men intimately. Second thoughts are likely to be fatal when there are no second chances. Gideon's purpose was to panic the enemy, not to let panic creep into his own small force through men insufficiently sound.

Gideon next combined "force and fraud" — as Hobbes characterizes war — to mask his deliberately modest capabilities. Dividing his men into three units of a hundred each, he set them to strike deep in the night just after the change of guard, before the new sentries had accustomed their eyes to the dark. He knew the time: he had sneaked close enough to the enemy to overhear conversation, an example of the hands-on quality of the special forces leader that has proved indispensable ever since. Gideon was confident that his force would be multiplied in the terrified minds of the enemy because of the contrast of fiendish pandemonium with the still summer's night, its impossible nearness at the moment of assault (achieved only by the band's being few enough to slip in), and its weird mode of attack. The assault would open with Gideon's men shattering their clay pitchers to reveal the glowing lamps within, thereby suddenly disclosing a terrible hostile presence, and then setting the Midianites' tents afire. His purpose was to make the night-splitting clamor seem not an act of war, but an invasion from the heavens. A small, disciplined, strictly vetted force discovering ways to horrify an enemy right from the start becomes a staple of special warfare.

Coordination was pivotal: the great Judge himself would give the signal. When he did, his companies sprang from three different points around the enemy perimeter to maximize confusion — leaving open an escape route to the east, where the Midianites would run upon the spears of Gideon's remaining forces holding the line of the Jordan. The Midianites drowned themselves in tumbling panic at the fords. Those not killed kept fleeing farther eastward, Gideon pursuing them indirectly by way of the far desert, living off the land, and finally surprising and slaughtering them and their plunder-rich kings. What worked, observes Yigael Yadin, with the double authority of a professor of archeology at Hebrew University and a former chief of staff of the Israeli Defense Forces, was not "the size or strength of an army but the offensive spirit and the capacity to extract every ounce of surprise from place, timing, method, and weapon."[4] The Midianites, ruined by Gideon's three hundred, would have made short work of his initial bewildered thirty-two thousand.

Although the record of Gideon is the exemplary tale of the founding of special forces, we have no reason to believe that he kept his three hundred together as a unit after the event. Such a stroke was not about to be repeated. (Large armies did not come the way of the twelve tribes for some time thereafter.) But thirty centuries later, a decade before the birth of modern Israel, Orde Wingate — a Christian fundamentalist, Zionist, commando genius — would explicitly invoke the great Judge in organizing his Special Night Squads on the same landscape, against Arab raiders. Founder of what was to become the Israeli army, Wingate achieved successes out of all proportion to his numbers: Gideon Force would be the name of one of his instruments, and *Gideon Goes to War* the title of the best biography of this short-lived phenomenon of nature.

The story of the fall of Troy, and of the night overthrow of the Midianites, each place technology at the heart of victory: the first passing off a troop inserter as a covetable offering to the gods, the second combining readily available household objects into portable engines of demoralization. You cannot kill someone with a jug and a lamp, but what does that matter if you can take his imagination captive? Over civil society's justly satisfied sense of achievement, there hangs the dark threat of what we might call the "Gideon effect," meaning that an opponent who can tell only that something terrible has befallen him (he knows not what) will energetically anticipate the worst.

There must have been more such instances than those of Gideon, since the Old Testament is largely a history of the wars of the Lord. But this is the only detailed narrative of all phases of a campaign. Otherwise, there is little interest in conveying the fine structure of war, as is apparent in the Book of Daniel. Having allowed ample space for the Prophet to pronounce the imminent doom of the great King Belshazzar and all his realm, the Book says suddenly and in its entirety: "In that night was Belshazzar King of the Chaldeans slain. And Darius the Median took the kingdom, being then sixty-two years old."[5] Nothing more. No mention, let alone explication, of what must indeed have been a most unusual venture as the Persians diverted the Euphrates — by night — and pushed their storming parties down the suddenly empty riverbed.

Instead, it is in the Greece of fifth century B.C., among the hundreds of city-states compared to which modern Luxembourg would be a superpower, that we can first get a more or less documented understanding of special warfare. The fortified cities of the time of Troy and the specialized warriors of whom we read in Homer —

chariot drivers, archers, and javelin men — had been products of a prosperous, centralized culture that foundered around 1100 B.C. Its collapse across the eastern Mediterranean seems to have been accelerated by raiders who exploited the shipping lanes. There followed several centuries of decay, in which writing vanished, trade, agriculture, and population shrank, in which no extended campaigns to conquer territory seem to have been fought. (Indeed, Homer — composing his work several centuries after the ruin of Troy — never really understands what chariots are for; the feudal anarchy of his era could not support such sophisticated technology.)[6] Around that time, however, the small but increasingly organized state (not always literally a *city*-state) was beginning to crystalize, bringing with it the practice of disciplined, heavily armored foot soldiers (hoplites) meeting in decisive head-on clashes over local autonomy. Using tricks to steal a victory went back far into the mythic past, if one thinks of Odysseus. But that was not the bold hoplite ideal, nor the ethos of Achilles with his fury and massive strength.[7]

‡

A GREEK *polis* was a largely rural territory, tightly circumscribed by mountains or sea, with an administrative center, often unwalled, analogous to those common names for county seats in Virginia that end in "Court House" (like Appomattox Court House), their sole reason for being that people met there to do public business (though some, probably, were refuges in times of disaster). By 700 B.C., such places dotted much of the coasts and many islands of southern Greece, as well as the western shore of what is now Turkey, and soon enough Sicily and southern Italy. Their constitutions varied, but their citizens felt a common identity, above all as Hellenes, despite specific complex identities as Ionians, Dorians, Achaeans. All Greeks regarded themselves superior to barbarians — that is, "babblers," non-Greek speakers — a fascinating arrogance that may have imparted much of the confidence enabling these small tribes from a stony peninsula to shake the world.

The sovereignties of these tiny states were islands not much larger than Manhattan and hill towns the size of college campuses. The entire region of Attica — a most substantial entity by the standards of the age — in which Athens was the primary city, was no bigger than

Rhode Island. From, say, 700 B.C. to the mid-400s, such modest scale combined with increasing innovation to produce an epoch of small but not necessarily petty warfare. In nonrepublican states, the king or despot offered a fabulous target. In states so compact as to have a single stronghold, authority might collapse before one clever blow. The most intellectually productive culture in history perceived a world of vulnerabilities; it also had the genius and spirit to exploit them. So often one of those promising little cities must have failed to detect the sudden move of a few determined men that brought it down. When the whole plexus of government was minute, the return on sufficiently precise strikes could be huge.

As myth begins to come together as history — itself a new discipline riding the slow return of literacy — we see the hero begin to pass from a superhuman figure such as Achilles into someone of extraordinary but rational skills. (Odysseus seems to be the only such figure of the preliterate age.) We also begin to see the systematic exploration of a society's array of vulnerabilities. The dynamism of a city can raise dangers for itself: "traders" within what walls exist may be enemies in disguise; water tunnels and aqueducts, indispensable to city life in hot, hilly Greece, were easy to sever; and even olive groves, a symbol of Greek well-being, were helpless before the axe in a day's raiding, not to be replaced for a good twenty years.

Probably the earliest coups d'état of which we have record do not entail soldiers in the streets and startled officials being hauled off under arrest, but persuasion, theatrics, and deception featuring guile from start to finish. Peisistratos, the adventurer scion of a great family laboring under a public curse for impiety, made himself three times tyrant of Athens. He first grabbed power during 561 B.C., by faking an attempt on his life, raising a bodyguard from a shocked citizenry, and then bit by bit expanding his force until he saw fit to seize the acropolis ("city height," or citadel).[8] After he was deposed several years later and run off, he recovered his authority by a "primitive and very simple ruse," Aristotle explains.[9] A rumor was spread that Athena herself, goddess of the city, would bring Peisistratos triumphantly home. A tall, beautiful girl was found from out of town, accomplices dressed her in armor, and Peisistratos arrived in a chariot with "Athena" standing patronly beside him. Even sophisticated

Athenians were awed and officialdom was bewildered: the gods still walked the earth. Such a fraud could not last, but under its fleeting spell critical moments might be gained for more enduring action.

Had Peisistratos made a stone-cold move — as the mistrusted, ambitious, pariah nobleman — to seize the state that second time, he would have stood an excellent chance of being pulled limb from limb. Instead, his charade reversed the terms of power, not by numbers, not by violence brought by hordes of followers who might have accompanied him and who could have been resisted, but by knocking the spirit out of his enemies and conquering the public imagination. To be sure, the third time he had to maneuver his way back with more force than fraud; mercenaries were hired and his opponents beaten in battle. But when he entered Athens to give a victory speech, he spoke so inaudibly that the city's still-armed citizens were lured to the acropolis, where he could be better heard. A group of his hirelings then gathered up and locked away the weapons imprudently left behind. In each case we see how that willful quality which knows what it wants can override honest quantity any day — which along with speed, insouciance, and a bit of muscle may make Peisistratos godfather of the coup d'état as special operation.

On the field, guile can combine with daring in ways at least as odd as Peisistratos's simple ruses. Around the same time as his seizure of power, in 525 B.C., the half-mad Persian king Cambyses invaded Egypt. The Egyptians, at least during the two millennia before Christ, regarded cats as divine. Cambyses collected hundreds of cats from surrounding villages the night before, and then had his cavalry throw them screaming and spitting into the enemy ranks when battle was joined. The Egyptians did not try to catch the creatures — these flying felines were regarded as too dangerously charged with mana — but instead scattered much as would twenty-first-century troops before anthrax, the decisive moment of this invasion being styled by Herodotus simply "The Battle of the Cats." Once more, we learn to make a study of one's enemy, as might be the case, say, in advancing behind a herd of cows when going against Hindu soldiers. One seeks what the enemy fears, and also what he is awed, disoriented, or disgusted by.

The mighty Persian Empire had a rougher time a generation later

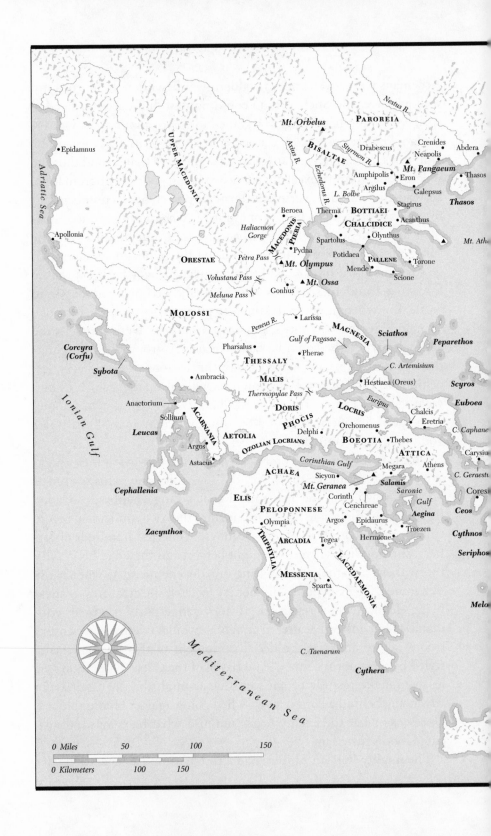

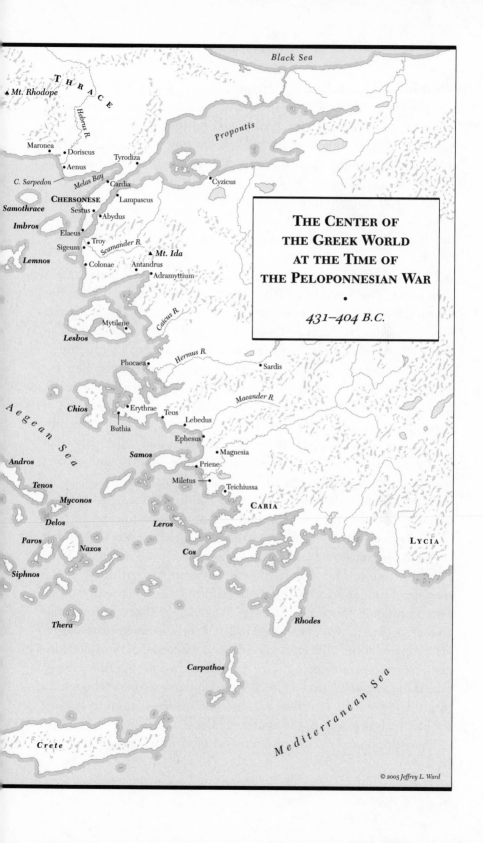

Black Sea

THRACE

Mt. Rhodope

Propontis

Maronea
Doriscus
Aenus
Tyrodiza
Hebrus R.
C. Sarpedon
Melas Bay
Cardia
Cyzicus
CHERSONESE
Lampascus
Samothrace
Sestus
Abydus
Imbros
Elaeus
Troy
Sigeum
Scamander R.
Lemnos
Colonae
Antandrus
Mt. Ida
Adramyttium

Caicus R.

Mytilene

Lesbos

Hermus R.

Phocaea
Sardis

Aegean Sea

Chios
Erythrae
Teos
Maeander R.
Buthia
Lebedus
Ephesus
Samos
Magnesia
Andros
Priene
Miletus
Teichiussa
Tenos
CARIA
Myconos
Delos
Leros
Paros
LYCIA
Naxos
Cos
Siphnos

Thera
Rhodes

Carpathos

Crete
Mediterranean Sea

THE CENTER OF
THE GREEK WORLD
AT THE TIME OF
THE PELOPONNESIAN WAR
•
431–404 B.C.

© 2005 Jeffrey L. Ward

when invading much less populous Greece (480–479 B.C.). Athens and Sparta led a heroic and successful united resistance, which did much to crown them as the preeminent powers at the center of the Greek world, the one stronger on sea, the other on land. But their interests increasingly clashed as they became the standard-bearers of rival alliances, which divided all Greece: Athens as the prime democratic power and dominant partner in a thalassocracy, the Delian League, nominally directed against Persia; Sparta the champion of the oligarchies and furthermore of a loose confederacy of states that felt themselves threatened by Athenian ambition.

The familiar polar opposition of Athens and Sparta is useful rather than exact. But it is still worthwhile to contrast Ionian Athens (inquiring, far-ranging, open, joyous, high-spirited) with Dorian Sparta (dour, plodding, ruthless — though no more so than Athens on a bad day). Athens was as close as the ancient world came to a high-culture democracy, albeit slaveholding and distinctly aristocratic, like the Virginia of Washington and Jefferson. Sparta in turn had a small, hypermilitarized elite, with men habitually eating in messes, not at home; profoundly austere, which may be why so many of their officials proved easy to bribe.[10] It was also as close to sexually egalitarian as any culture of the time, yet philistine and merciless, with a strict code of eugenics enforced to kill imperfect infants.

Paul Cartledge, the leading expert on this high-toned, vicious little tyranny, describes how it "acquired the reputation of being the SAS of the Greek world," always on the alert for enemies within and without. Spartans were enthralled by espionage, and "when the Spartans kill," wrote Herodotus, "they do so at night." All their young men spent time in a secret police, the name of which Cartledge translates as roughly "Special Secret Ops Brigade" or "Secret Operations Executive (SOE)," to control the Helots (a perhaps seven-times-larger Greek population subjected to serfdom), whose labors enabled citizens to concentrate on military excellence.[11] The Spartans maintained the best army in the Greek world, citizen-soldiers who were a byword for skilled effectiveness. Endless military training became the life, such as it was, of the Spartan male.

The Peloponnesian convulsion of 431 to 404 B.C., centering on the rivalries of Athens and Sparta, was "a fundamental departure from the traditional character of the Greek way of warfare," explains its preeminent scholar. Honor had previously required that men bearing swords and twelve-foot spears face each other on an open field in daylight, where "the braver and stronger army would naturally prevail . . . and march home, as would the defeated foe."[12] Courage meant staying in rank, with men pressed together for mutual protection. This had left little room in the wars of the Greeks for the deceit, guile, and surprise destruction of special operations. From the war's first year on, however, there appeared modes of combat significantly different from the traditional approach. The shift was likely due to the scope of the struggle, the variety of challenges, the need to rethink procedures if complex issues of all-out war were to be resolved. It built on Athens's intellectual hospitality and on the brutal primacy that Sparta gave to war as a way of life. As part of this adaptation, special techniques also moved front and center (this is an element of the Peloponnesian War nearly entirely overlooked by classicists).[13]

No manuals on generalship survive from fifth-century Greece, yet treatises on tactics do, and these are essentially bags of (dirty) tricks. They emphasize deception and guile every bit as much as do the writings of the nearly contemporary military philosopher Sun Tzu, who composed *The Art of War* during a similar surge of thought in China. The Greek approach also calls for the closest study of the enemy's character, attacking his mind before engaging his forces, exploiting his strength and momentum, counting on him to provide the means of his own destruction. That this great war would not be restricted by familiar, honor-bound rules was increasingly evident after its first year, when Athens was smitten by the plague and its citizens suspected that the invading Spartans had poisoned their wells.

Initial combat had begun when more than three hundred soldiers from Sparta's powerful ally, Thebes, pounced one night on the small, strategically positioned neighboring city of Plataea, long an ally of Athens. It was a sneak attack in peacetime far beyond any code of honor, abetted by traitors within, one of whom had guided the Thebeans through. Yet they were foiled in street fighting, the townspeople of Plataea showering stones and tiles from the rooftops on invaders flummoxed by labyrinthine alleys: 180 of them were taken prisoner and put to death. Certain of another attack, Athens sent in eighty soldiers and helped evacuate women and children.

Two years later it was the Spartans who built a ditched and battlemented double siege wall around the plucky little democracy to starve it to terms, a move countered with a resourcefulness unusual for this early stage of the war. Most of Plataea's 480 men volunteered to attempt a breakout, so Thucydides tells us. But sieges have a way of sapping a garrison's nerve: nearly half fell away as the moment approached. The height of the Spartan wall was calculated from a distance by elementary geometry, and ladders built. Two hundred and fourteen lightly equipped men with shortened spears, led by those who had conceived the attempt, waited for a nighttime storm, then advanced in groups of twelve, each man leaving one foot bare so as not to slip in the mud. Those who remained behind staged a distracting sally on the far side of the city. The first men scaling the siege wall were able to spear the sentinels and occupy the guard towers. With the Spartans' surveillance neutralized, nearly all the Plataeans who attempted escape made it out as the storm raged. They fled toward Thebes, their mortal enemy — precisely where their pursuers would least expect them to go — before cutting south again across the hills to Athens. Those unfortunates who had stayed put eventually surrendered, the 110 remaining women being enslaved and the men, including twenty-five Athenians, given a sham trial and put to death in their turn.

Plataea was a defining episode for what lay ahead, both in its reciprocal, ratcheting atrocity and its fostering of unconventional technique. The intrepid 214 had the transcendent self-confidence to climb out, and then the contrarian notion to head toward the seat of enemy power. It could have been an exercise in escape and evasion (E&E) taken from Fort Benning's Ranger School. The escape itself had to succeed or fail within minutes; the evasion had to affront common sense by the direction of its flight — all being special employments of stealth and deception by no means obvious to those untrained in E&E, as we know from the Spartans' inability to imagine how and where to intercept those who would get away.

That said, when goaded by more nimble allies, Sparta could offer its own surprises, as it showed that winter by a nighttime amphibious raid aimed at Athens's harbor-fortress of Piraeus, nerve center of the Athenian fleet and seaborne empire. "It was a golden opportunity," marvels a fine classicist from the years right before the British made such audacious raids routine in World War II. "No one in Athens had ever dreamed of an open attack by sea upon Piraeus. How was it conceivable?"[14] The Athenians, after all, claimed dominance of the sea — justified, for the time being, against an enemy fleet. For raiders to arrive instead by sailing straight in aboard someone else's boats was unimaginable to Athens but not to a combined outfit of Spartan soldiers and sailors who hiked across the Isthmus of Corinth — each carrying an oar and rowlock — to hijack vessels from the harbor of Nisaea, a bare twenty miles from target. Only a sudden loss of nerve by the Spartan commander saved an utterly rattled Athens from a roundhouse kick. And this was only the beginning.

Initially, in hopes of wearying the enemy, the Athenians had relied on a painful defensive warplan, checkered by "a protracted special operations campaign of pinprick raids against the Spartans and their allies."[15] After six years of annual Spartan devastations of their beloved farmlands, however, the Athenians emerged in strength from behind the city's famous Long Walls to launch a determined offensive. The years 425 and 424 B.C., for instance, become dense with all sorts of special actions, the result of desperation at a seemingly endless war — just the kind of struggle for which Spartan culture (which made the minimum distinction between war and peace) was eminently suited.

In the spring of 425 B.C. a newly elected, more aggressive Athenian general, acting despite opposition from officers and men alike, used the fleet to land a force well behind enemy lines, about forty-six miles from Sparta. Pylos lies on the southwest coast of the Peloponnese, a place famous since Homer for offering the only harbor on a rocky coast. Today, the Bay of Navarino is still shielded by an island roughly a mile and three-quarters long; this land lying across its entrance creates two mouths into the adjacent waters. The Athenians built a fort on the bay, preparing to garrison it and begin an irregular war of raids within Laconia (the region dominated by Sparta, which gave us the very Spartan word *laconic*), hoping to stir up a rebellion among the vast, sullen Helot population.

Dismissing the threat from this relatively small enterprise — nothing like their own main-battle-force incursions into Attica — the Spartans waited too long to counterattack by land and sea. When they did get around to what they perceived as a petty nuisance, they dispersed their forces, sacrificing an overwhelming assault on the fort to position a detachment (chosen by lot from the army) on the sparsely wooded island opposite. The purpose was to prevent the Athenian fleet from establishing a base, but the Spartans' position proved a treacherous perch. The Athenians held out until their fleet not only brought reinforcements but also cut off the 420 Spartan troops (plus Helot auxiliaries) who had taken the island, which offered no food and only brackish water.

Trapped, Sparta decreed huge awards (and freedom to Helots) to those daring enough to try to supply the isolated garrison. In response, what commandos today call "combat swimmers" slipped into the water from one of the horns of the bay, where the channels separating the island from the mainland are narrowest, pulling by cords skins containing food, wine, and a mixture of pounded linseeds and poppyseeds stirred with honey. The blockade was kept up for ten weeks, prolonged by these operations conducted by impromptu frogmen who crossed the channel mostly underwater, and by bands sneaking in aboard small boats at night from the seaward side, as if they were SEALs. The Athenians tried a landing to flush out the Spartans, burning what cover there was, discovered more of the enemy than anticipated, and rather gloomily expected them to fight to the death, for Spartans never surrendered. Yet here they did, their captain dead, his second in command suffering a nervous breakdown (probably the first recorded in warfare), leaving much of the force very much alive to pass into captivity: a tremendous blow to the mystique of Thermopylae.[16]

On went these critical actions laced with special operations. In summer 424 B.C., Athens, for instance, was convinced that it had to seize control of Megara, a nearby city on its western border, a gateway into the Peloponnesus. Sparta had already garrisoned one of that city's two ports, Nisaea, which was still seen as a springboard to attacking Athens's harbor. First, six hundred Athenians sailed at nightfall to an offshore island, only the leaders of this force being briefed on their mission. Double "walls" — essentially a fortified roadway — connected Megara to its ports, in imitation of Athens. Such a passage should have been the most economical means of deploying the garrison between port and city, but the Athenians realized the walls were actually a point of peculiar vulnerability.

Coming ashore on the mainland under cover of darkness, they concealed themselves by quietly slipping into a long trench from which the clay for the bricks of the wall had originally been dug. Meanwhile, a lightly armed detachment stole up to a shrine just outside a gate where the eastern wall met the port town. Conspirators within provided the third leg. This clever little cabal had established a pattern of going out each night through that gate with a wagon carrying a sailing dinghy, which they pretended to be using to raid Athenian shipping, always returning just before dawn.

When they came home this time, the gate was opened as usual by the guard within. But suddenly their wagon jammed the gate; the guard was cut down, clearing the way for the Athenians who had hidden closest to turn themselves into a storming party. Then up from the trench sprang the larger force to make the surprise complete. The long walls were taken; the next step was to consolidate victory with the arrival of an Athenian army of no less than four thousand, which had marched overnight across the border. (Or so it was planned: Megara itself was saved due to the equally sudden arrival of a Spartan general at the head of an army just as large.) The fall of Nisaea, the harbor town, was nonetheless a stunning example of simultaneous nighttime infiltration by land and sea, coordination between strike teams big and small, synchronization with a main force, and acute intelligence work in knowing how to leverage the cunning friends on the inside.

As we examine such fast and final encounters in the ancient world through the lens of special warfare, it is important not to neglect the fact that an operation can show itself as "special" in the brilliant deployment of breakthrough technologies by a daring few — now-or-never on-the-spot solutions, with little or no opportunity for rehearsal. Out of these tiny citizenries, an operationally adequate smattering of people (and perhaps a few of the cleverest and most trusted slaves) had to be found who could develop not only novel techniques but radical devices, and apply them fast — special warriors by definition being ones who both think and act a step or two ahead while being able to apply astonishing means of leverage.

That brings us, in November 424 B.C., to Delium, which also lay across the border from Athens. At Delium occurred the largest battle of the war's first decade. It was the last of the failed Athenian thrusts into Boeotia, the fertile country of plains and water dominated by Thebes to the north. Remnants of the defeated Athenians barricaded themselves into a temple sacred to Apollo. It was a desperate step and an outrage to traditional ways. To remove them the Boeotians — backed by the Spartans so recently dislodged from Nisaea — had to attack the breastworks. But frontal assault would go nowhere, and for once traitors do not seem to have offered their services. With no corps of engineers to send in, the next move had to be one of improvisation and fast thinking.

The attackers sawed and hollowed out an enormous log to act as a flute and overlaid it with iron, the immense contraption being brought into position by cart. A burning pot of coals, sulfur, and pitch was placed at the business end, at the other a huge bellows, which drove an enormous flame upward that swept the defenders away as they left behind some two hundred charred corpses. This tremendous primitive flamethrower played on the most elemental of human fears: fire (not cats), with its hideous, flesh-consuming, choking power. In our day of chemical warfare units and napalm, this may look routine. In the hands of a society yet to come up with windowpanes or metaled roads, it was special indeed.[17]

Within weeks the Spartans themselves brought off a remarkable exploit against Torone, in Chalcidice (the three-pronged peninsula on the northern coast of Greece, now famous for the monastery state of Mount Athos), which was also allied with the Athenians. A column slipped into position before dawn, concealing itself in a temple less than half a mile from the city. As happened so often in this war — or in the innumerable earlier quarrels among these passionate little polities — the assailants had allies within. A detachment of twenty volunteered to join the conspirators by infiltrating the hillside city at the point where its own wall met the sea. (These not being Green

Berets or SAS with years of preparation, it is unsurprising when Thucydides tells us that most of this impromptu commando team had second thoughts.) In the outcome, just seven bold spirits armed with daggers alone made their way up and over the wall. The main force moved quietly forward, an assault group of one hundred poised to storm in once the infiltrators dealt with the sentries and pried open the gate amid cries of "Fire! Fire!" to cover the noise of their killings, to bring in the attack, and to panic the town. Torone, that apparently well-defended capital, fell soon after dawn.

One reason surprises were possible was likely because reconnaissance had not been developed into a refined and familiar method of war. Previously, when two masses of infantry drew opposite each other on level ground, there had been little utility in chosen bands of scouts working independently of the main battleforce to perform such recon, let alone to bring off or to parry penetration missions.[18] (Homer only once describes a night raid, and Thucydides mentions just one such assault between large armies during the entire war, explaining that soldiers would have trouble recognizing their friends.) Indeed, the Greek vocabulary seems not to have developed any word for a surprise attack. But all this, too, was changing.

Ten years later, when a brief troubled peace unraveled, there came this war's ultimate special enterprise, choreographed by one of history's archmanipulators. In 415 B.C., Athens launched its mightiest force ever, transported by an armada against Syracuse, Sicily's largest city, more than eight hundred miles distant, and a capital soon to rival the older Greek cities in intellectual achievement. If Athens could dominate the Sicilian cornland — a deep reserve of money, ships, and political leverage — it would overturn the balance of power across the entire Greek world.

Handsome, rich Alcibiades — Socrates' most sparkling disciple — had been designated a joint commander of the expedition and was indeed its prime mover. He was then in his mid-thirties, a former ward of Pericles, a veteran cavalryman holding a crown for valor from Phormio, the unsung hero-general of the Peloponnesian War. With immense self-confidence and an intimidating capacity for violence, Alcibiades was also of louche character: too clever by half, said some; too charming by three-quarters, said others. He was the classic outsider/insider, walking the fine line up to this point between admiration and profound mistrust: the special operator forever swaying between decoration and court-martial.

Barely had the great fleet sailed, when this evil genius was recalled to stand trial for alleged complicity in the mutilation by night of the sacred phallic images of Hermes on display throughout Athens. The reason the phalloi had been mutilated remains a mystery twenty-four centuries later. It was the very creepy inexplicability of the act that made it so chilling. (If we are to believe Plato, Alcibiades and his drinking buddies had been on a tear shortly before embarking.) Such sacrilege would have been a dire matter in time of peace, let alone during the second decade of desperate war. Surely it would bring the wrath of the offended Gods down upon the embattled city. Alcibiades escaped from the ship sent to bring him back and defected straight to Sparta, anything but demoralized. Athens condemned him in absentia and offered a fortune to anyone who could bring him back dead or alive.

Having convinced his startled, often slow-witted hosts that he knew its enemy's deepest secrets, Alcibiades promptly set about formulating the simplest deadly ways of reducing his discarded country. It is revealing of that world of violent personal loyalties that he was readily believed, and that Sparta so rapidly acted on his advice. Like another highly effective traitor so many centuries later, Alcibiades could have simply described himself as "a patriot for me."[19] But he was much more than a turncoat. Any smart overreacher can ruin himself, go on the run, spill his guts to the other side. Very few, having brought about a huge strategic operation with oneself at the center, can expound the big-picture means of bringing down his whole country.

Alcibiades first persuaded the Spartan authorities to dispatch a military mission to help with the defense of Syracuse — a single, key person who could be even more valuable than an army: just one man would appear unthreatening to a suspicious new ally. Gylippos, a highly skilled operator, slid into the strategically decisive crack, carrying the attributes of "elite" and "light" force to the extreme. He was not an authentic Spartan in the sense of being a full member of the master race, since he was the son of a felon and perhaps of a Helot mother. A true edgy outsider with consequently more need to prove himself, neither was he fully invested in the Spartan way of warfare, or much else. As we increasingly will see, men with chips on their shoulders have set countless precedents in special operations; he would just be one of the first on record.

Gylippos reminded the Syracusans that their fame had been founded on having defeated barbarian invaders. Faced by a highly civilized enemy, they must rethink these methods. Had anyone before thought of deploying an advisory mission to instruct or mobilize an ally in need, as is second nature at the Pentagon today? Apparently not, otherwise the Spartans would have done so without prompting. Nor did it occur to the Syracusans to ask, even though it must have been as apparent to them as to the Spartans that Athens was assembling an armada — at the request, moreover, of some of Syracuse's jealous Greek neighbors. Alcibiades brought a new voice to the discussion and, in recruiting the crucial talent, took a step so very close to a single Green Beret in our era embarking on a "foreign internal defense" mission, of the type conducted by Special Forces Mobile Training Teams and comprising "one or more U.S. military or civilian [experts] sent on temporary duty."[20]

Alcibiades also suggested another way of undoing Athens: Sparta should seize and permanently fortify a post at Decelea, in the mountains fourteen miles north of Athens, which commanded the route from the vital silver mines at Laurium, Athens's prime sinew of war, over which food supplies and tribute money also reached Athens. What elevates this deep outreach mission to the role of special warfare is that it had to be accomplished by a fast-moving detachment springing forward in the teeth of Athenian power — without main battleforce support — to strike at the underpinnings of its enemy. This type of quick, piercing insertion is akin to a resourceful thrust in modern warfare that eviscerates an opponent's financial structure rather than confronts his soldiers en masse. Actually to hold on to and occupy Decelea turned out to be a splinter under the fingernail of the state — a threat to the mines (economic dislocation), a beacon to escaping slaves (social disorder), and a hemorrhage of Athens's imperial revenue as its allies began to waver. Again, this is leverage, keenly wielded. Alcibiades had put his native city doubly off balance by exercising leverage very close and very far away. Athens would be fighting two wars at once.

Over the next two years, battle as well as a combination of subversive operations in Sicily and on Athens's doorstep began to undermine the entire Athenian hegemony. The Spartan incisions were predicated not only on sea access, fortifications, and armies, but also on insurgencies, slave discontent, night raids, deceptions, and small-unit skills. The cumulative effect was horrific, compounded by the fate of the almost forty thousand soldiers and sailors whom Athens had set against Syracuse. "Having done what men could, they suffered what men must," Thucydides tells us. "They were destroyed, as the saying goes, with a total destruction."[21] Those not killed outright were worked to death in the quarries.

Alcibiades eventually defected *back* to Athens and, on returning, used an array of ruses to offset the Spartan successes that his counsels had brought about: hiding ships behind headlands to lure the enemy out; feigning negotiations within a strongly fortified city while his men took the unguarded walls; more night thrusts from unimagined directions, repeatedly appearing wherever opponents believed it impossible for him to be. In this highly personalized world in which war was like a fight between Dayton, Ohio, and Decatur, Illinois (everyone knowing everybody, cities of similar size, no ongoing institutionalized defense departments), the stage even of total war could be reset with every act.

Not that all this dexterity ultimately brought Athens more than additional exhaustion, and eventually in 404 b.c., defeat. Alcibiades, having betrayed his country yet again, was finally brought down by Persian assassins. In stripping Athens of its empire, its navy, its formidable Long Walls, and its independence, Sparta came to dominate the Greek world and with remarkable celerity found itself the object of widespread detestation. Thebes had been Sparta's ruthless ally against Athens and, indeed, had started the killing. Yet it soon grew weary of Sparta's heavy-handed primacy and eventually broke free, with the aid of a reviving Athens. The exiled leader Pelopidas and a few of his friends — in the manner by now so familiar, but so repeatedly effective — slipped into Thebes by night, dislodged the Spartan garrison, and overthrew its client oligarchy. The Sacred Band then made such short work of the Spartan army as had never before been seen.

‡

BY THE fourth century B.C., war had indeed made itself a violent instructor. A "marketplace of ideas" emerged as the Greeks adopted and refined military practices not originally their own.[22] Previously, subversion, ambush, assassination, and overnight seizure of power had percolated as standard pathologies — and had diminished after each specific event while outright war was conducted by those opposing ranks of spear-carrying hoplites facing off on a battlefield. But when all Greece divided itself in intercity and revolutionary intracity war for a generation — with uncounted citadels falling, innumerable governments overthrown — then such procedures bloodily codified themselves. Guile and improvisation that included all the practices above were emerging into a special means of war. By the end of this period, there was no need for warriors to sit around and brood for ten years when facing the city of a seemingly unbreakable foe.

This highly resourceful sort of "creative destruction" may accompany the overall advance toward more open societies that nurture individualized, special abilities. And yet the most vicious tyrannies have often been very good at these operations too, in the same way that in modern times such regimes have conscripted small children as potential Olympic athletes. Obsessed special excellence — the state does the obsessing, you provide the excellence — can fit well into the totalitarian world view. Moreover, as Thucydides reminds us, occasionally "the stupid [come] off best in intrigue," a step often to be found at the heart of the special operation: these individuals succeed because they fear being outwitted by more reflective people, so they do not hesitate to strike suddenly and sharply.[23] Thought and unfettered discussion help, but only so much.[24]

The triumphs and disasters of the worlds chronicled by Herodotus and Thucydides had the focus of describing remarkably small areas and populations — very often the lustrous smallness of a jewel, but smallness all the same. The enemy leadership was well known, frequently by face and house; death and captivity came in a flash;

gatherings of a dozen could be detected and broken up — or go on to conquer the whole polity. These quarrelsome, war-obsessed little cities composed a world white-hot with intellect, yet more often with fratricidal hatred. So while much can be learned about the spirit and consequences of special operations from the wars and civil convulsions of Greece, that place and time offers us minimal comfort in the exercise of power today.

In ancient times, smallness and the simplicity of a world in which policies might be enacted and revoked overnight made for surprise and often startlingly sudden conquest. In our day (jumping from a time of tightly held slavocracies gathering news, at best, at horse pace to one of twenty-four-hours-a-day CNN and Al Jazeera), the complexity of society stands as a defense against takeovers so speedy and simple. Some distinguished scholars nonetheless present us the insights of classical study as a guide to the management of our refractory planet. For whatever reason, the Peloponnesian War is a favorite garden of policy analogies as to how Washington can wield its might and manage allies in a twenty-first-century "American empire."[25] It is all too easy to be taken prisoner by a hungry quest for precedent.

"Empire" is a happily multiplex word that stretches in time from well before the designs of Athens to America's present powers of cultural assimilation and military preeminence. Fortunately, not much return offers itself today on seeking anything that smacks of it. Only a state that combines marked technological advantage with a much longer-term political vision than most modern societies find comfortable — and one believably and steadily prepared to be as exemplarily, terribly, ruthless as Athens and Sparta — can expect to be feared as much as it will certainly be envied and hated. In our world, unlike that of Alcibiades, the nation that is supremely powerful can beat its hands bloody against ostensibly weak opponents but — because it is the most complex society of all — has the most to fear from small, stealthy strikes aiming for its heart.

3

Birth of World Power

A Longer Reach, from Alexander to the Barbarian Invasions of Rome, ca. 356 B.C. to Fifth Century A.D.

"To impose the ways of peace, to spare the conquered and wear down the proud."
VIRGIL, AENEID, ON THE DESTINY OF ROME

THE EMPIRES of Alexander and of Rome were the successive superpowers of the Mediterranean world, and not surprisingly such geographically vast ambitions awoke an enormous range of enemies. To be sure, there had been sweeping movements of whole nations before, as of the enigmatic "Sea Peoples" against Egypt around the time of the Trojan War. Whoever the Indo-Europeans were, they had settled as triumphant conquerors from Ireland to Bengal, whose languages remain related to this day. But these were fragmentary, improvised conquests. The Irish and Indian settlement myths may be identical, yet neither place knew that the other existed. No one before Alexander had set out to put worlds unknown under systematic administrative reporting to a central authority thousands of miles away. Vulnerabilities had to be found in enemies never imagined.

Alexander's father was Philip II, ruler of Macedon, that inhospitable angle between Greece and Bulgaria whose name has been bathetically revived with Communism's fall, and whose flag derives from the fiery sixteen-pointed sun that was Alexander's standard.

Macedonians had been among the military contractors, or mercenaries, employed during the Peloponnesian War, sometimes fighting for the Athenians, sometimes for the Spartans. Philip raised his quarrelsome frontier realm to be the first country to dominate all peninsular Greece, employing a faster, larger, more flexible and mobile professional fighting force, open to synthesizing men's skills irrespective of class, race, or dialect, unlike the old city-state militias among which only Sparta had ever maintained a standing army, and that built around a tiny elite. It was Philip's genius not to close his eyes to the military excellence of the brilliant cultures on his doorstep, but instead to make the most of them.

In his palace at Emathia the scarred, dissipated, voracious conqueror studied the machines of war that the Greeks had been developing: torsion catapults that fired arrows, elaborate battering rams, wheeled assault towers, all set to their ruinous work by skilled engineers unequaled anywhere else in the world. After Philip's murder in 336 B.C., Alexander continued his father's emphasis on thinking and rethinking war — applying speed, leverage, stealth, new kinds of skills and people, all faster, subtler, and stranger as the years went by. Almost in a flash, the Macedonian powerhouse generated mountain units, amphibious siege trains, stone-projecting catapults, and light troops prepared specially against such of the age's heavy-weapons systems as battle elephants, which made a terrifying first impression but proved just as startlingly vulnerable to quick-thinking troops prepared well in advance for most any contingency.

Against immense hostile strength massed opposite him, Alexander had to move like lightning or risk not moving at all as he swept from the Balkans into the Indian subcontinent. And here is a key difference from the wars of the city-states: select men who undertook extreme missions of opening passes, scaling cliffs, or conducting ambush far ahead of his conventional forces were more or less an integral part of his army. Commandos came to be used routinely as an instrument of war, repeatedly making the vital difference.

As for Rome, it basically produced armies intended for fighting big battles, emphasizing what the second-century B.C. Greek historian Polybius simply termed "brute force." Generally relying on entrenchment rather than long-distance scouting to handle unforeseen dangers, it was as organized around the spade as Alexander's army had been around the horse. Of course, Romans, however loudly they propagandized their straightforwardness and good faith, could be just as tricky as the Greeks had been during the Peloponnesian War and as ingenious as Alexander.[1] For example, the audacity combined with special tactics of a small force facing hundreds of thousands in urban combat had pivotal outcomes when led by Caesar. But when iron Rome faced an enemy actually built around preparations for this way of war — one that understood the leverage to be gained by commandolike detachments or larger-scale ambush, ultimately by the speed and surprise of long-distance raiding tactics — the unhappy consequences of emphasizing brute force proved to be telling.

‡

STEEPED IN the classics that were to him the distillation of his civilization's supremacy, Alexander is credibly reported to have read the *Iliad* ("Tale of Ilium," i.e., of Troy) every night and put its special casket under his pillow, along with a dagger. But what befell Troy would be child's play compared to the accumulation of death and misery as a new — and surely ordained — supremacy asserted itself upon the earth.

Alexander considered himself heir to the heroes who had followed Agamemnon, high king of the Greeks, to Troy. He seems to have been of medium height, vibrantly curious, beardless, with tousled blond hair, and brown eyes. He was handsome, irresistibly charming, terrifying in rage, gallant in his loyalties, savage when crossed. He took various wives for politics' sake and seems to have begotten children, but the great emotional companion in his life was the even more impressive-looking young Macedonian aristocrat Hephaestion, who fought alongside him. (Alexander is said to have actively disliked ugly people — a certain narcissism probably being useful to someone whom any degree of rational doubt would likely have kept about 3,000 miles west of where he actually went.) With Philip's murder, a splendid fighting force poised for the conquest of the mighty Persian Empire had passed into Alexander's impatient hands. Its core was the redoubtable Macedonian phalanx, its striking arm a magnificent cavalry from the river meadows of the Vardar, beyond the means of the stony little Greek states farther south. Few men twenty years old have ever possessed the drive of the willful new king; lacking Aristotle as a tutor, far fewer have been intellectually prepared for the opportunity.[2] Many have been better suited morally.

He led from the front, with a passion that few generals have come near to matching — whether in death-filled minutes plunging forward at the head of the riskiest charges on his unmistakable stallion, or over the exhausting years as a wandering star, pushing his troops to the edge of the world. Alexander had to confront obstacles outside anyone's experience: fighting nomads in the eerie landscape of central Asia, enduring and conquering in the spirit-rotting Indian monsoon, tormented by snakes and yet defeating elephants. And he did this at the far end of his supply lines, where no second chances existed. Time and again, he had to seek the fatal cracks in a massed power the magnitude of which he could not gauge.

In a way, the whole adventure could be described as long-term, long-range special warfare, undertaken by a body of men minute compared to their objectives, rarely larger than the current New York City police department, subduing millions. It was an extraordinary force that developed yet sharper points to bring off special operations one after another at vital moments. Like a surgeon on the side of death, Alexander remade the face of battle, by routinely identifying an enemy's particular vulnerability and bringing such insight to bear on a larger scale, confident that the men behind him had the right technology and talent.

Alexander may have been the greatest of all patrons of special warfare and, at times, as he swept forth from the Balkan hills to venture halfway across Eurasia, one of the most effective captains of commando detachments ever. On scales both large and small, he revealed how the most decisive point in combat is not necessarily the weakest, as the world had assumed: taking the seemingly impervious mountain redoubt, striking into the worst parts of his enemies' harshest regions, making a specialty of winter campaigns, and conducting night attacks were among the most dangerous and unpredictable tactics of his destiny-fixated progress. Moves took shape around intelligence gathering, with shrewd synthesis of the details of climate, botany, hydrology. ("Combat weathermen" are the special operators offering these insights today.) As do the Green Berets, he had specialists for psychological warfare and civil affairs. Their use was unprecedented. Among his milder practices was "leaking" to the enemy the unsettling (and sleep-depriving) possibility of a night attack. His dexterity in melding indigenous peoples to his ends was similarly novel.

Well before Alexander there had been corps d'élite to achieve objectives that the best conventional armies of their time could not handle. The Sacred Band, whose power as the spearpoint of Thebes had first taught Philip to appreciate the value of a permanent body of chosen warriors, was the finest force of its size in Greece — which is why Philip took pains to wipe it out at the battle of Chaeronea. And Philip himself had raised a heavily armored cavalry of shock troops, about thirty-three hundred riders known as the Companions, three hundred of whom were designated as his Royal Squadron body-guards, and from the Companions sprung the *prodromoi,* who conducted reconnaissance missions and entered pitched battles ahead of the cavalry. Among the infantry were Philip's crack unit of three thousand Shield Bearers. But from the outset, Alexander relied on well-sieved formations for particular tasks well beyond shock tactics: Guards, Agrianians ("the Gurkhas of antiquity"), and archers described by the classicist, biographer, and novelist Peter Green as "his regular commando brigade," a specially picked mobile force driving fast ahead of the army.[3] The young king seasoned them and himself in some heavy fighting in the Balkans.

Once these troops had been toughened up, beyond even his father's demands, Alexander could aim higher. If Asia was to be conquered, the barbarian-haunted northern frontier of Macedon had to be pacified first. In the spring of 335 B.C., he ferried fifteen hundred cavalry and four thousand foot soldiers across the Danube at night by having leather tent-covers stuffed with hay and sewn into makeshift floats, a technique he would use in Asia. The startled Celts of the European plain did not bolt, but they did negotiate. He destroyed Thebes as a terrible warning, other Greek cities being quick to understand his exemplary savagery. Then, in May 334, he turned full attention on Persia, an empire extending in the east to what is now Pakistan and, in the west and south, to the Libyan desert and the Arabian Gulf. He knew the empire of the Great King was a pyramid balancing on its crowned tip, the present sovereign being Darius.

Proclaiming a new Trojan War, Alexander crossed the Dardanelles that May at the head of some thirty-two thousand men, making his pilgrimage to the shrunken little township of Troy, taking part in devotions at what was billed by the enterprising locals as the tomb of Achilles. He bested an awaiting Persian army strengthened by Greek mercenaries near the river Granicus, the modern Biga Cay, after a surprise night crossing. He used his siege engines to break open the largest Greek city on the Aegean's eastern shore, then rapidly pressed toward the powerfully fortified port city of Halicarnassus (modern Bodrum). His was a war of movement; Alexander could not afford to starve out cities while the huge lands to the east mustered against him.

The Persian commander in Asia Minor was the most famous Greek mercenary general of that generation, Memnon, who drew upon what Green emphasizes was his own "commando force" in a night raid to burn Alexander's siege train outside the city, dividing his picked troops into two groups of a thousand men each, lunging forward with torches and pitch-buckets just before dawn. Halicarnassus nonetheless fell in the August heat, the Persian garrison escaping by sea. Alexander was then able to sway the region of Caria (in present-day southern Turkey), conciliating the bandit-guerrillas who in the past had been able to inflict terrible casualties on all invaders' armies.

Having achieved his nominal objective of freeing the many Greek cities of Asia Minor from Persian domination, Alexander embarked on the unheard-of idea of conquering Phoenicia. Should these city-states along today's Syrian–Lebanese–Israeli/Palestinian coast be taken, it was a good bet that no enemy navy could ever again sail into the Aegean. Moving southward, he eliminated Persian naval bases that could threaten his supply lines. Special operations are famously ungentlemanly, now as then: at the still-unidentified town of Hyparna, a group of dancing-girls and their slave attendants were sent up into the acropolis as a present for the Persian garrison commander, with daggers hidden in their flutes and small shields in their baskets. After dinner, when the wine had circulated freely, they proceeded to massacre their hosts, and Hyparna fell without further trouble.[4] It was not the first time a sharp operator had recognized that some of the most effective camouflage comes from our social blinders. But the rule that servants are, to all intents, invisible, particularly in more oppressive societies, paid off here.

After taking Hyparna, Alexander maneuvered inland, sent ahead "a quick commando raid" to deal with the sentries guarding a narrow gorge leading to the citadel of Termessus, then headed relentlessly onward to roll up Persian power in Anatolia, the great core plateau of what is now Turkey. Anatolia subjugated, he swung coastward at a marathon pace to confront the Great King.[5] Alexander first led his archers and crack light infantry into a night storming of the Cilician Gates, a potentially impregnable cliff-lined defile through the Taurus Mountains. Then, on a November morning, along the Gulf of Issus, north of Antioch, the invaders at last came face-to-face with Darius and his army of some sixty thousand hardened professionals. Following another "quick commando assault" by light-armed troops against Persian detachments in the hills behind the Macedonian right wing, Alexander confronted Darius on the plain.[6] A man brave enough in single combat, Darius turned his chariot in headlong flight as he saw the terrible Macedonian cavalry, with Alexander at its head, hacking its way toward him through his disintegrating guards. With Darius's defeat, a way was open — not to his capitals in the interior, but down the Mediterranean coast and into Persian-occupied Egypt. Tripolis (Tarablus today), Beirut, and Sidon each surrendered at the approach of the twenty-three-year-old prodigy. But not proud and ancient Tyre.

The siege of Tyre may have been the most arduously intense until the industrial capacities of a newer world shadowed it with the dread epics of Leningrad and Stalingrad. Situated on an island two miles long and a little less wide, Tyre was the strongest port in the great curve of coastline running from what is now southern Turkey to Egypt. A half mile offshore, it was the base of the invincible Phoenician navy and home port to crews in the Persian fleet, holding a garrison and citizenry of perhaps thirty thousand. Windswept waters were only part of Tyre's protection. A coastal island, if held in such strength, is not about to be reduced conventionally by ladders, battering rams, or fire.

The siege began in January 332 B.C. and lasted seven gruesome months. Alexander vowed to join the city island to the mainland and set about building a causeway. (It was to become part of his mystique, that he overcame nature as well as human foes.) To proceed, he had to use assault barges to get to the base of the city's walls, towering out of a deep, choppy sea. The Tyrian defenders deployed steel-reinforced super-bows, dumped boulders into the water to impede his boats, and shattered incoming projectiles by using some sort of wheels that revolved on the walls. Alexander's version of Seabees had to drag away obstacles as the Tyrian bolts hissed straight through armored men and the further-improvised leather shields protecting the siege-works. Meanwhile, Alexander assembled the world's two highest towers, 180 feet tall we are told, the engineers making them collapsible for easy transport; and a wheeled borer that could bring a long stone-tipped pole against the walling.

Thoroughly resourceful themselves, the Tyrians launched their own commando raids. A vessel otherwise used to transport horses was turned into a fireship (i.e., packed with chips, pitch, sulfur, and other combustibles) to ram into the causeway that was bloodily reaching across the strait, its crew swimming away once alight. Another party slipped in to slaughter the men carrying rocks from the shore. Others set Alexander's siege equipment ablaze — including the ultimate prize, his towers — the entire attack being executed within minutes. The combined operations, multiplying the havoc, were risky, fast, and deservedly successful — blows to the gut of an enemy that had thought itself indestructible.

Nor was that all. Tyrian divers cut the anchor cables of Alexander's boats. Some of their fellows used a forerunner of napalm (heated sand and fine gravel spilled from above) that worked into the assailants' eyes and armor (essential, given the crossbow bolts) and was likely to cook the wearers alive. But Tyre was trumped. Given Alexander's power to commandeer the fleets of the Phoenician cities already in his grasp, a new causeway was extended. He deployed special assault craft crammed with shock troops, his dismounted Guards cavalry leading the way.

On the city's hideous last day in July 332 B.C., around six thousand Tyrians perished in urban combat; many of that constricted city's thoroughfares were so narrow that soldiers could easily cross by leaping from roof to roof. Two thousand male survivors were crucified on the beach, to signal victory and generate tremors ahead. "Cast into the sea, all that wealth of hers," Zachariah had prophetically gloated about Tyre's fate, "and herself burnt to the ground."[7] It was to be an example to other stubborn patriots, as, for instance, those at Gaza, 125 miles farther down the coast.

To move with such imperial drive and scope, in an era when most people died within ten miles of where they were born, one must do things never before contemplated. And one of those was to turn the use of terror into an unprecedented instrument of policy.[8] Speed married to atrocity conferred left-right punching power, as did Alexander's orchestrating of his commandos with the army. All were part of the central enterprise of a strategy that had no room for patience.

When Alexander came before Gaza, its inhabitants still thought their city impregnable. They were wrong but made enough of a point to enrage him. The adult male population was killed to a man; the women and children sold into slavery. After Gaza, he went on to Egypt (absorbed into the Persian Empire since Cambyses' Battle of the Cats), his army and navy in December reaching what is now Port Said. He installed new rulers, founded the world city that bears his name today, Alexandria, garrisoned it with Jewish mercenaries, consulted oracles, and, by late May 331 B.C., looped back toward Tyre. Within weeks, he had left the Mediterranean world behind him forever, to cross the Euphrates, then the Tigris in September, before reaching a killing field on the plains of Assyria (modern northern Iraq) chosen by Darius himself. There the Great King was again defeated in pitched battle and again fled eastward.

Darius's one hope was to directly knock off Alexander, assassination by individually dispatched operators or tiny hit teams being a staple of special warfare right through today. Without a dedicated band of killers honed for such stealth, he had to offer one thousand talents — say, twenty thousand years' pay for a skilled soldier or craftsman — to anyone who might succeed. Instead, it would be Darius who would be murdered, by one of his own ministers, after Alexander had hunted the throneless king and the remnants of his court to the strange lands of the Persian Empire's far east. After a pursuit south of the Caspian Sea, it was not an army that finally closed in, nor even Alexander's cavalry, but a specially picked, fast-riding nighttime detachment of some sixty hardened Macedonian infantry officers on horseback, with Alexander at its head.

By summer 330 B.C., Alexander had conquered all lands to the very eastern edge of the faintest civilized presence; indeed, some of that presence must have been Chinese. But at this moment, so close to India, he was unimaginably far from home, much farther than Caesar would ever be from Rome, or Cortés from Spanish authority. He was trying to impose order on the savage lands that threatened from the north, lands that we now call Turkmenistan and Afghanistan, only to hear of a rising in Sogdia (Uzbekistan/Tadjikistan) and Bactria. If Alexander lost control of the frontier territories, his grip on his immense conquests to the southwest could be imperiled. His movement had been so rapid that he had no established legitimacy to hold the resentful peoples before and behind. As Bonaparte would sigh centuries later, it takes very few defeats to unmake a self-made man. Alexander might be a king in Greece, but here he was just the latest of so many marauders.

Enforcing some sort of cowed peace on the mile-high Kabul Valley, Alexander came, probably in spring 327, to the apparently unscalable pinnacle known as the Sogdian Rock, a mountain fortress that was the rebels' impregnable stronghold and wherein Oxyartes, the principal chieftain of Bactria, had sought refuge with his family. At more than three miles high and fifteen miles round, it is east of Derbend, near Baysun-Tao, on the mountain border of what today is Pakistan and Afghanistan, now prowled again by Western special forces on the hunt.[9]

Disaster-inflicting frontiers have a way of dissolving imperial authority at the center — from the first Great King Darius, who had perished in these lands two centuries before Alexander burst into them to, say, the prolonged Soviet agony of less than twenty years ago. This time, the intruders' opponents enjoyed a position of unheard-of strength in this greatest of eagles' nests. No fewer than thirty thousand Sogdians had provisioned themselves with two years' worth of food from the systematically scorched and stripped countryside around, while Alexander's army was cold, exhausted, and hungry. Deep snow above provided the defenders with unlimited drinking water. From their battlements atop the sheer-faced cliffs, they could hold out indefinitely against an assailant unable to maintain an equally open-ended siege; delay, in this unpitying land, meant failure.

Alexander's men encamped before the mountain. With all his triumphant authority, Arrian tells us, Alexander demanded surrender to the conqueror of Darius, the Great King himself. (And Arrian is the one surviving classical historian of Alexander who had had military experience.) "Let your master find winged soldiers!" cried back the mocking heralds from their advanced posts — that, surely, being the only way this wonder of the world could possibly be taken.[10]

Alexander believed supremely in himself; but, like all great commanders, he believed equally in his men. He did not have actual mountain troops, although his army contained some experienced cragsmen. Mountaineering itself would be a Victorian invention, and Mount Olympus, less daunting than most of the Rockies, was first climbed only in 1913. But if he recoiled from the Sogdian Rock, the word of his retreat might go out across Asia and his conquests could unravel. In this, and in other crucial moments of history, we cannot embrace the counterfactual to assert what might have occurred had the Rock remained impregnable. But, as in examples to come, we can argue that commando action was indeed decisive in its fall.

Alexander needed men brave enough, skillful enough, and plain strong enough to go up, and against horrible conditions. His generals searched through the army. Offering immense rewards from the plundered treasuries of Persia to the first twelve men to reach the crest, Alexander prevailed upon three hundred to attempt the rockface, using iron tent pegs as pitons (those devices themselves being millennia yet to come) to drive into the solidly frozen snow and brief exposures of bare earth; the pegs would be tightly linked to strong flaxen lines. Compensation was in fame and coin: a man might earn a lifetime's pay for one night's work.

Of course, no one had ever done such work, whether by day or night. But by night it must be. The sheerest part of the cliffs would

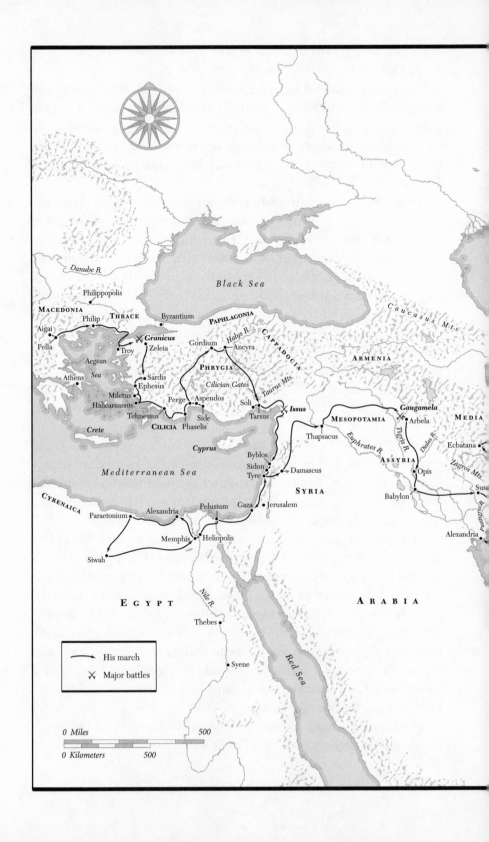

Black Sea

Danube R.

Philippopolis

MACEDONIA   **THRACE**   Byzantium   **PAPHLAGONIA**

Aigai   Philip   ✕ *Granicus*   *Halys R.*   *Caucasus Mts.*

Pella   Troy   Zeleia   Gordium   Ancyra   **CAPPADOCIA**

Aegean   **PHRYGIA**   **ARMENIA**

Athens   Sea   Sardis   *Cilician Gates*   *Taurus Mts.*

Miletus   Ephesus   Perge   Aspendos   Soli   ✕ *Issus*   *Gaugamela*   **MEDIA**

Halicarnassus   Telmessus   Side   Tarsus   **MESOPOTAMIA**   Arbela

Crete   **CILICIA**   Phaselis   Thapsacus   *Tigris R.*   Ecbatana

Cyprus   *Euphrates R.*   *Didas R.*

Byblos   **ASSYRIA**   Opis   *Zagros Mts.*

Mediterranean Sea   Sidon   Damascus   Susa

Tyre   **SYRIA**   Babylon

CYRENAICA   Pelusium   Gaza   Jerusalem   Alexandria

Paraetonium   Alexandria   Memphis   Heliopolis

Siwah   **EGYPT**   **ARABIA**

Nile R.

Thebes

Red Sea

Syene

→ His march
✕ Major battles

0 Miles   500
0 Kilometers   500

ALEXANDER THE GREAT

•

336–322 B.C.

Aral Sea

Jaxartes R.

Oxus R.

Tashkent

Maracanda (Samarkand)

Alexandria eschate (Alexandria-the-Furthest)

Sogdian Rock

Sogdiana

Cyropolis

Nautaca

Caspian Sea

Ochus R.

MARGIANA

Bactra

Drapsaca

Zadracarta

Hecatompylos

Susia

Khaiwak Pass

Hindu Kush

Kumar R.

Indus R.

Rhagae (Teheran)

Caspian Gates

PARTHIA

Alexandria Areion

BACTRIA

Dyrta

Aornos

Orthospana (Cabura)

Cophen R.

Taxila

Khyber Pass

Bucephala

Aspadana (Isfahan)

ARACHOSIA

Nicaea

Sangala

Farah (Prophthasia)

Lake of Seistan

Alexandria Arachosiorum

Hydaspes R.

Acesines R.

Hydraotes R.

Beas R.

Pasargadai

Zaradrus (Sutlej) R.

Hyphasis R.

Persian Gates

Persepolis

CRATERUS

CRATERUS

Alexandria Opiana

Indus R.

I N D I A

Sitacus R.

PERSIS

CARMANIA

Tarua

Anamis R.

Pura

GEDROSIA

Indus R.

Dotted line indicates probable course of the Indus in Alexander's time

Hormozia

Gedrosian Desert

Rhambacia (Bela)

Persian Gulf

Cophas

Strait of Hormuz

Pattala

ROUTE OF NEARCHUS

Alexander's Port (Karachi)

Coast line

Arabian Sea

© 2005 Jeffrey L. Ward

likely be the least guarded, and so it was there that the three hundred set out upward into the storm and darkness. Thirty fell "so that their bodies were never found in the snow," says Arrian, their screams lost in the howling storm.[11] Although such cries must have cracked the night every few minutes, the others did not turn back. They climbed on, inventing mountaineering as they went, until at dawn they could brandish fragments of cloth to signal frostbitten triumph to their comrades below.

Again, Alexander's heralds went beneath the unbroken walls, to the enemy's advance posts. "Look up! Look up! Our king has found his winged soldiers." And then 270 rock-bloodied, frozen, dagger-armed madmen rose along the crest, and the great gates creaked open in subjugation — even though the defenders may have outnumbered the mountaineers by something like a hundred to one. Perhaps they had *all* climbed up, trembled the Sogdians. It was a magnificent coup de théâtre, enough in itself to make a reputation to outlast the ancient world, the deception having been amplified by Alexander's hiding his main force from the enemy's sight far above.

To bind in alliance the peoples he left behind, Alexander got a queen, Roxane, one of Oxyartes' daughters, out of this victory, and, in time, a son. Today, Mediterranean blood groups exist in northern India (since the Greeks kept expanding in the Punjab) in no small part because Alexander did not try to throw his entire army against a rock — an order that would have been as futile as it sounds. It could not otherwise have been won.

Then a second rock well to the east was taken, about two miles high and six miles round, the rebels' final redoubt. The attackers were similarly mocked from above, until, in this case, a bridge could be built across a ravine to the mountaintop, and the laughter died. As he began his campaign into the subcontinent, Alexander approached the Indus near modern Palosi. Resisters fled to a mountain fortress called Aornos (to the Indians, "hiding place"; to the Greeks, "too high for birds"), modern Pir Sar.[12] The engineering behind his assault there was revolutionary (a great wooden cribwork between two peaks), but what is impressive for our story is that the man by now proclaimed "king of the world" did not hesitate to pull himself by rope up the rockface, leading an assault team of Shield Bearers, the cream of his troops, a feat comparable to the chairman of the Joint Chiefs commanding a Ranger company.

The last person to enduringly conquer Afghanistan, Alexander had intended to win his way east through India, the ultimate frontier, beyond which the world was thought to sink into the Eastern Ocean. What would have happened had this pupil of Aristotle found out that he was wrong, that there were lands beyond? What if he had pressed on through Assam, through Burma, Thailand, the vaguely known "Golden Chersonese" of the Malay Peninsula? North through Indochina to break upon the Warring States of the Middle Realm? But not even Alexander could exact those steps from his Macedonians (Philip's men, many in their fifties and sixties) and mercurial Greek mercenaries. So back he came: just over six months spent going down the Indus to its delta (taking time out to massacre everyone in an obstreperous city, including babies); then a deadly three-month march across the dread Iranian coastal desert long known to devour armies, as it did most of his own, and onward to modern Kirman, in eastern Iran.

Had his life not ended in Babylon at thirty-three, surely over the next ten years Alexander would have raised more troops, easily drawn by his victories and plunder, and gone on not only to overturn Carthage and undercut its empire in Spain and Sardinia, but to strike at the tempting Italian peninsula. And then who knew? But some spring broke — or was broken — and the overheated engine ran down, Alexander ultimately to lie near the Mediterranean, in a tomb still undiscovered beneath the greatest of his eponymous cities, Alexandria.

Imagination in war may be at its most potent, its most consequential, when it is applied in modes we have come to identify as special operations: precise targeting, self-reliance, breadth of technique, constant rethinking, an eye for vulnerabilities and leverage unknown to the enemy, and for resources never before uncovered in one's own people — all frequently at some distance from any hope of backup. We lack any account of how Alexander's commandos were able to reconnoiter an objective, determine the approaches, or get the generals to understand the specific problems their way. But with Alexander we see the special operation passing from a onetime act of crafty heroism into reasoned procedure, fostered by a sense of horizon-wide opportunities. He combined with it a belief that a certain kind of man can do anything if he is prepared to challenge the very limits of the possible.

With Alexander's death came the parceling out of his universe. Vast conquered provinces that had generally sound administration were exposed to the unchained ambitions of his all-too-energetic surviving marshals, their sudden new kingdoms falling into prolonged internecine war. None of those astounding warriors or their successors could replicate his drive and techniques: Ptolemy just had the good sense to seize the highly defensible lands of Egypt; and even Demetrios, son of another ambitious general turned warlord, still remembered in our day as "the Besieger of Cities," made his name mostly by starving out enemies.[13] A new science of war — and a grimmer, much more collective spirit — was required to place high enterprise again at the center. It would come, not from sparkling Greece, but from dour, sturdy Rome, a state of which it is by no means certain that Alexander had ever heard.

‡

IN THE densely populated Italian peninsula, an efficient engineering civilization was coming into being, only half noticed by the high seaborne cultures reaching out from the eastern Mediterranean, a civilization resting on roads, dams, aqueducts. Its philosophies were not debated in Alexandria; it fostered no philosophers worth reading for their own ideas. Its dramatists, when finally it got any, cannibalized Greek plays.[14] Museums do not compete seriously for its original statuary. But in creating the work of art that is a potentially universal state, Rome certainly had the skills. Today, five hundred miles outside Athens in any direction, no community speaks Greek as a mother tongue; Latin has left its mark on the planet, from Bucharest by way of Manila to New York.

As the comparatively unglamorous reach of Rome fastened itself on ever more alien peoples, it had to face many of the problems Alexander had solved, at least temporarily, with personal genius. Rome established dependable means of deploying superior numbers, instilling esprit de corps, of ensuring leadership in depth. If, as a consequence, the devil-may-care, crushed-hat commando dash was not nourished, that was the price of a system that pursued the welfare of the Republic over star quality. In doing this, Rome introduced a bureaucratization of war, an approach that tended to discourage brilliantly spontaneous operations. A new military formation evolved, superseding the phalanx of spears and overlapping shields: the legion (varying in numbers but around 4,500 men) became the most effective fighting force of its time. At its core were armored infantry units, fighting in closed ranks with short swords, confident of being backed by a competent medical corps. With minimal cavalry, let alone the "commandos" advanced by Alexander, it was a one-armed army for most of its existence — among its deficiencies being its unsuitability for fighting guerrillas or for meeting any finely crafted special operation turned against it.[15]

The Roman notion of the concentrated power of surprise came down repeatedly to extraordinary accomplishment in what today is called combat engineering: bridges thrown over impassable rivers such as the Rhine rather than paddling across (a conscious display of majesty, as Caesar makes clear, to intimidate the Germans, peering in awe out of their forests); other rivers dammed and diverted, tossed out of their beds like pillows, enabling the enemy to be hit en masse. If Rome also initially displayed little inventive genius in artillery, other aspects of military science were as powerfully systematized as could be hoped in a civilization without printing and the quantitative techniques we know as accounting.[16] Here we encounter the epitome of what in the twentieth century would be called "the business of war": large-scale operational thinking, repeatable, resting in confidence on well-trained junior officers and NCOs.[17]

What is extraordinary in the Roman way of war was not the sort of daring that sends three hundred men up a pinnacle in the howling dark. In the Roman world, the quick and the audacious were accomplished in more predictable ways — particularly employing the remarkable Roman science of drill to focus destiny into the ten bloody seconds that can mean the difference between success and catastrophe. To perform complex moves, however rote-rehearsed in peace, when one's life is at stake, is not robotic thinking. Indeed, sophisticated and rigorous practice could result in a deeper bench of potentially exceptional people. When the need for an unconventional mission did arise, a Roman centurion knew that if he looked in the right places he would find the right men and techniques. But the possibilities of special warfare were unlikely to be front and center in his mind, let alone in those of his superiors, as is seen when Rome encountered the one foreign master of war it ever feared before its final days.

The Carthaginian empire was the greatest naval power of the third-century B.C. Mediterranean, centered on a North African city near modern-day Tunis, founded centuries earlier by colonists from Tyre. From a land far more fertile than today, Carthage controlled the coast from western Libya to the Straits of Gibraltar; eventually most of well-populated central-southern Spain, in addition to the islands of Corsica and Sardinia; and the greater part of the huge island of Sicily, lying between the Carthaginian heartland and the southern tip of the Italian peninsula, then just falling under Roman dominance. Perhaps inevitably, this mighty power would clash with Rome, which knew the Carthaginians as Phoenicians, the word in Latin being *Poeni,* giving us the name for what followed: the Punic Wars.

The first war ended in 241 B.C. Carthage lost its holdings in Sicily, paid reparations, and was left too weak to resist Rome's snapping up Corsica and Sardinia not long thereafter. Twenty years later, twenty-six-year-old Hannibal rose to command in Carthaginian Spain. Already sworn by his implacable family to confront the menacing republic, he sacked a coastal city-state lying about halfway between the Ebro river and the Carthaginian capital of Spain (still known as Cartagena, "New Carthage," twenty-two centuries later) that had aligned itself with Rome. He was not turned over for punishment.

A hundred and five years after Alexander, Rome — with an approach to war that time and again fell short when the playbook changed — was hit by what one student of the times justly calls blitzkrieg, a lightning thrust by way of the barbarian North into Italy.[18] An invading army that lost perhaps 70 percent of its strength on the grueling march of more than one thousand miles over two mountain ranges set out to unravel Roman supremacy on a peninsula which, according to Livy, raised about thirty times as many men against it.

Hannibal, with a corps d'élite of Carthaginian officers, led a mercenary mixture of Libyan and Iberian infantry, Celtiberians, Balearic slingers, and North African Numidian tribesmen, the most skillful horsemen known. (He spoke at least four of their languages.) Once across the wild Pyrenees, he entered the unknown lands of the savage Gauls, an anarchic culture of forty or fifty tribes dangerously quick to learn. Brushing them aside, he then deceived two Roman legions and a host of their allies along the Rhone about the direction of his march. Before beginning the hitherto inconceivable venture of taking an army through the Alps, he overcame other tribesmen lying in wait along a deathtrap gorge by deploying "a commando force" perhaps assembled from Spanish mountain troops, which he led at night to the heights above, swooping down like eagles at first light to tear the would-be ambushers to pieces.[19]

Coming through the perilous immensity of the Alpine peaks (possibly via the Col de Montgenèvre), Hannibal emerged in November somewhere near modern Turin. Perhaps twenty thousand infantry and six thousand cavalry on bony horses survived the march from Spain and the final fifteen-day ordeal of avalanche, hacking roads at ten thousand feet, and the equally dangerous descent — as did thirty-seven small, emaciated elephants. When he chose the long way around, rather than nipping across the warm waters from North Africa to Sicily, Hannibal must have known that only a fraction of his men would live. Now a stripped-down force of the toughest faced Rome. It was special warfare from the start.

Sometime near the winter solstice, with ever more Gallic auxiliaries from the Po Valley rallying to his side, he slaughtered thousands of the shaken defensive forces in a spectacular victory along the river Trebbia, west of modern Piacenza, having entrusted to his youngest brother, Mago, "a commando group of 200 men, 100 infantry and 100 cavalry, whom he had personally selected during the day."[20] Each of these men thereupon chose nine others from among their comrades. The Romans were lured through the freezing water to confront Hannibal's cavalry and foot soldiers, only to be sliced into from behind by the selected men lying in ambush. Remnants of the consular armies withdrew into Cremona and other garrison towns.

Within two months this insolent young warrior controlled all of northern Italy. No need for elephants — just as well, since by now only a single pathetic specimen remained. Instead, the ferocious Gauls — equipping themselves with Roman shields and armor — who were to form the bulk of his army for many of the years ahead, were discovering the delights of mobility and plunder in a developed world much less secure than it had believed.

Pushing south, Hannibal annihilated an entire twenty-five thousand-man Roman army in an ambush in Tuscany near Lake Trasimene, intercepting and destroying four thousand reinforcements en route. Two neighboring towns still bear the ill-omened names Ossaia (bone-yard) and Sanguineto (bloodied).[21] After these defeats, significantly larger enemy forces (Rome was always able to call on more and more men for its citizen armies) shadowed Hannibal systematically, refusing to be drawn into battle as he bypassed Rome to cross the Apennines toward the Bay of Naples. Once the Carthaginians drove into the rich plain of Campania, the shrewd Roman commander suspected they would trek back across the mountains after they were heavy with loot. He blocked the crucial pass near Mount Massicus with four thousand men, the main force encamping on high ground overlooking the approach road. The Carthaginians riposted with a double bluff designed to be seen through at first glance.

One night the waiting Roman general saw thousands of lights moving up the hillsides above the pass, clearly a marching column trying to force passage. Expecting another trick of the slippery Semitic enemy (the Romans relished ethnic stereotyping), he once more refused to be drawn out, confident that his garrison at the pass would deal with whatever those lights moving up and over the crest might be. The troops at the pass, however, believing themselves outflanked, raced up the hill to intercept, only to be trampled by some two thousand oxen with burning torches tied to their horns, driven by a few dozen of Hannibal's scouts. A small force of Carthaginian light pikemen waited their moment in the shadows. The winded and disordered Romans obligingly delivered themselves among the beasts and fire into their enemy's hands, to be impaled or chased into the dark while Hannibal's main army silently slipped through the now wide-open pass below. At dawn, he sent up a contingent of Spanish mountain troops to finish the Romans off.

On August 2, 216 B.C., at Cannae in southeastern Italy, Hannibal enveloped and in noonday heat obliterated a Roman army nearly twice as large, bringing upon Rome the numerically largest catastrophe of its history, and inspiring generals down to the first Gulf War of our own day.[22] Just as in that brief, triumphant 1991 encounter, elements of special warfare made themselves felt. In the cautious maneuvering before proper battle was joined, Hannibal detailed some six hundred Numidian cavalry to feign desertion to the enemy. Surrendering their swords and shields, they were sent to the rear where, once the roar of combat arose, they whipped out hidden daggers, picked up the shields of the first soldiers cut down, and struck from behind the lines.[23] Not commando training or organization, but the right stuff.

Hannibal might then have marched on Rome, expecting to receive entreaties for peace that would reverse the humiliations inflicted on Carthage during his infancy. But sound as was his sense of day-to-day rulebook Roman culture, he had not gauged it in extremity — implacable in its will to endure, its iron ruthlessness even forbidding public mourning for the dead of Cannae. When he finally did bring his army beneath the heavily fortified walls of the Eternal City in 211, the Romans (according to the victors' history) contemptuously auctioned off to speculators the real estate on which he camped, while the Carthaginians milled around outside, unable to complete their siege. Surely that land would be valuable as the indomitable city grew.

The Romans gradually pressed the genius enemy back south, into a kind of troublemaker's war in the toe of Italy, where Hannibal was aligned with disaffected Greek city-states. He now exploited his long experience as an unwelcome guest by sending Latin-speaking infiltrators in local garb into towns across the Mezzogiorno (the hot, "high noon" Italian South); others disguised themselves as hunters carrying game to finagle their way into Tarentum (Taranto) — through a combination of "commando tactics," according to one of the many scholars who have studied the campaign, and betrayal from within that enabled his men to silently penetrate the gates of this bustling port city at night.[24] But the tide had turned.

Rome's rather rare ability to do the unexpected (doubling up the armies of two notoriously feuding consuls in a single camp) ensured the destruction of Hannibal's other brother, Hasdrubal, who had brought reinforcements through the Alps in hopes of joining hands in the south to form an army strong enough for total victory. This cost Hannibal his last possible margin of success; but even then he could prolong a debilitating war on the enemy's soil. Meanwhile, Roman forces took Cartagena, and with their naval superiority in the western Mediterranean pushed forward from Sicily against Carthage itself. Hannibal's ragged yet unbeaten army was recalled too late to face Rome's thrust to the heart and — without his cavalry — meeting greater numbers and superb generalship, went down before the gates of the home city. After that, it was just a question of the legions mopping up, Rome imposing a yet more devastating treaty, and, in time, having its agents track the exiled Hannibal to a remote kingdom in northern Asia Minor; his house surrounded, he took the poison he always carried with him, dying beaten but unbroken.

Hannibal had been able to push Rome to the edge by improvisation, hypermobility, and a repertoire of special assaults in a still slow-moving, rule-bound age. Increasingly outnumbered, he had maintained fifteen terrifying years' presence in Italy by floating light as a butterfly, stinging like a bee, while the provoked buffalo, great Rome, lunged always a second too late. But while the buffalo's bulk may be ridiculous against some of its enemies (one thinks of Indians with spears chasing them bareback), there are circumstances where its sheer strength is indomitable. Transforming itself from a regional power into an increasingly sprawling sea-basin empire, Rome provoked the third Punic War. Progress was brutal and, in its way, routine. In 149 B.C., the diminished but still energetic Carthage was subjected to a ruthless preventive war, which it yet was able to stall into an incredible three-year siege. Once its walls were breached, there followed perhaps the greatest block-by-contested-block destruction of a city's inhabitants, before World War II. Something like a quarter of a million people died in the reeking streets or helped pay off their conquerors' war debts in the slave markets of the Middle Sea.

‡

TIME AND again in our story we find ourselves having to look through the eyes of men instinctively alert to the weaknesses of others, who can find within themselves and put to work the crucial difference of speed, leverage, needlelike penetration, and means of destruction, who seek to command men solely of proven superior prowess rather than of birth or background, who expect them to demand and be able to endure the truth. We encounter such qualities in Alexander and in Hannibal — men for whom imagination and the unprecedented were ultimate facts of power, and their possession a kind of brotherhood — but also, now coming onstage, a much subtler, more flippant grandee.

Many war heroes become successful politicians; few successful politicians become war heroes, let alone conquerors. At the top of the list, from a family of his country's highest aristocracy, stands Caius Julius Caesar, probably born in 100 B.C. The date makes him two years below the legal age when he received the consulship in 60 B.C., which may indicate either that the year of birth is wrong or (more likely) his insouciant approach to the turbulent politics of Rome. Alexander was his model, to the extent that this unemotional man had one, much as Alexander had drawn on the example of the heroes of the Trojan War.

Busts of Caesar show an austere, intelligent, coolly authoritative face. We read of his keen dark eyes. He was likely of medium height for his class and, as a horseman who spent his later life in ceaseless movement, probably leanly muscled.[25] He shared some of Alexander's narcissism, being famously concerned about his receding hairline, but his character is far more interesting, given his immense library, his much respected poetry, and his world-class collection of cameos. He had an artistic sense, as well as a feeling for proportion — although not when it came to his deeply felt sense of entitlement to ultimate power. Such of his colossal indebtedness not arising from the sinister necessities of Roman politics was due to the breathtaking scope of his sculpture gallery. Immune to flattery, he knew his strengths and demanded ever more of his mind and body to enable him to fulfill them. Of his weaknesses he did not speak, but he was known to have epilepsy (adding to his aura in a culture that regarded it as a sacred disease) and once faked its onset to avoid arrest.

Caesar was already middle-aged when he came to exercise high command, having essentially none of the prolonged, hard military experience expected of the young Roman elite. His appointment was entirely due to political accident, the luck of the draw of provinces routinely assigned to an outgoing consul: he received the beleaguered governorship of Rome's then narrowly coastal Gaulish territories ("the Province"; now Provence) when its previous holder dropped dead of a too-ardent liaison. In the Roman system, the civil administrator on the imperial rim was the responsible field commander. Most men of Caesar's class had served their apprenticeship by soldierly stages, alternating with a rising career in civil office at home, before reaching the big jobs.[26] To be sure, Caesar had lived amid continuous upheaval as the old republic tried to digest its conquests and handle the conquerors nominally in its service. But for this assignment, while in his early forties — a decade that in the last century before Christ was closer to old age than it is today — he had to turn himself within weeks from, say, the type of smart lawyer who reads the medical articles in *Scientific American* into an emergency-room surgeon.

Caesar was much more a politician compelled to make war than a professional soldier reaching the test of his career. His tactics were mundane, his scouting poor, his handling of cavalry timorous — but his ability to turn an enemy's most fleeting moment of vulnerability into a fatal mistake was uncanny. Cicero, who rightly feared and distrusted him, nevertheless had to call him "a portent of incredible speed, application and insight."[27] In modern times, such high-risk politicians in the role of warlord would rather naturally set out to be patrons of special operations, like Churchill. In his hard-pressed world, Caesar was a counterpuncher of genius with an unsleeping faith in his own destiny.

His remarkable enterprises as a general were in the open field, especially when crossing, diverting, exploiting rivers, and, at last, in the imaginative use of artillery (lightweight arrow-firers) to defend camps or onboard ships to support amphibious landings. He had a corps d'élite, but it was only partway to a special force. (His Tenth Legion was a steely formation with a justified cult of being able to take punishment, a quality rather contrary to exercising guile.) He created German horseguard units, with men who were ceaselessly trained, fast moving, lightly armed, and masters at swimming rivers. But those warriors were notorious for being "carried away by emotions," according to the historian Flavius Josephus, not to be relied on to "reason about what they do." They may have been special in their functions and in their talents, but like the Tenth, they too lacked the guile of the special warrior, let alone the cool, careful honing of a modern commando force.[28]

From the outset, Proconsul Caesar faced colossal challenges both in the field and on the home front. His first years of command found him marching for the most part against the Gauls. He also dealt with the first serious manifestation of what our grandparents would know as the German Question, that swelling of Teutonic power into neighboring lands. Ambition spurred him to invade Britain, a place previously known to just a few wandering merchants. All this in the nine years from 58 B.C. to 50 B.C.

On the far side of the Alps, however, the Roman order was imploding. One complex of factions gathered behind Pompey the Great — Caesar's elder, friend, son-in-law, and for a generation Rome's leading general, elected "consul without colleague" in 52 B.C., in the interests of public peace. But Caesar discarded friendship to take arms against the Republican oligarchy with which Pompey had thrown his lot. Five years later, the western half of the empire was in Caesar's hands. He overcame Pompey's much-augmented army in Greece in 48 B.C. and chased him to Egypt, where, at the instigation of Ptolemy XIII's chief eunuch, Pompey was stabbed to death as he landed at Alexandria.

For more than a century, Rome had been closing in on cosmopolitan Alexandria, having consumed the other realms that stood successor to Alexander, imposing puppet rulers on the Jews to the northeast, on the Libyan Greeks to the west. The strongest local faction had hoped to gain Caesar's political support in a dynastic rivalry for their thirteen-year-old king's elder sister (and wife, in the old Egyptian way, Macedonian though the dynasty was), Cleopatra VII. Whether or not Cleopatra had herself delivered to Caesar rolled up naked in a carpet, he set aside his pursuit of the Pompeian diehards for subtler intrigues. When Caesar unearthed a plot against him (recalling the Alexandrians as "the fittest instruments in the world for treason"), he had the conspiring chief eunuch killed during a banquet. The next move was all too predictable: Alexandria rose against him. The fighting that followed may be familiar to graduates of the Special Forces Advanced Urban Combat Course, instituted after the Rangers and Delta Force commandos were cornered and killed in Mogadishu: but Caesar's cohorts had to learn on the spot.

With no more than two thousand troops, Caesar faced both an enraged population of about half a million and an Egyptian army described as a "countless host" — perhaps one rather more respected then than now, being fundamentally Greek, and including Roman veterans who had made their home in the country.[29] The small Roman presence found itself besieged in the palace precincts for nearly six months. Counterattack merely lost itself in a labyrinthine city that offered no scope for those deadly, disciplined powers of drill.

Immediately, Caesar had to fortify the Roman-occupied quarter, massing shields into mantelets, piercing walls for sniping and sallies, tearing down houses to build barricades, and constructing the torsion engines that served the ancients for artillery. The Alexandrians shut off all the avenues with a triple wall some forty feet high, dammed the canals, contaminated the drinking supply with seawater, called up vast numbers of soldiers, and thrust multiple-storied mobile towers against the Roman works to rake the ground inside. Caesar had succeeded in keeping the harbor entrance free, but escape by sea would likely have been suicidal. Had he allowed his terrified men to try to board ship, they would have been slaughtered by their nimble opponents, who knew the streets and could throw tiles, hot pitch, and spears from the rooftops: it would have been an antlike envelopment, as in Mogadishu.

Ordering his centurions to get fresh-water wells dug in the fore-shore, Caesar slipped dispatch boats to summon food, reinforcements, and like-minded predators — archers from Crete, cavalry from the Nabataeans of the Sinai Peninsula — urging the latter to raid at will, knowing that the speed and range of these desert fighters would shake the city-bred forces. The Egyptian fleet had far more and larger ships with which to sever his sea communications, but not enough strength to storm his hard-held position. By setting fire to the docks amid the scramble to keep the Egyptians at bay, this genuinely cultivated man thereby also destroyed warehouses of the world's greatest library. But still the Alexandrians swarmed. In the chaos of the amphibious fighting, Caesar found himself alone and about to be killed. He threw off his purple cloak and jumped into the sea. "The enemy hunted for him," the Greek historian Appian of Alexandria would write, "but he swam a long way under water without being seen, drawing breath only at intervals, until he approached a friendly ship."[30] He might have been the fifty-odd-year-old master of Rome, but this was the stuff of a SEAL "bullfrog" chief petty officer.

Cut off from the outside world, Caesar maintained his fingernail hold on Alexandria until relief arrived, including three thousand Jews from Cilicia and Syria. The tide turned, and he ultimately defeated the army of young Ptolemy XIII, who drowned as his rabble panicked in the Nile marshes; then Caesar reinstalled Cleopatra (the many times great-granddaughter of Alexander's marshal) as queen, and set out for Syria. Staying behind, she bore what she claimed to be his son.

His last and, he himself considered, bitterest battle came in March 45 B.C. at Munda, somewhere in central Spain, against a Republican coalition gathered round Pompey's sons. At least fifty-four years old then, he still could fling himself from his horse to fight on foot, showing his men he was not just there, but sharing their risks. The only contemporary account of this showdown is so short on detail as to make it impossible to fit into the known topography. But the anonymous author of the *Bellum Hispaniense* offers a glimpse of the transformation of a hideous attritional action by highly unusual inspiration. Strategy had availed nothing; everything had come down to a huge battering of legions, sword to sword, in the choking dust.

A raid by North African cavalry on the baggage train compelled the Pompeian commander to disengage some of his men and to deploy them rearward. But since those men apparently carried standards (both totemic objects of mystique and battlefield markers of organization), such a move was alarmingly visible to their fellows. Amid the screams of a desperate fight on the *meseta,* the Pompeian line held without difficulty. But this well-coordinated maneuver looked like flight. Caesar himself probably raised the cry, "They fly! They fly!" Down the disintegrating enemy battle line ran terrified mistrust and the urge to save oneself. Once confidence wavered, the reputation of the greatest of captains did the rest.

Taking ship for Rome, Caesar was made *dictator perpetuus* in February 44 B.C. But just weeks later, in March, the daggers came out from beneath the grandees' togas. He fought to the last blow, parrying the assassins' blades with a pencil knife. The mystique remained, his name forever synonymous with terms for sovereign power: Kaiser, Keyser, Tsar, right through the title "Kaisar-I-Hind" (Emperor of India) given up by George VI in 1947, only twenty-two years before the moon landing.

‡

THE OPENING scenes of the movie *Gladiator* give an impression of what a fascinating archeological study describes as "perhaps the most important battle in European history."[31] By 9 A.D., Germanic warriors, of all people, were held in contempt and considered thoroughly pacified (that euphemism for relentless application of the sword).[32] Special operations almost always involve a deadly combination of acute intelligence gathering and precision planning on one side, and a decided lack of imagination and humility on the other. In this case, the German warriors chose a perfect killing ground: the gloomy Teutoburg Forest, dense with late summer oak and birch, pocked with marsh, and threaded by a single long thin trail. Camouflaged ditches and walls had been built alongside. Bait had been set by news of a tribal uprising just beyond. On the march to respond, some eighteen thousand Romans — a two-mile column of crack professional infantry, plus cavalry and auxiliaries — would be at their most vulnerable while the lighter-armed attackers could move quickly with unique knowledge of the terrain.

The twenty-five-year-old chieftain Arminius (Hermann, to the folks back home) knew that "the most common beginning of disaster was a sense of security."[33] He also knew the Romans from the inside, having recently commanded one of their auxiliary units. In the depths of a west German forest that would be scattered with human bones for years to come, he exploited the flaw in the imperial war machine: when legions were stretched out for miles and then suddenly compelled to close in on themselves like an accordion, the troops could not shift to fighting mode and were prone to dissolve in panic. The trap perfectly sprung, the Romans were just about killed to a man. In fact, the single hour it likely took the relatively unscathed tribesmen to dispose of three legions was not much of a battle — precisely the outcome a special operation, no matter what the scale, intends.[34]

Despite a defeat so traumatic that it permanently cauterized all ambitions to push toward the Elbe, Rome rebounded, and continued to apply its storied precision in victorious sieges and pitched battles. Its lethally exact organization was terrifyingly apparent in Titus's destruction of Jerusalem in 70 A.D., commemorated by an arch at Rome under which no true Jew is supposed to pass to this day. Three years later, sheer above the western shore of the Dead Sea, the lofty fortress of Masada was taken from one thousand Zealot intransigents by some seven thousand legionnaires who built a huge ramp against the mountainside, as well as by applying ever-better designed artillery. Equally disciplined scouting preceded these victories, Titus himself having undertaken nighttime reconnaissance right under the walls of Jerusalem.[35]

Yet, at least on land, the methodical, high-engineering Roman way of war did not evolve to embrace Alexandrine commando operations — too clever, perhaps too brilliantly personal, not industrially reproducible, counter to legionary endurance and function. It was not that Rome was ignorant of the possibilities. They were thoroughly analyzed in the first century A.D. by Frontinus, one of the generals who reduced Britain to a province after 43 A.D., going on to govern it, subdue its Celtic tribes (who now survive only as the Welsh), then returning to Rome, twice serving at the emperor's behest as consul, and appointed to the by now quintessentially Roman, and probably more important, post of water commissioner. (His chief work was a study of the history, structure, and laws concerning the use of Rome's water supply.) A professional record that united counterguerrilla conquest on the rim of the world with megaproject administration at home enabled him to distill the experience in an unusually creative way.

Frontinus composed not only a treatise on military science (now lost) but an anthology of five hundred devices, ruses, and ploys that he intended as a checklist for the military commander: "On escaping from difficult situations," "On inducing treachery," "On ambushes,"

"On creating panic in the enemy's ranks," and — showing their author's full operational span — on "Contaminating waters" — an issue at the top of Homeland Security concerns today.[36]

It is on waters pure and in motion that we encounter the reappearance of established special operations forces in the form of marines, evolving from earlier years on Greek warships, as well as on those of the Persians and Phoenicians. The Roman adaptation drew on at least three refinements: first, use of small boats — fast sailing vessels with pointed prows, like cutters. We know from Vegetius, the principal surviving military philosopher of the ancient world, how such craft were deployed for reconnaissance, and, we may assume, for raids. Their sails and rigging were dyed a light bluish green (a color today known as Venetian blue) that, he explains, "resembles the ocean waves." A similarly dyed wax was used to cover these boats' sides, and their sailors and marines wore clothes of the same shade "to lie hidden with greater ease when scouting by day as by night."[37] It was the ancient world's version of a fighter jet undetectable to radar.

Another refinement was a special force of marines known as *lembarii,* who served on river craft — as on the Rhine and up those slow, westward-flowing tributaries — who could cut off the retreat of any barbarians tempted by the fair fields of Gaul. Third was the raising of foreign sea-soldiers, such as those Britons who likely served along with Romans under the "Tribune of British Troops trained for sea warfare," the emblem of which, Vegetius tells us, was a circle — which looks strikingly similar to the globe on the badge of today's Royal Marine Commandos. The shields of these cohorts (500–1,000 strong) were also colored sea green (according to a small drawing in Oxford's Bodleian Library) and their clothes seem to have been the same color as their shields — well suited for surprise.

Roman marines on rivers, coastlines, and at sea may have been as close as the ancient world came to an ongoing special capacity. But still none of these outfits were composed of self-reliant warriors specially expert in a range of skills: swimming, climbing, languages, urban and wilderness warfare, or indeed craftsmanlike handling of most any tool but the spear, sling, or sword. Rarely were they insightful about more than the immediate need to kill, capture, or conquer, on their own particular packet of well-practiced terms. The type of cool, versatile formation that could appear ubiquitous, that did not have to be embedded in the main army — being able to move unbelievably, undetectably far beyond it — would not take form until long after the last Roman dam had washed away.

Neither Rome's stalwart military traditions, nor its marines, nor intricately considered views of war, such as those of Frontinus, ultimately offered much help against barbarian horsemen who had little time to calculate the numbers they faced. What did work for a while was the ability of the late Roman army to adapt to "low-level warfare," as described by the historian Adrian Goldsworthy. Disciplined, regular soldiers began to use the enemy's own tactics of surprise and speed to defeat them, by resorting to "concealment, rapid movement and ambush." Scouting parties as well as somewhat larger units began to be used for such stealthy work, including the rather obscure *super-ventores,* which another scholar identifies as "rearguard commandos."[38] Yet by the mid-fifth century A.D., the barbarians had already carved out chunks of the western provinces.[39] Emerging from the island of Gotland off the Swedish coast, the Goths for a time were preeminent in the shadowy world of Europe beyond the imperial frontiers. Their horsemanship imparted an advantage of offensive mobility that, in 378, enabled them to annihilate a mighty Roman army, the terrified central government buying off the barbarians with huge subventions of food. The Goths nonetheless entered Rome in August 410, the first foreign invaders to do so for centuries.

The eastern realm of the Roman Empire, ruled from Constantinople, had already been dedicated the effective imperial capital in 330 as the emperors sought a safer base in their "new Rome." By this time, their power in the West was in deep decay, not least due to successive waves of pandemics that cut manpower and population at least a quarter beginning around 250.[40] Attila and his Huns had followed the Goths as the most formidable presence among the barbarians, indefatigable horsemen wielding bows, swords, whips, and lassos. Their long journey of conquest from the Central Asian steppes exemplified self-confidence and the ability to coordinate over endless terrain. Absent was any Alexandrine impulse to conquer in order to build. Like a cold wind, they blew through lands that the "king of the world" had overrun, not thinking of next year, let alone the next century. In 452 A.D., they broke into Italy, ravaging the Po basin. But by summer they were in retreat, Attila having parleyed a deal with Pope Leo I the Great, who offered gold for the barbarians' troubles, and the hand of Honoraria, the emperor's sister, who, sight unseen, had already proposed to the Hun in revenge for her brother having killed her lover — thereby jeopardizing the half of the empire owing as her dowry. Attila died within months, on his wedding night, although with a bride other than the tempestuous Honoraria. His sons warred for the succession, quickly ending Hunnic power. It is an example of how fragile a nation's fate can be when embodied in one demonic leader. Everything can unravel when he is removed from the scene, by whatever means.

Barbarians had been crashing into Roman territories or the lands uncomfortably adjacent for the previous seven centuries: they had been destroyed, defeated, deflected, or assimilated. Now they were coming in to stay, on their own terms. Following the Hun came renewed assault by the Vandals, who sacked Rome three years after Attila's death. As the Western world of cities and literature was torn asunder, fewer records were kept and yet fewer survive; we have ever less at our disposal to indicate how special operations were being applied. Probably the complexities of such undertakings fared poorly as life darkened. As always, however, courage and ingenuity persisted in some fashion. Diminished technology and organization may even have spurred initiative in new directions. Twelve hundred years later, Hobbes was to describe the Catholic Church as "the ghost of the Roman Empire, sitting crowned on the grave thereof," a reminder that ideas continue when stone crumbles, iron rusts, the grandchildren of kings become slaves.

4

A Terrible Few

Cracks in the Edifice, from the Fall of Rome to the Fading of the Feudal Order, 476–1300

> *"The number must be few, since your hope is in speed*
> *and secrecy. Had I a host, it would avail little."*
> J. R. R. TOLKIEN, THE LORD OF THE RINGS, *Iii3*

THE OUSTING in 476 of the last shadowy figure with any pretension to be emperor in Rome had been a belated symbol of its demise. In Gaul, fine Roman fortress cities such as Avignon, Bourges, and Nevers would endure, their high walls hard to penetrate by plain barbarian energy, and hundreds of monasteries would be built in the seventh century. But the fate of Arausio (Orange, in the Vaucluse) was all too common, as it shrank to occupy just the disintegrating hectare or so that had once been the racing and gladiatorial space of its glorious amphitheater. Dams washed out, roads were principally defined by the random absence of stones rather than the presence of street-metal, trade routes faltered.

If the "Dark Ages" (as described unfairly by Renaissance humanists seeking to connect themselves with a nobler ancient world) were not the primitive centuries long believed, they can at least politely be termed an epoch short on operational analysis. Many of the years in which the legacies of Greece and Rome retreated are chronicled insufficiently enough as to obscure most of the extraordinary feats that must have occurred in the more intricate of violent encounters.

There are features, however, that can be coaxed from coinage and from the conventions of poetry that explain what is expected of heroes, from the political geography in those much fewer writings which did continue, and then from annals that catalogued the military campaigns of the Carolingians, the sprawling Germanic-French dynasty founded in 751. Over time, societies were again becoming prosperous enough to encourage increasingly more capable raiders to turn into conquerors. Far-reaching Vikings (known all too bitterly as Northmen) eventually had the confidence to build a duchy on the mouth of the Seine in defiance of a king in Paris — with untold consequences for history — and five hundred Northmen raiders took Sicily from Islam, to turn it into a violently expansionist power in the central Mediterranean.

Militarily formidable in its way, the feudalism that emerged was closer in appearance to arrangements in Homer's day — when the state was the household of the king — than to Caesar's. As it spread through the societies of the West, with their castellans and knights, an intriguing question posed itself: where did feudal arrangements leave themselves open to being pulled apart most efficiently?[1] This system of closely held power, the castle as its focus of strength, was made to order for the special operation, certainly more so than in classical Rome, where the highest officers of the Republic might be killed and armies annihilated; yet a grim, self-renewing sense of impersonal public identity could carry the wounded nation through. Under feudalism, a conspicuous, politically potent strongman roistering in his castle, primed to face an army, could be surprised at a blow should infiltrators arise from the sewers. His troops of metal-clad hearties might lord it over the countryside, but how to contend with commandolike outlaw bands darting out of the forests?

If inventiveness was not yet systematic and ongoing, we nonetheless see how a very few combatants could bring victories or inflict outrages that defied armies, whether engineers tunneling under battlements or three hundred voracious and technically slick Christian raiders setting out to destroy the Kaaba at Mecca and the Prophet's tomb at

Medina. Meanwhile, among the Assassins, we meet the first institutionalized special operations force in history as it hunted Crusader kings and Moslem caliphs alike. Time and again, the most consequential of targets — chieftains, castles, cities, rulers — lay exposed to the informed hostile eyes of the daring few, no matter what their faith or the technique that brought these operators into the very last places an opponent would ever expect them to appear.

‡

By the sixth century, the *Völkerwanderung,* the southward and westward movement of entire Germanic peoples, brought to the British Isles the conquerors' languages that would fuse into English, imposed the German name "France" on Gaul, and saw the Vandals not merely add an appropriate word to a half-dozen tongues but also grind across Spain to build a final empire in Tunisia. The Lombards ravaged, then settled, northern Italy; the Burgundians came, and so too the Visigoths — all peoples who pushed aside much that was left of Roman ways.

Until the early Carolingians began building a military machine that would make it possible for Charlemagne in 800 to resuscitate the title of Roman Emperor, which had lain dormant in the West for 324 years, this was not a propitious backdrop for types of war much beyond wholesale slaughter. Twenty thousand Visigoths and then civil-warring Merovingians ravaging their way through Provence were unlikely to deploy — indeed to contemplate — carefully considered needlelike strikes against well-studied targets. For one, there were fewer worthwhile targets at hand — such as a city-state's acropolis or too-thoroughly-drilled legions with their vulnerability to forest ambush — that could be leveraged by such attack. Second, sprawling enemy armies might indeed have been at their most vulnerable if chieftains could be eliminated, but such decapitations might have been rarer in this period than one might expect. Societies that rest on display can be the most exposed to the commando's way of war: they offer markers on where best to penetrate and hurt them. Stealthy intruders can target a general's enormous tent, for example, or a potentate's procession. These early successors to Rome, however, were not culturally elaborate peoples. If we think of Attila some years before, known to sleep on the ground among his men and horses, it would have been difficult for a tiny force slipping in at night even to have found its victim in the field.

On the northern frontiers, darkening Britain, from which the legions had departed, suffered a far more complete catastrophe than the lands farther south — even losing its Latin language, as Italy, France, Spain did not. Yet out of this abandoned province arose a legend that put its spell over western Europe, that of the mighty Arthur and his knights. This magnetic figure was not, of course, the too-good-to-be-true senior prefect of High Medieval romance; but if he existed at all — and there is evidence that some warrior of this name did, around 530 A.D. — he was an improviser of iron will, perhaps a left-behind officer of mercenary cavalry, who upheld what pathetically little was left of the Roman order, buying time for a generation against the invaders who would nevertheless in the end leave their collective names, *English* and *England,* upon his foundering Roman civilization of Christian Britain.[2] The desperate marches and raids against the advancing hordes from across the sea — the Angles, the Saxons, and others from Germany, perhaps from the Danish coast — must have contained some extraordinary exploits of courage and skill against ferocious numbers. Yet of this we know little.

These years were undoubtedly marked by equally fierce clashes as in the days of Rome — and probably more of them, because Rome had been a rather severe enforcer of peace. But the centers of authority that existed were more likely to be concentrated on single dominating figures, such as Arthur. So, too, with the Anglo-Saxon invaders of England, who split themselves into fragmentary kingdoms. And what records may have existed of their deeds were generally lost or lyrically transformed.

One problem of heroic literature is its mingling of warrior experience with extravagant myth, as is instanced by the great body of poetry of ancient Ireland, going back to the beginning of the Christian epoch. We get tales about arms-bearing deities and a whole people cursed for having compelled a fertility goddess to race while pregnant. Yet there are real-world origins to many of these sagas, and strong evidence that bards would chant poems about cattle raids as both inspiration and practical example before such reavings were embarked on. The twelfth-century *Book of Leinster* carefully categorizes the poems that the bards should know, under headings like "Raids," "Sieges," and "Expeditions," indicating distinct modes and objectives that reach beyond mere havoc. From one of the greatest of Irish poems, the *Tain Bo Cuailnge* ("Cattle Raid of Cooley," ca. 200 A.D.), we can extract the discipline and subtlety of thrusting deep into enemy territory to steal a cherished possession (the brown bull). We learn of a raiding force moving forward in the face of crippling nightly counterstrikes, across highly specific countryside recognizable even today — a rapid, targeted attack, with orderly withdrawal, rather than warriors running amok. Details may be obscured, but even here we see operational cohesion and a political purpose, such as it was, to humiliate (or demoralize) the opponent by carrying off an item of supreme value.

As movable wealth, the place of cattle in our ancestral cultures at least since the Bible is astonishing: the very word is identical to *chattel;* they were the most interchangeable of prizes. Cattle were status, nourishment, and, with the Aryan conquerors of India, religion. (The Sanskrit for *raid* is, once again, "desires more cattle.") Raids — the swift penetration of and planned withdrawal from hostile territory — were extolled because they were hitting the enemy precisely where he was strong and rich. In Ireland, such raids must have been few, clever, and utterly disorienting; otherwise the chieftains of the age would have routinely posted layers of defenses, as in time they would do with more *bo-dhun,* cattle forts.

Among Indo-European peoples from Ireland to India, cattle raids were additionally a means of testing the skills and raising the character of elite young warriors — a process akin, say, to the exercise called "Robin Sage," the last grueling ordeal of the Green Berets' qualification course in which teams war over about a quarter of North Carolina. But the special qualities of combat leaders in the early tales of such long-ago raids remain more magical than real.[3] Enraged at the annihilation of a youthful troop, for instance, the mighty Cu Chulainn, "the hardest man they have in all Ulster," says *The Tain,* falls upon the slayers — with a beam of light being his sword, his jaws "going back," one eye folding like a flower, the other leaping out of his face, as blood geysers spew from his skull. (That may be a persuasive description of a drill sergeant, but hardly a presence to qualify for Command and General Staff College.) In W. B. Yeats's interpretation, Cu Chulainn finally perishes by hewing the ocean waves with his sword until overwhelmed by the sea. It is an unthinking fury, rather than the reasoned physical courage displayed by Caesar in the Egyptian harbor or Alexander reaching over the waters at Tyre. And its lesson to the warrior culture of Ireland set the highest value on implacable passion as opposed to cunning.

Out of the gloom where historic figures mingle with the demons which haunt the edge of firelight comes another and very different hero, Beowulf. In the earliest surviving epic poem written in English (sometime between the middle of the seventh and the end of the tenth centuries), the man-eating monster Grendel has for a dozen years been plucking the king of Denmark's warriors from Heorot, a glittering high-towered hall atop a fortified cliff. The threat to Denmark's order, in the heyday of its might, comes from within — the death shadow from the misty moors arrives each night to feed greedily. Grendel possesses immense strength, as well as magic against the warriors' whetted swords. These many seasoned fighters are sufficiently brave that they do not abandon Heorot, despite serving themselves up for supper year after year. Nor do they bother to discover how to eliminate the monster. We learn that courage unmediated by thought is more likely to get one killed than to bring victory.

Then arrives from across the water on his curved-prow ship the bravest of men, with just fourteen chosen companions in coats of mail. This champion who "dared against the unknown" carries no magic, yet determines to meet Grendel on the predator's own terms, hand to hand without swords during the long night, surprising Grendel by pretending to be asleep among the ranks in the grand hall. As Grendel lopes in to begin the nightly feed and reaches out for him, Beowulf pounces, wrestles, and rips off the monster's arm, wounding Grendel fatally. Yet the victory is incomplete, and Beowulf must "dare a terrible journey" to track Grendel's avenging mother, swimming down to her cave beneath the lake to kill her as well. There is a lesson here, for those who could see it: whereas the king's many warriors had all shown the endurance of Cu Chulainn before the waves, and had fought Grendel conventionally and hopelessly,

Beowulf proves able to wipe out the species by using guile and a sharp mind to multiply the gift of heroic daring.

Throughout these centuries there were tricks of warfare, to be sure — deception, ambush, indirect attack. Imagination always pays off, in war as in all else. But the skills evident in Alexander's commando assaults did not thrive among the warrior classes. Nor did the engineering knack of Rome. Few technological breakthroughs were to be expected amid nil developments in mathematics and an ongoing net evaporation of the body of literature that had illuminated classical times.[4]

By the days of Charlemagne (Charles the Great), who ruled from 768 to 814, we encounter a level of consistent offensive military success, combined with comprehensive planning and intelligence collection, not to be repeated until Bonaparte. At a muscular six feet four, Charlemagne had the presence and character to build further on what there still was of Rome's military heritage. He boosted the dynasty into a vast domain, stretching from the Spanish *meseta* to the German forests, including most of the Balkans, and reaching down the Italian peninsula. Well-paid professional soldiers were marshaled, including rigorously trained recruits advancing in formation along the old Roman roads, skilled personnel for sieges (with audacious ladder teams "able to scale the walls in the most daunting circumstances"), light horsemen expert in a variety of maneuvers, and elite household troops that performed as a mobile rapid-response force for search and destroy missions.[5]

The emperor's alertness to clandestine action from peoples still unconquered, and his biannual meetings that brought together intelligence specialists, senior political advisers, and military planners, were part of a process reminiscent of today's National Security Council.[6] Yet with all Charlemagne's passion for learning and intense organizational skills, it is at best unclear whether this prodigy could read. Nor, in his startling conquests, does he seem to have developed anything like commando units and missions. Perhaps, as the foremost student of the subject explains, that was due to his very success. There was no compelling need to seek battlefield alternatives; his formidable infantry and cavalry kept pushing outward. As a result, they were the more likely to be victims of enemy cunning, as when his rearguard was annihilated by a Basque ambush when he crossed the Pyrenean gorges in 778, a disaster that gave us the magnificent, if highly fictionalized, *Song of Roland*.

Charlemagne's death after a forty-six-year reign left an entity that crystalized roughly into France as one legacy, the increasingly incoherent central European ("Holy Roman") realm into another. Not until the later ninth century, as the empire he had built found itself fragmenting in turn, did the Carolingians turn to such special methods.[7] Yet once more, centralized power began to unravel; a warrior society with nothing better to do had plenty of time to turn its aggression inward.[8]

The violence that accompanied the decline of even provincial order likely brought about an array of small-scale operations, although they seem to have passed from making at least some political sense to instead being akin to smash-and-grab bank heists or third world embassy seizures. Less is known about how forces were organized by the later tenth century, but they surely did not combine the size, reach, and heavy equipment mustered by Charlemagne and by his father before him. Well-selected companies that needed to travel fast would have been compelled to sacrifice most of whatever hitting power they could cobble together; most of Europe maintained what little contact there was across wretched roads of bottomless mud. When the very word *travel* as an overland term derived (like its sister word, *travail*) from a term for *torture,* hitting hard and fast at a distance usually meant surprise from the sea. A squadron of small raiding vessels, if kept together and able to thread reefs and shoals, could pounce on a settlement and deliver an efficient force larger than what the defenders would be able to bring together from the immediate countryside.[9] As with airborne operations of a later age, such attack had to display immediate superiority at the point where it struck, lest the defenders rally to counterattack.

Beginning late in the eighth century, certain Scandinavian communities came to realize the possibilities of systematic adventure overseas. Originally they were little more than a few hundred warriors in search of food and loot; later they became mercenaries, conquerors, and then settlers over half of Europe. In what a recent head of U.S. Special Operations Command describes simply as "commando-type raids," the Vikings first struck England in 793.[10] Contemptuous of slow land power, however strongly it might be assembled, they undertook sorties even against the holdings of Charlemagne, their ships conferring a bewildering mobility that enormously multiplied the terrible visitors' strength. They were able to select a time and place to strike, to surprise without ever being surprised themselves. Just as important, they believed themselves unstoppable, so much so that they would sail into the unknown northern seas and leave the first European mark on lands not for centuries to be called America.

The Vikings ripped through eastern Europe (the very name "Russia" being Swedish, "the rowers' country"). They mastered the great rivers of the east and raised princedoms on the plains through which the waters flow. Vikings went on to bodyguard the emperors at Constantinople (or, as they sparely phrased it, the Great Kings at Mickelgard, "Big City"). They moved from hit-and-run coastal raids to beaching their ships, bringing in or commandeering horses, and setting off across country in loosely organized warbands that could break apart and re-form at will.[11]

Vikings shattered the Irish high civilization that had grown up alongside the cattle raiding. Their ships pressed up the river Seine as they mercilessly hammered France. Their raids and invasions of the ninth and tenth centuries imposed a great tract of "Danelaw" — and several Danish kings — on England. Progressing from indiscriminate pillage to more careful exploitation, the Vikings increasingly substituted conquest for the repetitive expense of lifting annual plunder. Armies could be formed, and with the arrival of the stirrup in the early 700s and its prevalence (along with the horseshoe) by the 800s, even untrained horsemen could become powerfully offensive warriors, able to swing their swords and, from a high-cantled seat (combined with double girthing, or breast harnesses), to couch lances. In north-central France, the "land of the Northmen," or Normandy, there arose a hybrid Franco-Scandinavian warrior aristocracy, soon converting to a rather muscular Christianity.

From the south, other indomitable warriors had been striking into Europe. By the early eighth century, Moslem herders turned raiders turned cavalrymen had already swept in on the wings of a fighting faith from southern Arabia, exploding across dazed Christendom to the Pyrenees, subjecting whole civilizations in the process. In one blazing century from the death of the Prophet in 633, Islam had reached out to bring all once-Christian North Africa under its sway, to conquer Spain and gouge into France, to push into Afghanistan, and even to disrupt with its revolutionary word the desert frontier provinces of China.

On the eastern reaches of Europe, roughly half the Roman Empire (Byzantium) held firm, its seat being on the narrows joining the Black Sea — into which run the immense rivers of Russia — to the Aegean, which opens into the Mediterranean. This chokepoint dominated the great saltwater route. At its slimmest passage between east and west was Constantinople, a Greek metropolis of culture and language ever less plausibly Roman. Shipbuilding and innovative means of warfare (including chemical weapons in the form of an incendiary cocktail to be known as "Greek fire") continued to evolve, and life rested on a still-literate, well-established tax system and bureaucracy.

War against the Arabs — and also against the Slavs encroaching from the north, Turks out of central Asia, ultimately against the Ottoman Turks, named after the founding dynasty — was still regarded as a science, one which could be practiced on several levels. It involved mastery of various writings on all known aspects of tactics and strategy. The Byzantines were adept not only at set-piece battle but also at conducting well-prepared, focused strikes delivered with "speed and secrecy" against the enemy's rear — in this case, by small detachments on horse and foot, "liers in wait" who, "if possible under cover," would hit suddenly and precisely where least expected.[12] When we return to the significantly more backward West, however, we find far fewer valuable objectives to attack, and no similar study of such stealthy behind-the-lines penetration.

A special operation that targets a well-organized society is by definition likely to be relatively small, sudden, and secretive. However, there have been moments in history when the impact of an entire nation on the move can be made most sense of through the lens of special warfare — in its enterprise, mobility, and means of assault on the daunting odds of entrenched power. In 1066, rival Northman entities invaded England from top to bottom. Those who had stayed in Scandinavia broke in near York, under a literally "ruthless" king,

Harald Hardraade, who had served as a mercenary in Constantinople, while the descendants of those Northmen who had conquered a home in France thrust up toward London from Hastings. Rarely has more proved to have been at stake.[13] By his own amphibious landing less than three weeks later, William became the Conqueror because he confronted an exhausted English army that had had to march two hundred miles down to the southern coast after destroying Harald. We have an extraordinary pictorial record of this great event, the 230-foot Bayeux Tapestry, embroidered by William's court ladies.

The tapestry shows much valor and, depending on a couple of stitches and one's perspective, perhaps even a crossbow, a technology for sniping as well as for the battlefield, the use of which had also ebbed and waned since Rome.[14] But apart from the portrayal of scouts, and of one just possibly feigned retreat that might have been decisive in its luring out of the enemy, all this courage is uncombined with subtlety, let alone guile. Except for knowing about the astounding amphibious assaults that lay behind all this, we do not see the more indirect skills that Byzantium — benefiting from that added creativity which can rise from a high urban and trading culture — had brought to war.

‡

"Fortune," Vegetius had warned, "tends to have more influence than bravery," therefore making it best to avoid battle when possible and to subdue the enemy not only by the famine of siege but also by "raids and terror."[15] The writings of this obscure Roman engineer were known at the time both to scholars and the more thoughtful of warriors. His work and indeed that of Frontinus had been among the classical military treatises copied in Charlemagne's busy scriptoria. In eleventh- to fourteenth-century records, we find no shortage of lively references to surprise attack, let alone to the repeated terrors of massacre. But as for most of the questions that interest us about the fine structure of war, it was no more likely to occur to chroniclers to document the answers than it had to the even fewer scribes of several hundred years past. A battle, the fall of a castle, the knocking off of a great lord, are likely to have been recounted by a monk who was not there, who had never borne arms, who did not know the terrain, or have it occur to him that such matters as stealthy small-scale actions were worth grasping. There was only so much space on the extremely expensive parchment. What the monks did know, they took for granted and did not spell out, assuming that they had been able to. We cannot consult the business files of war. Moreover, warrior cultures at any time with their brawn and boasting tend to be reluctant to concede that it is cunning which has brought triumph, in contrast to the bold tales of noisy combat told by the bard in fire-lit halls.

Greece and Rome had possessed institutions, such as the democratic assemblies and elected military commands of most of the city-states, or the Republic's iron administration and authoritative judicial system, which imposed constitutional government. Yet at the turn of the millennium, leadership was still highly personalized in the rule of great men (Duke William himself being "Mr. Big"), with the range of vulnerabilities as well as strengths of such individually held and flamboyantly visible power. A system of multiple levels of obligation, up and down, took hold, which would not only endure for several centuries but would be increasingly accompanied by the benefits arising from even a modest restraint on sheer mayhem.

During these centuries, "a class of specialized warriors" enforced such obligations, as Marc Bloch explains in *The Rule of Feudal Societies,* though a knight — except perhaps for the most determined of infiltrators — was far from being a special operator.[16] At least in theory, notions of chivalry were at odds with the spirit of "force and fraud" that reaches its most intense in the special unit, the maverick's outfit par excellence. Knights were also more likely than not to be diverted from pursuing the often subtler, certainly less personalized objectives of a focused, creative team to chase instead lucrative ransoms and finish private quarrels. Ransom was a most distracting influence in a mode of warfare where the purpose of coats of arms was to identify the grandest, and therefore most toothsome, warriors. It was entrepreneurial combat at its most basic: the more eminent the opponent captured, the more comfortably one could retire.

With no firm lines on any map that might have existed, who controlled what on a ground disordered by competing oligarchs could be anyone's guess. These were wars not just over real estate but were akin to Mafia struggles as to who was under whose protection. Henry II might rush around his dominions like an anxious landlord, dragging his wife, Eleanor of Aquitaine, behind him. But his authority lasted only as long as he could make it stick. "The skein of relationships between a lord — even a king — and his lieutenants could unpick with alarming rapidity."[17] Despite theatrically personal pledges of fealty, it might be imprudent to count on unquestioned devotion, let alone claims of divine right, when everyone was always squinting to see which way the cat jumped.[18]

Chafing against this feudal order were the people described in the rich medieval literature of outlaws and outlawry, legends altogether different from the three types of medieval romance centering on the tales of King Arthur, the exploits of Charlemagne, and the epic of Troy. The Robin Hood fable is rooted in stories set in England, Wales, Scotland, France, Flanders, and Spain, often featuring daring men returned from foreign wars, that seem to have formed from the twelfth to the fifteenth centuries. Nearly all celebrate vastly outnumbered bands which must rely on stealth, deception, and skill to outwit conventional forces of knights and men at arms. Horses are reshod with shoes pointing backward to mislead pursuers; disguised outlaws pass invisible through crowds; and the forest is their invincible home, which enemies are welcome to ride through in a fruitless chase. These outlaws employ "strategic tricks" to reconnoiter, gain entry, confuse or entrap the enemy. Such art certainly imitated life, as men on the fringe of society applied these techniques in the real world.[19] The hunted became the hunters. A fast-moving, self-reliant few were able to make the small but crucial moves that the strong proved unable to counter.

In this era, what we call special operations really meant quick, focused strikes against the human and material concentrations of political power — there were no lines to disrupt, of transport or communication, nor cannon to turn on their possessors. Authority rested on a scattering of fortresses and much noisy shifting of dignity. Modern special operators have a wealth of targets — who knows where and how the next blow may fall? In contrast, king, pope, marshal ("horsemaster") must have had a pretty good idea of what was at risk, although often not a sound understanding of how to protect themselves from what might slip out of the shadows.

Castles — as places of personal power rather than of any collective public authority — embodied the social structure of the time and were centers of vulnerability as well as of strength. Today, their spectacular ruins reach from the Scottish borders to east-central Europe, although well into the second millennium most were relatively simple structures of earthen ramparts, palisaded banks, and timber revetments, rather than the elaborate system of concentric stonework of high medieval fact and still more of Arthurian legend. The original Tower of London was not completed until the 1100s, and Dover Castle at the turn of that century — unsurprisingly around a Roman lighthouse, the legacy of the Caesars never dying away. Hundreds of castles were built after the Norman Conquest. France itself was "a country of castles," Louis VI being greatly preoccupied with the spread of his skein of fortresses.[20]

As the castle became indispensable to the continuous deepening exercise of power, it also became architecturally more formidable, steadily achieving higher levels of expert design, capable of cowing its countryside, wearing down any besiegers, exalting the castellan and his knights, and serving, much more than did the fortress of a later age, as a political center. Yet even at its strongest, the castle still suffered from the problem of all fixed defenses: once compromised, it became a prison for its own garrison. Its triumph represented a revival of the single inordinately valuable target, like the acropolis of a Greek city-state. Therein lay opportunity not only for the slogging unwieldy armies of the time but for stealthier overnight approaches.

On those relatively rare occasions when armies drew face-to-face on the field, the conflict was likely to have grown out of a siege, not necessarily of a castle per se, but perhaps of a fortified town, for towns were "the true masters of space" in the West of the time.[21] Even then, combat was on a limited scale: close-quarters battle (as U.S. Special Operations Command calls hand-to-hand killing) among hundreds rather than the clash of thousands. Outright battle might yield temporary victory but could consume hard-to-replace fighting men. "It is better to tame the enemy by hunger than by fighting," Vegetius had instructed his readers. Yet matters could be dragged out both ways. Sieges could be punctuated by the defenders' small, risky, "incursions, ambushes and sallies," and a besieging army could be worn down, especially once the countryside had been stripped bare, with foodstuffs hoarded within the stronghold's walls.[22] Time was often on the side of even heavily outnumbered defenders in that cold, wet, hungry, typhoid-ridden world.

Since the resistance of a castle or town could expose a besieger to the weight of an army coming to its defense, standoffs were often all the more a race against time. "Danger might come as much from within as without," adds Philippe Contamine, France's renowned medievalist, about the castle.[23] The "escalade" — a scaling by ladder of the walls — was likely to be suddenly effective if undertaken in the depths of darkness, should daring men seize brief opportunity, perhaps aided by treachery. Even the stoutest, best-provisioned castle might fall to a ruse, usually of the "Trojan horse variety," explains another scholar, "designed to effect entry by a small party." Knights were disguised as peasants, or smuggled in wagonloads of grain during a truce, or entered through a disused well or a sewer. Fortified towns had particular vulnerabilities, since outlying buildings, barns, and orchards enabled attackers to approach under cover, focusing on the gates.

As for actual conquest, time and again it can start as a raid, and finish in a presence far more enduring. The techniques of the raid are likely to have been developed for small-minded purposes, even when they are a testing ground for a young warrior-elite, but they hone the skills that sooner or later can be applied to a vision beyond the hit and run of snatching cattle, slaves, grain, even castles. For instance, the brothers Hauteville were tall, broad-shouldered, clean-shaven young Normans, with commanding voices, blond hair, and blue eyes. Venturing on the spring breezes of 1061 from southern peninsular Italy, they wrested Sicily from Moslem hands. After what today is called a "special reconnaissance" (i.e., scouting out the enemy's capabilities and the lay of the land before a strike), they inserted 270 horsemen at night across the Straits of Messina, clandestinely carried across a second group to bring the force up to about 500, landed in a place the much larger Moslem garrison at Messina did not suspect, and went straight in.[24] Five years before the Norman conquest of England, the brothers displayed clear assessment of terrain a lot more alien than the green lands on the far side of the Channel, careful appreciation of opportunity, lightning promptness, and an ability to exploit the defending garrison's blunder. This amphibious raiding operation unfolded to exploit huge strategic possibilities, laying the ground-work for what in two generations would be Europe's most effective feudal state.

Norman knights went ever farther afield, their energy being the prime force in recovering Jerusalem for Christianity in 1099, four centuries after the Byzantine Empire had lost it to Islam. By and large, these warrior pilgrims lacked the level of discipline and self-command — as shown by their incessant divisive rows — that might have brought them enduring success. Nor did they have the keen political understanding of their opponents that could have enabled them to take better advantage of no less fierce rivalries among the Moslems. Yet from the start, even on the way to Jerusalem, there was room for the few who thought and dared. Antioch, the capital of Syria, great from Biblical times, was far too large to surround, let alone to storm; European cities of the time were much smaller. And four hundred defensive towers were built into its miles of high honey-colored walls.

The Crusaders, many of whom had covered the almost twenty-five hundred miles from northern France by horseback or, in part, by sea, could not reach the Holy Land until Antioch was in their hands. Otherwise, there would be a huge power looming behind them. The siege starting in October 1097 lasted for eight grisly months through a winter during which the holy warriors of the Catholic Church for-aged, starved, and were compelled to beat back two large Moslem armies. To make matters worse, an even more formidable, well-organized army, including reinforcements gathering around Mosul, was preparing for a rescue.

Bohemund d'Hauteville (another strapping, handsome, blond-haired Norman marauder with cold blue eyes, as we learn from the diary of a Greek princess who knew and hated him) was finally able to corrupt an officer of the garrison with sackfuls of silver and prom-ises of more to come. Nothing new here, but what is interesting is that the Crusaders then made a show of withdrawing a large detachment of infantry and cavalry in full sight of the garrison, only for it to return stealthily by night and place itself near one of the wall's six large gates. Before dawn on June 3, sixty knights — described in our day as both a "picked band" and an "elite force" — gathered fearfully beneath the walls of the traitor's southeastern sector, not knowing whether they would be climbing into a trap. The traitor dependably lowered a rope, to which an oxen-hide ladder was promptly attached. Bohemund urged them upward, although having sense enough to stay behind himself. Some made it to the top, then the ladder broke, and the fall was high enough to kill.

Death cries must have been muted. The rest "managed to get in by using ropes," according to an Arab account. Silencing the sector's watchman, they raced along the walls to stab the sleeping guards at the three nearest towers, then descended swiftly into the city to help open one of the great gates, beyond which the returned detachment was waiting. Some of the Christian inhabitants remaining in the city rose up and opened other gates. In the house-to-house fighting and slaughter that ensued, the Crusaders barely distinguished between the Moslem enemy and the city's Christian families. By evening, the blood-soaked prize was in God's hands.[25]

What course might history have taken had Bohemund's commando action not cracked the city and brought in his starving friends? We can be pretty sure the First Crusade would have been eviscerated before it took another step toward Jerusalem. But as with the audacious success of Alexander's three hundred at the Sogdian Rock, or Arminius's destruction of Rome's legions before they could press farther east, it is anyone's guess what that might have meant regarding developments thereafter. The evidence nonetheless attests that at Antioch — as at those other points of history — the special operation was of its nature indispensable.

Antioch once taken and its Moslem would-be relievers driven back, pious chroniclers could record the appearance of Christ, St. Andrew, and a heavenly host in the clouds. Leaving aside the effectiveness of such air cover, we may at least note the significance of silent, intensely focused killing in which flat-out small movements against a crucial point — and more tangible personal assistance, as from the betrayer — transformed the grind of an ordinary siege that hung within a whisker of failing. Intrigue and bribery found a commando culmination. Of the hundred thousand or so Crusaders who had left Europe, perhaps

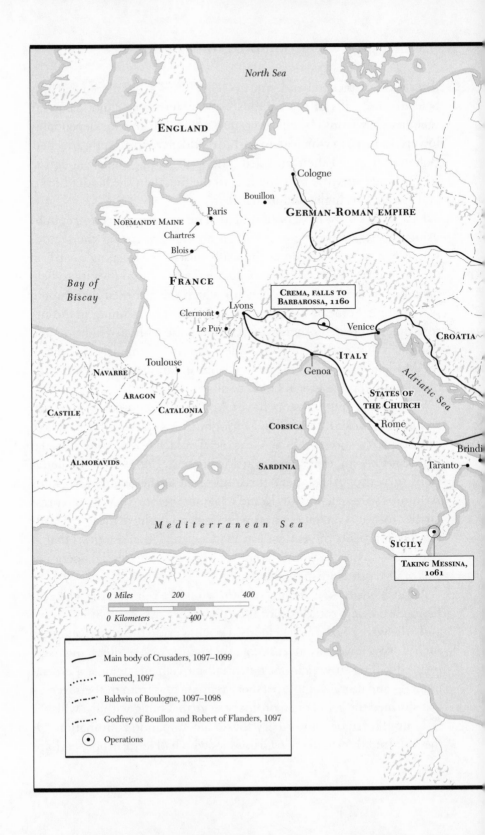

North Sea

ENGLAND

Cologne

Bouillon

Paris

NORMANDY MAINE

GERMAN-ROMAN EMPIRE

Chartres

Blois

FRANCE

Bay of
Biscay

CREMA, FALLS TO
BARBAROSSA, 1160

Lyons

Clermont

Venice

Le Puy

CROATIA

ITALY

Toulouse

Genoa

NAVARRE

Adriatic Sea

ARAGON

STATES OF
THE CHURCH

CASTILE

CATALONIA

CORSICA

Rome

ALMORAVIDS

SARDINIA

Brindi

Taranto

M e d i t e r r a n e a n   S e a

SICILY

TAKING MESSINA,
1061

0 Miles   200   400

0 Kilometers   400

———— Main body of Crusaders, 1097–1099

········· Tancred, 1097

·—·—·· Baldwin of Boulogne, 1097–1098

·—·—·· Godfrey of Bouillon and Robert of Flanders, 1097

⊙ Operations

PRINCIPAL ROUTES OF THE FIRST CRUSADE, AND SURROUNDING HOT POINTS

HUNGARY

Black Sea

Danube R.

ERBIA

CONSTANTINOPLE, THE "GREATEST CRIME," 1204

Adrianople

ASIA MINOR

Sea of Marmara Nicomedia

CAPPADOCIA

Durazzo THRACE Civetot

Nicaea

Anti-Taurus Mts.

BYZANTINE EMPIRE Dorylaeum *Seljuk Turks*

ARMENIAN STATES

Pergamum

ANATOLIA Tyana Marash • Edessa

GREECE PHRYGIA

Heraclea

Aegean Sea Smyrna LYDIA Iconium Aleppo *Euphrates R.*

Ephesus CARIA PISIDIA *Taurus Mts.*

Athens LYCIA Adana **ANTIOCH TAKEN, 1098**

Tarsus

Gulf of Attalia Maarat

Famagusta Tortosa S Y R I A

RHODES Tripoli

CRETE CYPRUS Beirut • Damascus

Tyre

Acre

Hattin — *Sea of Galilee*

Mediterranean Sea Jaffa **JERUSALEM, FALLS IN 1099**

Bethlehem —

Gaza •

Dead Sea **KERAK, REYNALD'S LAIR, 1182**

E G Y P T

Red Sea

© 2005 Jeffrey L. Ward

some thirty thousand of the toughest remained. Warriors, settlers, and priests could now go on to create a chain of principalities that would last for almost two hundred years in the lands between Baghdad and Egypt.

‡

ALEXANDER HAD sent picked men against targets never attempted by skilled mountaineers (the activity not yet existing); Francisco Pizarro would tear out the heart of an Incan empire that no Spaniards had ever even seen until he overthrew it; and Otto Skorzeny would rescue Mussolini from a mountaintop and then shake American nerve at the Battle of the Bulge. But for sustained effective effort, the deadliest special campaign in all history may have been that of the Nizar'ilyya, falsely called Assassins, or "users of hashish," "a company of most desperate and dangerous men among the Mahometans."[26] These warriors were agents of a hereditary leader known by many titles, such as the Grand Master or the Old Man of the Mountain. They were not random malcontents but the instruments of a powerful open conspiracy during the eleventh to the thirteenth centuries, operating from perhaps one hundred unassailable mountain fortresses stretching from Afghanistan to Syria.

In an earlier age of warring faiths, the Assassins were the most formidable of contenders, the spearpoint of a sect, not of a nation, defined by passion more than ethnicity or geography. Theirs was a deliberate program of terror, as the Old Man — a heretic from Islam — dispersed his movement outward, dispatching motivated, methodical young suicide killers able to live outside the cult for months or years. Cunning, mastery of disguise, immense patience, and knowledge of languages were not implausibly ascribed to them, though their myth was part of their power. One might never be sure when they were circling like vultures, or bowing (blade concealed) at the foot of a throne.

They always resorted to the knife, a weapon of sinister intimacy — and a more risky, less certain mode of attack than poison or the well-shot arrow — as they stalked the most difficult and protected targets.[27] Time and again, they brought home superlatively planned and highly publicized political murders: two caliphs of Baghdad; a roster of Moslem princes and ministers; even two attempts (the second by Assassins disguised as his own soldiers) on Saladin, the Kurdish pal-

adin who was the architect of Moslem unity. Two killers are remembered as having posed for six months as Christian monks until the
right moment came to stab Conrad of Montferrat, the Crusader king
of Jerusalem. The Assassins had a sense of the vulnerability of their
opponents to self-reliant, patient men for whom death in the cause was
the gateway to immortality. Their understanding went so deep as to
give a word of fear to most European languages ever since — and
an example of asymmetric special warfare we have come to know all
too well.

As the capacities of lone or small-unit killers flourished, so did
those of large and differently complex heavy assault. Whether in the
war of faiths, or in the recurring brutalities between fellow believers
in Christ, the siege itself drew upon new or revived technologies,
including mobile towers and rope-powered artillery, as well as upon
the more familiar skills of mining and fire-bombing. Chroniclers of
these great events could not ignore the presence of expert engineers.
We hear more about these specialists after the fall of Jerusalem, on
July 15, 1099, where their machines were powerful enough to fling
captured spies back into the city, and where a siege tower was
wheeled up against the walls to bring the assailants to the level of the
ramparts, despite the searing horrors of liquid fire, which must have
been particularly terrifying to men in armor. "Miners, pioneers, and
specialist craftsmen," including "wasters," figure conspicuously in
twelfth-century accounts, tasked to create machines as well as "to
ruin the economic resources of the enemy."[28]

Until gunpowder, artillery depended on the torsion of ropes and
then of counterweights, in both cases having to be moved close in.
What soldiers dryly call sharp-end forces — those tasked with the
ultimate execution of an undertaking — here required some degree
of unusual technical competence not only to handle artillery but to
get big, vulnerable engines into line. The unwieldy deadliness of all
these devices made it essential to have on hand units that would keep
their nerve — and, crucially, their loyalty to their machines at the
ugly part of an assault — when those around them, as Mark Twain's
Connecticut Yankee puts it, "find pressing appointments to the rear."

These technologies were in the dependable hands of a cadre
responsible for using them, as had been the case with the Byzantine

shipboard specialists who had manned their pumplike bronze flame-throwers and the Carolingian crews who had worked their own stone-throwing heavy artillery. Theirs was not the adrenaline-charged courage of wielding a sword, but intense endurance coolly combined with teamwork — an ability to absorb stress while hauling the machines forward as friends fell on all sides. Cooperation was all the more critical in an era when the elite fighter (the knight) was likely to be "an individualist jealous of his personal prowess and honour."[29] The ability of common soldiers to perform in these extreme circum-stances in some semblance of a team — on a ladder, in a mining squad, moving ahead a tower — was a whisper of things to come.

In 1158, for example, Frederick Barbarossa, by election imperial heir to Charlemagne at three centuries' remove, laid claim to the Lombard kingdom that included most of north-central Italy. Come July of the following year, he attacked Crema, a modest but well-fortified town allied to Milan, fifty miles away. At the time, the sci-ence of fortification may have been most advanced in Italy, where many Roman technical skills were well maintained. And, as a heritage of its ancient past, Crema was defended by a double wall. A citadel and a deep, wide ditch circling beneath the heights offered further protection, as did the river Serio, which ran unpleasantly close for any attacker's plan.

Barbarossa devoted immense effort to breaking Crema. Reinforce-ments had to be sent for from Germany. With ample supplies gath-ered in from its rich farmlands, the willful little city was able to hold out while Barbarossa faced winter, and the prospect that his feudal levies would be unlikely to stick around once enough time lapsed to let them whine about having fulfilled their obligations. Rumor seems even to have lurked that "Assassins" had been sent into his camp.[30] Meanwhile, he constructed a high movable tower of the sort used against Jerusalem two generations before. Hammered out of tree trunks, it could be rolled up to the walls, with soldiers packed inside to burst out and slice into the parapet's defenders. The tower must have been able to deploy pretty fast, otherwise the walls would have been impossibly well manned at the point of impact. In this instance, to get the tower up close, Barbarossa, the most senior secular figure in Christendom, had it pushed forth with hostages from Crema and

Milan bound to its front, hopefully to impose a more than mechanical barrier to enemy artillery. Instead, the defenders brought their own captives up to the ramparts and began to slit their throats in sight of their oncoming compatriots. For whatever reason (shocked sensibilities being unlikely), he pulled back.

After six months of desperation, the tower was worked near enough to lower its bridge, under the fire of yet higher-positioned archers. "Picked men" rushed across to the city wall.[31] Such walls often had their own strongpoints on top, with doors that could be closed to seal off a captured stretch. Thus, even the piercing of outer defenses could deepen the trap for an assault team dashing in, lightly armed as it had to be. Thrusts across the ramparts had to be done from murderously exposed positions, precisely and fast. Unusual endurance was, as usual, a mere suicide pact if not united with skillful timing. The lesson to be drawn for our more mobile and proficient age is the significance of speed and cohesion for the small force, working as a tightly loyal team. The final successful attack, however, did not end with just smashing into the city. Once the target was cracked, "street fighting was just as costly in the Middle Ages as at Stalingrad."[32] Probably more so. There were no automatic weapons to sweep windows or tanks to blast down buildings, nor any special training for urban combat.

Death did not just come from above the mud. Engineering was now counted on, as sufficiently akin to Roman days to make tunneling another, yet subtler mode of approach. Burrowing beneath city or castle walls could bring them down — at which moment an immediate assault would still have to be made through the breach. Mining was the most consistently effective procedure against fortifications, though the lack of precision in the days before fuses and shaped charges made it vital for a resourceful storming party to be able to seize the most uncertain moment. Tunnel builders (and tunnel fighters) would literally go on to carve out their own niche of special warfare — right through the Viet Cong's famed tunnels of Chu Chi (from which entire companies could emerge to fight) and the American "tunnel rats" who went down into the midnight maze right after them with knives and pistols.

In the thirteenth century, skilled specialists who engineered the tunnels and built the towers might be pampered as technological whiz kids. But the episodic nature of medieval war and the contempt of the ruling elites for all inferiors — which meant just about everybody else — stood in the way of even these valued bands developing into truly special units.[33] By the end of that century, clever specialists such as artillerists who crewed the trebuchets (using counterweights to propel and aim heavy stones) were being admitted to the military elite, and supplied with what they needed from royal arsenals. But the lords of war were still dominated by caste obsessions that precluded any concession of the faintest appearance of equality to hired technicians — and not just to such wonks. An impudent raiding band composed of common soldiers could take upon itself a mission as bold as attempting to seize Saladin's camp in the mountains east of Acre (today in the north of Israel) during 1191. Their betters — the knights who had refused to contemplate a move so enterprising — were delighted to see them slaughtered, no matter that snatching Saladin could have set off a succession war among the Moslems.[34]

Extreme, even lunatic, endeavors punctuated the storied clashes between whole armies when West met East. Reynald de Chatillon, for instance, had been held prisoner by the Moslems for sixteen years, and, once released during a truce, married himself into the lordship of Kerak, a castle crucial to the Kingdom of Jerusalem's eastern defenses. Its remains can still be seen five miles southeast of the Dead Sea — a position that, in its glory days, put it in tempting proximity to the Damascus-Mecca road. In the judgment of a noted medievalist, Reynald "was one of those men who rise from obscure origins and somehow change the course of history."[35] Sixteen years cried to be avenged: he was forever breaking truces and swooping upon Moslem caravans. This was not just another ambitious raider: Reynald's operations would doom Jerusalem itself by uniting Islam and enabling Saladin's declaration of war.

Caravans had been attacked since time immemorial. But no one had dreamed of assembling a band to venture eight hundred miles down the Red Sea, then to maneuver several hundred miles inland over desert to attack Mecca and Medina in today's southern Saudi Arabia. Starting not in some convenient Mediterranean harbor but on the shores of the landlocked Dead Sea, the master of Kerak first built galleys, then dismantled them into sections to be carried south for 150 miles, to be reassembled on the Gulf of Aqaba. In 1182, his band of no more than three hundred Christians, accompanied by perhaps several score renegade Moslems, ravaged southward, visiting depredations out of all proportion to their numbers on the somnolently secure Red Sea ports, getting as far as sacking the coastal towns from which led the roads to the holy cities, and stupefying the anciently secure peninsular Arabs merely by this unprecedented appearance in arms.[36] Sadly for him, the Red Sea was at all but its southernmost end a Moslem lake. Once Saladin's brother, the governor of Egypt, caught his breath, "Reynald's Raiders" (as World War II correspondents would have labeled them) were hunted down, their captain being among the few to escape.

"Who dares wins," says the SAS motto. But there are those who dare without a lick of judgment. When finally hauled to Saladin's tent five years later, after a Crusader army had been annihilated, Reynald — of all the noble captives — was so supremely insolent that Saladin, a man of punctilious honor, slew him on the spot.[37] Should we wonder at the thought processes behind Reynald's audacity, we can hear them voiced in the wisdoms of another intrepid warrior discussing a battle against a Moslem warlord: "I knew that my God was a real God and his was an idol," reflected a renowned general of U.S. Special Forces about opposing "Satan" in the current crusade.[38]

To be sure, displays of daring creativity against daunting odds were not confined to infiltrators, technical specialists, soldierly detachments in the mountains, or to the far-reaching raiders of a demented lordly operator. There was plenty of innovation and nerve — with a special twist — in the capture of Greek Orthodox Constantinople in 1204 by a Catholic army (woefully diverted from the Fourth Crusade), which had slipped well beyond control of the pope. Their attack on the greatest civilization in Christendom was orchestrated by Venice, helping gladly to put an end to the old East Roman Empire as a supranational state and, in the process, freeing the Most Serene Republic to build its own trading empire of bases dotting the coastlines of the Adriatic and the eastern Mediterranean.

With a population estimated at 375,000–400,000, Constantinople was vastly larger than any city in the West. The triangular metropolis was strong with natural defenses: the Sea of Marmora served as a moat, and the high walls along the six miles of perfect harbor that form the Golden Horn jutted straight up from the water. Miles of tall, thick, inner and outer land walls that can still be seen today were strengthened by terraces and ninety-six immense, well-spaced towers. "This barrier seems endless," explains a recent study of what followed, "at times stretching from horizon to horizon in front and behind."[39] Against an army of around only twenty thousand, the Greek defenders had an overwhelming numerical advantage. In April — once all the prostitutes had been cast out of the Catholic camp to ensure purity of motive — the final, long-awaited attack began.

A Venetian fleet of fifty battle-galleys positioned crossbowmen up front to establish fire supremacy over the beaches; the transports that pressed after them were constructed so that doors could be opened, gangplanks pushed out, and knights fully mounted on their stallions could spur directly forth into combat like tanks coming off an LST on D-day. Yet all was still a stalemated test of strength, with the Greeks proving capable of defending their city as long as the assault was fought in a more or less familiar way — with bolts, swords, fire, and lances.

Along the Golden Horn, however, galleys grappled the seawall crests with iron hooks, the swaying vessels covered with vinegar-soaked hides to lessen the impact of "Greek fire." Catwalks attached to the high masts of two of them were extended by tackles and counterweights, enabling men in full armor, balancing at least ninety-five feet in the air, to dash across these flying bridges and fight it out with warriors of the Varangian Guard atop the parapets. Greek morale began to crumble once ten knights and sixty sergeants gained a foothold. Performing like a "scouting party," they pushed inward. Flames lit in the face of the counterattacking Byzantine garrison — and the night winds predictably blowing off the sea, which fanned them — caused the emperor to shamefully flee, the people to lose heart, and the city to fall.[40] An army had hammered on the walls, but it was the pierce of a single strike team that created the breakthrough; the gates of the dying city were then crashed open and their fellows streamed in behind them. The murderous looting that followed has been described as history's "greatest crime against humanity," for which Pope John Paul II would apologize to the Greek Orthodox Church in 2001.[41]

‡

VULNERABILITIES OF civilizations come in many packages when faced by the unprecedented, and in the arrival of the Mongols from Central Asia we see a power and a practice that not even the Assassins could resist. The Mongols understood the special dangers posed by this peculiar enemy as they moved into the southern shores of the Caspian Sea toward the Arab financial and cultural capital of Baghdad. For example, a Moslem official at the Great Khan's court in distant Karakorum was found to be wearing chain mail beneath his clothes, and on being questioned explained that he did so for fear of the Assassins' stealth, knives, and terrifyingly long reach.[42] When Assassin hit teams were sent against the encroaching invaders, the Mongols had an answer. In 1256, bandy-legged horsemen turned themselves into mountain troops to scale the steepest cliffs of the Assassins' most formidable fortress, the Eagle's Nest, in northern Persia, surprising the defenders, laying hands on the Old Man himself, promising clemency as they used him for a year to induce other redoubts to surrender, then stomping him to death and exterminating whatever remained of the Assassins' field agents, the *fidain*.

The Mongols threatened Europe, practicing total war on a grand scale, to an extent not seen until Hitler ripped into Russia, which the Golden Horde had first overrun in 1237–38 before spilling onto the European plain. "Blitzkrieg by horsepower," as one scholar calls it, enabled them to take towns, castles, and river crossings by surprise.[43] The proud Western knights in their splendid but disordered thousands were as vulnerable as the tiny hit teams of the Assassins: they fell before these strictly disciplined mounted archers led by junior commanders who were encouraged to use their heads.[44] Hungary was shredded in just a year. Another year and Germany might have fallen; Italy lay open to the next vigorous drive. But the Mongols' vulnerability lay in the extreme and primitive personalization of their culture, a weakness we have seen before. All their success blew up in their faces when the Great Khan (heir to Genghis) died from a drinking binge. The khan's armies pounded five thousand miles home to contest the succession, quarrels consuming their energies on the steppes.

During the new millennium's first two hundred years, brilliant developments in focused, economical warfare that could harness special qualities had seldom been refined in the West beyond a single campaign or, at most, a lifetime. Each commander kept being an improviser much to himself, which meant that new ideas were unlikely to be applied to higher, ongoing levels of usefulness. It was not necessary to dismiss them as "not invented here"; few knew that something had been invented elsewhere in the first place. The force was more defined by its leader than its function.

It remained a time in which champions were still more likely to relish straightforward fights to the finish, as shown in the thirty-to-a-side formal bloodletting of Clan Kay against Clan Chattan, in a Scotland still between organized savagery and feudal conflict. Yet there were more purposeful exploits to be brought off, peeking out from the legends of the Round Table and in the conquests of Charlemagne. In looking at the infiltrations of castles and fortress cities, we glimpse a handful of silent men slipping into some position so vital they can only return from it alive if they dare to the point of triumph; or, in battle, we witness the specialized contributions of a well-prepared few at the point of contact. Throughout, the need to call on those who possess such character and skills never disappeared.

In the thirteenth century, a skyrocketing population, well-endowed universities, the absence of any major war between 1214 and 1296, and rising prosperity (assisted by long absence of crop failure and famine, as well as by fixed coinage and common weights and measures) was revitalizing cities and indeed creating others. With bustling cities came complexity, whether of financial instruments or modes of defense. And with complexity came new opportunities for targeted violence beyond killing a chieftain or knocking over a castle. Not merely might an opponent be diminished, but more supporters might be brought to arms, maintained, and rewarded with more than beefs. Prince Henry (son of William the Conqueror and soon to be Henry I) made good his claim to the English throne by seizing the treasury, right after the mysterious death of his older brother. Losing one's stash was crippling to any exercise of power, as happened to his great-grandson John (of Magna Carta fame), when the sea caught his treasure wagons crossing the Wash, that large outlet of tidal marshland deep into the east coast of England — a blow from which that shifty man never recovered.

Another advance in the ways of applying stealth, infiltration, and the small band is in the development of abduction as an instrument of political intimidation, rather than merely for ransom. At the high end stands the bloodless abduction of popes: the (soon-foiled) kidnapping of Gregory VII, as he was saying Christmas Eve mass in 1075, by the bravoes of the Roman city prefect; the more significant snatching of Boniface VIII in his palace at Anagni in 1303 by a detachment courtesy of France's Philip IV, which has the distinction of being the most high-toned such operation in history, because mentioned by Dante. It was an effrontery that paid off by cracking Boniface's nerve for life, proving to all that the secular power of a distant king could reach fast and far right into Rome.[45] Beyond bullying the Vicars of Christ, the kidnappings of sovereigns in centuries ahead would be undertaken by the slickest of special operations, with consequences felt to this day.

Our lives may seem far removed from the stealth of cattle raids, the penetration of strongholds, the snatching of treasuries, and even, one hopes, from a crusade against Islam — but less so once we think of our vulnerabilities to groups not altogether different from the Assassins (save for the degree of collateral damage within modern raiders' power), whose devotees were motivated enough to sacrifice their lives, who were not tied to any fixed public institutions, and who were able to unleash their deadly capabilities while hiding among their foes. The moment and the means are always at hand to greatly reward inventors of every sort, including them.

Part II

Part II

5

The Great Wheel Turns

When Nothing Else Works in a Time of Gunpowder, Learning, and Engineering, 1300–1500

*"By mutual confidence and mutual aid
Great deeds are done, and great discoveries made."*
Pope's Iliad

With the Renaissance, a culture was coming into being that drew increasingly on critical inquiry, rooted in the achievements of the twelfth and thirteenth centuries. Ever more people were beginning to assume that, where a technical problem existed, so did a technical answer, to be found by study, by searching for precedent, even by rapid analysis on the spot. Societies were thinking more deeply and effectively, whether in education, in administration, in commerce and finance, or in war. Toward the end of this 200-year span, for instance, Ferdinand of Aragon was rather hopelessly grinding away at a siege of Naples when, being a well-brought-up prince, he recalled an incident described in Procopius's *Gothic Wars* that enabled him to penetrate the city through an aqueduct.[1] One good reason to read, reflect, and ponder special methods.

During this period, warfare makes the technological leap from employing firepower as an occasional intensifier of siege or set-piece battle to applying it as the organizing principle of violence overall; wars of religion are fought savagely between Christians more than warrior. Their fierce reputation as Europe's preeminent infantry for hire by the 1300s arose from previous decades of fighting for independence from their Hapsburg feudal masters, in the kind of rough country that rewards initiative and improvisation. Perhaps also their lack of a class of mounted nobles increased their self-respect and stern mutual loyalty. Their distinctively long weapon, the eighteen-foot pike, and their ability to position themselves in deep, broad squares were strikingly similar to the signature weapons and formations of Alexander's infantry, a parallel that would fascinate Renaissance thinkers.

Soldiers who elect their own leaders are either so well honed that they can engage in a useful give-and-take with their superiors, or are as sloppy as a militia that chooses easygoing officers. The Swiss were anything but rabbles of dazed serfs kicked into battle by callous proprietors, the norm for any ordinary expanded infantry. These troops, even if draftees rented out by their fellow citizens, had community spirit, unit identity, and the hill-countryman's lack of awe of the gentry — a pretty deadly combination. There was room for initiative in the loose Swiss command structure; a freedom of expression within the ranks; and a self-conscious "glamour as sturdy, unshakable, non-prisoner-taking exterminators."[3] Their terrifying reputation was part of their stock-in-trade: war without grace-notes, aimed at the rapidest, cheapest victory possible. Such a force did not suddenly lose its nerve should its most visible captains be cut down — as could happen in any battle of that age, and often right through the nineteenth century.

In the simple terms of late-medieval warfare, this was the most mobile force in Europe, spurring imitation, as in the German mercenary infantry companies. With its pikes, halberds, and depth of ranks it was a strongly armed team that, by its nature, already had a special assignment. Those who survived its approach said that the impenetrable hedge of bristling points resembled a moving forest. "Engaging in battle as a pikeman [like the ancient Greeks] required an extraordinary state of mind," explains one scholar of the early Renaissance. "The security of each individual depended entirely on the solidity of the battle formation."[4] Risk had to be shared, and if done so with mutual confidence and mutual aid, paid off in a resourcefulness extraordinary for the time. Repeatedly able to tip the balance, as against Charles the Bold of Burgundy in 1477, their superb tactics were adaptable to the land over which they fought, as well as to the equipment and number of their opponents. The Swiss played their own hand, being too shrewd to meddle in their employers' politics. They could be trusted, although in an affectless way: it was the greatest of French tragic dramatists who coined the phrase "no money, no Swiss."[5]

In these fearsome democratic business formations, we see the mark not only of modern soldiering but movement toward the type of army that could contain the ingredients for special forces. However, even these troops did not possess the deeper talents of such forces as we think of them today. Swiss commanders were old soldiers "of the mental caliber of an intelligent sergeant-major," war-scarred veterans skilled in surprise and ambush, but lacking enlarged education or much imagination.[6] Almost nothing about their elaborately effective drill was written down, imposing further limits upon refining their skills. Moreover, the nature of society and war at that time prevented their pragmatic attitudes from being built on by others. The day was past when the hired help could morph into a warrior aristocracy. The Swiss had their place, and no more; they were set aside as soon as the job was done.

The Italian states had deployed the Swiss, but increasingly recruited mercenaries from their sunny peninsula through the condottieri (conductors) who, with their polyglot little armies, were the true warrior-entrepreneurs of the time.[7] The disorganization of lands fought over by what became known as the Holy Roman Empire, and the battles with the pope over the extent of church authority, had left Italy as a patchwork of largely self-governing city-states: Venice and Genoa, Florence and Pisa, Milan, also the kingdom of the Two Sicilies, and the Papal States themselves. Wealthy, bustling urban life by its nature offers a classic incitement to discreet means of predation. As in our day, cities that are generously open to trade and travel can overlook their vulnerabilities until too late, particularly at the hands of deadly conspirators working from within. As in 1377, when John Hawkwood got by the stout defenses of the rebellious little city of Cresna, victory here came less by keen infiltration than by traitors behind the walls. (Dante reserved a special place in hell for the betrayers of cities.) High culture, deep treachery, and quick, well-coordinated thrusts against targets worth coveting — we are back in a world in which Thucydides would have felt at home.

On the other end of worldly sophistication were numerous examples throughout Europe of small-action resistance against conquerors, as in Scotland and the Balkans. Guerrilla war waged by peasants and led by gentry had stalled English ambitions for supremacy in Scotland. Edward I — iron son of a feeble father, able to restore the imperiled fortunes of his dynasty in one exhilarating generation — had been able to cow even these fierce people by sustained, well-led savagery. However, the lessons of his campaigns still were not passed on, and his own son Edward II was way over his head when he moved against a patriot army loyal to Robert Bruce, the most plausible native claimant to the Scots throne. These were men who brought off night attacks and penetrated castles, camps, and towns in what, by any definition, are special operations.

In autumn 1313, for instance, a farmer loathing his English overlords "conceived the notion of elevating the familiar harvesting process to an operation of war and arranged the strategic details with his friends."[8] He let his hay grow high until the day when workers from the Linlithgow garrison emerged to cut the castle's own fields. Early the next morning, he loaded his crop. His men were hidden in a wagon driven by another tough Scot carrying a hatchet under his belt. The farmer himself walked idly alongside, right up to the castle gate and, when halfway through, suddenly broke into cries of "Thief! Call all! Call all!" In the ensuing chaos, the driver cut the harnesses, the farmer killed the nearest guard, his raiders burst out from under the hay, and the foreign occupier was quickly cut down or chased back through the fields.

On a February night the next year, the sentries of Roxburgh Castle, also in the Scottish borderlands, diverted themselves by scoffing at the stupidity of the halfwit crofters who had left their cattle to wander in the snow. Small cattle, perhaps, but in fact rather large men — sixty of whom were creeping in from the nearby forest with black gowns over their armor so as to resemble beasts from afar. Once unseen beneath the wall, the attackers cast high a specially made rope ladder with wooden steps and iron hooks, lodged it on the coping, and rushed up and over, bursting upon the soon-undone English. The following month it was the turn of Edinburgh Castle, which most everyone believed impenetrable to assault, irreducible by siege. Yet a small force scaled the sheer rock on the castle's north side, then used ropes to surmount the ramparts towering above. "Their nerves were dramatically tested," say the accounts, as they climbed hand over hand, up the cliff. The alarm was raised before all scrambled over, but a desperate fight left the enemy commander dead as the infiltrators sped to the south gate to admit a storming party.[9]

Against such reversals, the catastrophe at Bannockburn in midsummer 1314 should not have surprised the English, lulled though they were by three-to-one superiority. Their defeat came in a pitched battle after they had been severely shaken by a daring Scots raid the night before, which nearly killed Edward II, inflicted heavy casualties, shook morale, and, perhaps crucially, deprived the English of sleep and certainty. Two hundred raiders against a whole army — commando leverage again.

Thirteen years later, conspirators (likely minions of his wife's lover) finally got Edward. Power thereafter lay with the widowed queen mother, the "she-wolf of France," and with Mortimer, her paramour. All the while the new king, Edward III, fifteen at his father's overthrow, brooded and dissembled. Closely watched and being young, he had no opportunity to raise an army to hit such authority head-on.

Although Mortimer held no formal office, he enjoyed posts on the royal council and ruled indirectly, through the queen mother. He also found time to liquidate several of the old aristocracy, only a degree or two more principled than he, including the young king's uncle. Backed by his wild band of Welsh mercenaries, the ostentatious Mortimer was energetic enough to devastate the lands of his remaining rivals, while other malcontents chafed under his insolence for a rather astounding three years, their humiliation compounded by the rightful king's subjugation. Eventually, he would be accused of having "engrossed" every possible royal perquisite, including the royal dowager's favors, as well as conniving to have himself crowned and, along the way, shamefully enabling Robert Bruce to become king of an independent Scotland. But primarily Mortimer seems to have been preoccupied with his life of pomp and luxury, always busy setting up elaborate weddings on his estates for his seven well-married daughters.

Support for Edward III gathered around one powerful noble — William de Montacute, by the standards of the time a public-spirited citizen. The few contactable dissidents who were up to the challenge resolved to strike sharply and directly when opportunity presented itself in a court visit to Nottingham Castle in October 1330. Mortimer's Welsh security detail guarded every entrance. But the keeper of the castle, won over by Edward and Montacute, confided that a secret tunnel led under the walls. With characteristic cunning, Mortimer got wind of the plot — although not of the underground passage. He denounced Montacute (safe, for the moment, outside the castle) as a traitor and turned on Edward, accusing him of complicity. That same night, Montacute and his armed men slipped in, meeting Edward in the dark castle yard. The stakes were incredibly high; they had to move fast and certainly. There could have been no absolute confidence that the castle's governor was really on their side; if they bungled the operation, Montacute and his friends would die, slowly.

Moving with the speed of desperation, the group crashed in the doors of the upstart's bedroom, skewering two knights who got in their way. Mortimer was resolute enough to kill one of his assailants before being overpowered. The next day, Edward III proclaimed that he had finally taken over, then had Mortimer hauled back to London and the Tower. A month later, a kangaroo court condemned the fallen favorite to death, on charges as likely true as not of bribery and cruelties. He was promptly hanged, drawn, and quartered.

Edward went on to rule for the next forty-seven years, with Montacute and, undoubtedly, the castellan not suffering for their enterprise. Edward's coup raises not only the familiar question of castle vulnerability and the enormous rewards that might attend sudden, precise, small-force assault but also stands as a reminder that there were likely many other such ventures, although not so historic: the existence of secret passages in every stronghold enabled the castellan to play his own game, betraying whoever might place themselves in his web.

The common and by no means entirely unjustified view of later medieval war is that of a melee of posturing, arrogant, tournament-minded nobles, who, now and again, condescend to take the occasional gunner's or engineer's advice. If there was a certain lack of enterprise in maximizing the technological possibilities of an advancing age, we can be pretty sure that these titled ruffians were more than happy to adopt ever-better means of killing their neighbors. Clear heads and cold eyes existed aplenty to single out targets and opportunities for fast deft action, of which ambush and infiltration were just a taste.

Forty-odd years ago, Poul Anderson, contrarian par excellence, turned out an utterly convincing science-fiction extravaganza, *The High Crusade,* in which a company of English warriors mustered in 1345 for one more expedition of whoring and robbing in France gets scooped up by an interstellar predator culture.[10] By keeping their nerve, learning well, bluffing throughout, and particularly by fighting so differently from their self-satisfied opponents — midnight detachments slip through faraway forests, infiltrators hide amid an enemy armada, teams use undetectable wooden trebuchets to hurl captured "rocks" that go up in mushroom clouds — Sir Roger de Tourneville's Lincolnshire archers, huntsmen, and especially his knights, who are intimate with close-quarters battle, quite credibly raise a Catholic empire among the stars. The vastness of their achievement is as much a function of the imperial Wersgorix's previously unchallenged strengths as of the involuntary Crusaders' guile. "It doesn't have to be so" is as good a motto for any special force as it is for writers of science fiction, and in *The High Crusade* we have a marvelously instructive text for those embarking on extreme missions today.

Back on planet Earth, the final English struggle for preeminence in France was sporadically under way from 1337 to 1453, despite successive visits of the Black Death early on. The set-piece battles of what is known to us as the Hundred Years' War occurred largely in the first decade: Sluys (1340), Crécy (1346), Poitiers (1356), and — toward the end — Agincourt (1415) and Verneuil (1424). The full splendor of French knighthood had been shattered at the outset, including the capture of a king (Jean II le Bon) at Poitiers, and the intervening years did not go well for massed chivalry. Dramatically fewer knights remained to raise apprentices to the calling. We see the wasting of the countryside in the western third of France, the anarchy of private real-estate piracies that sprang up when so many great families lost their leaders, the burden of ransoms, and the desperate revolts of peasants taxed with mounting severity without even the crude benefits of protection.

A special warfare of small strikes and surprises emerged, much more focused and purposeful than the earth-scorching English raids (*chevauchées*) celebrated by Henry V (not Shakespeare's paladin, but the actual malevolent peasant-slayer and bigot) in a characteristically odious epigram: "War without fire," by which he meant devastating the French countryside, "is like sausages without mustard." And this form of war took hold until France arose from economic and social collapse, refortifying its cities and learning to "shadow" rather than to plunge upon an invading army.[11]

Some of the best descriptions of the intricacies of this generation-long maelstrom of small operations that make up so much of the middle part of the Hundred Years' War go unnoted even in today's military histories of this era. We instead find accounts in the never-translated memoirs of Jean de Bueil. He offers one of the most profound writings of the time because his book is both a highly original novel (distinct from courtly romances) and a firsthand military treatise that focuses on raiding, so different from translations of classical studies that had addressed the command of armies.

De Bueil thinly fictionalizes his own well-documented progress from being a poor child of the minor nobility to becoming one of France's chief generals, then Admiral of Cherbourg (a land force title for command of an immense region of France). Much of *Le Jouvencel* (*The Youngster*) is far removed from the sweep of great campaigns and the set-piece battles of chivalric war. *Le Jouvencel* depicts the special warfare of ambush and pinpoint exploits that spanned the decades of conflict between the French and English (and against England's allies, the Burgundians). The unnamed hero begins his career by stealing goats from a neighboring castle, then linen from a laundry to make himself a doublet, then a captain's cow, eventually winning a breastplate and a horse for himself with which to initiate a little band of young gentlefolk fighting by night with the bandit skills of avoiding roads, erasing tracks, and entirely sidestepping conventional combat. As the hero advances step-by-step to lead armies, he uses the graphically detailed tactics he had learned as a youth. In one assault, fifteen scouts are dispatched to draw out the garrison of "Escallon" into an entire web of ambushes.[12] We see another deft operation against the city of "Crathor"; the Youngster has studied its defenses while a prisoner; once freed, he leads his band against the city, choosing a night of half-moon, using the shadows projected by the guard towers to scale the walls, the ladders and tools of his little party wrapped in black fabric to ensure silence and invisibility. "Crathor" quickly falls to shock and fury.[13]

The struggle between the English and French groaned on until the most unconventional of warriors arose from peasant soil. As so often before and since, special approaches were turned to when familiar methods brought a string of disasters. In 1429, Joan of Arc revitalized the French cause in one season, knocking the English onto the defensive. Irrespective of gender, her low birth ensured that she could enjoy at best a sort of mascot role, while senior officers — including Jean de Bueil, in a meeting of minds — held the reins of actual operations. Yet her daring compelled her "companions" to the highest standards of performance, if only in trying to extricate her from the consequences of her precipitate forward dashes. The mystique alone of a passionate leader of relatively small forces — in this instance, of a royally certified virgin through whom God was apparently speaking — can pay off in exemplary, focused, and suddenly unstoppable actions.

The seventeen-year-old Maid (as legend identifies her) introduced a series of fast, successful, enterprising offensives, breaking through the English siege of Orléans at night, then reaching out from within at the surrounding forts strangling the city. The white heat of her example did more to renew the dwindling garrison's energies than the arrival of the few fresh troops she could bring with her — or, according to chronicles, her eerie brilliance in positioning her artillery.[14] Her aura arose from doing the exceedingly strange, in limited arenas where dramatic success could have extraordinary consequences. Equally important, word of her strangeness began to terrify the English.

Time and again, when a winning army is kicked hard by an unimagined assault, its triumphalism is shattered at the same time that the despair of the losers is erased: the contest can begin anew. The predictable attack may be able to shave away an enemy's strength, but a special operator such as de Bueil — let alone a warrior as alarmingly undefinable as Joan — understands the prick of a pin against the skin of a balloon.

Once Joan was captured and burned alive, the war's ultimate progress would be left to her mystique-charged but also very competent companions. The English were able to counter with their own daring displays, similarly driven by a desperate sense that nothing else was working — as at the capture of Pontoise castle, sixteen miles northwest of Paris, in February 1437. A small infiltration detail disguised as peasants seized a gate for just long enough to admit a powerful storming party, which had crept right up against the walls by wearing white sheets that blended with the snow, thereby enabling the attackers to sit unnoticed in the drifts for hours. This feat of skill, coordination, and endurance might have presaged the repeated use of similar, ever more clever assaults, by a force specially honed for the purpose. But it did not, probably because the storming of Pontoise, like the higher authorities' acquiescence in Joan's leadership and the turn to special warfare during the middle of the Hundred Years' War, was a last-ditch remedy at a critical moment. To an aristocratic warrior elite, such technique may have smacked too much of the vulgarly technical — and of the ingloriously bourgeois — to appeal as a pattern of innovation.

On the Balkan Peninsula, amid the overthrow of Serbian power by the Turks in 1389, a handful of young men (posing as Serb deserters to get into the enemy camp) had been able to kill the triumphant Sultan Murad (the "Amurath" of *Henry IV*) in his tent, pitched in Blackbirds' Field in Kosovo. Again, the ability to strike a hard-to-replace enemy leadership could do politically what battle could not. In this instance, their hit helped dislocate Ottoman power for a time and made Kosovo a Serbian holy place right down to our day. Yet the huge, decaying, Greek-speaking city of Constantinople, almost a country in itself, was always the true prize for the Ottomans. This 1,000-year-old relic of imperial Roman might — recovered by the Greeks from the piratical Latin crusaders who had taken it in 1204 — was the sole super-fortress facing Islam. With its fourteen miles of high walls, Constantinople still retained the most formidable defense system in Europe, while the city's fortified port enabled it to be supplied by sea. In case of siege, the Greek Christians might be able to call on the more or less neutral Genoese outpost of Pera, across the Bosphorus, whose artillery could help interdict any hostile shipping.

In the early spring of 1453, the Ottoman sultan Mehmed II's army of some eighty thousand troops was joined by perhaps another twenty thousand irregulars, comprising an odd assortment of adventurers from every country and race within earshot of the fascinating possibilities for plunder. The army camped before Constantinople's walls, while Mehmed's fleet, for all the Genoese artillery, rode at anchor in the Bosphorus (the channel that flows by Constantinople, from the Black Sea to the Sea of Marmora). The defenders still were able to resist the newfangled heavy siege artillery, and able to repulse Ottoman siege towers and fourteen tunnels penetrating beneath the walls — the miners being suffocated, drowned by letting in water, or met underground with spears and knives.

Ottoman ships could not prevent Christian reinforcements from slipping in by sea, nor could they break into the Golden Horn. That estuary formed a natural moat for one side of the great walls, which the defenders had closed with an immense iron chain between themselves and Pera, and about two dozen ships of their own.[15] Turkish chroniclers tell of the nightmares that obsessed the twenty-one-year-old Mehmed as he tried to find a way to take the fabulous city. The Greeks believed that their obstinate resistance had worn him down and that the city could not fall unless doubly attacked, from the harbor as well as from land. A keen student of history, fluent in six languages, Mehmed muttered about Alexander, who with a far smaller army had conquered half the world.

"In this perplexity," Gibbon relates, "the genius of [Mehmed] conceived and executed a plan of a bold and marvelous cast": he would haul his ships two miles from the Bosphorus into the upper reaches of the harbor, over a ridge that nowhere rose less than two hundred feet above sea level. A road was expanded, strong planks laid, and covered with cattle fat. Black smoke from the Turkish artillery hammering at the walls may have helped obscure the scheme. About seventy light galleys and brigantines were beached on the Bosphorus shore, placed on cradles, then drawn forward on rollers by teams of men and oxen, aided by pulleys.[16] Sails were unfurled to help. In a single day (though likely more time was required) it is said that half the Turkish fleet was painfully hoisted up a hill, rattled over the plain, and was launched behind the chain and the Greek ships guarding the Horn.

With fleet and army in place, Mehmed improvised a pontoon bridge formed of about a thousand barrels, linked with iron and covered by more planks, which he used to shorten communications around the top of the Horn; detachments balancing aboard this platform also brought their ladders up against the most vulnerable side of the walls. At 1:30 A.M. on Tuesday, May 29 (Julian style), Mehmed opened his final attack with horns, drums, and cymbals. Probably the best visualization of what this night was like is the assault on Minas Tirith in the movie *Lord of the Rings: The Return of the King:* the hopelessness of grievously outnumbered defenders, and the terror as felt by a cornered animal as bellowing hordes use artillery and muscle to bash down walls, splinter gates, and finally crash mercilessly through.

Emperor Constantine XIII, heir of that first Christian ruler who had given his name to the city itself, urged his people to be worthy of their ancestors, the heroes of the ancient world. Perhaps, they hoped in vain, they still had a chance if they could hold out until rescue from fellow Christians in the West. Yet Mehmed first threw in his irregulars to soften up the enemy. These were anything but a special force, many of them Christians fighting for booty and the Sultan's pay, and known to be effective only in their first onrush. As an encouraging touch, military police were echeloned behind them, bearing whips and maces. And behind the police were the Janissaries ("new soldiers") who were Mehmed's real elite — a deadly corps of infantry recruited by the five-yearly "levy of boys" from his Christian subjects, the children reared to a fanatical devotion to Islam. They were held in reserve to cut down any irregulars who might flee past the police. It was the Janissaries who were to plunge into the city once a breach was made in the walls by the age's weapon of mass destruction, a super-gun with reputedly a twenty-six-foot barrel drawn by sixty oxen.

But it was not the pounding of this monster (able to disgorge only seven times per day) that brought about the fatal penetration. Fewer than seven thousand frantic, exhausted Christians (their children and elderly huddled in prayer at small parish churches) furiously held off the Janissaries in hand-to-hand fighting as sections of wall tumbled down around them. What began the collapse was a little gate left unbarred after raiders had hurried back from a sortie against the Moslem flanks. In the early light of dawn, a party of Janissaries, some fifty strong, spotted the opening, dashed through, killed defenders atop the wall, and cleverly ran up the Turkish standard. Panic took hold. Then began a three-day saturnalia of rape, looting, and murder unmatched since the Catholics hacked their way in a quarter millennium before. Constantine fought to the end at the city walls, never to be found beneath the other corpses.

Mehmed's victory was the fruit of a combination of imaginative response to stalemate, an ability to coordinate his soldiers and ships, and, ultimately, an exploitation of the tiniest of gaps. To be sure, he had the advantage of numbers. But it is uncertain that what was quickly accomplished after two months' slugging could otherwise have been brought about: only days before the final assault, his most trusted councilor had urged him to give up. A truly strategic special operation of laboring a fleet across rough terrain, climaxed by pouncing on the kind of minute vulnerability that such immense walls must offer (but who knew where?), was rewarded with the highest of political consequences. As in 1204, the small but decisive move proved vital to victory. It brought the end of the free Greek world, and Christendom thereafter ceased to exercise even the glint of authority in the eastern Mediterranean basin.

Had either commandolike insertion of 1204 or of 1453 failed, the Christian East's destiny would have been unpredictably different. Particularly if Mehmed had indeed given up, who knows what an extra generation of survival might have offered Constantinople? Although one cannot play with the counterfactual, we will see the decisive and often conquering role of the daring few at other pivotal times to come.

Far to the Mediterranean west, a slower conquest was culminating against a different Moslem invader. As the Spanish Christian kingdoms stood on the threshold of victory over the Arabs who had swallowed most of the Peninsula, their armies came, in 1487, to the key coastal port of Malaga, in the highly civilized Moorish kingdom of

Grenada. A Moslem suicide assassin presented himself as a defector, claiming to have information for King Ferdinand, who was personally commanding the troops, and was taken to the quarters of Ferdinand and of his queen, Isabella, who had joined her husband at the front. Amazingly, the false defector was not adequately searched (a blunder that keeps repeating itself to this day, as in the September 9, 2001, slaying of Afghan rebel leader Ahmed Shah Massoud in his camp, by two Al Qaeda killers posing as journalists). Sometimes, however, inefficiencies have a way of canceling out. Speaking no Castilian, he mistook a Portuguese nobleman for the king, flipped a knife from beneath his robe, stabbed the wrong man, and was sliced to pieces on the spot — nevertheless leaving the lesson, if nothing else, that an incautious hunger to get information (or to share it) opens a way in for the one-way mission.

Not until the late sixteenth-century taking of Dumbarton Rock during the Scottish wars of religion do we encounter the next, and truly special, imaginative leap — turning an enemy's technology against himself. This is one of the earliest examples in which infiltrators were able to force a garrison to stare down the barrels of its own castle guns. Turning around the cannon transformed the other side's high-tech prowess into its weakness and was an introductory note on the value of discerning a different form of enemy strength. Outside Glasgow, this step may indeed be the breakpoint between medieval special operations and those of at least early modern times.

Dumbarton, the "Mount of the Britons," is a huge, red, vertiginous double volcanic plug, with nothing on its sheer face to hang on to. Two hundred and forty feet high, and a mile in circumference, the towering rock rises over the Firth of Clyde, only a marshy isthmus tying it to the mainland. Entrenched between its double peaks lies what had been the most famous fortress upon a mountain in the Dark Ages of Britain, a stronghold legendarily built by King Arthur's Merlin. On a densely foggy night in March 1571, a party of about 150 men and a guide silently scaled the cliffs at the north side. The garrison reasonably judged their bastion to be impregnable: the attackers knew that it would therefore be carelessly guarded. If successful, the operation could have the immense consequence of capturing the traditional port of juncture with France, which had been backing the recently deposed Mary, Queen of Scots, a fellow Catholic and the French queen dowager.

On the way up the rock, as we learn in a chronicle of the time, a man on one of the scaling ladders suffered an epileptic fit. He was grasped, gagged, tied up, and bound to the underside of his ladder. This immediate response is likely not one that could have been improvised in thirty seconds on a moonless night, nor simply accomplished by a group of picked men chosen hours before, nor by a technique drawn from civilian life. (It seems likely to have derived from a morale-enhancing means for helping the wounded in the hideous close quarters of breach assaults, where moats yawned below.)[17] Once the remaining force was on top, and the cannon suddenly turned, Dumbarton fell fast. And in its taking we are beginning to see another newly forming development: a fully prepared loyalty to one's casualties even in the extreme circumstances of a clifftop night attack, one that is akin to the maxim "no man left behind" that we find in today's crack units, which includes bringing home the dead. Special forces — even more so than armies themselves, which are likely to have reserves, redundancy, and possibilities of regrouping — cannot be drawn from callous, heavily muscled oafs, but from people as intense in their loyalty to the fellowship as in their commitment to the objective. "It takes an early Christian spirit of total self-abnegation and denial of individual material interest to create a truly effective killing machine," observes one of Geoffrey Household's characters in that gripping evocation of third world struggle, *Thing to Love*.

‡

FOURTEEN NINETY-FOUR is the most nearly appropriate hinge after which generally described medieval approaches to war start swinging toward oblivion, as they are replaced by recognizably modern techniques and procedures. We see the feckless young Charles VIII, king of France, known to those he did not lay waste as "the Affable," begin what would be France's sixty-year attempt to build an empire in Italy. Each side readily adopted any expedient to defeat the enemy: A detachment of the imperial Hapsburg forces would dress themselves in white for a snowy sneak attack to rout the French at Pavia; in turn, French men at arms donned the red cross of the Holy Roman Empire as a disguise to inflict their own surprise at Bicocca.[18] Ferdinand and Isabella had just united Aragon and Castile, thereby creating probably the best-balanced military force in the world, leading in mobile field guns as well as small arms. England, within the lifetime of those being born, would be pretty much cured of its ambitions for continental empire.[19]

Outreaching trade, war, and ever more distant conquest were enlarging ambitions for wealth and glamour. Greater stakes and possibilities particularly affected the special operation, always rooted in and drawing its strength from the condition of the society that undertook it, and perhaps yet more from that which it sought to break. It was the technological innovations of the fifteenth and early sixteenth centuries that made possible the military transformations of the next.[20] In the increasing development of specialized means of combat, in the readiness (albeit in extremis) to consider the eccentric, we see commando outliers emerging from increasingly formalized armies.

The Spanish kingdoms' excellent warrior cadres were poised for just such an outreach. The last Moorish power was overthrown five years after Malaga had added to a momentum both of technique and faith-driven energy. And here Spain got ahead of England and France. The Turks had been building a formidable empire in the east, although there remained determined pockets of resistance.[21] Now the Spaniards were about to leap the ocean to conquer much greater spaces far to the west — but not with armies of European scope. For centuries, only the boldest of Europe's navigators had ventured even as far as the bulge of Africa. Suddenly, the energy of the *reconquista* (reconquest from Islam) was distilled into armed bands, little more than landing parties, which burst on the formidable cultures of the New World mainland. This is the point in history where the smallest of forces had the greatest long-term effect, as the Aztecs and Incas were about to find out.

6

War of the Worlds

Where Only a Few Could Go: Aztecs and Incas Meet the Conquistadors, 1500–1600

*"So many cities level with the ground, so many nations
exterminated, so many millions of people fallen by the edge
of the sword. . . . Mechanic victories!"*
MONTAIGNE, 1585

MIGHTY CIVILIZATIONS of extraordinary achievement existed in
the Americas, enjoying excellent communications and a raw level of
power that stood for legitimacy in the hard world of virtually all preindustrial societies. Nevertheless, those civilizations had not evolved use
of the wheel, or any serious metallurgy, had never imagined cannons,
nor possessed any animals to tame for riding. The advanced qualities
that they did enjoy — such as centralized government — made them
vulnerable to forces small and rapid enough to pierce to the heart and
to immediately exploit initial success. Minute cadres of invaders
destroyed the Aztecs and Incas, even though each fielded well-organized armies in the scores of thousands, in less than twenty years.[1]
Nothing shows the poignancy of their defeat more than the Incas'
dazed acquiescence as they stood around once their conquerors, glut-
ted with mastery and treasure, fought to the death among themselves.
How could all this have been done, let alone so fast? Why could it not
have been accomplished by other, decidedly conventional military
means in a world still so empty and open to surprise?

The Conquistador parties tramping through the vast uncharted Americas highlight the profound dangers of distance for the special force. Men hundreds, if not thousands, of miles from the meddling hands of authority were equally far away from any resources that they could not cobble together or commandeer on their own. Here the challenge was to reach out and keep one's nerve in the face of the totally unknown — which was even spookier, perhaps, than what the well-tutored Alexander had encountered — let alone the great but at least well-understood dangers that any twenty-first-century special force might confront. The wonders of the New World — the Valley of Mexico, the mountains of Peru — were farther off than Mars is today: there were no photographs, no awareness of what terror might be mustering beyond the next hill. Yet these impoverished, unscrupulous hidalgos from the marches of Spain knew that God had willed the expulsion of the Moors and Jews from their homeland; surely, He would grant much more to these warriors of what the Spanish came to term the "New World." Particularly in Cortés, we see a thinking man and an unreservedly brave warrior, as well as a coalition-builder — a combination vital in modern commando leaders (perhaps more than in mainstream officers). These few conquerors were ravenous killers, but their genius for detecting the briefest moment of opportunity deserves a certain grim commemoration.

Ever since the blind Bostonian lawyer William Prescott published his gripping *History of the Conquest of Mexico* in the mid-nineteenth century, this tale of ruthless invasion and sustained triumph by a handful of adventurers almost as bewildered as their victims has fascinated readers worldwide. Distilling the conquest's voluminous records to highlight the vulnerabilities of an advanced civilization, however, and to examine what occurred in light of the special operation, offers a different perspective from those of past centuries.[2] So, too, does this approach when we consider the fate of the Incas. The destruction of both these New World cultures was by no means inevitable. Had either or both of them not been brought down fast, these sophisticated civilizations stood quite likely to adapt new methods as well as weaponry to resist, whereupon Spain's chance of a settled imperial claim would have disappeared as European rivals entered into the general struggle for empire. Only the lightning stroke of tiny, flexible, focused — and absurdly confident — forces could bring about so vast a change so soon.

‡

IN 1959, when people were still enamored with exploring the stars, Randall Garrett's space opera, "Despoilers of the Golden Empire," was published in the magazine *Analog*. After traveling in a vehicle "not equipped for atmospheric navigation," Captain Frank encounters a culture of gold users. In his first battle, he falls off his ground carrier, which (not being programmed to pick him up) returns to the rear lines without him; he nearly perishes. No matter; his men seize the celestial emperor, rule, and fall out among themselves. We read about the eeriness of the voyage so far from Captain Frank's home — the endless country, the cities and temples, the magnificent enticing riches. At the end, as he is finally cut down by his own people, he kisses the cross he has drawn with his own blood: "So died Francisco Pizarro, conqueror of Peru." The idiom of historic conquest and that of science fiction come so very close.

It was not the modest technological superiority of the Europeans over the builders of the pyramids of Mexico and the great highroads of the Andes that brought victory, though that interpretation has rarely been challenged ever since Montaigne, repelled by the vulgar Spaniards' defeat of these high civilizations, stigmatized the overthrows as "mechanic victories." His interpretation then became the controlling historiography of the nineteenth century, when technology (or "mechanics") was regarded as ever more significant against barbarian peoples. And it remains the established view, accepted today by military historians and even by Jared Diamond, a human geographer with profound insights into the relations of societies.[3] To be sure, the Conquistadors had important tactical advantages in their cavalry, steel, and (very early) firearms. But they carried more crossbows than crude, slow-to-load arquebuses and small cannon, the shock of which wore off fast. Their horses were usually a few dozen at most. Their swords of Toledo steel could kill by a swift thrust while an enemy who carried a weapon only sharp-edged or weighty was reaching back to slash or clobber. But a Conquistador who was busy stabbing opponent A could easily be sliced or crushed by enemies B, C, and D coming from every side. All such advantages only went so far, which is not far enough to give much credit to technology.

Indeed, the Spaniards would probably not have been able to accomplish what they did had they landed ten thousand well-equipped foot soldiers and cavalry on either the coasts of Mexico or of Peru. Such armies would have posed a threat so unambiguous that they would likely never have had the opportunity to snatch Montezuma or Atahuallpa. As they slogged forth to face these great realms en masse, the defenders would have had ample time to call out their levies, repair alliances, and devastate the countryside, if need be, to starve the invaders. Given breathing room, Aztec and Inca alike could have moved their crucial plexuses of power, decision, and authority out of harm's way, not to mention using passes higher than the tallest peaks in Spain to lay into such expeditions.

In fact, at the time, Spain had sent better-equipped forces into less exotic territory — and seen them wiped out. Having ousted the familiar Moslem enemy from the Iberian peninsula in 1492, for example, one would have thought that to defeat them in North Africa several years later should have been a cakewalk. Yet while penny packets of adventurers on the other side of the world triumphed against millions-strong societies deploying enormous armies, Spain and Portugal's main battle forces met disaster across the Straits of Gibraltar. (Afterward, it was said that the slave markets of Algiers were so overstocked that a Christian was not a fair price for an onion; Morocco would not fall for another four centuries.)[4] Disillusioning experience over the next five hundred years, from Little Bighorn to Dien Bien Phu to Mogadishu, has taught more advanced nations that the advantages conferred by repeating rifles or napalm-dropping bombers or helicopter gunships are no guarantee of ascendancy over simpler but more numerous people ready to fight to the death. At this moment in the Americas, other, very special means were essential to Spanish victory.

What got the Conquistadors into such fatally close proximity with their targets was, first, the sheer smallness of the forces that made these enormous states initially treat the invaders as curiosities, and then the

Conquistadors' ability further to exploit the virtues of small size to move straight in while improvising continuously (not the hallmark of most big battle forces). Nonetheless, the shock and awe by which a tiny, better-equipped outfit can induce panic in an entire disciplined army may work once or maybe twice, but the effect evaporates — all the more so against formidable imperial armies such as these.

"Both sides agreed," explorer and historian John Hemmings observes in discussing the Incas, "that a Spanish infantryman was inferior to his native counterpart"; and Hispanicist Hugh Thomas, as he describes epic showdowns with the Aztecs, reminds us that "superior technology did not count in street battles."[5] Indeed, soon after the first episode of urban combat in the Aztec capital, and barely escaping amid the horrors of *la noche triste* (the sorrowful night), remnants of Cortés's outfit had no guns at all. Faced with ferocious warriors who were fighting to the death, they raised only a few hundred swords and shields against tens of thousands of arrows, javelins, black obsidian blades that could slash like razors. Still, they prevailed. So we must look elsewhere than at technology, or even the sheer close-quarters abilities of the compact special force, to explain how attackers fewer in number than the households of the monarchs they snuffed out were able to bring down these empires.

What we see is complete self-assurance and an utter faith in one's fellows (if only in the heat of desperation) that multiplied the clout of constant improvisation, and the sense that such small numbers could win by piercing to the heart. It is the final, vital quality of any top-performing team and, in this case, one united around the will of an iron leader as was common in the early epochs of special forces. He made them believe that they could do it, and confidence, as always, was contagious. It was a confidence derived partly from the valor of ignorance, and partly from the *reconquista* spirit of implementing God's supposedly manifest will.

It is a spirit we see being proved to equally astounding effect during the same years by another small, extraordinary outfit working along military lines. That "picked force," so unquestioning before its general, was also prepared to "carry the faith by any means and at any personal cost into any land of the globe."[6] And it did, with absolutely no guns and steel required. Begun as a band of seven (later ten) by the Basque soldier Ignatius de Loyola, the Jesuits and their accomplishments help illuminate that final conclusive Conquistador advantage: a conviction that numbers are less important than purpose and will. Gladly including marginal people (initially those with Jewish ancestry), the Jesuits too would penetrate the Americas north and south, as well as Japan, China, and India, while charting, during the centuries to come, five of the world's eight major rivers and claiming more martyrs than any other Catholic order. All that should have been impossible as well, except for the combination of conscious, demanding attitude and extreme focus that distinguishes the special force throughout our story.[7]

Before Columbus, Spain's only possession of any consequence outside Europe had been the Canary Islands. Believing he was heading to India, the admiral — in his three little caravels with fewer than a hundred men on the most important journey in history — carried a letter to present to the Great Khan of China, and he had brought along with him a Jewish linguist who could speak Arabic. (Islam was known to have penetrated China.) Instead, on a continent that was not supposed to be there, Columbus encountered the Taino, whose means of self-defense, while alarming, proved insufficient — "their darts being wands without iron."[8]

By 1492, the population of central America and in the high valleys of the Andes alone might have numbered about forty-five million, encompassing more than fifteen distinct cultures and 160 linguistic stocks. Columbus's voyage kicked off a breathtaking sequence of discovery, conquest, and destruction. Hispaniola (the island which today embraces Haiti and the Dominican Republic) was taken; Cuba was completely occupied by 1511. A decade later, Mexico would fall in less than two years; then the core lands of the Incas even faster. Aztec primacy rested on a web of tightly held tribal states; the Incas were masters of a centralized empire. The Conquistadors nailed them both.

Hernán Cortés was from a family of honorable extraction (as it used to be said) but without wealth, in the Extremadura, still a desolate, dirt-dry region of Spain. At seventeen, he tried to embark on an early expedition to the Americas, but was injured during a fall while climbing into (or out of) a lady's apartment window, the ship sailing without him. Four years later, in 1506, he finally embarked for Hispaniola, then the center of Spanish predatory exploration.

In the simple agricultural life of the Caribbean, Cortés made himself useful by helping suppress an Indian revolt, being compensated in land and slaves, and by appointment as a magistrate.[9] He helped quell "rebels" in western Cuba, showing coolness of nerve, and acquired further estates — activities interrupted by jail time for seducing and then abandoning the woman he would ultimately get around to marrying.

From Cuba to the Yucatán is only 120 miles, but it might as well have been as many light-years. In 1510, the Spanish had founded an outpost at Darien (a name that dreamily echoed an ancient fairy tale) on the northeast coast of Panama. Nine years later, they had made at least two well-documented encounters with the coast of Mexico, and indeed yet other forays may simply have never come back. Cuba's governor determined to send a third, stronger squadron to the Yucatán as a holding action for his own interests.

Why Cortés could be captain, given his modest investment in the enterprise, is still a mystery. His grandly designated "armada" cleared Santiago de Cuba on February 18, 1519, Cortés knowing that the furious governor — appalled that the scale of his preparations looked far more ambitious than necessary — had rescinded his command at the last moment. The armada probably included twelve vessels, only four of any real size, the rest being brigantines (skirmish ships), which were essentially masted open boats.[10] He had with him about 530 Europeans, a few of them women, one or two of whom would show inspiring courage in the thick of the fight. Cortés was thirty-four, most of the others in their early twenties. Few of the men had military training; even fewer had seen war. Only thirty of this number had crossbows. A dozen carried arquebuses weighing about twenty pounds with thick stocks, a barrel about a meter long, and a cumbersome matchlock mechanism. There were ten brass guns and four smaller pieces of artillery, perhaps a few actual cannon. There may have been up to fifty sailors, as well as some two hundred Cuban Indians and a few African freemen and slaves. Their sixteen horses would prove vital, and a pack of mastiffs were terrifying executioners (as witness the fittingly Spanish word *aperrear,* to throw to the dogs). That Spaniards still depended on packs of war dogs may indicate how primitive was their other weaponry.

The rabble Cortés assembled cannot be described as a special force, as we think of it today. Except for a doctor, several notaries, and a half-dozen carpenters, these men were akin to the denizens of a Marine Corps brig: youthful poor whites who had arrived too late for the initial plunder of the Caribbean. But the winnowing-out process had been special enough — just getting from Spain to the edge of the world had been a self-selecting ordeal, let alone taking the decision to step off it. Patriotism and institutional loyalty are worn thin by isolation, remoteness, and empty bellies. Loot, however, can be a self-renewing motivator for precisely the kind of fellows who are unlikely to be inspired by regimental songs, spitshines, and by calling their betters "sir." These men were in the right place at the right time.

Cortés made first landfall on the large island of Cozumel off Yucatán. The Spanish also not being linguistically adept (now a key requirement for U.S. Special Forces), he had the immense luck to come upon the survivor of a Spanish shipwreck eight years before, kept alive after his companions had been eaten at a fiesta, who had learned the local Mayan tongue.

Advancing slowly along the Gulf, on March 4 Cortés landed on the shores of Mexico, in the present province of Tabasco, crushing local resistance with gunfire and cavalry and accepting, as amends, Indian maidens whom he courteously dispensed among his lieutenants. One was the gifted "Marina," who would be at his side for much of the expedition, providing espionage, advice, and eventually a son, Don Martín Cortés. Most significantly, she spoke the Aztec language as well as the Mayan tongues.

Sailing up the coast with his two interpreters, Cortés learned of a great ruling city in the middle of a vast lake, where sat enthroned a fearsomely powerful monarch. It was somewhere on the mountain plains of the interior, 250 miles inland, as the crow flies. He matter-of-factly landed his entirely all-too-modest outfit on April 21, near what is now Veracruz (True Cross). On Easter Sunday at this beach-head, he first encountered Aztec emissaries offering golden presents; he stated his determination to see their emperor Montezuma, and was pleased to stage military exercises with horse and his smallish cannon.

In the eyes of the Aztecs, concludes Thomas, these gaunt, bearded warriors were seen not so much as the popular notion of gods with thunderbolts but as "political terrorists."[11] As terrorists often do, Cortés was able to exploit divisions in the society he was attacking. What he initially considered an empire was more a confederation of about four hundred cities acknowledging some degree of subjugation to the Aztecs (or "Mexica," as they called themselves) and their capital of Tenochtitlán (which they often called "Mexico," or "Mexico Tenochtitlán"). He shrewdly recognized that much of the Aztec realm was kept busy oppressing the rest through fast-moving armies and punitive raids — the beating hearts of prisoners and slaves being fed to deities, with priests decked in the dried skins of previous victims amid the ceremonial devouring of arms and legs, and children being tortured for good measure to induce rain.[12]

Venturing ten miles inland, he witnessed a delegation of Aztec nobles extracting tribute from a surrounding town. He cunningly demanded that the hesitant Indians instead imprison the collectors, although he just as artfully took credit when setting two of the Aztec officials free, assuring them of his respect for their revered monarch in the capital. But word of the insult inflicted on Montezuma's authority swept the country. That reluctantly defiant town became the starting point for the thrust into the interior.

Cortés demonstrates the impact that a tight, lethal force can enjoy just with the first jolt of showing up from seemingly nowhere. He was still learning the tactics, but he had chosen his strategy: to fly blind if he could keep up yet greater surprises for the other side. Had the Conquistadors lingered on the coast for a year or two, gathering information and preparing their strike, the aroused power would have grown all too accustomed to these interlopers: accustomed to the point of annihilating anger. To be sure, an anthropological survey could have been useful before marching west, had anthropology existed. But the invaders were few, and time was against them. They had to act on the little that they knew — "ready, *fire,* aim" being one form of talented adaptivity.

Another ship with about sixty men and several horses beat its way in to his landing zone, somewhat offsetting the thirty Spaniards already dead from disease and combat before the main force, such as it was, had more than scratched the surface of empire. By now, some rational few must have been desperate to return to the coast and sail back to Cuba as fast as possible; conspirators in the ranks were planning to steal a ship and report to the governor that Cortés had already dispatched his own representatives to promote his personal interests in Spain. A special operation, however, does not, and usually cannot, pull back to hit harder. Cortés therefore seems to have ordered a cadre of faithful officers to slip back to the ships, drive nine of the twelve onto the sand, stripping these of rigging, sails, anchors, and guns.[13] Closing the door on retreat for all concerned was a classic example of small-force psychology centuries before the doctrine had been formalized anywhere but in the instincts of natural leaders. The venture must triumph or simply disappear. Armies can recuperate when they meet reverses, can call up reserves. A force of the absurd size of Cortés's — not only behind enemy lines but inside an enemy world — must bring off its mission or be consumed in the attempt. Cortés tortured and killed the core conspirators, while making it rather clear to the rest that it was preferable to follow.

In early August, somewhat over four hundred Conquistadors with war dogs and fifteen horses began the journey up to Tenochtitlán, accompanied by probably 150 Cuban Indians, perhaps eight hundred new Indian allies acting as guides, porters, and potential auxiliaries. They crossed the sleet-drenched passes, descending into open country still seven thousand feet above sea level. People along the way warned of Montezuma's huge armies, speaking with awe of his capital dominating the vast lake, only approachable by three long stone causeways interrupted by bridges of wooden beams, which could be removed to deny entry — or escape. The warnings were echoed by a little group of Aztec emissaries being dragged along.

Ahead lay the rugged lands of the Tlaxcalans, who worshipped the same blood-hungry Aztec war god (among others) but had long refused to pay tribute to His earthly representatives in Tenochtitlán. There was no open path through their densely populated cluster of little cities, about two-thirds of the way to the capital. Initially, thousands of warriors fought Cortés face-to-face, with guns and steel gaining some (but not necessarily decisive) advantage over spears, arrows, razor-edged clubs, and exceedingly strong shields. The vast confused mass of brave Tlaxcalans charged and recoiled, and charged again. "This was," says Prescott, "a repetition of the combat of the ancient Greeks and Persians" — it was the advantage of thought rather than of numbers.[14]

For two weeks the Spaniards slept with their weapons at their sides and horses saddled. The Tlaxcalans essayed one last attack, but had to do so under a full moon, and Cortés never allowed himself to be taken by surprise. Within minutes, the story goes, his men leapt to arms, and the enemy was crushed. Cortés could then offer peace, obtaining provisions and free passage. His purpose was not just to conciliate these tough fighters for the time it took to traverse their determined little commonwealth. He had also grasped their value as combatants.

His first Indian allies returning home, perhaps a thousand Tlaxcalans now joined his coalition of the willing for the march to Tenochtitlán. He gathered further intelligence, drew on Marina's deft, wide-eyed espionage skills to anticipate deception, and — by advantage of surprise — perpetrated at least one hideous exemplary massacre of some three thousand Indians at Cholula en route, which served further to terrify. Like many special operators since, he worked around his chain of command, such as that might be, sending what treasure he was collecting not to the governor in Cuba but directly to King Carlos of Castile and Aragon (grandson of Ferdinand and Isabella, and more expansively known as the Holy Roman Emperor Charles V). He also pledged, in a word that resonates through history, that he would "pacify" (*apacigar*) the country.[15]

The Valley of Mexico is a plain of some three thousand square miles lying midway across the great Mesoamerican isthmus, 7,800 feet above sea level. Mountain ranges hem it to the south, west, and north, the eastern peaks culminating in the 17,887-foot snow-capped volcano Popocatépetl. Through the intricate gorges of this Sierra Nevada, Cortés took his curious amalgam of early modern adventurers and High Stone Age auxiliaries, his slathering dogs bounding ahead. He sent word that he was coming as an ambassador.

The column spilled down into the valley nearly three months after

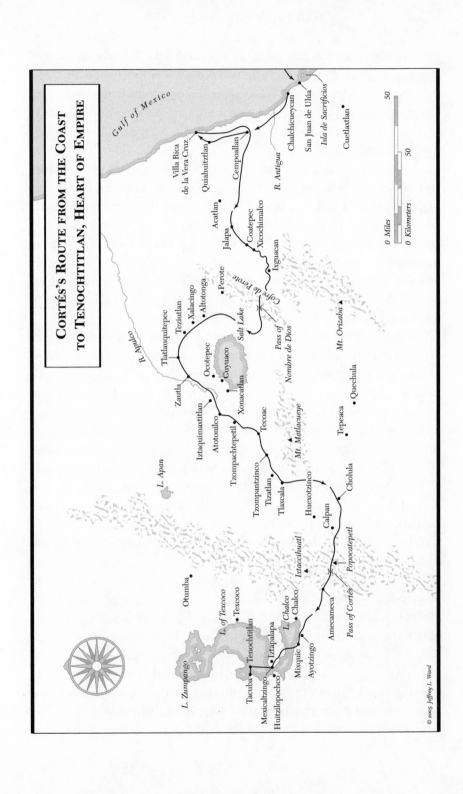

CORTÉS'S ROUTE FROM THE COAST
TO TENOCHTITLAN, HEART OF EMPIRE

Gulf of Mexico

Chalchicueyecan
San Juan de Ulúa
Isla de Sacrificios
Cuetlaxtlan

Villa Rica
de la Vera Cruz
Quiahuiztlan
Cempoallan
R. Antigua

Acatlan
Jalapa
Coatepec
Xicochimalco
Ixguacan

Perote
Coffre de Perote

Tlatlauquitepec
Teziutlan
Xalacingo
Altotonga
Pass of
Nombre de Dios

R. Apulco
Salt Lake

Zautla
Ocotepec
Cuyuaco
Xonacatlan
Mt. Orizaba ▲

Iztaquimaxtitlan
Atotonilco
Tecoac
Mt. Matlacueye ▲

Tzompachtepetil
Tzompantzinco
Tizatlan
Tlaxcala
Huexotzinco
Calpan
Cholula
Tepeaca
Quechula

L. Apan

Otumba

L. Zumpango
L. of Texcoco
Texcoco
Tenochtitlan
Iztapalapa
L. Chalco
Chalco
Ixtaccihuatl ▲
Popocatepetl ▲
Tacuba
Mexicaltzingo
Huitzilopochco
Mixquic
Ayotzingo
Amecameca
Pass of Cortés

© 2005 Jeffrey L. Ward

0 Miles   50
0 Kilometers   50

leaving the coast, having seen from the heights its lakes, cultivated fields, and cities — beyond measure intimidating, beyond imagination mouthwatering. Lake Texcoco was the center of six sprawling interconnected shallow seas, and the political, economic, and military seat of Aztec power. Upon an island in the lake there rose one of the world's largest cities, extending over twenty-five hundred acres and housing perhaps two hundred and fifty thousand people, with another million or so toiling on the shores to support its splendors. Of its pyramids, palaces, canals, and the daunting main two-mile stone causeway leading into the ominous maw of the city, eyewitness Bernal Díaz recalls, "It was all so wonderful that I do not know how to describe this first glimpse of things never heard of, seen, or dreamed of before. . . . Indeed several of our soldiers asked whether it was not all a dream."[16] It must have been like approaching Oz, or at least Venice, with which it was often compared. And Venice had never fallen.

On November 8, deliberately showing no apprehension, the array started across the causeway in elaborate order: four cavaliers actually in armor up front, then infantry with drawn swords, a few more horsemen, crossbowmen with plumed helmets, another party of riders, and finally the arquebusiers, with Cortés and his personal staff riding at the rear. With no more than a dozen cavalry at this point, the little party was far below battalion strength in all. Behind them in war paint came their Tlaxcalan allies. Such temerity remains beyond explaining; but it was true to the need to appear in complete control. In special operations even more than in war in general, "acting as if" is crucial: intimidation becomes part of the leverage exerted by the commando. He does not commence his thrust in a halting fashion and then escalate, as might an army: he begins by asserting himself as a superman and then presses the needle home. (We need only to remember how the Green Berets in Afghanistan 2001 set the indomitable tone from the start.) And act the conquerors did, the Aztecs having heard that they were clothed in armor made of silver and stone, although most merely wore padded cotton doublets.

Montezuma was fifty-two and had been an accomplished general before rising to the throne. He welcomed them in high state at the entrance to Tenochtitlán. Now decidedly fewer than four hundred, the Conquistadors advanced despite having been warned repeatedly by all the native peoples along the way that they would be enveloped as soon as they entered the city. "What men in all the world have shown such daring?" Díaz asks.[17] As a supposedly distinguished ambassador, Cortés and his brother aliens were conducted to its center and housed in a lavishly decorated palace, sheds being constructed in the spacious courtyard for the Tlaxcalans. Food was brought to the men, horses, and dogs. The new arrivals promptly passed from guests to garrison, setting out cannon and sentries. The Spanish knew they were in the belly of the beast: the Aztecs had only to bide their time. The scale of their hosts' craving for human sacrifice had made itself plain on a march that wound its way past temples, bloodstained altars, and architectural constructs of neatly stacked skulls. It must have been like passing through a Cambodia ruled by aesthetes.

Within a week of arriving, Cortés made his move. To preempt any centrally planned assault, Montezuma would be subtly kidnapped. An audience in the monarch's own palace was requested and graciously accorded. Cortés presented himself with five of his best men — leaving an escort of honor in the courtyard and small detachments to cover the converging avenues. Two dozen others were casually to stop by in knots of three or four once the meeting was under way.

Cortés, received with all due ceremony, was at the outset downright playful, bantering through Marina: but soon he changed his tone, accusing Montezuma of inciting vassals whom he learned had killed seven of his men left behind on the coast. Until this ugly incident was cleared up, surely Montezuma could understand why Cortés and friends now wished him, his family, and servants to live with them. The stunned sovereign finally yielded to hours of everheavier bullying, leaving under Spanish escort as if by choice, amid explanations that this was a visit for purposes of pure intimacy.

The kidnapping of Montezuma was a brilliant coup de main, literally a "blow of the hand," at a single whack. And it was accomplished by the insolent purposeful intimidation at which the modern special force so often excels. Days later, the chieftain responsible for the coastal attack, his sons, and fifteen officers appeared in answer to Montezuma's summons and were promptly turned over to Cortés, who had them burned alive in the central square while Montezuma's subjects watched in complete silence.

Cortés freely admitted, observes Thomas, that "a contrived use of terror played a part in the Spaniards' psychological calculations."[18] This competing savagery registered in a culture that was no stranger to it, although Cortés — seeing Montezuma's role in light of European feudal practices — misgauged the ease with which the realm could be decapitated and Tenochtitlán taken peacefully. Despite being heir to the single family to have ruled for more than a century, Montezuma was eminently replaceable.

Now that they controlled Montezuma, the Spaniards gained a measure of security by letting it be known that the exalted guest would not be harmed. But they were still in the middle of a largely hostile realm of millions, surrounded by divisions upon divisions of competently armed warriors trained to welcome death in battle. Meanwhile, struck by the Spaniards' obsession with gold, Montezuma was pressing it upon them, in the besotted belief that this would make them go rather than stay. Cortés and his men accumulated the bounty in their fortress-palace, but they also took time to busily construct boats. To control the city, Cortés had realized on entering Tenochtitlán, he would have to control the lakes, which the Aztecs policed with a navy of thousands of canoes, some carrying sixty warriors. And here we see another vital characteristic both of the leader of special forces and of the forces themselves: Cortés seems to have taken the problem of shipbuilding directly to his men, and he had the confidence to know that they would produce the suddenly required talent.

It was likely the soldiers, rather than their officers, who nominated the best person to supervise construction, an impromptu twenty-four-year-old shipwright; someone else was found to have been a blacksmith and could make simple tools. Over several months, four brigantines were built, each capable of carrying seventy-five men and supporting a small cannon in the prow. The whole unconcealable enterprise was being passed off as a project for pleasure cruising.[19] Who was fooling whom? Who was waiting for what?

Six months after arriving in the island capital, Cortés had more to worry about than revolt among a people whose fright was wearing off. The governor of Cuba had dispatched eighteen ships and nine hundred soldiers to arrest him for treason. That squadron had come ashore some forty miles south of Cortés's first settlement, its commander vowing to march inland to bear him off to the decisive justice of colonial Spain. (Clearly, the Spaniards were also divided, not that the Aztecs — perhaps consumed by the "fearful slumber" noted in their accounts — exploited this opening.) Cortés gathered intelligence on the new interlopers, then left about 120 of his men in the city to hold Montezuma while he pressed back to the coast, marshaling a total force of about 350 from the little outposts that he had strung behind. He improvised the weapons needed to withstand his pursuers' cavalry — long double-headed lances tipped with copper — weapons, in fact, that had likely been used against him by the Indians, although for this mission his Indian auxiliaries melted away.

Lulled by foolish confidence in their superior numbers, the fully alerted Spanish newcomers allowed themselves to be surprised in a nighttime thunderstorm. Cortés's raiders (for now this is what they were) slipped through the coastal town of Cempoallan, first impaling the artillerymen (the captain of artillery perhaps having been bribed to place wax in the mouths of his pieces) and, according to one account, cutting the girths of the cavalry — immediately eliminating the enemy's most telling advantages.[20]

When all was said and done, Cortés had defeated a much fresher force three times the size of his own, imprisoned its leader, and easily subverted his so-recent opponents with offers of gold. Here there were no supposedly decisive advantages of superior weaponry: the men he defeated had been far better armed. The attack is all the more extraordinary because Cortés may have benefited not only from a false cry that the opposing captain had been killed, but also from a species of large firefly that soon filled the air that night, perhaps looking to the governor's avengers like the matches of scores of Conquistador arquebuses pointed right at them.[21] Just as effectively as against the Aztecs, Cortés added bluff and imagination to surprise, focus, and insouciant courage in pulling off an audacious operation against these rough fellow warriors from the mother country.

But this smart, stealthy attack was only prologue to the truly special work that was to come. While in Cempoallan, Cortés heard that his oafish garrison had finally driven the Aztec capital to bloody insurrection and that his brigantines, the means of escape should the causeways be blocked, had been burned. He at once started back by forced marches, now at the head of well over a thousand men, most of them presumably as disoriented as the original force had been just months before, joined by at least twice that number of enthusiastic Tlaxcalans. As he crossed the great causeway to enter Tenochtitlán in strength for the second time, the midday city was silent. So much of his success lay in these quick movements, the Aztecs surrounding his men being appalled to see him so suddenly reappear to coldly confront imminent massacre.

Within twenty-four hours the great city exploded, its valleylike avenues filling with thousands of warriors. The Spaniards were besieged in the palace that they had transformed into a rudimentary fortress, which could hold out only so long against battering rams and fire. They cannonaded the Aztecs in the sprawling square outside, but were swept by almost as deadly slingfire from the higher rooftops. Montezuma, brought frantically out to plead with his people for calm, was met with screaming scorn and a hail of rocks, and stumbled back to his rooms, to die within three days, whether of wounds, chagrin, suicide, or by Spanish assistance. Cortés then probably liquidated, as a later age would put it, all the lords who had joined their ruler in captivity.

Fighting died away with nightfall, a respite that an enemy so much more numerous never should have permitted. The next day, Cortés led a sortie against the warriors regathering in the square. Spurring out on horseback at the head of his merciless infantry, he cleared the enemy — halfway between army and lynch mob — into the narrow side streets. It was hand-to-hand combat, the Aztecs wielding multipointed darts on cords for reuse, and plying the canals with canoes from which they could leap upon any isolated group of soldiers, to bundle them away for ritual expiation. In the end, the besiegers fell back, but the Conquistadors and their Indian allies were dangerously thinned, just as ever more levies from the mainland strengthened the enemy.

The Spaniards receded into their quarters as the undaunted Aztecs lapped back against the walls, employing their own form of psycho-logical warfare: night-long chants promising that the stone of sacrifice was ready and the knives sharpened, with the more explicitly refined pledge that the invaders were then to be cooked with chocolate.[22]

In a week of desperate fighting, the Spaniards sallied out from their fortress (nothing of a palace now) by day, the Aztecs reoccupy-ing at night what had been gained, and meanwhile learning — with the quick adaptation that desperation can induce — to disable the Spaniards' few serviceable horses by casting flat smooth stones beneath their feet. Hand-to-hand combat raged 150 feet up atop one of the great pyramidal temples from which the Aztecs had been showering arrows and shot into the fortress.[23] The Spaniards cleared those heights, but every hour fewer of their number remained.

And of course they were trapped. Cortés had to find a way to get his men, his allies, and their murderously hard-won treasure through the city, then across the multigapped causeway, and thereafter into a country the size of Castile, very likely to be in arms against him. He, too, was adapting fast, and had his people build out of beams and planks several early versions of a tank, pulled by ropes. These two-storied wooden mantles could shelter 20–25 crossbowmen and arquebusiers. At least something like it had worked in European siege warfare, and these devices just might smash their way through the boiling streets. But even that tactic could take Cortés only so far, since the Aztecs had demolished the bridges over the city's canals. As for getting across the causeway, a rough pontoon was hammered together which, it was hoped, could be shifted to fit breach after breach (there were eight of them all told) should the escape ever reach that stage.

Clouds and drizzle on one of the nights around July 1, 1520, pro-vided some element of cover. The city again seemed quiet: an earlier thunderstorm may have dispersed the sentries and put out their watchfires. Uncounted treasures were packed onto the strongest horses, their hooves muffled, the men allowed to help themselves to the fortunes in gold still strewing the palace floor. As many as 270 Spaniards may simply have been left behind in the confusion of what was expected to be a rapid, complete disengagement, in which the escaping force was supposed to march fifteen or twenty abreast over the shortest causeway, one that led westward out of the city. The surprise of such a move just might make possible an orderly retreat, as opposed to the more likely deadly melee resembling an audience fighting for the exits from a burning theater.

The signal was given soon before midnight. A vanguard of Cortés's toughest lieutenants led the way with about two hundred men, two priests, and Marina. Cortés would follow with the rest of the force, then the allies, and finally sixty horsemen. Some three thousand desperate people tried to tiptoe through a city having a population perhaps as large as Newark's. Silence had been strictly enjoined, and held for all too few minutes; then everything went wrong. The portable bridge sent ahead jammed in the first breach, by which time the alarm was well and truly raised.

The exhausted, gold-encumbered column blundered from causeway to gap to causeway, ever fewer, ever wearier, ever more terrified as thousands of canoe-borne Aztec warriors struck from both sides. Men bunched together at every breach, which soon choked with wreckage and bodies. Some tripped in the shambles and were cut up where they lay; others pitched into the water, to be drowned by the weight of their gold. Many had a few unwanted days more to live, being thrown into canoes and triumphantly carried away to atone on the apex of the Great Pyramid, along with those left behind. Horses were useless as cavalry but at least offered tails and manes to cling to as the screaming beasts struggled toward shore. Almost the entire rearguard perished. One of Montezuma's sons and a daughter, who were being spirited away, whether as hostages for ransom, as the nucleus of a Spanish puppet state, or because of Cortés's bizarre sentiment, vanished also in the blood and dark. About six hundred Spaniards never made it to the mainland; perhaps two thousand Tlaxcalans were lost. The lake consumed the treasure, artillery, and ammunition. Not an arquebus remained, the useless sodden objects having been cast away in the panic, and quite rationally too; this was a Stone Age battle.

Probably 347 Spaniards survived, along with twenty-seven horses. They set off before dawn along the north shore of the lake, Aztecs following like jackals to close over any laggards. At daybreak, pursuers could be seen massing behind those Spaniards who were left.

These pitiful remnants of intended conquest, themselves no friends to pity, somehow worked their way clockwise around the lake until they could head east toward hopefully still-allied Tlaxcala, then moved back into the mountains and starved.

Cortés now commanded the ghost of an army, without arms and ammunition, likely within days of being elaborately put to death to the last man. Within eight days of the escape he had to confront a real army, sent by Montezuma's successor to finish him off, so superior in numbers that the Spaniards were soon engulfed, ever more warriors swarming up as the fight grew even fiercer. What should have been a final encounter for all concerned turned suddenly once Cortés stood in his stirrups, spotted the so-obvious robed, feathered Aztec commander, borne in his litter at the center of his bodyguard, and led four of his fiercest killers to slash their way through the entourage and lance the chief. "For all our weakness we broke their great arrogance and pride," he related, "for they were so many that they got in each other's way, and could neither fight nor run."[24] In their blind terror, the abruptly leaderless Aztecs trampled one another. A great lesson is here. Once your enemy does not know what to do with his strength, it can become as useless as gold in the waters of a dark lake.

Subconsciously, we might deem such a reversal of fortune a truly mechanic victory, driven by horses and steel, perhaps equivalent to colonial wars centuries later in which machine guns swept away savages: except that the Aztecs, with sophisticated mathematics, a complex writing system, and a well-disciplined army typically divided into commands of eight thousand men, were anything but savages. And the Spaniards by this time were more like the survivors of a shipwreck than an expeditionary force, Cortés himself stoically enduring a fractured skull.[25]

Cortés understood that to show any lack of courage might compel the Tlaxcalans to turn against him as well.[26] Their cooperation reaffirmed, he was able to punish the ill-judging client states of the Great Valley (who still deemed the Aztecs the superior power), branding and enslaving his captives. Again, we see the special operator's essential skill when dwarfed by numbers in a hostile land: a faith that the enemy's disorder will undercut all his quantitative advantages, and an ability deftly to manipulate wavering allies.

Entirely in character, Cortés's one joy on the morning after *la noche triste* had been that the shipwright had made it through.[27] Having led his force into a mantrap, barely to emerge alive, even at that desperate moment he was now ready to urge the survivors to do it again. He knew these types intimately and, as he began constructing a fleet, drilled the Tlaxcalans from mountain warriors into sepoys of the matchlock era. Supplies from the coast were few. He ordered new arms made (mostly lances, as his men also feathered and put heads on arrows for the handful of crossbows that remained), and what there were of the old ones repaired.

Smallpox descended on what Cortés now called "New Spain of the Ocean Sea," and Jared Diamond, among others, believes "it gave the Spaniards a decisive advantage." That is unlikely. The Aztecs were ravaged, to be sure, but so were the Spaniards' vital Indian allies. The Europeans, most of whom were already scarred by the disease, were left relatively unscathed, but they were still so few.[28] Meanwhile, more Spanish ships made the journey, for one reason or another, to the beachhead on the Mexique Bay, and with no greater scruple Cortés recruited their men. With these additions, by the end of summer 1520 he may have had 550 altogether, including eighty crossbowmen and arquebusiers, plus forty horses and eight or nine guns, and, more vitally, sails, rudders, and a compass or two. "He was," Prescott tells us, identifying one of the key goals of a small force behind the lines, "receiving supplies he most needed from the hands of his enemies" — at least his Spanish ones.[29] Other men bore swords and the Indians' copper-headed pikes; still, the force was not much larger than what Cortés had originally brought in, and its enemies much more confident. Nevertheless, he could tell his men with no lack of earnestness that this would be a fight for Cross and Crown, and vengeance for those literally sacrificed — and, not incidentally, for riches and renown. As the patron of a grand alliance, he also probably had ten thousand Tlaxcalans at his disposal, who, we may be certain, were not up to doing any of this without him.

Cortés and his shipwright calculated that thirteen square-rigged brigantines would be needed to control the lake: these would be fifty feet long, led by a sixty-five-foot flagship. Cortés knew the brigantines were vital to what was to come.[30] How those waters were won may be the supreme example of the many smaller tactical special operations that make possible the overall strategic one, and also the step most overlooked today.[31] Four hundred and twenty years later, World War II made the term *combined operations* — meaning the coordinated thrusts of land force, seapower, and air — synonymous with commando attacks: here, at least, the first two joined in the most successful of Spanish Armadas.

Timbers were cut in the surrounding peaks, and the boats began to be built that fall near Tlaxcala — about seventy-five miles from the lake, depending on the route. The specifications were such that the Spanish gunners and archers would tower over their canoe-borne adversaries and, when grappled, would be able to slash downward with their swords.

The boats were complete by February 1521 and tested in a river that had been dammed to form a large pond. They then had to be knocked apart and carried plank by plank, mast by mast, to the base that Cortés had established near — but not dangerously on — the lake. In a well-guarded caravan five miles long, the brigantines slowly moved forth on the most amazing part of their voyage to traverse (or perhaps wearily skirt to the north) the mountain range that shields the eastern plains of the Valley of Mexico. Drums were used to encourage and give rhythm to the thousands of haulers tramping westward.

Once there, the vessels were reassembled near a riverbed about a mile and a half inland. Knowing what was afoot, Aztec raiders three times attempted to destroy the unfinished boats, even in this relatively inaccessible spot. To get the finally assembled craft from the overnight shipyard to the lake, the Tlaxcalans gouged a canal, digging in relays around the clock for seven weeks. There still was not enough water to float the ships down this damp arroyo, and so twelve more dams had to be built. Here is an engineering innovation and spontaneity that Alexander would have recognized, as the invaders drew upon machines and inventions whose nature we can only guess.

The armada finally moved into Lake Texcoco and was dedicated on Sunday, April 28. Cortés was "even by Spanish standards ruthlessly unconventional," adds Thomas.[32] For starters, there was no precedent for amphibious war in the Americas, and Spain has no lakes from which anything like this could have been learned. His opponents, in turn, lived and fought by rules — the perfect opportunity for the special operator. They never conceived of either a siege in the European style or an attack that would not allow for pitched battle, let alone of the fact that their pivotal means of defense — the lake itself — would be turned into a dreadful vulnerability.

Meanwhile, with two hundred Spaniards and a much larger number of Tlaxcalans, Cortés conducted a long reconnaissance around the great sheet of water. Most of the shoreline cities yielded, awed by the prospect of Tenochtitlán's fall; one city did, however, dare to breach a dike that nearly drowned the expedition and saturated much of the arquebusiers' gunpowder. The Aztecs themselves also made sorties, capturing and sacrificing several Spaniards, while they built entrenchments in their beautiful city, deepened its canals, stuck sharp stakes in the floor of the lake, mounted captured Spanish swords on the end of lances, and accumulated arrows and slingstones for a type of battle no one had experienced.

Within weeks, Cortés was ready: with him now were 86 cavalrymen, 118 bowmen and arquebusiers, 700-plus foot soldiers with swords and shields, three heavy iron cannon, fifteen small bronze fieldpieces. Three assault groups would fight on land, a fourth under his command on shipboard. Each boat carried 25–30 men, in a balanced complement of crossbowmen, arquebusiers, and swordsmen; Cortés distributed those with previous sea service evenly among the squadron. One student of this part of the story believes that the flat-bottomed brigantines resembled gunboats of the eighteenth century; perhaps, more accurately, they were functional versions of the SEALs' MKv special-ops craft, albeit with masts and paddles.[33] Bolts were feathered and distributed among the crossbowmen. Thousands more copper-headed arrows were made from a pattern that Cortés provided to his allies.

The attack began on the last day of May, and soon the Spaniards had demolished the aqueduct that supplied the city with fresh water from the forested hills of Chapultepec — a first step that Frontinus, the Roman water commissioner and strategist, would have applauded.

Swiftly mastering the brackish lake, the brigantines just as rapidly took the fight directly into the larger canals of the island capital. Each causeway was soon in Spanish hands; neither supplies nor reinforcements could break through. Then the attackers hammered steadily into fair Tenochtitlán from the south.

Months of unrelenting combat did not distract the Aztecs from sending processions up the Great Pyramid's 114 steps to escort Spanish captives and their allies — naked, adorned with feathers, carrying fans — to terrible ceremonial deaths. A great clamor of drums and horns alerted Spaniards and Tlaxcalans alike to each dismal pageant on the heights, which could be seen all too clearly from a distance.

Yet the agonies did not stir the impassive gods. The inhabitants of Tenochtitlán suffered the worst horrors of a siege — starvation, thirst, disease, inexorable fear — while the Spaniards at least could draw on a modest resupply of troops and weapons sent up from the coast. As gunpowder ran low, they were able to make it from sulfur hacked by the most reckless even of this lunatic fringe from the mouth of a live volcano. There were no explosives to blast down buildings, and the advantage conferred by sword or arquebus in street fighting was minimal if the defenders could drop things on the attackers' heads.

By early August, the end was only a matter of time. The last heroic stand has been called "an Aztec *Iliad*" as the fighting worked its way forward house by bloody house, street by agonizing street, while thousands of the defenders were slowly pushed to the north of the island.[34] To be sure, the ultimate erasing of a great city is only implicit in the *Iliad,* and the well-armed Trojans fell to superior numbers as well as greater cunning. But the historic doom of a mighty culture at the hands of relentless invaders comes close enough. The final day of battle saw, as had the first, combined operations as the land-assault forces smashed into the shrinking portion of the city still in Aztec hands, while the brigantines destroyed outlying buildings and patrolled the water for any fleeing chieftains. After seventy-five bitter days, the city fell on August 13, 1521. The new monarch and his remaining nobles were brought before Cortés, his mistress again interpreting.

The first need was to cleanse the city of perhaps more than a hundred thousand rotting corpses. The emperor would be kept alive, in hopes that torture would help him remember the whereabouts of his somewhat hypothetical treasure, until a frustrated Cortés hanged him four years later. A new Mexico City rose on the ruins of Tenochtitlán. Within three years, a choir school had been established, and by 1540 the metropolis was the core of Spanish America. The anniversary of Tenochtitlán's fall would be observed as a national holiday throughout the three centuries of Spanish rule, the Tlaxcalans receiving a unique tax exemption that lasted more or less into the nineteenth century.

As often happens with such idiosyncratic leaders, Cortés's triumph was followed by personal difficulty. He complained of insufficient reward, quarreled yet further with a Spanish authority that increasingly saw him not just as insubordinate but as a potential imperial rival. Lawsuits had to be answered and enemies overcome at court, including a highly plausible charge that he had strangled his wife. To placate him — or at least to buy time — he was appointed governor of newly conquered but much less materially rewarding territories, and clothed with empty honors just proportionate to his loss of real power and standing.

Cortés founded other cities in the New World, led a fruitless expedition to Honduras in 1524, and inspired the first expedition to the Baja California peninsula in 1536. Returning to Spain for good in 1540, he was allowed to fight his last battle in the disastrous Spanish descent on Algiers the following year, and died in Seville in 1547. When there had been no rules, he had ruled. Now each link in the chain of command constricted and suffocated. Shorn of his crazy miracle-makers, he became another worn-out grand old man unable to offer a serious contribution to conventional combat once under the eye of the brass, no longer free to create new ways of warfare beyond the old world's rim.

‡

MANY MEN of similar talents were waiting to step forward: it was Francisco Pizarro who struck it lucky. While Cortés was taking Mexico, this roustabout in his mid-forties, the insignificantly educated illegitimate son of an undistinguished officer in the Estremadura, had carved out a prosperous life in the town of Panama. He had arrived there by accompanying Balboa in crossing the Isthmus in 1513, to first set European eyes on the Pacific. Once another Conquistador had beheaded Balboa — standard operating procedure, as Pizarro would discover — he followed the fortunes of the new strongman to help subjugate the region's tribes.

There were rumors of places along the coast of the Southern Ocean that might possess treasures at least as immense as those of Mexico. Despite wranglings with established authority in Panama, Pizarro organized a private venture in 1524, with two partners, in the Conquistador tradition. The prospectus sounded so bizarre that the townsfolk called them the "company of lunatics."[35] The first expedition sailed roughly to what is today the border of Ecuador and Colombia, but returned empty-handed; the second, during 1526–28, pushed farther south. Pizarro's pilot, pressing ahead beyond the equator, made first contact with the Inca culture in the form of a trading raft carrying small amounts of gold, silver, and intricately woven fabrics. The Spanish encountered their first significant settlement at Tumbez, on the northwestern Peruvian coast. The cordial locals, perhaps just wanting the strangers to move on, promised a land of wonders even farther south. The Spaniards kept sailing, and two more landings confirmed evidence of a sophisticated, mysterious empire within. Returning elated to Panama after eighteen months, Pizarro was granted a contract for a third expedition to discover and conquer "Peru," plus the title of governor of the new lands, whatever those might turn out to be.

Even today, no one is certain where the Incas came from. Their empire — for such it was — by this time stretched north to south nearly three thousand miles along the Andean range (second only in height and harshness to the Himalayas) from Chile to the south of modern Colombia, and reached west to east from the coastal deserts to the steamy Amazonian rain forest. In 1530, it may have been the largest country in the world, though utterly ignorant of the Aztec power so near to its northern borders.

Although, so far as is known, this extraordinary realm was without writing, it disposed of a formidable professional army, well organized into the fabric of each of the four great provinces. All Inca men underwent military training. Warriors were armed with spears, maces, bows, and protected by helmets, leather shields, and thick doublets of quilted cotton — the form of armor also favored by

Cortés. Their slings were ubiquitous throughout the Andes, arguably with a level of personal firepower (in accuracy, impact, and speed of discharge) not reached in Europe for another two hundred years. Noblemen wielded halberdlike bronze axes. The size of this army may have been around eighty thousand, and the Incas' impressively solid fortresses bear an uncanny resemblance to low-slung European "star forts" of the seventeenth and eighteenth centuries.[36] However defined, given the disparity in numbers, only the most special of operations could overcome what the awed intruders must before long have deemed a hideous strength.

Two days after Christmas 1530, Pizarro set out from Panama back toward Tumbez, with one ship, thirty-seven horses, and 180 men, including four younger half brothers, who were similar toughs. Like Cortés's adventurers, most of his men were in their twenties. The advanced civilization they would penetrate was the last on earth utterly isolated from the rest of mankind: they faced it with an entire force deploying not much more hitting power than a single machine gun today.

Once there, after months of sailing, marching, skirmishing, and disease — plus a brief, fierce fight with a few remaining inhabitants — it was evident that Tumbez had been devastated since the last visit. The Indians who emerged from hiding explained that the great peoples of the interior were embroiled in the type of civil conflict that must have looked pretty familiar to Pizarro, given what had happened to Cortés and Balboa. He also learned that those people were reeling under a plague — probably European-brought smallpox creeping south from Mexico — that had killed both the powerful Inca emperor and his most likely heir. With one of the dead emperor's sons contesting the throne now held by a brother, there had befallen a disorienting moment perfect for a small number of men who knew their own minds, if not much else. One might question how clear the opportunity was at the time, but people with this level of faith in their star have a way of creating opportunities.

Pizarro recognized, as had Cortés, that to stay on the coast to gather intelligence and perhaps await reinforcements from Panama — one thousand miles to the north — would be rational, prudent, and disastrous. Establishing a base 120 miles south of Tumbez, Pizarro was joined by small contingents from Panama, including the dashing thirty-three-year-old Hernando de Soto, who began to reconnoiter the Andean foothills. He was coming at the outset upon at least the fringes of a great engineering civilization. The first glimpses of a 12,000-mile road network said to be linked by prodigious bridges over hundreds of rivers, capable of deploying large armies faster than on any highways in Europe, might have otherwise chilled brave men who lacked the eerie Conquistador confidence.

Although the outline of his actions can be reconstructed from the chronicles of his secretary and of some of his men, Pizarro's motivations at this juncture are unknown. He himself could not write. Prescott speculates in *History of the Conquest of Peru,* the companion work to his seminal book on Mexico, that Pizarro "may have meditated some daring stroke, some effective coup de main," as had Cortés in kidnapping Montezuma.[37] In any event, he decided to head straight for the highland city where, he had heard, the reigning Inca monarch was encamped with a large part of his army, ignoring for the moment what was reputed to be the splendidly rich capital of Cuzco.

Here, too, the secret would prove to be in going straight for the heart, although vast improvisation would be necessary. As the poet and military historian Hilaire Belloc says of the waterspider,

> *But if he ever stopped to think*
> *How he can do it, he would sink.*

Once a special operation is launched there can be no stopping to calculate the chances, only to exploit them — a very different form of analysis. Leaving about fifty men at the base, Pizarro struck forth with 62 horsemen and 106 foot soldiers, bearing just a handful of arquebuses and not even two dozen crossbows, and dragging four small pieces of artillery. The Incas would have reason to regret the excellence of their roads.

The emperor followed the Conquistadors' every move as they pressed from the coastal plains into the Andes toward his encampment near the upland city of Cajamarca. As with Cortés, the tiny force may have delayed the Incas' reaction time by conveying some vague impression that the Spaniards were gods. In any event, the emperor Atahuallpa was preoccupied by war with his brother, and rather than attempt to destroy the approaching strangers, he dismissed the Europeans' small numbers as an insignificant intrusion compared to the business at hand. Certainly, the invaders carried themselves as if they were invincible, though their advantage in weapons was minimal. The arquebuses, when they managed to fire, were likely more useful to shake morale (nevertheless a welcome advantage at the outset) than for killing: they could be reloaded faster than a crossbow, and their one-inch bores enabled them to be used as big shotguns, devastating several opponents at once, but they were not as accurate — and keeping their cords lit could be problematic.[38]

At this point, Pizarro refined his advancing force according to a manner of hyperselection reaching back at least to Gideon. He told his followers that none had to go farther, making it clear it would be no shame to return to the poorly garrisoned base; those who did so would still be entitled to the same share of plunder. Only nine departed. This was the equivalent of Cortés destroying his ships, with a yet more daring challenge to the individual spirits of weary men. Pizarro was concentrating rather than depleting his force. Only the most determined men would venture with him into the heart of power.

De Soto and a small party moved ahead to the Inca camp, returning more than a week later, having been courteously received, along with an Inca envoy carrying presents of vicuña weavings (tantalizingly embroidered with gold and silver). According to a part-Inca/part-Spanish chronicler, Waman Poma, the emperor had sent gifts of male servants and sacred virgins, the virgins also being offered to the Spaniards' horses because the Incas took them for a kind of intelligent being. (Already the science-fiction touch.) Despite seeing such large snorting creatures, the Incan envoy told his superiors that he was unimpressed by the fighting potential of the little band he had observed — which was the best possible response for the invaders.

All was being interpreted by two abducted Inca youths whom Pizarro, planning ahead, had educated in Castilian. The march resumed, accompanied by some friendly locals, ingeniously bridging torrential rivers, torturing information out of some Indians encountered, suborning it from others, and learning that the emperor was monitoring the party's approach, their few numbers, and was perhaps purposefully luring them into his golden parlor. Yet Pizarro went on, through a labyrinth of passes and defiles where ambush would have been a snap for a handful of hostile troops, then crossing a treeless savannah at an elevation of some 13,500 feet.

The fertile valley of Caxamalca is minute compared to that of Mexico, an oval merely twenty or so miles north to south, and about eight miles across; but over the next several years nearly as much blood would enrich its earth as had soaked into vastly larger stretches of Aztec terrain. As Pizarro descended into the valley through rain and hail on that afternoon of November 15, 1532, he could glimpse sophisticated irrigation and also Cajamarca, a solid little burg beneath the shadow of a stone fortress. Ominously, the slope of hills beyond was white with the war tents of many times the number of warriors who, with their emperor, were awaiting the intruders' arrival.

Making a show of good spirits, the cavalcade tramped straight into the city. Pizarro immediately sent one of his brothers and De Soto, attended by an interpreter and some three dozen horsemen, to the imperial encampment about two miles away. If a trap had been sprung, more than half of his mounted strength would have been gone at one blow. But Pizarro never balked at laying down a high stake for a higher one. Guarded by well-disciplined warriors, and surrounded by many thousands more in full battle order, Atahuallpa — known with formidable simplicity as "The Inca" — unsmilingly promised the interlopers that he and his warriors would indeed be pleased to visit them on the following day, more than enough grounds for moody speculation once the sufficiently awed emissaries brought back the news.

Here comes the point immensely significant for special operations, as well as for the practitioners of crime and terror. It is one of procedure and, yet more, of attitudes. Within moments, Pizarro proposed to his officers that the emperor be cut from his army and held captive. What was the alternative? They could not flee back through the mountains, whose tracks and passes the Indians knew intimately. To march out in gentlemanly formal challenge and make the fields between city and camp into a battleground would be suicide. To do nothing would merely borrow a few more days or weeks of life as the Incas lost the first startled impression of horses and guns. And, imminently, the rest of the Inca army would soon return to its emperor from triumphs over his rebelling brother in the south.

"Their only remedy," relates Prescott, "was to turn the Inca's arts against himself; to take him, if possible, in his own snare" — a classic move of the special operation in which the enemy's strengths are reversed. The assault would have to be so harsh and sudden as "alone [to] make a small number more than a match for a much larger one." Undoubtedly by now, Pizarro must have had Cortés's example in mind, "although the results in that case," Prescott adds wryly, "did not altogether justify a repetition of the experiment."[39] The literature of ancient and Christian warfare offered no precedent for bearing away an emperor from the head of his army the day after meeting him. But if successful, the kidnapping would both enable Pizarro to rule through the Inca and buy time until crucial reinforcements could arrive from far-off Panama. During that night, one of the Spaniards would recall, Inca watchfires on the hills were "as thick as the stars of heaven."[40] But had not the Lord of all the world stopped the sun itself for Joshua's warriors? These men expected the extraordinary. Such confidence goes far.

The town laid out as a stage for imperial dignity presented itself as a perfect theater for the deed. Its great square had three built-up sides, as can still be seen, lined by edifices each some two hundred yards long, within whose spacious halls cavalry could be hidden behind wide doors. The infantry concealed itself in another great hall. A few soldiers in the fortress tower accessible from one of the city walls could man the few small Spanish cannon; a shot and blaring trumpets would be the signals to strike. Meanwhile, Pizarro would greet the arriving army in the plaza, at the head of twenty chosen men, then close the trap with one sweep of a cloth. All was ready at dawn.

But the Inca presence took its leisurely sovereign time. By noon, the Incas could be seen beginning to advance in the distance. Some hours later, they came to a halt half a mile away. Messages were exchanged, the increasingly nervous Spaniards urging the emperor to enter and accept their hospitality. For all their fears, the Conquistadors must have exulted at being instruments of heaven when the emperor declared his intention not only to proceed but to spend the night. Accommodations, he commanded, were to be prepared, although he would leave the greater part of his force behind. All were playing cat and mouse. But the mouse was rabid.

The Spaniards, perhaps consulting their own intentions, expected a surprise attack. Yet surely Atahuallpa must have felt that he had all the choice and time in the world, visiting a few strange characters just arrived in one of his own cities, surrounded by his army. He therefore entered the town near sunset, accompanied by servants, guards, nobles, about five or six thousand men in all, apparently — whether in a display of goodwill or of disdain — unarmed. Few Spaniards were to be seen, most presumably hiding in fright. A Dominican priest advanced to the imperial litter with a cross and a Bible to offer a concise tutorial in the Trinity, the Crucifixion, the Ascension, the Apostle Peter, and the authority of his successor, the pope, as well as the place of the Spaniards' own king-emperor Charles in the earthly arrangements of these otherworldly powers — and to urge the emperor to subject himself to the service of Christ and king.[41] Atahuallpa, "his face a deep crimson," threw the Bible that he had been handed onto the ground; Pizarro's arm came down; the small cannon banged; cavalry and infantry burst upon the unexpecting Incas within the crowded square, slashing, stabbing, shooting. "The Indians were so filled with fear that they climbed on top of one another, formed mounds, and suffocated each other," wrote one of Pizarro's followers with professional dispassion.[42] The Spaniards ran down those able to flee through the streets or to get beyond the walls. Nearly all were annihilated in about two hours. There were no Spanish casualties.

Jammed in the middle of his household troops, the emperor had not resisted. With his capture heaping upon the overall catastrophe, his whole army disintegrated; Indian prisoners spent two days cleaning the city of bodies and gore. It was the very magnificence of Atahuallpa's power that had brought him into Cajamarca to gawk at the strange beings. Had Pizarro been facing some minor Inca chieftain, fate might have been quite different. Without such a magnificent army behind him, a mere Inca general would unlikely have been so reckless as to allow himself to be thus grievously set up. And knowing the relative weakness of his own position, he would have been far more inclined to pounce on the Conquistadors en route, in the mountains. Strength was Atahuallpa's undoing.

Over the next eight months Pizarro extracted from the dazed nation what may have been history's largest ransom for Atahuallpa's promised freedom. Once rooms were filled with the likely maximum of metal, the emperor was garroted in the public square, supposedly for trying to foment "rebellion." Those officials crowded with him in captivity were probably dispatched with arsenic-laced wine. A puppet ruler was then installed, as would be so common in colonial exploits three hundred years hence, to be followed by another whom the Spaniards mistakenly judged even more pliant. With the arrival from Panama of the expedition's venture partner, Diego de Almagro, and about 150 fresh troops, there were sufficient reinforcements for Pizarro to march on Cuzco.

Still with fewer than five hundred men — some nauseated by altitude sickness — he advanced along more than 750 miles of road that straddled the central Andes, traversing a half-dozen subsidiary ranges. He exercised terror (burnings alive, throwing captives to the dogs) and fought four pitched battles en route. Pizarro soon took the capital, along with its nearby terraced fortress, an imposing masterpiece of stone construction more than one-third of a mile long. Despite still possessing fine generals and tens of thousands of professional soldiers, once the initial blow had fallen the enemy could not recover its structure and common purpose. Their resistance could be overcome, at least for the moment.

Pizarro then preoccupied himself with building Lima, the suitably European capital for his new power, near the coast, the fitting seat of a regime that united brutal predation with amateur-night administration. But it was only a matter of time before the overwhelmingly more numerous, increasingly brutalized Incas were cornered into recognizing they had ever less to lose, whatever the Conquistadors' deadliness. In February 1536, they rallied behind the young emperor Manco Capac, who had come to despair of collaboration. His commanders used their genius for organization to secretly assemble, arm, and feed thousands of the country's remaining fighting men, who then arose to besiege what had been their own capital, Cuzco, setting it ablaze under a hail of burning arrows and red-hot stones wrapped in cotton, shot in by slings. Taking the great fortress of Sacsahuaman, they pushed down upon the city, devising *bolas* (three stones tied to the ends of connected lengths of llama tendons) to entangle the horses' legs, and digging pits and small holes to break them — a brilliant adaptation to a mode of warfare encountered only five years earlier. The technically inferior Incas had picked up not only on disciplined Spanish tactics but had also managed to equip themselves with some Spanish bucklers, helmets, and swords — a few even bestriding captured warhorses, as the Aztecs had never dared.

The Spaniards retook the fortress in a night assault with scaling ladders, and, after ten long months, the Incas slackened the siege, their army having barely held together during the harvest season, as the thought of their families' hunger must have bitten deep. Still, the Incas had succeeded in annihilating almost all the Spanish posts between Cuzco and the sea, wiping out even the well-armed and fully prepared relief parties of cavalry that Pizarro had rushed out to try to open the mountain passes.

News of the revolt spread so far as to galvanize Spain. But Manco overreached, ordering his victorious soldiers to descend on Lima, to kill everyone except Pizarro who, his back to the sea, thought the game was up. Manco broke in during the sixth day of the assault on Lima. Yet this was now conventional warfare, waged on flat ground at sea level; Manco was no longer playing to his strengths in the steep Andean terrain. As the Incas began to filter into the streets, the Spanish cavalry attacked. They had done this before; they were very good at it; and their victory was total. Almagro, who had embarked with his own column on an agonizingly fruitless quest for gold in the snows and then deserts of Chile, returned to Peru via the grueling Atacama wilderness. He and his men seized Cuzco in April 1537 from both the Inca besiegers and the Spanish defenders, and Almagro intended to keep it. The Incas were driven into the remotest corners of what had been their empire.

Released from the pressure of Incan attack, the victorious Spaniards unsurprisingly began quarreling over the spoils, and to murder one another at the first opportunity, if not earlier. Almagro asserted himself from Cuzco and the mountains, Pizarro from the coast. Within a year, the swords were out. The conquerors showed each other no more quarter than they had the Indians. A climactic pitched battle outside Cuzco in April 1538 saw Almagro defeated, to be tried for treason, and, by Pizarro's decree, garroted.

Manco established himself in a spectacularly defensible fastness in the deepest recesses of the Andes, but was soon enough dislodged even from there and compelled to seek further refuge in the Amazonian jungle, in which lay his legendary last capital. Unlike Cortés, Pizarro was locked onto a moving target. When Manco could be brought to battle, the Spanish would usually beat him, and hammer his soldiers in bloody pursuit. But then his realm's vastness always seemed to afford one more chance, even after he was assassinated in his refuge by a handful of Spaniards who had quite plausibly, given events, insisted that they too were among Pizarro's enemies.

Pizarro's response throughout was not just to inflict terror, but to stamp armed settlements upon the contested lands, as purposeful occupiers have so often done successfully before a beaten people can catch their breath. And settlers were steadily flowing in from the Caribbean, to exact what they could from the now-goldless natives. At the same time, several hundred embittered Spaniards who remained loyal to the cause of the executed Almagro scattered themselves through the expanding territory controlled by Pizarro, united only in hatred for the power-intoxicated conqueror. Holding a marquisate from the Crown and serving as governor, Pizarro was contemptuous of any threat these broken men might offer. But in June 1541, the seething dissidents, enough of whom were crowded destitute into a Lima that had already outlived most of its promises, struck home.

At noon on Sunday the 26th, around two dozen conspirators — once again, small numbers paid off astonishingly — simply marched through the city square to the governor's imposing palace, burst through the massive gate (open in arrogant confidence) into the residence, all the while shouting that justice was at hand. Most of Pizarro's entourage, softened by triumph and plunder, fled; but he and one of his brothers coolly started to fasten on their armor. They had the qualities of their defects: mass killers they might be, but steady in the face of being killed. The conspirators raged through the gilded chambers, to be met with long minutes of deadly swordplay. One against a dozen, Pizarro — now well into his fifties — brought down several of his attackers; until, run at last through the throat, he traced a cross with his finger on the bloody floor and bent his head to kiss it, as a final stroke ended the great adventure. It was the first of Latin America's murderous, yet often efficient, coups — the beginning of an apostolic succession of such compact, daring, occasionally brilliant acts only now fading from the continent they helped transform.

The insurgents became foolish enough not to exhaust their opponents but to attempt one last assault on a fully alerted Lima: they were crushed, their leadership comprehensively put to death. At the climactic battle in September 1542, with armored horsemen charging one another with lowered lances, a group of Inca warriors watched from surrounding hills as their destiny was being settled, descending only to strip the bodies of the Spanish dead.

After the worst of the conquest was over, two very different but equally revealing books appeared in Spanish, one barely known and chillingly practical, the other perhaps the greatest of all novels. Captain Bernardo de Vargas, brutally involved in smashing resistance in Chile, published in Madrid the first-ever manual of guerrilla warfare, *The Armed Forces and Description of the Indies* (1599), insisting that the pattern of European warfare with its familiar tactics, formations, and garrisons was useless in these lands. For the Americas, he urged creating what one expert on the period describes as "commando groups to carry out search-and-destroy missions deep within enemy territory," perhaps for up to two years at a time.[43] Vargas explained that such men had to know how to live off the land, treat tropical diseases, lay ambushes, and attack by surprise: shades of things to come as Europeans penetrated into North America, Southeast Asia, and Africa.

Soon after, and less than a hundred years since Cortés took Mexico, Miguel de Cervantes would write *Don Quixote,* the tale of a self-destructive, lovable fantast broken by an uncaring nation that has moved on from the bizarre adventures of the early sixteenth century.

But except for an essential decency, how far did Quixote differ in vision from the men whose loose grasp on reality changed the world? Quixote is made crazy by the novels he reads, two of them having been published in the early 1500s under such fanciful titles as *California* and *Patagonia,* names invented well before they were attached to regions of the Americas. If one is a bright, bored petty caballero who has heard about giant kingdoms falling to tiny bands of adventurers — no smarter or better informed than oneself — then amazing things are possible to those convinced of what they can achieve. We can imagine Cortés, Pizarro, and the rest of that unsettling brood saying with Quixote, "All things are possible — first the dream, then the fulfillment." As they even might be to those of us today who plan extreme missions.

7

No Peace Beyond the Line

Naval Special Warfare: Pirates, Buccaneers, and the Imperialists They Preyed On, 1522–1689

"If our number is small, our hearts are great; and the fewer persons we are, the more union and better shares we shall have in the spoil."
CAPTAIN HENRY MORGAN, NOTORIOUS PIRATE ON THE SPANISH MAIN, THEN DEPUTY GOVERNOR OF JAMAICA, 1667

CONQUISTADOR TRIUMPHS notwithstanding, the true military advantage held by Europeans over the rest of the world by the sixteenth century lay in their maritime superiority. These years witnessed revolutions in shipbuilding, navigation, and in war at sea. Ship design moved from a pattern that would have been recognizable to Caesar to shapes and sails that prevailed until the nineteenth century, when vessels propelled by steam overtook the speediest clippers. Powder-driven artillery heavy enough to smash an enemy ship now bristled from that crucial, though not obvious invention, the gunport. To reach into the unknown lands, the Portuguese had quickly realized that new types of ships were needed to replace their clumsy, square-sailed barcas, and they responded magnificently, with axled rudders and multiple masts bearing lateen sails.[1]

Trade and exploration could flourish. But so, too, did tightly bound bands of predators whose far-reaching missions could be at least as extreme as those of earlier arrivals in the New World: they faced not only perils of sea and jungle, but also equally tough opponents already in place, frequently better armed, and with little inclination to ask for or to grant quarter. Superlative navigation, boat handling, and deep amphibious-penetration talents were required, which elevated these marauders well above the level of ordinary thieves and into the realm of commandolike stealth, guile, and highly focused violence.

Piracy "is crime of a very special sort, demanding of its followers much more than boldness, cunning or skill in the use of arms," concludes a student of the profession.[2] It is a form of crime that shares many qualities with modern military special operations: the ability to handle boats and crew in the back of beyond, as well as frequent mastery of the diplomatic gifts found in the best of special operators. In this case, the aim is to win markets for looted goods, safe harbors, and impromptu allies along the way. At sea and onshore, such high-skilled theft has neither before nor since brought such profit, not only to the thief but to a nation's treasury.

The term *pirate* is like *terrorist* — it can mean many different things to those on the receiving end, who lump all such half-understood figures together. Regular armies and navies can also be so depicted by their enemies, as we see today when the military or even commercial activities of one or another Western democracy are denounced as piratical by the people aggrieved.[3] But in this age, the difference between the outright pirate and the commissioned regular officer could indeed be thin. And there are intermediate categories such as privateers and corsairs. The story of these sea adventurers — merchants with an eye for power, privateers stretching their commissions beyond the limit, explorers coining expertise into sovereignty — also shows the risks and benefits of operating at great distance, often with smaller numbers than even those disposed of by the Conquistadors.

Like the Conquistadors, these hard-hitting bands in distant spaces possessed the versatility and self-reliance so characteristic of the special force. Neither group had much to fall back on, which gave them few, if any, second chances. Conquistadors and pirates succeeded by detecting the vulnerabilities of the ostensibly stronger enemy — and how to get weapons and supplies from him, recruit their enemy's enemy, ferret out intelligence, do the unexpected. Each squeezed the most out of qualities, not quantities — speed, decisiveness, and daring so great as to constitute the sort of surprise that takes an opponent's imagination prisoner. Privateers, pirates, and buccaneers were self-selected in their mere presence on the scene, as were the Conquistadors who pulled down the Aztecs and Incas, if no more adequately prepared by actual training. They sailed into waters inhabited, as far as they knew, by sea monsters and creatures with mouths in their bellies. Even when privateers were supposedly working for the state, they also, like the Conquistadors, were forever clashing with authority.

Initially, Spaniards held sway in barely disputed lands larger than all of Europe. Their numbers south of the Rio Grande were huge compared to other adventuring Europeans who began to trespass. The Spanish looked strong, and indeed were so when England eventually gathered an army to throw against them; their fever-seasoned soldiers and settlers could additionally depend on the climate of some of the most pestilent regions of the continent to take a toll of invaders. The popular David-and-Goliath exhilaration of this era was knowing that small, often-solitary ships and daring captains were going up not only against the immensity of the oceans but also the full might of Spain — the global evil empire, in the eyes of its opponents.

To small, incisive, fast in-and-out penetration, however, Spain's treasures repeatedly proved vulnerable — not least because pirates of the time often appeared by night, were bound to their band of wicked brothers, cared nothing about blows or hardships, and relished their trade. Plus, they were second to none in seamanship. If not to the world-altering extent of the Conquistadors, naval special warfare in this era had its own impact on history, particularly if one considers Drake, as well as the interrupted treasure flow to Spain. In the hands of these characters, such tactics were also an example of technique not equaled until our own day.

‡

VIRTUALLY ALL wars, short of those for national survival, raise questions of who gets rewarded and how. Early-modern governments without remotely adequate mechanisms of taxation needed to make wars pay for themselves, a requirement that necessarily conferred huge opportunity on men prepared to risk their necks in the debatable realm between trade, plunder, and patriotism. If the Spaniards had seized much of the New World, the French, the English, and the Dutch were gleefully snatching a high proportion of the treasure-bearing vessels of the Most Catholic King. Then, as Dutch enterprise gained in the East Indies, their English fellow-Protestants ravaged like wolves among the bulky spice transports heading back to a continent whose winter-rotting foods desperately needed pepper, cinnamon, and cloves.

It was barely worthwhile to pirate for grain or cod. Better targets were gold from Mexico, silver from the mountains of Bolivia, Caribbean pearls, shining emeralds from Peru. The revolution in maritime technology brought conquest, riches, and more than a touch of irony. "By my faith," said Cortés in his declining years, "I carried on over there as if I had been a gentlemanly pirate."[4] To be sure — and the treasure hoard he shipped to Charles V after the fall of Tenochtitlán was waylaid between the Azores and Spain by French pirates, and borne off to Dieppe by seamen who exemplified what was to come.

Of course, pirates have existed since ships were built, and piracy fed off the maritime commerce of Phoenicians, Greeks, Romans, and Carthaginians. Like so much else, it had dwindled during the Dark Ages, only because there was less seaborne trade to steal. As robbery at sea rebuilt itself with the growth in commerce by the twelfth and thirteenth centuries, veritable floating republics had come into existence: the *Victualienbrüder* of the Baltic, an enduring pirate brotherhood operating in partnership with the brokers of Emden on the northwest German coast; and the curious nomads of the Mediterranean, like the losing side in the "Revolt of the Suburb," insurrectionists in coastal Morocco who had enough ships to flee the mainland en masse, then plunder the sea for decades. Leaders were frequently elected, and later pirate captains in the Caribbean and Atlantic might be voted into power by their ships' companies as well — a kind of legitimacy that could result in intense loyalty, at least as long as the prizes kept coming.

In the sixteenth century, and for at least 250 years thereafter, state connivance at piracy takes many remarkable forms. Ongoing maritime supplies and efficient markets for stolen goods required politically sophisticated relationships. Repeated attempts to punish North African corsairs were particularly fruitless, because the European powers kept dealing with these sovereign outlaws as if they were outlaw sovereigns.[5] Nod was met by wink, or simply by craven payoffs, in a form of accommodation not unlike those made by civilized nations today with rogue states, with drug lords seeking respectability, and, perhaps, with actual terrorists. In the Americas, official documents for centuries teem with complaints about faithless governors cutting deals with the people they were supposed to be running down; archives also abound in gaps that would otherwise record where higher authority had made its own adjustments. Elizabeth I may have regarded the initial slaving expedition of John Hawkins — one of the greatest mariners of the age, and probably the first Englishman to traffic in African flesh — as shameful business. But when she saw his profits, in short order he became "Queen Elizabeth's Slave Trader," embarking in her ship *Jesus,* thereafter striking forth against her enemies as a privateer, his coat of arms boasting an African in chains.[6]

Before what hobbyists call the golden age of piracy in the Americas, from roughly the mid-seventeenth to the mid-eighteenth century, the Mediterranean had been a pirates' paradise for millennia. It had seen centuries of North African slaving against Christian coasts and ships, Cervantes himself spending five years in Moorish servitude. Perhaps a million white men, women, and children ended up in the markets of Morocco, Algiers, Tunis, and Tripoli from the early seventeenth to the early nineteenth centuries, many of them seized at sea, but many more snatched from their homes in raids on the coasts of Greece, Sweden, England, and Spain. Even Iceland had to negotiate the ransom of its citizens carried off from among the glaciers to the sands of the Maghreb. And by the 1660s, a "steady trickle" of American seamen found themselves captured and enslaved in North Africa too.[7]

During this time, what Europeans called the Barbary Coast — that 2,000-mile shore of North Africa reaching from the western border of Egypt toward the Atlantic Ocean — was occupied by Islamic fiefdoms under the ostensible authority of the Ottoman Sultan in Constantinople. Very independent Morocco, for its part, had the infamous port of Sale, seventy-five miles up the Atlantic coast from today's Casablanca, and the emperor's slave pens inland at Meknes. In the slave-raiding that came out of Barbary (which sure looks like piracy, despite the hair-splitting of scholars), venture investors would outfit the ships of enterprising captains for 10 percent of the returns.[8] The exploits of the first of those famed pirate chieftains, Murad Rais (*rais* being the local term for captain), repeatedly show the creative focused enterprise that drives the special modes of war.

Born a Christian of Albanian parents but carried off as a child, Murad was groomed by his owner, an Algerian corsair, to fight at sea. His exploits would make him as renowned in the late 1500s as Francis Drake, then just returning from his circumnavigation. Fed up with the peculiar disciplines of the Ottoman navy, the young Murad began his career by deserting with his master's ship from the fleet, returning contritely to Algiers after initial calamities. Apparently, such fundamental talents were considered worth nurturing, and the headstrong youth was given another chance. He next went cruising off Tuscany with two galliots (light, swift, rowing vessels) and detected, towering over a rocky promontory, the tall masts of galleys at anchor, being the property of His Holiness Pope Gregory XIII (who gave us our current calendar). One was a papal flagship, its primary motive power being Moslem slaves and Christian criminals chained to the oars — including, said Murad, errant priests and monks.

How to attack these fully armed vessels with nothing more than a pair of big rowboats? First, Murad doubled his "force" by aligning himself with two other prowling Algerian galliots. But four of even these small craft could look suspicious if they all together approached the powerful squadron. So his second step was to tow the new arrivals on short stout ropes behind him. Approaching head-on, his group would appear half its size. To take ships of this magnitude, Murad must have counted on more than stealthy approach and sudden attack. Galley slaves are unlikely to feel any fond attachment to their overseers, and a flagship might have carried about 220 of them, by no means all emaciated. Unchaining these two-handed engines must have occurred in minutes: once again, a special operation could look for "friends in the garrison." The papal warships were suddenly boarded and subdued in a whirlwind of teenage violence, Murad's legend officially launched.[9]

The Christian powers responded only spasmodically to these depredations so relatively close to home, but when they did, it could be memorable. For example, Robert Blake had been an Oxford scholar and country merchant before the English civil wars and Republic, then became literally a revolutionary, open to seeing a problem anew, in matters of violence as well as of politics (a creative mix that we will encounter often in the special warrior). Practically overnight, this able impromptu general, as he first was in the civil war, began at fifty years old his eight-year career as one of his country's greatest admirals ever. In 1655, Blake was able to sail nearly straight into the high-walled harbor of Tunis and burn a collection of pirate ships — perhaps not exactly such a conquest against long odds as then believed, but daring enough. Twenty years later, it would be Tripoli's turn to see every ship in its harbor blown up at midnight by an English lieutenant and a flotilla of twelve small boats rigged with explosives.[10] But while piracy in the tideless Mediterranean would offer up ongoing special exploits, and the African seaborne hunters extended their attacks far into the North Atlantic, it was in the New World of barely charted oceans and unknown coasts that pirate predators set an interplanetary tone.

England, a nation that regarded fighting nine hundred miles away in the Mediterranean as an extreme long-range endeavor, suddenly found its star warriors in men operating three thousand miles from home, with no bases and no backup, living off whatever resources they could muster. High courage, extraordinary endurance, and considerable enterprise were mere entry-level qualifications. These men's reach was as astounding as their amorality. John Hawkins and his slaving, Francis Drake and his robberies, Henry Morgan storming well-defended cities — even William Baffin, the English navigator whose name stretches across the Arctic, and who died attacking a Portuguese stronghold in the Strait of Hormuz — all of them, in their way, were special operators who sharpened their swords for glittering and usually well-defended prizes.

‡

OF ALL THE oddities who emerged in this era, none could boast the accomplishments of the man known to the Spanish as *el Draque* (the Dragon). Many books tell Francis Drake's story, or fragments thereof. Yet details of his quests are often confused, not least by his own embellishments. There remains enough evidence to prove him a kind of seagoing Pizarro. His renown intensified the fear of his suddenly descending hand. Similar reputations today are exploited by as many elite forces as can get away with it, notably the commando ones: opponents quail when they know a SEAL or Special Boat Service team is on the hunt.

Drake was short, stocky, red-haired, strong as a bull, and brave beyond measure. He spent comparatively few years in actual service to the state. Despite the glory heaped on him in days when imperialism could still be sentimentalized, he was a shady character, akin to the shrewd nineteenth-century evocation of the seagoing Englishman of those later days as "half bagman, half buccaneer, with a sample of woolen goods in one hand and a boarding pike in the other."[11] In the ongoing similarity of commando skills and spectacular crime, Drake in his earlier years can be seen as "master thief of the unknown world," an opinion not just of the Spanish but of more than a few officials in London.[12] The special operations qualities demonstrated from the start of his dealings with Spain are woven into his hard, bloody life from beginning to end.

No one is sure when he was born in Devonshire, although it must have been sometime between 1539 and 1545. Depending on the source, by the age of eighteen he was either purser of a ship trading to Biscay or prowling on another along the French coast, picking off merchantmen. The two roles not being self-excluding, he graduated quickly to slaving in Guinea and Sierra Leone.[13] His first voyages to the New World were almost-honest business ventures (by sixteenth-century standards): trading slaves (mostly snatched from Portuguese custody in Africa) along with Hawkins, his cousin and mentor, then selling smuggled goods to Spanish colonists otherwise compelled to pay the king's sales taxes. (Also like skilled forms of bank robbery today, smuggling has long been among those undertakings whose techniques of stealthy insertion, speed, disguise, or ruse can parallel those of special operations.)

Short-circuiting royal monopolies could be profitable, although such of the Spanish authorities as had not been bribed attacked foreign vessels on sight, and usually hanged their crews. The pope, after all, had drawn a line in 1494: Spain was to control all territories of what subsequently became known as the Americas (the division was later revised). Drake's luck ran out in September 1568, when a storm pounded Hawkins's fleet of eight ships in the Gulf of Mexico, compelling it to refit at San Juan de Ulua, the harbor town for Veracruz, and no less than the principal port of New Spain. Drake was permitted entry, perhaps because his ships were thought to be the annual Spanish merchant fleet with its armed escort.[14] Unfortunately for the English, the real fleet arrived the following day. Spanish guns and deadly fireships soon laid into the already damaged, and distinctly smaller, enemy craft. Only the two now-overcrowded vessels captained by Drake and Hawkins made their way out and back to England, abandoning a hundred of their shipmates, who mostly disappeared on the Florida coast — almost three-quarters of the original crew lost altogether. Hardly one to fit in any chain of command, thereafter Drake rarely shared authority.

Drake's escape from Veracruz was thick with disgrace, yet he would spring back from what would have ended the career of a lesser captain. He appeared in the Caribbean three years later in a tiny twenty-five-ton vessel to team up with French pirates for an inland raid on the Isthmus of Panama, seizing assorted ships and riverboats. Returning to England with a respectable amount of loot, he took a few months off before venturing out again in May 1572 with seventy-three men, everyone but the sailmaker under thirty years old, and two little ships, this time carrying three disassembled shallow-draft sailboats known as pinnaces. He also packed muskets, bows, cutlasses, pikes, powder, and shot, but no artillery. Drake knew what he was about; they were going to travel light.

That July, he dropped anchor in a deserted harbor on the Caribbean side of the isthmus, where he built a small fort and assembled the pinnaces. Joined by a third English vessel, boats and ships slipped up the coast toward Nombre de Dios, a speck of a town, but significant as the transshipment point for gold and silver mined in Peru and brought to the port of Panama on the Pacific, seventy miles by trail across the isthmus. From Panama, mule trains would haul the treasure north to Nombre de Dios, where convoys from Seville would arrive annually to transport it to the king's ever-hungry mints. And the convoys at sea were just about impregnable.

The little fleet landed on an uninhabited offshore island. Leaving twenty men to guard the ships, Drake loaded his sailboats with fighting gear and pushed off, accompanied by an even smaller open boat, a shallop, carrying twenty additional men from the third English ship. The party hugged the shoreline (a procedure akin to flying under the radar) until they reached an islet, undertook a quick morning's drill, then sailed seventy-five miles farther to the mouth of the river that washed Nombre de Dios. Once the moon rose, the boats glided into the harbor, and two assault teams disembarked, Drake leading one, his brother the other. The incursion was quickly detected, church bells clamored, and half-awake but competently armed Spaniards tumbled out. Numbers may have been about equal, but the English took initial advantage by using drums, trumpets, and torches on their pikes to create the Gideonlike impression of a horde descending out of the early-morning darkness.

Drake's team made it to the marketplace before being checked by musketfire; but then his brother, whose men had looped around to assail the town from another direction, came storming in. Believing themselves truly outnumbered, the inhabitants of Nombre de Dios fled through the town gate. That was all very well, but the treasure house proved to be empty; the Spanish fleet had already left.[15]

Quickly things turned. Drake seems to have been spooked into believing that two or three Spaniards hiding in the dark with burning matches were a horde of snipers. He then had only to faint from a leg wound for his men to cave in; a Spanish counterattack quickly drove the invaders all to the boats. At this stage of the evolution of special forces, such brave little outfits rarely had depth of leadership.

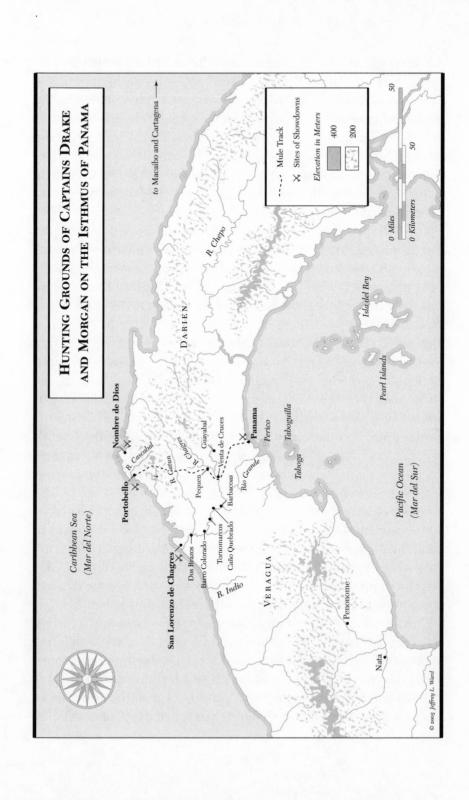

Hunting Grounds of Captains Drake and Morgan on the Isthmus of Panama

Caribbean Sea
(Mar del Norte)

to Macaibo and Cartagena →

Nombre de Dios

Portobello

San Lorenzo de Chagres

R. Cascabal

R. Gatun

R. Chagres

Pequen

Guayabal

Venta de Cruces

Barbacoas

Dos Brazos

Barro Colorado

Tornomarcos

Caño Quebrado

R. Indio

VERAGUA

Panama

Perico

Taboguilla

Taboga

Rio Grande

DARIEN

R. Chepo

Isla del Rey

Pearl Islands

Pacific Ocean
(Mar del Sur)

Penonome

Nata

Elevation in Meters

Mule Track

Sites of Showdowns

400

200

0 Miles   50

0 Kilometers   50

© 2005 Jeffrey L. Ward

The stealthy handling of small craft had been sound; but the few hours of last-moment tactical instruction were inadequate, the intelligence and follow-through even poorer. The whole business had proved worse than pointless, except as a deadly practice run for Drake's next efforts.

So the party limped back to their island base. Perhaps what remained of the entire group was now too small to crew Drake's two awaiting ships plus the sailboats — the third ship having left, unimpressed. Or perhaps Drake believed he would work better with just one (relatively) large ship. For whatever reason, he scuttled his second vessel, then went on small subsistence raids along the coast, soon snatching two Spanish *fragatas* (little vessels with one sail).

At least here the venture begins to reflect the qualities of special performance that Cortés and Pizarro had shrewdly displayed, which today keeps proving similarly vital: a small force deep in enemy terrain is augmented by discovering locals with more or less common interests. Drake was able to ally himself with escaped black slaves whom the Spaniards called *Cimmaronas* (Cimaroons), people of the hilltops. These resolute guerrillas so skilled in hunting and pathfinding lived in the jungle by raiding their former owners. On their advice, he moved his party to another island, receiving food and insight in exchange for weapons and goods.

In January 1573, Cimaroon informants told Drake that a Spanish fleet had arrived in Nombre de Dios, meaning that the treasure train would soon begin its trek across the Cordillera. He set out with eighteen Englishmen and about thirty black allies. After two weeks' slogging through jungle and over mountains, they penetrated to the outskirts of Panama and glimpsed the Pacific, on which no Englishman had yet sailed. Drake infiltrated into the town a Cimaroon spy, who learned that the treasurer of Lima and fourteen mules loaded with gold and jewels would be departing that very night for Nombre de Dios. The Cimaroons also helped identify the best spot on the trail for an ambush, which was duly set. Drake had apparently ordered all his men to wear white shirts to identify one another during the fighting, and — perhaps remembering the earlier effect of his drums and torches in magnifying his force — to add to the ghostly terror of the attack.

After hours of waiting in the dark, a horseman rode by on the trail (either an advance guard for the caravan, or a rider from the direction of Nombre de Dios, depending on the different versions). Again, the execution seems to have been poorer than the boldly simple plan. The men did not know when to begin moving from hiding, although bosuns' whistles had existed for centuries for similar purposes of coordination, and Drake was indeed carrying one. One man rose too early, a strange white figure in the undergrowth, but it was enough. The horseman passed the sighting on to the treasure-laden train making its way uphill, whereupon it prudently turned back, substituting a job-lot caravan of pots, pans, and odd clothes to test the trail. The bait was swallowed: the only people satisfied besides the Spanish were the Cimaroons, since such commodities were more valuable in the jungle than gold.

With the opportunity blown and anticipating an enraged colony in hot pursuit, Drake's party had to struggle back to the Caribbean hideaway with nothing to show for their suffering. Morale plummeted, but Drake reasserted his peculiar brand of leadership to convince them of imminent success. Over the following month they raided the coast for provisions, regained their muscle, and luckily encountered on the water twenty Frenchmen who, as privateers, were ready to join them. Most sustained special operations, it is worth remembering, are likely to be so slimmed down for the sake of sheer mobility and concealment that the warriors not only need to depend for supplies on the enemy, but also frequently have to gain fighting strength from previously unknown cobelligerents.

Strengthened by the Frenchmen and their firearms as well as by his Cimaroon jungle fighters, Drake pressed his light craft up the coast within six miles of Nombre de Dios, his original target, hiding the boats onshore, leaving a small guard behind, and heading inland to wait. The next slow-moving treasure caravan would arrive at the port toward the end of April. There it could be ambushed, rather than in the foothills outside of the town of Panama — even though this entailed jumping it virtually under the guns of Spanish warships.

So near to its destination within Nombre de Dios, the caravan would be pushing confidently ahead by day. Although it enjoyed triple the usual number of guards, these soldiers would likely assume that any threat was minimal; what troublemakers there had been outside of Panama City so many weeks before had probably been eaten by the jungle. The earlier attack on the then thinly held Nombre de Dios itself, after all, could be interpreted as a reckless blunder by roving freebooters. Can the average commandant or governor imagine himself surviving effectively in jungle, deserts, or mountain country? The comforting assumption of "out of sight, out of mind" is also a great ally of the special force.

The trap was sprung on April 29. Shots were fired, the stunned guards driven off in headlong flight. It has taken centuries for planners of extreme missions to recognize that achievement is consummated not at the point of impact, but at that of consolidation. In this case, Drake and company could take only what they could quickly carry, then simply bury another fortune in the jungle and fall back into the dense greenery as Spanish troops were heard approaching. He had to improvise a raft from unstripped logs to paddle his way out to an island where his sailboats had fled from a land patrol. Days later, he learned that the Spanish had dug up the treasure, its whereabouts likely known from torturing the captured French privateer captain. Still, what he had gotten away with was worth nearly eighty thousand pesos in gold. The Frenchmen took their share and departed. Drake and less than half the original crew survived to work their tiny, laden ship back into Plymouth Sound that August — he, at least, was an immensely rich man.

Drake bought a fine estate and set up as a gentleman, spending some months intercepting rebel shipping off Ireland. Four years later, perhaps restless for more profitable activities, he took the opportunity for an even more ambitious, relatively better-prepared operation, this time into the vast Pacific, an ocean over whose tens of millions of square miles Spain, on the strength of a few thousand tons of creaky shipping, asserted exclusive sovereignty. This time the investment syndicate that backed him included Elizabeth I.

The venture had to begin in secrecy so as not to further antagonize Spain — and was prudently opposed by powerful officials such as the Lord Treasurer. After all, England and Spain were not at war. But proceed it did. Drake dropped down-Channel in December 1577, aboard the flagship *Pelican,* little more than a hundred feet in length and twenty-one feet in the beam. Four smaller vessels followed, at the head of a company of only 164 men, boys, and a dozen young gentlemen-adventurers representing the backers. Purpose and direction were closely held. They moved down the African coast, snapping up small Spanish ships as targets of opportunity, recruiting a Portuguese ship captain turned pilot, then ran before the trade winds to the Cape Verde Islands, thence to the coast of Brazil in April, thereafter south toward the entrance of the Magellan Strait into the towering seas of the Roaring Forties.

He refitted at Port Saint Julian in southern Patagonia, the last safe anchorage where, in 1520, Ferdinand Magellan had wintered, and had tortured to death three of his mutineers — as Drake's men well knew. Mutiny was a recurring problem of the age — probably all the more so when challenging the myth-haunted, deadly Horn — and not by frightened individual malcontents but by entire ships' companies who yearned for kindlier latitudes. Continuing the tradition, Drake beheaded one of the gentlemen-adventurers, a former friend, whom he believed to be fomenting rebellion. The charge was doubtful. Exhaustion and malnutrition must have been rotting everyone's judgment, but the gratuitous quasi-judicial murder revealed Drake's habits of command.

He led by methods rare among leaders of a special undertaking, even for that time: fear, ridicule, and humiliation. To that end, Drake stood on the cusp of an age. He responded to immense new opportunities with merely a few score of fighting men, but as a backward-looking figure, a feudal lord at sea whose men (often unpaid once home) had to swear allegiance to him. He did not seek to maximize the best general qualities in subordinates, demanding instead unthinking obedience for his intensely personal aggrandizement. Without him, the operation would fall apart. A key characteristic of modern special operations, in contrast, is that they transcend such an approach; increasingly, men come to compose a self-reliant unit, rather than just a gang of courageous followers.

Approaching the tempests of the Strait, two of the lighter ships simply returned to England, and in September 1578, the remaining three headed in, monstrous waves bursting in white spray against the base of dark cliffs, men starting to die of cold. The smallest ship simply disappeared in the maze. Another, battered toward the Antarctic after making it through, preferred to turn back into the Strait, heading for England rather than face what would surely be even worse perils ahead. After sixteen days, *Pelican,* now auspiciously renamed *Golden Hind,* entered the Southern Ocean alone, with no more than eighty men and boys. There were no charts to guide her up the coast of Chile, stretches of which were still inhabited by Indians with excellent reason to attack any European coming ashore.

In December 1578, Drake pounced on Valparaiso, the port nearest the gold mines of Santiago, entering it at dark by convincing the crew of a Spanish ship in the harbor that he was a countryman — until the English sprang aboard. Perhaps twenty-four thousand pesos of gold were lifted, although Drake may have neglected to inventory what might have been ten times that amount. Those who steal are usually not those who like to share, and Drake had investors who would base their demands on his ledgers. He also found Spanish charts for all the ports along the coast.

Sailing north, by February 1579 he was down to a crew of about seventy, only thirty or so in any condition to fight. Again, Drake had prefabricated small sailboats stored on his heavily gunned flagship, essential for sneaking into the shallower ports along this fabled shore and, whether under Spanish flags or by skillful invitation, for ensuring surprise — a ruse he used repeatedly.

He gathered intelligence along the way and snatched treasure from ships in Arica, the outport (on today's Chilean-Peruvian border) of the famed silver mines of Potosí. Next was a raid still farther north — on Callao, the port town of opulent Lima, which lay wide open. After all, no European enemies (besides fellow Spaniards) had ever struck in this other half of the world. Once in, he learned that an immense wealth-laden argosy, the *Nuestra Señora de la Concepción,* had recently sailed for Panama, his old hunting grounds; he would run it down four hundred miles south of the isthmus. Altogether, the *Hind* enjoyed more than five months of uninterrupted plunder so far behind enemy lines that the designation is nearly meaningless.

To return by the same route around the Horn would risk not only prevailing winds from the south, but maybe running a gauntlet of two oceans' worth of angry Conquistadors along the way. So in a ship straining under perhaps twenty-six tons of stolen gold and silver, Drake and his dwindling band left Spanish waters during April, sailing farther north for wind. Despite the possibility that he reached present-day British Columbia, Drake's route from his last Spanish port to the Malay Archipelago, the fabulous Spice Islands in the seas for which German geographers would, centuries later, coin the name *Indonesia,* remains a mystery — in no small part because the route would be obscured for reasons of Elizabethan national security.[16]

Once across the world's widest ocean, he and his sixty-two remaining versatile bandits traded for cloves and cinnamon, made commercial contacts, and navigated brilliantly among the thousands of uncharted islands before crossing the Indian Ocean, rounding the Cape of Good Hope back into the Atlantic, hugging that part of the West African coast they had not touched before to return triumphantly to England in late September 1580, with fifty-eight men of the original company, after nearly three years and thirty-six thousand miles. Drake was knighted, despite frantic Spanish representations about piracy. His admitted profits paid a 4,700 percent return to the investors. "The booty brought back by Drake," explains the greatest of twentieth-century economists, John Maynard Keynes, "may fairly be considered the fountain and origin of British Foreign Investment."[17] Its profits led to the forming of the East India Company.

Except for one remark about "singeing the King of Spain's beard," there is little record of humor from Drake's mouth. Quite the contrary — although humor is indispensable when leading men in a pinch.[18] Also unlike other leaders of special forces, Drake disdained the opinions of subordinates, or even to involve himself much in details. Yet no matter how intimidated, perhaps only the private following of such a driven, unscrupulous maverick could have combined the destructiveness, readiness to improvise, and embrace of supreme risk that enabled his absurdly small force to cut through the limbs of the first world empire. And here is what distinguishes his operations from those of, say, a Pablo Escobar or the other global gangsters who still work out of someplace such as Cartagena in twenty-first-century Colombia. Drake's most extreme missions were, at least in part, subordinated to public purpose. They were also ones of nearly unprecedented technical skill. The farther he pressed, the more he was operating in truly a new world, so different from the smuggling of slaves then, or of cocaine and who knows what else today.

By 1585, after much importuning to be allowed to return to the Pacific, Drake instead received command of an amphibious expedition bound for the West Indies. Even then, the queen had doubts about letting the nation's favorite pirate take off at the head of more than a thousand soldiers and a fleet of two dozen ships. Perhaps she wanted him somewhat nearer as troubles brewed with Spain; perhaps an assault of this magnitude against Spanish holdings was thought too inflammatory; or perhaps there were concerns about leadership. Doubts were overcome by ensuring that the mission could be "plausibly denied," a convenience for governments ever since in handling secret operations.

Drake again used small boats and night maneuvers, surprising Santo Domingo, freeing galley slaves to join his men, and inflicting on the Spaniards "a debacle beyond anyone's imagination," although missing the treasure fleet by about twelve hours.[19] He moved on to Cartagena, the latest "New Carthage," on the eastward side of the Gulf of Darien, then one of the richest bastions on the South and Central American coasts, the by-now fabled "Spanish Main." Cartagena's more numerous defenders were fully aware of his presence. Indeed, he was casually rowed along the seafront — dressed in black, barely out of gun range, his ships draped in the same funereal color. Historians note that this may have been a signal to Cimaroon allies, who thereafter slipped aboard his flagship to warn about poisoned stakes planted by the defenders in the foreshore.[20] More likely, it was an instance of psychological warfare, building on Drake's ominous renown.

He finally struck at his preferred time of 2 or 3 A.M., and a simple order was issued. The men must capture the town or they would not be allowed back on board; anyone who retreated would be hanged.[21] This raid has been chosen by the U.S. Naval Postgraduate School to instruct rising officers about special operations in the age of sail — emphasizing Drake's techniques of amphibious action, talent for mobilizing irregular allies ashore, and his ability to split the Spanish land and sea defenses.[22] Yet, once more, there had been little thought given to outcomes and next steps. The ransom that the Spanish niggled down some 80 percent to 107,000 ducats was believed small for the loss of English lives, and what thought there had been about leaving an occupying force behind was erased by the hundreds dead from fevers that were endemic to this part of the world. Those hardy Spanish colonists who survived Drake's predations soon reoccupied their settlements.

Returning to Portsmouth after ten months, Drake had to rustle up more money from the investors to pay his crew, a third of whom had died since so recently leaving home. The voyage had been among the first acts of nearly open war with Spain, another being Elizabeth's dispatch of five thousand soldiers to aid Protestant Dutch rebels in the Low Countries. About a year later, in 1587, King Philip concluded that there was no alternative to invading England. As Spain's armada for its "Enterprise of England" gathered, Drake received ships and soldiers from the Crown. He and his business associates contributed four more vessels, and he brought along six pinnaces for inshore work.

A master of surprise attack, in April he sprang his most dazzling raid on the southwestern Spanish port of Cádiz, whose inner harbor is accessible only through a narrow channel that opens into a basin roughly four miles across — the Spanish therefore soon to rue their "confidence that no enemy would dare to enter the bay."[23] Castle guns commanded that funneled entrance and part of his fleet was traveling well behind, yet he swept straight in, by flying French colors, then led boarding parties to start an inferno, the rest of his squadron not to arrive for another day. Forty-eight hours after it began, some thirty-eight ships had been sunk or brought away, and warehouses full of cargo and supplies had been destroyed.

But what was war without profit? Drake soon left the enraged coast to close in on the second-greatest single prize that had ever been taken by pirates or privateers — a Portuguese carrack on the last leg of her voyage from India. (The greatest was his *Nuestra Señora de la Concepción*.) The ship was fair game on the high seas; seven years earlier, King Philip had overrun Portugal, traditionally an ally of England. No need for Drake to declare his ship's nationality until this

floating treasure was within gun range. And the carrack also produced what the more informed of special operators highly covet —
secret documents, in this case charts and papers that revealed the
long-hidden mysteries of the East India trade.

The Armada of some 130 ships carrying eighteen thousand men
that was finally able to make way against England the following year
was one of the largest long-range fleets in the age before steam —
"*La Invencible,*" "the greatest navy that ever swam the sea." Having
exchanged piracy for public service, Drake was now vice admiral,
commanding ships built low and sleek for what navy England could
assemble. To a degree often overlooked, he applied in conventional
combat the insights of surprise, improvisation, and espionage previously developed in his small operations. Hawkins (now Sir John)
joined him as an admiral.

Calais was the Armada's last chance to regroup before escorting the
Duke of Parma's invasion army on flat-bottomed barges from the
shallow waters of Flanders across the Channel to Kent. Had these
twenty-six thousand superb veterans, led by the finest soldier of the
age, been able to board, to combine with the men of the Armada, and
then to make it past about the same number of English vessels, Parma
would have held the desperate English militias in the hollow of his
hand.

Spain's army had already suffered from hit-and-run raids by
Dutch guerrillas in the shoals. Now Drake's scheming encouraged
fireships to be sent at night against the gun-torn Spanish fleet as it
huddled in Calais Roads after a tough fight up-Channel. (With
uncharacteristic generosity, Drake donated two of the fireships.) The
Spanish believed these eight terrifying objects to be the yet more
destructive bombships often used by the Dutch, which were timed to
explode and could not be deflected by lowering rowboats to tow them
away. It was "an exploit which with one hundred and thirty [ships]
they had not been able to do or dare attempt," marveled the Spanish
accounts.[24] Most of the enemy fleet therefore cut its own cables and
staggered out into the North Sea storms for a ruinous flight home.
Only half made it.

After an overly ambitious investor-backed attempt to finish off the
Armada's remnants at La Coruña on the Spanish north coast and at

Lisbon proved fruitless, Drake returned to playing to his strengths on a smaller, yet no longer tiny, scale. He led another descent on the Caribbean in 1595, at the head of twenty-seven ships and compelled to share command with Hawkins, with whom he quarreled violently. By this time, however, Spanish settlements were better defended. It was getting late in the day for simple smash-and-grabs, and the settlements had ample warning he was coming. Nor was luck any longer on his side: Hawkins died plain worn out, while Drake succumbed to bloody dysentery aboard his flagship and was released into the waters off Nombre de Dios. Given the means by which Drake had extracted obedience, it should be no surprise that discipline collapsed disastrously once he was gone. But in his last hour, he had gathered enough strength to rise and to attempt to buckle on his armor — a seagoing, world-changing Pizarro to the end.

‡

THE BYZANTINES had maintained fleets in their long struggle against the Moslems, and in the late 1500s, warfare in the Baltic had already involved state-owned ships sailed by government employees. But navies as professional institutions (even more so than armies) were truly a product of the early modern state. They were the more complicated organization, with permanent dockyards, gun foundries (though often run by the army), scientific boards, and primitive maritime casualty insurance. Until then, combat at sea had been a matter of the entrepreneurship exemplified by Drake and Hawkins, of calling up and refitting merchant vessels for war service.

It was the Dutch who first took advantage of the disintegration of Spain's domination of the sea after the Armada's overthrow, positioning themselves as the financial center of the world and building up what, for more than a century, was the world's largest merchant marine. They also first developed a high-seas fleet capable of long outreach, when England was still a second-rate power with no full-time navy or standing army.

Before the appearance of professional navies, with commissioned, reliable officers, adventurous spirits intent on "getting a ship and managing her" had a lot of room to make money (and be patriotic) in violent ways.[25] Drake may have turned away from Caribbean enterprise, but he left an inspiring example to people of a certain mindset, just as Cortés had served as an example for Pizarro and so many other adventurers. Unlike the outfits that had been under Drake's command in the distant hemisphere, these resilient marauding bands could not be beheaded, and, to that effect, they foreshadow the special forces of a later age, which perform superbly even if led solely by sergeants or chief petty officers. Time and again, they resorted to commando tactics not just for reconnaissance but for the main undertaking.

Among the first small-boat culture of raiders to emerge were the buccaneers (the word coming from *boucan,* an indigenous method for the smoking of *viande boucanée*). Originally, these were bands of poor French settlers on mainland Hispaniola, who burst out of creeks and coves in tiny craft pulled by oars, minimally equipped with a sail or two. In 1665, some of these raptors brought off what may have been their first significant attack against Spanish shipping. An overloaded boat with twenty-eight men had been fruitlessly prowling off Tortuga, an island northwest of what in 1803 would become Haiti, when it finally "spied a great ship of the Spanish Flota, separated from the rest" — the fatal vulnerability of an immense and confident galleon.[26] Hunger and general misery made it reasonable to seize the opportunity or die in the attempt. As darkness fell, the little party closed up astern. Then their leader (dubbed not unjustly Pierre le Grand) ordered that holes be driven through their own vessel's bottom. There would be no chance of the watch detecting anything tethered to the galleon; nor could there be any thought of failure and escape.

Barefoot and armed with pistols and swords, the twenty-eight climbed up the big ship's sides, killed the helmsman, burst into the cabin of the vice admiral of the Spanish fleet, where he was at cards with his officers, and demanded surrender while others took possession of the gunroom and cut down such opposition as they encountered in the passageways. A handful of men — about a third the number that merely stand watch on an aircraft carrier today — had overnight hacked their way up from little more than a dinghy to a sovereign of the seas. The leader of this band had the rare sense to sail the galleon straight home to Normandy, to retire in wealth. Yet the attack had not been a complete surprise. That same day, it is said, Spanish seamen had warned their captain that in the distance they could see a pirate boat. "What then should I be afraid of such a pitiful thing as that is," said he, in the ideal response for a special operator.[27]

Such a form of assault was a variation on "cutting out" a vessel, which entailed falling upon it with small boats, though usually while it lay at anchor, then working it out to sea. It was a never-ending practice until gunports became obsolete and warships were clad in steel — skills not so much handed down but rediscovered in every epoch of war at sea.[28] (This type of boarding, when used today against modern ships or oil rigs, requires intensive special training. But the fundamentals remain the same: "Not by Strength, by Guile.") To be sure, Spaniards could be equally skilled once the buccaneers began predations with larger vessels. For example, when anchoring off-shore and disembarking to "take, plunder, and fire" a city, attackers could, to their astonishment, be struck by Spanish swimmers able to float out on an inflated horse's hide to sneak under the stern of a ship, cram combustibles behind the rudder, and set everything afire.[29]

Henry Morgan was another inspired pirate leader, although he applied special tactics on a larger scale. Having left Wales as an indentured servant, then coming eagerly to seaborne theft, he also began work around 1665, this time out of Jamaica (which England had seized from Spain ten years earlier). He went on to win fame for attacking the capital of Mexico's Tabasco province; the silver-mining center of Nicaragua, 125 miles inland through dense jungle; and in an historic enterprise nearly a hundred years after Drake's positively last appearance, the city of Panama. It was not only the extreme daring of his operations but their administrative competence that marked them out. A higher order of numbers and sustained efficiency was being brought to bear through wilderness and rivers that even the Spanish had barely explored. A perfect example of this was the assault on Porto Bello.

Since Drake's unwelcome visits to the isthmus, the disease-ridden pesthole of Nombre de Dios had been replaced as the Caribbean transshipment point by this slightly more congenial town, twenty miles due west, shielded by well-garrisoned fortresses on either side of its harbor. Beyond lay blockhouses and sentry posts. Forty miles farther west was the mouth of the Chagres River, guarded by the Castle of San Lorenzo. The Chagres offered a passage that could be followed two-thirds of the way across the isthmus in the direction of Panama City, and today it feeds the lakes and fills the locks of the great canal. In the city itself, perhaps four hundred cavalry backed a garrison of some twenty-four hundred infantry; but the city's best defense really lay in the miles of surrounding jungle.

In late 1667, after nearly two years of successful raids along the Central American coast, Morgan received a vaguely worded privateering commission, the privateers being the "eyes and ears" of Jamaica's defense in the absence of any actual naval protection from London.[30] He was to collect information and to capture ships at sea, being specifically forbidden to attack objectives on land. Holding simultaneously a rather nebulous official appointment and the post, by election, of chieftain of a pirate community happily outside His Majesty's authority, he gathered nine ships and 460 men, to whom he disclosed nothing — and set straight out for Porto Bello, the best-defended place in the West Indies other than Havana and Cartagena. He anchored in a deserted bay on the Mosquito Coast, well to the west of the Chagres, and transferred most of the men to canoes twenty-three feet long, carried aboard ship. For four nights they paddled 150 miles northeast, slipping by somnolent castles on the way to the beautiful harbor. The raiders bore cutlasses, well-oiled pistols, and some of the best-made muskets in the world. Many of the party, explains a participant in these excitements, were superb marksmen whose "main exercises were target-shooting and keeping their guns clean."[31]

Morgan struck at dawn, his snipers picking off any of the garrison who showed their heads. Though he had no cannon, one of the city's fortresses fell quickly; the other held out, forcing Morgan (as good a Protestant as a pirate) to assault it using captured Catholic priests and nuns tied to his scaling ladders as human shields. This helped to do the trick. Tortures and massacres followed (repeated savageries that easily brand Morgan a criminal, even for the time), and a quarter-million pesos in ransom was raised before his additional ships arrived a month later, to exfiltrate what may have been the boldest, most successful amphibious operation of the seventeenth century.

The next year Morgan targeted both the city of Maracaibo, near the mouth of an inland sea that is today the center of Venezuela's oil industry, and another settlement on the far side of these five thousand square miles of fresh water. Each place had the good sense to allow itself to be looted without much ado. Getting into the giant lagoon, through its one winding channel, with eight ships — even small ones — and some 650 men had been tricky enough. When trying to leave, Morgan found escape barred by three Spanish battleships, and the adjacent fort rearmed, manned, and ready. The Spanish admiral offered (dubious) clemency. Morgan asked his men whether they wanted to surrender or fight. Fight it would be, and his outfit spent a frantic week in Maracaibo appearing to be refitting a big yet clumsy Cuban merchantman into a heavily armed battleship.

In the final showdown, at dawn on April 30, 1669, the bulky carrack proudly led the privateers' insignificant flotilla straight for the enemy, crashing into the grand flagship with what looked like a full complement of crew, the Spanish assuming the maneuver was an apparently pathetic attempt to board. Spanish boarding parties instead pounced down onto its decks before they had grasped that they were taking a ghost ship — but one packed with all the gunpowder, tar, pitch, and brimstone to be found in Maracaibo. It blew up, sinking one warship and firing a second. The dazed third was scuttled by the Spaniards. Only twelve men (who had rapidly dropped away in a rowboat) had worked the ghost ship against the Spanish, her decks lined with logs dressed up to look like English ruffians, other logs hollowed out to appear as cannon. Nothing like this had ever been done at sea, nor perhaps imagined.[32]

The seaward passage was still commanded by the fort's artillery. So, within sight of its garrison, Morgan had his men embark for shore in longer, forty-foot canoes, apparently concealing themselves in a mangrove swamp while the unloaded canoes returned to ferry in reinforcements. Clearly, Morgan was massing his raiders to attack from the landward side, and the Spaniards obligingly moved their cannon to blow him back into the mangroves. But those landing parties had never really gone ashore, returning instead on their bellies in the bottom of the canoes — a trick that had been used off and on since ancient times, known perhaps to book-learned military thinkers of the day but not necessarily to Morgan's less-than-literate band on the faraway Spanish Main, nor to the garrison. That night, the raider ships glided through on the tide before the bemused Spaniards could reorient their firepower.

Such operations brought fame and, in 1670, another commission to do all possible damage to Spanish shipping. As he sailed from Jamaica, Morgan also knew that the governor was about to revoke his orders — evidently an occupational hazard for such operators — on the pedantic grounds that a peace treaty had just been signed with Spain. Not delaying to capture any mere ships, Morgan aimed directly at Panama, still the vital relay point for Peruvian silver. That December he concentrated thirty-six sail at the mouth of the Chagres, having rallied no less than two thousand experienced raiders, one-third of them French. For the first and last time, virtually every privateer and pirate in the West Indies had gathered for a single cooperative outrage.

In January, this remarkable alliance took the castle of San Lorenzo by land, thereby nullifying the sheer cliffs that rise from the sea and the river. Around fourteen hundred men then headed upstream in canoes of various sizes, fearful of Indian ambushes, hacking through jungle, and stumbling out ten days later near Panama City.[33] Panama had not bothered to constrict itself with fortifications when one of the cruelest jungles in the world served as its glacis. The enemy once in sight, cavalry and militia made ready to defend their honor on the boggy savannah that separated the city from the jungle.

For Morgan, there was no possibility of retreat. His men had nearly starved in getting across; there were too many to live off the land. He first used his French sharpshooters (real buccaneers from Hispaniola) to pick off the cavalry that ventured out. The Spanish countered with another ancient tactic: stampeding two herds of oxen and bulls into the attackers' rear in order to drive the main force into the guns and pikes of the awaiting infantry, only to find the beasts dash away from the battle scene or be shot in their tracks.

In only three hours, this critical point of Spanish power was in Morgan's hands. Silver and coin were moved out on 175 pack mules, along with at least five hundred brutalized men, women, and children for ransom. There was, however, a hitch: England had by now indeed formalized its peace with Spain. Morgan was recalled to London and imprisoned for piracy. But one scoundrel (judging by the jolly decadence of his court) had a soft spot for another: Morgan was freed by Charles II, knighted, and appointed lieutenant governor of Jamaica.

Such success inspired one more new generation of predators, now seeing possibilities in the Pacific itself, although the Crown was getting tired of the European political price imposed by these ventures. In April 1680, for example, a smaller force than had been gathered by Morgan landed on the isthmus and, again using big canoes — three dozen this time — descended into the Pacific, almost immediately encountered and took two small Spanish vessels, and steered (canoes and all) for Panama. By then, the alarm had been given and three warships sent out, which the raiders nonetheless were able to surprise and board. These, in turn, they used to capture the far larger battle-ship *La Santíssima Trinidad* (The Most Holy Trinity), riding at anchor. "Thus in a few hours," explains one historian, they "had advanced from canoes to barks, then to small men-of-war, and finally became masters of a great ship-of-war" — one of the grandest lever-agings in the whole history of the sea.[34] Yet there was one advantage that the Spanish could deny to wide-ranging buccaneers. Spain's Indian slaves were ideal "friends in the garrison" for any attackers. Since the Spaniards feared revolt, as in the Chilean town of La Serena that year, they might kill most of their slaves as word arrived of approaching marauders.[35]

The last great buccaneering enterprise moved off in 1685: an unsuccessful attack on Panama by an English-led force of adventurers from many nations. When England returned to war in 1689 as part of the Grand Alliance, this time with Austria, the Netherlands — and Spain — to resist mighty France, many of the participants in this final raid on Panama were encouraged to shift gears and become legitimate privateers against the subjects of Louis XIV. Soon, regular officers of an emerging Royal Navy began to appear in Jamaica. Sensitive to mercantile opinion, European nations slowly came to enforce rules of international behavior, even if only in a form of cold war.

‡

LIKE THE swordsmen from the Estremadura and the farm boy from Devon, the buccaneering far-frontier opportunists displayed a strange assortment of talents: they were "physicians, naturalists, criminals, poets and broken men of fortune and title."[36] Eccentric backgrounds, chips on shoulders, mixtures of class and often of race provided sound, do-it-your-own-way preparation for these adventures — as they can still do for special forces. In the resort to small craft to achieve vastly outsized ends, moreover, we encounter a recurring technique of seaborne commandos, right down to today's SEALs. Such canoe operations by the privateers, pirates, and buccaneers are ancestors of the Special Boat Service (SBS) — "swimmer-canoeists," as they are known to the British — whose insignia of crossed paddles with a frog on top remind us of the versatility of all these deft amphibious warriors in rivers, harbors, and out at sea.

The increasing quality of coastline defense and the development of political objectives more refined than stealing bullion meant that such modes of operation would sooner or later have to be put on a professional footing in wartime. They came to be entrusted to men able to work hand in glove with a fleet for larger ends. Nonetheless, the piracy that spawned these techniques was not about to disappear. In North America, helpful harbors and obliging magistrates were to be found from Salem down to Charleston. The Gulf of Florida swarmed with people of whom it was better not to ask questions, and New England pirates infiltrated to the Red Sea and the Persian Gulf to prey on the Moslem trade with India. But Blackbeard, Captain Kidd, and their like are less interesting as forerunners of SEALs and SBS, or of France's Fusiliers Marins Commandos. They continued to display daring and stealth, yet rarely do the exploits of those later generations bear the mark of mind and endurance shown by Drake and by the men who came shortly after him into a world still being made. Nor do such undisputed outlaws make themselves felt as feisty bands of hard-hitting odds-defying rebels, such as we encountered in feudal times.[37] Instead, they are akin to today's ship-thieves in Southeast Asia and African waters whose expertise lies primarily in murder and insurance fraud.

A bigger change in the century after Drake fought the Armada was to be seen in how the new navies of Europe's Atlantic powers were taking shape. They were becoming means of projecting national ambition, whether against enemy merchantmen snuggling under the guns of a fortress or in the ability to unload troops on a hostile coast.[38]

In Drake's era and for nearly a hundred years afterward, there were no actual marines to fill this function of plunging ashore and striking inland, despite a few Elizabethan references to "sea soldiers" at a time when it was unclear whether the commander of a ship, a regiment, or an expedition was a soldier, sailor, or both together. Nor were there any distinct reconnaissance teams for stealthy penetration. At best, sailors took time off from hauling the bowline, heaving the lead, and manning culverins to swing their cutlasses in surprise attacks onshore, perhaps assisted by impromptu local allies and by gentlemen adventurers thirsting for excitement. Soldiers shipped in for the event — and unlikely to be familiar with boats, beaches, or how to handle heavy equipment — were expected to assault well-fortified coastal positions.

But if combined operations were to work routinely, they would require more than the cobbling together of landlubbers and sailors. To do it right, marines would emerge. As for the most specialized of giant-killers — teams of rigorously trained warriors able not only to arrive by sea but then also to slip ashore or up rivers or sneak up on ships at anchor or under way, men drawn from professional navies who possessed the shooting, raiding, and small-boat skills of the buccaneers — that step would have to wait until well into the twentieth century.

8

A Hazard of New Fortunes

Specialization and Enterprise: Europe from the Westward Discovery to the Zenith of the Sun King, 1492–1701

"He either fears his fate too much
Or his deserts are small
That puts it not unto the touch
To win or lose it all."
JAMES, MARQUIS OF MONTROSE,
BEHEADED AFTER MANY VICTORIES

THE YEARS from the landfall of Columbus on an unanticipated continent to 1701 and the outbreak of the War of the Spanish Succession saw the steady concentration of violence into the hands of the state. Permanent land and sea forces were emerging at different places and in different forms in each country of newly developing western Europe, and their overall growth was accompanied by the increasingly refined specializations that professional commitment makes possible. We see this not only in war — with the arrival in due course of written regulations, ongoing training (including firing practice), military academies, and military hospitals — but also, say, in surgery where, after a mere fifteen centuries of misleading anatomies, Andreas Vesalius finally began to map accurately the human body, and Ambroise Paré, after an accidental discovery, urged his colleagues to use emollients rather than simply to cauterize wounds.

Professional qualities of study and standards were appearing across the board by the 1500s. Previously, kings had dispensed justice, kings had made war — and often done both very capably. But not until there came onstage lawyers and military officers preeminently defined by their callings did the full creative possibilities of either discipline come into view. In these years it began to be assumed that the doctor, lawyer, and banker, as well as commander, had not just learned by doing but would be guided by some explicit reasoned principles. In one place or another, talent was able to percolate from below. We find Leonardo designing guns in Milan, Michelangelo sketching perfectly flanked fortresses, Galileo teaching classes in military mathematics. Results enterprisingly came to show themselves in combat.

While armies were becoming more professional, social development was offering fighting men an increased variety of promising objectives, including treasures of paintings and sculpture. Specialized capabilities were also evolving, such as dragoons and demolition squads, along with new rationalizations for pinpointed kidnappings and assassination. Tricks also became more widely known among Europe's professional soldiers as information was brokered between armies by diplomatic contact, mercenary service, and even reading — with a better understanding of how to leverage and follow through. Certainly, the ruses of war were becoming better documented.

Yet western Europe, with all its variety, was still not much more than a matrix of small areas of well-cultivated, road-served country (and those roads were dreadful) scattered amid great tracts of marsh, moor, mountain, and forest. On the one hand, increasingly professionalized armies with more men than in recent years met in set-piece battle, as on the outskirts of Vienna, where Christian armies won a stellar victory in 1683 against Ottoman invasion. On the other, Europe's undeveloped lands lent themselves well to embittered resistance, as in boggy Catholic Ireland or in the Protestant Netherlands' tidal waters and rivers or in dark German forests where audacious peasant bands ambushed marauding mercenaries. Here, too, can be found trickery and purposeful daring, and against undeniably greater strength. The concealment and camouflage that was by necessity second nature to such upstarts also came to make increasing sense to their betters.

The term *art of war* itself contained the ethos of the Renaissance, coming to mean not just creativity (which had long been valued), but its ability to embrace precision and efficiency, and to get to the heart of operational matters. The most intensely complex form of such art — the special operation — may have benefited the most. As in our lifetime, rapid growth of knowledge went hand in hand with improved means of defense and destruction, from stronger fortifications to deadlier firepower. And time and again, there were more efficient ways to negate such achievements than by blasting forth head-on, or even by making clever maneuvers on the flanks. As throughout our story, we encounter the contradiction of extreme risk when facing an ever more formidable opponent: the more extreme a mission, the less an enemy anticipates let alone prepares for it, paradoxically making the quest less risky and more reasonable to implement. Therein lie some of the biggest of opportunities.

‡

As THE Western world opened further to the powers of mind, there arrived a flood of books, including titles on every aspect of fighting: weapons, tactics, drill, siegecraft — most everything except keen explorations of strategy. The year Cortés took Tenochtitlán, Machiavelli published his systematic treatment of warfare, the first that tried to reconcile ancient and modern military practice; within nine months of Pizarro's snatching of Atahuallpa, his adventures were written up in a catchpenny bestseller that appeared in Spain, then in translation throughout Europe, and nearly as fast as instant analyses of the latest Iraq war.

In the 1500s, however, learning from the hard-won knowledge of the past was not always among the priorities of Europe's warring nobility. When Henry VIII dissolved the monasteries, in a move of Reformation exceedingly profitable to himself and his associates, the archives were sold to grocers as wrap for their wares. It was an age standing with one foot in a bleak era that did not merely persecute Galileo for his heliocentric doctrines but tended to regard lending money with interest as a mortal sin, and the other in a modernizing time of reviving populations, where a general might write learnedly about astronomy and where investment bankers backed, and sometimes led, ventures to conquer the New World.[1]

The early 1500s were years of upheaval not just in exploration but in religion as Luther challenged the Catholic Church. Yet much of life, including martial technique, remained burdened by tradition.

Books were becoming available to the still very few who could read or indeed purchase such luxuries, if the authorities allowed even this.[2] The ones that sold best had some aspect of chivalry (literally, the culture of the mounted man) as their theme. These were not just the fantasies that addled Don Quixote but also serious works, such as the influential book of manners, *The Courtier,* by an Italian war hero who, in a burst of bravery, had captured a troop of fifty knights at the turn of the century. Yet he insisted that a man should put himself in danger only when there was the likelihood that his bravery would be recognized and discussed. "For the warrior aristocrat," explains historian Thomas Arnold, "there had to be spectators" — an attitude 180 degrees opposite to the special operation that, to enhance the art of war, would have to first push through these enduring vanities.[3]

Old notions were gloriously if a little pointlessly embodied in the age's supreme exemplar of knighthood, the Chevalier de Bayard, most renowned cavalier of the predatory Italian wars launched in 1494 by Charles VIII of France. Think what one may of Bayard's plain military utility, as a man he at least seems to have been relatively decent. This warrior who, according to legend, held the bridge over the Garagliano single-handed against two hundred Spanish regulars was indeed a figure stepping out of the Arthurian romances, just before that book was closed.

His feats of arms were soon chronicled in a book, *History of Bayard the Good,* overlooking such details as whether or not a battle was won or lost.[4] He died more or less as he would have wished: in combat, as had most of the men in his family for two hundred years, having first fought in Italy in 1495, and falling there in 1524, his backbone shattered by an arquebus ball, fired from a weapon of the kind that he had long denounced as unseemly. (And he was known to hang even crossbowmen for shooting their cowardly missiles.) Bayard fell in a hopeless charge, his final hours attended by a guard of honor from his chivalrous Spanish captors — displaying a solemn respect for the greatest knight of the age. He was probably the last person everyone could agree was a hero from the past, a man to awe the practical technologists who were shaking his world apart. He was an inspiration, akin to the America's Cup captains whose races are followed by today's nuclear submarine commanders.

In the phrase of the day, Italy was the "school of war" for all Europe, in part because feudalism in Italy had shallow roots.[5] Conflict in the troubled peninsula helped originate new tactics and military architecture, besides which the condottieri had for a century been ripening means to stage unwelcome surprises in the most urbane and culturally advanced region of Europe.

As a republican enemy of the Medici dynasty, just as much as a student of violent power, Machiavelli was also never convinced of the importance of firearms. He additionally insisted that peasants made the best soldiers because of their familiarity with shovels, since digging was the task now most often required in the field — something their betters were not about to do. War was being transformed, but that barely changed who called the shots. The nobility retained an only slightly modified supremacy, with gradations of caste and class that lasted right into living memory, as in the British army, where the cavalry has always thought of itself as superior to the infantry, and marines were beyond the pale.[6] Innovation and tradition lived side by side. Yet, slowly, the knightly aristocracy began evolving into an officer corps, reining in the reckless bravery of the medieval cavalier, and the sangfroid of a Beowulf rather than the hot temper of an Achilles or a Cu Chulainn came to be the distinguishing virtue of the gentleman officer.

At the one end of the transformation now taking place lay cannon and their many modes of impact, whether against men or mortar. Gunpowder required new architecture to be adopted in western Europe and in the Spanish and Portuguese overseas empires. Fortifications featured low-lying, hard-to-hit sides with plenty of angled guns capable of raking assailants.[7] Among the consequences was that extreme missions would have to contend with harder to penetrate designer-brand fortifications. And should the few and lightly armed be detected in their approach, enemy fire would be all the more devastating. At the other end of gunpowder-compelled change there were appearing firearms that could be cheaper and easier to use than crossbows, especially when the extremely awkward arquebus of the type lugged by Conquistadors was at last superseded by the musket, a more potent tool — though still miles from modern assault rifles.[8] The appearance by the mid-1500s of actual rifled firearms, whose grooved barrels spun their bullets on a vastly more predictable flight, made reloading even trickier but introduced a new kind of specialist warrior. Ancestors of today's Marine Corps snipers used these rifles to start a special-unit tradition of their own, as when later in the century the Spanish besiegers of Dutch strongpoints erected musket-repellent wooden cages on tall poles, enabling their marksmen to pick off the enemy from above and afar.[9]

Actually breaching walls by cannonade exacted ordeals very similar to the attacks on walls by artillery using torsion and muscle power. If anything, the picked men intent on storming through the rubble had to endure worse; for instance, when Drake put seven thousand quick-in-and-out attackers on the beach in Galicia in 1589, his mines and cannon were able to split the wall of the fortress town of La Coruña. But blowback from a mine blast hit the besiegers, just before falling debris crushed the assault troops — and a rockslide buried those who raced in after them. Most of the ramparts remained standing.

Assault parties were also terribly exposed, and at point-blank range, to even a single cannon packed with a langrage of nails, small stones, shot, broken glass, or anything hard and small that made the artillery piece a giant shotgun. Open-ended sieges remained every bit as uncertain, costly, and disease ridden as in the past. Given a couple of months, desertion and typhus were likely to take a higher toll than the most brilliant commander on a single day. If anything, high-quality unconventional penetration gained in importance. And now there were ever more skilled, motivated, and resourceful people to choose from than just among the necessarily small cadre of knightly heroes.

Attackers had to exploit all possible vulnerabilities, and they did. "Commando tactics appeared," explains Arnold in his beautifully illustrated *The Renaissance at War* — or, perhaps better said, they were reemphasized, as in attacks on the artistically carved gates of Renaissance cities and fortresses.[10] Volunteers, well rewarded should they live, would place a bell-shaped bronze or iron pot packed with gunpowder against the mighty leaves, light a fuse, and scram — a type of lightning action that just might clear the path for an assault party only slightly less endangered. A safer approach was to break apart the iron grates protecting sewer outlets or aqueducts. Since Troy, cities had been vulnerable through their drains; now giant wrenches, crafted by awakening high technology, were used to tear openings.

Such an entry was forced right before the sack of Rome in May 1527, in which Lutheran soldiers of the half-Spanish, half-German but very Catholic Charles V (who in his civil capacity was nevertheless coercing the pope) took advantage of an early-morning fog. They discovered and pried open a badly barricaded cellar window in the city's outer walls, while others infiltrated through a neglected low-level gunport. These were just targets of opportunity. Moreover, there was nothing special about the soldiers from this ill-fed army on the verge of disintegration, other than their savagery in raping nuns once inside. But if such a ramshackle outfit could be so effective, what could a more select force do?

Answers can be seen in the importance of camouflage. An administrator raising English troops to fight in Ireland lays it down that the men must be dressed in russet, or patterned green, appropriate to the Emerald Isle.[11] Since they would be fighting in woods that covered much of the country then, this was a truly pioneering effort to adapt to the environment (so important against Gaelic warriors, who used firearms as well as blades in alternating heavy-infantry attacks with guerrilla-style operations). In even soggier terrain, we consistently see the uses of concealment and stealth combined with SEAL-like ability to make friends with that dangerous, indifferent power — water. "Sent yesterday," the military governor of Boulogne reported to Henry VIII in July 1544, "young Cotton, Spencer Bowes and William app Roberts, each with 100 men with their shirts uppermost that they know each other, [moved] over the water at low ebb opposite the Picards' camp to cut betwixt them and their ordnance."[12] Wading their way toward a greatly superior enemy amid the terrors of the dark, with a tidal sea behind them, these young officers were truly in command of special warriors, even if the formations only lasted a night.

In what is known as the Eighty-Year War of the Dutch, from 1567 to 1648, to assert their freedom from Spain, warfare involved not only a series of terrible sieges in an entire country of water defenses, but also the breaking of those sieges and sallying out through seas and rivers.[13] Spanish troops were superior in the war's early years, and we

see their fanatical bravery as well as cunning in the astounding operation by which they rescued their brethren at Tergoes in Zeeland during 1572.

The Dutch controlled all approaches to the encircled garrison by
road and sea. Having calculated the tides sweeping a ten-mile estuary
between their own position and Tergoes, known as the "Drowned
Land" in consequence of a flood years earlier, Spanish commanders
realized they had six hours in which the water would be only four to
five feet deep, rather than the usual ten. In the November cold, three
thousand picked men lined up on the shoreline to wade across, each
carrying his powder and some biscuits in a sack above his head. Any
delay meant a mass drowning. The crossing was completed in five
hours, in chest-deep water, in armor, at night; only nine men disappeared under the lapping waves. Like Alexander's cragsmen looking
down from the peak upon the Sogdians, when these men appeared
at dawn from the depths of the sea, the incredulous Dutch simply
caved.[14]

King Philip II and the duke of Alva, his commander in chief in the
Spanish-held south, were acting across the whole spectrum of possibility. Special warfare is defined by its techniques and use of leverage,
less so by the size of the force. And perhaps the most leveraged form
of attack can be found in dispatching a single, self-motivating, and, if
necessary, self-consuming assassin or a tiny hit team.

The fittingness of assassination as a legitimate instrument of state
policy has a strong intellectual foundation: Sir Thomas More (the
"man for all seasons") had published *Utopia* in 1516, a philosophical
satire in which an explorer-narrator describes a just-discovered
island somewhere in the New World. By striking directly at those
responsible for starting a war and by relying on cunning, he explains,
ghastly wartime carnage can be avoided. More's state of Utopia therefore deploys "a band of the bravest [or 'chosen and picked'] young
men, who have taken a special oath" to stick together. They are to
knock out the enemy commander "by every possible method,"
including traps, ambushes, and sniping (i.e., long-range archery).[15]
Its soldiers are trained in silent attacks and unseen retreat, and to
swim in light armor. Utopia also resorts to "secret agents" who post
placards in enemy territory, promising huge rewards to anyone

killing or abducting the enemy prince. Smaller but substantial sums are offered to those who help neutralize any of a list of other individuals whom they name, akin to the way America publicizes worldwide the 5- and 25-million-dollar rewards it offers for bringing down its fiercest enemies. If successful, the assassins or kidnappers are relocated to secure locations in Utopia or among its allies, as is U.S. practice today when offering rewards. In theory, the enemy becomes riddled with suspicion as to who will turn on whom.

Jesuit thinkers were reasoning along the same lines. Whatever their justifications, Philip and Alva chose not to find assassins of their own but simply to put out a 25,000-ecu contract on William the Silent, Prince of Orange, leader of the Dutch resistance. After several failures, William was finally shot through the lungs and stomach at the Prinsenhof in Delft in 1584. Yet as the Assassins (those original systematizers of small-unit terror as a political weapon) understood, there was little to gain in cutting down a prince if he could easily be replaced. The Dutch were fighting for religious and civil independence. They did not only weep for him; his death reinforced a stubborn anger. William's brothers and their descendants kept up the struggle just as determinedly through jagged truces and weary reversals to a final victorious peace.

Three years later, Dutchmen were using commando technique to try to take the fortress of Nijmegen on the river Waal by concealing themselves in turf barges to infiltrate the city, failing only because the lead barge grounded while the current carried the rest downstream. The Spanish defenders apparently learned little, or at least did not communicate details of this close call to their fellow garrison fifty miles away in Breda. The next year, what Arnold characterizes as "variations on the Trojan Horse" (although not sharing the mythic complexity of Odysseus's plan) were rewarded when eighty Dutch soldiers broke open that city by again hiding at the bottom of a barge.[16] The same commander who pulled this off, a condottiere venturing north, had recently succeeded in capturing the city of Warrel in Flanders by passing a select few of his men, concealed in salt carts, through the gates.[17] By now, that trick of compromising the main gate had been used so often through the centuries that one might have thought peasant wagons would be fired on at sight. Perhaps because the approach was so obvious (and because sentries were unlikely to be reading Thucydides in their off hours), it remained surprising and effective.

With a certain contempt, aristocratic warriors called these deceptions *ruses de guerre,* albeit rarely hesitating to resort to them. One of the first modern treatises on the overall theme comes from Blaise de Montluc, a war-loving petty gentleman who had fought his way up to the position of Marshal of France over fifty years of almost unrelenting violence. When finally too badly crippled to fight on, he was reduced to composing a memoir that includes nearly gleeful accounts of the particularly daring aspects of his life in the field — ambushes, escalades, surprises of towns, quick assaults — and much less so the ready organization of battles and sieges. But while Montluc may have brought real powers of mind to the business of war, as an upstart he still lacked the aristocratic flair to do whatever was in his interest, carefree of what anyone thinks. He splutters indignantly that no less than the duc de Guise, head of one of France's grand families, was betraying his class by actually *writing out* his orders. Such meticulous planning, insists Montluc, would have made the duke a good "clerk of the High Court of Paris."[18] (To call someone a law associate, in this age of picturesque blasphemy, was likely the ugliest epithet in the marshal's vocabulary.)

De Guise, a Catholic absolutist, was the finest improviser in that series of French internecine horrors known as the Wars of Religion, as we see in the "Day of Barricades" in 1588 — a moment when the fate of the continent hung in the balance. If France could be delivered to this power broker who was in league with Spain — as Spain was about to launch its great assault on England — there was a serious chance that Protestantism could be crushed in northwestern Europe, with likely consequences for world modernization.

During the last quarter of the sixteenth century, the coup de main, a classically special mode of action — sudden, small, hypertargeted — was as familiar as it had ever been and especially effective when conducted by a determined personality. That May, happily with no need to write orders, the duke simply "went into the streets of Paris in his doublet." (Here Montaigne, imprisoned for being loyal to the king, means without armor, cocky in civilian clothes.) This was a sudden, daring display of intimidation by a single warrior against the overwhelming force of the state, a move that was leveraged by a core team of sixteen bold conspirators who had positioned themselves around Paris, under the nose of royal might. The French Guard and the King's Swiss, let alone Henri III himself, were so shocked by the speed and brazenness of this action, and the citizenry so magnetized, that in hours De Guise had overwhelmed royal authority in a putsch by the Catholic faithful.[19]

De Guise demonstrated even in this cauldron of fanaticism what could be accomplished by focused, strong-armed enterprise, by acting in total command, and by creating a web of clandestine followers. The king did not need to be killed, and in De Guise's restraint not to seize the throne, we also see an emphasis on policy becoming uppermost over stellar individual acts of violence on the spot. But disciplined good sense has its limitations. Having held the destiny of France in his hands, De Guise could not be allowed to live once the English beat Spain by destroying the Armada. Before the year was over, the duke and then his brother, the cardinal de Guise, ended up on the blades of the king's efficient retainers.

‡

MILITARY TRANSFORMATION is now a Pentagon buzzword, but the term was originally applied by historians to the great changes in early modern Europe, such transformation (even what they saw fit to call "revolution") being consolidated during the wars of the mid-seventeenth century. It was when gunpowder, the compass, and the printing press had "changed the appearance and state of the whole world."[20] Today's changes include a move away from reliance on sheer numbers of fighting men and women, which is why we are experiencing a logical emphasis on special operations, whereas those transformations of the 1600s entailed big increases in manpower compared with the armies of a hundred years earlier. Yet both instances share an emphasis on smaller, more versatile devices (cannon, for instance, passing from a handful of gigantic siege machines to authentically mobile field artillery), greater maneuverability, and (only permitted to an extent in the 1600s) increased initiative from the ranks. Armor was sacrificed for mobility. To us that means gradually doing away with the tank; then it meant minimizing a horseman's protection to a breastplate and helmet, as distinct from the knight's metal cocoon, which became diminishingly valuable in a world where charging warhorses could easily be shot, smashing their heavily armored riders as they came down.

Four hundred years ago, the pace varied from state to state, depending on politics and geography, but all military transformation is driven both by an increase in technical possibility and by the ability of one's enemies to adapt. Resistance to change of this magnitude is predictable: we encounter it as U.S. Air Force generals remain determined to buy whoppingly expensive weapons conceived for the Cold War (e.g., new fighter planes); during the 1600s, it lay in the belief that generalship was not merely an aristocratic avocation but an aristocratic right. Yet then as now, transformation embraced new urgencies of rapid movement, preparedness, and reach. In both cases — and whether or not one's military expands or shrinks — such emphases can encourage the appearance of smaller, more select and focused units amid the mass of conventional arms.

Heroic improvisation, which was always necessary, since absolutely every contingency can never be taken into account, yielded steadily to a pooling of skills and experiences. Guards regiments such as the Coldstream (the oldest-serving regular regiment of the British army) became distinct corps d'élite rather than gentlefolk hanging around a sovereign's household hoping for some appropriate employment under arms. Commanders also came to have at their disposal not only diverse cavalry capabilities, but soon artillery and engineering corps — no longer the guildlike arrangements of the past.

Bridging the old order and the new were "forlorn hopes," point-of-the-lance companionships barely to be distinguished from suicide squads. "Forlorn hope" comes from the Dutch or Low German *verloren hoop* (lost troop), and it is the original sense that captures the phrase's real meaning rather than the mistranslation. They appear in accounts from European theaters of war in the late sixteenth century, as large-scale scientific fortifications raised new obstacles against their assailants. They were composed of picked men (voluntarily or not), increasingly drawn from crack line units, who plunged through breaches in a fortress wall or embarked on desperate midnight climbs up fortress scarps or cliff faces. At daybreak, or when the smoke cleared, their efforts would be witnessed by a heap of bodies at the crucial point of assault. They were overnight special units, defined by a special name, a special purpose. Yet they still exemplify courage rather more than technique: no practice required; often not enjoying or even seeking advantages of surprise; unguided by maps or diagrams.

In the days before medals were awarded, however, the knowledge that a man had been at such and such a storm served as his credential, as the king promises his followers in *Henry V* before the battle of Agincourt. Once medals came to be granted to exemplary units early in the seventeenth century, they were first bestowed on forlorn hopes.[21] These formations would endure in some fashion until the mid-nineteenth century, their tradition seen even today in those assault parties — or rescue missions — that embark with little chance of returning.[22] Committing a forlorn hope was different from Alexander deploying his commandos or Caesar his Tenth Legion. None of those warriors, let alone the Conquistadors or the pirates and privateers who followed them, expected to be wiped out. Nor do special forces today; this was trial by ordeal, the likely thinking of such men being echoed in our time. As General Holland M. Smith explained the triumph of U.S. Marines at Saipan, "Gentlemen, it was our will to die."[23]

The forlorn hope usually focused on sudden, direct, and supremely intense attack against a strongpoint. Should that require both speed and deep penetration, it had to be delivered by mounted warriors. Here richer specialization was combining with the increased mobility of seventeenth-century warfare enabled by slowly improving roads, drill books, and (occasionally adequate) maps. There was also the spyglass, the military significance of which Galileo had first demonstrated in Venice for picking out ships from afar: scouts on the battlefield could now climb church towers and take in at a sweep the scope of a day's march. Particular horsemen could adapt themselves not only as specialized cavalry but as far-reaching specialized strike forces. Heavy cavalry, with back and breastplates (cuirasses) as well as helmets — plus a few, derided as "lobsters," who still wore full plate — performed as shock troops atop big warhorses against mounted opponents or wavering infantry. The light cavalry, with crackling dash and the intense mobility offered by agile mounts, specialized in skirmishing, raiding, making contact between encampments, listening and watching, and holding off the enemy during withdrawals.[24] But the horsemen most unequivocally predecessors to modern special operations forces were the dragoons that were appearing by the early 1600s.

Dragoons were mounted infantrymen, their designation originating from the French *dragon,* the large-bore, and therefore closework, fire-belching short musket — the Uzi of the Baroque Age, a special weapon that came into its own for a small force committed to hanging on for a brief period, if it was to be useful at all. With different emphases, they fought from war to war, hitting hard at a distance, and being professional enough to do so as a matter of essential routine. A heavily armored man who has lost his horse is vulnerable; light cavalry may not have the strength for nasty impact. The point of the dragoon was that he was at his deadliest when dismounted, to seize a bridgehead, to push across a ford. Akin to today's airborne forces, dragoons struck fast, forcefully, and deep — expecting rapid backup if they were to succeed or being positioned at the flank of an army, flexibly employing their weapons against infantry and cavalry alike.[25]

The dragoon was crucial to the range and maneuver so characteristic of the apocalyptic event of the seventeenth century, the Thirty Years' War, a collapse of Central European order into a whirlpool of religious, ideological, and opportunistic conflicts that began in 1618. Here was Europe's first protracted "general war," as France, Sweden, the imperial Hapsburgs' Spain and Austria, and the 300-odd German states combined and recombined to gnaw on themselves for half a lifetime.[26]

Scholars debate whether the Thirty Years' War was in fact the all-destructive fury of legend. But the half-starved mercenary armies that marched, fought, murdered, and looted their way across Germany for decades showed fury enough. Daniel Defoe, the author of *Robinson Crusoe,* who was born twelve years after the war ended, brought those madhouse decades to life and wove a well-documented interpretation of their intricacies. His *Memoirs of a Cavalier* is a riveting tale that draws on the best contemporary accounts to chronicle the adventures of an unnamed English gentleman in "The Wars in Germany and the Wars in England: From the Year 1632, to the Year 1648." (Such was the original subtitle when the book first appeared anonymously nearly eighty years after the experiences described, persuading readers that it was a genuine memoir of that terrible time.) Because of its fidelity to historical detail, we perhaps do not encounter much of the Cavalier's character beyond a dry, dispassionate old soldier's view of the world. Yet particular forms of combat take on compelling vividness through his sharp eyes, elaborated by the thoroughly empirical reporter who created him.

For instance, the Cavalier signs up with the great Gustavus Adolphus, king of Sweden and hero of European Protestantism, who is occupying the rich city of Nuremberg in summer 1632, while the Imperialists (forces of the Holy Roman Emperor) have garrisoned a town a full twenty miles distant, stocking it with provisions and ammunition. The king receives intelligence about this supply base and resolves to take it before the matériel passes into the enemy's battle-line. There is no time to send infantry; it is a mission for dragoons. The king immediately summons the Cavalier, offering him "a Piece of hot Work," a rather mild term for how events proved in the actual attack against the town of Freynstat, on which this is based.[27]

Four hundred dragoons backed by regular cavalry approach the town at 1:00 the following morning. A sergeant leading twelve dragoons silently kills the guards on the town's perimeter. Ladders are thrown against an outer gate, and the dragoons swarm up and over, cutting to pieces some two-dozen foes within. Once the ravelin (a triangular structure protecting the main gate) is taken, they burst open the entry to a drawbridge, and the Cavalier moves in at the head of two hundred dragoons. Using a petard (an updated version of the iron pot packed with gunpowder), the town's main gate is then blown open; the rest of the dragoons roar in, supported by dismounted cavalry with light firearms. By three A.M., it is all over, enough supplies falling into the stormers' hands to last the king's army for a month. Fitting the ancient tradition of raids, where the more mobile the loot the better, a detachment is then sent to round up about a thousand head of cattle from the fields — fresh meat for the Nurembergers who, as the tables turned in this mishmash of wars, would later find themselves starved into surrender.

In what was already becoming a war of exhaustion, Defoe shows us something different: relatively small, highly mobile strike forces that bring off surprise at a distance while spinning off little commando actions (handling the sentries and leaping the walls). All is done in tandem with a bigger, more conventional unit. Other clashes even display the mix of infantry with cavalry in what would in subsequent years be called a "stirrup charge" — acrobatics in which infantrymen crash into a defending force at flat-out speed by looping their left arms into the cavalrymen's empty right stirrups, getting a lift from the horses, and running like blazes to slice into the enemy.

Gustavus would die when separated from his men in a heavy November morning fog at Lützen — easily stabbed by lancers after having chosen not to wear armor. His arch-opponent Wallenstein (commander in chief of the imperialist armies, whom the emperor was finding dangerously ambitious) fell sixteen months later. A handful of Irish mercenary dragoons stabbed Wallenstein's key loyal officers in black Eger Castle at dinner, then hunted him down minutes later on his sickbed.[28] It was a killing (or "special activity") with enormous consequences. Despite illness and dwindling troops, essentially no one in the Hapsburg camp dared for months to confront the still terrifyingly violent Wallenstein head-on. A megamilitary entrepreneur, he indeed was irreplaceable. Had he lived to change sides and join the Protestants, as the emperor feared, his weight could have brought down Catholic power in central Europe. Instead, he was efficiently erased and the war dragged on, the rampaging rival armies inciting bands of peasants to join the fray in the unmapped woods and marsh by fighting back with small-caliber muskets, pistols, knives, and pitch. It was stubborn, intelligent, and inventive low-intensity combat (including Germany's "first Werewolf group" of clandestine killing that drew on ancient fears of lycanthropy) while the soldiers kept cutting each other to pieces.[29]

At the other cultural end of anarchic central Europe there took shape unusual operations against "magnificence," the splendor of libraries and art being peculiarly powerful emblems of authority in an age of awakening intellect, as well as compact targets for high-speed attack and withdrawal.[30] Raiding forces were sent through the countryside by various sovereigns to bear off their rivals' collections of paintings and vertu. The failure of some prince or trembling city-state to hold on to the treasures that attested to political eminence was an enormously damaging humiliation, maybe more so, at truly refined levels of power, than an inability to protect one's subjects from fire and rape. The precedent of these operations is the more interesting because such delicate plunder had to be evacuated carefully, and that required preparation and special equipment. To capture a great pietà, or the manuscript of the Greek Anthology, was to capture a truly magical object, like the Palladium of Troy or the Brown Bull of Ireland's *Tain*. Its seizure was a zero-sum transfer of grandeur, glory, and authority. An assault force might be compensated for its casualties in splendor. The castles of robber barons could be tricked out in stolen opulence into the semblance of actual palaces. A couple of Titians were even better than stag heads on the wall — if probably, to half their new owners, less beautiful.

Eventually, with the peace of 1648, we see a sure sign that war was coming to be considered a public act, not an occasion for individual profit: the Westphalia treaties specified that all prisoners would be released without ransom. The captives of war would now be prisoners of the state rather than subject to a shifting marketplace of individual transactions. It is no coincidence that, within a generation, we see central banks coming into existence: first the Bank of Sweden, then the Bank of England. The state is thinking in large-scale rational administrative terms: strategy is as much dutifully financial as gloriously military.

‡

THE TREATIES that ended the war in central Europe were signed three months before Charles I became the only English sovereign to be formally tried and executed. In a world in which a king could do no wrong, he was sentenced like a common criminal. By the time he knelt at the block, the first cycle of English civil wars had largely burned out; the second, generated by his beheading and the triumph of the English revolutionary army, was about to begin.

What is often simply referred to in Britain as the "Civil War" (or among such of today's young fogies who are historically aware as the "Great Rebellion") had its roots in religious, financial, and political conflict — all of which culminated in 1642, once Parliament refused to entrust Charles with raising an army against troubles in Ireland. As a result, the king promptly set about gathering from nobles and landowners fighting men who were ready to take up arms against Parliament for treason. The supposed traitors drew on the loyalties of most of the country's militia and what there was of a navy.

The famous battles — Edgehill, Marston Moor, Naseby — show the usual bloody sophistications of "the art of war." Yet, once again, historians have focused on such pitched engagements rather than on the more numerous, more important, and even more vicious small operations under way in the troubled counties of England and Wales between 1642 and 1646.[31] Central to our story is the London Parliament's creation of a more effective means of fighting overall. From the start, Charles had recruited men from the type of people who could have been expected to prevail — those who rode to hounds, including "gentlemen, mounted on their favourite horses, and commanding little bands composed of their younger brothers, grooms, gamekeepers and huntsmen."[32] Yet Defoe's Cavalier, who had returned home to fight for the monarchy, notes how his opponents were soon busy "modeling" something new.[33]

This something new was championed by Oliver Cromwell, who rose from the provincial obscurity of a threadbare squire to become a gifted cavalry commander, then general of all parliamentary forces, and ultimately the austere Lord Protector of a rather improvised republic that was the logical consequence of beheading a king.[34] His army was based on a man's ability rather than social position. It was an army open to fresh ideas, to self-command, and to thought being valued in the lowest ranks. The Bible speaks of God's being "no respecter of persons," and even parliamentarian gentlemen were startled to find that one of their leading officers had been (in his trade, not particularly on the field) a butcher. "A few honest men are better than numbers," Cromwell wrote, and to him, the finest warrior was "a plain buff-coated captain [who] knows what he fights for and loves what he knows."[35] Here was the first instance since the ancient world of disciplined, dedicated, self-reliant, all-purpose citizen troops fighting far afield for a heartfelt cause, those of the Swiss being much fewer, from a simple society, and ready to segue into mercenaries at government behest — while the Dutch had so far fought on the home front, and could quarrel about entering another province.

Previously there had been no permanent army in England, the king and Parliament assembling what was needed in emergencies. What now emerged was an exceptionally well-trained, inspired force based on lightly armed cavalry, in which horsemen eschewed heavier armor for the sake of speed, often wearing those buff coats underneath their breastplates, or just thick leather jerkins, as well as long leather boots to protect their thighs. Attacks by formations four hundred strong, perhaps divided into troops of sixty or seventy men each, relied on surprise, hitting power, and the ability to move on to the next adventure very fast. Cavalry was the decisive arm; the new parliamentary troopers were styled "Ironsides" from their ability to hammer through the most determined of their enemies, mounted or infantry. This deadly combination of zeal and discipline showed itself particularly well in the use of dragoons, applied in the form of a 1,000-man regiment of mounted infantry initially equipped with the distinctive short-barreled full bore musket.

Cromwell and the New Model Army ensured victory for Parliament, effected the most complete conquest of Scotland ever achieved by the English, sent Blake (another overnight military wizard) to swat the Dey of Tunis, and killed perhaps some five hundred thousand among the "Antichrist" Irish. There his conquest left marks not yet forgotten, angers that are still used to justify the shedding of blood.

Cromwell refused the crown of England. After all, he had just taught the kings of Europe that "they had a joint in their necks."[36] When he died in 1658 from malaria contracted in Ireland, his eldest surviving son and nominated successor, Richard, did not have the mettle to stand for long in his father's mighty boots. Instead, the old monarchy was restored two years later. Despite the vengeance taken by the royalists — some executions, bodies (including Blake's) exhumed and obscenely displayed — most of the New Model Army marched quietly into civilian life and a different mode of achievement.

Curiously, service in the New Model Army quickly proved to have been a character-forming experience, somewhat like being in the U.S. Marine Corps. Or perhaps Cromwell and his colonels had simply attracted superior people in the first place to the rank and file. In any event, the veterans showed themselves to be every bit as independent-minded and enterprising in trade as they had been in battle. Best known to us for his diaries, Samuel Pepys had rejoiced at Charles I's beheading but, in the shifting political loyalties that were then about as common as today, ended up Secretary of the Admiralty under Charles II. Despite himself, he wonders why it is that so many of Cromwell's soldiers have attained financial success; he cannot avoid seeing something odd in a prosperity that was anything but guaranteed.[37] The restored Stuart monarchy endured for twenty-eight more years, one of its first acts being to obtain full parliamentary authority to maintain a standing army, certainly including dragoons — that fast, focused, and versatile force which might turn a raid into a decisive blow.

‡

As AMID the political jockeying and "national security" preoccupations of our own unsettled times, the truly significant events shaping the world were springing more from notebooks and laboratory experiments than from war and diplomatic dealings. It was not merely practical innovations that were arriving, such as better maps and, soon, chronometers; or, for that matter, the first watch with a minute hand, which eventually enabled generals actually to coordinate time, rather than depending, if lucky, on church clocks striking the quarters. The mighty breakthroughs of Newton and Leibniz in calculus, game theory, and gravitation would run on to shape ever-larger worlds down to this day.

Yet by the late 1600s, lines were being drawn in the sand left and right. France had usurped Spain's position as the dominant power on the Continent and was expanding vigorously in North America. Louis XIV, head of the House of Bourbon, King of France — the symbol of absolute monarchy and persecuting orthodoxy in this age — had built the largest army in Europe since Rome. The feebler of the Catholic dynasties, no less than the Protestant trading nations, cowered from his menacing splendor. Louis's fleet surpassed those of England and the Dutch provinces. Frontiers were expanded to the north and east, and he wanted more. At home, he had been pledged, ever since being anointed with the crown of Charlemagne, to protect the church and to exterminate heretics. These tasks of homeland security were to be assisted by dragoon units well fitted to rapid deployment and occupation. The English verb *to dragoon* and the noun *dragonnade* have had chilling connotations ever since.

In the Cévennes mountains of south-central France, Louis dealt with intransigent Protestants known as Camisards by deploying his special units to win, if not hearts and minds, then souls and bodies, with a strong instrument-of-torture budget to back up theological argument. Calling themselves "the Children of God" — never more than three or four thousand fighters but enjoying deep popular support — the Camisards were a "nation in arms" before Bonaparte coined the term. This was not another peasant rebellion against government or some brutal occupier but a response (often fought in guerrilla fashion) that had a rational, clear, and limited objective: being permitted to worship while remaining loyal to the king. Arsenals were stashed in the region's limestone caves; a baker's boy of seventeen commanded the Camisard southern army, deploying such methods as luring soldiers into a seemingly deserted village (Laguiole being an example) and then bursting out from every door and window. There was no time to go by rules; there were none worth following. Women marched as nurses and porters; the columns they supported tied down the Sun King's best marshals and twenty times their own number of combatants.

Among Louis's enforcers were junior dragoon officers. Their combination of cavalry range and infantry power also depended on rapid small-unit initiative. Only they could adequately deal with fighters driven by consuming faith and intimate knowledge of a rugged countryside. The Protestants (Huguenots) fought desperately against Paris's decision simply to erase them, a policy cleverly combined with building roads to move troops quickly in this demanding terrain. The outcome is seen not only in massacre and the number of men sent to the royal galleys but in the Protestants who fled to England and (to England's misfortune two hundred years later) southern Africa. Skills are often learned only when one has compelling reason. In the space of four years, from 1702 to 1706, these amateurs of war had applied techniques that the able, but too formal and dashing, French high command barely understood. The successes they had shown against the most ruthless of armies — spearheaded by some of the toughest of that army's special formations — were a telling demonstration of what even untrained civilians driven by a transcending purpose could accomplish when they knew their land, and fought smart, simply and fast.

What boiled up in the Cévennes introduced the peoples' wars that would make themselves a transforming part of the latter eighteenth century. A greater range of talent would be drawn on in that type of conflict, as first became manifest in these mountains. The self-confident personal initiative of farmers, tradesmen, and pensioned-off veterans comes into play to upend great armies of the old order. New ideas percolate, more sharp eyes are seeking out cracks in enemy strength. More brains are framing the next, often highly unconventional, steps. Perhaps most important, the best of the self-schooled warriors who volunteer to go up against the prevailing strength of established armies have shown themselves able to act daringly and cleverly without any officers, let alone officers holding rank by birth — each man then to know his role and purpose.

9

The Old World and the New

*Point of the Lance in Europe, India,
and North America, 1700–1775*

*"Uncommon parts need uncommon times
for their exertion."*
SAMUEL JOHNSON

WITH THE eternal exception of Alexander, the political goal of seizing and settling immense alien tracts of the world is not really a notion to be encountered in the West until the eighteenth century. Rome did not go off to India and was actually deterred from attempting the Elbe. Charlemagne stayed in Europe. Genghis Khan and his hundred thousand horsemen may have subjugated more lands in twenty-five years than did Rome in four hundred, and they may have shaped the Renaissance by conveying Eastern influences, but the Mongols were hardly builders or planters. Charles V had not been pacing around Granada worrying about whom he should send to subdue the Americas; indeed, it is startling how little support those who took the first great mainland enterprises received, and the extent to which the home government was forever suspiciously tripping them up.

As we move into the eighteenth century, however, we begin to see men sitting in big offices in London and Paris, soon enough in New York and Bombay, checking large-scale maps, exercising even bigger ambitions to extend their power beyond ever remoter horizons — and developing ever better means to do so. By mid-century, the world was so delicately balanced that war over bits of the present Czech Republic and southern Poland could echo violently through the Asian subcontinent and the depths of the virtually empty Ohio Valley.

In Europe, marines appeared as unconventional warriors, soon to be put on a permanent standing. Their shift in purpose off and on over the next three centuries — from emerging ad hoc, then to performing special operations, to being today masters of more familiar elite functions — is instructive. It is a reminder of how the "special" in war keeps changing. What is shockingly original in one era, such as shipboard shooting and professionally precise amphibious landings, has a way of being taken for granted — and being anticipated — in later years. The object of quality institutions is to make routine what has so very recently been astounding. As other fighting men discover that they can emulate and do ever more, the special formations will go ever further yet in their resourceful, highly leveraged creativeness.

The reach of nations stretched to the east, to the west, and just about all the way round. In India, a handful of British clerks, adventurers, and entrepreneurs came to believe they could go far beyond trading to pull down another sprawling empire, working ever more beyond the bounds than their boards of directors back home could conceive. In the East Indies, the Dutch taught themselves jungle-warfare techniques, to beat down other brave peoples who fought for the hearth fire and the home acre. Onetime farmers from Hilversum and fishermen from Vere found themselves replacing swords, bayonets, and gaiters with machetes and cotton clothing. All were added to the imperial skills of a far-flung seaborne nation.

In North America, "mere numbers could sometimes prove more of a hindrance than a help," as one student of the era observes about fighting in the bush, since "unwieldy armies were an embarrassment when it came to navigating the unsettled interior."[1] Whites born in the New World discovered the skills of living off the land, foraying afar on snowshoes and excelling at ambush against warriors who, for a millennium, had been masters of the dark forests. Only Indians were a match for Indians, it was said. Perhaps a mere ten on their home ground were the equivalent of a hundred soldiers.[2] Yet the wilderness would slowly prove to be a weapon that could be turned even against them. And in the formation of Rangers in North America we see an early example of what would increasingly make itself felt over the next two centuries: the part that marginal people — smugglers, forgers, political radicals, religious fanatics, all-around eccentrics — were to play in the growing sphere of special war. But also in Rangers emerges a degree of thinking constantly, of long-range penetration and rapid dispersal, of a new relationship between the camouflaged few among the force's officers and men, and altogether of a new discipline of irregular war.

Little of this was work for conventional soldiers and oftentimes not for soldiers at all. On both sides of the world, thousands of square miles began to yield before a few hundred men in a few key places who knew what they were about, could improvise fast, and were able to gather around them equally resourceful talents. As armies finally arrived on the scene — and learned rapidly to adapt to these ways — whole continents could change hands.

‡

WITHIN WEEKS of the death of the childless, inbred king of Spain in 1700, Louis XIV demanded the throne for his grandson. In response, there was a "cry for war" throughout England or, at least, among the moderately informed.[3] The huge American and Pacific empire of an increasingly weakened Spain could not, it was argued, be permitted to pass into the orbit of the already quite sufficiently mighty France. In less than a year, England reactivated an anti-French alliance, alongside the Dutch and the Holy Roman Emperor in his capacity as sovereign of the Hapsburg lands. To dispute the Spanish succession, there followed a twelve-year struggle from the Atlantic to the Vistula basin of central Poland.

England's unique ties to the sea as an island nation make it an excellent lens through which to view the reappearance of marines, fighting men who evolved into an elite. This is all the more so since England came to deploy such troops differently from the way other European powers did: France (which had the world's largest navy) heavily assigning them to garrison duty in its great naval citadels and colonial ports, German states to coastal defense, the Dutch less often than the English installing them as complements of oceangoing ships.

England became the only nation that consciously began to develop marines as a "special force," one that came to have very similar purposes as would emerge among its American brethren.[4]

One naval historian cautions how easy it is to overlook "links between the Admiral's Regiment of 1664 with today's Royal Marine Commandos." In part, that is because marines would not be put on a permanent footing until 1755. Moreover, the units that had first been styled "marines" some eighty years earlier came to excel at reinventing themselves as they resourcefully grew into their primary purposes of amphibious raiding and of seizing and defending beachheads, often against heavy odds.[5]

Operating on the principle that the best soldiers at sea are not seasick landlubbers, marines took on a mixed role akin to the "neither cavalry nor infantry" requirements of the dragoon and, like him, would be expected to perform with more versatility than the bulk forces behind. At the start, they were a special force only by the loosest definition. Nor, by and large, are marine units today special forces, despite being elite warriors. To be sure, for much of their history, the U.S. Marines have evinced many characteristics of the commando. With the exception of Recon and "special operations capable" units, the corps' infantry divisions, air wings, and armored battalions make it more of an integrated seagoing army, as was seen in Iraq, where the Marines made their longest march ever, driving far to the north, hooked into U.S. Army logistics.

Marines have always been seen as peculiar: "A kind o' giddy harumphrodite — soldier and sailor too," chuckles Kipling admiringly. Perhaps the dual nature of dragoons was easier for commanders to handle; after all, they were drawn straight from the armies of the time. As a hybrid force that performs special duties by land and sea, however, marines have repeatedly found themselves smack in the middle of the arm-wrestling of generals and admirals.

The term *amphibious* had first been applied to military uses in the seventeenth century to describe these peculiar duties, but only in the twentieth did it come to mean actual, systematized, ship-to-armed hostile shore operations. To be sure, soldiers and sailors had pulled off extraordinary landings at least since Caesar, defying wind and waves: William the Conqueror following suit from France; Venetian ships unloading fully armed and mounted knights at Constantinople; seamen disembarking in small boats with arsonist intent against a thousand harbors and forts worldwide.[6] Yet throughout time, no form of warfare has been more prone to confusion and failure, a point newly commissioned U.S. Marine officers absorb on the first day of Basic School.

Men recruited and organized for such double service had appeared nearly simultaneously among the English and Dutch, as they met in a series of hard-fought, purely naval conflicts from 1652 to 1674. As an emergency measure in 1664, the newly restored Charles II had raised twelve hundred men for service afloat, who became known as the Admiral's Regiment of "sea soldiers." Dutch marine forces came into being the following year; the powerful French raised regiments of their own; and the landlocked Swiss — never backward on profitable speculation that did not involve cavalry — got in on the act by hiring out a battalion of mercenary ship troops to France. The increasingly inadaptive Spanish navy fell that bit further behind.

At the beginning, marines had found themselves deployed not only at sea but far inland. England's marines adopted specialized equipment: flintlock muskets, when there were enough to go around, rather than matchlocks, which were less suited to ocean damp and the proximity of powder kegs; grenades (or at least the capacity to draw on grenadier support), while still being issued with pikes, the common weapons type alike of boarding ships and fending off cavalry. Several hundred marines fought alongside the French, with whom Charles II had forged a momentary alliance against the Dutch, and also ended up fighting near Strasbourg as what Churchill, writing of his renowned ancestor the first Duke of Marlborough, regarded as the equivalent of "island mercenaries" against Louis XIV's other enemy, the Holy Roman Emperor.[7] It was a depth of marine penetration into Europe not to be seen again until 1945.

The first forty years of experiment had been wholly unsystematic: regiments disbanded and reconstituted; a company of "bootnecks" idling in Virginia a hundred years before the Revolution after disturbances over taxes; another company sent to Flanders, this time to aid the Dutch against France; fighting those masters of ambush, the Moors, while defending Tangier (part of Charles II's dowry for marrying a Portuguese princess, her country now liberated from Spain); getting entangled in the ambitions of his brother, James II, to convert England to Catholicism. Yet from all this spluttering began to appear a focused mode of special warfare that reverberates today.

The colors of the Royal Marines bear, in addition to their proudly assertive globe, the single word "Gibraltar," a blazon deriving not from the Rock's capture in July 1704, but from its defense soon after against ferocious counterattack. The importance of Gibraltar's location — facing Africa at the eight-mile-wide entrance to the Mediterranean — is obvious. About two thousand marines dug in against a siege begun in October by perhaps nine thousand Spaniards, backed by at least three thousand French. As the determined assailants succeeded in breaching the walls, the marines — down to half their number fit for duty — were reinforced at virtually the last moment by ships bringing ammunition, rations, and the crucial margin of infantry.

The very confidence-building moment of reinforcement may prove a particularly rich double opportunity for a sufficiently stealthy and resourceful opponent. Learning from a goatherd about a dangerous path that perhaps could be followed by the sufficiently brave right up to the Rock's eastern crest, the Spanish commander sent in five hundred men under one of his colonels, as a forlorn hope. They took the sacrament — as such special forces had sound reason to do — and moved up the Rock at night, guided by the goatherd, using rope ladders to climb to St. Michael's Cave near the summit, in which they hid until dawn. As the sky lightened, a truly exceptional handful rushed the signal station on the crest, killed the guards, then frantically set to hauling up their comrades. Within moments, the alarm was given in the town below and a comparable number of marines were scrambling up to throw them headlong back down the steeps they had scaled.

For whatever reason, the main Spanish force did not open a conventional assault on the formidable forces at the mountain's base, which was likely deemed too well defended. Without such a disruption to pull away the English avengers, the forlorn hope — having been issued only three rounds apiece of ammunition for what was supposed to be a quick, cold-steel operation — was crushed: 200 killed, 190 captured.[8] That 110 nevertheless managed to get back down the cliffs is not the least indication that they came from a pretty extraordinary outfit.

Further English reinforcements arrived in December. Attacks were renewed, the Spanish trying to tunnel through the living rock, their French and Walloon allies ready with swords in one hand and hooks in the other to scale breaches opened by heavy cannon, other select men concealing themselves in the dead ground of the mountain's gullies, attacking at daybreak when they knew from English deserters that the guard would be changed. But sickness, hunger, and immense expense worked against the besiegers as guns, men, and food began to pour into the fortress from Portugal, whose hatred of the Spanish kingdoms had long made it England's most ancient ally. The siege was abandoned in April, after eight months in which rarely more than two thousand fighting men held out against an army better equipped, every bit as bold, and six times as numerous.

Following Gibraltar, marines in some form were spilled onto most shores assailed by the Royal Navy, spending the rest of the War of the Spanish Succession landing, re-embarking, and taking part in naval actions, such as they were in this land-power war. They helped seize Sardinia and Minorca, turning Port Mahon (so named since Hannibal's day, after his brother Mago) into a major naval base. And enemy gun crews and admirals on the open upper decks learned the effectiveness of aimed small-arms fire even from a swaying ship.

The most formidable western European soldier of the age, John Churchill, had been an ensign of marines at a time when many of these were simply drawn from Charles II's Foot Guards, and he had sailed with the fleet against Mediterranean pirates. In his campaigns — like the one culminating in the irreversible triumph at Blenheim on the Danube two months after the marines had taken the Rock — the first Duke of Marlborough avoided sieges to concentrate instead on mobility and energetic attack.[9] But when men on any side were thrown into action, initiative still went no lower than the battalion level; there was no capacity to disperse, or to engage systematically at the levels of small units, let alone to regularly dispatch well-prepared squads for stealthy special actions. One clear exception were the tiny parties of Huguenot officers — embittered exiles from France now fighting for the High Allies — who took it on themselves to venture out at night after a battle to harvest the disorganization between the lines. Prowling around the field in the dark, they would authoritatively call for the men of a given French regiment to rally around them: "*À moi Burgogne, à moi Picardie.*" As the stragglers and the lost stumbled toward what they thought were their officers, they would be rounded up. The French could not return the compliment because the exiles in their ranks were notably-accented Irishmen, Catholic refugees from English oppression.[10]

There is a convention, cautions Jeremy Black, the most profound of today's military historians, to see war in these years as limited in aims and methods, typecasting it in terms of soldiers robotically marched to attain chesslike aims. He reminds us instead of the extensive guerrilla upheavals in Europe: between invaders and resistants in Spain and Portugal; the later partisan warfare in Bavaria and Bohemia; in Italy against Franco-Spanish invaders; and by the Genoese, who rose against Austria, boasting workers' brigades and priests trained for combat.[11] Guerrillas may use the techniques of special operators (and vice versa), but we remember that such are not synonymous. In a Europe that, for the most part, resembled the third world without electronics, guerrilla uprising — without a wider purpose and imaginative cast of mind such as we saw in the Cévennes — could be more of a primitive rebellion that gets uncomfortably close to part-time banditry.

The leaderships of the most advanced nations knew all about predatory anarchy. Marlborough might smash army after army of Louis XIV, yet this notorious tightwad had to submit to losing five hundred guineas when held up by well-mounted, well-armed highwaymen five miles outside London.[12] Grandees of the time were likely to have all too many such encounters. And, in turn, they knew the value of dragoons in dealing with deft, insouciant highwaymen who preyed on the approaches to cities. Might they then have seen in these bands of free-flowing, self-reliant, nothing-to-lose daredevils — so very different from the deferential regular soldiers at their disposal — a certain potential if such men were introduced behind the lines in enemy territory?

Not quite yet. The pyramidal social order still projected a blind spot upon such possibilities — an almost complete refusal to believe in the resourcefulness of the common man. And why explore the prospect of road-agent-like bands severing commerce or preying on French dignitaries when the purpose of war, after the random devastation of the seventeenth century, was ideally for one army to nullify another in one day's battle, or at least in checkmating maneuver?

‡

FOR SOME reason, various commentators on U.S. foreign policy today turn to these years of the early eighteenth century to extract sweeping "lessons" about "naval reach" or, stranger still, about what the disintegration of Venice's imperial holdings might tell us about today's special operations.[13] Better just to state that this era's technological achievements rarely translated easily into administrative successes.[14] It did not yet occur to authority to try to find routine, enduring ways to handle extraordinary problems. So much was being done on the fly, particularly when it came to capabilities on the further side of that age's definition of the conventional.

For example, the heroism of the marines at Gibraltar did not prevent London from disbanding their regiments, which had to be formed anew when emergency recurred, as in 1739, after the outbreak of yet another war with Spain. Most of the new regiments were composed of men already in the army, the best-disciplined (and hopefully adaptable) corporals and privates being made marine sergeants; three additional regiments were soon formed in New York. Sailors already possessed an understanding of ropes and mechanics in ways that regular soldiers did not, and therefore it was men of the fleet who were expected to wrestle cannon onto land and then handle the batteries. But they had their limits. Marines were assigned tasks unsuited for sailors, whose characteristic "reckless individualism" was all too well known to the Admiralty. Such responsibility involved the steady use of small arms, orderly resistance to regular troops at close quarters, and, soon enough, "protecting H. M. officers from H. M. mutinous crews."[15]

Small-arms mastery was a prized skill. It is sufficiently difficult to hit a target at fifty yards with a smoothbore in fine weather when resting one's barrel on a stone wall. Try doing so on a ship swaying with every shift of wind, as sea-fetched gusts deflect each shot. In the 1700s, marine marksmen were expected less to pick off enemy officers from the tiny fortresses of the foretops than to drop enemy gunners, to shoot through the other ship's gunports, and to deliver volleys against any concentration (especially of boarders) on the enemy's pitching decks. And, unlike regular soldiers on European battlefields, marines were expected to take cover while reloading. The best line of fire was from the forecastle and poop, but sea snipers also had to have the gumption to keep switching positions in the clutter of an eighteenth-century man o' war — almost the equivalent of streetfighting tactics in so severely confined a space.

Peace with France and Spain in 1713 had allowed England to ship one consignment of goods annually into Spain's South American colonies and to sell the colonists four thousand slaves a year for thirty years — provisions as absurd as they were squalid. Tensions inevitably increased, with enthusiastic illegalities on both sides. English shipping was attacked by semi-piratical Spanish privateers claiming to be revenue collectors; dramatic charges followed in Parliament about brutalities toward English seamen. Even before the marines were re-embodied, six English warships already in the West Indies took the now well-fortified Porto Bello. Their commander's report was significant both for warning that marines would be required if the war escalated and for offering an account of his victory that quickly led to so many Porto Bello Roads and "Admiral Vernon" pubs (their signboards usually displaying six tiny ships knocking down gargantuan fortifications), still to be found throughout England.

However, the ill-founded belief that Spain could be strangled by severing it from its American colonies was coined into dangerous assumptions, based on a vast anachronistic popular literature glorifying the long-ago triumphs of Drake, Hawkins, and Morgan. If England struck promptly, it was argued, surely the Spanish Empire could be unseamed, and Spain itself ruined. Going by such a lightminded misreading of history (so common in today's defense debates), six marine regiments, strong land forces, artillery, plus two regiments of American marines, and 124 ships began to concentrate in Jamaica by autumn 1740, ready to roll up the conquests of Balboa, Cortés, and

Pizarro. The army would be responsible for operations on land, the navy for those at sea. But there was no remotely adequate coordination, and not for the last time in the annals of war, political abrasions between the command tent and the quarterdeck meant that marines would be dumped down as commonplace regular infantry rather than as a special force. Nor had any serious military intelligence been gathered, let alone any intelligence agency been set up to collect what anyway could be little more than rumors from various gentlemen who professed to know something about the "Spanish Main."

By early the following March, the fleet arrived off that much-attacked harbor fortress of Cartegena to disembark about eight thousand men. Yet warfare had changed far more than the elderly planners at home cared to admit. By now, combined operations really had to be combined. Enamored of Elizabethan legend, the English thoroughly underestimated their opponent. The Spanish defense works, so scorned in London, had been strengthened on the landward sides. A month after arriving, fifteen hundred English marines and grenadiers, backed by ladder-bearing Americans, set out to storm a well-gunned castle. Even had it fallen, it was just one fang of Cartegena's defense system. Nevertheless, only a few managed so much as to reach the ramparts in what proved overall a ghastly failure. Sailors "in specialist brigades" had been put ashore to work heavy guns in support of the marines.[16] Positioning cannon ashore was a task at which seamen and marines could be superb. For them to do so amid disease and the disorganization brought by ferocious squabbling at the top between army and navy brass over when, how, and even why to attack was another story. Slaves — perhaps better accustomed to the deadly climate than new arrivals from England — could not be counted on to work the cannon into position; that would entail committing already sparse manpower to guard duty.

As B.D. in *Doonesbury* once put it, "This war had so much promise!" If human quality could have overridden ignorant leadership, Cartagena would again have fallen. But there was no institutional memory when it came to missions so extreme that they required more the focused forces and singular leadership of a Drake rather than of a quarreling Admiralty and War Office. It was a textbook epic of throwing good resources — ever more precious because ever faster diminishing — after bad. The barely 3,000 survivors who could be taken off were pitched worse than fruitlessly into Cuba and the Panamanian jungles. Of the overall 12,000 or so who had set out on this expedition with such high hopes, 10,000 died, mostly from yellow fever (*vomito*), as mosquitoes swarmed around them both on land and between decks in suffocating, overpacked transports hovering offshore. Even getting to the Indies had been a trial — 600 Englishmen died just on the voyage to Jamaica. Out of the more than 3,000 Americans, 573 returned home (which would be like 300,000 of our people being left behind today).

The disasters of hidebound thinking even with marines deeply influenced the thoughtful, quietly authoritative Englishman George Anson. At sea by twelve and rising by rapid steps to lieutenant, commander, then post-captain on the North American station off the Carolinas (which is why there is an Anson County, N.C.), his most renowned voyage would inspire Patrick O'Brian's novel *The Golden Ocean*. Appointed commander in chief of a secret expedition in 1740, Anson received orders soon after the outbreak of war to sail down the eastern coast of South America, thence round the Horn, to attack Spanish settlements from Chile to Panama, as had the storied Drake. He was specifically to form an alliance with the unconquered Araucanian Indians of southern Chile, who had been holding Spain back since Pizarro's day. Plans for what should have been a clandestine "mission impossible" leaked almost immediately and were known in Madrid within weeks.

It might have been thought that a squadron of six warships and two supply vessels preparing to embark on such an operation would have received priority in the grand anchorage off Portsmouth harbor. Instead, Anson, still a relatively junior officer, was issued old rope, defective spars, puncheons of rotten beef, and peas and oatmeal already decayed, as we know from his unvarnished, characteristically fair-minded account.[17] Most revealing for how a government of that time could envision making war is what Anson faced when, ready to sail in June, he still found himself short some three hundred seamen. Instead of the sailors, he was allotted thirty-two old salts from the naval hospital, three dozen others from the fleet, and ninety-eight unattached marines. Instead of the regiment of infantry and three marine companies promised him, he received five hundred outpatients of Chelsea Hospital, true invalids sent to Portsmouth harbor from London. Those who had use of their limbs sensibly deserted before going aboard. The 259 others — including at least one who had been crippled at the Battle of the Boyne fifty years earlier — had to be hoisted on ship since none could climb the ladders; many could not stand unsupported.[18] Not a single pensioner would survive the voyage.

More or less to offset for the desertions, Their Lordships at the Admiralty drafted 210 marines into the squadron, men so raw they did not know how to load, let alone fire, their muskets. (For the melee of shipboard fighting, it was thought at the time, marines did not have to be as well trained as regular soldiers.) Their officers, who came under the War Office, not the Admiralty, would perceive no reason to defer to naval authority merely because they were several thousand miles to sea. Since Anson's squadron had to wait to depart with the entire fleet, his mission could not even embark until mid-September. In the Southern Atlantic, he was chased toward Cape Horn by the fleet of Admiral Don José Pizarro, descendant of the Conquistador and polished product of what had become one of Spain's finest families. Because of the late departure, which, Anson reminisced, "was the cause of all our woes," he had to round the Horn in the terrible weather of late spring when the westerlies are most fierce. Men froze to death in the ice-encrusted rigging as waves crashed over the decks below.

Dealt cards that could have destroyed his expedition simply over the long ocean route, let alone when action was joined on target, Anson carried it to success by sheer will and magnetism. He had to invent the type of war he would fight. (We have met this before.) Dispatched on one kind of special operation — supposedly secret, genuinely amphibious work on a vastly distant enemy shore, intended to raise indigenous allies — he adopted an entirely different one when ten thousand miles by sea from the big thinkers. Facing a well-alerted coast, hearing of the English disasters in the Caribbean (which meant that no home port would welcome them at Panama), losing most of his military stores aboard one of the supply ships wrecked in the still miserably charted Strait of Magellan, two other ships bolting, his infirm complement steadily dying of scurvy, he chose "to turn the expedition into a piratical raid in the style of the Old Elizabethans."[19]

Unlike Drake, George Anson was a well-liked commander who selected his officers with care. But they, too, were dying fast; aboard the three ships that barely made it into the Pacific, only 335 of the original 961 men were alive, and fewer further by the day. The merchant ships he captured were ransacked and then destroyed; there were too few Englishmen to sail them. Lacking any repair facilities, he also soon had to scuttle all but his sixty-gun flagship *Centurion*. Even then he did not have enough men to fire a broadside when he came upon an enemy. He supplemented his dying crew, he explains, by recruiting as eager warriors "some of the stoutest of the Negroes" aboard the ships he captured, the other prisoners being released on shore.[20]

Anson's predominant characteristic was a rational calm that nothing could shake. He was able to intercept the annual silver galleon from Acapulco to Manila (founded by King Philip's viceroys in the later sixteenth century, which is why the country is called the Philippines). Taking the fabulous treasure, he worked *Nuestra Señora de Covadonga* through the South China Sea with literally a skeleton crew, selling the ship at Macao before he returned home via the Cape of Good Hope, one of the few Englishmen since Drake to circumnavigate the globe. He arrived in Portsmouth in June 1744, bearing riches so vast that they were paraded through the streets of London on their way to the Tower, escorted by the remnant of a crew that had suffered far more from English neglect than from Spanish guns.

Anson used his prize money to finance a political career and eventually to marry the lord chancellor's daughter. But despite being extremely rich from his expedition, he also returned to sea, exercising his fleet in forming line against the French so as to execute "manoeuvres of battle till then absolutely unknown."[21] Like any good officer, he above all seems to have felt deeply the loss of more than two-thirds of his men, no matter how motley a crew they had been. On becoming a distinguished if rather cautious First Lord of the Admiralty, he set up a permanent marine corps and corrected the terrible habits that had brought needless death on so many in the conventional navy. An ever more rigorously honed amphibious force would be taken far beyond a level that had once been reduced to assigning septuagenarians to intercontinental special warfare.

Fifty-five companies of marines were ordered raised in 1755, as England prepared for combat, this time pitted against the French, Spanish, and Austrians. Disasters of the last war with Spain had not only laid the groundwork for an ultimately Royal Marine establishment but also for a versatile, rarefied way of war that would make itself felt around the world.

Yet even Anson's impatience with conventional methods did not go as far as the futuristic thinking of a Breton naval officer across the Channel, a visionary practically unknown to historians today. By mid-century, England was arriving at the takeoff point, as economists call the moment of passage from traditional society into sustained industrialization. Coal production, for instance, had already been booming by 1715, as the first practical steam engines began to pump water from the deepest mines of the time. Surely, immense havoc could be inflicted by striking at the still-almost-magical steam pumps (or "firemills") of the coal mines near the Northeast coast.[22] Only a generation old, steam engines held the remote mystique of nuclear plants circa 1950. Yves-Joseph de Kerguélen Trémarec perceived that destroying the coal, salt, and glassworks of rapidly industrializing England would be as crippling to the country's financial and political welfare as would be the destruction of London — or worse. Moreover, he proposed, this new center of industry could be wrecked in fifteen days, not long enough for the English to concentrate forces by land (across still-appalling roads) against seaborne attackers. Nor would an armada have to confront Anson's navy. But his imagination was far ahead of France's Ministry of Marine (as dull in such matters as the Admiralty), and the Industrial Revolution was left to ripen undisturbed.

‡

THE WAR of the Spanish Succession earlier in the century (in which England got Gibraltar) was followed by a dynastic quarrel in 1741–48, when there proved to be no Hapsburg male candidate to elect as Holy

Roman Emperor. This latter war dragged in nearly all the powers of Europe. Aside from the Tweedledum-and-Tweedledee alternation of obscure German princelings, the war is significant for demonstrating that Prussia now disposed of the fourth- or fifth-largest army in Europe, from a population that was among the smallest for a serious power, making it the most militarized society on the continent. Although there may have been more room for lower-level initiative in this juggernaut than is generally understood, the detailed instructions to harness the common soldier (once generals are simply instructed to accumulate "as many troops as you possibly can") document the extent to which initiative again was hardly welcome from the ranks.[23]

Frederick the Great was merely King *in* Prussia when he launched out on his career from this still-underestimated congeries of three hundred or so territories loosely stitched together over the sandy soil of northeast Germany. The last royal genius of war to trouble Europe, he was an odious man — predatory, treacherous to allies, privately vindictive, a rotten and lamentably fertile poet — unfortunately gifted with high intellect and astounding determination. His tightly controlled armies made his will felt and feared.[24] In voluminous writings about war, Frederick also saw fit to instruct his generals in the science of tricks, surprises, and even raiding, for which he had raised appropriate horsemen. Tactics of this type were indeed all part of his baleful repertoire, but to him "surprise" really meant little more than lulling the enemy into a false security by marching in unanticipated directions or shocking a city by the overnight arrival of an army.[25]

In the Seven Years' War, from 1756 to 1763, Frederick found himself surrounded by a coalition of vengeful enemies including Austria, Russia, and France, with England — previously his enemy — now his only strong ally. After a murderous shakeup in the imperial family, Russia (its army quickly improving along Prussian lines) finally took itself out of the war, opening his way to a victory that vastly expanded the borders of his kingdom. Prussia confirmed itself as the foremost military power in Europe and, in due course, combined with Russia and Austria to devour Poland, not for the last time. Fighting ranged from what today are Bangladesh, the Philippines, the United States, and Canada, to the Caribbean and Africa, beside and beyond the traditional killing fields of central Europe. The first truly worldwide war took perhaps a hundred eighty thousand lives directly, and many times that in "collateral" losses.

One of the notable military developments of this time was the appearance of light formations that probed, harried, and raided, most of these men having come to their calling "through natural habits of life, or through an enterprising and semi-criminal turn of mind."[26] (Not too distant, in fact, from highwaymen.) Among them were the storied Cossacks peculiar to Russia and the dreaded Prussian hussars, uniformed all in black, with the death's-head emblem on their caps. As for the light infantryman, he displayed similarities to the multi-talented marine, capable of performing functions akin to those the dragoons had originated. He was ever more likely to carry a trustworthy weapon, whose deadliness reinforced those special traditions of flexibility and resourcefulness that light forces steadily developed.

Like the marine and the dragoon, light infantry could appear suddenly where least expected. We see them in Jaeger or "huntsman" units, raised from the gamekeepers and foresters of wooded country, able to fight as motivated individuals from tree to tree, operating with stealth in Europe as did poachers, and then in yet bolder forms in America. Moreover, hundreds of free corps or companies sprang up during these European wars, loosely tied to armies and able to make it much harder for those of their opponents to stay in the field. Their roustabout leaders, who knew the terrain and often the different languages of their eclectic recruits, were capable of seizing opportunities and of independent thought and action. These were men who chafed against rigid hierarchies and bet their lives on speed and secrecy. They excelled at raiding convoys, took fewer prisoners than regular forces, and expected little mercy in return.[27]

The paradox is that as war was becoming more methodical in the vision of Frederick, so were the qualities of invisibility, vision, individual enterprise, and elite esprit able to coalesce in sharp and self-reliant outfits.

As usual, the experienced men who studied war formed a spectrum of opinion. Some concluded that victory was possible without fighting a battle, by precise moves and intimidation (perhaps a reaction in part to the holocausts of the 1600s); others addressed messier "small wars" and unconventional methods.[28] For instance, a French general who had fought against Italian soldiers in the Alps during the 1740s composed — albeit twenty years after the fact and without publishing it — a far-seeing treatise, *Principles of Mountain Warfare,* when there was still no mountaineering.[29] It was part of the piety of generalship that actually to divide one's main force in the face of a strong enemy was the eighth deadly sin. But the need for increasingly unusual, ever more independent activities on the edges of the big event could not be denied. And these activities were more like Corbett's daring form of tiger hunting than the cerebral maneuvers of chess.

‡

WARS OF the European heartland were now being ratcheted outward for increasingly higher stakes into distant India and North America. Certainly, there was a lot going on in even remoter lands beyond European grasp. Faraway Manchu China, for instance, possessed one of the world's more successful armies, kicking no less than the Gurkhas (the warrior master people of Nepal, the most distinguished of elite contract troops today) off the roof of the world in Tibet. For a while longer, China was effectively beyond Western military pressures, as was much of the East — Japan, Thailand, Vietnam — although the Russians were pushing their way across the Eurasian interior, eventually imposing unequal treaties on China.

It is Tokugawa Japan that offers us an epic which is the supreme instance of the special operation as implacable manhunt, an account that has become one of the dramatic themes of world literature. For two years forty-seven Rōnin ("wavemen," or masterless retainers of a ruined noble) plotted vengeance against a rival lord who had tricked their master into disgracing himself at court, for which he had been called upon to commit suicide. During 1701 and 1702, as every Japanese schoolchild knows, these stern keepers of the samurai ethic (which the Shogunate thought it had defanged half a century before) passed themselves off as demoralized roisterers. Yet all the time they were shadowing their prey, collecting intelligence, until the trap was sprung. On the snowy night of December 14, 1702, they winnowed their force from fifty-nine to the final forty-seven, divided themselves into two bands, infiltrated their enemy's stronghold, then stormed his house from front and rear, shocking more numerous warriors on guard. After exacting vengeance, they offered at their feudal lord's tomb the head of the man who had destroyed him and awaited with grave submission the sentence of the *Bakufu,* the military-turned-civil office of the Shogun that was the hand of constitutional authority. All except the youngest were compelled to disembowel themselves, while the highest in the land vied to give each of these heroes the honorable coup de grâce. This is not the stuff of empire-making, at least not yet. But the quest shows how a cunningly stealthy, supremely disciplined band of brothers hunted down one well-guarded foe in an unremitting effort not altogether different from the special forces hunts of our own time, be they for Che Guevara, Pablo Escobar, or Osama bin Laden.

By the 1700s in densely populated India — as open to trade with the West as Japan was sealed — the great Moslem empire of the Moguls (Mongols) was disintegrating, the center of its decaying power at Delhi beset by mountingly aggressive vassal states. The Moguls had originally been central Asian horsemen, descendants of Tamerlane's hordes, who had forced their way through the northwest passes as Cortés and Pizarro broke through comparable barriers on the other side of the world. Now the subcontinental jockeying between England and France got rougher as the rivalrous states emerging from the running down of Mogul strength offered unlimited possibilities for intrigue, momentary alliance, and ultimately conquest.

England possessed a foothold, having not only received Tangier (which it soon shed) from Charles II's marriage nearly a hundred years before, but also Bombay, gateway to untold ill-guarded wealth. Clever eyes could see that someone who knew what he was about and disposed of even a small number of disciplined adventurers — fast on the ground, ready to adapt — might change history. A few brave Frenchmen dreamed, but the culture in which Voltaire could dismiss Canada as just "frozen deserts, oceans of snow" never gave them remotely adequate support. It was England that would move in on India's treasures and then, mostly without realizing, turn them into European liquidity to accelerate the Industrial Revolution.

Again, it was not Europe's technological achievements that were decisive. In the late 1600s, the East India Company (the private London corporation with monopoly trading rights) saw its forces utterly routed by the Mogul emperor, and for some years thereafter the Honourable Company's directors dismissed the notion of conquering territories as impracticable.[30] As for Lisbon's last serious attempt to stand on its ancient imperial presence, that effort had been smacked down in 1737–40 by mounted Hindu warriors in southern and central India, nearly losing Portugal its major base at Goa, the Portuguese thereafter hanging on only in tiny coastal enclaves.[31]

As we saw with the Aztecs and Incas, however, domestic turmoil exposes an empire to even the smallest band of relentless, focused invaders, no matter the advantages of immense numbers, of knowing the land, even of having a sophisticated system of roads, armies, and government. India had become another example of sprawling vulnerability, despite having a far higher level of war technology than America's great civilizations. Its possibilities pushed a misfit clerk of genius, Robert Clive, toward the category of master of special warfare, against both the competing French presence and the various Indian princes whose cavalry, artillery, and infantry frequently outnumbered him about fifteen to one. Minimally understood by his superiors, this company clerk seized the opportunities of a fragmented continent to turn a merchants' war into imperial conquest.

Like so many of the type, he was full of contradictions — modest, brave, possessing a steady temper, yet likely afflicted, in this instance, with what nowadays would be called bipolar disorder, perhaps kept in the bounds of rationality by occasional use of opium. Having been the despair of his teachers, this restless eighteen-year-old arrived in the East as a pen-pusher for the company in 1743, three years later obtaining an ensign's commission in its corporate army. Amid the confusions of a war being improvised at six months' distance from the homeland, he soon shone forth among demoralized merchants and liver-rotted mercenary officers.

At twenty-five, chance came his way. The first to volunteer for a desperate expedition, Clive gathered seven other officers — like him, none having seen combat — and fast-marched about two hundred Europeans and three hundred sepoys out of company headquarters at

Madras, through the monsoon to strike against the enemy's heart, the capital of the Nawab of Arcot — a vital objective in the struggle to control the Ganges delta. The saga was not his sudden occupation of the city, but his ability to hold out for the seemingly hopeless fifty-three-day siege that ensued, a stand filled with surprise sorties and raids. "The action of a platoon in India," noted one of the officers, "may have the same influence on general success as the conduct of a whole regiment in Europe."[32] For two years, Clive triumphed everywhere, not only through head-on assault but also large-scale ambush, to then return to England to catch his breath. Soon sent back to the fray as a lieutenant colonel in the regular army and as governor of Bengal for the company, he went on to recover Calcutta, to win practical sovereignty over Bengal by opening every fissure in the combat and political capacities of his enemies (by shrewd bribery, conspiracy, and forgery). It all unfolds like a Hollywood epic and, indeed, became one in 1935, during the last years of the Raj — Ronald Colman and Loretta Young in *Clive of India*.

A great commentator on human destiny, Dr. Johnson, compared Clive to Charles XII of Sweden, the supreme general of the early century in his wars for the Baltic basin and eastern Europe — a world conqueror taking amazing risks against absurd odds. But it was no more foolish, after all, to think that England could subjugate India than to believe that Sweden might take over Russia, or the Bolsheviks replace the czar, or Israel survive the wrath of the Arab League. These judolike upendings by smaller, cleverer, fast-penetrating forces keep happening — to those who work for them.

Consolidating his position at home again in 1760, Clive bought a seat in Parliament and was ennobled, only to be sent back in 1765 as commander in chief for two further exhausting years. The wealth and conquest of "Clive of India" makes a walk today past his handsome mansion in Berkeley Square all the more poignant. In all the annals of worldwide British adventure, only "Lawrence of Arabia" won a similar nickname. Twice he had failed as a youth to snuff himself out, and then been soothed by glory. But his demons had their own upending strategies, and he ran a penknife across his throat at age forty-nine.

Only a few thousand Europeans got out to these lands before the

days of steam travel; they had to learn fast just how they could leverage themselves by imparting a mystique of drill and maneuver —
more than of technology — to adequate, hopefully allied, numbers of
the "martial races" of those teeming lands. That these daring interlopers relied on the loyalties of indigenous friends does not detract
from their achievement. Instead, it illustrates that recurring on-the-
spot quality of being able to exploit the talents (and susceptibilities) of
the vastly more numerous people against whom a certain kind of
adventurer sees fit to match his ambitions. England established a system that held for the next two centuries.

Since overthrowing Hapsburg authority in their own homeland,
the Dutch had meanwhile been busy moving into those of others.
This intrepid population of merely two million flexed its muscles,
acquiring significant points of the Americas and Africa, and above all
South Asia, where they briefly seemed about to succeed the Portuguese as the prime European power. Dutch pirates preyed on Chinese junks trading with Manila, with few complaints from company
directors along the Herengracht (Gentlemen's Canal) back in Am-
sterdam. Most remarkably of all, they conquered the Malay Archipelago (which today makes up the world's largest Moslem nation,
Indonesia), leaving the Portuguese two tragically destined enclaves in
Timor. By the mid-1700s, the Dutch had got beyond the coasts to
build an inland empire. They excelled in "exploiting the deep-rooted
antagonism which already existed between various groups," a pathology
of men and beasts common in island regions.[33] In islands where every
petty king had his jungle stronghold, Dutch soldiers nonetheless had
to fight it out in innumerable small actions against rainforest shadows.
Some of their opponents held out into the twentieth century: Dyak
headhunting in Borneo was only put down one long generation before
the Dutch were driven back into the sea that brought them.

‡

IN THE Western Hemisphere, resistance had continued in the cold
mountainlands of South America well after the conquest. In 1780 —
further away from the death of Pizarro than we are from the Declaration of Independence — a descendant of the Inca Tupac who had
fought the Conquistadors raised an insurrection serious enough to

take a hundred thousand lives (by far mostly Indian) before it was crushed, preserving the name for the Tupamaro rebels of two hundred years later. In the jungles, the Paiagua Indians, namesake of the river Paraguay, were able to release their arrows faster than troops from Portuguese Brazil could fire muskets and displayed a masterful use of canoes in river combat.

All this serves as a reminder that, until recently, technology was better at getting the more developed cultures to a contested spot than at overcoming the spot's particular dangers. From immunization shots to sand filters for engines, only the level of technique attained in the last lifetime has been of a competence sufficient to make hostile environments truly vulnerable to conventional military skills. And even then, those skills might not be enough for the task.

North America also demanded ways of fighting not seen in the home countries, so many of whose forests had been cleared in the centuries before firearms. Self-organized commandos took shape, in the word's original sense of small groups of intimately loyal men operating far afield. No one sitting behind some exquisite Louis Quinze or Hepplewhite desk in Paris or London was indenting for the frontier spirit. And no one in the New England woods or the swamps along the Potomac was waiting for them, either — least of all the type of men who would be known as "Rangers."

The term *ranger* reaches back to thirteenth-century England, where it characterized a far-ranging forester or borderer. By the 1600s, Border Rangers were contesting the debatable land between England and Scotland. The word (and perhaps some of the hard, self-reliant men) crossed the Atlantic with the early settlers, and it rang loud in the French and Indian War, in the American Revolution and on the frontier, then in Texas, and in World War II, and now in Iraq.

When King Philip's War broke over New England in 1675, the colonists were guided by a thirty-six-year-old Rhode Island carpenter, Benjamin Church. In loosely organized fashion, they fought in bands not unlike those of their Indian enemies. Church developed a creed of "march thin and scatter" against Indians, whom the British believed invincible in the bush.[34] Small units armed with hatchets, knives, and some quick-swinging muskets with sawed-off barrels fought a war that remains — proportionate to population — the bloodiest in North American history. After hunting down "Philip" (Metacom, the Wampanoag leader), hanging his chieftains, and selling their families to the West Indies, Church repeatedly turned his frontier skills against the French presence reaching south from the present Canadian Maritimes — although he had a tough time with the *habitants* themselves, skilled as they were in woodcraft and firearms.

The term *coureurs de bois* describes other Frenchmen far deeper inland, born in the New World, eschewing European dress and customs, blending into the endless forests as hunters and trappers. By the beginning of the eighteenth century, France had created formidable colonial forces, the *troupes de la marine* (under the jurisdiction of the naval ministry), which combined such special affinities with military discipline and (among its inordinately high ratio of junior officers) good breeding. There were no colonels; commissions could not be bought; troops were organized in small, independent companies rather than regiments. "The men who undertook raids against New England with Native allies," explains the distinguished historian of early America, Kevin Sweeney, "were in fact as exceptional as the raids themselves."[35] Perhaps no more than three to four hundred were qualified to carry out winter attacks deep into the English colonies.

At dawn in late February 1704, a party of 48–50 French — *troupes* and militia/trappers, commanded by thirty-five-year-old Lieutenant Jean-Baptiste Hertel de Rouville — and 200–250 of their Abenaki, Huron, Iroquois, Mohawk, and Pennacook allies had descended on the northwesternmost town of New England: Deerfield, Massachusetts.[36] Coming out of Canada on snowshoes, they were as mobile as they were merciless. A wind-raised drift alongside the village's ten-foot-high stockade and a sleeping sentry enabled a dozen Indians to vault over and open one of the three gates for the rest. Forty-seven among the mostly young families were killed immediately; 102 captives began the death march north.

The English settlers themselves had "snowshoe companies" to meet these raiders on their own terms. Nearer the coast, Benjamin Church, now overweight and in his sixties, was part of New England's rapid response. He compiled a detailed list of requirements for equipping the effective retaliation and for recruiting the right type of men to carry it out. By spring he was striking to the northeast, fitting whaleboats with leather loops and poles so they could be readily carried as his force penetrated the rocky coasts and river valleys of Maine. Whether slipping through dense summertime forests in loose formation or positioning snowshoe companies on the western frontier, both sides were embarked on modes of combat extraordinary in their resourcefulness, composition, and extreme objectives.[37]

In the early colonial epoch, the settlements' destinies were for the most part determined by the fortunes of war between the home nations in Europe. The scuffles of raiding parties in the unmapped lands and the juggling of Indian alliances counted for little at the conference table. Even when, for instance, forty-two hundred New Englanders in 1745 took virtually impregnable Louisbourg on Cape Breton — viewed as pivotal in controlling the St. Lawrence Valley — George II's diplomats soon returned it to France in exchange for territory lost in India.

By mid-century this had changed. In November 1753, Major George Washington of the Virginia militia — experienced on the frontier as a surveyor, and at twenty-one having stature as a gentleman — was sent by the colony's governor into the upper Ohio Valley to demand that the busily fort-building French withdraw. They were unimpressed. The following spring he was again ordered west of the Alleghenies, this time at the head of some four hundred soldiers and Indians, where he encountered a much larger French force, yet farther from home. His assertion of Virginia's right ended in bloody surrender and (though he was publicly vindicated) humiliation.[38] The collision of these often barely arrived Europeans on the edge of emptiness opened the early period of the French and Indian War.

European historians sometimes call this conflict, which lasted from 1756 to 1763, the "Seven Years' War in America." It was certainly a parallel colonial struggle stemming from a breakdown in international order, but the rewards, let alone the combat, in North America were radically different. Just as strategic special operations were passing virtually into eclipse in Europe, they began to come into their own amid the vast new stakes of empire. The French lunge to join "Canada" (Quebec) with "Louisiana" (the greater part of the Mississippi Valley) by a chain of posts — deploying perhaps a thousand men to hold down a domain five times the land area of France — could have left today's U.S. East Coast clinging by its fingertips to the Alleghenies. The title itself — "French and Indian" — catches the doubleness of the conflict. On one hand, the European colonial governments opposed one another with regular troops, well-uniformed and disciplined. On the other, they marshaled tough settler woodsmen as well as — in the yet-deeper shadows — the land's original inhabitants, taking sides as occasional "allies" of white men who were ultimately embarked on destroying them. While the woodsmen were evolving into actual buckskin-and-moccasins rifle units, the Indians were exemplars of skills virtually forgotten in Europe, now bloodily relevant. All practiced a warfare the savagery of which would have shaken even Alexander or Henry V.

From the outset, the two modes of war had to intertwine: the steady regulars and problematic militia were not masters of the forest; rangers were not (yet) the men to take citadels. Nor were the larger British forces shipped across the Atlantic necessarily decisive. The classic case in point is that of Major General Edward Braddock, sent from England to smack the French at the Forks of the Ohio, who began his march in April 1755, by way of what is now Wisconsin Avenue in Washington, D.C. Two British battalions, American recruits (including Daniel Boone), and locally raised militia headed toward Fort Duquesne (present-day Pittsburgh, which indicates who won).[39]

Braddock conducted his expedition of around two thousand men in European style, soldiers in brightly colored uniforms dragging a huge baggage train and heavy cannon with twenty-five hundred horses, and accompanied by a small city of camp followers. Provided with competent Indian scouts, he nevertheless held their advice in contempt. The outnumbered French (about one hundred soldiers, one hundred Canadians, and six hundred Indians) had laid the ground for an ambush in the tangle of forests along the Monongahela River. Instead, on July 9, Braddock's sweltering advance guard of

twelve hundred lightly equipped troops bumped into the equally surprised French, less than ten miles from the fort, and sent them reeling
back with heavy losses.[40] But the French were able to rally and, far
worse, to urge their Indian associates to spread themselves around
the flanks of the close-packed redcoats. "The whoop of the Indians,
which echoed through the forest, struck terror into the hearts of the
entire enemy," reported a French officer — for good reason, since,
when not shrieking, these Indians had for weeks been showing the
Anglo-Saxons their terrifying use of silence, plucking away any of
Braddock's men who had strayed from column or camp.[41]

Panic rolled back through Braddock's entire force, the most formidable one ever assembled in North America, but arrayed in a long
column, with little room to maneuver or retreat. He did what he
insufficiently could and was carried away to die three days later of his
wounds. Among the screams of other wounded being scalped, it fell
to Colonel Washington to get the wreck of this expedition back on its
last legs to Virginia. Long-range wilderness combat was the warfare
of another world; therefore to succeed one must, to use the title of the
epoch's most famous comedy, "stoop to conquer." And stooping
meant loosening up: the concentration of force envisioned by great
captains for regular war had to be relaxed into a dispersion of smaller,
flexible, high-endurance outfits.

In Europe, no groups so small had hit so hard at such great range
since the Vikings. In the Americas, to be sure, the Conquistadors had
indeed struck deep. But semi-continental distances did not wall off
their targets as they marched to actual cities, 250 miles up to
Tenochtitlán, ninety to Cajamarca: cities whose whereabouts they
more or less knew. Moreover, it was holy adventure, pure and simple.
They were not directly acting as political instruments of the home
government, to put it mildly. In India, as in New Spain and Peru, conquerors could frequently avail themselves of roads; they could levy
supplies from settled lands. North America's indigenous brand of
warfare offered no such advantages.

The North American campaigns became wilderness operations,
masterpieces of adaptation and movement through thick forests for a
larger military policy. More often than not, it boiled down to a fight

between men equally skilled and armed, including raiding parties of sharpshooting Native American riflemen (always a bewilderment to the whites) intent on making the cost of English settlement as high as possible.[42] Their warfare would begin to be defined for the Western world not in military texts but in internationally popular fiction — *The Last of the Mohicans,* one of the books of Fenimore Cooper's Leatherstocking saga. To be sure, Cooper had been a naval officer rather than a woodsman, and he is not particularly reliable for his descriptions of fighting in rough country. Yet, writing in the days of the early republic, he was able to dramatize a world ever more responsive to bold individualism, one that even understood the dignity of a type of life and combat that had so recently been dismissed as plebeian banditry. The hero's very name, Hawkeye, tells us how thoroughly he has become one with the Indian woodland culture: never trusting the treacherous quiet of the forest, leading in single file a little band of friendly Mohegan rescuers he calls "rangers chosen for the most desperate service" to track the evil Huron warrior Magua and save insipid Cora, the general's daughter, from having to choose between "the wigwam or the knife."

On a more gentlemanly level, Colonel Washington understood. His Virginia Regiment became "a truly special unit," according to his latest biographer, not only the equal of British Regulars (as they were called) in appearance and drill, but an elite force able "to master the mobile tactics of 'bushfighting' with Indian-like proficiency." However, their unmatchable combat operations while patrolling the Virginia frontier against the Indians' Six Nations confederation should not be confused with a "kind of guerrilla warfare." The woods-wise regiment that Washington recruited, trained, and led — and in which the enlisted men on patrol adopted what the redcoats called "Indian dress" — contained far more organization, discipline, reach, and simple effectiveness than can be expected from guerrillas. The Virginia "blues" became the professional model of such a special regiment, which the more enlightened of British officers sought to emulate, not that such imitation would help them match Washington's expansive views of war in the revolution to come.[43]

Today, when becoming a U.S. Army Ranger, a soldier is steeped in the lore of the frontiersmen, particularly of Rogers' Rangers, organized by a Scotch-Irish farmer and woodsman, initially as the scouting company of a New Hampshire provincial regiment. (Among the best studies of what Robert Rogers created is an account privately published during the worst year of Vietnam, titled simply *The First Green Berets*.)[44] Rogers was in and out of trouble with the law from boyhood to deathbed, beginning with a convincing accusation of involvement with counterfeiters. Come the struggle against French and Indians, his band of daring outliers soon earned favorable attention from the colonial authorities eager to carry the fight not only to the enemy but behind its lines as well. Rogers was ordered to raise additional units, being commissioned in 1756 captain-commandant of what would grow to ten full companies, including Indians, with Indian officers — a mix not just of local technique and expertise, but spirit.

The next year his "Ranging School" was authorized, incorporating cadets of promise from English regiments who would learn his methods and then go back to instruct others. It was to be an alternative for the British high command — something other than the heavy-handed conventional means that had brought disaster on Braddock. Rogers repeatedly praised the resolve of the men who ventured alongside him. Above all, the Rangers' long-range penetration groups embodied self-reliance that went well beyond even that of militia scouts, who were known to panic (despite their reputation as intrepid woodsmen) when they found themselves in forests of nearly impenetrable spruce.[45] We see such quality displayed in the SEAL-like attack by hatchet-wielding swimmers who surprised and overpowered the crews of five French warships on the Richelieu River north of Lake Champlain; of winter warfare, in blending white blouses among the leafless trees, substituting knives for rifles with frozen locks when assailing sled convoys in the snow or running them down over frozen lakes by strapping on ice skates.

To avenge the massacre of the British garrison at Fort William Henry (also vividly depicted by Cooper), this six-foot-tall, burly, blunt-featured, twenty-eight-year-old major took about two hundred Rangers — "carefully selected from amongst the fittest, keenest, and wiliest fighters in the great British-American army" — up from the foot of the lake through two hundred miles of uncharted, mostly enemy-held wilderness on a search-and-destroy mission right into Quebec.[46] During a half-hour of an October dawn, a venerable Jesuit mission village full of Abenaki warriors, as well as of their women and children, was surprised and incinerated.

To newspaper readers in Boston, New York, Philadelphia, and London, the epic fifty-day raid proved that Indian methods of woodland stealth could be matched by frontier-conditioned European and provincial troops — a special force that just might return even when the going got rough in horrifically unforeseen ways. (As in this mission, amid starvation, shooting, and scalping during the long pursuit home by French regulars, Canadian militia, and vengeful Indians led by the French captain who, not long before, had disposed of Braddock.) Yet the raid had stunned the French as well as the Indians. It proved that the English could strike deep at what should have been the safest of spots. Not that the French hesitated to apply the talents of their own warriors in the vein of Church and Rogers — Jean-Marie le Marchard de Ligneris, Charles Philippe d'Aubry, and Joseph Marin.

The frictions that arose between the military hierarchy and the first iteration of Rangers are not unknown to their twenty-first-century descendants: regular officers who demand that Ranger patrols serve directly under them, and army bookkeepers who grouse about the costs of supplying Rangers with nonstandard gear and apparel. But Rogers's companies had other, more immediate concerns. If they were taken alive, the Indians could be counted on to inflict the grisliest of tortures on the most enraging of their enemies — the intruders who stalked the forests every bit as adeptly as did the Indians themselves.

On the edge of civilization lay another sort of backwoods fighter unconnected with the Rangers or the French. These were the "white Indians," deserters, former captives, and all-around renegades who roamed and fought as members of Indian war parties, appearing in their own bizarre way where no one expected.[47] As for the actual Indians, their disciplined use of firearms could, for a time, extend the power of their unseen presence. Men who faced the soundless skewering brought by well-aimed arrows might find this prospect more demoralizing than musket balls, but the guns that Indians mastered could prove even deadlier. One veteran who survived an Indian ambush recalled that the Indians would surround an enemy "by a circle of fire, which, like an artificial horizon, follows him everywhere."[48] But, skilled even with rifles as they may have been, theirs was not a culture with the technology to maintain firearms efficiently. Moreover, the fewness of their numbers was telling, decade after decade.

A fine writer conversant with French whose *Journals* and *A Concise Account of North America* became bestsellers in the colonies and England, Rogers drafted a collection of twenty-eight tactical insights, which he called his "Plan of Discipline." Irregular war was to be turned into a science, with additional instruction on what wild fruits and berries to eat, on using ice skates (Rogers and his men were known as "the swiftest skaters in the world"), on how to survive blizzards without lighting fires.[49] The plan is considerably better thought-out than the semiliterate if distinctly entertaining "Rogers' Standing Orders," which appeared in the 1936 novel (and ensuing movie) *Northwest Passage* and thence passed, amazingly, into the 1960 *U.S. Army Field Manual 21–50, Ranger Training and Ranger Operations*.

The original plan's discussion of scouting and skirmishing furnishes sufficient detail to guide special operators today. Leaving aside some perhaps dated points, such as when to rush an enemy with one's tomahawk, we learn how to fix sentries with "profound secrecy and silence," "take a circle" to ambush pursuers, and how best to sneak up on "forts or frontiers for discoveries."[50] Those original rules form also the first field manual to be written in North America, in the days before formulating military doctrine had become the responsibility of much-loved staff officers.

The companies that Rogers created fought not just northward toward the heart of enemy country but also diagonally west in innumerable short, sharp actions memorable (even in that pitiless struggle) for brutality. These operators became part of the forests, although no less so than the French Canadians who were accompanying Indian raiding parties into the Virginia and Pennsylvania backcountry. When uniformed, the basic Ranger requirement was for a "good hunting coat" (green, chocolate brown, or drab, as worn by the New York Provincials) and "a pair of Indian Stockings." Rogers's Indian units were "to be dressed in all respects in true Indian fashion," he insisted.[51] No need for *them* to adapt to the woods.

Along the frontier, even once peace finally arrived between the European powers, the Indian presence was there to be reckoned with, as on the Straits of Mackinac at the northernmost tip of Michigan's Lower Peninsula, where the British had won from France the wooden fort established to command the narrows. Soon the Chippewa (no French allies needed) came visiting, to bring off an action exemplary for detecting the blind spot that it is the job of the special operator to exploit.

The British did not want to borrow trouble; so when the Chippewa turned up, they were treated with wary affability, combined with genuine interest in their odd amusements. It was June 4, 1763, George III's birthday. There were suitable ceremonies, and the Indians initiated, in their apparently primitive fashion, a noisy game of lacrosse just outside the fort. Despite midwestern heat, the squaws standing along the palisade also watched the game, heavily wrapped in blankets. Twice the ball went over the walls and into the fort. Perhaps the first, maybe even the second time, as excited players dashed to retrieve the errant toss, the British spectators put hands to their sword hilts. When the ball flew over for the third time, players pursued it inside, this time pausing only to snatch their weapons from under the blankets of the lumpish, unnoticeable women. Few of the garrison had the time to unsheath or shoot before the tomahawks came down.[52] Fifteen redcoats fell in the rush; those who tried to escape were quickly tracked and captured to join the prisoners. The Indians held the fort for more than a year, its little community of merchants unmolested.

Between the British and the white-coated French professionals was fought primarily a war of regularly organized soldiers, focused on capturing fortified positions, led by officers compelled into originality by terrain so different from that for which they had been schooled. The critical moment came with the audacious taking of Quebec City in 1759, by the thirty-two-year-old Major General James Wolfe, a slight, red-haired, bookish, exceedingly difficult man. Wolfe had held his first commission in the marines at fourteen, and nearly accompanied his father — one of Marlborough's veterans and by then a colonel — on the disastrous Cartagena expedition. Wolfe loathed Americans, when that was by no means a common attitude among English officers. He particularly disdained Rangers as "the worst soldiers in the universe," yet repeatedly deployed Ranger teams for raids and deep nighttime reconnaissance. One suspects it was their irreverence that grated, as it can today. "The Pow-wow and paint, and howl operate too strongly upon the Rangers," he snorted, contempt from the heart since he considered Indians fit only to be exterminated.[53] In his refined way, Wolfe was as strange (and skilled) a man as Rogers. Whereas Rogers knew little of the conventional means of war, concentrating on the problems posed by his environment, Wolfe set out to rethink war in the New World and was justified in his final achievement, which he sealed with his life.

Wolfe had previously demonstrated his keen understanding of amphibious operations. By June 1759, he (and the navy) had succeeded in bringing a battle fleet of five frigates, seventeen sloops, and twenty-seven troop transports two hundred miles up the St. Lawrence — the swiftly flowing artery leading into France's Canadian empire — to confront a city that squatted like a medieval fortress atop the 180-foot cliffs that edge the headlands where the St. Lawrence meets the St. Charles. Impassable tidal flats defended the city to the west.

There ensued long weeks of fruitless bombardment and siege (only slightly relieved by general orders permitting regiments to send back downriver for one woman per company). Wolfe's senior officers were nearly all under thirty: their 7,500 men, mostly on the river's south bank, confronted a substantial French army of 15,000 on the north bank in and around Quebec's massive walls. About a thousand Indian warriors had rallied to the French, and Wolfe had no Indians at Quebec. Instead, he offered five guineas to any soldier who chose to go out into the woods and lie in ambush for the savages, the achievement to be substantiated by a scalp — proof of truly special skills — should one return.[54]

The hard months ground on to September as Wolfe suffered from fever and quarreled with his brigadiers. There was time for just one last attempt against the city; the fleet's captains rightly feared being iced in.[55] Indian canoes patrolled the river to detect any attempt to cross by the main English force; Canadian militia patrolled on land; French pickets guarded the cliffs. Wolfe searched through his spyglass for the slightest concavity that might yield his army a foothold. How he finally decided on one particular cleft just two miles from the city nobody knows. He had no confidants, but his luck was so astounding that we cannot dismiss the possibility of a chatty deserter, or treachery within the French garrison.

An assault party of twenty-four "picked men" was selected to scoot up a path winding through cliffs that here rose about 175 feet above the St. Lawrence. (Eight were actual volunteers, each of whom was ordered to select two others among their fellows.)[56] Taking advantage of an ebbing tide and a perfect quarter moon on the night of September 13, the stealth attack was launched with precision timing. The initial flat-bottomed landing craft bluffed their way past sentries along the northern shore by claiming to be French provision boats that had slipped through the English blockade. Wolfe himself went in with the first wave; yet, from the river's edge, the way to the top looked daunting. This apparently sparsely guarded underbelly could also have been a trap.

As so often before, brave men with their backs to the water set themselves against a dark and unknown obstacle. "Where a goat can go, so can a man," was a saying of the time, "and so can a gun." The twenty-four — bold and skillful enough — led the way, crawling up, slipping and sliding and clinging to branches. Others soon followed. Once over the edge, a small camp of sentries was taken, but a runner had just enough time to race away and blurt out a warning to the main French forces. Yet, surely the cliffs west of Quebec were invulnerable; the initial report was dismissed as "incredible."[57] Perhaps the crackle of musketry was a probe or a feint. A landing must be underway from another direction. Meanwhile, Wolfe ordered the second wave out of their boats, then up and over. By sunlight, some forty-five hundred redcoats were massing on the Heights. What ensued saw parade-ground tactics riding on the looser methods of New World warfare. The English soldiers lay full-length in the deep grass to escape the Canadian snipers and French cannonade, as well as to deceive the enemy; then they rose into line, waiting until the slowly advancing white-coated regulars got within fifty yards' range. The French took the volley and broke, but snipers covered their flight. It was likely one of these who sent a bullet through Wolfe's chest. The French commander, Montcalm, was also mortally wounded within ten minutes, his army shattered, its will to fight gone.

Two dozen men at the spearhead in mountain shadows, superb coordination among an amphibious force beneath the cliffs, all in a stealthy climb where the opponent knew himself to be "invincible" — it was the most dramatic operation of the eighteenth century, the most consequential of victories, and a combination of skill and audacity in the extreme. Throughout it was the redcoats — campaigning stolidly from Canada to the West Indies, prepared to freeze or die of fever in places they could not find on the map — who adapted too, and did the most to win the war.

The less exciting fall of Montreal (150 miles farther upriver) the following year signaled the collapse of French resistance in North America. The British expedition had by now (not least through Wolfe's death) learned to use its Ranger brethren more effectively. In 1762 — after more victories in India and Africa, as well as at Martinique — hard-bitten British veterans of North American combat took Havana from Spain (allied again, too late, with France) in a startling amphibious move aided by American troops. As the Seven Years' War wound down, Britain gained all of North America east of the Mississippi, Canada, as well as Florida, which Spain's diplomats traded to get Havana back. Neither the French nor the Indians sat idle. The Indians organized themselves over vast distances under the daemonic leadership of Pontiac; the French (sourly aware that their overthrow in Canada removed the threat that had compelled colonial attachment to overbearing England) seem to have begun infiltrating curious talents into their opponent's prize imperial possession.

The covert operator excels at learning from — and pitting against each other — historically and geographically different groups of people. The French were making this an art form during the eighteenth century as they exploited their enemies' internal divisions. Early in the century, the Protestant-persecuting regime of Louis XIV had allied itself with Calvinist Hungarian squires against the Hapsburg emperor. More predictably thereafter, twice French fleets inserted Catholic Stuart pretenders into Scotland, backed by enough regulars to be the nucleus around which the marginalized might gather — Highlanders, Jacobins, bankrupts, whoever — to explode against the satisfied classes of what, with Scotland and England placed under a single parliament, had become Great Britain.

Now France was more than ready to secretly inflame republican resentments. "What then is the American, this new man?" asked St. John de Crèvecoeur, the Norman-born visionary of the emerging nation, who was farming in upstate New York: "Americans are western pilgrims ... whose labors and posterity will one day cause great changes in the world."[58] To be sure, but it may have taken someone perhaps rather close to French political intelligence to explain the future so clearly.

At stake was country of a size inconceivable in Western Europe since states began to consolidate in the Middle Ages. Men were learning more about unusual forms of war from the Indians in these decades than anyone in Europe had gathered from primitive peoples in two thousand years, except for the stirrup. Step by step in this sprawling land, the special operation was passing into undertakings that were, of necessity, entire campaigns in themselves, often performing at arm's length from headquarters, generals, and meddling staffs. With the American Revolution as with the Conquistadors, we are about to see again how small elements of warriors can multiply thought and skill to recast the fate of continents.

Part III

10

To Try Men's Souls

A Continent to Make and Few to Do It:
The American Revolution and Its Enemies,
1775–1807

"The way to be safe is never to be secure."
BENJAMIN FRANKLIN

WITH ACCELERATING innovation, relative tolerance, and new sources of capital came the initial surge of industrial revolution. A month before Cornwallis surrendered at Yorktown, the first factory chimney in England (or anywhere else) topped out. More enduringly than the eighteenth century's political convulsions, the Industrial Revolution released new possibilities for talents that had been sat upon for centuries, for all sorts of specialist skills, and for the confidence that grows from them. Fertile minds of the new age also seized on engineering and industrialization for less salutary pursuits, including the development of the rocket, the armaments factory, and the ever more deadly personal firearm. Change was irresistible.

And everywhere. The assistance given by Louis XVI to the American revolutionaries was intended not to advance republicanism but to cripple Britain. No good deed going unpunished, such help instead precipitated the insolvency of his monarchy and let strange ideas loose in his kingdom, thereby opening the way to France's own revolution with which, yet more ironically, the new American democracy soon came to blows.

Armies that have to invent themselves within violent months must rely on new talents and on extraordinary means to pursue victory — a seedbed for unconventional measures, as is apparent among those as different as Cromwell's Ironsides, the southern Confederacy, and, lamentably, the Nazi Waffen-SS. In the American revolution can be seen not only the determination of the fledging Continental Army but an ability to work closely with small-boat operators who enabled radical maneuvers, backwoods hit-and-disperse bands, long-range columns, captains of fishing smacks used for offshore ambush, and "market-stoppers" cutting off British supplies. These seemingly meager forces (composed of citizen-warriors able to function with the loss of their capitals, to display huge resourcefulness without aristocratic leadership) confronted "the most powerful and efficient machine for waging war in the world."[1] With fewer numbers amid hunger and disease, time was by no means on the side of the Patriots. The odds appeared overwhelming. No wonder that rebels who could be dismissed in London as "cowards" and "bandits" were expected to fold in short order. But it was not so easy to calculate weakness and strength, particularly when much of the "weak" embraced a harrowing web of democratic small-force operators along a front thirteen colonies wide, a Patriot army able to exploit such space in coordination with these outfits, and naval raiders ready to extend their hands into the British homeland.

New developments percolated, including ever more far-reaching bodies of riflemen-rangers and light infantry. Special warfare on so vast a scope had not been seen since the days when Alexander married it to a single, far-going battle force. With victory came new enemies from without and within: the former met with a one-two punch of naval might and devastating special force offensive in North Africa; the latter by arrest and trial of a smooth operator who put the American continent itself into play.

‡

FROM THE start, the role of Benedict Arnold exemplifies much of the American effort: unfanatic courage against daunting odds of numbers and distance, resilient optimism amid defeat, divided loyalties, brilliant exploitation of the military advantages inherent in the immense backcountry stretching from Maine to Georgia. Considering his achievements in the first five years of war, it is no wonder that a French historian who began to write a history of the Revolution in 1780 (the news of the treason not arriving until late fall) devoted his first volume to Arnold, whereas Washington received only a footnote.[2] However, after eight generations, the place of Arnold as a backwoods warrior, and the skills he drew on that complemented the larger conflict, have yet to be put in proper context. He brought off two riveting achievements at the head of small, tough outfits, even before he went on to be the decisive figure at the world-changing battles of Saratoga — first at Ticonderoga and, more astoundingly, then at Quebec. Both occurred well before independence was declared.

Arnold was born to a strong mother with a respectable inheritance and a father who apparently weakened as disease took four of his six children. Overreaching business deals and consolatory alcohol then spiraled what was left of this eminent Connecticut family into debt. Pulled from school at thirteen and apprenticed to cousins in the apothecary's trade, the boy was likely bequeathed a lifelong sense of frustrated embitterment. Herbs and poultices must have been a maddening confinement for a youth already adept at riding and shooting, as well as at picking up the habits and skills of the nearby Mohegan Indians. When sixteen years old, in summer 1757, he may have served a stint with the town militia during the French and Indian War, but otherwise had no military training. In the 1760s he was in booming New Haven, his sister his assistant, running a high-risk, high-return venture in which, as partner of another prospering merchant, he acquired ships that he captained to Quebec and the West Indies. Threading the tangle of foolish restrictions that hindered the expanding trade of the Atlantic basin involved certain misunderstandings with customs authorities that some might call smuggling — no bad education for a future adventurer.

Before the outbreak of revolution, Arnold was also drawn to what were regarded as the terror tactics of the Sons of Liberty, measures such as effigy burning, stone throwing, and tea dumping, which are rather mild in today's light. By 1774, he and sixty-four other men had organized themselves into a militia company, grandly designated the Governor's Second Company of Guards, Arnold elected captain. Within a day of the news of Lexington and Concord, the Guards set off for the American lines — no matter that New Haven had voted neutrality the night before, or that he had to threaten to tear down the doors of the town's powder magazine to take what they needed.

Less than two weeks later, he proposed to the Massachusetts Committee of Public Safety in Cambridge a rough plan to capture Fort Ticonderoga. This star-shaped bluestone bastion stood about a hundred miles north of Albany, starkly secure on its peninsula at the foot of Lake Champlain, adjacent to the portage to Lake George, and thereon to the Hudson. It was a crucial strongpoint, commanding the continent's chief military thoroughfare — the passage to Canada that Indians knew as the "Great Warpath." Despite having been partly demolished by the retreating French during the last war, Ticonderoga could still choke the waterways that a British invasion from the north would have to take. Moreover, it disposed of scores of cannon, some of which might be put to good use against the redcoats occupying Boston.

The Committee of Public Safety appointed this overdriven Connecticut colonel for a "secret service," providing he agreed to use no more than four hundred men.[3] Riding westward with only a handful of captains who were expected to do the recruiting, he immediately found himself caught in a political crossfire between the colonies. In what is today southern Vermont, the hulking, bragging, thirty-seven-year-old Ethan Allen was asserting himself not just as leader of a buckskinned militia company (or, opponents would say, vigilante gang) but for some time, and for quite separate reasons, as a practitioner of low-level violence to keep this area known as the New Hampshire Grants from becoming part of New York. New York obliged by putting a price on his head. Complicating matters further, Allen had linked up with a Connecticut raiding party (backed by cash from Hartford's treasury) that believed it, too, had official authorization to seize Ticonderoga.

It was an example of the antagonisms that so easily bedevil special bands as they awkwardly serve on theoretically the same side. To be sure, regular army officers have their jealousies and confrontations. Bitter feuds between senior commanders plagued the Continental Army throughout, as they did the British. But like all else, tension can be magnified among small, sharply honed, supereager forces looking to different centers of support.

Impeccable in his red, black-collared Guards uniform, armed only with saber and pistols, Arnold hurriedly arrived at the rallying point along the eastern shore of Lake Champlain on May 9, and immediately tried to wrest command from Allen. If there was to be an attack, Arnold believed the committee had authorized him to lead it. The Green Mountain Boys were half savvy operators, half hard-drinking hooligans, a not-unusual mixture in these years when special forces were ad hoc and eccentric. Yet they were better equipped and skilled than most militia, able to dash through rugged country while maintaining a startling level of secrecy, not hesitating to pounce at dawn on a mighty (if undermanned) fortress. Feeling they had paid their dues after a hard march from Bennington (its Catamount Tavern declared the capital of Vermont, which no state, let alone the king, recognized), and having completed reconnaissance by infiltrating one of their own into the fort, Allen's 230 men began stacking their rifles and threatening to quit. Furious, Arnold agreed that he would issue no orders, provided he could march with Allen at the head of the column.

The slapdash forty-eight-strong British garrison in Ticonderoga may not yet have known there was a war on, despite vague warnings from the confused authorities in Boston about a rebel foray. Allen and Arnold shipped across Lake George before dawn in a thirty-three-foot scow. Two slow, rain-drenched trips over a mile of heaving water brought eighty-three men into position. There was no time to ferry the rest; those that got over crashed in upon the sleeping garrison. Allen, who had his lifelong differences with God as well as government, would say that he had demanded surrender from the violently awakened captain "in the name of the great Jehovah and the Continental Congress." It is equally likely that he just shouted "Come out, you old rat!" — the difference being a reminder of how respectable people on the coast preferred to apply proper faces to the rough-hewn frontiersmen who would make the difference against the yet more proper imperial enemy.

Whether or not history was fast rewritten, we can be sure that Allen convincingly promised to massacre all the defenders, and their twenty-four accompanying women and children, if surrender was not immediate. Immediate it was, and the Boys started in on the wardroom's ninety gallons of rum. Once sober, they also took the Crown Point fortifications sixteen miles north.

Working around Allen in the ensuing mayhem, Arnold seized a forty-ton schooner at the head of Lake Champlain from a Loyalist landowner. Impromptu marines were recruited. Knowing how to handle a ship, he gathered more boats and took the fortress town of St. Jean at the lake's northernmost angle, thirty miles down the Richelieu — well into Canada. Scouts had penetrated at midnight in birch-bark canoes. Arnold's landing at daybreak with three dozen men in rowboats stands not only as the emerging nation's first naval attack but also its first foreign invasion; he had stretched orders nearly to the breaking point.

Allen's invidious version of events was first to be heard in Cambridge. Arnold came to feel that he had received insufficient credit for the overall expedition — only the start of an accumulating list of grievances — and quit his Massachusetts commission. But he was far from done. Ticonderoga was a bauble when the real prize could be Canada. Allen and Arnold both wanted to go after it, but the Continental Congress wavered.

By June 1775, Congress selected Washington, then forty-three years old, as commander in chief. He was soon in Cambridge, overseeing a ramshackle army of some sixteen thousand that held an arc of fortifications around the landward side of Boston and perhaps seven thousand British Regulars. He too eyed Canada, and endorsed the obvious route and means that the tireless Arnold had originally proposed to the Congress in June. It would be a quick-hitting, preemptive invasion by a well-disciplined militia force from New York, capable of pushing up from Ticonderoga through Lake Champlain and the Richelieu to Montreal, then northeast down the St. Lawrence to Quebec. Surely, thousands of French Canadians would rally to the cause — the perennial hope of invaders who, knowing the dislike in which most of a population holds whatever alien or sectarian rulers grip it, believe that they will appear as liberators. It is a mistake we have seen since.

Congress accepted the plan, and initiative suddenly became urgent when Canada's royal governor took steps that indicated it might be he who would do the preempting. Even worse, the American plans passed smoothly into British hands thanks to Dr. Benjamin Church, surgeon general of the army, grandson of the seventeenth-century pioneer of frontier warfare, and superbly placed to be a spy as one of the highest-ranking Massachusetts revolutionaries.

Speed in a world without electricity was a relative thing. Suddenly widowed, Arnold returned to New Haven to make arrangements for his three little boys, then rode back to Massachusetts in July, to be hounded by Church and the Massachusetts authorities over his personal expenses during the Ticonderoga raid. Amid all, he proposed directly to Washington another route, by a second force, which just might be unanticipated. It would use an obscure map and journal of a British officer's extraordinary passage from Quebec to the Maine coast and back during the French and Indian War — following a nearly pathless course used by French Jesuit missionaries a century earlier, one well known only to Indian war parties. No need to sail the well-guarded St. Lawrence; a strike force could make an opportunity out of extreme difficulty by journeying overland from the coast of Maine via rivers, Indian trails, through virgin forest — to combine for a double envelopment with the rebel soldiers conventionally dispatched from New York.

Like that tireless land-speculator Washington, Arnold understood the importance of looking far inward at all the possibilities of America's wilderness. This viewpoint was remarkable in a New Haven trader whose previous life had been going out to the sea. Washington approved the plan and appointed its creator a full colonel of Continentals (as the army would be known by year's end) despite complaints of insubordination from Arnold's seniors. Wrangling continued. Delays mounted.

Allen, for his part, was still at the northern tip of Lake Champlain — holding no army commission but successfully recruiting Indians, an extraordinary skill in itself. He was not about to wait longer. Allen was all drive, no patience. What he could do, he did at once, without the willingness to wait, plan, and think — indispensable qualities for the small-unit leader aspiring to accomplish more than to hit, plunder, and run. In September, he staged an impulsive attack on well-prepared Montreal, was promptly captured and shipped to England, where he was lucky not to be hanged.

Outside Boston, Washington called on his army for experienced woodsmen or men competent with small boats. Further information would be shared if chosen. Around four thousand came forward, Arnold further requiring that volunteers be under thirty and relatively tall.[4] In two days, 786 officers and privates were selected. Washington personally assigned an additional three hundred Pennsylvania and Virginia riflemen, frontier killers indeed, whom he wanted out of his camp anyway, and fast. (Only later would he come to dignify them as "the Corps of Rangers.") Among the other talents was nineteen-year-old Aaron Burr, a brilliant Princeton graduate, fluent in French, and grandson of America's greatest theologian, who would make himself useful on this expedition as a courier, thereafter as a daring night raider in New Jersey.[5] It was a determinedly citizen force, drawn from an army mostly signed up on what the founders still hoped would be steadily renewed short-term enlistments. Arnold would have to exercise leadership by strength of will.

But an army, had it been available, could not have been sent on so ambitious a mission through the wilderness. Having sailed from Newburyport, north of Boston, and barely dodged British patrol boats, Arnold's outfit disembarked from eleven sloops and schooners in Gardinerston, Maine (then still a province of Massachusetts) on September 21. The initial difficulty was the map. By standard, if remarkably advanced, British practice, it may have been subtly altered for purposes of national security, a ploy that the United States itself would apply to sensitive, publicly available charts once it replaced Britain as a superpower some hundred and seventy-five years later.[6] Moreover, a surveyor whom Arnold had asked to refine the map likely distorted it further, again perhaps intentionally. The

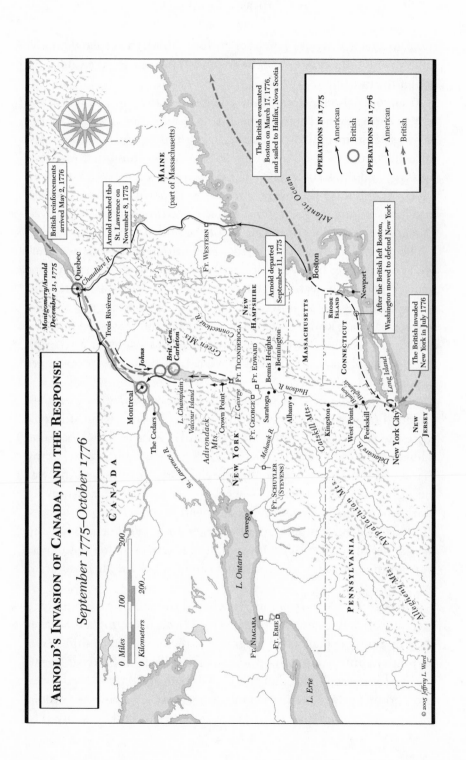

ARNOLD'S INVASION OF CANADA, AND THE RESPONSE
September 1775–October 1776

OPERATIONS IN 1775
American
○ British

OPERATIONS IN 1776
American
British

The British evacuated Boston on March 17, 1776, and sailed to Halifax, Nova Scotia

British reinforcements arrived May 2, 1776

Arnold reached the St. Lawrence on November 8, 1775

MAINE (part of Massachusetts)

Montgomery/Arnold December 31, 1775

Arnold departed September 11, 1775

After the British left Boston, Washington moved to defend New York

The British invaded New York in July 1776

Quebec

Chaudière R.

Trois Rivières

Johns

Brit. Gen. Carleton

L. Champlain

Valcour Island

Crown Point

L. George

Ft. TICONDEROGA

Ft. EDWARD

Bemis Heights

Bennington

Saratoga

Ft. GEORGE

Albany

Mohawk R.

Hudson R.

NEW HAMPSHIRE

Green Mts.

Connecticut R.

MASSACHUSETTS

Boston

RHODE ISLAND

Newport

CONNECTICUT

Long Island

Hudson Highlands

West Point

Peekskill

Kingston

Catskill Mts.

New York City

NEW JERSEY

Delaware R.

Ft. WESTERN

Atlantic Ocean

Montreal

The Cedars

St. Lawrence R.

Adirondack Mts.

NEW YORK

Ft. SCHUYLER (STEVENS)

Oswego

L. Ontario

Allegheny Mts.

PENNSYLVANIA

Appalachian Mts.

Ft. NIAGARA

Ft. ERIE

L. Erie

CANADA

0 Miles   100   200
0 Kilometers   200

© 2005 Jeffrey L. Ward

route to Quebec would be closer to four hundred rather than 180 miles through the Maine woods, giving ample time for the Canadian winter to close in.

As anyone who has canoed the Allagash — the surrounding lands of which are now a benign national park — understands, such a journey in Maine in the best of weather is a toiling series of portages, upriver poling, long carries from pond to pond through bogs, deep muskeg, and thick undergrowth. On top of this comes soaking rain, which in this case the men's late-season departure ensured would turn into stinging sheets of snow. These woods are not to be compared to gentler forests of western Europe or the mid-Atlantic region.

The boats that Arnold obtained were entirely ill chosen: two hundred cramped yet heavy (400-pound) so-called *bateaux,* terribly constructed and easily waterlogged, potentially deadly in fast water and all too readily soaking provisions. Each man carried a gun, a tomahawk, and a long knife. Each had been issued a pair of woolen trousers, a woolen jacket, a short fringed coat, a round hat with a snap-up brim, and a blanket. Compared to what L.L. Bean now supplies for Maine winters, this was nearly beachwear.

As for the riflemen, their weapons might pay off in accuracy — provided they got long enough drops on the enemy — but still took twice the time to load as the flintlock muskets carried by less exotic soldiers. The rifle was seen, considers military historian Jeremy Black, "essentially as a weapon for special units." In any case, this was the first time that riflemen — working as a body of fast-moving sharpshooters — had ever been used together in such large numbers, let alone as a substantial part of a larger force. Rather oblivious to the fine points of tactical innovation, the rest of Arnold's volunteers were amused by the riflemen's "silly fashion . . . to ape the manners of savages."[7]

Whereas the Rangers of the French and Indian War had operated in small bands with few supplies, "Arnold was inventing a new kind of army unit," explains one biographer: the long-range amphibious raiding column. And Arnold knew that he was innovating, as we read in his journal, and that the British had no comparable formation.[8] Some of this invention came of necessity. The riflemen would accept orders only from their own officers and insisted they would be slowed down if encumbered by his less woods-fit companions. At least by going ahead, they could clear trail and might intercept attacks from the brutal and presumably hostile Abenaki. To that end, they were to shoot the chief of this tribe on sight — an early American instance, as it would turn out, of ill-conceived assassination orders being given to a special force.

Arnold estimated the march would take twenty days as his scouts ranged even farther ahead in canoes. The route was up the Kennebec and Dead Rivers, into Canada by way of the Chaudière (cauldron) River, which spills into the St. Lawrence within four miles of Quebec City. At the start, everyone had enough to eat. But before long, the woodcrafty scouts themselves began nearly to starve and then hunger ravaged the far-larger force trudging behind. It is never easy for a sizable body of troops to live off the land, as too many operators reaching through an unforgiving wilderness have found out. A third of Arnold's force deserted (taking half the remaining provisions) while he was several miles ahead, perhaps carrying a boat or supplies, as he repeatedly did to set an example. Those who remained attempted to survive on shot pouches, belts, moccasins, a pet Newfoundland dog. Two of the wives accompanying their husbands were among the first to die. Stragglers risked being irretrievably lost within less than a hundred yards of the column in the barely penetrable timber and brush.

Arnold streamlined his detachment by selecting fifty men to race to the Chaudière. Those too sick or feeble to advance were to be given three days' food and left behind.

The scouts kept holing their birch canoes on the rocks and snags of the tumbling rivers or bridged them on the steep banks, endlessly patching and sewing. Finally, an imprudent moose provided just enough calories for them get through, barely, to the first French settlements on October 20. Eleven days later, Arnold and his first body of men struggled out of the forests. Fed and clothed by French Canadians, Arnold sent cattle for slaughter twenty miles back up the trail. The scouts in their canoes followed with grain, mutton, and tobacco. Another biographer speculates that Arnold's column had been only days away from cannibalism.[9] Just bringing his men through the howling Maine wilderness would make Arnold known in the colonies as the "American Hannibal."

By the time Arnold and 675 men emerged on the St. Lawrence on November 10 (the day the Marine Corps was being formed in the capital of the Revolution, at Philadelphia), they had lost any chance of surprise. But Arnold had gotten them there, in the end with perhaps only forty to fifty dead. None of the men he led were by any means as deferential as the bands of adventurers we have encountered previously. They were politicized, sectarian, mostly literate, a far cry from the heroic but ignorant followers of Cortés, Pizarro, Drake, Morgan, Anson.[10] But he had held this all together, uniting inspiration (which any leader of such extreme activities must possess) with discipline.

The next challenge was to get across a mile of river guarded by warships, the British having burned or confiscated every boat in the vicinity. It was as he emerged from the wilderness that Arnold learned — in a story nearly too uplifting to be true — that the British-hating Abenaki and their chief had been shadowing his column all along, rescuing and feeding the stragglers. By interceding with local Indians, the Abenaki now helped secure forty canoes in which Arnold slipped his weary but still determined command across the river at night to Wolfe's Cove, where the great general had landed to take the cliffs. He followed the same footpath upward, but history would not repeat itself. The defenders refused to be lured from the mightiest fortress in North America, particularly once Arnold finally linked up with a 300-strong detachment of the other American force that had followed the predictable route from Ticonderoga, having already taken Montreal.

Arnold's call for "fellow subjects" of the king to surrender was ignored. Moreover, disease was breaking out on both sides, and the British may also have practiced germ warfare by sending smallpox victims into the American lines.[11] Now early December, the cold made life even more ghastly.

Since many enlistments would expire on New Year's Day (and in this already lawyerly civilization, such matters were important), a siege could not be dragged on. Instead, there would have to be an all-out assault, certainly at night, given the defenders' two-to-one superiority. A fierce snowstorm on New Year's Eve provided further cover: the attack at 4 A.M. on January 1, 1776, was both tactical (seeking to bring off a coup de main against an unprepared city) and political, since it might be even harder to keep the little army together by later afternoon. Arnold led what he himself called the "forlorn hope" of twenty-five volunteers, being among the first to fall as a bullet sliced into his leg.[12]

General Richard Montgomery — a former British officer and a veteran of Wolfe's expedition who then married well, into the Livingston family of Hudson Valley patroons — had led the main force up from New York and then the even more daring three hundred who volunteered to head farther north from Montreal. Rushing a blockhouse with the eager Aaron Burr right behind him, he was torn apart by grapeshot. Scaling ladders were thrown against the outer walls; the stormers' grappled hand-to-hand, only to be driven back. Sixty were killed, more wounded, and 426 captured. Pallet-ridden with the wounded and knowing that he merely held segments of the city's outskirts, Arnold pleaded for reinforcements from Montreal as soldiers began wandering home.

Come June, the British had landed some eight thousand troops at Quebec and forced back the remaining Americans. Like the retreat of Xenophon's Ten Thousand, defeat would turn into legend. The worn-down force made a scorched-earth rearguard action — felling trees, setting traps, destroying bridges, scuttling boats, burning anything that might prove useful to the pursuing enemy, and finally shooting their own horses before pushing off into Lake Champlain as they evacuated St. Jean. Arnold was the last one out. Falling back to Ticonderoga, the Americans decided to make their stand on the lake. Over the summer, they amateurishly built seventeen boats. The showdown came in October, on the waters west of Valcour Island.

What the British called the "Rebel Fleet" — more like Arnold's quickly created backwoods Special Boat Service — faced at least twenty-five vessels constructed by experienced British shipwrights, plus a serious naval assault force of more than one thousand seasoned marines and redcoats. The fight's significance is best summed up by

Admiral Alfred Thayer Mahan: "The little American navy on Champlain was wiped out; but never had any force, big or small, lived to better purpose nor died more gloriously, for it had saved the lake for that year" from the British attempt to sweep south by water.[13] Arnold and most of his men managed to escape to Ticonderoga, which would not fall until the following July. But the fortifications at nearby Crown Point had to be abandoned and were immediately taken, one of the victors reported, by British "Rangers & Indians," the army to follow "two or three days afterwards."[14]

Arnold's story thereafter unites both cold-steel heroism with angry irresponsibility: raised to brigadier general; hounded by legal inquiries over malicious charges of looting in Montreal; a hairbreadth escape during hand-to-hand combat in western Connecticut; then passed over for promotion by Congress in favor of politically connected mediocrities; quitting once more in 1777, to return to a haunted double destiny as a major general once an embarrassed Congress reversed its decision.

As second-in-command at the two battles of Saratoga that September and October of 1777, he faced an opposing force of around seven thousand (including some forty "English Marksmen selected from the different Regiments, & called Rangers") marching south from Montreal.[15] The redcoats were the finest troops in the world. At Saratoga, they were led by a Coldstream Guards playwright general known for fast-moving, bloody, cut-and-thrust attacks adapted to bush fighting — reminding that originality has a way of showing up in several forms. Arnold planned the defense and sent out skirmishing parties against the approaching enemy and "its primary instrument of terror," its Indian allies.[16] He led a raiding party at night to snatch prisoners for interrogation from the enemy camp and, when the first battle was joined, directed the riflemen from his Quebec expedition to the crucial points. They worked in "small detachments . . . shifting ground . . . plac[ing] themselves in high trees," and, the defeated general would report, picking off his officers with single shots.[17]

Again, it was Arnold who inspired, who rallied militia to the field, unit by unit, man by man. He seemed to be everywhere when needed, recruiting men incited by a not particularly nation-creating emotion: rage at the stripping and butchering at Indian hands (as Arnold luridly kept repeating) of a supposedly exquisite beauty, Jane McCrea, daughter of a frontier clergyman, no less. Shorn of his command during the eighteen days between the battles for insultingly trying to goad his commanding officer into action, he charged into the front lines anyway during the climactic engagement. His black stallion was shot out from under him; he rolled clear, to be hit once more in his left leg. At the end, the Patriots had won one of history's most decisive battles, finally ensuring the vital, out-in-the-open assistance that could be brought to bear by France's soldiers, sailors, and treasure.

Not even gross jealousy among his superiors could conceal that it was Arnold who had gained the margin of victory at Saratoga, in no small part due to his riflemen and his recruiting.[18] But he was in much pain and justly angered at the acclaim that went to the wooden grandee who signed the victory dispatches. Frustration, remarriage into a Tory family, Congress's demand for a court-martial over the latest charges of shady financial dealings, and the prospect of twenty thousand pounds and a British commission lured him within two and a half years after Saratoga to set about betraying the vital bastion of West Point, covering a narrow curve on the Hudson River. Part of the plot was to grab General Washington as well.

It is surprising that there were not more Arnolds in the Revolution. Had West Point fallen, there might well have been. Barely getting away from West Point in September 1780, to a British warship in the Hudson before Washington arrived on an inspection visit, he went on to fight with individual deadliness against the cause he had kept alive. The fuming American high command entertained plans for a special operation against one of its least conventional of warriors. Some wanted him assassinated. Washington personally drew up orders for his abduction — preferring to see him tried and hanged — and infiltrated into the armed camp of lower Manhattan a tough, twenty-three-year-old sergeant major posing as a deserter, who was to meet an agent in place. It was eighteenth-century "rendering" to justice: Arnold was to be jumped during his customary midnight walk, gagged, and dragged to a waiting boat on the Hudson pier.

Only luck in the form of troop-embarkation schedules kept Arnold out of the hands of his former countrymen, preserving him for a long, financially embarrassed, morally oblique exile in London.

Arnold was not so different from Alcibiades, a man brilliant at a pivotal point of history and thinking not just outside the box but outside the confines of loyalty, perhaps of all virtue itself. Just as such men are removed from the familiar assumptions of war, they can stretch far beyond the common assumptions of civil society — their first devotion always being to themselves. Deploying mavericks of this sort for the extraordinary tasks at which they excel so creatively may be unavoidable; it also brings a higher likelihood that the guns will be pointing in unexpected directions.

‡

WASHINGTON HAD kept backing Arnold and seems to have felt genuine warmth toward that very different man, likely arising from respect for quality if not qualities. Rich, tall, lean, and strong, one of the best horsemen known — a man in his prime — Washington is not quite the "old English gentleman" that Andrew Johnson once called him. Instead, he is better seen as standing between two worlds: one that of Louis XVI and of Jefferson, George III, and Alexander Hamilton, with its formal governments and yet more formal armies, the other that of the beckoning wilderness, which the only great national leader to be a surveyor contemplated with shining eyes. Comprehending Washington's intentions as a strategist is an exercise in mind reading. But we can be sure that his sense of America's largeness and the use thereof — going back to frontier days with his Virginia "special unit" — surpassed any understanding by generals Howe, Burgoyne, or Cornwallis. If overpowered, he said privately, he was willing to retreat behind the Allegheny Mountains to carry on a "predatory war" against the king's men.[19]

More so than Arnold, Washington encountered recurring problems of discipline in making soldiers out of his volunteers, including those from militias in which officers were customarily elected.[20] Such is the tradeoff: the more that a commander must rely on soldiers who are full members of a consensual society, the more he is likely to face unruly skeptics as well as men from whom he can extract extraordinary achievements. Therefore, Washington's officers had to be acknowledged by their men as exceptional enough to merit obedience; they could not depend on superior rank alone (or on good-hearted convincing) to ensure they would be followed. And therein was a way of leadership that really only survives today in the give-and-take of the special force, that in fact is essential to its success.

Washington felt a gentlemanly disgust at the use of Indians and spies (though use them he did), let alone of assassins, which is why he gave "express stipulation and pointed injunction" that Arnold be brought to him alive.[21] Not that the Continental ranks were pictures of decorum. Like British soldiers, they included many of society's losers. In the American case, however, there was a larger element of people whose strengths lay in the newly created modes of war, not necessarily the frontiersman (himself a misfit), but farmers and shop-keepers for whom the self-reliance of overcoming big obstacles of huge spaces and harsh climates in this new land might not be unfamiliar.

Of course, these qualities of adaptivity and initiative are human, not uniquely American. They would develop in different times and in different circumstances with all armies. It was in America that they were first blended into an army of the line, no matter how bedraggled. The possibilities of the modern citizen-soldier came to demonstrate themselves in many ways, from corporals proving able to lead decimated companies in battle to the uncanny surprises that fathered a slew of special operations. As for the officers of this new army, they were largely self-taught military men — "hunters, lawyers, physicians, clergymen," according to a startled Hessian's diary — who began to consume texts and handbooks of war.[22] The British had to destroy them all, a task made trickier as France, since the start, had been covertly shipping arms to the insurgents via a "false-front" company (Hortalez & Cie.) working through Saint Dominique (Haiti) and Martinique.

Initially, the British had the aid of Robert Rogers himself. Years earlier, British army paymasters had tormented him for the Rangers' haphazard bookkeeping, joining the creditors who threw him into debtors' prison. Once he had been redeemed in 1765, with appointment as the commandant of a restored Fort Mackinac, he then stirred the vengeance of two powerful British superiors who accused him of treasonous dealing with Indians. Imprisoned in chains, with long delays before acquittal, he eventually sailed to England to seek redress. Instead, he drank himself into debt and, again, prison, to be salvaged by friends who got him placed on half pay as an army major. Returning to America, Rogers made vague attempts in summer 1776 to join the Continental forces, but Washington instead chose to arrest him for suspicious, though likely innocent, contacts with Loyalists.

A prompt jailbreak in New Jersey enabled the forty-four-year-old frontiersman to offer his services to the Crown. Fortunately for the Revolution, the ranger units he formed were pale imitations of his earlier achievements. Few of his veteran backwoods fighters joined that cause.[23] Rogers was elbowed aside, and the British themselves began to revitalize what became the Queen's Rangers, turning it into effective yet incongruously well-uniformed battalions. Once more imprisoned for debt, he would die in London after the American victory, drunk and destitute, but leaving an indomitable legacy.

One indirect way of corroding Washington's army, the British believed, was to stage a series of coastal raids on New England, inducing recruits to hurry back to defend their homes. But the general responsible — later the commander in chief for North America — Sir Henry Clinton, as well as the Royal Navy, had enough on their hands. Massachusetts patriots from Marblehead, the colonies' foremost fishing port (and the town to suffer proportionally the most dead), were skilled people undertaking what they did best — and an example of the small-unit enterprise that the likes of Clinton had to endure throughout the war.[24]

Under the leadership of a stocky Salem merchant, John Glover, these blue-jacketed fishermen of the Grand Banks operated as a form of special ferrying command. At the Battle of Long Island, in August 1776, Glover and his men were vital to winning a race against time, tide, and wind to silently extract Washington and nine thousand nearly doomed Continentals with horses, supplies, and cannon across the East River from Brooklyn to Manhattan in nine hours, in pitch dark and, at dawn, under cover of fog and rain. At Trenton that Christmas night, it was the other way around. Backed by longshoremen and riggers from Philadelphia and ferrymen from New Jersey, they made possible the crossing of the thousand-foot wide, ice-clogged Delaware River in the middle of a nor'easter's violent snow and hail, thereby restoring the reputation of Washington and his army as fighters. Both at Long Island (on the defensive) and Trenton (on the offensive), Washington surprised the enemy at night as he used heavily loaded rowing boats to turn waterways rapidly into highways.[25] "Enemy advance," said Mao, "we retreat; enemy retreat, we pursue" — continental thinking against island peoples, whether British or Japanese.

Other unusual talents mobilized in this mind-stretching war included African Americans, slave as well as free. The First Rhode Island, three-fourths of whose soldiers were black, included exceptional fighting men. One of them is to be remembered for his role in the Patriots' most dramatic abduction of the war, an enterprise that by all definitions was a commando raid. Major General Richard Prescott, "infamous in the annals of that war as one of the meanest of petty tyrants when in power, and of dastards when in danger," as an American chronicler would immortalize him not long after the peace, commanded the redcoats in Rhode Island and beyond during 1777.[26] On the night of July 10, he was quartered in a well-guarded house about five miles from the British base at Newport. A lieutenant colonel of the Patriot forces in Providence led "a few chosen men" (about forty) in four whaleboats with muffled oars across Narragansett Bay, as they threaded through three British frigates and assorted guard boats. On land, the men were divided into squads, some penetrating silently through a surrounding company of light horse, others approaching the general's house from behind. The sentry at the door was jumped and bound. "Four strong men" made the final entry, one of them being remembered as "a powerful Negro."

In a short obituary of November 3, 1821, the *Providence Gazette* would write of "Prince [once the lieutenant colonel's 'confidential'], a negro man, aged about 78 years" and note what followed that long-ago July.[27] "The door of the General's chamber was fast closed. Prince, with a leap, plunged against the door, and knocked out the panel" as the three others stormed in behind him. They dragged Prescott to the shore, along with a British major who got underfoot, and the prisoners were hurried back across the bay to an awaiting coach, which spirited them to Providence by sunrise. (In latter years, "Prince" would be more respectfully known as Jack Sisson.) Although the Revolution would be won with an army more racially integrated than any American military force until Vietnam, the talents of such unconventional warriors as Sisson caused familiar anxieties; surely there were dangers in letting these people become acquainted with means of making war, let alone this type of war.[28]

Throughout, there were operations on both sides reflecting these special qualities: that of Captain Allan McLane, for example, whose "market stoppers" managed a small, cunning thrust into Philadelphia by melding their shooting into the fireworks with which the British were staging a ball.[29] Even Prescott's abduction was nearly replicated in January 1781, this time against Clinton himself. Under orders from General Washington, another team of about forty men apparently came down the Hudson at night on a flatboat, English colors drooping from the stern. They rowed through enemy ships at anchor in New York harbor to land near the commander in chief's quarters where, at the last moment, an alert sentry sounded the alarm, and they were rounded up. Wise at least after the fact, the less complacent British command ordered that distinctive uniforms had to be worn and troops were to be "on watch in the city with combed and powdered hair," presumably to set themselves apart from wet and muddy infiltrators.[30]

Washington understood, as did Benjamin Franklin, that partisan warfare with its characteristic hit-and-run raiding is only effective up to a point. So did that most brilliant of American generals (at least of those who stayed true), Nathaniel Greene, a self-taught soldier and birthright Quaker, turned out of Meeting for too great an interest in arms, and, in 1777, a burly thirty-five-year-old with a pronounced limp from a childhood accident, a man whom lesser ones saw as an embarrassment on the parade ground. (Again we encounter the flawed, the different, the outlier who grasps creative alternatives, as did Greene, who commanded the southern army in a brilliant campaign of guerrilla attacks complemented by field forces constantly in motion.) Yet sharp little strikes against a serious opponent, even delivered by the hundreds, rarely compensate for an ineffective army.[31] At the birth of the Republic, final victory lay in the ability of regular Continental officers to tie partisan audacity to strategy. Open-ended rangering and special warfare alone was not an option if America was to be taken seriously abroad, among enemies and allies alike.

‡

ON MAY 12, 1780, Charleston, South Carolina, fell to a skilled amphibious landing and siege by Clinton and Charles, Earl Cornwallis, the next senior British commander. For the Patriots, it was the war's worst disaster. Clinton returned to New York, believing South Carolina to be in hand, leaving Cornwallis with eighty-five hundred men responsible for that most populous of the thirteen states, and the one that would suffer the most deaths during the war. (Georgia, where the British had even been able to elect a legislature, was a second foothold.) But to knock the South out of the war, the British needed to subdue South Carolina, which meant not just taking Charleston but subjugating much of the backcountry. Only then could British power dare to turn north and on to Virginia. And it might have worked. When Washington sent Greene to take charge in the south, he confessed it was like dispatching a "forlorne hope" to near-certain death.[32]

The consequences of what followed, at least, are well presented in Mel Gibson's movie *The Patriot*. A well-off farmer outside of Charleston, expert with rifle and tomahawk, shadowed by rumors of having butchered French prisoners in the back-of-beyond Ohio Valley during the last war, leads his sons through the Carolina forests and swamps, pursued by Cornwallis's hypermobile special forces. If particular atrocities are historically unfounded (such as herding townspeople into a church and burning it), and, indeed, outraged British opinion when the movie was released, we nonetheless get a good impression of the dark struggle of ambush and terror that did go on, far from the cities, behind the polished generals' backs.

In Gibson's Hollywood version, Cornwallis's elite dragoons are called "Tavington's Legion." In real life, six companies of light dragoons (and five of foot) were led by Lieutenant Colonel Banastre Tarleton, a muscular redhead, son of a prosperous mayor of Liverpool, who had studied law at Oxford, then spent a year blowing through a £5,000 inheritance when his father died (equivalent to about $400,000 today), and finally prevailing on his mother to buy him a commission in the

King's Dragoon Guards. At the age of twenty-five, he was in the Carolinas at the head of a green-clad, fast-moving, stomach-punching
outfit, as much at home in the saddle as cavalry, as much at home on
foot as riflemen.

Tarleton was a horsemaster who learned the terms of the game real
fast. He was already famous for, in 1776, having pulled off an astonishing fifteen-minute raid that captured General Charles Lee —
second-in-command of the Continental Army — at a New Jersey
tavern. In the Carolinas, he undertook the duties of reconnaissance —
tracking, raiding, some tough pitched battles — and repeated, sudden retribution. He was an advanced liberal in his views (as he would
show after the war in Parliament) and a relentless, no-holds-barred
killer. Like so many independently minded operators, Tarleton was
utterly unconventional in political opinion: vicious in war, when necessary (and often when not), yet enlightened in civilian life because
capable of thinking so creatively. There is absolutely no inconsistency.
Meanwhile, the term *Tarleton's quarter* (no quarter at all) commemorated his outfit's way of fighting against a frontier culture, it must be
said, which had gone to school in its own way of vicious combat with
the Indians. The barely spoken of savageries from the earlier war that
haunt Gibson's film character "Benjamin Martin" are far from fiction.

"What if there is a context of time and place in which the rules do
not apply?" asks the leading historian of the war in the Carolinas.[33]
The answer is that then anything goes until new rules are formed
from experience, and in war, this can be the ideal environment for the
type of fighting in which special warriors of all sorts thrive. We can
put guerrillas into at least two types — those who defend their villages, perhaps venturing no more than a day's journey away; and
those who come to think bigger — exploiting range, taking the
offensive, having the unit spirit of special warriors to disperse and
reform, connected (however tenuously) to the large forces on which
usually hinge victory or defeat.

It is the second type that appeared in the South. American children
of the late 1950s remember the television series *Swamp Fox,* with its
jaunty theme song. It, too, was not far-fetched in portraying that war.
Francis Marion, the lead character, was in fact a wiry operator superb
at killing from ambush, shameless about violating flags of truce, and

constantly suspicious. He deliberately recruited a limited number of men: rarely less than twenty, never more than several hundred. Drawn by his victories, they had wandered into his camps deep in the Carolina swamps, spent a few weeks campaigning, and then left — perhaps enriched from a plundered corpse, perhaps just having had the experience. Marion did not even try to hold them in the ranks, the war being so fierce that men left for home to protect families, to rally again once the typhoon had moved on. And what elevated him above just being a guerrilla leader was his ability to accept authority and work hand in glove with Nathaniel Greene.

Also pushing out, retreating, and springing back in classic adaptations of Indian woods wisdom were the "Over Mountain Men" from, literally, over the mountains in what is today east Tennessee. These Scotch-Irish deep-forest hunters, traders, and Indian fighters bore craftsmen's weapons and displayed a flexible deadliness that chilled their opponents, who still expected to see the men who would kill them. Their skill was decisive at remote Kings Mountain, on the border between North and South Carolina. There, during one terrible hour on the rainy afternoon of October 7, 1780, the Patriots achieved what may be the turning point in the South, buying time for Nathaniel Greene to reorganize the Continental Army. All equipped with rifles, hunting frocks, and moccasins, about 240 Over Mountain Men formed the spearhead of an 850-strong force that also included more formally trained militia from the Carolinas, Georgia, and Virginia. The Patriots hunted down and trapped roughly eleven hundred fellow Americans on the mountain's heights.[34]

These Loyalists were Provincial Regulars and also Carolina militia commanded by the single British soldier to be present at the battle — Major Patrick Ferguson, one of the Crown's own keen backcountry fighters, a twenty-year veteran at age thirty-five with special warfare experience against rebels in the Caribbean and himself the best shot in the service.[35] Had he met the Patriots most anywhere else, he probably would have won. Here the thick forests were against him. Yet Ferguson was still confident; surely the summit of Kings Mountain was too steep to be scaled in the face of defending fire. Over Mountain Men led the Patriots up, tree by tree, rock by rock, finally yielding before desperate bayonet charges, only to thrust upward again.

The Loyalists were torn to pieces. Afterward, one of the survivors observed that the hasty shallow burials after the battle had attracted wild hogs to dig up and scatter enough bodies on which to grow fat, the men who stayed around quickly losing a taste for pork. Ferguson, at least, lies undisturbed where he fell.[36]

General Cornwallis's orders to Tarleton and his legion were simply to get Marion, as well as the frontiersmen whom Ferguson had imprudently called the "backwater men . . . a set of mongrels." At Cowpens, South Carolina, in January 1781, the Patriots well knew whom Cornwallis would be sending against them, and how to fight him. Tarleton had made himself predictable. Supremely confident on his distinctive black stallion, he "came on like a thunderstorm" at the head of a some eleven hundred men, as one of the Patriots would remember — against a deftly maneuvered force that included veterans not only of Kings Mountain, but of Arnold's operation in Canada, and of Saratoga, led by an Indian fighter who had been at all three, and who had also survived Braddock's defeat twenty-six years earlier.[37] The dragoons were shellacked, and the Patriots were on the move again within two hours.

Partisans largely sustained the revolutionary cause in the Carolinas through 1780, and from partisan war arose an unremitting cycle of vindictive cruelty. Beneath the storied battles of the big war, operations flourished that can be deemed special, not only against the British but between Patriots and Loyalists: kidnappings, ruses, artful modes of well-considered guerrilla action. And we are reminded that the Revolution's Patriot militias were at least as important for stomping down Loyalists as for fighting the British. While Washington, Adams, and Jefferson looked at the ceiling, people one or two steps down were doing things in their own corners — enterprising, heroic, grotesque. By this time, the war's overall fury was so intense that Congress debated sending a letter to Benjamin Franklin in Paris, instructing him to hire arsonists to burn London, a city of nearly a million souls and the largest in Europe.[38]

Except for Tarleton's unhappy encounter at Cowpens, Cornwallis by 1781 had driven every force he met from the battlefields; he sent Tarleton raiding deep into Virginia during that summer, Jefferson only escaping by ten minutes from Monticello. Turning his back on the Carolinas, he set out with approximately one-quarter of the British army in North America to join hands with the fleet and reinforcements at Yorktown. Blood kept flowing behind him. "We fight, get beat, rise and fight again," Greene said laconically.[39] Elite-force attitudes, when defeat was assumed to entail mass desertion, complemented the special-force procedures in the swamps and woodlands.

In the 7,500-man army that Cornwallis surrendered on October 17 were six companies of Royal American Rangers, about eight hundred marines, as well as sailors who had landed from the British fleet that had failed to keep the seaway open against decisive French assistance, and German Jaegers, along with the conventional regiments. Also surrendering were Tarleton and the remnants of his dragoons. He had been marked for death by the Patriot militia, at least once barely escaping a midnight hit team.[40] For good reason, he and his dragoons, as well as these Rangers, were evacuated on a safe ship — not to be searched — that the terms of surrender permitted the British to sail to still-occupied New York. The greater war was about establishing sovereignty and peace, not perpetuating vendettas, and Washington was not prepared to stomach what would likely occur if these fiercest of combatants were included in the general surrender.

‡

As in the shadowy struggle between Loyalists and Patriots on land, American privateers worked on both sides of the Revolution, driving up insurance rates for all and forcing merchant ships into convoys.[41] Far-going Patriots, like their more explicitly piratical predecessors, brokered their winnings and supplied themselves through friendly foreign ports, Bremen on the northwest German coast being particularly favored.[42]

Since Britain had the world's largest navy, the best approach for the barely forming American fleet, as John Paul Jones insisted, was "to surprize their defenceless Places and thereby divide their Attention and draw it from our Coasts." He meant not simply pouncing on enemy commerce at sea but using "terror" against civilians on land — beginning by raids against Britain with landing parties and green-uniformed Continental Marines from his (appropriately named) sloop USS *Ranger*.[43]

Only Arnold can compare to Jones in the drive, resourcefulness, and scope with which he led his self-designed operations, Jones taking into combat at the outset even worse people than Arnold had had to deal with among the Green Mountain Boys or the deserters in Maine. With every American patriot of the time regarding himself as an authority on "tyranny," Jones was throughout this cruise muttered against as a "tyrant" for requiring the mere basics of discipline. He had been compelled to make an approximation of a crew out of quarrelsome locals from around the seaport of Portsmouth, New Hampshire, men who were far from being heroes. The heroes had gone privateering (and still can, since the U.S. Congress continues to enjoy the constitutional authority to grant "letters of marque and reprisal").

Jones began his "diabolical work," as the *Cumberland Packett* would report that month, in April 1778, by sailing around Scotland and down into the Irish Sea from France to strike Whitehaven on the northwest Scots-English border, the port from which he had shipped out eighteen years earlier as an apprentice on a merchant vessel. Thirty reluctant volunteers were lowered at midnight in two overloaded boats packed with gunpowder and tar. Hours of hard rowing brought them into the harbor by daybreak, the plan being to surprise the twin forts guarding the mouth: one team to start burning some two hundred vessels anchored in the upper harbor while Jones and the second party scaled the southern battery to spike the guns. Dozing redcoats were surprised, and that part of the mission at least came off. But the ships resting on the tidal flat could not be burned: most of the other team, such as it was, had broken into a tavern and gotten drunk, and — they groggily explained — the flames they had tried to create with canvas and pine-cone "candles" had flickered out.

The lack of a flame (whatever the reason) is significant of a larger story. Most anything that involved technological foresight before well into the nineteenth century tended to be haphazard; stevedores, for instance, routinely loaded gunpowder while smoking pipes. Not being able to start a fire or ignite the powder shows the technical limits of the time, let alone how poorly men were equipped to execute a complex operation. By the time Jones could produce a flame, perhaps from the burgled pub, the sun was over the horizon. One collier was fired, but hundreds of townspeople began to rally, awakened by a deserter from Jones's landing party. Everyone else hit the boats, the men's cheerful willingness to leave their captain behind foiled by one of the few loyal officers. It attests to Jones's strength of command that he could accomplish what he did with a crew that would just as soon have seen him dead.

Once on the *Ranger* by midmorning, Jones took another bold step — striking immediately across Solway Firth to kidnap the Earl of Selkirk. For Jones, the son of a gardener on a great estate nearby, these were home waters; naively he assumed that the local VIP could serve as a hostage whom Lord North's government would be eager to exchange for American prisoners in Britain. To that end, he led a dozen men with muskets and cutlasses ashore in early afternoon, passing them off as a Royal Navy press gang to scare away any able-bodied men among Selkirk's retainers — only to learn that the earl was away. (Operators can count on gaining even more leverage by impersonating enemy authority figures, whether authorized kidnappers or police.) Jones turned to leave. His prize-hungry detachment demanded to loot the manor house, and the only way for Jones to preserve Revolutionary respectability was to limit them merely to lifting the mansion's silver, for which they duly offered the countess a receipt.

By now, the region was aroused; but rather than running back to France, Jones was determined to offset his spate of bad luck with a real success, and this he accomplished by sailing directly west to Belfast, where he knew HMS *Drake* was riding at anchor — intelligence, the press would say, that he got from a fishing boat. Never hesitating to use deception, he displayed a British flag, wore a British captain's uniform to get in close, and kept his marines below decks. He lured the *Drake* out to sea; the classic duel that ended at sundown was the first between an American naval vessel and a comparable British one, and the first American victory.

And yet it was Jones's two unfulfilling amphibious raids that brought more turmoil to the British home front than the loss of the *Drake*: the theft of Selkirk's silver was found particularly outrageous. It was not war, cried the ruling classes, but cowardly crime. All strangers in major seaports were hauled in and grilled; everything went on the equivalent of Code Red alert everywhere; the Admiralty dispatched half a dozen warships after the "Yankee pirates."[44] It was a good example of the way a force small enough to be invisible, capable enough to be extremely unwelcome, frightens the enemy into overreaction.

Jones's near-mutinous crew accomplished what they did despite themselves. Once they reached Brest, on the western tip of the Brittany peninsula, all their quarreling had to be sorted out by the American commissioners coordinating the new allies' war effort in Paris. Most of the seamen headed home. Jones stayed in France, to inflict, during three short months on the North Sea, in 1779, a rather higher level of pain with a small squadron built around the *Bonhomme Richard* and including 137 marines from the Irish Brigade of the French army. By the time he returned to America in February 1781, marines had demonstrated their importance as raiders, at least as valuable as in their familiar duties of boarding and picking off officers in ship-to-ship actions. Not that this would prevent U.S. Marines from being disbanded with the peace, along with most of the Continental army (including all ranger companies) and the entire navy — whose one battleship had only just come down the ways when it was given, in fitting gratitude, to France.

Focusing on its first exercise in "nation building," the United States had no navy department until 1798, when republican, vaguely deist America, once the glad ally of Catholic, absolutist France, found the now-republican, deist France to be a much nastier customer. An act of Congress then reestablished the marines on July 11.

Nevertheless, the founding legend of the U.S. Navy, and of the Marine Corps, would come into being not from the 1798–1800 Quasi War (its official name) with France and its Caribbean privateers, but from confronting real pirates in North Africa. Without British protection, American ships were now thoroughly exposed to Barbary. Washington and Adams paid tribute, following tradition and because it was cheaper than war to keep these outlaws' predations in some sort of bounds. Jefferson was a harder case. He was a bad man to cross, and a deadly enemy. There are reminiscences even of Washington that show warmth of heart but few, if any, of Jefferson. Since his diplomatic days representing the new republic in Paris just after the Revolution, he had been insisting that the civilized world put an end to the piracy, proposing in 1786 a Barbary Fund for the purpose, which might underwrite a perpetual blockade by an international fleet — a pioneering, but fruitless, initiative of international security. Once president in 1801, he acted.

A half dozen years before, Congress had authorized six frigates to be built to protect commerce from "Algerine corsairs." Three splendid vessels were laid down — the USS *United States,* the *Constitution,* and the *Constellation,* to be followed (due to the difficulties with France) by others, including the USS *Philadelphia,* as well as smaller craft suited to Mediterranean warfare. However, the unfamiliar waters of the Pirate Coast took their toll. Sailing out of Gibraltar in 1803 as part of a U.S. squadron trying to enforce a blockade, *Philadelphia* was in hot pursuit of a shallow-draft raider when it struck an uncharted reef, to be captured and worked back into Tripoli harbor. Three hundred and seven Americans were now held hostage.

The U.S. commodore operating out of Syracuse gave orders to destroy the mighty *Philadelphia* — there was no hope of extracting her. The "enemies of the human race," as pirates are described in maritime law, could not be permitted to add so ultramodern a weapon system to their strength. The following February, twenty-five-year-old Lieutenant Stephen Decatur Jr. took advantage of a new moon to enter deep into the harbor with eighty-four well-rehearsed raiders. A surgeon's mate had previously examined a host of volunteers for fitness: Decatur had selected the toughest, carefully briefed them, and organized squads each commanded by an officer with a specific assignment. Silent throat-slitting would delay detection. Their captured Tripolitan ketch flew English colors; the half-dozen men on deck were dressed as Maltese sailors (Malta then being under British occupation). Jammed below around barrels of gunpowder were sailors and eight marines. Decatur had also recruited a Sicilian pilot who hailed the watch on the *Philadelphia.*

In Lingua Franca, the pilot explained that his little trading vessel, bereft of anchor by a storm, needed to run a line to the largest vessel — which just happened to be the *Philadelphia* — to make fast for the night. The ruse was convincing until someone on the *Philadelphia* (nearly inevitably in an operation this complex) detected a flaw — something was amiss on the deck, and the cry of "Americans!" went up. But by then lines had been thrown, and the boarders were close enough to spring out, up, and over. For silence, only edged weapons were used: cutlasses, swords, boarding axes, knives. Resistance proved slight as the squads scattered to their assigned positions. In a total of twenty minutes the fires had been set, a blaze taken hold on *Philadelphia;* the men regained the ketch and shoved off. They ran not only the gauntlet of the shore batteries but through a convulsion of double shot from the *Philadelphia*'s guns, loaded for harbor defense and now set off by the flames. The men's escape was assisted by oared boats from the USS *Siren,* which, disguised as another merchant vessel, had been hovering outside the harbor to cover the retreat. Not a single man was lost, and all were soon making for Sicily. It was the "most daring act of the age," said Horatio Nelson, who would have known.[45]

This classic commando strike offered exemplary preparation — detailed operational intelligence (about *Philadelphia*'s mooring), a special means of delivery (a small vessel turned into a concealed troop carrier), as well as of penetration (disguise, language skills, a false flag). Plus, the infiltrators were able to rely on thoroughly coordinated backup when the deed was done. More enduringly for the new nation's reputation, the assault also confirmed that the Republic, like Cromwell and Blake, was not going to put up with tradition-encrusted civility for old times' sake. The United States would use all methods, of which this was a taste.

In September, thirteen volunteers tried to replicate Decatur's piercing of the harbor, using the same ketch, this time rigged as a floating bomb: fifteen thousand pounds of gunpowder, overlaid with 150 cannon shells. A line (or "train") of gunpowder (since fuses were still too quirky for precise timing) was calculated to give the crew fifteen minutes to race away in two fast rowboats before the blast ripped into the pirate fleet at anchor.

A special operation may succeed once: the odds against successful repetition of an undertaking against any remotely competent enemy mount inexorably. Clandestinely escorted almost up to the harbor's mouth, the ketch went in around nine o'clock on the night of the fourth. The Americans on the most closely inshore vessel could dimly discern its movement among the Tripolitan patrol boats. About forty-five minutes later, a volcanic explosion shook the harbor, strong enough to rattle the rigging of American warships well offshore. They waited until dawn, but no one returned. What had happened remains a mystery: an accident; a direct hit on the infiltrators' boat from the shore batteries; or, as the American commodore concluded, the vessel's captain, Richard Somers, had hurled a lantern into his magazine, as he had vowed to do if intercepted.[46] The Tripoli Memorial, America's oldest military monument, stands at the U.S. Naval Academy to honor this sacrifice.

Through the next year, the United States remained at war with the entire North African coast except for Egypt, a more closely held part of the Ottoman Empire. In 1805, negotiations were opened. Simultaneously, William Eaton — already at eighteen a veteran of the Continental Army, thereafter a Dartmouth graduate speaking French and some Italian — undertook the self-conceived and White House–authorized operation that survives in American memory as the Marine Hymn's "shores of Tripoli."

Having some political connections, Eaton had recently served as U.S. consul at Tunis, where he ran up a huge unauthorized government debt to nobly rescue an Italian slave girl. Now he was ostensibly under orders of the navy. He sailed to Cairo with eight marines (out of an entire USMC of five hundred) to begin assembling with promises and a bit of money what in our era is called a long-range penetration group. Also as is common in our time, its purpose was regime change as well as hostage rescue. His land assault against Tripoli became the first U.S. overseas clandestine operation. There were to be no compromising documents showing ties to Jefferson.

The mission was built around a deposed pasha of Tripoli (to be restored to his throne in consideration of a treaty), some artillerymen of various nationalities, Moslem cavalry, assorted Arab street rabble, and an intact troop of thirty-eight competent Greek mercenaries — about four hundred adventurers, camel drivers, and cutthroats in all. An always-prickly subordinate, Eaton — a muscular five-foot-eight with deep-set blue eyes — began going remarkably beyond his remit to appoint himself "commander in chief of land forces." Posing as tourists, the Americans found their reluctant potentate well up the Nile in what is called Upper Egypt. Wearing an inventive home-sewn uniform, Eaton then rallied his motley caravan near the Mediterranean some thirty miles west of Alexandria. Tripoli lay a thousand miles in front of them across parched gullies, ridges, and plains.

Increasingly thirsty, hungry, and quarrelsome, they began to march 520 miles westward through Cyrenaica, the Libyan coastal land that takes its name from the ruined Greek city of Cyrene. Bedouin nomads, who were familiar with this type of unstudied war, would be recruited to offset desertions and expand the group.

From this curiously special force, Eaton distilled a truly elite squad by selecting the best riders and rifle shots as his "special Janissary Unit."[47] Since his service at Tunis, he had developed skill with the scimitar, to an extent only equaled by real Janissaries — and he was ready to demonstrate when quelling mutiny as well as breaking up showdowns among his Moslem and Christian irregulars.

Six disorienting weeks later, this polyglot but determined enterprise made it to the well-fortified Tripolitan port city of Derna. At the head of an assault detachment outnumbered ten to one, Eaton charged the town's southeast walls assisted by a well-timed bombardment from three awaiting U.S. warships. For the first time, the fifteen stars (and stripes) of the American flag were planted in battle on foreign soil. Benghazi, three hundred miles farther west, was to be next, then the city of Tripoli itself. Like Somers, "General" Eaton let it be known he was going to succeed or die.[48] But an utterly unnecessary and all-too-temporary peace agreement was reached in Tripoli between eager U.S. negotiators and a ruling tyrant held by the throat. Eaton was prevented from pulling the Dey off his throne, let alone from subduing the entire region, as he believed was eminently possible were he furnished with enough cash to rent tribal loyalties. His force was compelled to disband, on the very "shores of Tripoli." Betrayal and tragedy followed: the Americans, other Christians, and the tame pasha were sealifted to Syracuse; the hundreds of Moslem fighters who had rallied to Eaton were left to the mercies of the now secure and vengeful Dey of Tripoli.

Ransom paid for the freedom of *Philadelphia*'s brutalized crew was rationalized as humanitarian necessity. Decatur would be back with U.S. gunboats in 1815 to again deal with the menace, thereby encouraging a British fleet of eighteen battleships the following year, backed by a smaller Dutch squadron, to shatter Algiers and its pirate vessels, and to send a terrible signal to Tunis, Tripoli, and Morocco, before the North Africans renounced Christian slavery forever. Without libeling the Barbary Coast's most respected calling, or taking away from the British thrust, we might regard Jefferson, in his Age of Reason optimism, as at least having initiated the opening U.S. response to international terrorism, and in a way that enabled the U.S. Navy to launch two undeniably extreme, well-coordinated, and at least militarily effective missions.

‡

IN EATON's march we see the precursor of a host of nineteenth-century colonial ventures in Africa, Asia, and the American West: rapid improvisation by bands of skilled, disciplined men far removed from backup and constituted authority, overcoming harsh environments (mapping them for the first time in the process), recruiting local allies when needed, and compelled to go in for the kill because they lack the numbers to exact attrition or impose piecemeal occupation. What such bands encountered may not have been as otherworldly as the empires of the Aztecs and Incas, but the numbers they deployed were frequently less even than Cortés's or Pizarro's original companies.

These adventures are also a step up from Clive's, and closer to the special operation of today. Clive had worked in India for years as part of a more or less enduring British presence, with the organization, muscle, and plain experience of the East India Company lending him a certain weight. With fewer marines than nowadays patrolling the main gate at the Washington Navy Yard, Eaton had to improvise from the ground up. It was one more headlong stretch in a life that, after the Revolution, had climbed from being an infiltrator under "Mad" Anthony Wayne (a good master for such technique) in the Indian wars of the early Republic, to court-martial, diplomacy, and to practically overnight recruiting the strangest of people to lead across a coastal wilderness. Except, unsurprisingly, for Jefferson, it was all a bit beyond the imagination of higher authorities, which is precisely the realm in which the special operator thrives.

Yet the United States themselves remained fragile, particularly to this type of disruption. The largest republic in history lived with an amazing set of contradictions: Puritan New England and the slave South; a frontier expanding away from the earlier American culture of seaports; weeks being required to communicate among the states.

A brilliant political tactician with formative experience in small-unit operations — a man able to see possibilities in these fissures that others did not — just might be able to hive off a chunk of the continent for himself and a few friends. In the back of beyond, empires could be juggled if one could command a relative handful of rough cases holding only notional allegiances to a national government merely sixteen years old since the arrival of its constitution.

At the same time that Eaton was on his trek in 1805, Aaron Burr began heading west. He was in the mold of Arnold and Alcibiades, but with the political standing of having just stepped down as the vice president of the United States. First with Arnold in Canada, then as a lieutenant colonel of New Jersey horsemen "fighting Indian-style" against the British through the wild forests around Paramus, he had cut his teeth on a way of war well suited to the frontier, confronting larger, less nimble forces of a distant power. Jefferson's restless imagination was also quite up to seeing the possibilities Burr was envisioning. All that is known for certain is that Burr had some huge plan in mind — whether to invade Spanish territory to make himself emperor of Mexico, or to erect a western sovereignty altogether independent of Washington and Madrid alike. The president could be certain that once Burr made his first move, he would be able to make his second and third extraordinarily fast — with little time for federal authority to react, weeks away from the scene of action. It was utterly believable to Jefferson that the history of North America could be transformed through an adventure no less bold than Arnold's, and every bit as resourcefully led against land much less firmly held.[49]

What was now the American West had undergone fast swaps in Parisian salons and Spanish palaces, the United States ending up with 532 million acres from Bonaparte. But this purchase meant little more than buying acreage on the moon today. (At least we have *seen* all of the moon.) Burr did not have to try to raise an army, nor was there any likelihood of his doing so, or really any need in such terrain. On one hand, Jefferson would later say that he had never expected Burr to get the support of more than five hundred men, which was about right.[50] On the other, five hundred men joining with Burr might prove more than enough to create some, however speciously, glittering kingdom. It was a time and place when one temperament like Burr's, so open to men of unusual talents — men like Eaton, embittered at not being allowed to take Tripoli, and whom Burr tried to recruit in 1806 — might bring off only God knew what. Jefferson was not going to wait to find out. Burr, too, understood whom he was dealing with and, before his arrest in present-day Alabama, feared assassination by that frighteningly intense genius in the muddy community that was by then called Washington.[51]

Burr would be acquitted of treason by the end of 1807, though left in disgrace following the most celebrated trial of the early republic. He had made his move too early. Had he waited five or six years, until America had been swept into the vortex of Bonaparte's wars, such a small, determined operation would have enjoyed gigantically multiplied chances of success. Instead, the United States would be left to expand into the most fruitful river basin in the world, having faced down the special forces elements that, a generation earlier during the Revolution, had helped bring about this unprecedented nation in the first place.

11

The Fate of Glory

Special Operations in the Biggest War Yet: The French Revolution and Its Aftermaths, 1789–1830

"From this place and this day forth commences a new era in the world's history, and you can all say that you were present at its birth."

GOETHE TO YOUNG GERMAN OFFICERS THE NIGHT AFTER THE FIRST SUCCESS OF FRANCE'S REVOLUTIONARY ARMIES

THE CITIZEN resourcefulness so recently seen in an almost empty continent across the Atlantic now appeared not only on Europe's battlefields but in Breton woodlands and Tyrolean valleys, along the roads across the harsh Spanish *meseta* and on coastlines where infiltrators could take a boat with muffled oars. Revolutionary passions, however, produced a type of warfare not experienced in North America, or anywhere else that could be remembered. France pushed beyond its national frontiers, driven by ideals of liberating supposedly enslaved nations, consolidating the homeland, and by the less exalted need to restock the treasury.

From below there surfaced a fury that previewed the fanaticisms of the coming two centuries. Now all France's citizens were subject to being requisitioned for national defense: young men to fight, married men to forge weapons and transport supplies, women to make tents and serve in hospitals, old men to be carried to town squares to rail against kings and extol the Republic. It was a vision that sees all one's neighbors as fellow warriors, as well as seeing all the people of one's enemy as targets, once they had been so foolish as not to rally when a new order was proclaimed.[1] This zeal inaugurated the mass armies, complex administration, and megafinancing that France's enemies by necessity had to emulate.

The spirit of the age also drew upon other emerging technologies like the semaphore telegraph and the balloon, each conceived as a technique for war. In 1783, the brothers Montgolfier had already used hot air to send a balloon up to six thousand feet after debating how to outflank impregnable British lines at Gibraltar (Louis XVI's support of American independence having brought Britain to war both with France and with Louis's Bourbon cousins in Spain). Within a dozen years, balloons would be used on the battlefield for observation; another fifty-five (lightspeed in those early industrial days) and the Austrians would employ them to bomb rebellious Venice.[2] From fantasy to operating procedure in a lifetime. It was a portent.

France was the largest country and most populous nation in Europe other than Russia, and it had discovered the ideological and patriotic secrets of raising immense armies. Its most relentless opponent, Britain — a land of traditionally small, disliked armies and a large navy — meanwhile ran up a remarkable list of failures on the continent for more than fifteen years even when fighting alongside the big conventional forces of its allies. It was an appalling record wherever Britain tried, with little effect, to match the French with simple manpower — until it aligned itself with a guerrilla war in Spain that came to bleed Bonaparte's occupation dry. But as its armies rotted from fever or were pushed back to the sea, Britain excelled against the French colossus by small, high-speed insertions and eviscerating surprise attacks enabled by command of the oceans. It also developed to outsized effect the first special operations bureau on record and let loose a handful of extraordinary officers who lifted naval special warfare to new heights made possible by cumbersome French giganticness — Bonaparte eventually to blame one of them (the only man so credited) for altering his entire destiny.

C. S. Forester, creator of Horatio Hornblower, made most of a brilliant career by dramatizing how strategic impact can be achieved with tactical, relatively tiny numbers deployed with imagination and skill — whether remaking Baltic politics, cutting out a mutinous warship deep in enemy waters whose success might unmake the discipline of the whole Royal Navy, or depriving Bonaparte of the margin of victory at Waterloo by raising the French west country. It was art imitating life — and of course magnifying it, given that such things had happened, though not with just one heroic officer. But in the all too real world, as France swallowed the greater part of Europe, minute incisions by rebels, guerrillas, outright special operators, and intelligence agents, including a shady civilian figure who brought about the most consequential security leak in history, cumulatively undermined France as ventures of vastly leveraged malice made war pass from years into decades.

‡

AFTER A fumbling start, the new French Republic was by 1794 able to unleash armies of unprecedented size against Austria (which ruled over what is now Belgium), Spain, Prussia, and an unimpressive British expeditionary effort in the Netherlands. They were commanded overwhelmingly by a galaxy of young talents who would have been lucky to be sergeant-majors under the ancien régime. The startled forces of the old order were struck by seemingly endless columns of hard-charging youths who — at least for a few white-hot years — seem to have thrilled to the urgings of their generals that "only through cold, hunger, filth, and exhaustion could [they] hope to die gloriously for their country," as commander Jean-Baptiste Jourdan is quoted as saying. It was long enough to unravel two coalitions of the great powers that could have stopped any Bourbon in his tracks.

Strength, however, begets resistance, and the worst can make itself felt at home. A century after Louis XIV's dragonnade in the Cévennes, another regime, far richer in manpower, found itself hamstrung by rebellion, on different principles but marshaling similar skills. As France became a "nation in arms," passions blazed up in the country's western regions against the Revolution, ones every bit as implacable as those which at Paris were turning dreams of equality and fraternity into the Reign of Terror. In remote, not always French-speaking Brittany and in the Vendée there arose loosely organized resisters drawing on the resentments of an overall population of more than a million. They were energized by historic hatreds of military service and bitterness at the Republic's suppression of established religion. While Republican battle forces made headway against foreign armies along France's eastern and southern frontiers, they took heavy casualties in the sleepy woods and narrow roads of their own country.

Alienated, loyally Catholic poachers, gamekeepers, peasants, weavers, unschooled countrymen (and thousands of women) led by a few far from religious squires and naval officers with their own agenda, tied down forces desperately needed in the Rhineland and in Flanders. As in the ferocious backcountry fighting we encountered in America, these plain people also elected their leaders, going to and fro between their families and farms. Honoré de Balzac, greatest of the nineteenth-century French novelists, would see the New World parallels and later make his book about this partisan war, *Les Chouans* (the local word for owls, whose call was imitated by smugglers), an explicit homage to Fenimore Cooper.

Unlike the American rebels, these forces never had sufficient guns and ammunition. Nor for all their extraordinary enterprise (such as using the arms of windmills to signal across country) did they take their implacable resistance into the realm of systematic special warfare, fitting into long-term plans or long-range operations, or establishing well-organized ties to a main army. Their key difference from the Americans lay in a tragically parochial perspective. It never occurred to them, at their strongest, to strike outward from the territory in which they were entirely comfortable and directly to the heart of heavily centralized power in Paris. They could dramatize local anger; they could not see themselves as part of a wider war that alone could fully resolve their grievances.

When the insurgents massed themselves into the Grand Royal and Catholic Army, they achieved only momentary success, before getting clobbered by main forces of the Republic. When they resorted to the more rational alternative of blending themselves into the environment from which they were drawn, they played to their strengths. Yet a terrible consequence follows on such effectiveness. The more daunting such fighters prove to be in technique so close to ingenious private murder, the more they inflame their enemies into dropping any civilized restraints.

The passage of spontaneous atrocity into a considered policy of state terror may indeed have been history's "first ideological genocide."[3] A third of the population perished, including the "wolfcubs," whom neutral observers would have called children. Masses of the doomed were made to dig their own graves, then stand within them to be shot, a scene now so familiar from documentaries and newscasts. Paris toyed with exciting plans to use poisonous gases, which were tried out on sheep, but at least that leap into the future proved too awkward, given the technology of the times.[4]

In due course, the central government's unorthodox commander, Lazare Hoche, a former corporal, pioneered a sensible counterguerrilla war of concession and manipulation — along with authentically counterforce, not counterpopulation, procedures. These included establishing strings of compact strongpoints, linked by heavy fighting patrols, while fast-moving, hard-hitting "flying columns" remained under the main commander's hand. His actions proved a point often ignored by more conventional minds: with the right leadership and perspective, the state can be every bit as adept in applying special methods as are the rebels who have the temerity to defy it. But little of Hoche's creative response would be drawn on to confront an even worse guerrilla challenge to come.

The British had backed the insurgents (through half-hearted efforts to supply weapons and, in time, taking some steps as modern as permitting an exile training camp to be organized in Hampshire).[5] In turn, bewildered French troops were landed in Wales during 1797, and, more seriously the following year, in genuinely disaffected Ireland to encourage both Catholics and Presbyterians to revolt. But these forces were conventional, too weak to have much effect. Paris's grander, more ambitious enterprise of 1798 was to send the promising twenty-nine-year-old general Nabulione Buonaparte against Egypt — a first move in his avowed intention to threaten British interests by targeting Syria. If he dominated the Middle East, only Persia stood between him and India.

Americans who feel sentimental toward France as our oldest ally can be dismayed by the glory surrounding the memory of Buonaparte, or "Bonaparte," as he would make himself known, to fit into a France with which he was never really at one. The supreme angel of death in European history between the central Asian invaders and the dark stars of the century just passed, he discharged continuous blinding energy from a lean, perfectly proportioned physique, giving him a commanding presence before which the toughest quailed. The distinguished British historian Correlli Barnett convincingly portrays him as above all a demagogic politician, the effective general being a distant second. (He compares him to a modern "take-over king," which, coming from a Fellow of Churchill College, Cambridge, is unlikely to be a compliment.)[6] Bonaparte's career displays an endless need to keep moving, to achieve quick wins (no matter how unenduring) with an eye to the home front. His bold agility looked impressive, as today do the maneuvering of Wall Streeters who, say, take a leveraged buyout to its extreme. Like those wheeler-dealers, he time and again only escaped disaster by last-moment infusions — in his case, of more bodies rather than of more cash.[7] Yet his compelling qualities remain astounding — phenomenal tactical insight, resourcefulness when cornered, immense administrative grasp — which made it all the more tempting to overreach.

By June 1798 he carried the dilapidated defenses of Alexandria itself, having by simple good fortune evaded the powerful Mediterranean squadron of Admiral Lord Nelson. Within weeks he shattered the charges of brave but medieval Mameluke horsemen in the Battle of the Pyramids outside Cairo, turning muskets and artillery on cavalry that still thought it honorable to close to the sword's point.

Horatio Nelson destroyed the French fleet at the mouth of the Nile ten days later, thereby marooning Bonaparte in his new possession. Marching on the further Ottoman holdings of Palestine and Syria the following winter proved disastrous, as thousands of youngsters from the Morvan or Armagnac perished in his futile siege of Acre, that ancient fortress on a rocky peninsula north of Haifa. Back in Cairo after massacring prisoners and poisoning his own wounded, Bonaparte might declare victory, but few were convinced.[8] A series of crippling special operations — again undertaken by a Britain grown desperate by conventionally accomplishing next to nothing on land — stopped him in his tracks and shunted him in new, ultimately disastrous directions.

A shrewd Royal Navy officer/diplomat/intelligence expert, specifically assigned by handlers in London to remove the French from

Egypt by subtler means, shattered Bonaparte's eastern dreams. In a combination of force and guile, Captain Sidney Smith moved from conducting piercing strikes on France's Atlantic and Channel coasts to become one of the era's most dramatic special warriors. As so often before and since, he was an operator at loggerheads with his uniformed superiors, including Nelson, for appearing to have stretched his authority. But Smith, as an historian of the Royal Navy explains, was "charged with secrets not known to admirals or even cabinet members" — precisely why special operators can drive superiors in their chain of command batty.[9]

Smith had just escaped from the Temple prison in Paris, where he had been cooling his heels under the guillotine's shadow after his ship was boarded during a still-mysterious mission up the Seine — his "servant" at that time being a leading royalist agent in disguise. Now, at thirty-five, he launched into his legend by undertaking what he described to his multilingual liaison officer with the Turks as a host of "our old Chouan practices": forging correspondence and proclamations; recruiting a thousand Balkan mercenaries paid as Royal Marines to bolster Acre's ferocious defense; capturing vital French siege guns en route; using a posse of French royalists (also carried as marines on navy paybooks) to infiltrate Bonaparte's army; finally enabling Bonaparte (for better or worse, the reasons still debated) to slip through the British blockade and to return to the explosive state of affairs in France. Thereafter, it was relatively easy for a British expeditionary force to soon round up the abandoned Army of the Orient.[10]

"With Acre captured, I could have reached Constantinople and India," Bonaparte bitterly reflected in exile. "I could have changed the fate of the world." (To his mind, taking India would have unraveled the British Empire, the stern entity that ultimately did the most to bring him down.) But by blocking him in Syria and subverting his effort overall, relatively tiny intrusions on the ground had deflected his Alexandrine visions for the East. He held one man responsible. "Sidney Smith is a brave officer," Bonaparte would reminisce. "He is active, intelligent, intriguing, and indefatigable." Yet there was another element about Smith that Bonaparte recognized and that has been said about other daring, imaginative operators before and since. "I believe he is half insane," added the head of the profession from the

Thirty Years' War to the present. "Had it not been for that, I would have taken Acre in spite of him."[11]

When Bonaparte used the army to seize power in November 1799, to install himself as First Consul the following month, he enjoyed one powerful advantage over the European old order. It was an era when even George Washington had been uncomfortable with officers who were not sons of gentlemen, when Arthur Wellesley (later to carve the dukedom of Wellington out of his role in Bonaparte's overthrow) loathed meritocracy, believing that an officer not derived from the ruling class might be tempted to turn against it. Yet Bonaparte inherited a system that had opened top command to the best young male talent: sons of a grocer (Massena), a cooper (Ney), a steward (Murat), a mole-catcher (Serurier), a peasant (Lannes), a barber (Bessières), a notary (Bernadotte), a ruined aristocrat (Davout). Equally important, there was an incomparable cadre of junior officers and *sous-offs*. Even the sons of generals found it impossible to enter except through the ranks.[12]

Bonaparte enlarged the classic main battle-force's crack units, the sovereign's household troops, into the Imperial Guard, virtually an army in itself — an elite famed for endurance, for executing the most demanding of orders on the battlefield, though not with an ethos that encouraged the hiving off of commando squads to, say, infiltrate an outlying strongpoint or create chaos in the enemy's rear. It was an elite, but one that moved on well-trod pathways. Nevertheless, Bonaparte understood the effectiveness of having such big stellar formations pressing forward among clouds of self-confident hit-and-run sharpshooters whom he had also inherited from France's brilliantly improvising war leaders of the 1790s. In Egypt, he had put them on horseback.

These *voltigeurs* ("flutterers," who formed the special skirmishing companies attached to each regiment) swayed back and forth along the battle line. Influenced by the tactics of Americans and Indians, they were expected to be able to run considerable distances at the speed of a trotting horse, to seize opportune points of cover, pick off enemy officers, and pump fire into the opponent's cumbersome ranks. We get a sense of their enraging insectlike ubiquity from repeated references to their coming in "swarms."[13] But like the Imperial Guard, they too might be special units with special skills but were not trained to act at long range or to exploit some barely visible weakness. *Voltigeurs* left bloody nicks all over the enemy's hide; they penetrated no vital organ. Tactically, France had developed an elite small force, but that is where it stopped.

Instead, Bonaparte's wizardry was apparent when he took fifty thousand men in May 1800 to fight in Italy by traversing the Great St. Bernard Pass, to emerge behind the unwary Austrians; in beating two emperors deep in enemy territory at Austerlitz in 1805; in crushing the Prussian military machine in a single day at Jena the following year (the Holy Roman Empire by then specifically liquidated). All this thrilled the imaginations of a romantic age. All appears superhuman. But the lightning moves — and murderous losses — were accompanied by repeated, and revealing, breakdowns of his commissariat. Little of Alexander's forethought or meticulous scrutiny of a problem is evident in the self-exalted figure who crowned himself Emperor of the French in 1804.

In contrast, his generals were drawn from the type of men not above delving into grimy details, Murat, for instance, spiritedly disguising himself as a peasant for a spying mission. With those attitudes, one would have thought that the special operation might have been applied more widely. Perhaps part of the reason it was not is that the immense increase of magnitude in all aspects of warfare was consuming the attention of the highest command.

To Bonaparte's top officers, the achievements of speed, cunning, fraud, and spontaneity were most interesting when directly relevant to their ever-larger, ever-further-reaching main forces. Faced with stalemate when deep in enemy territory at Austerlitz in 1805, for example, Marshals Murat and Lannes had no qualms about how to seize the bridge at Spitz. They announced an armistice, put on their dress uniforms for the alleged negotiations, and then rode charmingly among the Austrian forces while their grenadiers sneaked forward to back them up in a sudden rush. This was not work for gentlemen, and it fitted them to a tee. Unlike them, Bonaparte was a military academy man less inclined in such ways. The best of artillerists, he used raiders less than did his revolutionary predecessors. He despised guerrilla warfare and anything that smacked of it.

Bonaparte did, however, make one rather medieval exception for a particular kind of special operation: abduction and the killing that went with it — not surprising in a Corsican who traced his ancestry to the vendetta-loving nobility of the tenth century. His interest was encouraged by attempts on his life, like his narrow escape from the first truck-bomb. That was a barrel of explosives charged with fragments of scrap iron in an apparently harmless horse-drawn cart, the killers paying some sad little girl a *sou* to hold the reins. The detonation at a bend in a Paris street nearly changed history as well on Christmas Eve, 1800, as Bonaparte passed in his carriage on the way to the Opéra.

In 1804 — whether for reasons of self-defense, brutal example, or both — he turned on the thirty-two-year-old Duc d'Enghien, a collateral member of the former royal family, in British pay, and imprudently living only seven miles across the border in the independent but cowed German state of Baden. Bonaparte decided on an act of exemplary shock to deter the royalists once and for all. During the night of March 14, as part of a larger operation against counterrevolutionaries, three hundred dragoons and a detail of Gendarmes d'élite crossed the Rhine on rafts, the gendarmes galloping into Baden to seize the duke at 5:00 A.M. D'Enghien was hauled back to the forbidding Château de Vincennes east of Paris, his grave perhaps having been dug before the formalities of a trial. Though not a party to assassination attempts, he was convicted, sentenced, and shot. The royalist assaults promptly stopped, though killing D'Enghien was nonetheless indeed a blunder, to the extent that his youth, high station, and supposed innocence personalized for the courts of Europe the anything-goes ruthlessness they confronted and was one factor in raising another coalition against France.

D'Enghien's fate was just part of a secret war underway. The historian and former operator Alistair Horne discerns in London's efforts "the precursors of modern British intelligence agencies, of the Secret Intelligence Service and the Special Operations Executive of the Second World War," SOE's purpose in 1940 having actually been to direct its eclectic talents to apply throughout occupied Europe what had once been brought against France.[14] Local elections were rigged, attempts made to subvert the Vendée and Brittany, renegades likely backed to assassinate Bonaparte himself — much of it choreographed by an English magistrate out of an office set up, for sake of deniability, in Switzerland. Britain was putting highly specialized political-military operations on a habitual, well-organized basis, whether handling men such as Sidney Smith or supplying money, documentation, training, and swift cross-Channel passage by night. The Scarlet Pimpernel is himself much less a fictional character than a composite of several well-placed daring Englishmen who were busily infiltrating France.[15]

A less incendiary but creepier example of the "special tasks" (as the Soviets would come to call assassination) on the increase is a still-unresolved disappearance five years later. In November 1809, the British envoy to the court of Vienna, a Mr. Bathurst, raced northward across the front of mobilizing French armies to return to Britain, probably to brief his government on Austria's war planning now that the Hapsburgs had again turned on France. Bathurst was traveling light — a sign of extreme urgency in those days — but, between Berlin and Hamburg, had still to pause for his coach to change horses at an inn. The proper young Mr. Bathurst got out of the coach, stretched, strode forward, and was never seen again. (A science-fiction tale of our own day, "He Walked around the Horses," has him stepping into an alternative universe.)[16] Had Bathurst indeed walked through a crack in time, it must have had an opening in Lützen, fifty miles away, where his breeches in fact showed up. Neither his body nor the documents he was carrying were ever found.

Europe was a cauldron of such operations, the acute intelligence gathering that accompany them, and the unusual characters who execute these missions. Bathurst could have been eliminated by any of the players from either side, many of them having furtive ties with an array of people of totally opposed interests. We see one of the most alarming in the Comte d'Antraigues — an early advocate of the French Revolution, thereafter the most dangerous of royalist secret agents, acquiring both Russian and Spanish nationality, drawing salaries from both governments, finally being offered the title of "Director of British Intelligence."[17] And it is he who likely brought about that immensely consequential security leak.

Two years before Bathurst's disappearance, Bonaparte and Czar

Alexander, each suspecting that he could not destroy the other, had met at Tilsit (now in the westernmost region of the Russian Federation, on the Nieman River). The purpose was to make a virtue of necessity by partitioning the civilized world. Part of the deal was that France, slowly outbuilding British naval capacity, could seize the Danish fleet. With that increase of margin, Bonaparte could probably have held the seas long enough to invade — and, given his skills and his army — to conquer Britain. But somehow this tightly held secret reached London, and an amphibious operation bore away the ships of the justly indignant Danes. Everything points to the sinister D'Antraigues, who was serving as an interpreter. Without this foreknowledge, and given the chance of knocking Britain out in 1810 or 1811, Bonaparte would have had no major enemy to his rear when he turned on Russia, which could have granted him the time and the scope to crumple the czardom. The destiny of nations seems truly to have hinged on this escape of two or three pieces of paper.

Such intrigue was undoubtedly a fraction of D'Antraigues's mischief. But his end underlines the ongoing tie between intelligence and secret, messier means of national defense. Five years after Tilsit, three years after Bathurst vanished, a discharged servant murdered the count and his wife in London. In those days, as in ours, "wet work" could indeed be a form of special operation, D'Antraigues falling in a fog of culpability. Bonaparte, Louis XVIII (brother of the guillotined monarch), or British intelligence itself — it was anyone's guess who had "placed" the servant; the flunky conveniently committed suicide within twenty-four hours of extinguishing D'Antraigues's busy career. As happens in this line of work, D'Antraigues possessed "papers" likely to have been highly compromising. The Home Office scooped them up, to be soon examined by the foreign secretary. To such ends, Britain's Foreign Office may still keep as classified several curious files from the Napoleonic wars.[18]

Whereas intelligence, abduction, and assassination have always intertwined themselves with special operations, in the eighteenth and early nineteenth centuries such targeting was by no means as acceptable as it had been several hundred years earlier, or as it is today. At least to officers and gentlemen, the notion of identifying and killing specific opponents lay as far outside decent international conduct as it ever has (which is one reason for the outrage over D'Enghien's death and for the minimal documentation of such moves).[19] Such professional courtesy had seeped in during the Enlightenment. But secret war had its exceptions, and that is where gloves really came off, although the operators employed to "terminate with extreme prejudice," as misguided Green Berets some 160 years later would use the term, were unlikely to have been trained specialists in the art, beyond being adept with the knife or garrote. Those professionalized talents would have to wait to flourish in our day.

☦

BONAPARTE'S CONTINENTAL System attempted to ruin Britain by closing Europe's ports to its shipping. His design encountered the unintended consequences that usually bedevil big ideas of economic warfare. First, it ensured that smuggling got an enormous boost all along the French-dominated coasts of Europe, with even Americans joining in. And when smuggling thrives, the special operation has all the more routes to follow, thanks to dodgy entrepreneurs who are just as pleased to slip people as well as products across wartime borders. Second, to enforce a boycott required Bonaparte to seize and administer every coast in reach.

If a nation dominates the sea, as did Britain once Horatio Nelson shattered the main Franco-Spanish battle fleet off Trafalgar in 1805, it has an option to exploit its enemy's uncertainty as big as his sea-coasts: the more land he occupies, the more points on the periphery where he can be made to feel pain. Nelson, who gave his life at Trafalgar, had been the supreme fleet commander of the age. With Nelson gone, the greatest seaman alive was a very different sort, a captain who accentuated the fraud rather than the force of war, and who was convinced that he could cripple France altogether by small, keenly focused strikes along its coasts and short, sharp operations inland.

Of necessity, navies have been more hospitable to unusual cunning initiative than armies can afford to be. The degree of resourcefulness expected of even junior ship-handlers is often not remotely expected of their peers on land, who at most command companies or perhaps battalions. This is a recurring feature of service life, owing to the complexity and unforgiving quickness of the sailor's tasks and, in earlier days, to being frequently days if not weeks out of contact with the higher direction of the war; moreover, ocean and storm make naval operations even more unpredictable.

Thomas, Lord Cochrane, later tenth Earl of Dundonald, was — in his fighting, technological vision, and sense of the land's vulnerability to the ocean — more than a great captain. His brilliant mind united into a temperament of command to make him the greatest of all special operators by sea. His exploits off and upon the coasts of France and occupied Spain combined the small-force, quick-hitting, imaginative daring of the privateers with the disciplined seamanship of the highly professional Royal Navy. His thrusts were efficiently precise, and he was so careful of the lives of his men as to deserve a reputation to this day as one of the fathers of a new mode of war. But he destroyed no fleets — so unlike Nelson, whose fame still stands against the sky — and Cochrane is barely known to warriors today.

Cochrane is instead more familiar as the model for nearly two hundred years of riveting naval fiction: notably as Frederick Marryat's Captain Savage (Marryat having served with him), Forester's Hornblower, and "Lucky" Jack Aubrey in Patrick O'Brian's novels. He figures also in C. Northcote Parkinson's extensive historical fiction, including *The Fireship* and *Dead Reckoning* — the shrewd academic mocker of bureaucracy (formulator of Parkinson's Law) having appreciated an efficient man. But none of these novels comes close to portraying what was actually achieved.

Cochrane's father had made himself even poorer by indulging in ruinous scientific experiments at his crumbling seat of Culross Abbey, introducing new processes of distilling tar from coal and of manufacturing alkali — which would have made him fortune upon fortune had this fine practical scientist done anything with them. Cochrane's inheritance, other than a gold watch and a muscular six-foot-two-inch frame, was this gift for invention, which he applied on the spot in war: kites with delayed fuses to spread propaganda leaflets over enemy coasts, a form of barbed wire sixty years before its formal invention, a type of manned torpedo. He would be among the first to promote steam power in ships, as well as the screw propeller. And he concocted chilling plans to use fumes of burning sulfur against French naval bases, the crumbling documents being studied by

Churchill during a later war, right before Germany introduced poison gas in 1915.[20]

Cochrane's first command was the converted brig *Speedy,* which shipped out of Port Mahon in May 1800, with ninety-two men and only fourteen small cannon, but still captured fifty ships within a year. The truly legendary engagement of the cruise was with a large Spanish frigate the following May, when he took the offensive at the head of a crew by then reduced to fifty-four men and boys, bumping, firing, shearing off, pulling back against the *Gamo*'s towering sides. Eventually his men scrambled ten feet up to storm the main deck and pull down the Spanish colors to deceive the enemy (their captain having been killed) into the belief that the ship was surrendering.[21] Three hundred and nineteen dazed survivors ended up under hatches, a triumph whose fictional descendant is the taking of what was vulgarly called the *Cacafuego* in O'Brian's *The Far Side of the World.* In the movie *Master and Commander,* it figures as the boarding of the *Acheron.*

The *Speedy* had employed the hardnosed ruse de guerre of hoisting an American flag to delay the first enemy broadside, which would have blown her out of the water before she could close. Cochrane resorted to deception throughout his wild career — painting the *Speedy* to resemble a Danish coastal brig, even finding a Dane to be passed off as a Danish officer; dropping overboard a tub containing a lantern to distract the nighttime chase of his slower vessel; disguising his boarding parties as demons in order to panic superstitious Spanish crews. Above all, his night attacks won him his original reputation; these were a kind of assault never performed or apparently thought of before, because of the perils posed by treacherous coasts in pitch darkness. "In the day time we are usually out of sight of land," he wrote, "with the men fast asleep in their hammocks."[22] Such a combination of cunning, quickness, and midnight hunting wrung from Bonaparte himself Cochrane's historic nickname, the "Sea Wolf."

Cochrane's work was imbued with originality, precision, stealth, speed, and the advantage of using outrageously small numbers against surely impossible (and therefore unexamined) odds. He created a new type of bombship that panicked French vessels into running ashore along the Biscay coast. The effect of these devices, he reminisced, "depended quite as much upon their novelty as engines of war as upon their destructiveness."[23] And that is the point relevant to special operations — relatively minute, often improvised, deadly new efficiencies that bring chaos to an unsuspecting opponent.

By 1808 Bonaparte attempted to overrun Portugal in order to tighten his trade blockade of Britain — which meant deceiving his ally Spain into permitting a French army to pass through. When he installed one of his brothers on the throne in Madrid, revolt broke out, the insurgents appealing to London for assistance. For ten generations the Iberian peoples had fallen in supposedly holy conquest upon the world from Manila and Angola to Mexico and Brazil. Now they were returning to the medieval predicament of having their lands torn apart by foreign troops. But they would make the incomers pay. Bonaparte would lament that the "Spanish ulcer" ultimately destroyed him, as it would more literally destroy around a million people over the next six years.

With Britain controlling the Mediterranean, Cochrane was ordered to assist his very recent enemies, focusing on Catalonia, that northeastern region having quickly been overrun by the French. To incite an uprising in its principal seaport of Barcelona, only a hundred miles from the French border, was too obvious, too unlikely to pay off. Instead, Cochrane and his men slipped ashore to instruct guerrillas, supply crucial engineering skills in the blowing up of bridges and in ruining the coastal road connecting Barcelona with France (forcing the French to swing inland into terrain that made them even more susceptible to the attentions of guerrillas), and, throughout, leveraging the talents of the type of tough people who had fought the Moors on the outposts of Christendom.

In time, Cochrane moved against Barcelona itself, to show the flag to the civil population and to alarm the French garrison. Throughout, there was the leveraging of guerrillas, so common to the special operator. He struck the coastal fort of Mongat, combining a landward assault by Catalan allies with amphibious assaults by British seamen and marines. As eight hundred Catalans rushed a key position guarding the harbor, his landing parties wrecked the road by which French reinforcements could arrive — the terrified garrison surrendering to the British and being evacuated by sea rather than being exposed to rightly dreaded guerrilla vengeance.

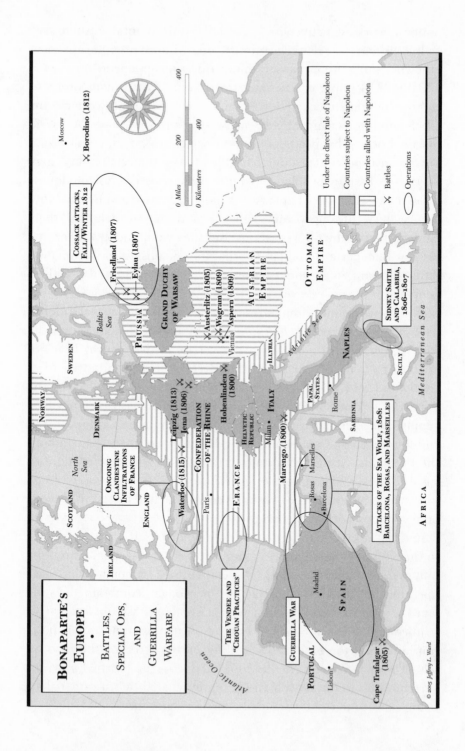

BONAPARTE'S EUROPE

BATTLES, SPECIAL OPS, AND GUERRILLA WARFARE

Under the direct rule of Napoleon
Countries subject to Napoleon
Countries allied with Napoleon
✗ Battles
◯ Operations

0 Miles 200 400
0 Kilometers 400

COSSACK ATTACKS, FALL/WINTER 1812

Moscow
✗ Borodino (1812)

✗ Friedland (1807)
✗ Eylau (1807)

NORWAY
SWEDEN
DENMARK
North Sea
Baltic Sea
SCOTLAND
IRELAND
ENGLAND

ONGOING CLANDESTINE INFILTRATIONS OF FRANCE

PRUSSIA
GRAND DUCHY OF WARSAW

✗ Leipzig (1813)
✗ Jena (1806)
Waterloo (1815) ✗
CONFEDERATION OF THE RHINE
Hohenlinden ✗ (1800)

✗ Austerlitz (1805)
✗ Wagram (1809)
Vienna Aspern (1809)

AUSTRIAN EMPIRE

THE VENDEE AND "CHOUAN PRACTICES"

Paris •
FRANCE

HELVETIC REPUBLIC
Milan • ITALY
✗ Marengo (1800)

ILLYRIA

Adriatic Sea

OTTOMAN EMPIRE

Atlantic Ocean

PORTUGAL
Lisbon •

GUERRILLA WAR

Madrid •
SPAIN

Barcelona •
Rosas •
Marseilles •

ATTACKS OF THE SEA WOLF, 1808: BARCELONA, ROSAS, AND MARSEILLES

PAPAL STATES
Rome •
SARDINIA

NAPLES

SICILY

SIDNEY SMITH AND CALABRIA, 1806–1807

✗ Cape Trafalgar (1805)

AFRICA

Mediterranean Sea

© 2005 Jeffrey L. Ward

The French had recently deployed a visual telegraph system of giant semaphore towers that now carried the most urgent communications of the empire. Discerning that targeting these towers could unstring the French coastal convoys while denying the French command any knowledge of British ship movements, Cochrane took them out in raids between Perpignan and Marseille in summer 1808. But the stations were by no means always easy, unprotected targets, instead having frequently been installed near shore batteries and garrisons. To hit them required night raids by marine commando detachments set ashore by small boats, not only to destroy the stations but to spike cannon and blow up barracks. The boats mounted nine-pound guns to cover retreat against cavalry galloping up too late for anything but reprisal. Cochrane led these raids himself, along with his officers. No other naval officer of the age had so envisioned the light-like-a-butterfly, sting-like-a-bee possibilities of seaborne action against land communications. "It is wonderful what an amount of terrorism a small frigate is able to inspire on an enemy's coast," he would observe. "For real effect I would prefer a score or two of small vessels well-handled to any fleet of line-of-battle ships."[24]

Cochrane's night raids captured not the semaphore stations only, but their signal books. He intentionally would leave charred papers behind amid havoc wrought by fire and gunpowder, as if the books had perished with everything else. But it was a feint; the codes themselves were carried away and dispatched to the commander in chief, Mediterranean, whose frigates could then read ruinous information from the semaphores still standing — both about what the French knew regarding the whereabouts of British ships and about the location of their own. It never occurred to the French to alter their codes, since it was so apparent that this pirate firebrand had lacked the sophistication to commit more than arson when treasures of information lay before him. It took a long time before the higher management of war could believe that special operators were more than oafs who had somehow missed being born into the criminal classes.

In corrupting such newfangled communications (ones nearly instantaneous for the time), Cochrane was seeing additional possibilities that the conventional warriors missed. With eminent sense, he conceived of raiding operations as assaults to maximize assets destroyed, not enemy killed. Better the efficiencies of the special operator against the larger enemy system, he realized, than just adding up body count. But tellingly, Cochrane never received command of a squadron from his superiors. Throughout, he performed independently from the fleet, only occasionally encountering a like-minded captain, working with whom he would be able to increase the scope of his actions and hack away at the tentacles of that system. By November 1808, he had returned to interdicting enemy use of the coastal road to Barcelona, this time by recasting himself as a garrison commander. On the border, the town of Rosas was the key to this route — dominated by a citadel and a massive fort whose walls towered 50 feet above steep seacliffs, while behind the walls rose a bastion of another 30 or 40 feet, crowned with a tower about 110 feet high, a memorable structure altogether resembling a cathedral turned fortress. Both strongholds were for the moment in the hands of Catalan patriots, but six thousand French reinforcements were on the way.

Two British captains senior to Cochrane had dismissed the prospect of aiding the Catalan holdouts as illusory before he nonetheless sailed the *Impérieuse* into Rosas Bay. Coming close inshore, he first used a broadside from his thirty-eight-gun ship to rake the besiegers already gathered before the citadel. Then he was rowed ashore for reconnaissance, entering the fort from the seaward side at the head of fifty sailors and marines. Working with the Catalans and about fifty Irish Catholic exiles in Spanish service, he made this awe-inspiring bastion nearly impregnable: by hideously entangling a breach with linked chains salted with fishhooks; constructing what he called a "huge wooden case" above a deep pit as a mantrap; suspending live shells of grapeshot from ropes against the outer walls.[25]

The reinforced French captured first the town, then the citadel, finally turning against the fort. In the furious assault that followed, scaling ladders were raised but flung desperately down, laden with men; bodies piled up at the foot of the walls. The French retreated, to regroup as their artillery and sharpshooters blistered the ground outside. Cochrane routinely made such near-suicidal defiances as venturing from the fort with several young officers to nobly (and insouciantly) bury the French dead, then, once the French and their deadly Swiss snipers began firing on the burial detail, ordering his men to run back to the citadel while he followed them very, *very* slowly through a shower of musket and rifle balls, "a funereal pace after the funeral was over," recalled Midshipman Marryat, the future novelist and short-story writer.[26] Such seemingly casual conduct confers a sort of warlock authority on those leaders who survive.

Further resistance would have been pointless against what, with reinforcements, was building up into an entire army, so Cochrane decided to evacuate the fort under cover of the *Imperieuse*'s guns, strengthened by those of two other frigates, the only way out by now being a rope ladder to the boats on the beach below. First went the Catalans (who had, he explained, served longest in the fort), then the Irish, then Cochrane's sailors and marines. Although a Royal Navy captain, he and a gunner were the only men to remain as the French surged forward. But he had set powder kegs to blow the fort sky-high, and now he lit the kegs' ten-minute trains as he and the gunner slid down the rope, jumped into the last boat, and were rowed fast to the *Impérieuse*. Up went the charges as the French poured in.[27]

Cochrane had held out with a polyglot outfit of at least three nationalities for two weeks against an increasingly superior foe — while incurring only six casualties. His feat stands as one of the most extraordinary combined operations on record, and by an officer trained exclusively for war at sea. Not that the admiralty was impressed, although the fleet commander sent dispatch after dispatch to London, reiterating what was no more than the truth, that "his resources for every exigency have no end."[28] And here is summed up the role of leadership in special operations forces: little landing parties along the Mediterranean without Cochrane's deadly mind to guide them would have been just little landing parties, scragged regularly by the French.

It was Sir Walter Scott whose novels taught the Western world that the past was truly a different country, with immense consequences for politics and law, as well as for scholarship and literature. And it was Scott, too, whose great family had spent centuries plundering England and being plundered in its turn, who introduced into the English language the unhappily indispensable word *raid*. By the time he made that term well known, his countryman Cochrane had given it amazingly practical meaning on half a dozen enemy-held coasts.

But *raid* is a word of the land, not of the sea. It derives from *ride* or *reiving*. For a ship captain to embark repeatedly on such descents was regarded as the indulgences of a local hotshot, as more than a few in the admiralty were concluding. So much that Cochrane did or envisioned — from needlelike commando assault to weapons of mass destruction — had to be reinvented in another bloody century. As for his brother officer Sidney Smith, his form of terror was to fight along the coasts of Calabria with ships and small craft, bringing muskets and shot to mountain guerrillas — then going on characteristically to combine gumption, decency, and romance by creating a little group he called the Society of Knights Liberators, which pushed for the 1816 showdown with the white slavers of Barbary.

‡

WHAT ALSO stands out in the Peninsular War (as the struggle consuming Spain and Portugal was simply known) were the ways it was being fought inland. There we encounter two dramatic developments on some of the least hospitable terrain of Western Europe: British rifle regiments, with their autonomous small-force deployments and cultivation of initiative among junior officers; and the role of guerrillas, so significant that the word spread to Latin American upheavals and then entered English.

The British dispatched an expedition to back their traditional but feeble Portuguese ally in 1808, beginning a long series of seesawing campaigns. The army that Sir Arthur Wellesley would quickly come to command never had more than forty thousand troops, with perhaps half as many Portuguese allies and what there were of useful soldiers from Spain. On the other hand, Bonaparte's forces never fell below two hundred thousand, but the web of rivalries and open hatreds among his marshals nullified much of this advantage.

Young Colonel Wellesley had served in the Low Countries at the outset of war against Revolutionary France, then spread his wings in India where, from 1794 to 1805, he fought under his eldest brother, who had succeeded Lord Cornwallis (fresh from Yorktown) as governor general. The fifth son of an earl who was a professor of music (meaning a practically penniless aristocratic Anglo-Irish colonial family), he was known for a warm heart as a youth but increasingly became a cold, enclosed, frighteningly strong-willed careerist. "Do the business of the day in the day," he would say, which was impressive, considering what was on his plate when conquering large parts of India and then pressing his way through Spain.[29]

On the peninsula, his grim common sense could see that some newly applied approaches were imperative to parry a much bigger foe. At hand was a corps of riflemen clothed in dark green, its soldiers expected to be intelligent individual marksmen, "trained to act in separation to a common purpose." They had been raised in 1800 as a countermeasure to Bonaparte's shock tactics, based on his sudden use of overwhelming numbers of diehards. At the time, the army's only other rifle regiment was the 60th Royal Americans (later the King's Royal Rifle Corps), which had been created in 1755 to confront the marksmanship of French Canadian backwoodsmen: this new outfit was more sharply honed. Their officers boasted they were deploying "the thinking fighting man," soldiers who excelled in isolated, fast-moving groups that could contest rough country inaccessible to cavalry.[30] These type of men did not need the comforting reassurance of regimental colors and tradition.

On the peninsula, they provided reconnaissance, conducted night attacks, covered retreats, and would engage swarms of *voltigeurs*. The emphasis on two-way trust between officers and men, and on initiative down to the smallest subunit, combined into the vision of a new weapon and a new role; this was another step toward the modern special force, though still in the form of a regular army regiment. Yet there were limits to how far the "new" could go in the British army of the time, especially where it came to opening the path to talent. As for sappers who were similarly innovative and specialized, such miners and engineers were the type of people to be disdained by their betters as "all mad, married, or Methodist" — meaning wonks, risk averse, or lower middle class. No encouraging military culture for the commando.

In Spain — "where small armies are cut up, and big armies starve" — the polar opposite of Britain's disciplined light forces, and the determined forlorn hopes that so often sprang from them, was the guerrilla. This most famous of all guerrilla wars has been studied ever since by strategists, at staff colleges, and even compared to Russia's late twentieth-century debacle in Afghanistan to show "what can be accomplished by arming a people."[31]

Our interest in this horror, as in the previous guerrilla fighting we have discussed, is what the guerrilla of a particular time and place reveals about special operations warfare, a more sophisticated form of combat. Up to fifty thousand Spanish guerrillas accounted for about 145,000 dead over these years, a staggeringly painful drain of roughly eighty men killed a day, 10 percent of Bonaparte's army of occupation a year.[32] In a country six times the size of South Carolina, they caused extreme disruption — ambushing couriers, setting supply wagons and food caches afire, compelling the French to put ever more heavy escorts on convoys — by fighting in many ways so similar to the enduring tactics of commandos. Not surprisingly, Bonaparte's bravest officers were shaken by the ferocity, as chronicled in their memoirs; this was terribly different from, say, being at war with the Germans, "to whom it never occurred to attack a French messenger."[33]

The French responded by offering fruitless amnesties, bribing turncoats to track other guerrillas, and conducting countless bloody sweeps of guerrilla-ridden high country — which, of course, raised comparable numbers of new opponents. France's ambassador may have declared that guerrilla terror required "special treatment" at the hands of "units set up for this sort of service."[34] But it is curious that the French never applied focused, mobile, longer-range deadly operations, that they could not repeat Paris's ultimate success in the Vendée barely ten years earlier, or come up with an answer as ruthlessly precise as the not-so-long-ago use of dragonnades in the Cévennes.

Probably the key reason for no special counterforce being developed against the guerrillas (even after they bragged that they had sawed one French officer in half and boiled another in oil) was that, by 1809, Bonaparte's officer corps was thinned out of the type of smart, fearless twenty-five-year-olds who could lead in the back of beyond, who are the indispensable cadre of such formations. Such hard-charging types were needed for main battles insofar as by this time Bonaparte had drawn down terribly both on his overall talent bank and on his individual genius, not least by the very invasion of Spain. The ever fewer such talents coming to his armies were more than badly stretched for conventional operations and could not be bled further in order to pioneer special ones. Since success in the Vendée, after all, France (with a population little more than that of

Texas today) had suffered at least half a million fatalities in its apparently never-ending wars. Another reason for such failures of counterinsurgency (as we will see in Vietnam) is that promotions in Bonaparte's armies were granted for bravery in big-picture battlefield combat, not for small, barely visible actions requiring patience and political sense.[35]

The other interesting question — and one recently canvassed by historians — is whether at least some of these brave, terrain-wise bands that fought the "little war" (the meaning of "guerrilla") could have been better used as actual soldiers by the allies joined against Bonaparte. These banditlike rabbles enjoyed much closer ties to military and civil authorities than has generally been understood. And the guerrillas deployed only a fraction of their potential to effect, even when supplied by the British. But this does not mean that any of these diverse outfits could have been cast as soldiers, let alone been raised to the hypercapacities of commandos. Nor were these people likely to follow the ongoing leadership of some beef-fed British heretic, however skilled, had any been plunked into their midst in the interior as a nineteenth-century version of a Green Beret "foreign internal defense" adviser.

The guerrillas were racked by different motives and identities — mountaineers who suspected (or hated) anyone from more than ten miles away; lowland peasants smoldering with anger at watching their children starve; bandits pure and simple, whose horizons were enlarged by greater traffic on the roads. Yes, among them were also to be found former army officers now severed from disintegrated commands, as well as the never-resting smugglers whom at least one French general believed were the bedrock of the entire resistance.[36] But these were not people open to wider cooperation. What Cochrane had been able to achieve on the Catalan coast and Smith in Calabria, with guerrillas, was short-lived and rare.

Although more Frenchmen died in Spain than in Bonaparte's June 1812 invasion of Russia, thanks largely to the guerrillas, it was this latter demented overreach that was the beginning of the end.[37] Well-populated France could also drag to the front ever more bodies from the dazed satellites it dignified with the title of allies. If Spain proved an ulcer for Bonaparte, Russia was a slash across his throat as probably the largest army in history to date followed him east only to disappear into the heat, and then the cold and dark. Stendhal (Commissioner of War Supplies during the retreat from Moscow) would later provide grisly details of men sucking their own blood, eating their own severed fingers. But it is Tolstoy who best presents the invasion as disordered slaughter. Death is as random as a road accident; Prince Andrew's regiment at Borodino, for instance, not even firing a shot or moving from where it stood, yet losing a third of its men to French shellbursts. This is war about as far removed as we can get from the piercing and purposeful special operation.

By December, a fraction of the six hundred thousand or so men who had entered Russia emerged in any semblance of military order. Stragglers followed, the entire retreat having been tormented by Cossacks, the "special operations forces" of the Russian cavalry, as described by a prominent descendant.[38] (The French referred to Cossacks as vultures of the battlefield.) Like Arnold trekking into Canada, Bonaparte had expected his adventure to be all over in twenty days.

In burning their towns and villages as the French advanced into Moscow, and then in picking up the cudgel of well-directed, professionally led guerrilla action as they withdrew, the Russians had thrown away what rules there were in war for killing people. It is a point Tolstoy makes explicit and that Stalin, 130 years later, would hark back to in repelling the Nazi invader.

Bonaparte finally turned up in Paris on December 18. He had abandoned his army nearly two weeks earlier to rush back soon after learning that his grossly overcentralized state — one in which, for instance, he had just personally reorganized the Comédie Française from the Kremlin, and in which authority hinged on a capital city from which he was weeks out of touch — had nearly been snatched away from him by a focused, tightly knit coup. (A dozen men performed a superb bluff in the heart of power, led by a general who had just broken out of a lunatic asylum.)[39] Once in Paris, Bonaparte astoundingly began to raise three hundred thousand more men. Yet all of Europe smelled blood. The Allies would be parading down the Champs-Élysées by late March 1814, with the emperor soon exiled to preside over the tiny Mediterranean island of Elba. When he slipped back to France a year later to rally the army once more in his cunning use of mystique and daring, events came full circle. The inheritor and subverter of the Revolution, the ultimate practitioner of mass war, found his hope of victory at Waterloo lost to revived insurrection in the Vendée and Brittany, where he had diverted seventy-five thousand men.[40] The remaining six years of his life were spent on St. Helena, a bleak, windswept island in the south Atlantic, which is where he reflected on Smith and what could have been.

‡

BONAPARTE'S WARS — particularly the devastation of the peninsula and the economic blockades reciprocatingly imposed by France and Britain, and in due course by the enraged United States — reverberated in the Americas, bringing the Republic into war with Britain to defend freedom of the seas. Those wars also precipitated revolution in South America against Spanish and Portuguese authority. President Madison and the congressional war hawks counted on Britain's being tied down by Bonaparte, which to an extent it was, although not sufficiently so as to prevent it upending U.S. ambitions against Canada at the very outset, as well as to limit the extravagant hopes of privateers.[41] The war declared exactly three years before Waterloo was at best a draw. An invasion of British settlements along the Detroit and the Niagara Rivers was dashed, the familiar route through New York and down the Richelieu to Quebec and Montreal being impractical because of New England's anger over the war and with much else out of Washington. The British and their Shawnee allies under Tecumseh then took Forts Detroit and Mackinac before American victories afloat on the Great Lakes in 1813 — to be followed through in Canada by forces under William Henry Harrison, with his mounted Kentucky Riflemen known as the "Forlorn Hope" — helped even matters up.

Significantly for us, backcountry fighting was here a business for line troops. The Americans barely used rangers in this war, although Congress authorized six companies to protect settlers from Indian raids on the frontier and (despite regarding them as an extravagance) would call on rangers again twenty years later in the Black Hawk War. Yet against the British, scouting and raiding operations by frontiersmen were poorly coordinated, compared to those of the Revolution. Why? Perhaps, in part, because Americans, at least along the coast, had come to regard themselves as part of an established, re-spectable member of the family of nations, with a correspondingly respectable army. Not that there was much to that army, which had been oozing to the sclerotic, as seen in the loss of nerve by faded eld-erly generals such as William Hull at Detroit, and by the besotted James Wilkinson, the one man to be the senior general in the U.S. Army while in foreign pay (Spain's "Number 7").

Humiliating American reversals — yet without a strategic setback — compelled the resurrection of radical methods in the form of small-boat amphibious operations and the deadly individualist riflemen and unconventional warriors (Baratarian pirates, free blacks under black officers, a band of Choctaw Indians) who won under Andrew Jackson at New Orleans in January 1815. But it may be the British who took the biggest step in the creative use of talent for small, hard-hitting, well-prepared operations. Once the war had wound along the southern coasts and into the hinterlands of Wash-ington and Baltimore, London secretly but explicitly forbade its com-manders to incite slave revolts. No one was up for that form of warfare, as the French had accused the British of doing in the "exter-minating war" just passed in Haiti.[42]

Instead, the British raised three very special companies into the Corps of Colonial Marines, a disciplined, well-trained body of fugi-tive black Americans transformed into fearsome sea soldiers. Escaped slaves (deemed to be free as a measure of war rather than of idealism if they could reach British ships and posts) were recruited into the invaders' service from Georgia, Maryland, and Virginia.[43] Initially sent in pennypackets to serve as guides to landing parties and pilots to British warships, they developed into a solid fighting unit, their spirited first sergeants leading bands of scouts and skirmishers. These were truly amphibious troops precisely suited to hit-and-run assaults along the Atlantic coast, men who also saw action in the cap-ture of Washington and the *Star-Spangled Banner* attack on Balti-more. Come the peace, they and what families they had with them were evacuated, mostly to Trinidad, where their descendants in the south of the island are still known as "the Merikens."[44]

And where, during most of this time, was the world's greatest of special operators? While Britain was still at war with France and, after 1812, with the United States, the thirty-nine-year-old Cochrane, its most unconventional of warriors, had been cashiered from the navy and lay in prison for a bold, simple, clever stock-market hoax. His accusers insisted that his raid on the market — the Victory Fraud of 1814 — was all too much in character with his famous ways of fighting, replete with ruses, disguise, subverting communications, and haunted by curious associates aplenty.

An undertaking as elaborate as this fraud, let alone during wartime, was unprecedented. People whispering in corners, forming cabals, or bribing one another had previously been the means of manipulating markets. Now the financial center of Europe was struck by a scheme of inordinate imagination. The drama reflects the growing vulnerability of another, newer, impersonalized form of centralization, a system that was geared to put a premium on suddenly accumulated knowledge and fast response, and that was made to react uncritically to suitably emphatic input, whether of goodwill or malice.

The fraud involved a bogus report of Bonaparte's death at the hands of Cossacks. (Then as today, welcome political news could boost stock markets.) A laurel-decked post-chaise raced over London Bridge to authenticate the news, carrying three putative French officers conspicuously displaying the white cockades of the Bourbons in their hats. False rumors delivered fortunes to a clique of insiders at Omnium (a name that today could have been pulled off the listings on the NASDAQ, and a company in which Cochrane was an investor) who had bought low and sold high — "the practice in all countries ever since stock-jobbing began," he recalled sardonically.[45] National defense was impacted (a reason for the Crown's fury), since a prime immediate consequence was the flareup and fall of government securities.[46]

It took an original mindset to see such fundamental weakness in a financial system, a remarkable temperament to carry it out — and a still more unusual one to bring others onboard to share the risks and, theoretically, the rewards. Given the perspective of two centuries, an argument can be made that Cochrane was guilty of nothing more than surprising credulity and of having created a few too many resentments, in no small part due to radical political views he found time to share in Parliament with the raucous Major General Banastre Tarleton. Indeed, those who defended Cochrane insisted that the damning mistakes involved in the fraud's execution were utterly contrary to the precision of his wartime planning. But he certainly understood the compressed vulnerabilities of a nation — and of its finances — as it grew more complex, points that he argued publicly.[47] Such experiences were making it all too clear how devastatingly resourceful operators of very different stripes and motives could turn their talents on advanced civil society, whether in London or Paris. Luckily for the developed world of the time, from here on Cochrane's talents would be applied on the rim.

Once released from a punishment cell (into which he was thrown after an astoundingly acrobatic jailbreak), Cochrane turned down a lucrative offer from the Spanish navy, to put himself instead at the disposal of national liberation in South America. Beginning as Admiral of Chile, then of Peru, and using a similarly tall, tough, and humane twenty-three-year-old major of Royal Marines as his right-hand man, he embarked on seven years of what a biographer styles "commando operations" that gave the deathblow to both Spanish and Portuguese naval power in that quarter of the globe.[48] Most anything seemed believable to the world when it came to Cochrane's skills as a raider — including a rumor that he intended to spring Bonaparte from exile on St. Helena.[49] The masterpiece in fact came at the end of his time in the New World, as First Admiral of Brazil. In the one fleet action of his life, he threaded his ships at night through a supposedly unpassable channel at Maranaho, thereby demoralizing and going on to beat a far stronger force of thirteen Portuguese warships by conveying an impression of uncanny power — not least by letting a captured enemy officer "overhear" some of Cochrane's people discussing the impending arrival of an imaginary armada and then artfully letting him escape.

Cochrane's last supreme command was as Admiral of Greece, in a massacre-filled, twelve-year war that caught up just about every Western liberal in a wave of philhellenic sentiment before Greece wrung its independence from the Ottomans in 1832. Inspired by the examples of the U.S. and French revolutions, and by the wars of liberation that Cochrane had just helped succeed in Latin America, the

Greeks were conducting their revolution like "pirates" — or so the British foreign secretary weighed the term in deciding whether to back them.[50] Operating from their country's thousands of ports and hundreds of islands, they in fact were more like privateers, as every coastal village fought its own little war for profit and freedom. Turkish commerce and even warships in the Aegean were ravaged in nighttime raids. The most unlikely people joined in with their idiosyncrasies and unconventional methods: Byron dying with the guerrillas at Mesolonghi in 1824; yet another English aristocrat, Richard Abney Hastings, like Cochrane booted out of the Royal Navy, trying to relieve Athens by startlingly entering its harbor with the first steamboat to appear in the eastern Mediterranean; the medical pioneer Samuel Gridley Howe leaving Boston to spend three years organizing the Greek army's medical staff.

The war and its participants spotlight a generation in which an amazing range of dissidents bedeviled governments through half of Europe, from roughly the fall of Bonaparte to the revolutions of 1848.[51] The extolling of untrammeled will that is Romanticism was manifested not only in poetry, painting, music, and sculpture, but in politics and subversion, giving rise to uncountable small, bold enterprises. We see this spirit in the outbursts of nationalism and in such audacities as that of Alexandre Dumas who, armed only with pistols and leading exactly two students, took the arsenal at Soissons in 1830, during the three-day uprising that deposed Charles X, King of France. It requires a lot of imagination to bluff that boldly, and it is no coincidence that Dumas is the author of the first novel plausibly to recount a special operation.[52]

Eighteenth-century elites had seen the years between the peace of 1713 and the fall of the Bastille as the Age of Reason, decades constrained in objectives religious or political and ones more or less stable in social order. Wars also of relatively limited scope had taken a correspondingly tactical view of special undertakings — the capture of a fort, or the cutting out of warships. Except for what was being rehearsed on Europe's colonial fringe, there had been no room for the overthrow of whole governments, of demigods swooping across continents. Then came a time, in Europe as in the Americas, when exceptional men were expected to embrace the exceptional opportunities that were breaking through the smooth walls of eighteenth-century order — first an obscure Virginia squire to become the most famous man in the world, then catastrophically a penniless Corsican with Europe at his feet to make into family kingdoms, a marshal's baton in every foot-soldier's knapsack, but also operators such as Cochrane and Smith, Eaton and Burr. It was not just fitting but natural that Dumas should single-handedly capture an entire arsenal in romantic exaltation.

Chemical and industrial revolutions no less than political ones were adding possibilities that reached even further beyond human vision. ("Soon they will discover how to live forever," reflected Rousseau's mistress, herself an intellectual presence, on seeing the Montgolfiers' balloon over Versailles.) Anything seemed accomplishable if one were daring enough to seize the moment, and to leverage even what minute resources or fleeting chances might be at hand. Some twelve malcontents using elaborate bluff could come within a whisker of seizing France's imperial capital; handfuls of swashbucklers in India might scramble across gold-floored Oriental treasure houses. Great egos and, fittingly, great adventures filled the horizon. Burr might have moved too early, and Bonaparte be driven to overreach, but there was no necessity to their setbacks. Next time someone would get it right.

12

New Frontiers
Where Special Talents Apply: National Revolt and Global Ambition, 1830–1861

> *"Give us Rangers in Texas. . . . They are men who are acquainted with action. They are efficient. They are athletic . . . and they carry with them a spirit that is not to be found in the troops that are generally collected in the regular army."*
> SAM HOUSTON TO THE U.S. SENATE, 1858

AFTER THE convulsions that stretched from Lexington and Concord in 1775 to the elevation of the bourgeois King Louis-Philippe in 1830, continental Europe settled down to a remarkable international, if not always domestic, equilibrium. Between 1815 and 1914, the five canonical great powers of the time (Britain, France, Germany, Austria-Hungary, Russia) were only at war among one another (and never more than three at once), for a total of four years. There were, of course, many smaller wars, and great-power combinations pummeling lesser nations, such as Austria and Russia crushing Hungary's rebellion against the Austrian emperor in 1848–49. But these shootouts rarely exacted high initiative.

In the space of this 1830–61 generation, however, three of the five powers dominating Europe (Britain, France, and Russia), together with the United States, were going all out in territorial expansion: Britain fighting a series of wars from China to Latin America to consolidate its interests; France pursuing ambitions from Vietnam to Mexico, conquering Algeria as a colony and organizing the Foreign

Legion; Russia overrunning Central Asia; the Americans turning themselves into a transcontinental power with the Mexican War.

Armies had no monopoly on this type of work, and, as is so often the case when out on the edge, necessity was the mother of invention — of new types of Rangers; of Guides and of horse regiments; and, ultimately, a largish raiding party in the bleakest part of southern Europe that proved decisive in building a state. On the far frontiers, more often than not, the small unit had to face the violence of nature as well as of combat: ordeals of trekking through hundreds (or thousands) of miles of desert, jungle, prairie, or mountains before even seeing action. Great endurance was the merest price of admission for such ventures, ones for which armies were often unsuited given their slower pace, heavier supplies, and often the requirements of other business. Where armies were used to cement national ambitions, such as on a much shorter trek to the Halls of Montezuma, or when they were dumped on the Black Sea coast, success could hinge on how well they did in adopting unconventional methods. In Mexico, the U.S. Army succeeded with reconnaissance engineers, marines, rangers, amphibious innovation, and bands of spies; the armies of Britain, France, and Russia consumed themselves in the Crimea by solely and ceaselessly smashing into each other head-on.

It is the mark of modernity to get things right not just in light of experience but in the absence of such practical (and often painful) occurrences. And that requires planning ahead for things that have never been done before. During these three decades, that would entail special operations as part and parcel of efforts to expand nations, build others, and organize empires.

‡

THE ALAMO is held in the national memory as that rare American, let alone Texan, event — a glorious defeat. At the time, Mexico — independent for barely two decades — angrily maintained its Spanish-derived claims to much more than present-day Texas. At dawn on March 6, 1836, about 200–250 colonists and U.S. volunteers fought to the death against some twenty-six hundred Mexican troops. In a desperate hour and a half, the little fortress' largest cannon was turned inward by the stormers to blast away men and their last-ditch obstructions, making possible the swift elimination of resistance. Perhaps Davy Crockett did defend the ramparts with clubbed rifle against scores of Mexicans in the old mission's last agony. Perhaps Jim Bowie, so bedridden with fever in the infirmary as to be unable to use his fearsome knife, did empty his pistols into the unstoppable waves before the bayonets pinned him to the floor. But all this was more akin to the final heroics of a Cu Chulainn warring to the death against the sea than of soldiers fulfilling their public duty of harming the enemy. Recklessness had gotten the defenders into this mess in the first place: holding an absurdly too far advanced strongpoint against the orders of General Sam Houston, commander of the Texan army.

The siege at least afforded time for Texas to declare its independence and gave its soldiers (along with the memory of the later massacre of 350 Texans at Goliad) a vengeful battlecry the following month, when they swept the Mexicans away at San Jacinto, in the climactic engagement of the Texas Revolution and the next step to the continent-transforming events of ten years later.

The previous November, Texas's provisional government had authorized the recruitment of a force of twenty-five Rangers, soon increased to three companies of fifty-six men each, built on the example of the paramilitary units — half citizen posse, half cavalry patrol — that had fought Mexicans, bandits, and the Comanche for at least fifteen years. The "Ranging men" skirmished with Mexican troopers as well as Indians foraying over the Rio Grande. Contrary to stereotypes, friendly tribesmen as well as Hispanic volunteers served with the Rangers during much of the brief existence of the Republic of Texas. (Nothing so dictates enlightenment on a predatory frontier as shortage of manpower.) Under the complex militia laws of the United States, the Rangers, as they had come to be called, whatever their official title, were practically the only armed units in Texas that ultimately could be mustered into the U.S. Army for wartime service.

The war declared in May 1846, following Texas's entrance to the Union as the twenty-eighth state, was one of the costliest in U.S. history, in terms of dead among those who served. At the start, as is often forgotten today, it was by no means certain who would prevail. Mexico had the much larger army — thirty thousand regular soldiers, officers well trained in formal warfare, unsurpassed companies of lancers,

peasant recruits used to obeying orders and enduring hardships —
and they would all be fighting on home ground. Facing Mexico were
two conventionally constituted main U.S. forces, mostly composed of
brand-new recruits: a grandly named Army of Occupation, already
positioned on the Rio Grande to defend the southern regions of
Texas; and a more substantial force, which the following year would
march in Cortés's path from the sea to Tenochtitlán, now Mexico City.

Initial exploits underscore the roles of endurance and distance in
special warfare, such as small fighting units surviving two thousand
miles of deserts and mountains en route to California, and the thirty-
five-hundred-mile epic of the Missouri Mounted Volunteers, 856
troopers spurring across northern Mexico in December 1846. Lacking uniforms, pay, or supplies, at their head a little-town lawyer with
no military experience, the volunteers won two small-scale yet sensational victories before emerging on the Gulf Coast the following
June, to be evacuated by steamboat, their exploits riveting the nation.[1]

All the while, the Rangers provided critical assistance to the U.S.
Army as scouts and raiders deep into Mexico, and they were equally
effective in the role of highly irregular light infantry. "Many were
doctors and lawyers," observes a close student of what is today that
elite of 116 law enforcement professionals, "while a notable number
had college degrees" — a reminder both of the strange talents drawn
to special forces, and when college degrees were much rarer than are
Ph.D.s today, that education hardly stands in the way of undeniably
brutal killing capacity.[2] Since this was the first war reported daily,
and more or less accurately, in newspapers, the Rangers also became a
sensation. (Special forces always make good press.)

The Rangers had their own methods of fighting fast and dirty,
adapted from Mexican vaqueros and the Comanche, the latter perhaps being the finest light cavalry in the world. Rangers were specially armed, with the first Colt revolvers. Sixteen had used these in
1844 to successfully attack eighty Indians, who "up to this time,"
according to a captain, "had always supposed themselves superior to
us, man to man, on horse."[3] For good reason, a Ranger preferred to
carry two of these five-shot Colt-Patersons rather than a saber in his
outfit's fierce, high-decibel charges. And, no surprise, they took pride
in flouting military procedures — their encampments, for instance,

Accompanied only by his spaniel, Jim Corbett stalked the man-eaters, which large expeditions of shooter, beaters, and elephants could never destroy during the final years of the Raj. Against the longest of odds, he used stealth and surprise to turn the predator's natural advantages in the deep jungle to his own deadly favor. *Courtesy of Oxford University Press India*

"The sound of struggle roared and rocked the earth," says Homer, as the Greeks fought inconclusive pitched battles on the plains of Troy. Achilles, portrayed here, was the stongest and fiercest of their warriors. Yet it turned out to be Odysseus, the night raider and "man of wiles," who brought down the proud city through his "twists and turns." *Prometheus Imports*

Gideon's destruction of the predatory Midianites is the exemplary tale of the founding of special forces, to be revisited three millennia later during the birth pangs of modern Israel. The Midianites were as numberless "as grasshoppers," says the scribe. Although Gideon had only three hundred warriors, they were carefully sieved and imaginatively led. *CC-Art.com*

Alexander (356–323 B.C.) may have been the greatest of all patrons of special warfare and one of the most effective captains of commando detachments. Some two centuries later, he would be venerated by Rome, as shown by this bust. Caesar, too, revered him, though Caesar usually fought so differently — but not when embroiled in Alexandria's insurgency.

Invading the densely populated Italian peninsula through the Alps, Hannibal spent fifteen years (218–203 B.C.) eviscerating Rome's finest legions. Large-scale force and fraud were combined repeatedly with commando tactics, including infiltration, disguise, ambush and the rallying of indigenous peoples.

The First Crusade would have withered away without the decisive commando assault at Antioch in 1198. (And such an assault brought the misguided Fourth Crusade over the walls of Constantinople two centuries later.) Weary, uniquely toughened warriors walked and rode 2,500 miles to build the Kingdom of Jerusalem, only to encounter years of raiding and assassination, as well as battle.

During 1520–22, thirty-four-year-old Hernán Cortés and several hundred brilliantly led ruffians brought down the Aztecs, one of the world's most advanced civilizations. This ferocious entity of millions possessed a well-organized army in the scores of thousands. How the conquest was possible has long been misunderstood.

Beginning in 1572, Francis Drake's daring night attacks in tiny boats and through jungle, his immense reach with the smallest of units, and his big payoffs epitomize naval special warfare early in the Age of Discovery. Drake's SEAL-like tactics would be applied by pirates and buccaneers on the Spanish Main.

In 1740, Englishman George Anson was appointed commander in chief of a secret mission to sail down the eastern coast of South America and around the Horn to attack Spanish settlements from Chile to Panama. Deprived of adequate supplies and manpower, he invented his own type of war. Few survived, yet the treasure was immense. In contrast to Drake, he was an enlightened, modern leader for impossible missions. *Portrait attributed to Allan Ramsay © National Maritime Museum, London BHC2517*

Robert Rogers (1731–95) is the father of the U.S. Army Rangers and the embodiment of the special operator as a daring outlier in nearly constant friction with a stern military hierarchy. His woodland Indian methods, long-range penetration groups, "Ranging School," and lucid writings also introduced Rogers' Rangers as "the first Green Berets."

Well before the Declaration of Independence, Benedict Arnold was lauded as the "American Hannibal" for his deep-wilderness warfare. Along with the Green Mountain Boys, he took Ticonderoga and then led an epic mission through the northern forests to attack Quebec. His small boats halted the British on Lake Champlain, and it was he who deployed the riflemen and carried the day at the decisive Battles of Saratoga.

After Admiral Horatio Nelson was killed at Trafalgar in 1805, the greatest seaman of the age was an utterly different type of warrior — Lord Thomas Cochrane, the "Sea Wolf," whose night raiding, deadly inventions, coastal incursions to back guerrillas, and use of fraud against towering opponents place him in any pantheon of history's special operators. *P. E. Stroehling © National Maritime Museum, London PU4567*

The "Ranging men," as they were called originally, had skirmished with Mexican lancers and Comanches for fifteen years before the Republic of Texas was founded in 1836. When Texas entered the Union ten years later and war broke out with Mexico, the Texas Rangers were mustered into the U.S. Army, where they excelled at deadly reconnaissance.

Like the Texas Rangers, the young men who fought through northern Virginia with John S. Mosby, the "Gray Ghost" of the Confederacy, looked the part, though these superb horsemen were a step up in military discipline. They too eschewed sabers for revolvers but had no camps, and preferred to strike at night and in foul weather. They demolished the hunter-killer teams sent to run them down.

The British Empire had never confronted such mobile, nearly invisible riflemen who ranged so effectively over a large expanse as these Boer farmer-warriors on the South African veldt. Their hard-hitting, democratic, weather-exploiting units were the original "commandos." Yet the Empire counterpunched fast with its own special formations. *TopPhoto*

Oskar von Niedermayer, shown here in Persian disguise, was one of the young German officers expected to set the Moslem world afire in an anti-colonialist jihad against Britain and France. During World War I, he led his clandestine operators from Turkey through the Great Salt Desert to Kabul, with several spin-off missions, including one against the Royal Navy's oil facilities in the Persian Gulf.

T. E. Lawrence, archeologist as special operator. Two of Lawrence's brothers were consumed on the Western Front, inspiring him to fight a different war by heading advisory groups during the Arab revolt against Ottoman rule. A romanticized figure who carried the *Odyssey* and Mallory's *The Death of Arthur* throughout the campaign, he was further acclaimed by Churchill. *TopPhoto*

David Stirling (1915–90) went from training to climb as-yet unconquered Mount Everest in 1939 to joining the Scots Guards at the outbreak of war and then seguing into the newly constituted Commandos. While in Egypt with this elite force, he formed the nucleus of Britain's Special Air Service (SAS), which he intended to be even smaller and better skilled than Britain's existing unconventional units. "Who Dares Wins" remains the SAS motto. *TopPhoto*

Louis Mountbatten of the Commandos, and of much else. A global entrepreneur of special operations, he reported directly to Churchill and then fostered further small-unit violence while serving as Supreme Allied Commander in Southeast Asia until the end of World War II. Thirty-four years later he fell to IRA terror. *Getty Images*

Gideon goes to (twentieth-century) war. Orde Wingate styled himself after the great Judge, and fought similarly. He was a truly strange man, like more than a few others among the special operators. His Special Night Squads in Palestine during the 1930s, his Gideon Force in the Sudan, and his 9,000-man Special Force in Burma during 1944 attest to the success of this British officer buried at Arlington National cemetery. *TopPhoto*

Recon Team West Virginia in North Vietnamese uniforms. Commando operations during the Vietnam War were undercut by the enduring ignorance and still-unresolved turf quarrels in Washington that plagued the U.S. effort from beginning to end — compounded by the emphasis on hopeless attrition warfare into 1968. The U.S. Army would have much to repair. *Photo courtesy of Ron Knight (rear, center) and John L. Plaster*

Recon Team leader Ben Thompson of the Studies and Observations Group (SOG), a composite elite and secret U.S. unit of the Vietnam War. Army Green Berets, Air Force Air Commandos, and Navy SEALs joined in, along with South Vietnamese commandos. All was way behind the lines, including valuable reconnaissance and targeting of the Ho Chi Minh Trail in Laos and Cambodia. *Photo taken by fellow operator John L. Plaster*

Today the United States possesses the largest, best-equipped, and most varied special operations capacities in the world. Finally the commandos are here to stay as a recognized arm of warfare, and here U.S. operators are shown in Afghanistan. Yet vital questions remain as to how they will be shaped and deployed. *Photos courtesy of Special Forces Association Chapter 79*

said by one annoyed regular officer to resemble "a collection of huts in a Hottentot village."[4]

As war approached, it was California that was becoming what defense planners today delicately call "unstable." Democrats in Washington, including the powerful Missouri senator Thomas Hart Benton and James K. Polk, president since March 1845, saw opportunity; it could be to U.S. advantage should matters destabilize further.

John Frémont was no polished West Pointer but the hungry illegitimate child of a French émigré. He had been fortunate enough to marry Benton's daughter after joining the Army Corps of Topographical Engineers in 1838, and had already headed two surveying expeditions along the Oregon Trail during 1842–44 (the Oregon Territory soon to be carved out of the debatable land of overlapping U.S. and British interests). The year 1845 found him leading ostensibly a third survey, this time into California. Four rebellions had broken out against Mexican authority in the previous dozen years among some only ten thousand white inhabitants. There were even rumors that Mexico might try to sell the whole place to Britain.

Frémont's outfit hardly appeared to be on a scientific quest. His men were mountaineers, soldiers, engineers — each having been issued a Hawken rifle as well as a brace of pistols — and well-armed Delaware Indian scouts; sixty-two horsemen altogether, with no less than Kit Carson as guide. They embarked on their own 2,000-mile adventure, leaving Missouri in June 1845, across to the Great Salt Lake, then over a desert that no one was ever believed to have traversed. The outfit divided, most to enter California from the south while Frémont and fifteen others headed into the Sierras, through the Donner Pass (as the following winter would make it known), to ride down the western slopes in early December, right before the snows fell, eventually to reunite with the southern party near San Jose. Whatever instructions he might have inferred from his father-in-law or the president, Frémont quickly embroiled himself in the violent ambiguities of Californian independence. In February 1846 — months before war was declared — he built a crude log fort on Gavilan Peak outside Monterey, the little white, red-roofed adobe town that was still California's provincial capital, holding it for three days before slipping away from the gathering Mexican forces. He then ventured north, scattering mixed signals of U.S. support to the hunters, trappers, settlers, fugitives, and assorted troublemakers who were uneasily coalescing into the Bear Flag Republic.

Frémont reorganized his men into a "Regiment of Mounted Volunteer Riflemen," essentially taking steps to precipitate a revolution. With the happy arrival of actual war, and Commodore John Stockton's proclamation in August that California was now U.S. territory, he collaborated with the navy's five-ship Pacific Squadron to snatch the quiet little pueblo of Los Angeles. It did not stay quiet for long as its Mexican citizenry rose up. To quell the U.S.-created disorder, sailors from the squadron had to transform themselves into a sort of naval brigade with muskets, carbines, and boarding pikes. California's chaos was ideal for Frémont to fill the role of territorial governor, his Delaware Indians serving as a personal bodyguard. By December, the arrival of the coolly authoritative Colonel Stephen Kearny, the Great Plains explorer and "father of the U.S. Cavalry," would bring Frémont's arrest for insubordination and mutiny in having failed to turn over California despite explicit presidential orders.

The contrast between these two regular U.S. Army officers leading missions similarly extreme reflects the changing times. The impetuous Frémont had the character of a filibuster in Latin America, a daring hothead out of the dime novels that were becoming popular. In Kearny, we are beginning to see the disciplined professional operator hardly preoccupied with fame and money, full of enterprise to be sure, but also with a sense of the limits of his authority. He had already undergone epic ordeals before locking horns with the excitable topographer: pressing down the Santa Fe Trail with his grandly named Army of the West (in fact never more than 1,458 men, mostly the Missouri Volunteers, and 459 horses) to take possession of New Mexico, then (mistakenly believing California to be pacified) pushing on with only a hundred dragoons while the Volunteers headed to Mexico proper. Finally, his expedition made it through the Colorado Desert, to be met by a posse riding in from San Diego, around sixty miles away — insufficient added strength to prevent the exhausted column from getting mauled by awaiting Mexican lancers, in the bloodiest battle of the California campaign.

With a third of his force dead or wounded, Kearny willed himself and his weary command onward despite two ugly spear wounds, trying to keep moving toward the coast for another forty-eight hours before all were trapped. Kit Carson, known to the Mexicans as *El Lobo,* had signed on when he encountered Kearny while racing east with a message from Frémont prematurely announcing victory. He and two volunteers performed the desperately heroic act of sneaking at night barefoot through the cordon of lancers, not even carrying canteens, lest in their long painful crawl these should clink against the stones, to meet up with a rescue party of 215 sailors and marines thirty miles out.

What Carson's tiny team accomplished in passing through that deadly circle epitomizes commando technique. We now take for granted that even a long-range patrol is in continuous contact by radio or satellite. But in Carson's day, just communicating between far-apart forces (even when not surrounded by vengeful lancers) could still require Rangerlike stealth and endurance well beyond those of even highly qualified conventional soldiers.

Frémont, for his part, got court-martialed in Washington, then pardoned by Polk, to go on to apply the entrepreneurship shown in his curious mission to bold forays into business — a not-unusual step for such irregular warriors. He would enjoy big successes (a railroad fortune followed by the first Republican presidential nomination in 1856) and, in character, suffer bankruptcy from corner cutting that included shady dealings on the Paris Bourse.

As with Pizarro and Drake, these were still days in which someone like Frémont could pull off amazing feats thousands of miles from controlling legal authority — the farther, in fact, the better. On the other side of the Pacific, for instance, "Mad Jack" Percival, a pioneer special operator of the War of 1812, who had disguised a stoutly armed fishing smack as a grocery boat to jump a British warship, had just taken it on himself to have his marines seize Tourane, the Da Nang of our day.[5] Once a small force was out there in the pre-Marconi era, it could (and often did) ignore diplomacy. The State Department took two cautious years to apologize to Vietnam; no one was about to do so to Mexico.

Well to the east-southeast of California's birth pains in summer 1846, Major General Zachary Taylor saw opening before him the grand opportunities that would bring him the presidency two years later. This rugged, sixty-two-year-old former Indian fighter pushed into Mexico to win impressively at Monterrey (sixty miles southwest of the Rio Grande) in September, against superior numbers behind stout defenses, followed by bitter house-to-house fighting, and, in equally brutal combat at Buena Vista the following February, against an army that outnumbered his four to one.

A crucial part of Taylor's hard-won victories was another element of special warfare — the use of previously unconsidered technological capacities, in this case unusually mobile artillery whose firepower was akin to future machine-gun support sections. These were small, fast-moving, hard-hitting batteries of little bronze guns, their barrels about four feet long, slung low between a pair of oversized wheels. They served as part of a newfangled "flying" unit, drawn by teams of six fast, well-trained horses ridden by artillerymen, the rest of the guncrew bouncing atop the caissons to stabilize them. None of this came from the War Department. These spirited formations were the brainchildren of a young West Point–educated major who believed that they would transform warfare — over the doubts of senior commanders whom the War of 1812 had left comfortable with solid conventional artillery. True to the dictum that a special enterprise is best led by whomever designs it, the major commanded one of Taylor's three batteries, and was killed directing it.[6]

Taylor was equally skeptical of the Rangers, while wise enough to put them to use as well, sending reconnaissance teams behind enemy lines through the thick chaparral, to slip back at night past the "friendly fire" of nervous sentries. The risks were even greater because the Mexican scouts knew the terrain as well as the Rangers. Neither gave quarter. Regular U.S. forces had strict orders not to molest a disarmed enemy. When the soldiers came across Mexicans "hung up in the chaparral" after a Ranger reconnaissance, recalled one of these operators, "the government was charitably bound to suppose" that they had committed suicide.[7]

Convinced that northern Mexico no longer offered strategic advantages, and worried by Taylor's mounting political popularity, in November 1846 President Polk approved the plan of the army's com-

manding general, Winfield Scott, for an amphibious assault on Veracruz. Once taken, it would open a passage for the army to follow
Cortés's route of three hundred years earlier through the mountains.
Prescott's *Conquest of Mexico,* published three years before, had
already fired American imaginations — including those of the more
literate of Scott's officers, who saw the parallels throughout and who
expected resistance every bit as tenacious.

The landing was the largest amphibious operation in history until
then — when amphibious work was still special indeed, whether
small or large scale. There were no courses at Marine Corps Base
Quantico. Indeed, this landing would establish war doctrine that
held well into the next century. The challenge was how to get 12,250
soldiers quickly ashore from transports, against who knew what
opposition from a walled city protected by a complex of fortresses.
The navy had designed flat-bottomed, double-ended, so-called surf-
boats (the USN reemployed the word in 1942), constructed in three
different sizes so that they could save space aboard ship by nesting
tightly inside one another.[8] Once the fleet had taken position off
Veracruz on March 10, sixty-five of these novel landing craft were
lowered and then lined up abreast of the landing beach. Disembarka-
tion commenced, twenty-five hundred men in two initial waves.

The "Gibraltar of Mexico" fell by March 26, after three days of
punishment. Two weeks later, Scott ordered his army to advance into
the mountains that back the coast, up the long steep road to the halls
of Montezuma. The march followed what was already then the
National Highway — Cortés's route — as Scott and President Polk
feared that the Americans could get swallowed up in a guerrilla uprising driven by the furies of religion (i.e., Catholicism).

Not for the last time, Washington thought that its interests would
be served by returning from exile a man of supposedly moderating
influence. To that end, the U.S. Navy shipped back General Santa
Anna, the savage victor of the Alamo, from his refuge in Cuba. Once
in Mexico, Santa Anna instead vowed that this time he would make a
greater hash of the gringos, in passes deadlier than the plains of San
Antonio. When Scott drove inland against much greater numbers,
none less than Wellington insisted that the Americans were doomed.

To cut loose from the doctrine of one's time, as did Scott, is not necessarily in itself special warfare, but it has a continuity with such thought and ability. Not that Scott's push inland was a surprise; much of Europe as well as the Mexican army was watching his every move.

Two parts of Scott's accomplishment are truly special-operational: first, employment of highwaymen, here meaning the bandit chieftains who beset the road from Veracruz to Mexico City and, once safely in U.S. pay, were given a vital yet secret standing as the "Mexican Spy Company." Heading the recruiting of never more than a hundred men, Ethan Allen Hitchcock (that eminently respectable West Pointer, Inspector General of the Army) paid out lavishly to retain the services of the type of ruffians who in a different time and place might have included his grandfather, Ethan Allen of Vermont, and indeed for similar purposes of back-country warfare, guiding, couriering, infiltrating. "All business was to be transacted without papers and without signatures," he wrote in his diary about these "indispensably important agents." They were the communication network for Scott's advancing army. This nineteenth-century expedition was also working in ways not altogether different from those by which the United States has hired influential — and temporary — loyalties in Afghanistan and Iraq. Hitchcock says that if he had not employed the bandits, Santa Anna would have.[9]

The second special mode was the formidably effective reconnaissance of this empty, ill-mapped land by West Point-trained engineers. At the very outbreak of war, the U.S. Army had the foresight to dispatch a covert topographical team into Mexico to map terrain likely to be contested — no adequate maps of Mexico existing.[10] Today, special operators know this as "battlefield preparation activities." Then, the emphasis on practical cartography just reflected the extent to which West Point was ever more fulfilling the vision of its founder, Mr. Jefferson, as the polytechnic for a new nation. Officers were properly thinking as graduates of an engineering school. No one, though, was considering using a secret team to, say, abduct the president of Mexico.

Now the engineers had to know precisely what could be moved through dangerous country, how, and indeed where. This required not just the courage of other infiltrators, such as the Rangers and the Spies, but the more modern special-force characteristic of having to apply brains and immediate calculating ability to the mission. Small teams went out, only occasionally accompanied by dragoons. Forty-year-old Captain Robert E. Lee took command of the engineers, beginning a legend that would only grow when he hid for hours beneath logs and rocks at a spring, within touching distance of a lolly-gagging enemy patrol, while finding a way around the passes through mountains Santa Anna thought impenetrable.

By early September, Scott's dispatches were singling out Lee's "daring reconnoissances" (*sic*) before the assault on Chapultepec, a castle overseeing the western causeways into Mexico City, the chosen route for a final assault.[11] Chapultepec sat two hundred feet up a rugged hill behind walls so thick that bombardment could not breach them, and it was protected further by unscalable cliffs on its northern and eastern faces. Held by some nine hundred professional soldiers, including military cadets determined to fight to the death for their country, it looked impregnable.

For all the tactical brilliance of the invasion to date, there was no way to avoid a direct attack. A "forlorn hope" (as the soldiers called it in one of the last uses of the term) was raised, all who volunteered being guaranteed immediate promotion.[12] Ultimately, two teams of about 250 each, including a company of Marines, levered themselves upslope with pickaxes in the face of intense enemy fire to fling ladders against the ramparts from different directions in an assault so startling and bloody that the stronghold fell within an hour and a half.

Scott had already infiltrated into the city men from his Spy Company disguised as peasants to report on its defenses. So informed, he pushed in over two of the causeways on the morning of September 14. Within minutes, a party of Marines ran up the Stars and Stripes over the National Palace.

William Prescott would conclude that this "second conquest," which had seemed at the outset likely to be as difficult as the first, had proved otherwise.[13] But it was not over. Throughout, formally established Mexican partisan units had been striking the supply lines that connected Veracruz to the advancing U.S. Army. Once Mexico's capital was in his hands, Scott still had to deploy 25 percent of his troops against these insurgents who fought on into 1848.[14]

It was victory nonetheless, though one that for the first time made U.S. troops a genuine army of occupation, with all that this entails — enforcing martial law, hunting guerrillas, the soldiers restless, the proconsul edgy, along with squabbles between the field and Washington. There could be no withdrawal until a treaty was negotiated and ratified, which came only the following June. The Mexicans conceded half their country — in addition to Texas, the lands that are now California, Arizona, New Mexico, Nevada, Utah, and parts of Colorado and Wyoming.[15] The United States had sought, in a phrase of the time, "to conquer a peace." It had. But here the question of which, if any, of the spoils would be slave or free arose to break apart the Union, just as Hitchcock had anticipated when first ordered to the border.[16]

‡

WELLINGTON SOON acknowledged that Scott had achieved the greatest feat of arms for a generation, the end of the previous generation to him being, of course, Waterloo. But in India — the land where he had made his name — exploits every bit as high in initiative and daring were being brought off by forces closer to the size of Frémont's than of Scott's. By mid-century the East India Company — that private, publicly regulated business paying a dividend for governing a subcontinent — was still the face of the British presence. The company had three armies (one for each ample "province") and a fleet, along with a substantial backing of British regulars. The French had been defanged, although they held onto several coastal enclaves and would keep them until after the British were gone. There was still no policy in place declaring that Britain itself had to dominate the entire area that today also includes Pakistan, Bangladesh, and Burma. But a lot was happening on the steamy ground and, taken all together, was adding up to something prodigious.

The British never thought they could run India alone. By this time — despite the horrific 1842 setback, when 16,500 British soldiers, women, and children were killed in Kabul over six days — they still had only thirty-four thousand European troops in the subcontinent. These generally worked through local rulers supported by British bayonets, and some quarter of a million British-officered native soldiers were raised from India's many warrior peoples. The most renowned of the local units, the Corps of Guides, began with a picked force of three hundred men created in Peshawar during 1846.

The unit's purpose was long-range mapping and intelligence collection in a land of some four hundred languages and about as many states. It had been conceived in the first few days of the Afghan War by Henry Lawrence, "Uncrowned King of the Punjab" and probably the most open-minded political officer ever to appear in the relatively minute but remarkably high-quality British presence in India. Its tone was conspicuously elitist: high pay offered, high caste required. The men were to be good fighters, he insisted, but also ones who could disappear and live unnoticed "while they hunt secretly for information of all sorts." Sent out in ones and twos, they were to get a habit of doing things quietly.[17] It was an organization markedly subversive of the military shibboleths of the age. The effects of the Guides' slender capacities — a troop of cavalry and two companies of infantry — were wholly unmatched to their numbers. Men would be chosen for fidelity but above all for initiative and brains.

There was nothing of the dog-loyal simpletons of imperial fiction about the volunteers who served in the Guides. Instead, they offered just that high-octane mixture of talents that astute organizers of special forces welcome. Only two years after the Guides were created, they showed their guile in an assault on Gorindghar, a supposedly impregnable bandit fortress in north-central India.

Gorindghar commanded the crucial line of communication between Ambala and Lahore. To the British, it appeared more than strong enough to tie down a large part of their never large enough forces. Rasul Khan of the Guides was sent ahead with 140 men to reconnoiter. A small strike team took the next step, as the rest of the Guides hid outside. Shabbily dressed so as not to appear connected with the main regular force a good day's march over the horizon, Rasul Khan proceeded to insinuate himself into dinner with Gorindghar's chieftain, presenting himself as a Moslem freebooter in Sikh service, carrying three prisoners with large prices on their heads to the Durbar.

Might he borrow the fortress cells overnight? And might he — these were valuable captives, he would understand anyone being tempted — post his own sentries over them? The Exalted Presence, all too gracious, further allowed Khan to assign his own men to strengthen the chieftain's night guard. These were dangerous times, after all. . . .

The chieftain had hundreds of men and bristling artillery — facing outward. Rasul Khan had, all told, three "prisoners" and a handful of sentries, but these were inside and ready. Hours before dawn, the guards were overpowered, and the rest of the Guides let in. When the main British column trudged up next morning, it was greeted with a Union Jack snapping over the ramparts, and a guard of honor for the commanding general's rather bemused entry into a stronghold that he had expected to penetrate only after weeks of butchery.

Nine years later, in 1857, when the terrible Indian "Mutiny" burst upon overconfident British authority, the Guides showed their sheer capacity as fighting men, as at the Residency in Lucknow, where Henry Lawrence fell. Less than eighty loyal Guides were on the scene and held out against an enemy in the thousands, with artillery. Before the last of the Guides died fighting, they had killed at least six hundred of their besiegers. Special forces are not just infiltrators and tricksters, it must be remembered; they rest their particular strengths and mystique on superior mainstream soldiering.

Not just in the Guides do we encounter special qualities, but in a growing roster of fast-moving, intrepid, and frequently brutal irregular outfits, such as Hodson's Horse. Its thuggish major, William Hodson, is best remembered for his pivotal role in subduing Delhi during the Mutiny: with fifty men in the face of many but disorganized thousands, he seized the puppet Mogul emperor, a dazed front man for the mutineers. The next day, with "a hundred picked men," he grabbed the emperor's three sons from their refuge at a sacred tomb, took a carbine, and shot them one after another as a vast mob circled around — cowing the masses who looked to the imperial house for leadership.[18]

Europe's war ministries could understand the ruthless, reactive courage of small outfits such as Hodson's, but the initiative shown by the Guides did not filter back. In this age of innovation, few were the qualities of special warfare that rubbed off on the antagonists at home, no matter that enormous returns could have been won by small investments of men, money, and thought once European powers clashed head-on.

Certainly, the will to seize radical possibilities was in the air. We see it in the era's supreme special warrior as the Crimean War got badly bogged down after Britain and France had lumbered into the conflict to protect the fading Ottoman power against Russian encroachment. By the outbreak of war in March 1854, Cochrane's commission in the Royal Navy had been restored for twenty-one years. At age seventy-nine, admirers in the admiralty and the Cabinet turned to him to command the Baltic Fleet. As for the seemingly invincible Russian base at Sebastopol on the Black Sea, he had a cheap, efficient solution — suffocate it with poisonous fumes. The Admiralty dismissed the plan as "infallible, irresistible, but inhuman."[19] There were also reconsiderations in Lord Aberdeen's cabinet about Cochrane taking charge in the Baltic: surely, the Queen was advised, he would embark on "some desperate enterprise" (likely something short and sharp against Russia's capital, St. Petersburg, if not the czar himself) that would make a messy international situation worse.[20] Cochrane was left on the sidelines to die quietly four years after the peace, in 1860, and is buried in Westminster Abbey, among plenty of other unrespectable geniuses.

No one fighting in the Crimea had Cochrane's understanding of the small, fast, focused, and devastating.[21] The strangest example of the absence of such thinking concerns the immense supply bases on the coast, as sixty-odd thousand men got into position to take Sebastopol the hard way. Substantial Russian relieving forces could assault the allied lines from without; and the garrison could try large, brave sorties from within the siege lines. If an assault was worth making, the thinking seemed to be, it was worth making big. Although the Russians knew the terrain, and had maybe the greatest military engineer of his generation, Todleben (oddly meaning "living death," in German) inside Sebastopol, it never seems to have occurred to them what a commando team of, say, thirty, slipping through the Black Sea fog, could have accomplished more effectively than entire divisions rolling up the valleys. Nor did it occur to the allies.

No more than five miles away from Sebastopol, the French anchorage at Kamiesh Bay alone was jammed with thirteen hundred vessels:

troop transports, supply ships, men-of-war. It was easy enough to recognize its vulnerability to a hurricane, a nasty one having just blown through in November 1854. The prospect of man-made disaster was far higher, yet ignored. It took a sharp Yankee skipper to detect what to us seems the obvious horrifying risk.

Captain John Codman's *William Penn* steamed into Kamiesh later that month, having been chartered by the government of Napoleon III to haul a cargo of provisions, ammunition, and a contingent of French troops. The danger was immediately apparent, at least to him — and, unsurprisingly, to various Greeks working in the harbor. "There might have been some Russian spies who could on any night simultaneously have set a number of ships on fire to windward," he would reminisce. Once that occurred, as he was certain would soon happen at the hands of saboteurs, little afloat could have cleared the crowded flaming harbor. He therefore berthed the *William Penn* as near to the mouth as possible, and kept his boilers fired. But nothing so clever as a commando-induced conflagration blazed up in this war, and for the rest of his life Codman would find it "strange indeed that this means of doing more injury to their enemies than could have been caused by battle was not improved by the Russians."[22] It would take a different mindset, as well as countless deaths in trenches and cavalry charges, before belligerents set out to detect such opportunities as could have left Kamiesh Bay a sea of flame.

Against this backdrop of obliviousness are highlighted other imaginative failures of the time, such as our successors will undoubtedly spot all around us today. Consider the procedures of handling steamships — the practice then being, when these encountered fog, to increase speed rather than to slow down, the sooner to get out of the trouble. Otherwise able people seem to have missed the point: accelerated passage through the fogbanks could be achieved only at the cost of increasing both the likelihood of disastrous collision and its intensity.

Yet fog not only shrouds shipping lanes, as it famously does war, it also conceals dangers right at home. While the disease-ridden armies kept slugging it out in the Crimea during spring 1855, there took place in the rolling green fields of Kent a radically innovative operation by a team of no more than six. Here the target was the twelve thousand pounds in bullion (nearly $1 million today) conveyed monthly to the British war effort on the Black Sea. Using "skill, dexterity, perseverance and ability" — and that said by the police — this little group applied inside information, reconnaissance, disguise, and deception to pull off "The Most Sensational Exploit of the Modern Era," or at least "The Crime of the Century," as headlines labeled the achievement.

A moving train had never been robbed, let alone as it raced along at fifty-four miles per hour. Despite escorts of guards from the London banks to the South Eastern Railway station, then more security at the Channel ports, and ultimately at the arrival point in Paris, where the loss was so belatedly discovered, all the gold in the ironbound strongboxes had been replaced en route by equally heavy lead shot. Only found out because the perpetrators turned on themselves, this technically complex performance is chronicled step-by-step in Old Bailey court records — where the insouciant bandit in command apparently contrasted his slick operation with the "rank stupidity" of the bloodletting in Crimea, where both armies kept grappling toward mutual destruction until Sebastopol fell piecemeal. Because one mode or another of assault has never occurred, master thief Edward Pierce might have advised the narrow-minded generals, that fact hardly means an utterly novel scheme won't spring out of the gloom to indeed bring far more injury than battle.[23]

‡

I N O N E theater of European warfare, however, we do encounter the full possibilities of small-force initiative of that epoch: Giuseppe Garibaldi's liberation of the Mezzogiorno, that part of southern Italy somewhere between the first and third worlds of the time. Significantly, Garibaldi was a leader seasoned in the hypermobile small wars of South America's Rio de la Plata basin, where he learned to live rough and fight dirty. He left Montevideo in 1848 with sixty-three men, intending to start a revolution.

In the mid-nineteenth century, the Bourbons (part of a junior dynastic complex of that family which long ruled France, and are back to being kings of Spain) lorded it over southern Italy, as the "Kingdom of the Two Sicilies," from their seat in Naples, the third-largest city in Europe. Garibaldi proposed to expel them and unite the nation. But timing was not yet right. Liking to fight against impossible odds, he was dismissed as a "buccaneer" by the Italian authorities he wished to serve.[24] Years were spent on the run, seeking work in the United States, before returning to Italy to await the main chance.

By the night of May 5, 1860, a "picked body of seamen" carrying pistols clambered up from rowboats to hijack two paddle-wheeled steamers in Genoa's harbor.[25] Nearly 1,150 would-be fighting men ("The Thousand," and one woman) then boarded the steamers from small boats at sea. These volunteers were of all sorts: "a hundred doctors and a hundred and fifty lawyers . . . students, journalists, gentlemen adventurers, labourers, tramps and artists."[26] It was an eccentric mix of determined people for extraordinary ends of a sort we have seen before, and for whom Colonel Colt would supply revolvers.

Two days later, and barely missing two Neapolitan warships, they landed at undefended Marsala on the island of Sicily's west coast. Garibaldi stated his hope of starting an avalanche, tiny successes to roll into greater ones. He seized the electric telegraph office, sent off false messages, rallied peasants and clergy, and led his poorly armed irregulars through torturous hill-country paths northeast toward the Bourbon garrison of twenty thousand soldiers in Palermo. "Skillful diversions and clever use of mock campfires," plus the deadly silencing of sentries, caught the soldiers off guard.[27] It was all a ludicrously impossible assault. Yet he leveraged speed and the enemy's certainty that nothing like it could be pulled off to transform his effort into supremely effective sustained combat: he swept the island to face an overwhelming superior enemy across the Strait of Messina. Then he won Naples. The impossible could indeed be accomplished by resolute spirit, for starters. Shock at his astounding military achievement had its political effect; the army of Victor Emmanuel (monarch of a modest realm in the northwest and of Sardinia) moved down to cut through the turmoil and to unify most of the peninsula into what was to be the new Kingdom of Italy, the sixth power in Europe.

By this time, the high commands of the industrializing nations were observing one another's procedures closely: military attachés and observers were being exchanged. General Winfield Scott himself would be lionized on a stately tour of Europe. Studies were made of the successes and failures of one's counterparts.[28] The *Times* reported every detail of Garibaldi's landings; Dumas, sitting on his yacht off Palermo, immortalized in the Paris press the romantic adventure of how a band of rebels led by a man "acquainted with action" could take on a notoriously oppressive kingdom. A waiting world had finally heard of what a small, highly motivated force could do against a hidebound (however heavily equipped) European army conventionally led and of indifferent morale.

What Garibaldi had accomplished may have been one step up from banditry (and that step only established because his side won). Yet in 1861 he was a hero on both sides of the Atlantic, and to both sides in the Civil War; a hero of liberty, against a loathsome old order, to abolitionists and slave owners alike; a nation-builder, to Federals (with New York's "Garibaldi Guards"), who saw themselves as preserving a country, and to Confederates, who were confident that they were bringing one to birth. More than most such figures raised up by a revolutionary movement, Garibaldi presented a credible embodiment of new forces in the world, a prodigy of enterprise and small arms, with a sense of the opportunities offered by modernity. The nineteenth-century transformation of communications — of transport, telegraph, and press PR — was enlarging the vision not just of individualistic adventurers, but of generals and political leaders. New forms of raiding against ostensibly overwhelming armies were just a start. It would be a view of war that took fire over a quarter of a continent in vast, improvising, innovation-rich America.

13

Strange Fulfillments
Newer Tasks for the Daring Few as Steam and Machinery Transform the Struggle, 1861–1902

"It is just as legitimate to fight an enemy in the rear as in the front. The only difference is in the danger."
JOHN SINGLETON MOSBY, "GRAY GHOST" OF THE
CONFEDERACY, REMINISCENCES

THE PROCESS of sustained compounding industrialization that had gotten underway in Britain in the 1700s had, by the middle of the nineteenth century, reached out to the United States and western Europe. First coal, steam, and machinery — then the telegraph, rail networks, and soon the undersea cable — were reshaping life. Less apparent was the fact that industrialization was a sword that could be swung back upon its creators.

By the start of the Civil War in 1861, railroads, for instance, could deliver armies to the front with unprecedented speed but would also come to be at the mercy of raiders setting trestles afire. Telegraph lines became the nervous system that could summon the foam-flecked cavalry but could be tapped to send spurious messages. The great cities that were the age's proudest boast served as the centers of ever more complex financings and trade deals, but were therefore inviting places to destroy — not only with armies, as in *Gone With the Wind* Atlanta, but by secret cells able to horn in on a grander and much less reachable city, as all of New York (then being just Manhattan) came amazingly close to going up in flames. The Civil War became the tipping point toward the modern special operation, which appears in forms all too familiar today.

Of course, for three thousand years daring, stealthy, and often skilled men had zeroed in on targets that could exert strong leverage against the enemy being struck. But it is in America that special warfare took on the tasks appropriate to an industrial age. The Civil War was also the first war in which serious people — though nonetheless conspicuously aberrant from sound regular soldiers — beat nearly nonstop on the doors of the high commands with credible proposals for employing such techniques. More relevant to us than the raising, training, and combat deployment of thousands and then tens of thousands, for which the West Pointers were pretty well prepared, are the small, novel, intense clawings at the margin.

Rapid transport and communication might be recasting nations of the West while making them more vulnerable to incisive penetration, yet it was on the developing world's advancing frontiers, at least as much as between the thirty-four warring states, that the special operation was being put into place as a matter of course. There was no shortage of adventuresome mavericks or imaginative professional officers ready to work far beyond the book.

Under stress of imperial conquest and wars of independence, title to some 70 percent of the earth's land surface and to perhaps 50 percent of its population changed hands between 1776 and 1914. One vital instrument in all this shifting of ownership was the small, well-armed band, prepared to pit effrontery and skill against superior numbers, venturing into the remotest places, betting lives against immense potential rewards. Now such hyperfocused, fast, and inventive professional forces were truly coming into their own in places where regular armies might meet with disaster from disease or aroused, implacable peoples. The chieftain, the war party, forays of encroaching colonial rivals — these were the main targets of imperial war, not hardened positions or technically sophisticated objectives, as prototype commandos were required to extend pacification and profit-making. Of course, such audacity could also work both ways, as the British Empire would discover at the hands of the Boer commandos who made the term famous in the biggest colonial war of all.

‡

WHAT COMPELS our attention in the first year of the Civil War is not only the creation of American intelligence services, with their ongoing close ties to special warfare, but the appearance of the first English-speaking fighting formation to bear the designation "special." There shambles onto the stage the 1st Louisiana Special Battalion, "Wheat's Tigers," whose brief and eccentric history did much to establish the stereotype of out-of-control adventurers that so many regular army officers still find it easy to splash over units of this genre.

The Confederate Tigers enjoyed the entirely deserved reputation of being composed of murderously effective sociopaths almost as dangerous to their comrades as to the enemy. In seemingly reckless attacks, they proved their deadliness at First Bull Run in July 1861 and around the five-times-taken battery at Port Republic in Stonewall Jackson's drive into the Shenandoah Valley the following year. Of their personal qualities, it may be enough to mention that one company was largely composed of ex-convicts, and most of the rest had been found a little too rich for the blood even of cosmopolitan New Orleans. As for their elected commander, Major Chatham Wheat, suffice it to say that his law practice before the war had been interrupted by endeavors to overthrow various Latin American republics, and he was just returned from distinguishing himself in Garibaldi's Sicilian expedition.

Once Wheat was killed at Gaines' Mill in 1862, the Special Battalion (which he had barely kept on the appropriate side of the thin line between sedition and general criminality) had to be disbanded and merged, a few to each unit, with the rest of the Army of Northern Virginia. But Wheat had blazed a trail that even the most trig of West Pointers would have to consider. He had selected by type, choosing real misfits and marginal people who could bring special levels of harm, and who could show a peculiar indomitable spirit. At least ever since Alexander's captains picked the three hundred at the Sogdian Rock, men had been chosen for bravery and skill. So too here, with the added dimension that these ferociously effective warriors were not only the type to think outside the box, but were alienated from most any structure at all.

By spring 1862, there began to emerge exploits that drew on a new kind of analysis and forethought — because the vulnerabilities they played on were also new. Certain officers and shadowy civilians were regularly taking steps toward procedures that look ever more like part of a twenty-first century, special operations consciousness.

In the 1860s railroads had functioned for barely thirty years anywhere in the world. In the South (industrially much less developed than the North), the Confederates were still sufficiently impressed by rail power to frequently name battles after railheads, whereas the Union would name the very same actions for rivers: Manassas/Bull Run, Sharpsburg/Antietam, Murfreesboro/Stones River. And every main line was strategically crucial for the Confederacy, notably the Western & Atlantic, a State of Georgia–owned artery joining Atlanta to Chattanooga, connecting thence to the Carolinas and Virginia.

In the Georgia hill country, there happened to be working for the Union a secret agent who called himself James J. Andrews. He was to be remembered as soft-voiced and pensive, tall, carefully dressed, and always carrying a concealed revolver. There is no record of his existence before 1859; he was one of those precursors of an age of disaster, a self-invented figure coming out of nowhere — perhaps in flight from an abandoned family, a failed bank in the Panic of 1857, which did much to bring about the war, or both. Andrews was the clever operator with nothing to lose but his life, who at this stage of the discipline's evolution was the classic type of player.

Andrews had been smuggling in quinine and other goods for the Confederacy in exchange for military information from rebel sources. He had obscure ties to the generals commanding the Union forces in middle Tennessee as they tried to push into the eastern part of the state — a properly vital offensive in the eyes of President Lincoln.[1] In March, one of these generals had sent him on a mission with eight men to burn railroad bridges west of Chattanooga, a promising effort that only failed for lack of coordination. (Such sabotage, let alone what followed, may have been more than a little disconcerting to the many West Pointers who had been railroad executives, such as Generals McClellan, Meade, and Sherman.)

After secretly visiting Atlanta and scouting the Confederate rail network around the city and northward, all the while collecting timetables, Andrews returned to propose a second, far bolder attempt.

It would begin with another clandestine penetration of enemy territory, but this time would truly turn the enemy's strength against him by seizing a train, using which the raiders could burn the bridges on the northern part of the Georgia state railroad and another bridge on a line to east Tennessee, thereby completely isolating Chattanooga. By harnessing a passenger and goods train, Andrews believed, such a raid might leave enough destruction as to open the door for a Union offensive into Alabama.

Andrews was authorized to gather two dozen volunteers. He knew none of those he picked up, and had only the slightest role in their selection. Privates, corporals, and two sergeants came forward from out of three Ohio infantry regiments. Two had some experience on the rails. All dressed in civilian clothes and carried revolvers. The group first met its leader, only days before the operation, at nightfall on a roadside about a mile east of Shelbyville, Tennessee. There were no well-concealed long-term training areas "somewhere in Scotland," as in World War II, or "at Bragg," as today: you heard about it, and you did it.

Andrews laid out his plan. The men then dispersed by threes and fours to head the two hundred miles to Marietta, Georgia, starting east into the mountains, working their ways southward, traveling by rail once within Confederate lines. Two were arrested; two failed to show up; one vanished. The remaining nineteen regrouped with Andrews early on Saturday morning, April 12, in his room at the Marietta Hotel.

In a shrewd, binding stroke of leadership, Andrews offered each of them a final chance to withdraw. None did. They then boarded a Western & Atlantic train, drawn by a soon-to-be-famous locomotive, *The General,* heading to North Carolina. They allayed suspicion by buying tickets to different destinations up the line. When all the crew and most of the passengers got off at Big Shanty (now Kennesaw) for breakfast, the raiders uncoupled the engine, the tender, and three boxcars, and sprang abroad. A sentry stood twelve feet away, amiably watching the funny things people did on railroads. The train lurched, picked up steam, and rolled off, only slowing to let its hijackers cut telegraph lines after passing each station. The raiders launched upon what destruction they could as they headed north, but they only had a

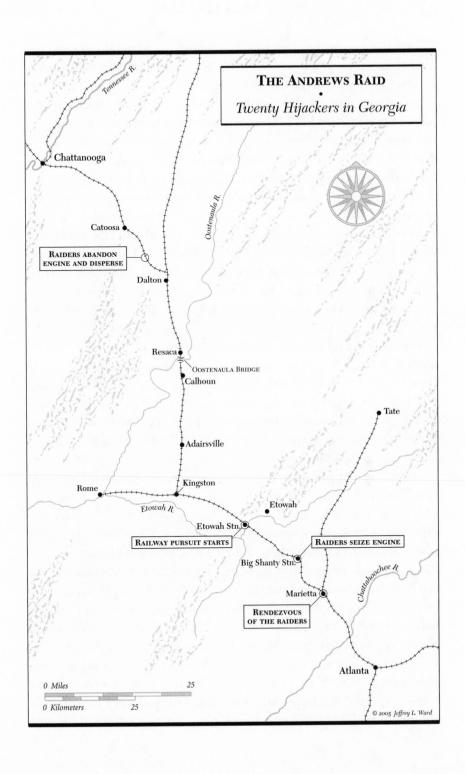

THE ANDREWS RAID
·
Twenty Hijackers in Georgia

Tennessee R.

Chattanooga

Oostenaula R.

Catoosa

**RAIDERS ABANDON
ENGINE AND DISPERSE**

Dalton

Resaca

OOSTENAULA BRIDGE

Calhoun

Tate

Adairsville

Kingston

Rome

Etowah R.

Etowah

Etowah Stn.

RAILWAY PURSUIT STARTS

RAIDERS SEIZE ENGINE

Big Shanty Stn.

Chattahoochee R.

Marietta

**RENDEZVOUS
OF THE RAIDERS**

Atlanta

0 Miles   25

0 Kilometers   25

© 2005 Jeffrey L. Ward

few crowbars to attack the rails, no explosives to cave in tunnels, and the bridges proved too wet to burn. One of the survivors nonetheless remembered the fun they were having.

Special operations are a sphere of human endeavor where one just has to ignore Churchill's injunction not to argue the difficulties, the difficulties will argue themselves. In special operations, the difficulties have to be dissected. Great ideas have one weakness: they convince the people who articulate them that their fine thoughts are unique. Had the abandoned train crew of *The General* simply walked away; or had Andrews's plan included capturing them; had the raiders possessed better equipment to pull up rails; had the raid fallen on Friday, as originally planned (when there was less rail traffic and no rain), the blow could have been devastating. Instead, the mission failed for two reasons: the Law of Small Numbers that bedevils special operations, and a lack of sufficiently rigorous and pessimistic thinking-through.

What happened was that the Confederate crew gave chase, first by a handcar, then by grabbing an old locomotive whose progress had been blocked by a lifted rail, finally by intercepting the southbound *Texas*. The intrepid party in pursuit was also able to slow down long enough to take aboard armed men en route. (There was no way to turn it around on the track, so throughout the great chase *Texas* was running in reverse.)

Once they realized they were being pursued, the raiders' fun ended fast. They threw rail ties onto the tracks, but the speeding *Texas* simply brushed them aside; they set fire to two of the three boxcars (the other being torn apart for fuel), and slammed them back down the track; *Texas* just shunted them onto sidings. In the mad dash, the two engines may have set world speed records for that era, certainly above sixty miles per hour. Each time the raiders halted to try to lift another rail, the smoke of the hurtling *Texas* could be seen around the last bend, its shrill whistle, as another of the survivors would recall, sounding "like the scream of a bird of prey."[2]

Finally, all fuel and water gone, the Yankees saw their mission lost ninety miles from their starting point, and they did not even know that one partial telegraph message had already alerted Confederate troops ahead. There was no fallback plan. Andrews ordered his men to leap from their gasping engine, disperse into the dripping woods, and try to make it back separately. All were rounded up within ten days; eight, including Andrews, were hanged in Atlanta for espionage, the secret of his true identity dying with him. The survivors, after a saga of escape, recapture, and exchange, would become the first recipients of the Medal of Honor.

One wonders what further havoc Andrews could have accomplished had he been better prepared, let alone if a force specially organized and trained for this purpose had been sent in. One also wonders what might have happened to Andrews and his followers had they been successful. Probably the men would have been lionized for a few days, then returned to the ranks. Andrews, unless he feared further attention, might have parlayed his achievement to more ambitious mischief — or have quit, right after the raid, to be married the following week, as he intended. Only later in the war would rail destruction be put on an undramatic businesslike basis by the Union cavalry. But Andrews' Raid, as it came to be known, was a sign of things to come: behind the big moves of men and matériel that the generals afforded lay new opportunities for those who thought in terms of the small and silent.

By early 1864, few strategic rewards seemed to be coming from the bloody grapple of armies. Time, however, was against the Confederacy, and influential men in Richmond were open to desperate measures as the Union's naval blockade began to grip. Jefferson Davis, President of the Confederate States, had designated three "commissioners" that spring, with offices in Montreal and in Toronto, to oversee clandestine operations against the Union that were to be staged from the pro-rebel but formally neutral Canadian colonies.[3] The senior conspirator, a former U.S. Secretary of the Interior and more recent lieutenant colonel C.S.A., was hardened enough to declare that "the way to bring the North to its senses is to burn Northern cities." Even apocalyptic schemes of bioterrorism took root. The cause of the disease not yet being understood, clothes of yellow fever victims were shipped in from Halifax.[4]

The so-called special service operations (Confederate jargon for secret action) staged from Canada were at least imaginative, but, once more, startlingly unrehearsed for objectives so complex. Nearly all failed, often from betrayal, for which the Union paid generously: raids on Maine, ships seized on the Great Lakes; attempts to free thousands of prisoners from Midwestern internment camps (including the audacious capture of a steamship on Lake Erie to break into the military prison on Johnson's Island off Sandusky); an uprising planned in Chicago; perhaps ties to the fraudsters at the New York *Journal of Commerce,* who conspired to push up the price of gold with alarmist news, which, had they been successful, would have devalued U.S. government securities; and a raid by twenty-two Confederate cavalrymen (infiltrating as gun-carrying members of a Montreal sportsmen's club) on St. Albans, Vermont, which proved little more than a murderous bank heist, with grave international overtones for the British colonial authorities.

What beckoned, for reasons of vengeance as much as strategy, was New York City. Insurrection was in the air, as shown by the appalling Draft Riots the year before, and a plot had been laid to set off something even worse come election day. A broad front of defeatism, ranging from quasi-treasonous secret societies to tides of disillusion among war-weary citizens, was there for those skillful enough to draw on it. By Tuesday, November 8, Union counterspies had put the authorities on the alert, and thirty-five hundred additional troops had been moved into town.

In the Great Fire of 1835, hundreds of Manhattan's buildings had burned — and that only by accident. Now, with a densely packed population of seven hundred thousand, as well as structures towering eight stories high, the still largely wooden island was even more prone to fire. And fire could only be fought by the notorious 125 rival clubhouse volunteer fire departments, so well depicted in Martin Scorsese's film *Gangs of New York.*

Exhaustion in the field might prove exploitable by terror at home. Eight Confederate raiders had been sent in separately from Toronto in late October, under different covers — a step up in special-force procedures from the eager Ohio doughboys who had raised their hands for they-knew-not-what before Andrews' Raid. Now at work were hardened, embittered officers, most of whom had ridden with Brigadier General John Hunt Morgan in his drive deep into Ohio as he had eliminated the Yankees in darkness and ratcheted up the fury of war. Most had been tough enough to escape to Canada from the living cemeteries that were both sides' prison camps. And they were led by another hard-bitten colonel. These men knew what they were about. Registering in different hotels and boardinghouses, they stayed in seclusion, changing locations frequently to avoid suspicion, communicating through personal ads in newspapers, and quietly contacting key Confederate sympathizers. They bided their time after Lincoln's reelection.

Had their plan "been executed with one-half the ability with which it was drawn up," concluded the *New York Times* the day after the fizzled outrage, "no human power could have saved this city from utter destruction."[5] The terrible civilian fatalities of 9/11 would have been a traffic accident compared to what so nearly came to pass in the space of roughly four hours on the night of November 25–26. The saboteurs planned to set fires in eleven large hotels, housing about five thousand guests altogether, and in wharves, hay barges, a lumberyard; all were nearly given to the flames. Even the stairway of the busy seven-story Barnum Museum was thought worth burning.

Hotels were the easiest, most horribly concentrated targets. For instance, the Astor House, on Broadway across from Barnum's, boasted a thousand rooms for four hundred guests, and fire laws were still in their infancy. To ensure that the blaze would rip through the heart of the city — at prime time, starting around 8:30 P.M. — each of the hotels had been selected so as to stand well apart from the others, extending along Broadway from the Bowery well over a mile to Twenty-fifth Street, the other points of ignition being dispersed citywide. Furthermore, November 25 was a holiday, Evacuation Day, the eighty-first anniversary of the end of Royalist occupation in 1783. It could be counted on that theaters, museums, hotels, and Broadway would be packed.

The fires were set off by a phosphorous compound, which the raiders incorrectly called "Greek fire." The mixture was supposed to ignite spontaneously on contact with the air, after several minutes of absorbing atmospheric moisture, just time enough to let the arsonists escape and, indeed, to press on to their next target. But they were unfamiliar with their nostrum's idiosyncrasies — another example of failing to follow through systematically. They had collected the 144 vials, each filled with four ounces of what looked like water (innocuous enough to pass through airport screening today), from a Manhattan chemist who was in on the plot and was also supposed to provide instruction on the use of the elixir. The saboteurs had taken away the vials in twelve satchels and had given themselves time for some practice in Central Park, but not enough, nor in operational conditions. Each took rooms in one or more of the hotels, piled furniture on top of beds, added sheets and curtains to each pile, then saturated all this with the mixture, in some cases adding turpentine and rosin. On the wharves, in the lumberyard, they simply cracked their vials against the wood.

But while alarms clanged from one end of the city to another, every fire was quickly checked; the blazing barges spread no conflagration. It had not occurred to the raiders to open their hotel rooms' windows on that cold November night. Absent any current of air to draw the flames into a self-sustaining blaze, alert guests and chambermaids had the vital minutes to detect the sources of the smoke seeping into the hallways. At the sold-out Winter Garden Theater, part of the structure of the Lafarge House on Broadway, Edwin Booth — appearing with his brothers Junius and John Wilkes in *Julius Caesar* — appealed from the stage for calm. Panic at other theaters and at Barnum's Museum incredibly killed no one, nor were any lives lost in the hotel fires.

It was city and federal authorities who understandably panicked, or at least came down like a hammer as the military took over. The city was blue with troops. Today's Patriot Act would have looked mild: all southerners in the city immediately had to register with the military; anyone suspect was hauled in for bare-knuckle interrogation; in Washington, guards were doubled on all government buildings. Amid the type of situation-normal chaos that bursts over the landscape when the authorities are taken off balance, the raiders could count on making it back to Canada by train.

Further ventures from Canada were soon body-blocked. New York detectives and federal secret agents thereafter seemed to infest every corner in Toronto and Montreal. Only one of the raiders would be caught, however, when he tried to return to the South on a false passport. Shadowed from Toronto, he was jumped at Detroit's train station before he could reach for his revolver. Captain Charles Cobb Kennedy — having been expelled from West Point for being "extremely inattentive to regulations," having been wounded at Shiloh, then having fought under Morgan — was hanged in New York the following spring, in tears, but carrying to the grave the names of his comrades.[6]

‡

As in Andrews' Raid, the petty bungles of the hugely conceived New York plot show an absence of any disciplined operational perspective — whether for a bold commando mission or a terrorist outrage. In the New York case, failure also resulted perhaps because full, prepared commitment to such a horrific project would have required authorization by the forbiddingly honorable Jefferson Davis. Truly deadly enterprises may need to be wrapped in a double secrecy, against the responsible leadership at home at least as much as against the guardians of the target.

To be sure, the war was being shaped more by actual battle, and by fights at sea and along the coasts. Rising from an unpromising start (bilged from the Naval Academy), William Barker Cushing made his way by amphibious skill and daring, going on to be portrayed in a marvelous book co-authored by Charles Van Doren, *Lincoln's Commando,* for running what was close to a Special Boat Service along the sheltering inlets of the Carolina coast. Lieutenant Charles Read won the sobriquet "Sea Hawk of the Confederacy" for his spectacular disruptions of Union shipping lanes. And in 1863, the first submarine to sink a warship, now known as *H. L. Hunley* for its courageous builder, was laid down, with close ties to the Confederate secret service.

Commerce raiders and the infiltrators of "special service" may have their uses, but ultimately "War means fightin', and fightin' means killin'," as said a champion of special warfare, Confederate general Nathan Bedford Forrest, that slave trader turned self-taught apostle of mobility known as the "Wizard of the Saddle." In a curious effort to put irregular ways on a basis of modern legality, the Confederacy passed a Partisan Warfare Act (before thinking twice and disbanding the barely controllable outfits that sprang up) while at the same time accelerating the deployment of electric signals interception and submarines. The aged and the new, even today so absorbingly juxtaposed in the Old Confederacy, entwined as the South fought for its existence. American inventiveness and individualism rarely burned so high.

In 1962, Edmund Wilson, the most distinguished of his generation's literary commentators, observed in his absorbing book on the literature of the Civil War that John Singleton Mosby was its best-known figure, at least for the half century after Appomattox. It is a reputation that has endured, by fits and starts, down to our day. *The Gray Ghost* TV series riveted American boys during 1957–58, though it was quickly shelved against the travails of the civil rights struggle.[7] What interest Mosby holds for our story lies in the ability of his Rangers to float through Union lines like angry phantoms, to infiltrate, strike, and disappear again. For more than two years, they were vilified by the humiliated Yankees as "marauding highwaymen" and idolized in the South as knightly free spirits. Mosby was the precursor of the Lawrence of Arabia myth that would arise some sixty years later, both legends being conditioned by the main-front slaughters of their times.

Mosby formed his Rangers in 1863, the year that the Union promulgated the first full code of military conduct: General Order 100.[8] Not that laws or standard practice of any kind influenced this sandy-haired, twenty-nine-year-old Virginia captain of five feet, eight inches, 128 pounds — the perfect build for a steeplechase jockey. Although he had studied law at Mr. Jefferson's University, Mosby's intellectual life was above all as a reader of the classics: "I was born a Greek."[9] And what he emulated of the Greeks was not their original honor-bound approach to war, but their later deviousness. At the university, a far bigger student had picked a fistfight. Mosby pulled out a pistol and shot him — sound preparation for a career in which anything went, by a man with no military experience before 1861.

Mosby's Rangers tormented the Union war effort by seeming to be everywhere. In convincing the enemy that he could strike often enough and shrewdly enough, he vastly multiplied his effectiveness by being able to tie down troops a hundred miles from where he actually struck — the military value to be reckoned (then as now) "by the number [of opponents] he keeps watching," as Mosby put it.[10] The point was to throw away the rules, never to fight "fair."

The men he chose personally to gather around him had, for the most part, found even Army of Northern Virginia regulations too much. They were similarly prime horsemen, superbly mounted on hunters — and they were operating in what is still the finest hunt country in the United States. What he created was more effective, focused, and ambitious than a band of partisan guerrillas, which his force (officially, the 43rd Battalion, Virginia Cavalry) was not. These were skilled enlisted troopers under military discipline.

All was by stealth. They used hand signals, and preferred to strike around 4 A.M. Sometimes they passed themselves off as Union cavalry, more by the effrontery with which they rode about under cover of darkness or foul weather than by wearing U.S. uniforms. They had no camps, as the hunter-killer teams sent to run them down would discover. Unlike his opponents, Mosby was not bound by any traditions at all. Like the Texas Rangers, for instance, he and his men had no faith in the saber, to them an obsolete weapon. Why engage close in with an equally skilled horseman, where any rabbit hole could put you at his mercy, when he could be neatly shot down at ten feet with a finely balanced .36-caliber Navy Colt?

Mosby's initial coup was to take twenty-nine of his men through the perimeter of the Army of the Potomac on the drizzling night of March 8, 1863. Unlike less adept raiders, part of his astute preparation was to see that everyone ate and slept before heading out; exhaustion (because of the greater intensity that can come from moving fast against worse obstacles with fewer people) is even more a hazard of special operations than of war in general. In turn, he was convinced that his enemies' rage — and with it decay in judgment — was vastly compounded by the sleep he made them lose.[11]

Twenty-five hundred Union troops lay within a mile of Fairfax Court House when he blew silently between their campfires to spirit away a brigadier general, a captain, thirty men, the unit telegraph operator, and fifty-four horses without firing a shot — the reward of superb operational intelligence, of secrecy so tight that not even his men knew their destination. "The safety of the enterprise," he recalled, "lay in its novelty."[12] There is much to admire in his technique. It is nonetheless worth remembering how he would defend his torching of a train that same year: "There was nobody but soldiers on this train; but, if there had been women and children, too, it would have been all the same to me."[13] Throughout, he claimed to have been tormented by "martinets" and "red tape" in Richmond, but there are frequently good reasons why higher military authority is usually at odds with its rule-breakers.[14]

The Union struck back with predicable fury, deploying its own special force to turn Mosby's techniques against him. A hundred volunteer scouts were armed with seven-shot Spencer carbines, but were soon cornered by the Rangers near what is today Myerstown, West Virginia, with the loss of fifty-five men, their captain clubbed to the ground with the butt of a pistol before being sent south to internment.

The other approach was more familiar. The bitter history of partisan warfare forever comes back to the common fact that an occupier will, sooner or later, drop any restraint in rough proportion to the increasing effectiveness of resistance. In this case, draconian orders, soon amended, came down from Ulysses Grant personally: to destroy all the forage in northern Virginia's Fauquier and Loudoun counties, intern every man under fifty, take the families of known Rangers hostage, and hang any Rangers captured. Major General George Armstrong Custer, part of the force Grant sent to desolate the Shenandoah Valley, hanged or shot seven. Other prisoners were acknowledged to have been quietly "disposed of."[15] Mosby just as summarily ordered seven of Custer's troopers to be executed (four escaped from the half-hearted effort), and matters quickly equilibrated to the *status quo ante pendendum:* a dialogue of action and response that has yet survived.

Both sides continued to refine their special operations right up to the end, for instance, in the Appomattox campaign, which brought Lee and most of the Army of Northern Virginia to capitulation. Union scouts from a fifty-eight-man unit tapped enemy telegraph wires to misdirect vitally needed supply trains. As for the Confederacy — given its capacity for raiding, "special service," and clandestine organization — no wonder that U.S. prosecutors looked beyond John Wilkes Booth and his tiny band of incompetent malcontents to try to pin responsibility for Lincoln's assassination on a far more elaborate plot crafted at the highest levels in Richmond. Only a year before, after all, a Union cavalry raiding force had nearly penetrated the Confederate capital with the probable intention of killing Davis and his cabinet — and had done so, the entire South believed, at Lincoln's explicit orders.

It takes no abuse of the "logic trail" of modern professional intelligence analysis to see Lincoln's death as a desperate, unintended outgrowth of a well-organized kidnapping plot terribly recast by its operatives on the spot. The original preparations may have drawn on the range of resources at the disposal of what, by war's end, had finally consolidated into the rebels' Special and Secret Service Bureau, with the objective of abducting Lincoln from Washington, rowing him across the Potomac, and then rushing him through Mosby country with the aid of the ghostly operators who, even as the Confederacy died, still ruled the nighttime. There is evidence that Lincoln was to be brought into high Confederate hands, whether for trial or negotiating advantage. When the events that preceded the catastrophe at Ford's Theater on April 14, 1865, are examined in terms of technical knowledge, support structure, precedent, motivation, and documented fact, a compelling case can be made that the Confederate leadership had launched a special operation against the President of the United States.[16]

Booth, as such analysis sees it, began as just one of the participants. While plans were coming together in fall 1864, for instance, he had obtained pistols, handcuffs, and two hard-to-acquire Spencers (while coordinating with other operatives more directly linked to "special services") during his November theater appearance in New York. That this rather elegant scheme was corrupted into cold murder (and, had it been more competently handled, the temporary beheading of the U.S. government with the killings of Vice President Andrew Johnson and Secretary of State William Henry Seward) was likely due to the Confederacy's implosion in early April. The responsible people at the top of the chain of command were isolated from the brooding drunkards and nihilists on the ground in Washington — which should not obscure the subtle planning that seems to have framed the original enterprise.

Had it been brought off, Lincoln's abduction could have been one of history's most shattering special operations. The murderous outcome was more significant still, as the nation ended up without a strong president to manage the tremendous complexities of victory. The attempt was a preview of secret warfare that began to go far beyond what, say, Jack Sisson and friends had done in the American Revolution, or what Bonaparte's henchmen pulled off against an unessential figure like d'Enghien. Such special-warfare techniques of assassination and abduction would not come into their own until World War II, extending from there to the most classified of all types of missions undertaken by shadow warriors today.

‡

WELL BEFORE Appomattox, the war was being studied by European powers for its novel uses of rail and telegraph, and its mobilizing of mass forces and supplies. It is these destructively creative examples of industrialization that so impressed the Prussians. What went right past the military thinkers of the time were the small, dirty, technologically leveraged features that had been shown to be intertwined with modern war, some of which would resurface spontaneously, with no further preparation, in Europe fifty years later.

In his younger days, Prussia's Field Marshal Helmut von Moltke had been one of the first railroad executives in Germany (that mid-nineteenth-century theme again). He was a thinking man, a distinguished novelist and geographer, whose office began developing a rail bureau before the American Civil War had finished showing what locomotive power could do. By throwing half a million rail-borne troops against the French frontier before the enemy could get half that number into place on their own soil, he won the crucial early victories that were to determine the six-month conflict of 1870–71.

The Franco-Prussian War upended Europe's assumptions about comparative power. Among its humiliations, France lost its eastern province of Alsace and parts of Lorraine. The war's brevity is likely one reason for a lack of special enterprise much beyond the guerrilla. (It had taken a year, after all, for Andrews to gear up.) What existed was in the form of *francs-tireurs,* originally based on rifle clubs in eastern France and on the model of similar ones in Switzerland — men without uniform who, in the German advance on Paris in 1870, operated as auxiliaries by blowing up rail lines and bridges, launching themselves in small bands against German troops, and sniping at marching columns. Even Garibaldi's presence on the side of France in command of an army of some ten thousand *francs-tireurs* (the revolutionary outcasts and downtrodden of half a dozen nations fighting around Dijon and Autun) was of little help.[17]

It is thereafter in German planning that we see the concept gaining a foothold of well-crafted special warfare aimed at other major nations: planning that involved not only combined land and sea offensives against the Low Countries and France, as well as the insolent United States, but also steps to incite Holy War among the Moslem peoples of rival colonial powers. All of which adds up to a warning that visions of conventional and unconventional warfare alike float out of control without endless reality checks.[18]

Particularly impressive is the first realistic modern plan for strategic special warfare. It was formulated at the improbable initiative of the Russian admiralty, always a little anxious to show itself alert in the councils of the biggest land power. Their scheme serves as a rather telling reminder of the unusual initiative that the endless challenges of the sea can bring out in naval officers. Drafted during the 1885 Anglo-Russian crisis over Afghanistan, the plan gives context to the island-kingdom's nightmare of the time — a "bolt out of the blue," as it was phrased — the British coming to fear that the compactness and accessibility by sea of their homeland now left them particularly vulnerable to surprise in the swift era of steam.[19]

The Russians, who governed the greatest continuous imperial entity in history, discerned Britain's unique weakness as both the world's most developed nation and farthest-flung empire. A generation previously, during the Crimean War, superior naval power had enabled Britain and France to strike at will (if not always effectively) against Russia in the Black Sea and the Baltic. Now Russian naval planners proposed literally to disconnect the British Empire by moving against its long-range electrical communications, technologies that made possible the efficient use of Britain's dispersed strength and, for that very reason, could undercut it if unplugged. Raiding parties and grapnel ships were to strike relay stations and undersea lines, thereby enabling Russian forces to mass unparried against the wealth of British colonial targets exposed in the sudden silence. Czar Alexander III blinked, however, and the plan was not implemented.

Still, ever more aspects of war were drawing on the inventive strengths of nations. The international telegraph was among the heralded breakthroughs of the time, and we know from experience how technological advances great and small both enable special undertakings and offer new targets for them to destroy. By 1875, Alfred Nobel had discovered how to convert unstable nitroglycerin into safe, easily deployable dynamite. Mining and civil engineering would benefit, but so, too, could strike teams now able to carry explosives powerful enough to act against the new age's constructive marvels of Portland cement and structural steel. By 1887, Charles Parsons's turbine had made possible small raiding craft that could outdo the speed of much larger steam-driven ships sent to chase them down once the telegraph lines had warned of an assault by sea.

All these advances offered fine possibilities to the special warrior, but it was still on the edge of exploration and settlement — rather than in conflicts between industrializing nations which kept pursuing maximization of numbers — that he thrived. Time and again, this alternative to armies would show what a few brave men could do, adding to the small-force mystique for the future. Old-fashioned rigidity and contempt for an opponent destroyed Column No. 3 at the hands of the Zulus in 1879, but a fragile outpost in Natal at Rorke's Drift the next day held off a Zulu enemy thirty times the size of its garrison. There was also a compelling administrative reason why certain proven, well-prepared outfits came to be valued far beyond their numbers and firepower. If Spain is a country "where small armies are cut up and big armies starve," much of the theater of nineteenth-century imperialism occurred in lands where small conventional armies were wiped out and big, slow-moving ones died of fever. In the 1880s, it cost the French some five thousand lives to conquer Madagascar; of these, a few score may have been killed in action. Nor was Vietnam a health resort as the French in those years pushed up to Hanoi from the south.

In fact, a tiny French presence had briefly grasped Hanoi some years earlier, in 1873, and by a fast-moving, hard-hitting, well-executed feat in the heroic style. One headstrong ensign, the cartographer Francis Garnier, brought no more than a hundred sailors and marines straight up the Mekong, brushed aside the forces of the Vietnamese emperor, took Hanoi's citadel against greatly superior numbers, and imposed himself upon this ancient seat of imperial power. French authority only had had to recoil because, within a month, the emperor called in a band of the Mekong's river pirates, themselves operators of a sort we have met before.

At least no one was succumbing to malaria on the Great Plains, where Indian fighters had adopted their enemy's speed and stealth into cavalry routine in open country. One of the standouts was that thoroughly unregimented frontiersman Frank J. North, who never held a regular U.S. Army commission, yet perhaps just for that reason was able to create the Pawnee Scouts. He was fluent in the language and led in six extremely persuasive campaigns against the Pawnees' far more numerous tribal enemies (by now also those of the United States), losing just one man killed. It is hard to see the railroad going through Cheyenne country remotely so fast without North's thrifty effectiveness.

The horse peoples of the Plains were certainly predators, but not without the kind of grievances that have made resistance elsewhere the stuff of patriotic myth. These lands and the Indians' way of life were being cut into by campaigns that combined the qualities of special warfare with the terrible twist of making the entire ecosystem a strategic objective. This meant more than killing the buffalo. Another Indian fighter, Ranald Mackenzie, was an army officer but, significantly for us, also a crippled cavalry phenom whom the Indians called "Bad Hand" — again, the outlier. During the 1870s, his operations against the Kickapoos included a raid right into Mexico, and a devastating one in the Texas Panhandle against the Comanches, Kiowas, and Cheyenne that involved driving some fourteen hundred of their horses off a cliff after a surprise attack. Mackenzie showed not only a gift for striking at the heart of Indian society but an understanding of strategic consequences once native warriors were deprived of the capacity to maintain a running war.

Garnier was done in by the river pirates. North would die from injuries after being trampled while performing in his friend Buffalo

Bill's Wild West show. Mackenzie went mad while still a serving officer, dying at forty-nine after being removed from a New York asylum. These were among the men who chose to place themselves in extreme circumstances with shared qualities of resourcefulness, speed, and little concern for being outnumbered — all for what other combatants would have been a worrying distance from backup. They were not men to fade away at the Old Soldiers' Home.

‡

JUST AS the French first seized Hanoi, British imperial clout had reached out across almost equally ill-known distances to put down insurrection in northern Manitoba against the newly imposed Dominion authority.[20] The outbreak was too far from the center of power in Ottawa for the six-year-old central government to quell. Instead, the mother country mobilized the man who for a generation would be its worldwide military fixer, Garnet Wolseley. He took a 1,200-man canoe-borne force, maximally adapted to the country in which it would make its presence felt, six hundred miles from Lake Superior toward the Red and Assiniboine rivers within weeks rather than months. It was a model of how to move far and fast, by a colonel who recognized that he had a lot to learn quickly, right down to adopting the better New World ax heads used by the locals. Showing up so suddenly and confidently melted the rebellion.

Faced by another waterway problem eleven years later — but this time in the Sudan — the by-now General Wolseley worked out a comparable solution. The rivers of Manitoba are hardly like the Nile, but Wolseley's sense of the similarities nearly paid off. Four hundred French Canadian *voyageurs* with specially made boats were called in during 1884 to race a task force upriver from Egypt in a desperate effort to save Major General Charles "Chinese" Gordon and his garrison at Khartoum. This hard-drinking religious eccentric had made his reputation as a foreign expert in a colossal Chinese civil war, the Tai Ping Rebellion. After having been dispatched into Sudan to evacuate British-commanded Egyptian garrisons, he found himself trapped in a ten-month siege by the Mahdi, the greatest rebel leader in all Islam at that juncture — and, in the eyes of some in London, a religious fanatic only a little more peculiar than Gordon himself. Gordon's friend Wolseley moved the lessons learned north of the 49th Parallel, across half a dozen climate zones, to direct an operation that, only because of political-military screwups (reinforcements sent too late, the rescue commander mortally wounded, his replacement overly cautious) made contact just two days after the entire Khartoum garrison had been destroyed to a man.

Gordon's head may have been paraded on a pike through the streets, but other men kept transplanting their peculiar talents from one side of the globe to the other. For example, Frederick Burnham, another renowned Indian fighter in the closing years of the American frontier, had gone on to be useful as a hired gun in an Arizona range war in the 1880s. Captivated since childhood by tales of Africa, in 1893 he was to be found in Matabeleland, part of the present Zimbabwe, as a scout for Cecil Rhodes's British South Africa Company. He became famous for his magnificent but unsuccessful attempt to assist a cavalry assault party (the Shangani Patrol) disastrously overextended while seeking to capture the Ndebele king. As a gunman-cum-politico-military operator, however, Burnham is best remembered for the part he played against the subsequent Ndebele rebellion three years later, at the head of a daring raid that tracked one of the most provocative of the movement's prophets to a sacred cave in the Matopo Mountains, an eerie terrain even for a hiker today. Burnham himself strode in and killed the man — the coup that likely ended the uprising.

Using special warfare techniques for often dubious purposes is a reminder that high warrior qualities, though admirable to contemplate, are no better than the cause in which they are enlisted. We can be in awe of how only sixty thousand Boers of two sovereign republics fought to uphold their independence from the British Empire for nearly three years during 1899–1902, while giving the word *commando* to at least as many languages as the Peninsular War has given that of *guerrilla*. That these Boers' descendants in white-supremacist South Africa would use their superb Reconnaissance Commandos later in the twentieth century to crush black African nationalist guerrillas is another matter.

The British tried to make sense of how simple farmers (*boers,* in Dutch) could inflict so many setbacks on the 450,000 seasoned regulars and other well-equipped volunteers who poured in over these years from throughout the Empire to subdue them. The easy answer was to give much of the credit to the racial origins of these rugged settlers, whose forefathers in the Netherlands had for eighty years held off all the might of Spain, and who in southern Africa had inter-mixed with the bloodlines of French Huguenot refugees.[21] Of course, the real reasons had more to do with local culture, environment, and the fact that handling horses and repeating rifles was second nature for so many of a people who, in the 1820s and 1830s, had left the British-ruled Cape Colony to conquer new territories on the south-ern African tableland.

The war was unlike any other of the Victorian era. The Boer farmer-warriors (they hated to be called soldiers) had no experience in fighting big forces of well-equipped Europeans; the Empire had never faced mobile, nearly invisible riflemen ranging so effectively over so large an expanse. The Boers pulled themselves together in "commandos" — fighting units cut loose from any base, with a mobility and a cohesion rarely found in conventional armies. True bands of brothers, each man came and went as he pleased, used the weapons he preferred, and fought in the most democratic of loosely structured formations. They wore no uniforms, and frequently appropriated the khaki ones now adopted by the British army, which had only given up on scarlet two years earlier (for wearing which cap-tured Boers would be shot). These hard-hitting, weather-exploiting raiders were not fighting by the book — except, to their misfortune, at the start.

The Boers opened the war with a heavy, blundering offensive. They mired themselves in long ineffective sieges of large rather than strategically useful cities, possibly losing the opportunity for a knock-out blow by denying the British their vital ports. The Empire resumed its own rudely interrupted offensive once the sieges of Ladysmith, Kimberley, and Mafeking were lifted. Troops arrived from Britain, Canada, New Zealand, Australia, and British units in India (no Indian troops; this was "a Sahibs' war"). Surely, it was believed, conventional methods would in turn knock out the obsti-nate farmers, undoubtedly demoralized by the loss of their capitals, Pretoria and Bloemfontein.

Instead, the British found the sea of grass that extended over much of the contested terrain a deadly ocean for Boer commando units that had now begun to fight as mounted corsairs. The Boers' effectiveness became legend, but even in this type of war they were not fully playing to their strengths. Their militias may have been organized as commandos, but they fought as spontaneous guerrillas, not as honed special operations forces. We read of them, for instance, blowing up rail lines, not seizing trains the better to harm the whole system. Their stealthy bands were not infiltrating deep into British-held territory to sabotage and assassinate in what veterans would long remember as "the last of the gentlemen's wars" for the relative decency with which white opponents in the field still treated one another, if nobody else.[22]

For three years after what might have been a quick Boer victory — perhaps opening an opportunity to make a deal — the resistance of these farmers drained millions from the British treasury. The British were compelled to change: to rethink the nature of surprise; to arm roughly ten thousand black African combatants and concede their peculiar skills as native scouts; and to rely on the masterful reconnaissance of Highland ghillies shipped in from Scotland — the latter known as Lord Lovat's "Scouts," formed by the chieftain of the Fraser clan. Australian Bushmen were used as infiltrators, and Australian cavalry strike forces, as unconventional in their mode of war as in their culture, swept across the veldt. Except for the natives, these were not local people who had any particular knowledge of the land, but in their own domains they had felt the discipline of heat, thirst, and the need to blend into the terrain, absent anything but their own resources to rely on. Not that British victory held joyful news for London. If a few thousand heroic throwbacks like the Boers had been such a bellyful, a few hundred million subject people or a few hundred thousand technically sophisticated adversaries from the industrialized world might prove much, much worse.

‡

AMERICA'S OWN bite at overseas imperialism — seen in the war of April to December 1898 against Spain — contained even less originality. It was yet another bulk delivery of an ill-prepared big force, this time dumping volunteers from throughout the then forty-five states to die far more from disease and festering provisions than from enemy shot in Cuba. Dishonest "embalmed-beef" contractors alone may have killed more of their countrymen than did King Alfonso's soldiers.

There were legendary actions to be sure: the Rough Riders at San Juan Hill (the more legendary because African-American "Buffalo Soldiers" had already cracked the Spanish position); Commodore George Dewey's steaming through mine-infested Manila Bay and past the Spanish batteries to sweep Montojo's fleet from the water; Richard Hobson and seven volunteers scuttling the collier *Merrimac* in Santiago de Cuba harbor while attempting to bottle up the Spanish fleet. What is most significant for our story, however, is a minute fourth operation, the covert nighttime penetration of the Cuban coast under presidential orders by Lieutenant Stephen Rowan, USA, who was to be paraded before the world as the war's true hero.

A Message to Garcia, the poorly chronicled depiction of Rowan's exploit, became "one of the most extraordinary documents ever issued in the United States," or perhaps anywhere in light of its immense global distribution.[23] It may have sold forty million copies in at least twenty languages, including Chinese, Turkish, and Hindustani. It is a parable of prompt, high-initiative individual action — in mean-spirited contrast to the author's almost pornographic caricature of industrial workers as lackadaisical, responsibility-fleeing louts. Dashed off one night in February 1899 by the poisonous Elbert Hubbard, a crackpot philosopher, soap salesman, moralist, and corporate cheerleader, to be included in his appropriately titled monthly *The Philistine,* it was bought in half-million lots by the New York Central and by the Russian railways. It was distributed within the Japanese bureaucracy. And it was made into a dreadful 1936 movie starring Wallace Beery and Barbara Stanwyck.

At the outbreak of war, President McKinley wanted to communicate immediately with the supposed head of the Cuban insurgents, General Garcia, somewhere in the island's mountainous interior. There was no telegraph, certainly no radio, but neither were there layers of Pentagon E-Ring bureaucracy to cut through. (There was no Pentagon.) One of the unscheduled visitors who popped in on the White House in those days seems to have let it drop that "there's a fellow by the name of Rowan who will find Garcia for you, if anybody can." Once identified and handed the president's letter, Lieutenant Rowan put it in an oilskin pouch, wrapped it around his chest, landed four days later on the Cuban coast from an open boat, and disappeared inland, to emerge three weeks later.

Rowan and Garcia may well have met in more salubrious circumstances at a beach hotel rather than in the depths of rebel terrain. And, for all the title, the message in question was actually *from* Garcia, outlining his plans to McKinley. But the point is that Rowan allegedly did not ask his superiors who Garcia might be or how to get to him. He was some kind of unstoppable robot.

The immensely influential author of the account — whose shaping of the mythology of the American business culture only ended when he went down sixteen years later in the torpedoed *Lusitania* — concludes that civilization is one long search for individuals like Rowan, the man who can be expected to get things done, to get a history-changing message through. To that end, *Garcia* is the first inspirational essay to be written for industry, in fact the beginning of a business literature nine years before the founding of Harvard Business School.[24] "Look at what your employees could be like," is its premise, as it rationalizes leaving anyone less enterprising (or docile) in the cold. One wonders what Mosby, by now a deserving Republican taking a break between high consular and Justice Department service, made of it.

More than a generation after the Gray Ghost had haunted northern Virginia there began to unfold in the West an ever-widening sense of self-demanding human possibility, not only among resourceful officers such as Rowan, but among many people of similar character who set out to attain a higher level of achievement for its own sake: racing to the Poles; developing the riskier forms of bullfighting; or making the first climb up Mount Olympus. Indeed, the Olympic Games had been revived in 1896, with the new twist of setting records (rather than just vanquishing one's opponent) and the pentathlon revised to include riding, shooting, fencing, running, and swimming — the staff officer's repertoire of the times.

After a hundred years of technical miracles, this competitive drive for various excellences was also a new part of life and culture. The more one expects of oneself, the more one accomplishes, and the more one gets beyond externally imposed standards of what is possible. When we are continuously trying to exceed our personal best — when self-command makes us the severest judges of what is an operational success — that is when the world can be startled. It is the attitude of people who find discomfort stimulating, and it is one to be found among men who scale cliffs to reach a fortress or rappel down office towers to smash in windows as they "clear a room." Extreme athletes and amateur adventurers who embraced key qualities of the commando were adding themselves to the human-resource pool of war.

Such highfliers are to be found in any nation, and it is a reason why open societies that give free vent to individual creativity and assertion have no monopoly on bringing together the astonishing, outlying talents who compose a special operations force. Shadowing the individual's quests for heroic achievement, after all, was the power of the state and of the big organization to co-opt these energies for the heavy-handed purposes of the collective. We get a good preview of that in the use Hubbard's essay makes of the dutiful Rowan. While the crude, still unreformed capitalism championed in *Garcia* was pushing forward, there soon arose far worse "isms," inflamed by their coercive visions of the future of man: socialism, syndicalism, communism, and fascism, with the latter two enabling precisely these kind of men to come together in superbly capable special forces — a contribution to making the twentieth century the bloodiest ever.

14

From Spark to Flame
Alternative Means: Kitty Hawk to the End of All Wars, 1903–1918

"If it works, it's obsolete."
T. E. LAWRENCE

A HUNDRED years ago, practical people could look at the new century and anticipate a future of worldwide progress. It was a time of rapid industrialization, peace among the great powers, exploration of most every corner of the globe, booming international trade, the dawn of flight. If one were, say, an insurance executive in New York or London, Paris or Berlin, St. Petersburg or Tokyo, one might comfortably assume that accidents and deaths would happily continue, but in rationally predictable numbers. As usual, there were intellectuals anticipating strange and dangerous events: Jack London foresaw world trade carrying world-annihilating plague; H. G. Wells described some ghastly ironclad land vehicle of war; E. M. Forster envisioned a narcissistic planetary culture that fades out of existence because it has lost the gumption to maintain itself. But then, intellectuals always seem to see the worst in life. In the words of an eminent socialist Member of Parliament speaking of the future, "Up and up and up, on and on and on."[1]

Yet at the turn of the century, the world was far more perilous than most people understood — or than is now commonly believed by those who speak of a chimerical "Pax Britannica" since the overthrow of Bonaparte.[2] Well before World War I, significant voices could be heard urging what is today called "preemption." All this advancement could be seen as ultimately winner-takes-all, with room only for so many in the sun, whether of empire or industry. Surely this or that opponent had to be stopped before one's country was hopelessly outclassed. What might be the implications of Germany's steady industrial displacement of Britain — or, as seen from Berlin, of Russia's slower but even greater possibilities? As for the French, pioneers in aviation and the internal combustion engine, they dwelled on "revenge" for the disasters Germany had inflicted on them in 1870–71. And Germany's only true ally, Austria-Hungary, was offering no encouraging sign of being able to hold itself together once the old emperor died.

Already by 1912, enormous numbers of men were under arms backed by yet-greater reserves of former conscripts: France and its ally Russia possessing a total of nearly two million men; Germany and Austria-Hungary assembling around 1.25 million; with Britain's high-quality, long-service army by far the smallest.[3] (The British Army was merely "a shell to be fired by the Royal Navy," it was said at the time, about the only contender without compulsory military service.) All were ready to lunge into huge expansion.

There may have been peace since 1871 among the great powers, but an unprecedented arms race was accelerating. The Royal Navy was the world's largest, but never as omnipotent as fantasts of a twenty-first-century "Pax Americana" argue today; it was being challenged by the German naval buildup, and perhaps even that of the Americans as well.[4] Here, too, the emphasis was on the big and heavily armed, in this case the battleship, undergoing its fourth complete metamorphosis in forty years.

To add to life's uncertainties, Japan had risen meteorically to formidable military clout in two decades, passing from feudalism to state-of-the-art weaponry and organization in less time than it had taken the West to move from the repeating rifle to the machine gun. Tokyo applied its skills and Bushido spirit in surprise attack — a tradition the world would get to know well, first against China in 1894, then, shockingly, crippling a Russian fleet in 1904 without bothering to declare war. As for the United States, it kept relatively remote from the quarrels of the industrializing world except as a conciliator, but had taken a taste of extracontinental empire from Spain and was concerned not to be dealt out of vast, decaying China.

When war ministers and generals pondered the years ahead, the extraordinary payoffs that might result from small, focused operations were hardly the first thing to come to mind. General staffs concerned themselves with moving armies the size of nations, with how to take fortresses not by forlorn hopes (let alone by commando raid) but by pummeling them with gigantic railborne artillery, untried but awe-inspiring. This was the logic of early coal-and-iron industrial revolution: ever bigger, ever more centrally controlled. Only when desperation would come to take hold, as the huge resources of opposing armies brought stalemate, would warlords search for relatively minute means of leverage on the sprawling battlefront. But small things were creating big instabilities even during the run-up.

In the colonized world, young Indians and Vietnamese were envisioning their nations set free — and in Ottoman-controlled Arabia, a violently potent step toward that end was taken in five minutes, as we will see. The vainglorious Kaiser Wilhelm II was just creative enough to imagine how he might assist downtrodden peoples elsewhere in the Moslem world. Militant Islam could be a powder keg under the far-flung realms of his great opponents: Russia, France, and above all Britain. Germany fortunately having no Moslem colonial subjects, he had already noisily proclaimed himself, while in Damascus during 1898, as protector of the world's three hundred million true believers. This was a step of applied ethnology that would have been inconceivable as soldiers' work in 1870. However, his Chief of the General Staff at the outbreak of the next war also thought it a splendid idea to harness "the fanaticism of Islam" to the German war machine.[5] And the British would fuel Arab insurgency in turn. Once the war arrived, the farther away we get from its main battlefronts the more we encounter small improvising outfits with big impact. Maybe the edge *could* help consume the center.

Another source of disorder at the start of the century was terrorism, generating consequences and institutions still with us. As with today's killers, its practitioners were of many different types driven by as many different motivations. Some movements made war on constitutional governments, such as anarchists who threw a bomb into France's Chamber of Deputies in 1892, and did the same to fancy cafés, or to a Barcelona theater. Others came from genuine oppressed nationalities striking back at their overlords, as did the Armenians against their harsh Turkish masters, and the Irish, who would soon bring a successful fight for independence into the very capital of the world's biggest empire (eliciting London's "Special Branch" in response).[6] Relentless efforts by revolutionaries against the czardom had included bombings and assassinations: a mine blew up much of the Winter Palace in a deadly inventive operation before the revolutionaries' bloody three years' hunt finally got Alexander II in 1881, and before systematic terror, as so well evoked in Conrad's *Under Western Eyes,* revived in the early 1900s. Could gargantuan, semi-feudal Russia endure such seemingly low-level strain imposed by cabals of tenacious destroyers?

Indeed, Europe's actuarial tables did not contain many good life risks after all.

‡

BY THE early twentieth century, more fiction was being written than ever before that sought to bring home the earth-shaking possibilities of a world being remade and remade again by war scares, politics, and science. Scientific detectives, aeronaut heroes, and colonial demigods offered easier instruction than the usual heavy texts on chemistry, engineering, and geography were ever going to provide. So, too, in special operations. We see in G. K. Chesterton's 1904 story, *The Napoleon of Notting Hill,* an early revelation (with a light twist) of how a small band might use a great city's infrastructure to coerce the state.

By 1984, his story goes, the old hereditary monarchy has disappeared. Amiable kings are chosen at random under the brisk administration of technocrats. For our interest, the megaplan to put a highway through a quiet London neighborhood is thwarted by an opposition of lovable cranks, who nullify the grandest ambitions of their (in the end) worthy rival, Councilor Buck. They seize that exemplar of modernity, the waterworks, and rather symbolically threaten to wash him and his overwhelming municipal forces away. Buck concedes, compelled by "all the power of his great sanity" to acknowledge that a handful of clever people cannot merely obstruct the supremely rational state, they can subjugate it. Chesterton could see that the more magnificently steel-clad and technocratic a society, the deeper the chink in its armor.

Who else was looking at the possibilities of so efficiently crippling an industrialized enemy? No one other than creative writers thought in these terms. Surely the big and powerful, not the small and ingenious, would forever hold the secret of dominance. The uneasy exception possibly lay in a rare sense of vulnerability to sabotage. In the war scare of 1911, for instance, the Home Secretary wondered "what would happen if twenty determined Germans in two or three motor cars arrived well armed . . . one night" to blow up the magazines where all Britain's reserves of naval cordite were stored. Essentially no one else was concerned about such a bizarre possibility. But the Home Secretary was Winston Churchill and he demanded guards of Royal Marines.[7] As for the more elaborate approaches of the waterworks variety, those were to remain fiction for a while longer.

Thus the special operation was still a curiosity to be applied less in the industrialized world than to subdue restless natives in the back of beyond. To this end, the experience of the U.S. Army in the Philippines from early 1899 into summer 1902 is significant, particularly when twenty-first-century pundits speak glibly of "small wars" and "imperial policing."

Comparisons of current U.S. military dilemmas to what was long known as the Philippine "Insurrection" — along with supposed parallels to whacking the Barbary pirates, the 1900 intervention against the Boxer Rebellion in China, the various curious experiences in Russia during 1918–20, and subsequent U.S. counterguerrilla efforts in the Caribbean — first became popular during the Vietnam War.[8] However, such comparisons soon break down, rooted as they are in too many far-fetched analogies, and all the more so today, given the utterly different capacities of engrained, often anonymous enemies: for starters, their communications, hitting power, and reach. Discussing America's small wars of the past may pep up the cheerleaders: "We did it before and we can do it again." But these treatments usually offer worse than misleading conclusions not only for policy but for what (other than the very basics) they tell us about the nature of the beast — special operations and their prey. This is the least likely of subjects on which undigested history is a guide for anything more than, say, affirming the need for soldiers to be resourceful in exotic lands.[9]

Ironically, the U.S. Army in the Philippines started out with its own unhelpful analogies. The army still remembered fighting Indians on the Great Plains, and surely, it believed, those wars were full of instruction for the jungles of Luzon, the most important island among the seven thousand in the vast Philippine archipelago. By casting the *insurrectos* as Comanches, commanders were confident that they could write the script for trouncing nationalist guerrillas in tropical mountains.[10] What lay ahead became far more costly than expected. Operations against highly mobile mounted combatants in thinly populated, wide-open country offered little relevance for tropical warfare. One would need to go no further than children's books to learn that Sitting Bull was no jungle fighter and that Custer was not handicapped by the rainy season.

With the signing of the Treaty of Paris in December 1898, the United States moved to take over the greater part of the Spanish Empire. Troops finally arrived in Manila that month, around eleven thousand men at the start, to find themselves by February in a vicious fight with the brave, far larger following of Emilio Aguinaldo, a twenty-nine-year-old firebrand whom Commodore Dewey had originally brought back from Spanish-paid exile in Hong Kong to help bring down the existing colonial government. As Americans spoke of lifting up the Filipinos, of marrying them into the family of nations, etc. — and moved to annex the islands — Aguinaldo declared independence and became president, and America's first experience in strong-armed "nation-building" began.

Of course, the Philippines was not yet a nation — a point to keep in mind when dealing with a pastiche like Iraq today, or any number of African states tomorrow that are little more than colors on a map. For the first nine months, the *insurrectos* dutifully tried to fight like soldiers, serving themselves up on toast to the Americans. As had happened so often, much blood had to flow before a headstrong movement learned to play to its strengths: familiarity with jungle-crowded valleys, a peasant population into which warriors could blend, an inchoate mode of warfare that spindled out time against an opponent eager for fast results. U.S. commanders were put off balance by these stealthier opponents, who fought in a kaleidoscope of alliances, raiding and ambushing in bands scarcely ever more than fifty strong, collecting taxes, setting up shadow governments, bullying their own people, and sometimes taking and torturing U.S. prisoners, although heaven only knows which side began that.

To this extent, the Philippines provided a preview of later twentieth-century special warfare. As more U.S. troops arrived, the next stage of the fight compelled them to build on very recent experience in the Philippines and to use those commonsense forms of combat we know as counterinsurgency: long-range patrols, night attacks, small dispersed garrisons, and highly targeted strikes. Here, exemplary massacre was thrown in for good measure.[11] Headway was finally made when junior army officers adapted their tactics to the different geographies and political situations in which they found themselves — by improving intelligence, using native guides, and merging themselves into the local cultures, for instance gambling at cockfights. Each small detachment was linked with "its" cluster of villages throughout the countryside. Lieutenants could modify overall directions as they thought best but were firmly held to finding the guerrillas in their areas. Real benevolence was crossbred with extreme violence, including torture — a practice more recently condoned, with civilized regret, by authors of the many "small-war" books stemming from Vietnam and 9/11.[12]

The mission that finally captured Aguinaldo, thus doing so much to take the heart out of the insurrection, was a special operation of a classic kind. Walking in the shade of Rasul Khan, a thirty-five-year-old brigadier general of Kansas Volunteer Infantry (i.e., National Guard) who already held the Medal of Honor for battling the *insurrectos,* proposed an extreme step to the military governor, Major General Arthur MacArthur. One of Aguinaldo's trusted lieutenants had defected, pinpointed the location of his leader's faraway headquarters, and also handed over dispatches that requested reinforcements.

Here was an opportunity, explained the National Guardsman, to take, say, eighty Macabebe Philippino Scouts and a few indigenous deep-country guides posing as insurgents straight into that redoubt. He and four other officers would accompany them as prisoners. MacArthur approved, though convinced he would never see any of his men again.[13]

Getting so far into the wild from the northeastern coast of Luzon meant being dropped on a distant shore by gunboat at night and ultimately approaching the village of Palanan through drenching jungle along a single, well-guarded trail. An outright raid on such a remote, well-defended place would have been impossible. For ten days the American "prisoners" and their captors hacked through the appalling terrain, sleepless in the soaking wet, their food soaked to ruin. On March 22, 1901, they arrived to find Palanan bedecked to celebrate Aguinaldo's birthday, a band playing. The Scouts (clad in nondescript insurgent dress and carrying rifles) strode into the settlement of some eighty thatched-roof huts arrayed around a square. The Americans hid in the bush.

The President's fifty-man bodyguard presented arms. Two of the infiltrators were taken into Aguinaldo's residence to report. While Aguinaldo was congratulating them on their achievement, one signaled to the men outside, who immediately blazed into the insurgents drawn up a few yards away, just as Aguinaldo's guests shot two of his aides and told him that he was now a prisoner of the United States. By the time the officers entered the town a few minutes later, all was in hand, and the little party with Aguinaldo in tow was exfiltrated by the gunboat back to Manila.

Beheading a political movement, as by the taking of Aguinaldo, could still be decisive in highly personalized political cultures but less so in the industrializing world of the time. The early twentieth-century example of piercing to the heart of power that has had the longest-term consequences was about to be enacted on the other side of Eurasia.

The angry Wahhabism combined with Saudi wealth, so familiar to us, stems from five frantic minutes in a Riyadh gateway in 1902. What took place there was again not some guerrilla ambush but a focused operation of high politics against a remote and well-armed enemy stronghold. It had to be brought off perfectly. If accomplished, all might fall into the laps of the Saudi raiders. If they failed, within the first few moments of making their presence felt in the enemy-held town, they could count on the consequences being worse than death, although probably not much worse than procedures in their own kingdom today.

Abdul Aziz, "Ibn Saud," came of a princely dynasty whose ancestors had joined forces with the religious reformer Muhammad Ibn Abdul Wahhab to command, by the late eighteenth century, a realm that encompassed nearly all the Arabian Peninsula. But the rising family of Al Rashid pried loose the grip of the House of Saud. By 1891, Ibn Saud's father had been driven from Riyadh to drag out his days in Kuwait. There the boy learned the bitterness of the bread of exile and the steepness of going up other men's stairs.

Ibn Saud was twenty-one when he decided to vindicate his family's right to Riyadh — a mud-walled speck in the wilderness 250 miles from the Persian Gulf, but nevertheless an historic seat of authority. An imposing six feet four inches, he rode and shot at a level to leave an impression on distant people who had rigorous standards in such matters. A British intelligence report would describe him some years later as "of kindly face and simple manners; intelligent, energetic and warlike."[14]

The account of his infiltration of Riyadh with around forty men on the night of January 15, 1902, and the death of the Rashidi governor early the following morning, is an exploit straight out of the Middle Ages by a man who would lead his reawakened nation into the era of the hydrogen bomb.

The details that bright bloody morning are as nearly encrusted in myth as the fall of Troy. Yet enough can be gleaned.[15] At sunset, Ibn Saud's forty slipped out of the desert into the fringe of ancient Riyadh, where the palm trees met the sand, carrying only swords, daggers, and a few rifles. They were all that remained of a much larger force that had left Kuwait some months earlier but had turned back in discouragement. Here, Ibn Saud picked just six men to take on a scouting mission, with the rest to follow. This little group likely used an old palm trunk to climb the wall on the town's northeast side (though another version says that they had grappling irons), then crept through the dark streets. Their objective was to place themselves near the well-garrisoned Mismak Fort, which brooded on its own square (commanding a clear field of fire) in the heart of the town.

Sneaking into the house of an astounded Saudi loyalist, the little band sought intelligence on the whereabouts and habits of the governor, whose nearly adjacent private residence stood opposite Mismak's strictly guarded main gate. These indeed being dangerous times, the governor was known to spend each night within the fort, emerging half an hour after sunrise through a postern (a two-by-three-foot hatchway in the gate, as was used in medieval castles, allowing access without the gate having to be opened). He would then cross the square to breakfast with his wife, or to go riding. But there were no nighttime sentries on his house.

Ibn Saud and his desert commandos climbed onto the roof of the loyalist's home, then onto the roof of the one separating it from the governor's, where they tied and gagged a couple found sleeping. Once the two had been secured, the commandos stood on the shoulders of others to reach the roof of the govenor's taller dwelling next door, then worked their way silently through the rooms, pinioning and gagging his wife and sister-in-law. A hole was broken in the rear wall of the ground floor to enable the others to slip in unnoticed from the palm groves.

All waited inside during the long hours before daybreak. Some slept, some read the Koran. Prayers were said at daybreak, facing Mecca to the southwest. On time, a bustle in the square signaled the governor's appearance. Whatever exactly occurred, Ibn Saud is known to have tied back his sleeves, knotted his headdress around his neck, and giving a terrible shout, plunged rifle in hand into the square, straight at the governor and his guards, the forty pouring behind him. Faced by this apparition, the guards bolted back to the gate but, frustrated by their own security, could only get through the postern one by one. Ibn Saud tackled the governor, who scrambled up, drawing his sword. Sentries began firing from the ramparts, probably doing as much harm as good to the indistinguishable melee below.

As Ibn Saud parried blows with his rifle butt, the governor suddenly turned to run for the postern. He seems to have been shot in the arm but, in any event, got himself halfway through the gate, shielded by guards tugging on his shoulders from within, the Saudis on the outside trying to hold on to his desperately flailing legs. Ibn Saud went down with a kick to the groin. In a final frantic heave, the garrison jerked their chief inside. Had the governor lived, the raiders would have been doomed. But in the very moment in which he seemed to have reached safety, someone stretched through with a knife and left him dying.

Once fear takes hold, it is amazing how fast and thoroughly one's worst nightmares are believed to have come true. What was essentially an elaborate assassination operation had fallen upon the garrison with such force, suddenness, and audacity as to convince them that they faced an entire army. The leaderless garrison surrendered without the raiders having to attempt the far more severe test of trying to scale the fort.

Year by year, Ibn Saud fought on to regain the Saudi realm, using Bedouin warriors as shock troops in the speedy camel-borne ways of Central Arabian warfare. Of course, the Riyadh garrison could have ended it all in minute six of the morning of January 16, even after the governor's death, by cutting down with similar dispatch the raiders milling in the square below. But the surprise had been too extreme, and Riyadh's elders were soon gathering to swear allegiance to the returned hero. Not that the world beyond the Nejd Desert would know much about this adventure, other than vague reports picked up via British gunboats in Kuwait Bay, or better-translated accounts that may have drifted home from German merchants doubling as intelligence agents in Bahrain. Only a few Western explorers had appeared in Riyadh in the nineteenth century; the next European would not even arrive until 1912.

At least Aguinaldo's capture ten months before had been cheered throughout the United States, Vice President Theodore Roosevelt exclaiming that "no single feat" in U.S. history could compare and, in character, advising the intrepid Kansan to turn his thoughts to Germany.[16] Yet even if these exploits had been discussed for more than a few minutes among the great powers' general staffs, what significance could they have had for warfare between civilized peoples? Surely the question — come what German militarists called *Der Tag*

(The Day) — would be how to assemble a hundred thousand men in hours and then move millions by rail.[17] The notion of sending a commando team behind the lines to abduct or kill an enemy leader would have been dismissed as close to a war crime.

Ignoring the possibilities of such leveraged operations in part reflected a lack of experience. The generals who would soon be fighting one another in Europe (the British excepted) had little practice in colonial warfare. Only two out of five future French marshals would have served outside France. Neither Ferdinand Foch nor Philippe Pétain, the two most famous French commanders to emerge from the coming war, would have had to contemplate other than rather archaic notions of the defense of Lorraine. As for Germany, few of its officers had served with the small, white, regular forces within the nation's barely settled colonies — and those who did, as in South–West Africa, had simply exercised a genocide surpassing in brutality even its imperialist peers. In Austria-Hungary, which possessed no colonies, only a handful had served against China's Boxer Rebellion. Italy had suffered successive colonial disasters, despite conquering Libya in 1911–12, so overseas colonial service was even less respected than in other armies.[18] Russia had built an empire over brave and skillful enemies in Central Asia, but neither the economic nor the political return had paid off. And the only reason that the British would have well-practiced commanders in that war was that the country's entire volunteer professional army was so comparatively small. Not that experience in having fought Boer commandos would prove enlightening on the Western Front. Since Field Marshals French and Haig were cavalry generals who had made their names in South Africa, it would be said in gloomy mockery, they seemed to expect the Front to open up into a limitless veldt across which they could gallop forever.[19] Limitless instead would be the hammering of armies on both sides of Europe.

‡

As we review the run-up to August 1914, sadly knowing what is to come, we ask ourselves how these extremely capable military professionals, these thoughtful and well-informed civil administrators, could so unquestioningly set themselves up for disaster. Did they not guess that the thirty or forty years after Prussia's 1871 victory —

decades that had changed the world more than any others — were likely to offer even greater surprises?

As always, a few sharp people were as skeptical of conventional practices as, say, Captain Codman had been at Kamiesh Bay. One did not have to be a special operator or even a clever sea captain to look askance at all this confidence. In a fine example of the banker's mind at work, the Warsaw financier Ivan Bloch had foreseen the possibility of a total deadlock caused by the amount of mutually nullifying fire-power that could be brought to bear. (Those who back — or with-hold from backing — grand visions requiring investment know that bigness and certainty can have unhappy consequences and that such visions may be far riskier than they seem, despite universal expert endorsement.) But not even Bloch had anticipated transcontinental battlefronts. The deceptively stable century of peace, punctuated only by swiftly resolved clashes, had not produced those periods of pro-longed international disorder that demand alternative ways of look-ing at the world.[20]

Senior officers with responsibilities for the lives of large numbers of men are rarely the most intellectually open-minded of people. Gen-eral staffs, like boards of directors in Detroit or trust officers in Boston, are sober, serious citizens whose very awareness of their weighty responsibilities can actually get in the way of meeting the unexpectedness of the modern world. "That's good sport," said Gen-eral Foch, the ultimate promising French officer, at the 1911 Paris Air Show, pointing to a Farman biplane, "but for the army the aero-plane is of no value."[21] Around the same time, one of the abler senior officers in the British army was informed on maneuvers that his tri-umphantly successful field exercise would have disintegrated in actual combat: his men would have been wiped out by a mounted machine-gun unit that had notionally opened fire from where it had galloped onto his flank. The general simply roared at the offending detachment's lieutenant, who was explaining this to him, to run up his stirrups and *walk back* to barracks.[22] Such incidents are often quoted to illustrate the military's resistance to innovation and its catastrophi-cally romantic attachment to old ways. Yet it is worth remembering that Thomas Edison, no technophobe, had made a similarly dismis-sive observation only fourteen years before, having denied during the mysterious "airship scare" of 1897 that flight was unlikely to be of any practical use but was something akin to fairground spectacles.[23]

So much that was antithetical was working against the spirit of special operations, of trying to convert the enemy's visible strength into his infectious weakness. The problem was not that these huge mass armies possessed no elite units. There were plenty of them: Britain's Guards regiments, France's Marine Fusiliers, Germany's Guards Rifles battalion. But these were corps d'élite of dash and endurance not bred to versatility or creativeness. Arguably, one reason for France's self-immolating offensive of summer 1914 was that its army had too many elites, or at least units that thought of themselves as such — magnificent, but just better at doing the usual — which under 1914 war doctrine had a way of meaning getting killed.[24]

French staff planners, driven by the disastrous combination of brilliance uninterrupted by experience, carried the fantasy of elite capacities to absurdity. They envisioned a headlong assault at all costs inspired by an *offensive à outrance* to sweep the doughy German army before it. After all, they puffed, France was the greatest nation; she could impose her unique shattering courage on mere vulgar technology. Their monuments are the military cemeteries where many of them lie. *"Le feu tue"* (bullets kill), as Colonel Philippe Pétain, one of the few expert marksmen of field grade, had muttered when this doctrine of moral ascendancy at bayonet point was expounded to him before the war.[25]

Even before the slaughter ended, horrified observers would speculate on what should have been done to avoid the calamity of August 1914. What indeed might have been the alternative to the Austrians declaring war on Serbia? Could other steps have been taken once Serbian suicide-squad nationalists (undoubtedly having contacts with elements in their little kingdom's government) assassinated the Hapsburg heir and his wife five weeks earlier, over the border in Bosnia's capital city of Sarajevo? Looking back, it is tempting to ask what if the Austrians, in whose empire Bosnia sat, had possessed a form of the special operations forces capability (say, SAS or Delta) with which we are now familiar? What if it had been deployed to pick up the loathsome "Apis," the Serb chief of military intelligence, and a couple of his irredentist pals? Given half a chance, though protesting loudly, Serbian ministers would have shed no tears over a covert step into their country to erase the "terrorists" killing in their name or, better still, to bring them before an Austrian court.[26] It is the sort of move one anticipates from a great power today. But not then.

‡

THERE HAD been earlier clashes that could be called worldwide wars, but in 1914–18 belligerence was to be found across every meridian. The Germans, for instance, were messing in Central Asia, and their seaborne raiders went straight for British cable stations. In turn, a single British ship immediately ripped up Germany's five undersea telegraph cables and momentarily isolated Berlin from much of the outside world.[27] Before the United States intervened in April 1917, the war had even hit New Jersey, when German saboteurs blew up munitions stored on Black Tom Island and then, a half-year later, destroyed the munitions plant in Kingsland.

Although the Eastern Front gave us the Soviet Union, the emblematic battleground was that in the West. There, the essence of the Great War belongs to the artistic revolution of its time — with tortured, obscurely communicative shapes, endless ruin and ravaging. The war's enduring tragedy is captured by F. Scott Fitzgerald's image in Tender Is the Night, of one empire moving forward a few yards a day up a slope of the blood-soaked Somme Valley, another empire falling back, both dying at the edge, when "a century of middle class love was buried here."

The political systems of the time were almost incapable of graduated military response. Yet, in a way, they were more civilized than today, or at least more mannered. With the outbreak of war, for instance, the Serbian general in chief, taking the waters at a spa in Austria, had been courteously escorted to the border. The following year, the Hungarian government, half of the Imperial-Royal Austro-Hungarian state, tried to pay the coupons of its enemies' bondholders. (Old habits, like the distinction between public and private obligations, die hard.) Throughout the next four years, generals would drive about in open cars; it would take another war before squads would be sent behind the lines to kill them. Such almost-personal violence was not part of the bulk-packaged way of war in 1914–18.

A conflict meant to be a three-month chess match — to be won by sheer élan and the genius of rail-transport officers — turned into a siege along 470 miles of excavations, which soon stretched from the North Sea to the Swiss border. On the plains of Flanders, the uplands of Picardy, amid the low hills of Lorraine, it became a war of long, deadly obstacles. There were no flanks to turn, as when armies had met on battlefields that spread within eyesight of one man on a hill. Rarely were there even battalion-level surprise attacks, although almost equally slogging raids on each side's trenches were the nocturnal dimension of the horror. Where were the alternatives to desperate frontal assaults across No Man's Land, a term that, not surprisingly, originated from the ground at the foot of a gallows?

Clever men of lesser rank were looking for them. Early on, the officer coordinating what British strategic planning there was had circulated a paper on how deadlocks had been broken in previous wars. Special devices had been provided, he observed, or attacks had been launched from some other direction.[28] His analysis laid out not only the principle of the tank but the "strategy of the indirect approach" — the unlikely way around — which is the hallmark of any mastery in battle, but so notably of special operations. Novel assaults by gas and armor had no adequate doctrine, however, to enable troops to exploit the breaches once made.[29] One enormous coordinated mine detonation might tear a hole in the line, as the British succeeded in doing with the million simultaneously detonated pounds of high explosive that reshaped the hills beyond Arras in 1917 — mining by then having attained the theoretical status of a routine, rather than its own form of special operation as in centuries past. But that surprise 3:10 A.M. eruption, which immediately entombed ten thousand Germans, took much time and luck. Stalemate would be broken only for a moment.

In Eastern Europe, the Germans initially enjoyed a succession of victories. Bulgaria sided with the Central Powers in 1915; then the following year Romania rallied to the Allies, soon to be overrun while Germany kept wearing down its great enemy, Russia. Against the Ottoman Empire, the bold French–imperial British attempt to circumvent the Western Front by pushing through the Dardenelles to capture Constantinople (thereby enabling them to join with the Russians from the rear) ended at Gallipoli in evacuation and forty-three thousand Allied dead; the attempt to push up the Tigris to take Baghdad led to the largest British surrender since Yorktown. Whole nations that did not know how to stop — that were too great to compromise — were becoming physically and emotionally exhausted.

Against such a backdrop of deadlock and reciprocating disaster, the Allied and Central powers groped for ways to cripple each other's empire. Perhaps, observes an historian who has studied one of the responses, "a few highly motivated agents, aided by friendly and sympathetic tribesmen, could accomplish what would normally have required several infantry divisions."[30] The British came to rely on their own unusual people — men part soldier, part political officer, part intelligence operative — who might more deftly unravel the Ottoman sultanate. Germany, for its part, remained alert to the ferment of political disaffection in an Indian subcontinent of 315 million. In the half-dozen years before 1914, a string of assassinations in that vastest of colonies had actually reached into the heart of London, when a high imperial official was killed in 1909. Then, in 1912, the British viceroy was terribly lacerated in Delhi by a bomb packed with nails, screws, and needles. Indian exiles were creating a network of overseas cells from headquarters in California, at Berkeley; a shrewd British secret agent was dispatched to San Francisco to monitor, but was rapidly uncovered and shot. Global terrorism was coming to be a price of empire: the opportunities offered to Germany appeared colossal.

Among them, Wilhelm II implemented his dream of raising militant Islam to drive the Russians from the Caucasus and Central Asia, and the British from India, home to by far the largest Moslem community in the world. His plan was to work through the Sultan (Caliph of all Sunni Islam, with authority to issue *fatwas*) in Turkey, the Shiites (with their spiritual capital in Baghdad), and to win the support of the young Shi'a Shah of Persia (Iran today), which had declared neutrality. The amir of Afghanistan was to be persuaded to push south. There was no precedent for a jihad in modern grand strategy — so here, as always on the frontier, special operators would have to be sent in from the start, to fight a shadow war between each side's colonial and intelligence services, their officers carefully chosen, smuggling arms and funds, and appealing to ancient passions and distant centers of authority. (The kaiser's Foreign Ministry specialist for revolution schemed to abet the effort through Germany's Jewish community, also expecting these patriots to line up against the pogrom-practicing Slavs.)[31]

Barely had war broken out when thousands of leaflets in Arabic (to be read and relayed by mullahs and imams) were run off in Constantinople, to be smuggled into India and Egypt, the Caucasus and Central Asia. They flamed with religious hatred, crying for the slaughter of all Christians except — no coincidence — Germans. The task of infiltrating these bales of sedition into lands still for the most part village societies was special work, but so was blocking them from being shared among the scores of millions in the empires.

To reinforce its printed presence, Berlin dispatched wide-ranging missions, not just of scholars and orientalists, but of tough, ruthless, hand-picked officers in their thirties — fluent in the relevant languages, whose political and military skills might be more helpful for gunrunning, bribery, and strong-armed persuasion. Both sides deployed their hard cases, but the imperially astute British — who, until alliances shifted, had had to contain Russian ambitions in Central Asia — may have possessed an edge. What occurred was a "New Great Game" (the original being the incessant late nineteenth-century intrigue and predation along India's northwest frontier), albeit with fewer innings.[32]

Germany gathered a secret mission of around eighty to head overland to Constantinople — the fit young men initially passing themselves off as a traveling circus company — then to make its way from Turkey's Ottoman Empire into Persia. Persia was to be rallied for a Holy War against British India; the rest of the force would go on to Afghanistan with promises of abetting historic vengeance against the British, that empire having twice seized Kabul, but for the moment keeping the amir on retainer for the sake of peace and quiet.

The foreign ministry and general staff in Berlin jointly controlled the operation, each designating a leader: at the start, Wilhelm Wasmuss, a rugged, aloofly handsome prewar career diplomat (in fact probably an intelligence officer on secondment) fluent in Persian and Arabic; and an army captain, Oskar von Niedermayer, well traveled in Persia and India (also probably for intelligence purposes), summoned from the Western Front, and reputed to be "the kind of man who made the German army almost invincible."[33]

The Turks, who had second thoughts about contributing troops to this curious exercise, made it exceedingly difficult for the Germans to cross over into neutral Persia. Wasmuss decided to hive off part of the force and make his own way south to incite holy war. He conducted a faltering yet indomitable three-year attempt to direct tribal wrath against the Anglo-Persian Oil Company installations along the Gulf — oil was by now a crucial resource for the Royal Navy.[34] Niedermayer and the rest moved on to Baghdad; from there, the German minister to the shah's court got them across the border into Persia.

Reinforced to a strength of about a hundred men by German soldiers escaped from Russian POW camps, Indian Army deserters, and dubiously loyal Persian mercenaries, Niedermayer made Isfahan, the old Silk Road caravan town due south of Tehran, his jumping off point to the east. An edgy twenty-nine-year-old diplomat, cavalry officer, and intelligence operative was sent in by the foreign ministry as the new political presence. By now, in April 1915, the British and Russians knew most every move.

In July, at the height of summer, Niedermayer's group began a 700-mile trek to the Afghan border, which meant traversing the great Kavir Salt Desert, an epic in the annals of special operations. Its crossing had never been recorded. In this wilderness between two worlds, they had to slip past Russian probes from the north and British patrols searching for them from the south, while riding at night through indifferent desolation, with little water and less food, slithers of venomous snakes felling their horses. After a seven-week ordeal, a band of walking skeletons stumbled into the relative safety of Afghanistan, into which neither Russian nor British cavalry dared trespass.

British intelligence had been following this venture all along through a network of agents that it had had a long opportunity to develop in the region. So had been the kaiser, who meanwhile was employing other operatives to try to smuggle thirty thousand rifles and pistols, plus crates of ammunition, to Indian and Burmese revolutionaries by way of the Pacific and what is now Thailand, everything picked up in the United States. Ultimately, the impressive skill of British intelligence was able fatally to enmesh all these grand efforts

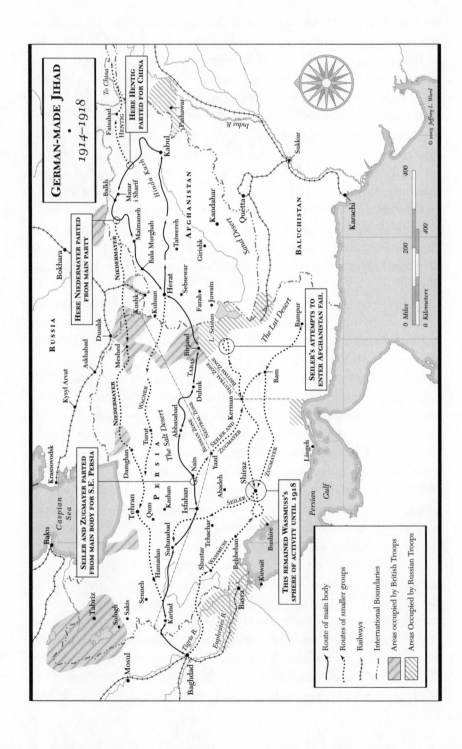

GERMAN-MADE JIHAD
· 1914–1918 ·

HERE HENTIG
PARTED FOR CHINA

HERE NIEDERMAYER PARTED
FROM MAIN PARTY

SEILER AND ZUGMAYER PARTED
FROM MAIN BODY FOR S.E. PERSIA

SEILER'S ATTEMPTS TO
ENTER AFGHANISTAN FAIL

THIS REMAINED WASSMUSS'S
SPHERE OF ACTIVITY UNTIL 1918

© 2005 Jeffrey L. Ward

RUSSIA

AFGHANISTAN

PERSIA

BALUCHISTAN

Caspian Sea

Persian Gulf

The Salt Desert

The Lut Desert

Sand Desert

Hindu Kush

Indus R.

Euphrates R.

Tigris R.

To China

Faisabad
HENTIG
Peshawar
Kabul
Balkh
Mazar i Sharif
Maimaneh
Bala Murghab
Taiwereh
Kandahar
Quetta
Sukkur
Karachi
Bokhara
NIEDERMAYER
Kusht
Kuhsan
Herat
Sebsewar
Girishk
Dusahk
Meshed
Farah
Juwain
Birjand
TABAS
L. Seistan
Bampur
Askhabad
Kysyl Arvat
WAGNER
Turut
Abbasabad
Duhuk
Bam
NIEDERMAYER
NEUTRAL ZONE
BRITISH ZONE
SEILER AND KERMAN
ZUGMAYER
RUSSIAN ZONE
Krasnovodsk
Baku
Damghan
Nain
Yazd
Shiraz
Lingeh
Tehran
Qum
Kashan
Isfahan
Abadeh
SEILER
Sultanabad
Shustar
Tehachar
WASSMUSS
Behbehan
Bushire
Tabriz
Subogh
Sakis
Senneh
Hamadan
Karind
Kuwait
Basra
Mosul
Baghdad
ZUGMAYER

Route of main body
Routes of smaller groups
Railways
International Boundaries
Areas occupied by British Troops
Areas Occupied by Russian Troops

0 Miles   200   400
0 Kilometers   400

in its century-old assets worldwide. The agitation was effectively confronted in southern Persia; the gunrunners were intercepted off the Netherlands Indies, and the machinery of British justice in India was provided with evidence to begin hanging the revolutionaries. At Kabul, the amir (in no rush to stake his future on newfound Lutheran enthusiasm for Islam) was mellowed to the status quo by receiving a raise in his ongoing bribes from the British, while the little party of Germans was made to pointlessly cool its heels for eleven months before it split up to begin further odysseys to return to the Fatherland. In our day, with recurring intelligence failures, it is instructive to consider how the British service was different from, say, the CIA: it had genuine lifetime experts in a given area, deep "humint" derived from long and patient penetration of the obscurest sects; money put into precisely the right personal bank accounts; and not predominately well-meaning, unworldly recruits amiably working undercover out of U.S. embassies and, at home, within the most notorious of bureaucracies.

Herr Wasmuss, who had gone on to lead his small force against the British in southern Persia, has been seen as the "German Lawrence," although during Wasmuss's most effective months the actual Lieutenant "Lawrence" was still an archeologist-turned-intelligence officer at General Headquarters, Cairo, having come a little late into what he jauntily called "the show." As the most star-quality figure of the Great War, T. E. Lawrence would emerge as the champion of a mode of combat that was the antithesis of what he also described as the "murder war" by which Europe was destroying itself in the mud of the Western Front (two of his brothers being consumed). Eminent thinkers on strategy have placed him among the Great Captains: Alexander, Caesar, Bonaparte, and only a handful of others.[35] That is likely an exaggeration, though at the time he was known as "Drake of the Desert," and his methods acclaimed as those of privateers.[36] He can best be remembered for the way he enlarged the place of special warfare in the Western mind by his heavily fanciful writings (*The Seven Pillars of Wisdom*), the immense publicity that soon hypertrophied his exploits, yet also by providing the right wing as British forces pushed into Palestine.

This unsettling man had been born into deception: on his mother's side the illegitimate child of an illegitimate child, his father to become the seventh baronet of his line, the surname "Lawrence" derived from having to explain away a second family of five sons. Coming down from Oxford in 1910 with a First in history, Thomas Edward, or T. E. as he preferred, served as an assistant at a British Museum dig in Iraq, then still known as Mesopotamia, uncovering cities and mapping crusader castles westward toward the Mediterranean. He had an astonishing grasp of detail, as his intelligence reports would show. He became fluent in Arabic and tribal slang — competency in the language of the indigenous people among whom one presumes to be a special operator being a basic prerequisite for effectiveness, if we think of men as different as Robert Rodgers, Frank North, Niedermayer, and Wassmuss.

Lawrence had volunteered for the army at the outbreak of war but been rejected. No Peter O'Toole, he was five feet four inches tall, with a disproportionately large head that made him look yet shorter. By 1915 he nonetheless had been commissioned and posted to Egypt (then under Britain's thumb since a nationalist outbreak some thirty years earlier), serving as an interpreter and cartographer for army intelligence. In autumn 1916 he persuaded his superiors to assign him as liaison officer to the sharif of Mecca, whose followers were poised to hamstring the Ottoman garrisons strung out over the Arabian desert, their cause to expel the Turks from all Arabic-speaking lands. (The farseeing Ibn Saud, loyal to Britain yet grossly underestimated by Lawrence, was sitting it out in Riyadh and letting the sharif do his dirty work.) Lawrence began creating a much greater role for himself as he pumped gold, explosives, and automatic weapons into the fight — resources probably more precious than his leadership, the Arabs as usual having too much of that already.

Lawrence had brilliance and courage — and equally real personal troubles. He lied compulsively, never able to transcend a confusion of identity — as shown by a need to fabricate ominous authority figures, like the young men he hired to beat him, and, after the war, by his desire to change his name and submerge himself in the ranks. Yet above all, this strange, tiny man possessed the range of political as well as warrior talents — plus deep cultural understanding — to tie down thousands of enemy troops by applying "a highly mobile, highly equipped striking force of the smallest size" at the farthest place, as he recalled.[37] The Turks always had to be alert along their whole overstretched lines: like the Union army arrayed against Mosby, they never knew when or where he would appear.

Contrary to myth, Lawrence was never himself a Bedouin commander, having authority over no one but British soldiers and his bodyguard. In fact, this was all the more impressive because his operations in raiding and mining the Medina-to-Damascus railway, and his taking of Aqaba far up the Red Sea by reaching across the desert and surprising it from inland, were accomplished as an adviser, albeit a very influential one. Here are two further significant steps in the evolution of special warfare: the unambiguous impact of the advisory mission focusing on turning disordered locals into well-directed fighters; and the fact that no longer were small expert forces with up-to-date weaponry just imposing themselves on the timeless passivity of the world's poor. For the moment, Western operators were now in place to share the magic of new powers and spirits with the long oppressed.

In the desert, the clean-shaven Lawrence wore elaborate Meccan robes of the whitest silk, with a golden head-rope. This was certainly not to deny any conspicuous identity to sharpshooters, as is popularly believed, but to acquire trust and intimacy, as well as to show himself to his lawless men.[38] The amount of money and weapons he brought in was in fact modest compared to what was being squandered elsewhere; rifles and machine guns could be taken from the Turks. In the struggle, just as valuable as those weapons were a handful of other British experts. All served to harness ancient desert enmities against the city dwellers, whose defeat offered golden opportunities to Lawrence's plundering camelteers. Like Frank North channeling the warrior ways of the Pawnee, Lawrence did not try to make regular troops out of quasi-nomads. Whereas North in effect worked for the railroad, Lawrence was fighting a more historically complex war, conspicuously *against* the railroad, that epoch's classic instrument of state power. He wrote that the whole performance was "heaven." Why? Because "there aren't any returns, or orders, or superiors, or inferiors;

no doctors, no accounts, no meals, and no drinks." He knew that his superiors "could not make out how much [of me] was genuine performer and how much charlatan" — all of which explains why so few regular officers could tolerate him.[39] Once more, successful special warfare was a chapter as much of diplomacy and bluff as of strategy, exercised by an extraordinary warrior unlikely to fit in anywhere else.[40]

‡

THE REAL victories of the Great War, as always, had to come from killing, capturing, and demoralizing large numbers of the other side on the main battlegrounds. Gas, flamethrowers, and ultimately tanks were the most technologically dramatic responses to the mud, water, and vermin of European trench warfare. But the Germans had been developing a novel means of using small groups of men and light weapons that would prove able to rupture whole sectors of the Western Front. Indeed, such innovation was applied in strength for the first time in the counterattack that quickly regained the ground taken (and more) when the British brought off history's first major tank offensive, at Cambrai in France during mid-November 1917.

The loathsome practices of some years later have defiled the name of "storm troops" (even creepier in the German, Stosstruppen, "thrust teams"), but these remarkable bands represent a crucial point in the evolution of small, high-initiative, hard-hitting, specialized combat units. Special assault units would move into position to break up Allied lines already shaken by brief but intense bombardment. Fighting in platoons that were further distilled into independent squads, the storm troopers developed a matrix of deadly technologies: machine pistols and the first effective submachine gun, in addition to their ample array of mortars, grenades, and carbines. These outfits were profoundly different from the heroic but less impressively armed rifle companies of 1914. The British and French had also improved their tactics under years of bloody schooling, yet they barely comprehended this level of integrated innovation, entirely appropriate to Europe's most effective industrial power.[41]

Storm troopers, however, had not yet attained the operational subtlety of the special forces that would emerge during World War II. They were still elite infantry, whose methods lay somewhere between those of the forlorn hope and the SAS. They emphasized the outright assault, or "storm," rather than guile. Indeed, while these units were in their first stages of development in 1915, the designation *hunt command* (Jägdkommando) was considered and dismissed, as was the designation *raid troops*.[42]

To be sure, they had a mission of unique intensity; they had patrons in Berlin; they eschewed tradition, proudly lacking regimental colors or any affiliation with the historic regiments going back to Frederick the Great. They wore special uniforms and benefited from special training, which included live-fire rehearsals against full-scale mock-ups of their objectives. Yet when storm troopers penetrated too far behind enemy lines, they were in trouble: they were not working from adequate maps; nor had they been prepared to identify valuable targets well to the rear, such as enemy headquarters. By late 1917, they were nonetheless romanticized throughout Germany, and not only in the press. Earlier in the war, propaganda posters for selling bonds and picture postcards for raising morale had dwelt on chivalric themes of mounted knights, with sword and shield. In the war's last year, those themes gave way to inspiring depictions of the lantern-jawed, steely-eyed storm troopers, gas masks ready around the neck, grenades at the belt, pistols in hand.[43]

By 1918, the high command's ambition was to raise all infantry divisions to storm-trooper standard, an impossible goal even to contemplate had the storm troopers been operating at an authentically special level. Instead, they had most in common with German mountain troops and Austrian Jaeger light infantry, each of which naturally had to employ the small-unit tactics demanded by Alpine combat. Before radio it was primarily mountain warfare that offered wide-open opportunities for special skills, improvisation, and enterprise by rifle and machine-gun units, led by young officers who knew that top commanders smiled on their initiative. In such theaters, war had maintained much of its mobility, becoming less a matter of back-and-forth assaults than of mastering steep terrain, of dodging and climbing up long wearying slopes.

Independent tactical judgment had been stressed as a principle of German infantry training before 1914, and it was in the Romanian Alps that the twenty-six-year-old first lieutenant Erwin Rommel — future commander of Hitler's Afrika Korps, an expert deerstalker during the interwar years — made his name. His mountain troopers, as he would write, moved "like hungry wolves," exploiting every facet of the ground.[44] They proved themselves conclusively in the devastating German offensive in October 1917, at Caporetto (today remembered in English-speaking countries only as the setting in the Trentino plateau, from *A Farewell to Arms*), which nearly knocked Italy out of the war. The rapid, focused, and fluid performance of these specialized formations — akin to the work of both blitzkrieg and *Kommando* units two decades ahead — did not go unnoticed, particularly by other fast-rising German officers.[45]

Early the following year, an outnumbered Germany knew that the spring would afford it the last throw of the dice, even though Russia had quit the war in March. Artillery artistry and fierce storm-trooper thrusts tore apart chunks of the Western Front, followed by unprecedented penetrations from March through July. The French, bled white by their own battering-ram tactics, had meanwhile been experimenting with far stranger means of breakthrough: paratroopers.

Previously, the technology, adventure, teamwork, and heroic drama of air combat had been a riveting contrast to the trenches — but with little relevance to special operations. Pilots fought duels in the sky, much less rule-bound than those on earth. Now there was something different in the air. The American pioneer, Brigadier General Billy Mitchell, born in Nice during his parents' three-year tour of the Continent, had learned quickly from the French. Only the Armistice and U.S. commanding General "Black Jack" Pershing's cavalryman incredulity prevented him from attempting to drop elements of the 1st Infantry Division into the conventionally impregnable fortress city of Metz in Lorraine. The British, who had in April just created an independent air force, were gearing up to bomb Berlin. The Germans, in turn, had recently brought off the first capture of a ship by air.

After an epoch dominated by the rigidities of mass warfare, new means were arriving to restore the ancient qualities of mobility and surprise, at a significant level of advantage to the truly enterprising. In the huge counterattack of August 8, designated by Erich Ludendorff, the nearest to a mastermind of the General Staff, as the "Black Day of the German Army," British armored cars broke through the lines to race far enough in to shoot up corps headquarters.[46] All the civilities of an earlier age (meaning four years before) were being abandoned, as we see in Faulkner's chilling tale "Turn About": an American aviator without orders — enraged, not coincidentally, by the death of a deceptively schoolboyish British friend, a brilliant small-boat operator — bombs a chateau "where the generals sat at lunch." Such young men as survived to exercise higher, often decisive authority in the next war would display few of the professional courtesies of 1914, and they would strike fast, with raiders and hit teams.

‡

THROUGHOUT THE war, as so often before, it is at sea that we encounter many of the richest alliances of force and fraud. For Britain, the key purpose of its fleet was not to replicate Nelson's daring and to destroy the German navy in its own waters. The gigantic clash of battleships in the North Sea off Jutland in 1916 had been inconclusive and fraught with command misapprehension, operational failure, reconnaissance accident, and inability to grasp intelligence. It was certainly no Trafalgar. Instead, the Royal Navy's more numerous ships concentrated on blockading German ports in order to both prevent the kaiser's High Seas Fleet from breaking into the Atlantic and starve Germany into submission. Germany, in turn, waged its own war of starvation against island Britain, turning fatefully to unrestricted submarine warfare in February 1917, which would finally push the United States into the fight two months later.

Submariners are certainly part of a special undertaking, but one very much their own. Deftly used by Germany, U-boats both gnawed at the world's richest sealanes and targeted warships — one determined craft sinking three heavy cruisers patrolling off the Dutch coast in less than seventy-five minutes. That early shock of September 1914 showed the full offensive potential of this weapon. The submariners themselves had the ethos of the hunt — in the next war as prowling "wolfpacks," as the Allies would call them, in this one mostly as single predators. Their crews were picked men in a corps d'élite, relying on stealth and surprise, able to sink far bigger vessels and drowning much larger numbers of men, leveraging the latest specialized technology.

A quarter century later, submarines of both sides would insert commando teams on vulnerable shores, as U.S. submarines do today for Navy SEALs. And now that the Soviet Union has fallen, astounding operations of the next order of skill have come to light, in which American fast-attack submarines are known to have worked with specially trained combat divers to tap the undersea communications cables of Soviet naval bases. Yet in the Great War the role of submariners was nearly exclusively to torpedo enemy ships or, once surfaced, to sweep their decks with such firepower as they could carry, originating the expression "sunk without trace" (*spurlos versenkt*).

From the struggle with the German menace beneath the waves, there emerged something closer to the force, fraud, and quick-moving flexibility of the special operations force. These are the British "Q" or "mystery" ships — slow-moving, apparently unarmed vessels disguised as tramp steamers or fishing boats that served as live bait for unsuspecting U-boats.

Rarely in war have deception and destruction been taken so systematically to such a consistently effective and unprecedented level. Always on the sharpest lookout, a Q-ship (flying the "red duster" of the merchant marine, or perhaps a foreign flag) might narrowly dodge a rushing torpedo off, say, the southwest coast of Ireland, or take a hit but be kept afloat by its deliberately buoyant cargo of wood or cork. Then a conning tower would break the surface as the hunter came up to turn its deck gun on the victim. All the while the Q-ship's captain and crew would be trying to lure the killer in closer, whether by appearing to tack frantically, or seeming to abandon ship as "panic parties" of stokers and spare men lowered lifeboats and pulled away. The surfaced U-boat would steadily close in as its officers prepared for the terminating shots. Yet concealed behind canvas or cargo, an entirely different exercise was underway, the captain perhaps lying on the bridge peering through a slit in the coaming. As the big fish glided in for the kill, its men on the casing, down would come the Q-ship's screens and the white ensign of the fighting navy would break out within seconds. The porpoise turned into a shark, twelve-pounders, machine guns, torpedoes, and depth charges laying into the suddenly vulnerable assailant.

The Q-ship response was formulated in December 1914, as German submarine warfare was already proving itself effective, and as such countermeasures as destroyers, mines, and camouflage were proving lamentably insufficient. The British Admiralty had rejected the notion of escorted convoys on the grounds that merchant captains were too inept to keep station over a long run. Naval officers of various ranks instead seem to have conceived the idea of the Q-ship, not the brass around Their Lordships in Whitehall (though the navy's civilian chief, Churchill, signed on enthusiastically). Eventually, sailing smacks, schooners, and brigantines would be drafted to add to the deception — the challenge being to find officers who could sail them, as in the days of Drake. Within two years, forty-seven decoys were going in harm's way.

Q-ship captains, recalled a Royal Navy officer who patrolled the Atlantic with them, had to possess the virtues of "the most patient stalker, the most enterprising big-game hunter," along with the steady nerves of the best seaman.[47] Brains and bravery had to be matched with imagination. Officially, these unarmored decoys were "special service" ships, their identity kept so secret that, in harbor, Q-ship officers and crew came and went, usually at night or early mornings, wearing plain clothes. The guns on these slovenly civilian-seeming craft (which could be made to appear as riding heavy in the water) were so well concealed that a Q-ship might lie in harbor a few yards' distance from too-curious neutral vessels without revealing its true nature. Even regular officers walked their decks unable to detect the masked gun mounts.

Disguise was essential to offset the enemy's advantages of submerged surprise and torpedo speed against the lumbering bulk bearers that wove along the North and South Atlantic sealanes, into the Channel and the Mediterranean. The Q-ship captain also had to possess an intimate understanding of his submarine counterpart, as well as of the U-boats' speeds, how many hours their batteries could keep them operational underwater, and their tactics. He saw the submariners as worthy opponents rather than as cowardly sneaks (which was Churchill's view) and was mindful that to die by inches in a sinking iron coffin is, even for war, a hideous way to go.

By early 1917, a special department in the Admiralty was selecting possible ships, screening personnel, and arranging disguises. So novel a mode of warfare could neither be made routine nor improvised

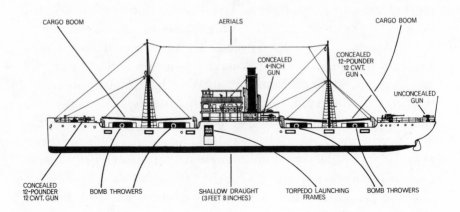

CARGO BOOM

AERIALS

CARGO BOOM

CONCEALED
4-INCH
GUN

CONCEALED
12-POUNDER
12 CWT.
GUN

UNCONCEALED
GUN

CONCEALED
12-POUNDER
12 CWT. GUN

BOMB THROWERS

SHALLOW DRAUGHT
(3 FEET 8 INCHES)

TORPEDO LAUNCHING
FRAMES

BOMB THROWERS

from action to action. The whole four-year experience never lost its continuously experimental quality. By 1917, German submariners were seeing Q-ships everywhere; the most seasoned ship-hunter could never be sure whether the wallowing freighter he was closing in on would suddenly pounce on its pursuer.

Of course, the U-boat captains were getting craftier, too, in their underwater ambushes. The slightest indication that there might be more to the rusty tramp or tuna boat than met the eye — some faint departure from normal outline, some obscurely detectable lack of anxiety about venturing on the wartime seas alone — could bring a much deadlier attack. By the time Q-ships received the legitimizing formal designation "HMS" (only in the war's last year), their effectiveness had already peaked. Triumph at sea ultimately was dictated by sheer weight of armament and change of policy: more destroyers, magnetic mines, and — finally — convoys.[48]

Although the U-boat offensive had been contained, it remained a threat to Allied shipping — all the more galling because its key bases were just fifty miles across the Channel. That final year, so marked by frantic search for alternatives, saw what our friends at the Naval Postgraduate School call the "commando raid on the German submarine base at Zeebrugge," as well as against the nearby port of Ostend.[49] Here, indeed, was a recasting of tactical surprise. Never had a landing been launched against a position so heavily defended, the object being to neutralize the bases and to block the eight-mile canal connecting them to the secure inland harbor of Bruges, where more submarines were berthed.

What ensued in the early morning of April 23, 1918, has been deemed, "for concentration of power and sudden startling violence," greater than any other clash in that war.[50] The landing of seventeen hundred men from about seventy vessels involved an orchestration of novel procedures, from smokescreens generated by chemicals injected into the exhaust of dozens of fast patrol boats to concrete-solidified block ships. Some two hundred marines landed as a diversion near the entrance of the canal (at the mile-long Zeebrugge mole) while the block ships got into position. A British submarine full of high explosives maneuvered under the viaduct connecting the mole to the shore, its skeleton crew picked up by patrol craft before the charge exploded, shattering the viaduct and cutting off the characteristically fast-arriving German reinforcements from reaching the end of that massive breakwater protecting the harbor.

The fruits of this elaborately planned attack were mixed (German operations from Zeebrugge resumed a few days later), but it showed that a war of hopeless deadlock could suddenly flare into one of mobility, innovation, precision, and surprise — and on a scale large for a raid, yet so much smaller than the mindless frontal assaults elsewhere in the West.

At the end, at the eleventh hour of the eleventh day of the eleventh month, the consequences of such mass industrial warfare had become all too clear. A French poet cried that the Gare du Nord (the Paris train station delivering the armies to the Western Front) "had eaten our sons." The war had separated courage and devotion from intellect, consuming much of a generation. It showed how the high commands of not only the Russian and Turkish despots but of modern democracies could become anesthetized to casualties once they thought of how many "bayonets" rather than bodies they had at their disposal. "Never again," concluded idealists who had embraced this as the war to end all wars. Harder-headed people said the same thing, but with new visions of combat in mind.

Part IV

15

Sinister Twilight
Dangerous Young Men: The Unreal Peace, 1919–1939

> *"You think that a wall as solid as the earth separates civilization from barbarism. I tell you the division is a thread, a sheet of glass. A touch here, a push there, and you bring back the reign of Satan."*
> ANDREW LUMLEY IN JOHN BUCHAN'S THE POWER-HOUSE

THE MEMORIAL at Verdun, where 150,000 Frenchmen died from February through December 1916; the Cenotaph in London, with its single line "To Our Million Dead"; even the stark slabs on the hillside overlooking the town of Chateau-Thierry, which commemorate 1,811 Americans who went to their deaths in dark Belleau Wood during June 1918 — all are heavy, brooding structures conveying profound sorrow, each reflecting the massive mechanical repetitiveness of that war, like monuments to an industrial process. Neither architects nor families could say outright that the losses were unnecessary, but the designs show well enough that these are remembrances to the death of a civilization, when the lamps were indeed put out all over Europe.

One monument notable for its light, comparatively high-spirited touch does stand in London, commanding a good sweep of the corner between Hyde and St. James parks, diagonally across from Apsley House — one of the splendid rewards that a grateful nation bestowed on Wellington. It honors the Machine Gun Corps, and appears to have been built for people who had little doubt that they had won.

"Saul hath slain his thousands" is stated confidently on the marble, "but David hath slain his tens of thousands" — an invocation of the mass shedding of blood by one singularly chosen of the Lord. To be sure, shrapnel and high explosives had taken more men on all sides. But it was the machine gun — its workings not much more complicated than those of a factory clock — which provided the cheap, easily learned, literally industrial-strength means of wholesale killing.

More than young men had died. Twenty-odd dynasties had been shaken off in Europe: the Hapsburgs, the Hohenzollerns, the Romanovs who no longer ruled "all the Russias," as well as that of the Ottoman sultan, the dissolution of whose empire would help bring about the Middle Eastern turmoil with which we live today. As for the victorious British and French, their success had been perilously narrow, and cripplingly expensive. The Americans might have come home to tickertape parades, but they anxiously recoiled from world power. And the war had given Japan confidence to reach for empire as the nations that had once blocked its ambitions deliquesced or licked their wounds.

Most terribly, 1914–18 made a much worse war almost inescapable. During early 1917, the kaiser's government had introduced Lenin into Russia, as Churchill put it, "in the same way that you might send a phial containing a culture of typhoid or of cholera to be poured into the water supply of a great city."[1] The episode remains a ghastly example of how little things can make a big, terrible difference. Once the precedent of totalitarianism was set in Russia, the next likely step was for it to be countered by its alleged mirror image in a rival tyranny. Lenin became Hitler's alibi. Within sixteen years, Communism enabled Hitler ("a human nothing," as he would see himself right after the Armistice) to invoke ultimate danger and to pose as the savior of Germany. It was increasingly understood that a single sharp move by a few men might alter history.

What to call this cataclysm just past? By 1919, Colonel Charles à Court Repington, a perceptive war correspondent of the *Times* (no need to add "of London" in those days), had an idea of what was coming. Knowing that war begets war, that indeed world history is the history of war, he bluntly called it "the First World War." Before Repington's book of that title was published in 1922, plenty of skeletons were digging themselves out of the earth to confirm his foresight. Word was about, in imaginative literature and among the professionals of war alike, that new techniques had to be drawn on should the Great War turn out not to have been the last. How to exploit vulnerabilities in enemy armies and societies rather than horrifically trying to smash such opponents head-on? Part of the answer lay in means that could be as fast, stealthy, and penetrating as needles, whether these involved bands of warriors able to adapt radical technologies or hidden operatives to work from within.

The biggest war to date was being coined down into a multitude of little conflicts: seizing cities in Europe, ideological back-country warfare in South America, high-stakes plays in Central Asia by political exiles ranging from a fallen Turkish dictator to White Russians. But something huge and ghastly was slouching forward.

‡

WHETHER OR not their influence can rightly be compared to the leverage found today among little groups ready to release pathogens in subways and reservoirs, the Bolsheviks had been a not particularly numerous faction of the Marxist Social Democrats. By November 1917 they had seized St. Petersburg in an almost bloodless spatter of rifle shots and blank naval discharges. Three months later, the Red Army came into being. What might happen next, as nationalities all around the perimeter of the Russian empire separated from the center, with noisy declarations of independence?

The Japanese had some ideas, such as inserting a presence of what would peak at seventy-two thousand men to try to gnaw away a chunk of eastern Siberia. So did the British and the French, dispatching troops to northern Russia, seizing Archangel on the Arctic Ocean in August 1918 to support a puppet government opposed to the Bolsheviks, sending troops to Vladivostok on the Sea of Japan, the British also intervening in September in the Transcaucasian region of southern Russia (between the Black and the Caspian seas). After the Armistice, the French and the British took the Black Sea ports of Odessa and Batum, again in an attempt to back ideologically broad-front White Russian armies against the Bolsheviks. Even the Chinese pushed into Manchuria, much of which they had some historic reason to regard as theirs. However reluctantly, the Americans had weighed in during

September 1918, plunging expeditionary forces into Archangel and Vladivostok, becoming entangled in a civil war that Churchill would also call one of "few casualties and unnumbered executions."[2]

Early in 1918, the Russian-speaking Major General Lionel Dunsterville had set forth from what was at last British-held Baghdad into the Caucasus. The original purpose of his "Dunsterforce" (also to be known as the Hush-Hush Army) was to try to constitute the broken units of Russian, Georgian, and Armenian soldiery against a Turkish invasion of the collapsed Czarist empire from the south, and then to put on its feet an independent Trans-Caucasia, including the key oil port of Baku on the Caspian. The reputation of this perceptive British officer, a childhood chum of Kipling's, survives not for this effort but for his already having been heroized as "Stalky," the resourceful main character of the most fascinating of all school stories. (At the end, as Stalky does brilliantly in India, we see that schoolboy scheming is excellent preparation for the deviousness and disregard for procedural niceties needed to run the empire.) Dunsterforce was less than a thousand strong, half of them officers and NCOs, "chosen for special ability," its founder relates, from the toughest of (white) veterans from throughout the British Empire — Canadians, Australians, New Zealanders, South Africans, British.[3]

Before his force's grand objectives were blocked that autumn, not only by some fourteen thousand Turks but by many fewer (but hot from the furnace) troops of the new Red Army, Dunsterville had made an art out of what he called "moral camouflage" — the aggressive deployment of very small, well-armed, hypermotivated, and self-reliant units. Since they moved fast and rarely concentrated in one place, their hovering could create an impression equivalent to that made by several entire by-the-book brigades, although bringing to bear at most the strength of a few platoons. It was also a leveraging of reputation. When what had so recently been a handful of crank revolutionaries was proving itself able to change the world, who knew what a special battalion of Anglo-Saxon empire-builders could pull off?

Much was forcing itself to the surface among the passions of a world less made new than one in which so much that was old had been consumed, leaving curious forces free to act. Relatively small outfits that understood what they were about — Bolsheviks, fascists, revolutionaries of all sorts — could find a colossal advantage, not only in sheer, suddenly released will power but in the ability to pull off, often overnight, what everyone had thought impossible.

The Bolsheviks — inspired by Lenin's prodigious military improviser, the war commissar Leon Trotsky — raised armies on every front in the civil war and took resistance behind the many enemy lines. By November 1920, they had won in Russia proper and would soon recover much of the old empire. That year the nine thousand American soldiers who had been tossed into Siberia were pulled out (the final Allied forces having already left northern Russia in fall 1919). Their intervention prefigured the political-military "peacekeeping" roles in which relatively modest numbers of U.S. troops can find themselves today, their professionalism encumbered by the usual ignorances back in Washington about the specifics of who-what-why-where — conflating the bloody enmities of centuries within the horizon of the next election. Having faced Bolshevik guerrillas and the resolve of the tough, versatile American general on the spot, the Japanese army reluctantly departed Siberia two years later.

The Soviet empire was rising in parallel with the emergence of fascism, both offering a beau geste of commando characterization: the determined well-prepared few against the irresolute many, a disdain for rules, a sense of structural vulnerabilities, and the objective not just to seize a town or capital but to capture a national imagination. The renegade socialist Mussolini organized his fascists in Milan during 1919, combining with the at best partly employed veterans of Italy's distinctively uniformed shock troops, the *arditi*. The 1922 Kapp Putsch (so styled after a senior Prussian administrator proclaimed as chancellor) briefly overthrew the German government. It, too, was an example of the short, sharp work of marginal people, carried off by a naval brigade without a navy in landlocked Berlin in the name of a man born in New York. It was also a precursor of the street battles that would make many World War II Nazi SS officers "personally familiar with the potential of small units aggressively handled."[4]

Of the seven principal European states as of 1910, two had simply disintegrated, and three more undergone revolution. For the first time, fiction was articulating truths about how delicately balanced a nation and a political order (or perhaps a civilization) may be when unknown, determined, malignant organizations are working with deep purpose inside a sleepwalking society. One brilliant anticipation of events is John Buchan's *The Power-House* (1914), whose hero suddenly sees how an innocent might disappear from the quiet summer streets of Mayfair after stumbling across the existence of a spidery international cabal, its operatives thoroughly blended into daily life. Ten years earlier, it would have been considered paranoid to think like this. (Sherlock Holmes, after all, faces Professor Moriarty, the well-bred Napoleon of crime, a gentleman who gives him time to write a letter before their final grapple; Erskine Childers's *Riddle of the Sands* (1903) had featured a single British traitor plotting to open his country to German invasion.) But Buchan warned that people chillingly different were moving from the shadows, quietly injecting themselves into the system, and he presents an entire culture of secret evil — the equivalent, say, of an intelligent young New York lawyer in summer 2001 discovering by accident a hidden worldwide network trafficking in nuclear devices, laundering billions of dollars, or even (impossible for sensible people to believe) plotting to devastate lower Manhattan, the Pentagon, and White House.

This Scots visionary of the otherness that awaits us around the corner did much more than invent the genre of the modern spy thriller and inspire films by Hitchcock. Even in then rather datable style, his writings are more ominous and timely than the sardonic, distanced stories of Somerset Maugham, Graham Greene, and Le Carré. Indeed, Buchan's other work introduces an additional phenomenon emerging from that decade when immense political stakes rode on small but alarming movements: the actual special operations novel, a logical extension of living in a world like that of *The Thirty-Nine Steps* (1915). Having already published *Greenmantle* (1916), which envisions a rivalry of conspiracies around the German attempt to suborn Islamic passion with a holy man who can energize it against the corrupt West, Buchan offers in *The Courts of the Morning* (1926) a convincing portrayal of operations conducted by an isolated group in a fictitious Latin American republic not unlike Peru. The country has fallen under the well-concealed control of a mysterious international entity whose grip can only be broken by small-boat raiding, espionage, resourceful mountain and desert warfare, for the most part relying on arms and supplies won from a better-equipped enemy army ("our Q[uartermaster] side"). Shades of things to come.

In highly ideologized but no less convincing form, the Russians (whose international operatives for the next half century aspired to exercise just such control), had their own widely read special operations novel — *The Band,* about a Bolshevik outfit behind the Japanese lines in Siberia, the little group never giving up and going it alone. By the time we get to Geoffrey Household's *Rogue Male* (1939), about a British big-game hunter stalking an obvious Hitler figure in the plentitude of his power, a whole bookshelf had emerged to illuminate nearly all the possibilities of the commando and secret operator ready to come to life should the world crack up again. It did, and on they came.

‡

FOR THE first time in history, planning for the next war was approached in ways thoroughly discontinuous from the past. Just about everything was examined anew: bombers, aircraft carriers, paratroopers, tanks, marines (even the ultimately unpursued option of "tank marines"). Speculations brushed away as fantasies just two decades before at the turn of the century — voices coming out of the air (radio); the plump bourgeoisie zooming through clouds (airplanes); moving, talking pictures (films) — were becoming part of daily life. Being so open to the unprecedented played directly into the search for alternatives to the mutual destruction of 1914–18. New approaches to war between industrialized nations were explored, and here appears another crucial difference from centuries past: a reversal of the sources from which special operations are being pioneered.

Previously, as we have seen at least since the eighteenth century, such operations sprang up along all the far frontiers of imperial contact, just as they were slighted on the newly hyperorganized battlefields of Europe. In the 1920s and 1930s, the opposite occurred: few were the colonial problems that the white man could not handle more effectively with bombers, rapidly dispatched battalions of regulars, armored cars, rail networks (as in India), or naval bombardment. In contrast, innovations that included streamlined, focused operations were now being thought through in the staff committees of the industrialized world. Enterprising actions being worked out for the well-equipped, fast-moving few were not to be applied against the poor and backward, but against the rich and advanced.

Consider the conflict that finally broke out between the British and the Afghans in May 1919, the latter having picked up, a mite late, on the dire trouble in which the Empire had found itself only shortly before. A new amir finally declared jihad, letting his ill-trained, more-or-less regular forces and their Pathan allies off the leash. They were swatted in a quick punitive campaign in which the Royal Air Force bombed Jalalabad and Kabul. Rather well-advertised bombers were also handy against tribesmen in central Iraq in 1920. Wahhabi raiders threatening Iraq and Kuwait in 1928 sustained further unhappy surprises from the air, and the RAF made itself just as expeditiously felt in Somaliland and Yemen. The Dutch, French, Spanish, and Italians underlined their authority with similar heavy-handed responses from Morocco to the East Indies.

Undoubtedly, the underdeveloped world was still furnishing epics of special warfare, although not by foreign adventurers. In 1924, there arose from Brazil a large-scale manifestation in the Western Hemisphere of these qualities of speed, mobility, novelty, reach, and extraordinary leveraging of relatively few numbers. It unfolded across more and harder terrain than the Conquistadors had marched on, and it provided exemplary, inspiring defiance that would resonate among the continentally minded in faraway Washington for a long generation — and for good reason.

After a mutiny by lieutenants within Brazil's fractious army, twenty-nine-year-old Captain Luis Carlos Prestes — the "horseman of hope," soon to be a leader of Brazil's Communist Party — retreated into the remote interior at the head of about a thousand rebellious *tenentes,* soldiers, and state policemen, who all served as carriers of peasant revolution. What they accomplished between late 1924 until early 1927, in one of the most extreme of endeavors, was simply, by any previously established standard — of logistics, of mobility, of what small malcontent cadres could accomplish on the move — impossible. Opposed by the largest army in Latin America and pursued by the more terrain-savvy militias of regional strongmen, the Prestes

Column's day-and-night forced marches swept through thirteen for the most part roadless, railless, and, more happily for it, telegraphless Brazilian states, covering almost sixteen thousand miles before it finally wore out the enemy and six hundred survivors sought refuge in Bolivia.

Here was a nucleus of infection, combining a truly memorable dismissal of the odds with the apparent ubiquity that is the mark of a special force, however self-selected. An intrepid body of men prepared for the worst, directed by a leader of genius (less literary but probably more formidable than Lawrence in deriving strategic strength from range and space), and one of the world's six biggest countries was changed forever, though not in the ways anticipated. The shock to the old oligarchies, the demonstration of the power of the terribly poor, had much to do with the destiny of tolerant, accommodating twentieth-century Brazil: the neofascist supremacy of Getulio Vargas, who was to be the prime figure in Brazilian politics for a quarter of a century, was around the corner.

Previously, it had been easy to stereotype guerrilla upheaval as parochial mischief, carried out by sullen locals who were deadly, no doubt, in their savagely defended corners but possessed no strategic thought nor long-range impact. (The Brazilian example is the Jagunco insurgency of 1896, memorably fanatical but wholly unstrategic, best known through the Portuguese-speaking world's *War and Peace,* Euclides da Cunha's *Rebellion in the Backlands.*) The Prestes Column brought insurgency into areas where this type of well-led dissent had never occurred, sowing defiance and moving on. It asserted by will and endurance a strategic dimension to peasant revolt — awakening and consolidating the sheer masses of strength from below. And it is a feat still examined as a supreme example of special warfare by officers in China's People's Liberation Army, an understandable interest since the founding epic of Beijing's Communist regime — Mao Tse-tung's much shorter Long March from southeast China to Yenan in the northwest to escape Chiang Kai-shek's Kuomintang armies — was written in sweat and blood only ten years after Prestes had set out.

Impressive as were these exertions, the aspects of special warfare they display are not those of the superfast strike at the tiny targeted plexus; instead, it is the ability to accomplish the unprecedented by exploiting immense distance and delay against the larger, better-equipped enemy — with consequences to be felt ever since. Peasant revolt was passing into mobility, with a continental scope that combined itself with guerrilla qualities (speed, flexibility, striking where the enemy armies are not) to create a novel threat to bewildered yet seemingly unshakable central governments.

At the same time, more insidious revolutionary inroads were being made in the ways that Buchan well understood. Handfuls of talented Soviet political-military advisers and secret operatives, ranging from China all the way to the Americas, were working to revamp the world for "the new socialist man."[5] In the developed world, they were creating curious tunnels of influence and subversion, whether in usually democratic labor unions or, as diplomat George Kennan suspected, in the U.S. State Department.[6] The Soviet Union took another step forward in shadow war when it established the Administration for Special Tasks, whose operators and professionally manipulated agents routinely killed or kidnapped enemies of the state, no matter how distant from the motherland: Trotsky, forced to flee the Soviet Union in 1934, hacked to death with an ice axe in Mexico City; Party member Juliet Poyntz, among others reckless enough to raise questions, vanishing in New York; the curious end of Soviet defector General Krivitsky, whose body was found in a locked hotel room near Washington's Union Station, with a most unconvincing suicide note; the White Russian exiles who ended up in the crematorium beneath the Soviet embassy in Paris.

Bolshevism had originally assumed industrial Europe to be the heartland of revolution, but sufficient numbers of the working classes had simply failed to rise to the dream. And in Europe it was understood that — if war was indeed unavoidable at this level of human achievement — it must be so shaped as to deliver victory on less than civilization-wrecking terms. Insights from the Great War were, of course, differently applied (or neglected). The main point was to avoid the terrible slaughter just seen. Each of the European powers during the interwar years — Britain, France, Italy, Russia, and Germany — was wrestling with alternatives, and, among the last three, additionally putting in place units sufficiently small and secret as to be barely detectable until their sudden blows were felt.

Already in the 1920s, British planners had formulated a vision of what were explicitly called "guerrilla raiders," small bodies of troops able to move quickly and go anywhere, unencumbered by the weight of numbers or bulk logistics, yet armed with outsized destructive powers. In the 1930s, the War Office carefully studied the Boers, examined the work of Lawrence (dead in a 1935 motorcycle crash), and the strange difficulties met on the Northwest Frontier. But little was pursued. Such steps were regarded as wasteful draws on tight postwar military budgets. Nor could senior commanders go quite as far as seeing a place for anything like guerrilla units in the British Army, whose mandatory twelve-year enlistments produced a level of training that earned it the ungrudging nickname of "the perfect thing apart" from no less than the German officer corps.

Already before the Armistice, the British had also been examining the possibilities of utterly rethought large-scale tank offensives, this time to be supported by aircraft. The advocates of this more refined "indirect approach" sought to break through at selected points and zero in on the opponent's "brains" — divisional, corps, and army headquarters.[7] Why despairingly wear down one's enemy layer by layer when there were modern means to unhinge him overnight from within? Pandemonium could be set loose behind the lines.

Such thinking sowed the seeds for the special forces that would appear at the start of the coming disaster; although, during the 1920s and 1930s, the prospect of decapitating an opponent was still conceived as a mechanic marvel for tanks and planes, confined to the all too obviously traditional battlefield. Ultimately, Britain brought neither form of assault to an operational level. But others in Europe were listening, and going quietly to work.

As for the French, they had been seared by the loss of 1.4 million dead and the maiming of many more in a war fought largely on their own ravaged soil — about equivalent to a nine-million–man loss for the United States today. They built interlocking high-tech fortifications from the Swiss to the Belgian frontiers that have since become a symbol of head-in-the-sand defensive foolishness but appear less so given that France possessed what was widely considered the best army in Europe, with more tanks than anyone else even in 1940. The Maginot Line (as the fortification became known after the war minister) was meant to be the pivot of a bold offensive — an impregnable forward position from which France could lash out should Germany again push west.[8] For the good reason of avoiding Brussels' becoming an appendage of Berlin, the line was not extended to the Channel coast. Instead, some thirty-five French divisions were to counterattack through Belgium. The army would not only need to be highly maneuverable to fill that gap, political decisions would have to be made quickly in Paris. But when war came, there would be no enveloping maneuver, at least by the French. As the saying goes, a hole is nothing, but you can break your ankle in one.

Italy's military capabilities (like its sports cars) have been most impressive when they resort to the few, fast, and elite. In the recent war, the Italian navy had excelled at naval special warfare. It had developed 244 small, fast PT-like boats ideal for the shallow waters and rocky islands of the enemy's Adriatic coast — thirty-eight of them equipped with electrical engines for stealth.[9] The Italians had also pioneered the use of divers walking on the sea bottom to attach mines to the hulls of targeted ships, then combined the two notions of fast boats and diver insertions to create piloted, drivable torpedoes — a clandestine special means that accounted for two Austro-Hungarian battleships.

When one matches this against what it had cost the British in tonnage and lives to take out German battleships, the ratio of effectiveness is stunning. By the 1930s, with Mussolini declaring the peninsula a natural aircraft carrier in *Mare Nostrum* (Our Sea), Italy's admirals clamored for large warships, which got the attention of the Royal Navy's Mediterranean Fleet, pleased to make friendly port calls.

The Italians were justly aware of their navy's fragility before such a behemoth, and of their vulnerable lines of communications to imperial holdings in northern Africa. Elements of the Italian navy therefore also made time to further develop hyperindividualistic special operations craft: remarkably small (slightly under two tons) powered by Alfa-Romeo engines, capable of speeds above thirty-two knots, which would explode at the moment of impact against a ship after their daring crews had ejected.[10] The brass would treat these innovations of *mezzi insidiosi* (naval guerrilla war) cavalierly, and Mussolini's characteristically inflated beliefs in what Italy's air force could accomplish from his natural aircraft carrier were fanciful — all of which set up the navy to be creamed by a very small British air formation at Taranto. But what was secretly under way between the wars would prove out in the cataclysm ahead: frogmen-saboteurs, the exploding speedboats, and two-man "chariots" (like jet skis that could be steered close enough in to enemy craft for diver-crews to attach limpet mines) would endure to blast Gibraltar's main dock and then to bring havoc on the British fleet in Alexandria. Conceptual descendants of Decima MAS (the 10th Flotilla, "MAS" being an acronym for both the boat type and the motto "Remember Always to Dare"), and its Special Underwater Raiding Force, can today be found in the SEALs.

It is nearly always the defeated of the last war who do the hardest thinking. They are the ones truly open to radical steps, determined to do it better the next time without any lulling memories of success. It is chilling to remember that here the defeated meant Russia and Germany — daunting enough, anyway. By 1935, each of the two great tyrannies was promising that a future war would have several ingenious new components.

The Soviets, ruling the world's largest state, were thinking continentally, probing the Arctic with skillful icebreaker crews and aviators (small teams, again, whose dividend would be to make easier the passage of Nazi raiders into the Pacific in 1940). They were also thinking like revolutionaries. War planning was pursued on "unalienated" Marxist terms, stressing combat as *voinii trud,* ("war-like labor"): not a bad approach to radical innovation. The war doctrine of such an entity must be able to impose conquest over immense distances and varied terrain. It pioneered the development of airborne special forces: small detachments used against the Moslem *basmachi* ("bandits" or freedom fighters, or both) in Central Asia as early as 1927; inserting a small but heavily armed airborne force into Tadzhikistan in 1929 to repulse an Afghan incursion; dispatching fifteen parachutists with a machine gun behind a large band of *basmachi* in 1931.[11]

In 1930 the first permanent airborne units were created, and within five more years the Red Army was astounding military attachés by being able to insert no less than 1,800 men by parachute and then, as they spread out, reinforcing them by air transports on fast-cleared ground to disgorge another 1,765 "locust warriors" (*sarancha voin,* went the slang), fully armed with heavy weapons. These armies filling the air were a display of what tomorrow's opponents could expect behind their lines. If the Red Army was to be an exporter of revolution, perhaps abetting insurrection in foreign capitals, airborne forces operating well in advance promised to employ special-purpose battalions trained to link up with insurgent workers.

From the first, as in Central Asia, the growth of airborne armies ran parallel to the development of much smaller, parachute-qualified spetsnaz units (a composite word from *Spetsalnaya Naznacheniya,* meaning "special purpose" or "special designation") also to descend behind the enemy but to reconnoiter, sabotage, and strike right into headquarters. In a foreshadowing of bureaucratic quarrels in most every country about the command and control of special operations forces, the army and the secret police raged over who would direct them.

Spain's atrocity-filled fratricide from 1936 to 1939, in which Moscow backed the leftist government against fascist-supported rebels, gave spetsnaz a laboratory, with "immense relevance to the course of the war."[12] Many of the most highly skilled Soviet operators performed secretly in Spain as hands-on advisers in deep reconnaissance, guerrilla warfare, prisoner snatching, and assassination — presaging Soviet special operations in World War II, Czechoslovakia in 1968 (seizing Prague's airport and abducting the uncooperative party leadership), and Afghanistan in 1979, while enabling several Soviet officers to amass unprecedented thirty-year careers in the discipline.

But the Bolsheviks were passing fast into Orwellian orthodoxy. The combination of five airborne corps and tiny commandolike units was perhaps the last flareup of genuinely radical thinking in the manner of 1917. Too revolutionary, its dashing innovators such as civil war hero Marshal Mikail Tukhachevskiy (suspected of putschism), and most of the other Soviet high command (three marshals out of five, hundreds of generals) were shot by Stalin, history's all-time massacre-maker, just between 1937 and 1939. Swallowed as well in the Great Terror was the former chief of military intelligence (the GRU's Jan Berzin), whom Stalin had dispatched to run special operations in Spain; his counterpart in the state security forces (the NKVD's Alexandr Orlov), which ran its own "special activities," escaped to the West to survive.

As for Germany, its enemies loomed to the west and — despite rather short-sighted military assistance by Russia, Europe's other pariah state — to the east. (Von Niedermayer was directing Moscow Central, the liaison office, and would die in the Gulag in 1948.) Still not as rich as the industrial democracies, and lacking the sheer manpower of the Soviet Union, Germany had the most incentive of all to explore rapidly precise means of breaking up numerically superior foes. The Versailles Treaty had skeletonized its army and navy — and prohibited any air force. The German military machine nonetheless evolved surreptitiously between the early 1920s and the mid-1930s.

One ensuing innovation was blitzkrieg — an assault spearheaded by tanks and colossally backed by Stuka fighter-bombers that would be a total shift from the bulk movement of troops to railheads, taking advantage of every capillary of the road system. The likelihood of success would be boosted by preliminary unconventional steps, such as securing road crossings and bridges, wiping out strongpoints behind enemy lines, and undercutting enemy resistance by confusing all apparent distinctions between friend and foe. Berlin was also intrigued by the exotic possibilities of what the Soviets were doing with airborne. Therefore, two other developments ensued: sudden large-scale airborne descent, as well as *Kommando* infiltrations at the outbreak of war.

In circumventing Versailles, Germany was encouraging young men and women to learn how to fly, with much of the effort devoted to fostering the still-extreme sport of gliding. Civilian glider clubs flourished and competed, building a talent pool of pilots. By 1933, such expertise with sports gliders evolved into the handling of much larger ones, each capable of carrying heavy loads of equipment or, perhaps, ten combat-loaded troops able to sail down on their targets at a speed of 180 miles per hour.

Hitler attained power that January. He was not loath to expand and flaunt Germany's armed forces, so the well-incubated Luftwaffe was able to unveil itself in 1935. By the following year, a Luftwaffe jump school was in full swing. Not only might armies arrive behind the battlelines by air, as the Russians were demonstrating, but the Luftwaffe similarly saw immense potential for smaller units to appear out of the blue by parachute or glider. With newly devastating explosives, they might be used to hit hardened positions. "Oil-drop" insertions were also explored, in which parachutists, concentrated at points of groundfall, would expand outward to form a clinging, destructive surface over what was likely to already be the disorder of a combat rear area. The very appearance of these superbly trained cadres of storm troopers from the sky in their skull-tight helmets and strange archaic/futuristic apparel of leather jerkins signaled the wars of tomorrow.

In 1938, a year before Poland was invaded, all of this innovation was coming together at Berlin's Tempelhof airport, under the auspices of a full-scale divisional command, the Flieger Abteilung, with its own regiment of "flier-hunter" (Flieger-Jaeger) warriors. The Flieger Division united paratroopers, glider-borne troops, a cadre of experienced, specialized pilots with their own training structure, and follow-up regiments arriving fast by air transports built for rough landings. Major General Kurt Student, a Prussian World War I aviator turned light infantry officer, was named commander.

Parallel with an ability to strike at enemy nerve centers through blitzkrieg and airborne troops, there emerged one more truly special unit, rather different from the "flier-hunters." Its origins lay in the East African combat of the Great War, where a small, inventive German colonial force relying on captured weapons — several hundred whites and some twelve thousand loyal Askari warriors fighting in a supremely mobile fashion — had tied down British imperial troops ten to twenty times their number by thrusting out of today's Tanzania into Rhodesia and Kenya.[13] A perceptive veteran of this outfit, Theodore von Hippel, found himself among the junior officers during the interwar years who were trying to figure out why Germany had lost the Great War despite its enormous preparation and ferocity. He examined not only his own experiences with irregular forces but T. E. Lawrence's exploits in penetration and sabotage.

Von Hippel recognized that a particular sort of highly skilled, elite formation could be the very point of the spear in the European war certain to recur. Such "special soldiers," as he called them, would form an established unit utterly different from guerrilla-style raiders, parachutists, "hunters," or in fact, anything ever seen. He envisioned them as tough, resilient volunteers fluent in other languages, men who may have lived abroad, who understood foreign cultures well enough to master disguise. The traditionalist German army had no interest.

Yet, as German military counterintelligence also came to flourish by 1935, *Abwehr* officers began to create detachments not of spies but of "soldiers with specialist aptitudes" — men who could disguise themselves to seize bridges, tunnels, crossroads, and armaments plants before the arrival of armor and infantry. And were able to do so at night.[14] Their companies would be open to a variety of people, including Germans returning to the Fatherland from living in the Baltic Republics and in Russia, as well as emigrants coaxed back from South America and Africa, and also Slavs, mavericks of various sorts, and men with don't ask/don't tell Jewish ancestry. All of them could be at home in surprising places. The first groups had been trained by summer 1939, their cover name being No. 1 Construction Training Company, soon to grow into many special units known collectively as "Brandenburgers."

German operators were also again looking well beyond the Reich's frontiers. In the years up to 1938, intelligence officers traveled covertly to Syria and Palestine, to Iran and to Iraq, to establish contacts with underground nationalists. Hitler personally agreed that an "Afghanistan story" would once more be pursued at the outbreak of war.[15]

The happily distant United States, for its part, was not even maintaining much of an army during the 1930s (roughly one soldier per eight hundred citizens, the ratio to be found in Luxembourg), nor did it have a separate air force. Had the U.S. Army been more robust, it is likely, given its continental responsibilities and trans-Pacific functions, that it would have taken similarly innovative steps at least toward an airborne capacity. Instead, for reasons of Depression-era economy, Congress in 1933 dropped from both the War and Navy departments the position of assistant secretary for air. The interwar army offered no room to explore anything like spetsnaz or "flier-hunters," let alone Brandenburgers, for which the multiethnic, vibrantly creative republic would have been ideal.

Nonetheless, after barely two generations removed from Indian fighting, the role of the modern hunter-warrior had grabbed public imagination and, indeed, soaked into the culture. We see it during these decades in the ongoing acclaim of the barely literate Tennessee mountaineer, Sergeant Alvin York, the best shot in Fentress County and the *New York Times'* "biggest hero of the war," who in the last weeks before Germany fell had pushed out alone in the thick Argonne Forest, sniping and then shooting 25 tough German veterans face-to-face before rounding up 132 more who surrendered as he closed in.[16]

We can also find curious allusions to special-force qualities in the fiction of the interwar years. Scott Fitzgerald, for instance, presents them winningly in "Dalyrimple Goes Wrong": a young war hero returns to his hometown, winds up jobless, toils in a stockroom, and then employs his special talents to expand his life as a daring night-time burglar. His success is believable because we are told at the start that he had "played the star in an affair which included a Lewis gun and a nine-day romp behind the retreating German lines." He then goes on to raid a high-toned district among whose residents are a family bearing the name of Fitzgerald's old company commander, the "Eisenhauers." (Fitzgerald could never spell.)[17] But the Philippines were pacified, the Indians crushed. The American generals had gotten their stars for positional warfare in Europe. Bush fighting and deft little actions by intrepid individuals behind the battle lines were not the concern of the army of an industrial democracy, a talent-packed conventional force shaped by the Academy, a school rooted in engineering and complex administration.

It was the U.S. Navy — with a fleet confirmed by the Washington Treaty of 1922, an early effort at arms control, as second to none — which was assigned to protect the continent. This was a service that was thinking of the breadth of oceans, as the Red Army thought of continents, and thereby was compelled to envision how to establish bases and to destroy its enemies far away. If a navy of this size had not yet found the need to develop the small-boat and frogman capacities of Decima MAS, it was enabling an ever more specialized form of amphibious warfare to move front and center.

Japan, the only exclusively Pacific power of the early twentieth century, was increasingly regarded as the most likely opponent. However, such of the American leadership as contemplated another world war was puzzled by the future role of the still-daunting British Empire. Was it a bosom Anglo-Saxon partner or a fearsome rival? Right into the 1930s, deadly serious planning by sharp minds on the U.S. general staff could imagine no more probable danger than that of six million British imperial troops rolling down from Canada to destroy the intolerable competitive challenge of the Midwest as Japan locked the arms of American power in Asia.[18]

If Japan should indeed be the more likely source of menace, it would not be enough for the United States merely to defend its island waystations of Guam, Midway, and Wake. Japan's rather minimal and coolly profitable participation in World War I had yielded it through League of Nations mandates a belt of strategically crucial Central Pacific islands in Micronesia that lay across the main U.S. sea route to the Philippines and China. Should Tokyo turn them into outlying bastions, it might be able to at least hold the United States at arms' length while it expanded its power on the mainland into some form of Fortress Asia.

The marines, who themselves often forget they are part of the navy, were meanwhile busy undertaking police actions in Central America and the Caribbean. The flavor of their operations against nationalists and bandits (the two also often being the same) is caught best in the only fiction of current American war between 1919 and 1941, the stories of Major John Thomason, USMC (*Fix Bayonets!*, *Salt Winds and Gobi Dust*), including vivid accounts of highly political small-force warfare. Better known to us (because dog-eared copies have been taken to Iraq) is the Marines' *Small War Manual*, compiled by 1940 to explain the Corps' techniques against guerrillas, a useful handbook today not so much because of its excellence but due to the absence of anything better.

The Marines, however, were regarded at the time less as an elite specialized force than as a "simple, rough-and-ready gang, which could fight banana wars."[19] It was an opinion that changed fast once a new specialty of war emerged, one they quickly mastered while, not incidentally, emancipating the U.S. Navy from having to depend on the U.S. Army for ground assault against fortified positions.

In their 140 years before World War I, the marines had never fought in such size, nor, as in that war, had their brigades been a segment of a large U.S. Army division. Success jeopardized existence; what was their distinct purpose if they were performing U.S. Army functions? Yet if there was now to be a war for the Pacific, if the navy had to break down modern hardened ground defenses, the corps had to be more than just the navy's landing force, Caribbean policeman, or adjunct to the army. Even the visionaries of that generation, such as H. G. Wells, the patron-prophet of tankers, never got around to rethinking the role of marines. Had not Nelson said "never fight a fort" after he had lost his arm at Tenerife in 1797, when his landing force was smashed on the beach by the Spanish? Had not the bloody sinkhole of Gallipoli seemed to show that defending soldiers, given the backup of fortifications, could contain and wear away the highest-quality troops thrown against them even when supported by a powerful fleet?[20] But with the United States and Japan glaring at each other across the Pacific, and with China's future apparently at stake, something had to be done.

Soon after the Armistice, while America was still embroiled in Siberia, a brilliant Lieutenant Colonel of Marines, Earl "Pete" Ellis, wrote an astonishing paper for his commandant, Major General John Lejeune, outlining most every move the United States would gear up to make in countering Japan twenty years later. It explained how heavily fortified islands might be stormed by landing craft and envisioned the likely new roles of aircraft carriers, submarines, and torpedo planes. All had to be preceded by trained demolition specialists using wirecutters and explosives to break up obstacles on the beach — the most advanced of units, said he, which included "skilled water men and skilled jungle men."[21]

While Japan considered the Pacific an impregnable moat, the corps would have to be redesigned as an entire compact army of special forces — whose strategic function resonated with the naval doctrine that the oceans are the longest highways, not the widest barriers. For the first time, the corps would not just defend advanced positions; it would conduct immediate offensive land operations from the sea. It was being positioned as the point of the lance for a twentieth-century navy that would seize or neutralize bases on its way to the enemy heartland in a war of vast oceanic distances. The marines would be the "buckle" connecting sea, air, and land power.

That Ellis was a "mustang," a man commissioned from enlisted service, when such an advance was a huge achievement in itself, may have somewhat isolated him from his fellows despite his record. He had won the Navy Cross for distinguished conduct in France and made himself a longtime student of Japan's rising power, about which he was not reticent in voicing his conclusions.

With Lejeune's backing, the forty-one-year-old Ellis booked out in May 1921 on an intelligence mission to discover the extent to which the Japanese were fortifying their Pacific islands. Though always on active duty, never on leave, he posed as a businessman to travel to Australia, the Philippines, and then to Japan itself. (He spoke and wrote Japanese well.) In Yokohama, he was soon checked into the U.S. naval hospital with acute alcohol poisoning — to walk out on the night of October 6, 1922 . . . and from there much is blank. Still presenting himself as a business traveler (though his identity was already blown), he is known to have made his way to the Marshall Islands, then, after several months, to have taken a Japanese ship even deeper into Tokyo's far island possessions.

In May 1923, Japanese representatives let it be known to Washington that, to their deepest sorrow, an American who was apparently a U.S. Marine officer had — it could not be imagined how — been found dead at Palau in the forbidden Carolines. As a macabre footnote to the mission, a pharmacist's mate was sent from the Yokohama hospital to retrieve the body, which he instead is said to have had cremated — the sailor to then courteously be returned to base utterly insane and unable ever to explain anything that had occurred.[22] Among marines, Ellis came to be regarded as a human sacrifice, a name and a face on the fury building up against Japan in the long, teeth-clenching years before December 1941.[23]

The Japanese were also thinking about oceanic outreach, whether

to erect a sea barrier against the United States while they were conquering into Asia, or to extend their holdings southward into the
British, French, and Dutch empires. Go forward or go back — after
their mainland ambitions were shatteringly checked by the Soviets at
Nomonhan on the Manchurian border in 1939, they had either to
dominate the western Pacific or be cut down to size. In the 1930s,
they were already driving brutally deep into China, carrying out their
own world-class holocaust. Meanwhile, they developed airborne
troops, and they trained sedulously in Okinawa (the current location
of the U.S. Marines' Jungle Warfare School) and on Taiwan, seized
from China in the war of 1894–95, for an alien tropical form of warfare that no one had ever seen.

‡

So MUCH was in play worldwide. So little was nailed down. It was
as if a great paperweight had been taken away, to borrow Wells's
metaphor, and everything was blowing everywhere — and much of
the world knew it. So much that had been inconceivable was now
readily believed, including a fraudulent 1930 newspaper claim that
Germany had been able to project motion-picture images of spirits on
the cloudbanks, hoping to terrify British troops during their retreat
from Mons (and had only inspired them with an illusion of angels);
and that there were invaders from Mars in 1938.[24]

The First World War had been the generals' war; the Second
would be the politicians', as radio and the lost illusions of 1914–18
enabled them (many being distinguished veterans) to lean over the
shoulders of their uniformed experts. And it is easier for political
leaders to feel the lure of special operations rather than of conventional ones — fewer lives and less money lost; more publicity; often
more hands-on involvement. By the late 1930s, there was a chaos of
clear ideas, lacking the hideous total-war context in which properly
to place them: blitzkrieg, paratroopers, marines, special operations
units for land and sea, secret political-military operatives, jungle warriors. To be sure, people in the democracies realized that the next war,
should, God forbid, it come, was going to be even worse than anything before. Most everyone (except planners in Berlin and a few survivors of Stalin's purges) looked on airpower largely as a means of
bombing cities, probably with gas. But should The Day dawn again,

there might be better ways than creating Western Front hecatombs for the privilege of holding one more devastated village or leveled wood.

Special warfare, for all its quality, must take into account that it confronts superior weight and numbers, and therefore must emphasize the unexpected. Little indeed had been unexpected, say, on the first day of the Somme, other than the top British commander's surprise that his cavalry could not get through. Every big move had been signaled by artillery bombardment. By September 1939, as so much of the world was squared off, people realized that virtually everything that lay ahead would be surprising. And this was nothing to what arrived.

16

So Far, the Main Event
Anything Goes: The Stakes of Totalitarian Conquest, 1939–1945

"And now set Europe ablaze."
WINSTON CHURCHILL, 1940

THE WAR that opened with an order to British officers to sharpen their swords, and that climaxed as proudly modern Germany blitzed into Russia with nearly two hundred times more horses than tanks, ended in a heave of nuclear ash — from a bomb that came into its terrible existence only sixty-one years after the invention of a device as simple as the ammunition clip. The world was being harshly remade by factories that could assemble aircraft faster than Model Ts had until so recently been clanged together, and then by cruise and ballistic missiles, finally by jets and computers, propelled into development by demands of war.

On the Russian plains, where the steam locomotive was a marvel less than a long lifetime before, the greatest of tank battles ground away the world's two mightiest armies like whole species of dinosaurs trying to exterminate one another. Slavery was reintroduced into the middle of Europe; Tokyo and Berlin each coolly administered genocide. Firestorms burst from the air. Fleets that never saw each other ship-to-ship clashed over huge areas of the Western Pacific. Names to puzzle geographers became fulcrums of the world: El Alamein, Kursk, Tarawa. Armies crossed the English Channel like huge boarding parties. Toward the end, starving millions stumbled across borders, shedding children and the aged. Only the gas- and germ-bearing winds were granted a surcease. God, in Churchill's words, seemed to have wearied of mankind.

In this fight to the death among industrialized nations, special operations for the first time assumed an ongoing strategic importance: German commandos landed atop the elaborate Belgium fortress system to secure the northern flank for the blitzkrieg race to the Channel ports; Britain determinedly penetrated occupied Europe within days of France's surrender; and Mussolini's rescue from high up the Gran Sasso massif renewed his authority after Italy went over to the Allies in 1943. And more, including pivotal hit team assassinations. Techniques and their usually strange visionaries, small efficient actions and their often-unsettling practitioners, were combining around the world.

Previously, weapons and equipage had defined one form or another of fighting force. A warrior's appearance reflected his function and often his social standing. Men were archers, dragoons, marines, grenadiers, jaegers, riflemen. With the arrival of actual commandos, however, we begin to see units whose implicit purpose is open-ended. They do not just improve themselves, as all good enterprises do, or make one gigantic innovative leap, as did the founding generation of tankers and paratroopers. Instead, by their nature, they set out to be uniquely versatile, adapting themselves to mountains, sea, jungle, or desert as well as using a breadth of weaponry in singularly extreme missions.

Nonetheless, much remained improvised: many British amphibious Commando Raiders could not swim; Nazi *Kommandos,* formidable in themselves, were repeatedly hampered by the monocled perspective of the Wehrmacht's high command despite the Führer's erratic patronage; the U.S. Office of Strategic Services raised (almost overnight) heroic but so often amateurish operators of the likes of Nick Carraway, from venues such as Wall Street bond departments in the days when selling securities required little more than the breezy New Haven manner. But now the need for the other kind of right stuff — the hunter's eye and ear — was making itself indispensable.

Four influences that shaped this greatest of wars also worked to push special operations forces toward the way of life we see today.

One was simply geographical vastness and variety. In a war that spread over Europe, the Middle East, a third of the Western Pacific, and huge areas of China and Southeast Asia, even the most modern nation could not quickly deliver, say, a quarter-million troops (men likely to be just a quarter-way prepared) to every theater in which it needed its presence felt. Furthermore, bulk for bulk's sake might prove downright counterproductive in the sand seas of North Africa, the Norwegian fjord country, and in Burma's mountainous jungles. The high commands themselves acknowledged there were crucial steps that would have been hard to take in traditional modes. Special operations were being coordinated more than ever before with strategic objectives.

Second were the double-edged possibilities of technology, both as an instrument and as an objective of the commando. Radio communications, for instance, made it possible to injure the inner organs of enemy territory, not just to gash the skin. Infiltrators with powerfully compact explosives could penetrate in the inspiring hope of being exfiltrated by precisely arriving submarines or light aircraft. And there was now an abundance of vital targets that lent themselves to pinpoint destruction, in the days before precision bombing: electric grids, chromium processing plants, the Third Reich's heavy-water facility in Norway (most identifiable point in the nuclear weaponry chain), blown up by twelve men of the resistance who climbed an "unscalable" (and therefore undefended) gorge, then other commandos sinking the railroad ferry carrying away to Germany what remained of the isotope.

Third was the eruption of resistance movements, barely calculated before 1939, across Europe, Ethiopia, the Philippines, Burma, anger there to be leveraged. Ever since Gylippus steeled the nerve of Syracuse during the Peloponnesian War, we have seen what a small amount of professional encouragement and specific effective advice can accomplish. Now the price of Axis conquest was to be raised.[1]

Fourth, and perhaps most important, was the decentralization of authority that accompanied war among ever more developed nations. Awareness mounted of what individuals could achieve without the top command scrutinizing every move of every company. We see this ever-expanding scope for lower-level initiative in the accomplishments of small combat forces working nearly independently from main armies — carrying on right through the U.S. Special Forces take-down of the Taliban in 2001, known as "the sergeants' war."[2] Moreover, at the start of World War II, even the most uninvolved of people understood what the fast, focused, and comparatively few could pull off against the strong: the Prestes adventure, "fifth-column" subversion in Spain had all been popping up on the front pages. Hitler himself had grasped the importance of street fighting and putschist confrontation in rising to power.

This was a war in which everyone realized that enemy headquarters might at any moment be visited, and not by noisy frontal formations making themselves heard ten miles away, but by silently delivered, soot-faced marauders, or by hunter-killer teams flying out of the sun or stepping from suburban hedgerows. Just as the wholesale slaughter of civilians reasserted itself in war, professional courtesy was breaking down into a practice of targeting individuals — by "band[s] of chosen and picked young men . . . sworn to stick together" — that might as well have come out of Utopia, or at least the Dark Ages.

‡

THE SEPTEMBER 1, 1939, attack on Poland that dragged Britain and France into war two days later was, as might have been expected from National Socialist Germany, covered with macabre deceit, including leaving bodies of murdered concentration-camp inmates, armed and dressed in Polish uniforms, on the German side of the border. (Berlin could claim to the world that the warmongering Poles had struck first.) As the Wehrmacht (German armed forces) raced east, their way was eased by several hundred lightly armed operators who had infiltrated days earlier, dressed as miners or businessmen, to prevent the Poles from blowing up their own tunnels and factories, then to disrupt Polish communications and troop movements. Within three weeks, the Red Army joined hands with the Wehrmacht to divide the spoils, although, farther north, badly led Soviet divisions (the best generals having been shot) were about to encounter a harder time against a series of sharp, quick actions waged far across snowbound terrain by the small democratic republic of Finland, invaded at the end of November.

A naval war was under way, which included the sinking of a battleship by a U-boat startlingly able to penetrate the Scapa Flow base in Scotland. Otherwise, Germany made no further attack until pouncing upon neutral Norway and Denmark on April 9, 1940. As for the United States, it was becoming ever more "neutral against" the authentic axis of evil: Germany, Italy, and Japan.

War had broken out even though it might involve what are now known as weapons of mass destruction: nations chose to fight despite the likelihood that cities would be bombed not just with conventional high explosives and incendiary weapons but also with poison gas — a prospect which failed to exercise a deterrent effect every bit as persuasive as the nuclear one that came on stage a decade later. At the other extreme of violence, all were concerned about imminent sabotage, which can be at its most effective when intertwined with the clever targeting, infiltrations, and efficient destructive technologies of the special operator. We see such awareness in fall 1939, as the British anticipated a novel form of information warfare, as the technique is now called in the glossary of U.S. Special Operations Command: the BBC directed its previously anonymous radio announcers to identify themselves by name to prevent German impostors from taking advantage of the lack of identity to spread defeatist news or instructions that might assist an invasion.[3]

The news was bad enough when Hitler snatched Norway and Denmark. Troops sprang off merchant ships at night to take Copenhagen by early morning; people going to work passed field-gray columns and thought they were watching a movie being made about the fall of Poland. Speaking the language perfectly, Brandenburg units disguised as Danish soldiers seized a bridge across the Grosse Belt that enabled tanks to race north into the island ports of the kingdom. Simultaneously, task forces grabbed Norway's major ports from Narvik above the Arctic Circle on down and around the western and southern coastline to Oslo, while well-practiced airborne troops dropped inland, and Brandenburgers created chaos by posing as Norwegian soldiers. Seven German divisions were in Norway within forty-eight hours.

Ten days later, on the other side of the world, German operators went to work with obliging tribes along the Afghan-Indian border. Backed by the German embassy in Kabul, they established a unified command as the "Afghan Company" and — before carrying out the first attacks — traveled through the country under cover as a research group studying leprosy. Crossing the northwest frontier, they pushed twenty miles into India to blow up a bridge, destroy a radio station, and strike a telegraph office before finding themselves in a deadly firefight with British patrols. It was the RAF and brand-new British paratroopers that retaliated decisively, acting as a pincer to kill the commander, take prisoners, and scatter German survivors back to Kabul from where — as in World War I — the would-be insurgents began the long journey home.[4]

Churchill, again at the Admiralty (Neville Chamberlain was still prime minister), pressed hard for a response to the far-graver attack on Norway. The Allies' commando-style units first appeared amid the British-Canadian-French-Polish–exile effort to aid Norway. Neglected proposals in the War Office for army "guerrilla raiders" boiled up to the attention of the shaken leadership. "Striking companies" modeled deliberately on the Boers were raised largely from Territorial volunteers (halfway between the Reserves and the National Guard) still in Britain. The men dispatched by the end of April to join conventional formations possessed nothing that can be described as commando training; even their maps were torn from holiday tour guides. The amphibious riposte would fare badly, occurring exactly twenty-five years after the disaster at Gallipoli. But this time dissatisfaction fastened on the luckless Chamberlain, while Germany kept showing it was far better prepared for special warfare.

Adolf Hitler was the most lethal crank to imperil the Western world since the wars of religion, Bonaparte at least having troubles of ego rather than of mental health. But cranks are not stamped from a single bent cookie-cutter. The same megalomaniacal vision that guided Hitler to become chancellor before he was forty-four and when he had been a German citizen for fewer than two years would do much to destroy the Wehrmacht in Russia. The same temperament that let him be hospitable to visions of clever new destruction posed by junior officers made him at home in the ruins of a civilization. As a brave soldier from the trenches of 1914–18, he understood the possibilities of Valkyrie assaults through the air at dawn. It was likely he who initiated what came next.[5]

Belgium's elaborate defense system centered on a bastion in the northeastern tip of the country that had been built into and atop 150-foot cliffs sheared off by blasting that had gouged the Albert Canal, which flows into the Meuse near Maastricht and is a crucial waterway for both trade and protection. Biggest and strongest in the world, the fortress of Eben Emael (named after the nearby town where a strip of the Netherlands hangs down between Germany and Belgium) was more than half a mile long on its canal and inland faces. Almost as long on its north side, its honeycomb of thirty miles of rooms and corridors and superb internal railroad system promised a confident redundancy against any bombardment. Its casements and cupolas were constructed like the turrets of a battleship. Immense guns with a twelve-mile range commanded the approaches, enough to cover three vital bridges over the Albert Canal and to interdict any force seeking to rebuild them once well-placed charges underneath were detonated at the moment of invasion. The fortress complex was considered impregnable, and bombers of the time could not offer the precision to destroy a structure this solid, particularly when well protected by antiaircraft batteries.

Berlin believed it essential not only that the fortress be taken but that the bridges should pass intact into German hands. The British Expeditionary Force and the First French Army had to be lured here to Belgium while thrusts drove farther south through the Ardennes, through Luxembourg, and against the center of France's defenses. Even a plan as radical as deploying paratroopers offered no solution. The Belgians were fully alert. The droning of approaching transports might be detected, and since this was when chutes could not be steered, paratroopers would have found themselves too dispersed to implement the audacious scheme of landing not only near the bridges but atop the fortress roof — easily giving the few minutes that were all the Belgians needed to blow up the bridges and to put the fortress into full battle mode. For Germany the answer lay in cheap, silent, precisely landed gliders, released from their tow planes approximately thirteen miles from target.

The fragility of the plywood craft, which had never before been used in combat, was offset by soundless descent, a minimum landing run, and their enabling the commandos to bring along flamethrowers and heavy satchels of explosives — a simple means of silent insertion surpassed only recently by helicopters with muted engines. It was a marriage between the storm-trooper formations that Germany had created a quarter century before to crack the Western Front and the new, almost sportive capabilities of the Luftwaffe's *Fallschirm,* or Parachute Division. Seasoned sport pilots would take these air force "flier-hunters" (also known as Para Assault Engineers or *Pioniere,* soon to receive the name *glidermen*) to the roof.

Rather dated aerial photos were available, but any unidentified plane sent overhead now might telegraph the plan. Otherwise, research had been exhaustive. The Belgians had been sufficiently shaken by the sandcastle fate of their defenses in 1914 to have thereafter piled up those state-of-the-art concrete casements and steel cupolas at Eben Emael. But he who thinks defensively must also think about the enemy's many forms of offense. Here the dutiful Belgians failed on several counts — not only regarding the famous vulnerability of the roof but, as we have seen before, in holding a misplaced faith for what is gigantic. "The great size of Eben Emael," observes a student of the attack, "meant that its gunners were largely isolated and couldn't provide covering [or supporting] fire."[6] Berlin had obtained blueprints from the two German construction companies that Belgian thrift and lack of hard feelings had employed to work on the fortress in the early 1930s.[7] While the Belgians put their faith in steel and concrete, the nation that led the world in chemistry had developed economical hollow (shaped) charges able to burst the seams of such a colossus — a device also never before used in war.

It was no surprise that an attack of some sort was coming. There had been many alarms, which was part of the problem. A month after Hitler invaded Norway and Denmark, the 650 men of the Belgian garrison, with 233 more well-armed troops about four miles away, and others guarding the bridges, were ready to defend the narrow strip of land separating these key points from the Reich. With high morale, the Belgians were technically prepared to turn back the worst — of a predictable kind of menace. But to the men on the wind, they were vulnerable. Had they envisioned so technologically delicate an assault, a few score *chevaux de frise* on the fortress roof would have disemboweled any landing, the passive weaponry of the fifteenth century (stakes joined together crosswise) trumping the extreme sport of the twentieth. But they were not looking to the future, let alone the distant past.

At beginning of morning on May 10 (a night landing being impossible), nine German gliders made their final approach. The Belgians had known for at least half an hour that some aerial attack was afoot (hardly enough time for them to rethink their fundamentals), and they opened up with antiaircraft fire against these "planes" in the sky with their engines apparently turned off. Six gliders were hit during the descent, but none of the attackers were wounded. The gun crews stood dumbfounded as the black aircraft with no insignia skidded to a stop on the roof within seconds of each other. Because two of the gliders had snapped their towropes soon after takeoff, there was only one officer among the sixty-nine men who sprang out and dashed through machine-gun fire to stick magnetic packs of hollow charges to the metal plates of the gun turrets. It made no difference. "The officers had trained all of the men so well that the officers were expendable," recalled the mission's twenty-three-year-old lieutenant in charge, who still got himself to the scene two hours later by road. (Less flatteringly, one of his platoon sergeants reminisced that the men were inclined to behave like "bandits.")[8]

The German glidermen were able to incapacitate enough of the fortress guns within fifteen minutes to enable the rest of the 493-man assault in forty-two gliders to take the three bridges. With gas masks and machine pistols, they then pursued the defenders — initially ten times their number — down into the fortress' galleries, clouded with discharge from the explosives and packed with crushed bodies from tons of falling debris. The position was held until the main battle force smashed its way through the frontier, dive-bombers helping to thwart Belgian counterattacks against the glidermen.

This devastation of a suit of armor by eggshells played against the defenders' every human and technological vulnerability. Of the men who descended on the roof, just six were killed and twenty wounded. It was a modest price for what the best analysis of the drama (written by a U.S. Navy SEAL commander who interviewed survivors and walked the ruins) concludes "was one of the most decisive victories in the history of special operations."[9] A point vital to the Allies' hopes had been erased in hours while German troops poured into Belgium across the intact bridges.

The ability to insert a small force against deep or hardened positions had until this time been an essentially supportive tactical move, unless some vital objective was vulnerable from water. Now surprise attack by the relatively few against the thoroughly entrenched many could have staggering consequences. Not until the gliders were assumed to have touched down did the overall German offensive get the final go-ahead. The lock had been blown; now the vault door could be shoved open.

With Parliament having despaired for weeks at the way events had been falling apart, Churchill finally got his chance, coincidentally becoming prime minister within hours of Germany's attack against France and the Low Countries. Then the Netherlands surrendered in five days. Like the French behind the Maginot Line, the Dutch believed themselves safe behind their dikes, which were set to be broken to flood away any invaders. The men commanding the watery defenses of "Fortress Holland," however, had not given enough attention to German paratroops, hydroplanes, and deception. The Brandenburgers were first in, wearing Dutch uniforms stolen months before. Fifteen combat teams were sent to take Dutch bridges. Against a crucial railroad bridge over the Maas, they appeared as German deserters "guarded" by friends dressed as well-armed Dutch frontier police, the prisoners' unbuttoned greatcoats (which might have looked suspicious in May) concealing machine pistols under their armpits and grenades in their pockets.[10] The ignition wires cut and Dutch demolition post once taken, a German armored train rolled through.

The Germans broke farther into the West, with Rommel at the head of his panzers exulting at "the flat countryside [that] lay spread around us under the cold light of the moon. We were through the Maginot Line!"[11] Actually, he was around it, the French and British still not understanding what had hit them. The RAF was ordered to strike the rail lines, as if this were 1918, even as the tanks were racing to the Channel by road. All Allied forces were withdrawn from Norway in early June, right after the British pulled off the miraculous nine-day evacuation of a third of a million men from Dunkirk's shell-pocked beaches.

With the fall of Paris imminent, an assault team of Brandenburgers disguised as French, Dutch, and Belgian refugees drove into the city, straight to an annex of the French intelligence service. (It was June 9; the government would not abandon the disintegrating capital until the next day, and German troops would not enter until the fourteenth.) The raiders held the staff at gunpoint. Captured were the central card index and files of France's domestic security agency, the *Sûreté Nationale,* and the prize was soon crated and sent by train to Berlin.[12]

Finally determining which side was the stronger, Mussolini got around to declaring war on the Allies, and Hitler's Soviet partner opportunistically swallowed up the Baltic republics of Latvia, Lithuania, and Estonia.

On the seventeenth, France pleaded for an armistice, some 124,000 of its soldiers dead and 200,000 wounded in six weeks; Britain and its celebrated but not industrially enormous empire faced the continent alone. Within forty-eight hours, and only nineteen days after Churchill had further urged the generals to come up with volunteers of the "hunter class" who could fight in independent units — outfits significantly harder than those of the brave Territorial irregulars — Britain began launching commando raids across the Channel.[13] The British had been in this spot before, as they kept reminding themselves, when facing Revolutionary and Bonapartist France as alliances formed and collapsed between 1793 and 1809. Churchill ordered one of his most extroverted ministers, with a good World War I record, to "set Europe ablaze" as the head of the Special Operations Executive, the next step being to create means of "ungentlemanly warfare" to defeat the Nazis at their game.[14]

Launching special operations into occupied Europe demonstrated that there remained an aggressive democratic redoubt practically within sight. Only such actions on the ground could fuel indigenous resistance and also be a precise means of striking at German strength in France without the collateral damage of aerial bombing, which Nazi propagandists were so cleverly able to spin.[15] If the British were again facing a ten-to-fifteen-year struggle, they could at least attempt knife thrusts into what Hitler would call "Fortress Europe." No one could foresee that the Nazi-Soviet nonaggression pact would break apart or that America would enter the war. Once Hitler turned on Stalin the following summer, these thrusts could additionally be a way of keeping Europe's liberation movements from falling entirely into Communist hands.

On the night of June 23–24, 1940, a force of 120 men (carrying half of the 40 Thompson submachine guns then in Britain) used small rescue craft from the RAF to stage an offensive reconnaissance on the French coast south of Boulogne–Le Touquet. With no particular target, little was accomplished besides killing two sentries and tossing a couple of grenades. But Fleet Street headlines were tremendous. Other raids followed, though shortcomings in training, intelligence, equipment, and specific targets quickly told. These "special service" companies were still the most improvised of heroic bands against an enemy very strong indeed. By mid-July, Churchill was denouncing such "silly fiascoes" and demanding immediate reorganization.[16] What followed became the most variegated, innovative, and active collection of special operations forces ever seen until today.

Churchill was the first British prime minister since Wellington to have served in the military, and the only one ever to wear a uniform while in office, his choice being an honorary one from the Royal Air Force. As a subaltern in the 1890s, he had experienced hand-to-hand combat against the Dervishes in Sudan and indeed had made his name during the Boer War by taking more than his share of risks as a war correspondent. He entered early into Parliament in 1900 on the strength of his sensational escape from Boer captivity. Curiosity and high energy compelled him to qualify as a pilot — reflecting a fascination with technology and gadgets apparent at least since his strange 1907 notion of installing a giant turbine to harness Victoria Falls as a source of electricity.

By 1921 Churchill was simultaneously Secretary of State for Air [Force] and for Colonies. After having been a midwife to the tank during World War I, he became a pioneer of airpower well before World War II. Twice he nearly ruined himself in politics — over Gallipoli and then, in the 1930s, by a backward view of Indian independence and misjudgments of economic policy. But he was known for his comebacks, his largely principled switches between parties, from Conservative to Liberal then back to Conservative, and his noisy exuberance. In war, he was always pursuing ways to substitute mind for blood, spirit for numbers. Shut up on his besieged island, he was a dangerous man when entrusted with the powers of recoil.

As Britain awaited invasion in late summer 1940, U.S. assistance had reached the point of shipping over deer rifles donated by a well-armed citizenry to support the guerrilla warfare Churchill promised, once Englishmen were driven back from their bloodily contested beaches.[17] Busy clearing the decks for action by dismissing or re-assigning senior officers, U.S. Army Chief of Staff George Marshall prudently insisted that America concentrate on its own defenses.[18] The Axis could move awfully fast; island Britain was not, on the evidence, a reliable front line. To be sure, it was in the Battle of Britain from August to November that "the few" of the RAF, outnumbered in planes and pilots four to one by the Luftwaffe, blocked Germany from attaining the air superiority that would have made invasion feasible. Of interest to our story, however, are the other few on land and in small boats, who with hunters' endurance and fortitude, stalked, struck, and, if lucky, returned to strike again.

In early August, "commandos" (battalions with about five hundred men each) were being formed under the direction of the admiral who had led the path-breaking Zeebrugge raid of 1918 against the U-boat pens in Belgium. A school for officers was helpfully opened on the Scottish estate of Lieutenant Colonel Lord Lovat (son of the founder of the Scouts), a tall, handsome, twenty-three-year-old whose second in command would recall him in the thick of combat wearing "corduroy slacks, a gray sweater, and carrying a Winchester sporting rifle."[19] Training remained haphazard. Lovat's ghillies, for example, taught the arts of deerstalking to men who, within weeks, were expected to come from the sea like a "hand of steel which plucks the German sentries from their posts," as Churchill dramatized their work.[20] Today, well-choreographed close-combat skills have been displayed ad nauseam to whole nations of moviegoers; suburbanites practice karate and tae kwon do at studios in the shopping mall. But martial arts and quick-fire pistol shooting were novel even to army officers of the time. The commandos would be taught Judo 101, with nasty street-fighting moves stirred into that relatively polite discipline by a hulking cop from the Singapore imperial police.

Churchill was always looking beyond the moment. Commandos were not just to go in to eliminate sentries and to raise morale but, by coming back, to be deployed when needed in substantial strength. He demanded ten thousand such men — including five thousand paratroopers, when landing atop an enemy position was still special warfare indeed. Commandos had to perform together not only in small teams, but with the capacity, should opportunity arise, to fight in the hundreds, maybe thousands, as do U.S. special forces today. And this fact is crucial to our theme: special warfare need not be conducted by only nineteen recruits, as on the Georgia railroad, or by several dozen, such as on the roof of Eben Emael. It can include forces the size of Cortés's or Morgan's, or ones much larger. Yes, they were to be men "accustomed to work like packs of hounds," envisioned as "small 'bands of brothers' who will be capable of lightning action."[21] But such men were also of the kind able to pull off a raid at least on the scale of Zeebrugge or, before long, of spending months operating at brigade strength behind the lines of an entire army, to the distress of the highly efficient Japanese in Burma. It is here, in 1940–41, that we see the origins of British Army commando units per se, and of their many variant forms, some of which still endure as SAS, SBS, and the Royal Marine Commandos.[22]

While the toughest of volunteers began to be shaped into hopefully versatile raiders during summer 1940, Churchill backed an even stranger organization, distinct from both the military and intelligence services. Initially working from the fourth floor of an obscure London hotel, then out of an office block on Sherlock Holmes's Baker Street, the Special Operations Executive (SOE) grew into a global presence of ten thousand men and women, claiming as its purpose to "encourage every form of terror."[23]

On the Allied side, what we think of as terror today — indiscriminate carnage inflicted on civilians to make a political point — would be left to the strategic air forces over Hamburg, Dresden, and Tokyo: SOE's purpose was rather to equip, train, and coordinate patriots within the occupied nations, and to dispatch agents to sabotage and assassinate. Its Destruction Section hit deep. SOE began its own abrasive relationships with the army, the navy, and the RAF, as well as with the Secret Intelligence Service, better known as MI6 — all institutions not only skeptical of men they derided as "amateurs," but by now stretched desperately thin and loath to hand over boats and planes.

Improvising by the week, SOE provided the grains of sand that would coalesce into pearls of resistance (or *terrorism,* as the Nazis called it).[24] Its operatives were recruited by word of mouth, trained in a bootstrapped fashion similar to the military commandos. They leveraged themselves in groups rarely more than five or six behind the lines in France and, in the Netherlands, with merely pairs of men (a radio operator and a sabotage expert). There was little modern precedent on which to draw as SOE partitioned itself into country "desks," such as one for France (infiltrating 393 operatives before liberation), another for Yugoslavia (SOE's even more active terrain after the Wehrmacht invaded in April 1941), and, indeed, a "desk" for Germany itself. SOE had laboratories that spun out a variety of necessary customized devices: tailored forms of explosives, poisons, silenced (or "suppressed") firearms, and advanced radios.

SOE launched its first mission in February 1941: a low-altitude fourteen-hour round-trip flight to Poland to night-drop three Polish parachutists who were to infiltrate occupied Warsaw. (The "Dark and Silent," these patriots were called.) By this time, agents were emerging from training to begin other penetrations by parachute, submarine, and — "in the buccaneering tradition" — small boats.[25] All was makeshift, although frequently no more so than the schemes of MI6, which possessed its own intelligence networks and agent-saboteurs.

It shows how hastily these capabilities had been brought into being that so many different special and irregular outfits, as well as lots of little private armies, sprang up, all pursuing "the commando idea" and dedicated to extreme missions. They lived in uneasy alliance not only with the regular army and navy, but occasionally with one another. Yet all worked as commandos, despite an array of designations — warriors able to face extremity well ahead of the reassuring reach of their nation's fleets and divisions. They had by this time gone beyond being just heroes intent on "showing the army how to mount a breach," as in the Peninsular War, or insouciant daredevils such as the Texas Rangers, or for that matter, elite parachutists and engineers even as expertly deployed as at Eben Emael.

‡

As an imperial power, Britain considered the Middle East every bit as vital as the European continent. If anything, the prospect of losing Egypt and the Suez Canal was believed to be the more calamitous, and would remain so in war planning for at least a half-dozen years after 1945.[26] It was here, across one of earth's most desolate regions, stretching some fifteen hundred miles from the Nile Delta to the frontier of Tunisia, that the empire began to strike back in strength. The Western Desert Force of thirty-six thousand men already in Egypt (another 27,500 in Palestine) was reinforced fast to shatter the Italian colonial army in North Africa in the second half of 1940 and, after February 1941, to confront Rommel's daunting Afrika Korps as it arrived to bail out the Italians and try to push across the canal all the way to the Iraqi oil port of Basra at the top of the Persian Gulf.

Right away, in June 1940, the British commander in chief at Cairo set up the Long Range Desert Group (LRDG), conceived by a major who envisioned its small independent columns of 1.5-ton Chevrolet trucks reaching undetected from Egypt to Tripoli, thus accomplishing the collection of the deepest of intelligence in the limitless expanse. Based in the caves of the Siwa Oasis and later in Khufra on the Egyptian-Libyan border, maintaining daily contact by some of the best radios in the world, LRDG may not have been designated as a commando outfit on the organization charts. But these bearded men (the best of them said to be New Zealanders) were performing as "packs of hounds" if anyone was, and this pack included former professors, archeologists, sailors, and shepherds.[27] They specialized in not being seen, and a feature then thought notable was that every man could drive. Yet in their hundreds of missions, the temptation to move beyond road watching into raiding was irresistible, as in mingling their trucks with an Italian convoy at night until the perfect killing site was found to pull to the side and ambush the line of vehicles behind them. It was an enterprise that would be readily adapted beyond the desert into Europe itself.

The Desert Group worked intimately with another new formation, the Special Air Service (SAS), which at the start was not much of an air unit beyond its twenty-something founders stealing parachutes from headquarters in Cairo and taking it upon themselves to try jumping out of a plane. But its purpose was unambiguous attack delivered in four-man patrols of warriors who were cross-trained in demolitions, signals, languages, and emergency medicine. Thrown together in Egypt during summer 1941, around a core of sixty-six men who already possessed commando experience in the Channel, the SAS grew to master insertions by air, land, and sea. Like its founders (and distinct from many of the Allies' ad hoc commando outfits), only men who had already been specially trained were welcomed into this versatile fraternity where skills would be further honed. They were to be clandestine operators distinct as well from the now two-thousand-strong Army Commandos, whose much larger combat units SAS's founders regarded as cumbersome. Instead, minimum demands were to be made for men and equipment. In the desert, the SAS were guided by LRDG navigators, to turn up like a thunderbolt far in the enemy's rear in jeeps with twin Vickers machine guns and then vanish, striking like pirates on the seas. Port towns in German and Italian hands along the entire North African coast could be hit from land or water.

In character, David Stirling, SAS's six-foot-four Scots Guards officer visionary — incessantly complaining about having to fight two enemies, his own general headquarters and the Axis — would eventually be captured after doing what he was told not to do (trying to cut through terrain stiff with Germans, including a force trained for operations against commandos). But Stirling had laid a strong foundation before being imprisoned for the duration at Colditz Castle. He wrote down four famous guiding principles for the SAS: engage in the never-ending pursuit of excellence; maintain the highest standards of self-discipline in all aspects of daily life; tolerate no sense of class; all ranks to possess humility and humor. They compose an enduring personal code as well as core instruction for any demanding venture.

Stirling was succeeded by a former second-row rugby forward for

Ireland who, before joining, had to be pardoned for having struck a commanding officer and who collaborated with the LRDG to destroy (on the ground) more enemy bombers and fighter planes than any Allied pilot of the war. Revealingly, this was accomplished with the Lewes Bomb, a device named after its creator, a recent Oxford rowing Blue from the science schools. It was invented for such purposes by the men who would use it, no matter that experts told them it would take forever to develop. Throughout, these operators worked to damage enemy morale, which was accomplished effectively when the throats of aircrews were unsportingly sliced in their sleep. As the Allies came to win in the desert, the SAS itself would be expanded to nearly two thousand warriors (integrating French Régiments de Chasseurs Parachutistes and Belgians), who would ply their craft not only along the Italian peninsula, in the Balkans, and during the Normandy invasion, but also against the Japanese.

As for German enterprise actually in oil-rich Iraq, Berlin dispatched Brandenburg infiltrators and Luftwaffe operators to play the card of Arab nationalism. The British military presence initially suffered some one hundred casualties at their hands but responded with overwhelming force in mid-1941 — as the United States exerted pressure on Iraq to change its wavering government. The small Brandenburg combat unit pulled back to Syria and then made it home. Imprudent Iraqis went to the gallows.

Other bands of elite Allied desert warriors were building on the exploits of both the Desert Group and the SAS, including the Special Identification Group (SIG) of German-Jewish volunteers from Palestine, who disguised themselves in Afrika Korps uniforms to mingle with enemy convoys and messes for eavesdropping and sabotage. An even smaller unit in the British force was, by happenstance, "Popski's Private Army," known at times as PPA, or No. 1 Demolition Squadron. It roamed through the wilds of Cyrenaica, leveraging Senussi Arabs against Italian colonial occupiers and German reinforcements, raiding the enemy-held coasts out of the inner desert, its mission to spread "alarm and despondency."[28] Remembered both for their precision and their windshieldless Jeeps equipped with Bren guns and mortars, this handful of hyperselected volunteers covered much of the terrain over which William Eaton's own "private army" had marched in 1805, Major Vladimir "Popski" Peniakoff infiltrating Derna itself (the port city taken by Eaton a century and a half earlier) in disguise to rescue POWs. Peniakoff demanded exactness laced with imagination and self-reliance. He concluded these were the qualities of seamen more than of soldiers. Like the desert, the sea never makes allowances.

German officers could not make sense of so many loosely linked outfits dashing about with so few apparent ties to any centralized command. Army units specifically titled "Commandos" — rather than "Independent" or "Special Service" companies, and wearing a hunter's green beret — had begun their own raids in the Middle East in 1941. But war in the enemy rear could still show blunders enough: the breakdown of small craft, dysfunctional compasses, landings on the wrong beach, wishful thinking passing for intelligence, and outfits disastrously tripping over one another once the Army Commandos, the LRDG, SAS, SIG, and the Royal Marine Commandos, among others, tried to cripple Tobruk as a Cyrenaican port for the Afrika Korps. A culture that valued the gifted amateur was still feeling its way through the start-up phase.

In May 1941, when Britain and still-neutral America were just laying the foundation for their serious airborne capacities, Crete would be taken by history's first invasion from the sky. Hitler regarded mountainous Crete — 150 miles long and about 20 broad, the great isle lying between the Aegean and Egypt — as the next step in an Eastern Mediterranean island-hopping strategy that would take German power to the Suez Canal by another route than just the Western Desert. After the expeditionary force that Churchill had sent to Greece was driven from the mainland, some forty-two thousand resolute British, Australians, New Zealanders, and Greeks were in place to defend the offshore bastion. They were fully alert; codebreakers in London and a paratroop coup at the Isthmus of Corinth twenty-five days before had given them some idea what was afoot. Plus, the British had captured a copy of the training manual for these self-described "German warrior[s] incarnate."[29]

Yet, like giant bats at dawn, the cream of the Luftwaffe's Eleventh Air Corps silently swept in on fifty-three immense square-fuselaged gliders launched from the Peloponnesus and outlying islands. Nearly simultaneously, two thousand camouflaged parachutists leapt from low-flying Junkers transports in waves of two hundred at fifteen-minute intervals. Most carried just pistols and long-handled fighting knives, their tommy guns, sniper rifles, and heavy weapons being dropped separately in rubber-padded canisters. Jaeger and Alpine regiments then quickly arrived as the paratroopers secured runways — about twenty-five thousand invaders altogether. Lieutenant General Kurt Student's planning had been meticulous. His paratroopers, for instance, had been taught to handle British trucks, which were to be gathered and used in the breakout from the landing areas, when it could not be taken for granted (as requirements for the British LRDG reveal) that even these skilled fighting men could drive.[30]

The "oil-drop" tactics and sudden thrusts by Jaeger and Alpine regiments subdued the island by June 1, as the defenders crumbled. Thirty-seven-year-old Evelyn Waugh fought there as an Army Commando, his novel *Officers and Gentlemen* — with its commando protagonist Guy Crouchback disgusted at the mayhem — best evoking the disintegration of morale not under horrors half so much as amazement. Yet victory came at a price that startled even Hitler: every third man killed, every second survivor wounded among the Flieger division's point-of-the-lance Assault Regiment; at least 60 percent casualties for the invaders overall. Germany would not use airborne forces again in their original big-picture role, although the prospect of a descent right into London for some time haunted Churchill's War Cabinet.[31]

From here on, successful airborne assault would be performed nearly exclusively on a huge scale by the Allies as parts of enormous offensives, such as the sixty-seven hundred men of the 101st Airborne "Screaming Eagles" and more from the 82nd who dropped into Normandy right before the D-day armada departed from England.[32] Such coups as seen in Crete were already passing out of the realm of special operations: they had lost the element of surprise. And resistance to them — as to chariots and elephants, gas attacks and tanks — was becoming part of the trade of the well-prepared soldier. Paratroopers, for example, descending on strongpoints could be shot like ducks; those who made it down were now known to be terribly vulnerable until they could regroup.

Using the most stripped-down of tactics, the British would extract a modicum of revenge before retaking the island in 1945. Dispatched from Egypt, two men of the Army Commandos with tommy guns were put ashore by motor launch, signaled in at night by "a convicted murderer, a couple of 'wanted' sheep-thieves, and a sprinkling of rogues" of the brave if louche Cretan resistance, as one of them recalled. They hid out in caves with a British parachutist who over several months had made himself indistinguishable from these *andarte*. The target was Major General Kreipe, Germany's divisional commander near Knossos. Confident in his seemingly subdued fiefdom, Kreipe was being driven alone at night after a game of cards, his chauffeur sufficiently at ease to stop at a turn in the road when flagged down by two fair, fine-looking young men in German uniform.

The getaway, with Kreipe bound on the backseat floor, was only possible because his brand-new hijacked Opel flew pennants and the new driver simply barked "*Generals Auto!*" at each heel-clicking sentrypoint.[33] A ninety-minute dash took them deep into the mountains, where the car was abandoned. Lugging their distinguished captive, the commandos and a little party of guerrillas climbed their way west through snowy mountains, evading the manhunt, before being exfiltrated by sea more than two weeks later. That these commandos waiting on the dark beach did not know enough Morse code to respond correctly to the signals of the returning launch ("We're not regular soldiers," they shrugged) barely hindered the adventure.[34]

When we look back, it is startling how so many of the basics that we take for granted in special forces today were often lacking, no matter the heroism of the operators. Among the daring Special Boat Squadron raiders who came to haunt the coves and inlets of the Aegean, for instance, night signaling was likely to be made with a flashlight covered by a sock. We see an absence of the right training combined with addled intelligence as London sent Army Commandos to kill Erwin Rommel, whose advance into Egypt from Libya had, by November 1941, given him a dangerous mystique of invincibility; rubbing him out would strike at what Churchill regarded as the brain and nerve center of the Afrika Korps.[35]

In a conflict so different from the battering and attrition of World

War I's Western Front, getting rid of one man just might make an amazing difference. And battalions or brigades could not accomplish it. In targeting Rommel, we see the special operation reflecting the very old and the very new — eliminating the chieftain, arriving by submarine. On November 10, two subs left Alexandria to deliver the commandos to the Cyrenaican coast at a point 190 miles behind the German lines. Through the dark, they saw the signal of a lone British intelligence officer who, disguised as an Arab, had been dropped in weeks before by a Long Range Desert patrol. But high seas extended the rubber boat landing to seven weary hours: two of the fifty-three men drowned; others struggled back to the submarines; thirty-one made it through the surf. Those who got to shore lay up for a day in a wadi. The depleted force split into two — the first detachment to set off over twenty-odd rugged miles to the Italian settlement of Beda Littoria, to zero in on Rommel; a second smaller one to cut the telephone and telegraph wires at a crossroads south of Cyrene. The cool Royal Horse Guards colonel in charge (now an Army Commando) remained in the wadi with three men to form a beachhead and be there should the rest of the team be able to land the following night.

Instead of assailing what MI6's intelligence officers had determined to be Rommel's villa, the raiders found themselves attacking a supply headquarters manned by Germans who were anything but just clerks and mechanics. Although no sentries had been posted so far from the front, stealth was quickly lost; the detachment's leader fell in the sudden firefight, his second in command wounded by friendly fire. The hunters turned at a blow into the hunted. Eighteen altogether made it back to the beach — to discover that their boats had been washed away. Frantic signals out to sea eventually brought the *Torbay* to surface eight hundred yards offshore. Many of the men could hardly do that distance in the most placid of waters, and others could not swim at all. Yet this was still a commando unit: all or none. The survivors remained on shore, hiding in caves. But a map that marked the pickup point seems to have been dropped by one of the raiders in the villa shootout, and a running battle developed until, before long, their colonel ordered them to evade back to British lines by twos and threes. Just two returned after a forty-one-day trek — most captured in the dragnet, at least five murdered by Arabs. Rommel had, in fact, been at the front with his soldiers, as might have been expected, and had never used the supposed villa anyway.

Nonetheless, a peculiar spirit shows through in this mission's calamities. It is telling, for instance, that the officer in overall command was reading a soggy copy of *The Wind in the Willows* while awaiting the return of his detachments, and then read it aloud over and over to his sergeant as the two of them struggled successfully east to Alexandria.[36] For commando units nearly out of boys' books, this dreamy English pastoral offered a sense of what might be accomplished by courage, goodwill, and stealth. The tale is the first fantasy special operation ever written — the expulsion of the Wild Wood hosts of stoats and weasels from Toad Hall by a secret-tunnel assault party led by Badger, brilliantly potentiated by disinformation released by Mole. (Like the Midianites fleeing Gideon, the stoats and weasels do not pause to count, but fall into panic and drown one another in the river.) It was not as if there were staff college texts to prepare and motivate men for missions such as these.

That fall, Churchill brought forty-one-year-old Lord Louis Mountbatten to London as chief of Combined Operations, promoting him to vice admiral and thereby making him head of the Army's Commandos and the rest of the increasingly special operators. Significantly, he was to report directly to Downing Street. Mountbatten was rich by marriage, a great-grandson of Queen Victoria, a champion oarsman, and the author of the standard work on polo. He was about to be heroized in Noel Coward's movie *In Which We Serve*. His seniors might dismiss him as a sports-star lightweight and publicity hound, but that was rather hard to square with his astounding expertise in signals and his bravery commanding a destroyer flotilla. It was a fascinating mixture of skills with character, and in 1941–42 he was in the right place at the right time, cutting through bureaucracies further to professionalize a raiding arm still teetering between enticing possibilities and humiliating failures. A Commando Training Center, also in Scotland, finally opened in early 1942, as did an Operations Development Center that included some of Britain's most imaginative scientists and engineers. The whole was becoming greater than the sum of its parts.

Raids grew more ambitious, with better interservice cooperation: a well-coordinated amphibious operation in late December 1941 against a small Norwegian port; 119 paratroopers soon thereafter joining with amphibious raiders to hit the French coast near Le Havre to remove German radar equipment before being evacuated by sea. This was followed by the complex night assault on St. Nazaire in March 1942 that was, Mountbatten explained, "not an ordinary raid" but "an operation of war," with 611 men using small boats and a destroyer, loaded with four and a quarter tons of explosives cemented below decks, which rammed itself into an enormous dry dock expected to berth the giant battleship *Tirpitz*. This exploding Trojan Horse was timed thoughtfully to detonate the following morning once curious high-ranking German officers could be counted on to have come aboard.[37] And then, in August 1942, Combined Operations visited Dieppe in the biggest raid of all.

Nearly five thousand Canadian troops hit France's northeast coast to test the defenses of a major port and to compel the Luftwaffe to give battle. They were supported crucially by 1,075 other warriors, who included even newer arrivals than the Army Commandos to special warfare: Royal Marine Commandos, an Inter-Allied Commando unit (German-speaking, many of them Jewish), and forty-nine U.S. Army Rangers, most of these tasked to destroy gun batteries overlooking the harbor. Dieppe's bloody nine hours saw the last of the great Channel raids, though tiny penetrations with big payoffs continued. In December of that year, for instance, ten Royal Marines in specially designed canoes (called Cockles) would be delivered well offshore in the Bay of Biscay by submarine. The mission was to paddle by night thirty-five miles up the frigid Gironde estuary to blow up enemy ships lying in the docks of Bordeaux, then to make their way home by land. The Germans considered anything like this fantastically impossible. Two commandos were immediately swallowed by the roaring tide. Six would be captured two by two and shot. The two who survived to see England helped build the Special Boat Service.[38]

Dieppe's ferocity and the immensely publicized daring of the "Cockleshell heroes" bore a promise that the democracies would be returning to the Continent for keeps. Since early spring 1942, the

Americans had begun to develop their own strike force, initially a battalion hand-picked by a West Point artillery officer from the two U.S. divisions and smaller units being readied in Northern Ireland. Volunteers had to be at least five foot six, in shape, not over thirty-five years old, of excellent character — and white.[39] Dieppe was the U.S. Army's first meeting with the Wehrmacht.

Other battalions of approximately five hundred men each would follow, some of them only to be deactivated within months as the crusty general most responsible for U.S. Army training believed commandos to be a distraction — they brought administrative problems; they absorbed too many of the best junior officers; they had to seek out strange peripheral missions to justify their existence. But also coming to life in 1942 was the First Special Service Force, a combined U.S.-Canadian brigade trained in Montana and designated as a separate branch of service of the U.S. Army. Men were not only parachutists and commando-skilled in close-quarters battle and demolitions, but also skiers and mountain troops, and in the final iteration of this variegated outfit, amphibious warriors. These "supercommandos," who would fight in the Aleutian Islands as well as southern France and Italy, are one of the three roots of today's U.S. Army Special Forces, signalized by the same crossed-arrows insignia.[40] Arguments from among the top brass that it was better to deploy well-trained regulars for special tasks were ever less convincing, at least while the war lasted.

Three months after Dieppe, Rangers would precede the awaiting fleet during the Allies' November 1942 landings in Northwest Africa, while another new U.S. outfit, joint army/navy "Scouts and Raiders," cut through protective booms and antishipping nets in North Africa's Arzew harbor. As the United States threw itself into action, Rangers were being run through the Commando Training Center at Scotland's Achnacarry Castle. The wheel had come full circle: an outfit bearing the name of formations that had taken such toll of one King George's soldiers was being polished by the fighting men of another King George (and great-great-great-grandson), to assist in America's passage to world power.

‡

IN A wheelchair in the Oval Office sat a man who understood the special-force ethos as did few others. Cousin and nephew-by-marriage of Teddy the Rough Rider, Franklin Roosevelt had fewer than forty years before been the fastest man in the world as a champion ice yachtsman on the Hudson. Nearly until his death, he was proud of his muscular biceps. He had served as Assistant Secretary of the Navy, coming to love the service and to understand it as an instrument of far-flung power — then, after being stricken by polio, had pulled his way up the greasy pole of New York state politics, to escape five bullets shot at him a month before the 1933 presidential inauguration. He was a master of small-group skills who knew extreme circumstances.

Tricksy as Ariel and with all the might of Prospero, Roosevelt since 1939 had been maintaining a private diplomatic arm of favored agents as he maneuvered his country toward a showdown. He had personally insisted that the Marine Corps adopt commando battalions; and his eldest son, James, had served as executive officer of "Carlson's Raid" that first August of the war when 219 Marine Raiders were brought two thousand miles from Pearl Harbor by submarines to hit the Japanese deep in the Southwest Pacific.[41]

Pearl Harbor had been a name unknown to most Americans, but the shock may have been worse than that of 9/11; at the time, there was nothing for the country to match it with. Like today's predators, the Japanese had been making destructive surprise sufficiently familiar for an attack "out of the blue" not to be that surprising at all. The Philippines, Hong Kong, the Dutch East Indies, and finally Burma all fell within five months. Thailand and French Indochina silently became satellites. Singapore, one of the most heavily defended places in the British Empire, was taken in February by a masterstroke of special warfare that not only introduced main-force, modern jungle operations but used them to exploit the fatal vulnerability of the world's preeminent naval base. The British believed their island-fortress to be impregnable — as it well might have been, had the Japanese come by sea. Instead they came, outnumbered more than four to one, through rain forests, swamps, and mountains (as well as on some of Malaya's fine roads) to attack it from behind, using the bush as a highway rather than regarding it (according to conventional wisdom) as an impenetrable barrier.

There could be no set-piece battles in such terrain. People who had never fought a jungle war sent troops in a month-long dash five hundred miles down the length of the peninsula — the size of England itself — by using new methods of cumulatively effective short-range penetrations that disregarded fronts and flanks.

No one had seen anything like it; certainly not the British, holding racist assumptions about little myopic invaders in shorts and sandals, comically pedaling thousands of bicycles. The Oriental Mission of the Special Operations Executive threw together behind-the-line units, led by a celebrated mountaineer.[42] But it was too late, and the secret infiltration parties stopped nothing. By the final days on the Strait of Malacca, after the British had dynamited Singapore's causeway to the mainland, Japanese swimmers sketched maps of the best approaches to this glittering outpost of European civilization. In the short term, the victory totally altered the balance of force — more than 130,000 British, Indian, and Australian troops rounded up and the fate of the Dutch East Indies sealed; in the longer, what Churchill calls the "authority of the white man" (i.e., European colonialism) in Asia never recovered.

Australia and India were in the crosshairs, the Australians making their stand in the "green hell" of New Guinea, as they called the flesh-rotting gloom of jungles that reach from the slopes of thirteen-thousand-foot peaks to the sea. It was the very springboard to their homeland, and they would turn the sprawling island's defense into the war's only campaign in which the artfully organized bushcraft and muscle of local people, superbly leveraged by Australian Army units, were vital to success.[43]

Meanwhile, in the Philippines, remnants of the American forces fled into the mountains, making their mark as regular soldiers turned guerrilla leaders. On the great southern island of Mindanao, for instance, a former mining engineer, Lieutenant Colonel Wendell Fertig of the Army Reserve, grandly appointed himself "Commanding General, United States Forces."[44] He backed up his insouciance by working with an army captain, a lieutenant, a chief petty officer, and a private to build a guerrilla army (operating as an actual military formation) that would grow to some thirty thousand strong, developing its own commando school, demolition section, and makeshift navy — uniting Catholics and Moslems, eventually rallying the Moros by showing photos from *Life* magazine to convince them that King Ibn Saud had allied Islam with America's cause.[45] The U.S. Navy had stemmed the tide at Midway, and the marines had stopped the land advance at Guadalcanal. But the strategic impact that can come from shaping indigenous resistance — the original purpose of today's Green Berets — is seen in Fertig's ragtag force.

Fertig was among the unintentional "stay-behinds" whose obstruction did so much to prevent Japan from establishing a single major defensive position in the Philippines to resist the return of General Douglas MacArthur, Supreme Commander of Allied Forces in the Pacific and son of the former military governor. On these and yet farther-flung islands, American and Australian "coastwatchers" were embedded in the local cultures, working with natives as low-tech radar, their sightings relayed to distant generals by radio — and themselves capable of taking the offensive in little boats against the Imperial Navy. Altogether, as MacArthur acknowledged, these heroes were saving thousands of Allied lives.[46]

Hitting the Japanese directly where least expected in Southeast Asia were Australian "Z Special Unit" commandos, an offshoot of the dominion's own SOE, much of the rest of their work on Timor, the Solomon Islands, and Borneo being backed by U.S. submarines and PT boats. In order to disrupt Japanese shipping while Allied divisions moved against the Japanese in New Guinea, a converted freighter brought six raiders within twenty-one miles of Singapore's great harbor. They stained their bodies black, loaded three rubber "canoes" (again, more like kayaks or shells) with limpet mines, machine guns, rations, and water and paddled off to spend a week reconnoitering likely targets. On the night of September 26, 1943, mines were attached to the hulls of freighters and tankers in the harbor; the raiders were able to watch the fireworks from a jungle base camp before slipping back to safety through a net of frantic Japanese air and sea searches. Who would be looking on the oceans for something as microscopic as canoes anyway?

Similarly precise, stealthy vengeance by the few inflicted a personal payback for Pearl Harbor as Roosevelt authorized the killing of Admiral Isoroku Yamamoto, commander in chief of the Combined Fleet of the Imperial Japanese Navy, and the visionary proponent of naval airpower most responsible for the sneak attack. Thanks to an intercepted radio message, eighteen carefully chosen U.S. Army Air Corps pilots in P-38 fighters with .50-caliber machine guns, .20-millimeter cannon, and augmented gas tanks embarked on the longest-ever overwater fighter mission: "Don't come back until Yamamoto is dead," a marine officer had directed.[47] Mechanical failure compelled two to return from what all suspected to be a 492-mile wing-to-wave suicide operation — the pilots ready to ram the prey, if necessary, should their planes even get that far.

On a two-hour flight to inspect forward positions in the French Pacific islands, Yamamoto was in a bomber bristling with machine guns escorted by six Mitsubishi Zeros. An assassination at several hundred feet never having occurred, and Americans assumed to be safely distant, the formation was flying low. It was minutes from landing at Bougainville Island: a perfectly timed setup for the "Killer Section" (four fighter planes covered by the others) to shed their external fuel tanks, dive out of the sun, and shoot their way through the Zeros to send Yamamoto's transport flaming into the jungle. All then made it to American-held Guadalcanal.

The killing changed the course of war in the Pacific. Among the many instances of a special operation shaping history, this was the latest, and is unambiguous. There was "only one Yamamoto," all Japanese writers would admit, and, in time, Americans would come to understand. After his death, the Japanese never won another major naval battle. Tokyo would likely have fought a better war had this superb, English-speaking, Harvard-educated strategist lived.[48] He was the one senior officer with an intimate knowledge of America's industrial might, and shrewd enough not to have played into the American purpose by trying to keep hold of every inch of conquered territory, instead certain to have put up obstacles by clever retreats and consolidations. But it was not to be.

In a war full of surprise attacks, commando raids, and assassins appearing from skies and deserts, Americans were even more attuned to the possibilities of sabotage than had been the British in 1939 — which is why Japanese Americans were rounded up at the start in California, without any evidence of treason, as to a lesser extent were

Italian and German immigrants on the East Coast. One might have thought it more likely that saboteurs from the Reich would have exercised their skills in the United States, yet essentially no such efforts were experienced during this war. The infiltration of two groups of profoundly incompetent agents by submarine onto the Long Island and Florida coasts was the sole attempt, the missions being so clumsy as to be memorable mostly for how fast they imploded. Instead of fulfilling plans to cripple aluminum production, destroy New York City's waterworks, bomb Penn Station, and dementedly set fire to Jewish-owned department stores, six of the eight terrorists quickly ended up sitting in Washington, D.C.'s jail-house electric chair.[49] It is unlikely that Berlin was deterred by the thought that J. Edgar Hoover was on alert; his manhunt was similarly inept. Rather, the best special operators that Hitler did have were otherwise occupied.

Five months before Pearl Harbor, and under pressure from London, Roosevelt had started moving toward a capability that could sow far more effective mayhem behind enemy lines. It was a civilian enterprise akin to SOE that, nearly a year later, was renamed the Office of Strategic Services (OSS), its mission to direct the nation's excursions into sabotage, subversion, and guerrilla warfare. "Special" assistance was to be provided to the army and navy.[50] Not that either welcomed OSS being added to the administration's alphabet soup of New Deal agencies. Nor did the Wall Street lawyer and World War I Medal of Honor winner at its helm (name partner of what remains the eminent firm of Donovan & Leisure) have much patience with the service academy men.

OSS branches for Research, Secret Intelligence, and Special Operations would, William Donovan promised the president, enable America, "the bush league club," to go up against the "big league professionals" of Germany by deploying operators highly trained at "stealing the ball and killing the umpire."[51] Unlike in later years, there would be no "stovepiping" of information among several independent agencies, and special operations were to be fully integrated with a nine-hundred-member Research and Analysis Branch that originated the bulk of OSS intelligence. Donovan was to report directly to the president. The first group of operators was trained at a secret school set up by the British outside Ottawa; such assistance, at this stage, was probably vital to OSS's survival.

Donovan welcomed every imaginative approach to war in the shadows, whether plans to set up airbases behind Japanese lines in China or to abduct Reichsmarschall Hermann Göring, head of the Luftwaffe and theoretically Hitler's "number two." By word of mouth, Donovan gathered around him an assortment of amateur secret warriors not unlike those of SOE: labor activists and professors; men and women with essential skills whether of mechanics, forgery, or seduction; clever businessmen and socialites who had never had such fun in their lives. Like the Special Operations Executive, OSS also had no hesitation to recruit in jails and underworld hangouts. This, of course, did nothing for the standing of either one of these marginal forces in the officers' messes. Exaggerating slightly to make a point, as professors often do, the one from Harvard who was responsible for psychological matters would reflect that "the whole nature of the functions of OSS were particularly inviting to psychopathic characters; it involved sensation, intrigue, the idea of being a mysterious man with secret knowledge."[52] Once again, the strangest of remarkable talents were being pulled into the invisible line.

OSS ultimately enlisted over thirteen thousand Americans, although not quite around the world: J. Edgar Hoover jealously fenced off Latin America for FBI counterintelligence; MacArthur excluded "Donovan's Dragoons" from the Southwest Pacific. Nor was General Dwight Eisenhower's staff enthused by OSS plans to assassinate commanders of Rommel's army in advance of the 1942 North Africa invasion. (That sort of "special" assistance was dismissed out of hand; they would either get in the way or start a chain reaction that could lead who knew where.)[53] And given the Roosevelt administration's naiveté about Stalin, espionage was not about to be permitted within what remained of the mangled Soviet empire. But gradually heroic deeds came to eclipse the eccentricities, and to quiet the worst of the quarrels.

Only recently have oral histories from the last surviving participants filled in the details: OSS commandos destroying critical bridges in Greece to disrupt Germany's chrome supply; fifteen-to-thirty-man

Operational Groups as well as three-man parachute teams called "Jedburghs" (a meaningless code word) to meld before long with railroad-sabotaging partisans in France, Belgium, and the Netherlands. Frogmen of the Maritime Operational Swimmer Group sabotaged harbors; a cadre of officers linked "Commanding General" Fertig with the outside world; a Special Force Detachment severed German phone lines behind Utah Beach on D-day. Eventually 102 missions were sent right into Germany; agents were poised, at the very end, to deploy some fifty German hitmen (volunteers from POW stockades who were mostly Student's disillusioned paratroopers) to kill or capture Hitler, Reichsführer-SS Heinrich Himmler, and whatever SS diehards might flee Berlin to a National Redoubt in the Bavarian Alps. Here, too, was a cumulative effect that helped undercut the Reich, as well as a second root of modern U.S. Special Forces.[54]

Like their British counterparts and the patriots of the occupied nations who were trained in covert operations and dropped back into the continent, OSS operators rarely went up against such relatively civilized people as Rommel, known to treat even captured commandos with decency. The German renaissance had perhaps become the most powerful intellectual force of the preceding century. Yet it had metastasized into a totalitarian phenomenon in which the black-uniformed SS lurked as a state within a state, responsible for Reich internal security and also possessing an army of its own, the Waffen (armed)-SS, for which murder was an essential part of war. In a shrewdly apt phrase, Himmler's chief of personal security, later one of the deadliest leaders of that sinisterly formidable line division Das Reich, described the elite bodyguard under his command as composed of "the most *piratical,* brave, and experienced warriors in Germany."[55] Like pirates, the Waffen-SS, with its peculiar equivalents of military rank, adhered to no rules of war, and its effectiveness man for man was unsurpassed (more is the pity).

The head of the Reich's Security Service (and therefore, after Himmler, of the Gestapo) was thirty-eight-year-old Obergruppen-führer (Lieutenant General) Reinhard Heydrich, a paragon of evil even among his own SS. Together with Hitler and Himmler, he had planned the mock attacks that were a pretext to invade Poland, and of all the Nazis, he was most thoroughly acquainted with the answer to the "Jewish Question." But it was his savagery as Protector of dismembered Czechoslovakia that spurred its government in exile to target him, with British intelligence and the SOE providing training and parachute insertion.

On May 27, 1942, in the appropriately named Operation Anthropoid, two Czech parachutists ambushed the Protector's wide-open Mercedes convertible with antitank grenades, a Sten machine gun, and .32-caliber Colts at a crossroads in Prague's northern suburbs. Heydrich died of wounds ten days later, and the agents turned their pistols on themselves two weeks thereafter following an epic eight-hour stand alongside five other parachutists in the catacombs of a church. He was the highest Nazi official to be assassinated, and the effects (beyond the fifteen thousand Czechs doomed in retaliation, combined with the ongoing death-camp gassings in Poland named "Operation Reinhard" in his honor) were profound. Amid pagan funeral rites in Berlin, Hitler compared his death to having lost a battle. Even that was putting it mildly, since Heydrich may have been most likely to end up at the top should tragedy have befallen the führer.

Knocking off the man portrayed in Germany as the Nazi ideal of the "blond beast" — the very symbol of Nazi occupation in Europe — riveted the Allies, the Reich, and everyone under the jackboot. In America, Fritz Lang and Bertolt Brecht quickly turned the assassination into the movie *Hangmen Also Die*. And finally Britain repudiated the 1938 Munich agreement that had betrayed Czechoslovakia in the first place. Hitler spat out how "stupid" Heydrich had been to disdain escorts and armor plating. "It is the opportunity which makes not only the thief but also the assassin," he added.[56] Here the opportunity was taken by a handful of operators from the shadows — backed by an organization dedicated to secret war — who had reached deep into an occupied capital far from the nearest battlefront.

The closest front in Europe was still far away in what the Nazis called the "Wild East," stretching over 3,060 miles from the Baltic to the Black Sea. Some 228 of Hitler's divisions were facing the Russians (compared with 58 in the West after D-Day) as the German Army colluded with the SS in mass murder. They kept thrusting forward, despite having suffered their first million casualties by March 1942, and the Red Army smashed back, to rack up more than 6 million German casualties three years later, while burying altogether somewhere between 28.3 and 35.3 million Soviet dead before the hammer and sickle flew in Berlin.[57] Perhaps the Communist security apparatus itself accounted for 7 million of that number, whether by firing squad, in cattle-car deportations, or in the Gulag death camps.

That Stalin had been imposing on his own country a body count equivalent to a Holocaust about every six years is significant for our story. It is extremely difficult to conduct clandestine operations against a system whose internal controls are so ruthlessly proficient that it does not think twice about such steps as dropping a battalion of NKVD political-police paratroopers dressed in German uniforms near its own population centers — those foolish enough to show sympathy then being shot. Behind the Russian lines lay a deep, ever-adapting, deadly "prohibited zone" and a maze of checkpoints manned by the NKVD's special army of enforcers, periodically swept to examine complexly crafted personal-identity papers. Square miles of inhabitants could be rounded up at the mere scent of infiltration. And the NKVD understood intimately the techniques of deception, disguise, sabotage, and subversion in what the Germans called "camouflage operations": those, after all, had long been the Bolsheviks' own.

Hitler had presented the attack on Russia to his generals as preemption — perhaps, for instance, Stalin's airborne corps would otherwise suddenly drop into the Reich. Instead, the Operation Barbarossa invasion had been preceded by special measures, while the bulk of Soviet paratroops were killed fighting as infantry. The Abwehr had obtained Red Army overcoats, helmets, and rifles from the Finns. Short-range missions by Brandenburg operators had been conducted ahead of the panzers, taking bridgeheads and crossroads, German machine pistols stowed at the bottom of their equally deceptive Russian-made trucks. All along the front, Brandenburgers — assisted by so-called East Legions of ethnic Russian and Baltic volunteers — kept slipping ahead of Germany's three army groups to assassinate Soviet commanders, capture documents and cipher equipment, and pull off relatively close-in sabotage. They took the Dwina bridge in Latvia while disguised as wounded Red Army soldiers. With the exception of the Luftwaffe's secret KG 200 formation stalking on

France's Vercors Plateau southwest of Grenoble, they were also the only special operations force in World War II that hunted partisans.[58]

As the Red Army in 1942 began disemboweling the Wehrmacht and the Waffen-SS, the Germans made repeated attempts to work ever farther behind the lines: parachuting in radio-equipped teams to at least try to establish the number of Red Army divisions endlessly arriving at the front; SS teams hot to rescue what Soviet disinformation led them to believe was a German column lost five hundred miles beyond the swiftly shifting front in Byelorussia; dispatching at least twenty operational groups, as in the Caucasus, intending to raise anti-Soviet guerrillas; sending another group of twenty-eight men into Russia disguised as members of a Soviet mining brigade in hopes of blowing up bridges and warehouses.[59] Most such hyperambitious ventures failed.

In contrast, Soviet penetration often enjoyed better odds against the Wehrmacht's poorly equipped Rear Area Security Divisions.[60] The NKVD, for instance, deployed its Special Department operational groups well behind German lines, not only for sabotage but to kidnap and kill individual German intelligence staff in what was the most extensive spy-vs.-spy contest in history. And to shoot collaborators. Spetsnaz commandos (termed *guards minelayers*) within the Red Army cut into the enemy's rear, operating with partisans in the sprawling "War of the Rails" that during 1943–44 destroyed 582 trains, as well as more than three hundred rail and highway bridges.

It was more than propaganda when Stalin harked back to the professionally led guerrilla exploits against Bonaparte. The 1812 military journals of the young poet/officer Denis Davydov — who had received 180 men from a reluctant marshal to kick off the crippling raids on the *Grande Armée* and is immortalized as Tolstoy's Vasili Denisov — were reprinted in bulk. Some 250,000 partisans were mobilized by the Kremlin and run by a "Central Staff" to hit the Nazis with these techniques of penetration and surprise. Instructors were parachuted in, and Red Army officers took over guerrilla training and leadership.

Russian and German operators were superbly matched in cunning, skill, and equipment, not — at the risk of sounding invidious — as it is today, when a modern force honed to stunning effectiveness goes up against such less impressive foes as Iraqi insurgents or Palestinian guerrillas. All of which makes what Lieutenant Baron Adrian von Foelkersam accomplished with eighty-six men deep in the Caucasus during a single week of August 1942 one of the most astounding extreme missions ever.

Von Foelkersam had been born in St. Petersburg, where his father had served the czar as curator of the Imperial Hermitage Museum. He had fought in Poland, then with the Brandenburgers in the Netherlands. And he had been at the siege of Leningrad, where the battalion's Special Missions and Sabotage Company targeted the rail line to Murmansk (the artery for U.S. Lend-Lease supplies to the Russian front) on foot, skis, and boats, while its Coastal Hunter Company worked the seas. He was already known for having ambushed the headquarters of a Russian division in the north. Operation Maikop was to be von Foelkersam's masterpiece, exploiting the quivering submission that regular Russian soldiers, like all Stalin's subjects, accorded the NKVD.

Impersonating an enemy's soldiers, let alone his elite regiments, requires an unsurpassably high level of performance. Should a special force be disguised as an enemy security or secret police unit, it can venture not merely behind the lines but throughout the enemy's military apparatus. Just as a double agent can eviscerate an intelligence agency from the inside, a special operations force able to impersonate police enforcers can cripple an army.

In East Prussia, von Foelkersam prepared for the operation by placing his men in a totally secret, totally Soviet environment, subjecting them to an exact replication of NKVD training, discipline, and procedures, which included the wearing of Russian uniforms, practice with Russian weapons, and speaking Russian at all times. Abwehr officers handled this part of the preparation, using stolen NKVD manuals and instructions, and monitoring the smallest detail in subjecting the men to total immersion, practices akin to Soviet spetsnaz preparations against Western Europe during the Cold War.

Rehearsals were exhaustive, including vodka-drinking ordeals among von Foelkersam and his subordinate officers to prepare temperate Lutherans for NKVD boozing bouts, the mastery of NKVD jargon, and learning the anthropologically fascinating different modes in which NKVD officers addressed their peers, their dreaded superiors, and ordinary soldiers — particularly the hectoring manner that Red Army soldiers reflexively expected from people who could get them shot out of hand. One wrong gesture, misinterpretation of the slang, stiff behavior under pressure that smacked of an intelligence-school cram course, or the simple inability to engage in alien yet casual conversation could bring immediate exposure, torture, and death.

Such sangfroid, von Foelkersam and the Abwehr came to recognize, could best be found among not-so-young university graduates, most of whom had followed civilian occupations before the war. This quality of mind was above all vital to success. To achieve true effectiveness required an understanding of the enemy's psychology that only the best of intelligence officers are likely to possess. Moreover, these eighty-six men were warriors who had been in combat together before.

"Maikop" actually comprised two special operations, conducted by separate units. Von Foelkersam and sixty-two Russian-speaking Brandenburgers undertook the primary attack — a long-range mission tied to seizing oil installations near the city of that name on the Kuban steppe, with the object of destroying the Soviet demolition squads poised to blow up wells and pumps before the main German offensive broke through. The secondary attack was a short-range strike by a team twenty-four strong to capture the only road bridge across the Bjelaja River; once taken, a panzer division could race across and consolidate the oilfields kept intact by von Foelkersam's party.[61]

The group led by von Foelkersam infiltrated the Soviet front on August 2; the tanks were to follow seven days later. Disguised as an NKVD detachment, they slipped by night into a Kuban village in which Cossack and Ukrainian deserters from the Red Army had sought refuge. The false enforcers rounded these up, and von Foelkersam harangued them in style; then they were separated into ethnic categories and marched off as if for the customary mass executions. At one end of the village, where the Cossacks had been collected, the "liquidators" discharged their weapons into the air — the Cossacks then being convinced to defect en masse and smuggled back to the German lines. The remaining deserters, mostly Ukrainians, were ordered to board their trucks and return to Maikop under appropriate escort for more refined disciplinary procedures.

Once von Foelkersam and his prisoners arrived at the real NKVD headquarters in Maikop, he presented himself to the general in charge as "Major Truchin." News of the Cossacks' liquidation had preceded him and he was greeted warmly, assigned billets and duties for his detachment, and invited to a reception that evening.

For the next six days, von Foelkersam toured the Soviet defenses with the general; his men, still disguised, meanwhile inspected the oil installations and double-checked the Soviet scorched-earth plans. As the day of the panzer attack approached, von Foelkersam divided his men into three supposed NKVD groups: one to wreck Soviet communications along the battlefront; the second to occupy the military telegraph office and to answer all inquiries with "official" instructions; the third to abort demolition of the wells by issuing false orders, pretending to carry out authentic ones, and wiping out the real demolition squads.

When the German conventional attack began, von Foelkersam personally positioned the first group at a key strongpoint — normal NKVD procedure being to shoot any retreating soldiers. "Major Truchin" issued orders first for a Russian antitank unit (lying effectively in ambush) and then for an infantry division to pull back, setting off a chain reaction that carried ever more Soviet units into disorderly withdrawal. Meanwhile, infiltrators on Maikop's other blade at the Bjelaja bridge appeared in the Soviet rear aboard four captured trucks. Feigning terror and flight, they swooped among the Russian troops with shrieks of *"Tanki! Tanki!"* panicking entire disciplined columns. Commissars attempting to stop the rout were swept aside in the chaos, which allowed the infiltrators to dash over the bridge, remove its demolition charges, and hold the structure until the panzers rolled up.

This amazing action would have been impossible without the NKVD's terrifying reputation. Set above the main body of Russia's military hierarchy, their graveyard mystique enabled von Foelkersam to drive a wedge between state and army. His mission rested not only on flawless disguise, but on knowing intimately the minutiae of the enemy's equipment, daily routines, documentation, and jargon. To that end, his planning had to be intertwined with the Abwehr's intelligence expertise. Panzer divisions entered Maikop on August 9, but there the German advance to the east was brought to a final halt.

Hitler had the tyrant's animal sense of how people quail when faced with bullying. To the more cerebral surprises of his opponents, ones that might create targets inside his own realm, he responded in character, with indignation and violence. In October 1943, he issued his notorious Commando Order, aimed at the British raiders — in his lights, unlawful enemy combatants outside the protections of decent nations. "Our opponents have been employing in their conduct of war methods which contravene the International Convention of Geneva," the führer mournfully declared. "The members of the so-called Commandos behave in a particularly brutal and underhand manner." Therefore when captured, even in uniform, they were to be delivered to the Nazi Security Service for execution. After all, these were "terror and sabotage troops," the Wehrmacht's chief of operations added, in circulating twenty-two secret copies, assistance for which he would hang at Nuremberg.[62]

‡

THAT MONTH, von Foelkersam and ten of his officers petitioned Otto Skorzeny to let them join a new independent unit that this six foot four, thirty-five-year-old dueling-scarred Haupsturmführer (captain), a bloodgroup SS tattoo under his left armpit, was creating at the authorization of his superiors. An ardent Nazi who within a year would be responsible for all German special operations, Skorzeny had been educated as an engineer and was known as a keen sportsman (car racing, in addition to fencing) and a ruthlessly effective officer on the Eastern Front. Earlier in 1943, he had found himself sick in a repair depot on the outskirts of Berlin, when SS chieftains were searching for an adventurous, unscrupulous sort to assemble men and initiate what he would recall as "the birth of the [German] commandos."[63] With Hitler coming to doubt the loyalty of the Abwehr, Skorzeny's SS Special Formation was to be smaller, tougher, harsher, more focused, and even more inventive than the now division-sized Brandenburgers, whose talents were being squandered as they were flung as shock troops into the deadliest gaps on the battle line.

Skorzeny's first step, as he relates in his memoirs, was "to ascertain how a small band of resolute men might, with a reasonable chance of success, storm the most vital enemy centers." To him, industrial plants, headquarters, canals, communications all had their "heels of

Achilles."[64] Sten guns, silencers, radio sets, and other tools of the trade could come from the many SOE and OSS airdrops to the Western European resistance movements that instead fell into waiting German hands. Skorzeny's was a concept of special operations as strategy and of a special force built on what he correctly believed to be the British model of independent raiding companies not tied to conventional army divisions.

Skorzeny pored over a huge file, including prisoner interrogations, which documented the exploits of British commandos in France and the Middle East, concluding that Mountbatten had created something superior even to the Brandenburgers. (He was able to keep at bay Himmler's more delusional schemes, such as using the two new companies against Soviet factories deep in the Urals.) In July 1943, at his "Wolf's Lair" headquarters deep in a primeval East Prussian forest, Hitler selected his fellow Austrian thug to assist General Student in rescuing Mussolini, whose fed-up fellow Italians, it would be learned, had imprisoned him in a heavily guarded mountaintop hotel after they had turned against their German ally.

How Mussolini was found and then spirited away from a small, rock-strewn plateau sixty-three hundred feet up in the Central Apennines forms one of history's classic heists. No amount of army divisions could have pulled this off. Once Skorzeny's espionage efforts pinpointed Il Duce's confinement on the Gran Sasso, the problem was how to liberate him without giving the guards ample time for an execution. A climb from the valley would be detected; the funicular railway from the base of the Gran Sasso to the plateau was the obvious way up for any rescuers, but therefore diligently watched; and the altitude too high and wind too harsh for a parachute drop, even assuming that approaching transport planes might not be heard. Again, gliders were the solution, built this time of canvas, while German paratroopers coming by road concurrently attacked the funicular terminal in the valley to prevent the arrival of Italian reinforcements. Aeronautical experts pronounced the planned role of the gliders to be technically absurd; the landing run was far tinier than atop Eben Emael, and the severe updrafts among the seventy-five-hundred-foot peaks made navigation difficult, at best. What Skorzeny claims to have been his retort sums up the thinking of special operators through the ages: "The safer the enemy feels, the better our chances of catching them unawares."[65]

Early in the sunny afternoon of September 12, twelve gliders set off on the harrowing hour-long flight from an airfield outside of Rome. Only 26 of the soldiers were Skorzeny's commandos; the rest of the 108 men were Student's paratroopers. Nine gliders succeeded in swooping down from twenty-one thousand feet to land yards from the hotel-fortress. The men who burst through the canvas had been ordered not to shoot; silence was part of the shock as the remaining Germans confronted about 250 stunned carabinieri. Success lay in the ability to appear from nowhere and in the moments gained by pushing a terrified Italian general forward as a frontman to befuddle the guards. Touchdown to grabbing hold of Mussolini took four minutes. Skorzeny gave the Italians sixty seconds to surrender. Even once this was conceded, exfiltrating the prize proved equally perilous.

The paratroopers who had secured the terminal had by now brought themselves up the railway, finally giving the rescuers numerical superiority. But a radio link reported that the transport plane expected to

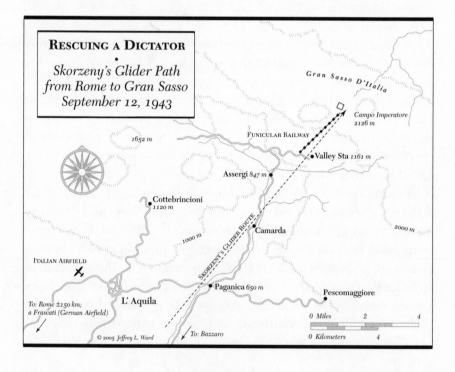

RESCUING A DICTATOR
·
Skorzeny's Glider Path
from Rome to Gran Sasso
September 12, 1943

Gran Sasso D'Italia

Campo Imperatore
2126 m

FUNICULAR RAILWAY

Valley Sta 1161 m

Assergi 847 m

1652 m

Cottebrincioni
1120 m

Camarda

1000 m

2000 m

ITALIAN AIRFIELD

Paganica 650 m

Pescomaggiore

To: Rome ±150 km;
a Frascati (German Airfield)

L'Aquila

SKORZENY'S GLIDER ROUTE

© 2005 Jeffrey L. Ward

To: Bazzaro

0 Miles   2   4

0 Kilometers   4

arrive at a landing strip in the valley had not appeared. The danger of Mussolini's being intercepted by his unhappy countrymen if he accompanied the German troops on their ninety-mile drive back to Rome was deemed too great, so boulders were pushed aside to create a makeshift airstrip on the plateau for a two-seater monoplane to fly in. The hulking Skorzeny and the bulky Duce crammed themselves behind the pilot, creating a combined weight of four; the grossly overloaded *Storch* raced its engine as paratroopers held its wings. Once released, it bounced forward, got momentum, and essentially fell off the edge, to slowly, slowly gain altitude. Thirty minutes later, it landed on the same field from which the gliders had departed and where Student awaited. Skorzeny insisted that he personally escort his charge on the awaiting flight to Vienna.

Mussolini had been a pricked balloon, but his rescue was a tremendous deflation of the Allies in turn. Fascism claimed to be the wave of the future, and rescue by gliders and escape by a light plane was a totally futuristic display that Nazi propaganda spun artfully to assert German superiority and the führer's steadfastness toward his friends. With Mussolini in hand, Germany could create in the north an Italian social republic to keep on fighting the Allies. At the price of only ten men killed or injured in a glider crash, the rescuers had provided Hitler with a huge strategic success.

Skorzeny's unscrupulousness also ensured that he, his commandos, and the SS reaped the glory, rather than Student and the Luftwaffe paratroopers and pilots who truly composed the mission. The old-line officer corps came to hate him; this was someone who could have come out of the Chicago mob.[66] But he had been on the mountain, his glider by mistake being the first to land, and he had first announced the success to Berlin. His press was marvelous.

Now Sturmbannführer (Major) Skorzeny's Special Formation would be handed an array of missions: he and von Foelkersam assigned to lead the arrest of the French government should the Jew-deporting quislings in Vichy also think of tipping to the democracies; to help abduct the Regent of Hungary as it dawned on this East European weathervane that he had pointed in the wrong direction; and Skorzeny's men to push themselves on the navy to help train Germany's own "sea commandos" who were — thanks to its admirals finally having accepted advice from Decima MAS and learning from British example — doing OK on their own. And it was likely Skorzeny who put Himmler onto the notion of launching V-1 rockets against New York from submarines. But time was running out. The central Eastern Front imploded in June 1944, and in the West, the Allies began their sweep to the German frontier and beyond.

Skorzeny shuddered at the prospect that the Reich's "Achilles' heel" was Berlin itself. Several Allied airborne divisions, he suspected, might land at the city's gates, move right to the center of the Nazis' political jungle, and pull off the supreme coup d'état. "There is no possible doubt," he recalled, "that these troops, making a lightning attack, could have seized all the nerve centers of our army."[67] Awe of the British commandos, and by mid-1944 of the OSS, made him imagine that they could choreograph such an endeavor and — what they never did — scale up their commando operations to a strategic level in combat.

Instead, that threat came from within. On July 20, thirty-seven-year-old Colonel Count Claus Schenck von Stauffenberg, a wounded Afrika Korps veteran and recovering ex-Nazi, planted a briefcase bomb ten feet from Hitler in the less heavily constructed of the Wolf's Lair conference rooms. He then quietly departed to fly the 350 miles to Berlin, where he was to assist conspiring generals and signals officers. It is worth remembering, in our own information-laden era, that the operation that was said at the time to be a "revolution by telephone" was being plotted very simply, over common landlines. With Hitler dead, the conspirators were to commandeer the army's radio transmitters, as well as its telephone exchanges and teleprinters. Orders could then be issued throughout the Reich, their authority unassailable.[68] They were also playing at judo: Operation Valkyrie, a contingency plan to crush insurrection against the Nazi hierarchy, would be flipped over to eliminate instead Hitler's surviving henchmen.

Speed, coordination, and the certain death of the tyrant — vital in this form of the special operation — were imperative. Full control of government had to occur within six hours. But the plotters hesitated fatally; Hitler lived; and it was by telephone from the SS offices at the Hotel Prinz Albrecht that Skorzeny, by chance in Berlin, alerted von Foelkersam to speed in from their suburban barracks. With no direct role really required from either of them, and with General Student at nearby airborne headquarters incredulous that a putsch was under way, an elite Wehrmacht unit (the Berlin Guard regiment of the Grossdeutschland division) had just enough time to descend on the dithering conspirators.

The signals officers were high on the death list drawn up by the regime's most reptilian elements. While entire armies were being devoured in Russia, Hitler was barely more prepared than Bonaparte had been for what tiny parties could achieve in his capital. Again, well-primed conspirators just about succeeded where huge enemy divisions were still unable to reach. Yet the führer's protective measures could not be faulted, investigators concluded. The Reich Security Service was more than ready to counter a revolt or such predictable attempts from, say, a skilled shooter, as in *Rogue Male,* prepared to "hunt an animal in its habitat." It had just never conceived that a general staff officer summoned to this fortified encampment might be an assassin, let alone tied to a deadly venture right in the heart of empire.[69]

By late August, Paris had been liberated. "We, who were conquered by William, have freed his homeland," proclaims the inscription at the Bayeux Memorial Cemetery in Normandy, where lie twenty-three young men of the SAS who had parachuted into France with heavily armed jeeps to cause chaos behind the retreating Germans.[70] In the east, Poland's underground Home Army burst forth in Warsaw, after pulling off a spectacular assassination (or "execution") of its own six months earlier — the car of Gruppenführer (Major General) Kutschera, one of Himmler's most trusted, vicious, and now heavily guarded SS officers, ambushed by a tiny hit team at 10 A.M. a few steps from Gestapo headquarters. The uprising was crushed in sixty-three days of block-to-block combat (Stalin holding back the Red Army on the east bank of the Vistula) as the Nazis eliminated Poland's toughest surviving patriots, much as they had done the youths of ZOB (the Polish acronym for Jewish Fighting Organization) in the Warsaw ghetto a year before.

The ring growing ever tighter, Hitler ordered Skorzeny to prepare for the final desperate December 1944 offensive in the Ardennes, to be known as the Battle of the Bulge. Since a U.S. detachment had slipped through the lines wearing German uniforms, the führer delicately explained, he was obliged to order Skorzeny to assemble small groups of commandos who would wear enemy uniforms in turn to get themselves among the advancing Americans and British.[71] From the start, this scheme of issuing false orders, cutting communications, and otherwise creating havoc was hampered by the blunders of exhausted Wehrmacht commanders. For instance, an essentially unclassified recruiting appeal was circulated throughout the army calling for volunteers for an unusual task who spoke English with "American dialect terms," as U.S. intelligence could not help but discover.[72] Even worse, only a handful of volunteers, rather than the necessary hundreds, could be identified who possessed such fluency. Few convincing American uniforms and even fewer U.S. Army vehicles could be rounded up, though Skorzeny's commandos were given chewing gum to help make them look like GIs.

In contrast to special operations practice today, where the unit commander who plans the mission must actually head it, Skorzeny was this time instructed to remain behind. And here we see what reputation can accomplish. Through the line of fire went nine of his four-man undercover teams, von Foelkersam being part of a larger assault force of German panzers converted to resemble American tanks. The commando groups cut phone lines, removed signposts, blew up an ammunition dump with results far beyond expectations. The Americans convinced themselves that a huge, fiendishly disguised sabotage and assassination enterprise was under way: authentic American officers were arrested as infiltrators, a British general hauled aside by MPs to be minutely examined; for his own protection, Eisenhower was sequestered in his headquarters for days, all because the man who had taken Mussolini was said to be on the hunt.

Not that any of this staved off the fiery end. Every able man was needed on the lines. Skorzeny was given command in January 1945 of a conventional division, containing a smattering of commando elements, on the ever-closer Russian front; fighting near Posen, thirty-year-old von Foelkersam took a bullet in the head, his SS Jaeger Battalion being completely destroyed. By April 30, the day Hitler chose to shoot himself in his bunker beneath the Reich Chancellery, Skorzeny with another small detachment had gotten himself to the

Alps of Obersalzburg. Eisenhower and his Special Force Headquarters (SOE, OSS, and SAS now grouped under him) took seriously the prospect of a far-fetched but not mythical National Redoubt, the *Alpenfestung,* or mountain fortress, of which Skorzeny was to command the northern approaches.[73]

Instead, there was a great calm. It was the disciplined surrender of a warrior nation: Germany's ominous *Werwolfen* resistance organization almost completely shutting down with zero Allied casualties once the ultra-respectable new führer, Grossadmiral Dönitz, capitulated. It would be for a later American generation — that of the defense secretary and the national security assistant at the time of the Iraq War — to witlessly create the legend of "SS officers" and "diehards" as *Werwolfkommandos* staging implacable resistance during Germany's occupation.[74]

Skorzeny, like all too many of the SS, went on to prosper — acquitted at Nuremberg, then literally escaping a second prosecution once friends disguised in U.S. Army uniforms helped spirit him from custody and send him on his way to Argentina. Yet his reputation lingered. Even in the early 1950s, rumors circulated among the convicted Nazi war criminals who had not been hanged at Nuremberg that a Skorzeny helicopter attack on Berlin's Spandau prison would spring them as well.[75]

With victory in Europe, different special missions remained for the winners: Churchill ordering commando hunter-killer teams to secretly dispose of Nazis who had executed British soldiers; tiny bands of young, uniquely toughened Jews arming themselves to track down their bloodstained tormentors; and units from the NKVD and Smersh counterintelligence operating in Norway, North Africa, France, Belgium, and the Netherlands to kidnap and murder White Russians, Soviet POWs, Cossacks, and other defectors whom the Allies did not force into trucks and return to Stalin. Shameful as these betrayals were, it was unlikely that the democracies would be so obliging much longer to Moscow's security apparat.

‡

ON THE other side of the world, what remained of the Japanese empire had barely five months to live. The U.S. Navy's Pacific commander, Admiral Chester Nimitz, had as little interest in the OSS as did MacArthur. His marines, particularly the Marine Raiders — less than 2 percent of the corps, honed even sharper for recon, demolition, jungle tracking, and ambush — could rightly insist that the "commando spirit," let alone commando skills, had been second nature for about 170 years. On the Asian mainland, the commander of American forces in China, Burma, and India — the abrasive Lieutenant General Joseph "Vinegar Joe" Stilwell — had simply concluded that guerrilla tactics were not much more than "illegal action" and "shadow boxing."[76] Yet the geography was too big, the tempo too fast, and the peoples of the farther side of Asia too strange not to turn to special warfare as part of a reconquering strategy. Seas and jungles were as cinematic as Lawrence's desert sands; islands in the Pacific offered opportunities that would have thrilled Cochrane.

By the start of 1944, on a speck off the southeast tip of New Guinea, one of MacArthur's top generals (a Texan) had begun personally to form the Alamo Scouts, extremely proficient men trained to reconnoiter hostile beaches, to call in air strikes from the enemy's rear, and to equip and lead guerrillas. Those who passed six grueling weeks of tests were winnowed yet further, selecting by secret ballot the men with whom they would most like to serve. Ten teams of seven or eight Scouts carried out 106 known missions by war's end.[77] They never lost a single man. From New Guinea's mists, an Army Ranger battalion was also emerging.

At a time when special operations, as we now know the discipline, was still in its infancy, Ranger exploits were tantalizing the home front on both sides of the globe. On D-day, June 6, 1944, for example, 230 Rangers became known forever after as the "boys of Pointe de Hoc." What they accomplished there, the French would remember on the sixtieth anniversary, "was like scaling a fort in the Middle Ages."[78] In an invasion preceded by thirteen-man navy demolition units to destroy underwater obstacles, they used grappling hooks and waterlogged ropes smashed into place by rockets to climb under withering fire up the hundred-foot cliffs of a Normandy peninsula that jutted out to the west of Omaha Beach. "It can't be done," intelligence officers had said.[79] Wrong. This, after all, was the first war in which techniques and technologies were being applied before most thoughtful members of the profession of arms knew they existed, or even knew them to be possible.

In the invasion of the Philippines four months later, Captain Arthur "Bull" Simons and half his company scaled imposing cliffs to take a Japanese-held lighthouse well in advance of the actual landings. And the 503d Parachute Infantry Regiment dropped onto the fortress island of Corregidor. By the time MacArthur waded ashore on Luzon, the landing beaches had been reconnoitered by navy Underwater Demolition Team swimmers, and he had at hand eight hundred smart, self-reliant Rangers prepared for lightning assaults. One hundred and twenty-one of them plus fourteen Alamo Scouts ventured thirty miles ahead into the jungles to save 513 of their countrymen from a hellish camp before the retreating Japanese could burn the POWs alive. These were recruits from farms and ranches, who only fourteen months earlier had been muleskinners for a pack artillery unit struggling up and over the Owen Stanley Mountains.

It is the huge stretch from the Indian Ocean to the Yellow Sea — that designated China–Burma–India — in which OSS and SOE played their role in the East, more or less in tandem with British and U.S. soldiers and airmen who embarked on some of the era's most ambitious episodes of special warfare. The landscape Stilwell described as one of "rain, rain, mud, mud, mud, typhus, malaria, dysentery, exhaustion, rotting feet, [and] body sores" seemed made for this kind of combat, as he came to understand.[80]

Well before Pearl Harbor, America had been supplying Chiang Kai-shek's Nationalist government with Lend-Lease matériel to resist the Japanese. China's future was regarded as that of a great power; with America in the war, its manpower was seen as crucial to victory. But the Japanese by mid-1942 not only dominated China's coasts but also Burma (roughly the size of Texas), through which supplies had previously been sent overland from the port of Rangoon via the miraculously constructed, U.S.-built Burma Road. Moreover, the Japanese could block any new engineering effort to build another route to China from the India-Burmese border, as well as hack out airstrips in the north for their fighter planes to shoot down U.S. transports flying supplies from India's Assam Valley over the "Hump" of the Himalayas to Kunming.

Needing all the help he could get in his deteriorating China–Burma–India theater, Stilwell accommodated OSS eagerness to conduct sabotage and intelligence gathering in the enemy's rear. By early February 1943, minute U.S. and Anglo-Burmese teams had begun parachuting into northern Burma, setting up radio stations, seeking to recruit and train guerrillas among Kachin tribesmen, hitting Japanese outposts, relaying the location of Japanese movements and installations beneath the jungle canopy, and rescuing Allied fliers. Altogether the famed OSS Detachment 101 (designated with a ludicrously big number to deceive the Japanese) was never more than some 120 men.

More significantly that month, Britain's wise chief of the general staff dispatched one of history's classic special operators from the deserts of Ethiopia to India, "where he might prove useful" against the Japanese in neighboring Burma — not that more than a handful of people who knew of this strangest of warriors thought him fit to command anywhere at all.[81]

Forty-year-old Orde Wingate had been the unhappy child of dour, prosperous parents whose notions of childrearing were dictated by the stern tenets of the Plymouth Brethren. "His ability to create violent antagonism against himself by his attitude to authority," as his second in command in Burma and fellow cadet recalls, had already been displayed at Woolwich, the British Army's technical academy, the rules of which Wingate, ever the loner, made clear he thought stupid.[82] But there he encountered horses and, three years after passing out in 1923, had ended up at the army's School of Equitation, where his slight physique, passion for detail, uncanny intuition in the saddle, and arrogant fantasizing as a cavalier made him an Olympic-quality rider. In character, his long speeches comparing Jesus to Karl Marx, slovenly hygiene, and contempt for the commandant also made him insufferable. Only family connections enabled him to land relatively softly, being sent by the army to study Arabic in London, at which he excelled, thereby obtaining secondment in 1927 to the Sudan Defence Force.

Wingate shone on expeditions in this moonscape, where he was noted for extreme powers of observation and vivid reporting. By late 1936 he was in Britain's League of Nations mandate territory of Palestine, where a rebellion was under way, some three hundred Jewish settlers already dead that year at the hands of Arab raiders —

the two British infantry divisions in place responding ponderously at best, and all too often with malignant slowness.

Wingate was drawn to Zionism by his Christian fundamentalism and genuine admiration for the accomplishments of the persecuted Jews of Eastern and Central Europe who, as immigrants, were fulfilling the biblical promise that the desert should blossom like a rose. It was an attachment at odds with general British sympathies.[83] He offered his services to Chaim Weizmann, the great chemist turned prophet, to organize underground forces for the quietly forming framework of a Jewish state. Given the British position, this bordered on mutiny, if not subversion.

Today, Wingate is regarded in Jerusalem as one of the founders of Israel, certainly of the Israeli Army. Already in 1937 he had composed detailed plans for independence, resting on the need to make settlers in Galilee and rural areas secure. As Arab guerrillas fighting for their own land and freedom not only hit the settlements but Britain's oil pipeline, railways, and telegraph, Wingate was permitted to create what he called Special Night Squads. With a cadre of British officers and NCOs, the squads embedded themselves in settlements, these volunteers dressing as colonists, collaborating with Jewish police, traveling in civilian trucks, and turning the tactics of ambush, reconnaissance, deception, and fast-moving night assaults against the guerrillas. It was a mobility and economy of force that had results out of all proportion to numbers, dislocating the network of violence and initiating the Israeli tradition of excellence at operating in the same conditions as the guerrillas themselves — albeit against opponents, then as now, who had little benefit of special training, military discipline, and the best modern weaponry.

Come the war, Wingate's desert-fighting skills with small units had landed him in Ethiopia. There, in early 1941, he had assembled what he called with biblical appropriateness Gideon Force, two battalions from which small teams of officers and NCOs would venture into enemy-held territory to instruct and coordinate native resistance against the Italian Army, now numbering a somewhat demoralized three hundred thousand troops. An actual invasion using guerrilla methods of daytime ambush and nighttime strikes was something new in modern warfare, building on Wingate's theory that the enemy is weakest far behind the lines — if he has troops that far back, they are likely to be the poorest, and a small unit could wreak outsized havoc. He named his tactics "Long Range Penetration," convinced that what he offered was more effective than the desert doctrines of T. E. Lawrence, about which he made informed mockery. Rather than foreign advisers dispensing gold and weapons to self-proclaimed tribal leaders, he argued, "you must send in a Corps d'Élite to do exploits." And he would supply the elite, including Jews from Palestine, knowing that "a thousand resolute and well-armed men can paralyze 10,000."[84]

These dazzling maneuvers were soon bringing in thousands of prisoners and enabling him to grab center stage in Britain's rapid Ethiopian victory. His triumphant presence on a white horse at the head of the victors' procession into Addis Ababa in May 1941 had added to the loathing felt for him among staff officers at General Headquarters Middle East. Gideon Force was disbanded with no allowances or awards for its members, and Wingate himself hustled out of Ethiopia. His appeals for further active service ignored, suffering from malaria and taking dangerously potent medication, he plunged a knife into his neck that summer in a Cairo hotel, but he recovered to avoid dismissal and write a lucid report of what long-range penetration against larger numbers could accomplish. Churchill saw it and was fascinated. As with so many of his kind, Wingate's genius for alienating generals was offset by his almost unconscious mastery at magnetizing politicians.

Of course, once in India, his superiors argued that Colonel Wingate's plans — to apply in Japanese-overrun territory on a larger scale what his Long Range Penetration patrols had done in Ethiopia — were impractical, at best. Hadn't he noticed that the environment was rather different? But as we have seen so often before in the story of special warfare, creative approaches are forced upon the most cautious and procedural of army staffs once alternatives have been brutally eliminated.

Come 1943, the Chindits — 3,000 British, Indian, Gurkha, and Burmese troops, men from the Empire's Bush Warfare School distributed throughout the brigade — were at work within Burma. Their size was dictated by the task: large enough to strike, small enough to vanish, innovatively supplied by jungle airdrops as they targeted roads, bridges, and rail lines. Their romantic name came from a mispronounced Burmese word for the winged stone beasts which protected that culture's temples. Wingate had demanded "the cream of everything: the best men, the best NCOs, the best officers, the best equipment" from the army.[85] But at the same time, with that faith in his troops that marks the first-rate modern commander, he insisted that men did not have to be exceptional to accomplish the extreme. Given the right leadership, he argued, fit, determined soldiers could be brought up to a level of accomplishment previously deemed almost superhuman.

They would also benefit from his fanatical attention to detail. On the sparsest of daily rations — little more than twelve biscuits, two ounces of cheese, four ounces of dates, onions, and a few cigarettes, otherwise trying to subsist off the land — the Chindits moved through Burma west to east and east to west. Even Japan, which was justly proud of its offensive thrusts over distances and through jungles, was astounded at the raiders' ability to traverse the grain of Burma's north-south mountain-and-river system. The Chindits disrupted Japanese plans for most of 1943; but 27 percent of them did not return, a staggering loss.

The British press was riveted by the adventures of this "Clive of Burma." While Wingate was briefly in London during August, Churchill dragged him across the Atlantic to present his Long Range Penetration approach (and probably yet more his mystique) to Roosevelt and Marshall. The Chindits thereby obtained the collaboration of the U.S. Army Air Corps in the form of the 1st Air Commando — the Americans deploying "commando groups" built around a one-of-a-kind assortment of 348 fighter planes, bombers, light liaison aircraft, transports, and gliders.[86]

The scale, mobility, and audacity of these operations increased accordingly. Wingate's effort was designated "Special Force" and was the largest such force of the war, this time advancing in conjunction with the army. Now, as a major general, he was leading thousands of men and envisioned establishing a "stronghold" deep in enemy territory (akin to the Jewish settlements in Galilee) from which would set out marauding columns. Guerrillas, lightly armed, gain immensely if they can provoke the enemy into striking back into "their" territory. "The Stronghold is a *machan,* overlooking a kid, tied up to entice the Japanese tiger," Wingate explained.[87]

By March 1944, Wingate and the Air Commandos launched an incredibly complex two-step operation: first moving 539 soldiers, 3 mules, and 33 tons of supplies into central Burma, using eighty gliders taken up by RAF and U.S. Air Corps Dakotas, towed in the dark over a 7,000-foot mountain range to land in clearings more than two hundred miles behind the lines — which, it was hoped, would not be occupied by the enemy; second, once secured by the glider wave, airstrips could be built for troop transports to bring the total force to 9,052 men, 175 horses, 1,283 mules, and 250 tons of rations, jeeps, weapons, and ammunition.

Barely had this leap been accomplished than Wingate's plane went straight into a mountainside. The brass had never been reconciled to their self-styled Gideon, but he had restored offensive capacity and spirit against a dangerously confident enemy over a vast territory, months before any main-battle-force success could have been contemplated. Still, Britain's official history of the war in this theater perversely denies that Wingate's operation possessed any strategic value. He is buried in Arlington National Cemetery, alongside the American crew members of the flight in which he perished.

At least that global entrepreneur of special operations, Louis Mountbatten, understood. Since October 1943, he had been Supreme Allied Commander in Southeast Asia. He felt a certain patrician amusement toward the earnest, evangelical, middle-class Wingate, but he took the Chindits and their doings seriously. Mountbatten was additionally backing an array of other special forces in the theater: Small Operations Groups of Royal Marine Commandos and SBS, Sea Reconnaissance Units, Combined Operations Pilotage Parties (COPPs) specializing in beach landings. Within his command, American special warriors in numbers much greater than the OSS teams were also reentering Burma. Having trained in long-range-penetration tactics under Wingate in India, they went into action in February 1943. Their epic was codenamed "Galahad" — like Gideon, an invocation of a legendary warrior past — and led by Japanese-speaking Brigadier General Frank D. Merrill, a former sergeant who had graduated both West Point and MIT. A *Time* correspondent quickly coined the alliteration "Merrill's Marauders"; 2,830 very odd infantrymen soon found themselves the war's most publicized U.S. irregulars.

Perhaps not surprisingly, U.S. Army recruiters in the South Pacific, the Caribbean, and in the United States could come up with few jungle-tested veterans who had any inclination to volunteer for an unspecified "dangerous and hazardous mission." Not for the first time in the story of special warfare, divisional commanders took the opportunity to unload misfits. What resulted was a "provisional unit" — embodied for a single major undertaking — to flank the Japanese far-rear areas while Stilwell advanced eastward at the head of the Chinese infantry divisions he had turned into competent warriors. This improvised outfit, one of its officers (a former book reviewer) would write in his classic of war literature, *The Marauders,* was composed of men "so recruited as to ensure they would exhibit the extremities of human character, the worst as well as the best."[88]

From February to August 1944, including most of those months that see one hundred inches of monsoon rain, this improbable fraternity fought across six hundred miles of northern Burma to open land communications with China. They stalked and were stalked themselves; staying off trails in a terrain where the horrifyingly persistent enemy simply had to hide and wait to hold on to his conquest. Dysentery racked them, leeches bulged with their blood; wounds were cleansed by maggots; safety was only to be found when men could huddle into the nighttime forest. Success was possible because of a combination of superb leadership, a "what-the-hell-did-you-expect-anyway" spirit in place of conventional morale, and Japanese American (Nisei) Marauders, who crawled out by night to eavesdrop on the enemy and then to scream false but convincing orders in vicious combat by day. Indispensable assistance came throughout from the local forest people — Kachins whom OSS operatives had already organized as guides and potent little armies they justifiably styled "Rangers."

Much of their purpose fulfilled in one lightning-fast daylight attack on the only all-weather airstrip in northern Burma, directly on the route to China, the emaciated survivors evaporated as a unit even before Stilwell could get around to disbanding them. Many were physically broken. Having more than its share of "drunkards, derelicts, guardhouse graduates, men of low [but undoubtedly crafty] intelligence, and out-and-out bad men," the Marauders self-destructed once their worst tendencies were no longer held in check by training, marching, and killing.[89] Yet, as they no doubt would have said between scratching and spitting, who cared? They, too, had gotten it done and — if one overlooks the aberrations — provided in their astounding resilience and deep penetration the third root in the lineage of U.S. Special Forces.

Special operations may have offered a decisive push toward victory in the China–Burma–India Theater, but competition among already independent-minded participants — Stilwell and his determined Chinese infantry, British imperial divisions, SOE, OSS, the Chindits, and the Marauders — "led to grotesque situations." In the bush, for instance, forward units of their brother main-battle infantry might be advancing within miles of special operators, neither aware of each other's reciprocating presence. At times, as one of the Marauders observed dispassionately, "the United States Army and the Office of Strategic Services were fighting independent wars in Burma." And out of its habits of energetic improvisation, OSS developed a reputation for inefficiency that would extend right into the CIA.[90] Failures to coordinate paramilitary operations were not to be resolved during this war. Americans would try to sort all that out — instructed by an entirely new breed of foulups — the hard way in Korea five years later, then during the Vietnam War, and again today.

But no matter which theater of war, much evidence was already accumulating about the value of special operations and the startling qualities of the units required for them. Close study of skills and methods indicated more was needed for success than surprise, daring, and disguise. In the immense body of new experience that was so terribly compressed into 1939–45, there was present a frequency, clarity, and awareness of special possibilities across a breadth of terrain and culture as had never been known. The framework of special operations as we understand it today had been hammered into place:

the need for them to work meticulously with the sources of military and, likely, political intelligence; to be further aligned with the objectives of armies, navies, and now air forces; to thereby have specific command and control procedures, and to avoid a host of competing outfits clawing over each other. The need was recognized to radically develop specialized trainings and to ensure that operators be able to use all possible means of transport, often in peculiar ways; to have the same officers both plan and lead the versatile, unpredictable missions; and, finally, to deploy special undertakings repeatedly, broadly, reinventingly in order to benefit from compounding effectiveness.

Other conclusions could be drawn from the hundreds of different actions in Europe, Asia, and the Pacific. To those who looked, the personal qualities of commandos themselves were most apparent — and how these qualities mixed to suggest new ways to approach the terror and extremity of war. Today, that understanding of the human element is simply part of the doctrine of special operations forces. At the time, it was novel to emphasize the different types of reasoning and imagination that distinguish this kind of war from conventional combat. Finally it was understood that the most originally effective leaders may fit uneasily into military life; and that the men and women who succeed when pushed beyond their limits of isolation and disorientation will be more self-reliant than even the good, determined soldiers of a modern warring democracy.

17

Dawn Like Thunder

Here to Stay: New Strengths, New Dangers, 1945–1961

"The need for quick reaction in emergencies does not deny the requirement for a well-thought-out and applicable [foreign] policy."
DWIGHT EISENHOWER, THE WHITE HOUSE YEARS

BY 1945, Lenin's arrival at the Finland Station to take over the Russian Revolution was closer in time than the end of the Vietnam War is to us today. The organizers of victory during that bewildering autumn easily remembered that a handful of Marxist dogmatists had within years pummeled a sixth of the world into strange new shapes. Under the iron hand of Stalinism, it became increasingly clear that civilization faced another "odious apparatus," as Churchill had called Nazism, and that there was a real possibility of such a deadly ascendancy again casting itself over Western Europe.

"Neither war nor peace" Leon Trotsky had cried toward the close of World War I. Whereas that situation seemed unlikely to be endurable, or, in the longer run, even sustainable, by the democracies, the East/West antagonism that was soon to be styled "Cold War" was not a new experience for oft-invaded Russia or revolutionary Bolshevism. For Stalin, the prospect even possessed a certain homecoming quality. Perhaps the sheer luck that had so largely brought the democracies to victory against the last cycle of tyrannies had been used up.

Inspecting Germany's devastation, a high U.S. official described it as "unparalleled in history unless one goes back to the Roman Empire, and even that may not have been as great an . . . upheaval."[1] On the other side of the world, China's Communist moloch Mao Tse-tung was parroting Stalin in policy as well as rhetoric, soon to drive Chiang Kai-shek's Nationalist government pell-mell 115 miles offshore to Taiwan and to exult in Tiananmen Square that subject peoples everywhere were ready to "stand up."

So the world quickly began to bleed again. Starting on the day of victory in Europe, French authorities in Algeria's eastern cities saw fit to kill some fifteen to twenty thousand locals rioting for independence. In Southeast Asia, the French navy under Thierry d'Argenlieu, a fine-drawn Carmelite priest in admiral's uniform, killed five thousand people by shelling Haiphong after the equally brutal nationalist revolutionary leader Ho Chi Minh (having been saved from deadly malaria by an OSS medic in the war's final months) had declared an independent Democratic Republic of Vietnam. Retaliations were not slow in coming. In India, the succession states to the British Empire became independent in 1947, their emancipated citizenries killing a couple of million of their own inhabitants along the way. In Palestine, a minority within the Jewish settler population was inflicting exemplary radical terror on British and Arabs alike in a conflict that also presaged worse to come. In Europe and in America, the suspicion was abroad that the Nazis' V-2 rocket was all-too-soon likely to be merely the Model T of ballistic missiles, its high-explosive payload little more than a firecracker among warheads.

The special operations forces of the two greatest democracies, the United States and Britain, were dissolved with the peace, but they would come to be revived as permanent, ever-more-deadly arms in a world drawing closer together through upheavals of technology, culture, commerce, and rising expectations. By 1960, in the strongest democracies as well as in the worst of dictatorships, permanently established and highly professional commando units were here to stay.

In following our theme from now on, we focus largely on the American experience. This is because of the country's strength and global presence, because its greatest twentieth-century political-military blunder was shaped at the start by hopes of what special operations could achieve; and because it was America that, in time, brought its array of commando capabilities to the most numerous and well crafted deep outreach capacities ever achieved. There is another reason too: the United States also exemplifies the difficulties of joining such sharp instruments with a nation's more hammer-and-mace-like means of argument and with its intelligence services.

As the disorders that would stretch the Cold War over nearly a lifetime began to grip the nation's attention, Americans came slowly to accept the political and military involvements that a few well-placed leaders increasingly saw as inevitable. But as a cheerfully techno-pragmatic, business-oriented people, they hoped that they could face the world's turmoil from a distance through proxies (alliances, client regimes), high technologies (intercontinental bombers, missiles), and, if necessary, consigning the secret overseas dirty work of government to covert fixers who had refined the means of promisingly cheap, surely efficient paramilitary solutions. The new CIA would conduct such operations, increasingly in tandem with even newer U.S. Army Special Forces. OSS veterans were drawn to both.

The dangers posed by Moscow quickly grew far greater than anyone had anticipated. But the country would come to place hope in, then to ascribe alarming clout to, and finally simply to tolerate an intelligence agency that would compile a record in operations as well as in analysis that is striking for its chronic failure. Here is a record of failure that has rarely been examined as a whole, to the concealment of which the CIA seems at times to have devoted more energy than to establishing, say, the state of affairs in Russia, Iran, or Iraq. Contrary to popular and even professional belief, an unsettling degree of incompetence has always existed, by no means limited to the embarrassments surrounding 9/11 or Iraq. And the record is one that bears directly on our story because, from this time forward, special operations forces became the action-arm of the agency and because, in the early twenty-first century, these endemic shortcomings in intelligence will limit the effectiveness of U.S. commandos.

So often since 1945, U.S. foreign policy has found itself burdened by short attention spans. Impatience has equally been the secret of America's adaptivity and the cause of grave problems abroad when trying to manage issues not susceptible to American speed. For a lifetime, we have seen an amazing gamut of fits and starts — as in the swings of enthusiasm for foreign aid, Pentagon spending, language studies, or "nation building." The knack for extraordinary accomplishment (rebuilding Europe, winning the Cold War) has also found itself, more often than not, offset by having to relearn the already obvious. This would also be the case for the use of special operations, as Americans stormed into the world to block a different version of totalitarian ambition.

‡

THE MOST striking feature of the two years after 1945 may not be the vigor of Communist pressure but the weakness of the American response to it. In not wanting to appear as if it were ganging up on Moscow, President Harry Truman's new administration, for instance, refused to sell army-surplus Garand rifles to Denmark, of all places, and tried to block the founding of an Anglo-U.S. Old Comrades veterans' organization.[2] No consensus bubbled up that the nation would turn outward and assume global responsibilities, as the usual writing-backward of great historical junctures now depicts it. Being newly instructed in totalitarian horror, Americans were intent on keeping several steps away from the world's abysses. Many believed they could do so not only through UN resolutions and an unexpectedly brief monopoly of the atomic bomb, but by relying on the British Empire as an "outer fortress," the archetype of a "super power" for whose worldwide presence the term had just been coined.[3]

To that end, sending home within a year all but 1.2 million servicemen from a military of 12.1 million once Japan had surrendered was not so precipitate a reversal as it would later appear.[4] The services were squaring off against one another for shares of a defense pie that was withering to a crust.[5] Dissolved were Rangers, Marine Raiders, Alamo Scouts, all three Air Commando groups that had entered the inventory, most anything resembling a special force. It took legislation to prevent the U.S. Marine Corps from being winnowed away. The OSS — the need for its talents surely gone — was disbanded, too. The war had probably seen more man-years of special operations than in all previous history, but it was unlikely that such units would be maintained while their professional seniors within the army, navy, and (less so) in the newly hived-off U.S. Air Force were being stripped to the bone.

Britain dissolved its SAS, Long Range Penetration Groups, Sea Reconnaissance Unit, COPPs, SBS, and its whole startling range of other special capabilities as it also demobilized. The original Army Commando amphibious raiders were dissolved, and it was left to the Royal Marine Commandos to carry on with what remained. The intelligence establishment finally swallowed SOE. Only France among the war's major democratic powers kept up a level of special operations forces — a demi-brigade of parachute commandos for colonial war, plus elements of the Foreign Legion, newly transfused with tow-headed veterans from somewhere or other of whom career questions were rarely asked. ("Danes," or "Dutch," they would mutter unpersuasively.) And those energies were soon heavily committed to what the French called Indochina.

The biggest empire of all, now covering twelve time zones from the Pacific to the intra-German border a hundred miles west of Berlin, made its own reductions after the war. Stalin's tyranny may have been troublingly familiar, but its secrecies and cruelties ensured that virtually no one knew what was happening within. The Red Army still was presumed to be a massive 175 divisions. Although its spetsnaz units practically ceased to exist, the special talents of the NKVD were treated gently, essential if only for purposes of internal repression.

During the initial two years, it took Britain's tough new socialist government to set a firm example for the United States and indeed to lay the groundwork for NATO by decade's end.[6] But for all its blustering to Moscow and its struggles to keep presenting itself as a great-power equivalent to the two continental behemoths, it became increasingly apparent that there was only so much Britain could do as it faced crisis after financial crisis. Washington responded with hurried improvisation once Britain abruptly ended financial aid to Greece and Turkey in early 1947, London adding that it also intended to withdraw its eight thousand troops amid a civil war between a thuggish Greek monarchy and Communist guerrillas. Speaking to Congress that March, Truman pledged his country "to support free peoples who are resisting attempted subjugation by armed minorities."[7] Significantly, as has been forgotten, this precedent for un-thought-out commitments to unassessed regimes in ill-defined places was made not against Communism or Stalin explicitly but to oppose "terrorism" and "terrorist activities."

In any event, there was not much that the United States could do beyond writing checks and offering modest training and planning to the hapless Greek National Army. Theorists might be speaking of "containment," and the Marshall Plan would set about transmitting foreign aid on such a scale as had never been seen before in history. But America neither looked nor felt ready to contain anybody — certainly not at the keenly prepared, precisely targeted level of violence that might have dealt with terror in Greece before the "monarcho-fascists" (as the left called Athens, not without reason) finally drove the guerrillas into the neighboring Communist nations of Yugoslavia, Albania, and Bulgaria.[8]

By the fall, Washington was embarked on a government reorganization of the kind that habitually follows a convulsion. Twelve new agencies and departments were created, all organized around national security, including the CIA and the National Military Establishment, which within two years received the less-oppressive designation of the Department of Defense. By then, the *New York Times* could assert that the Americans were facing a test as real as that after Pearl Harbor.[9]

Within half a year of the CIA's being set up as an intelligence-gathering body, George Kennan of the State Department — "a footnote of the Truman presidency," according to Secretary of State Dean Acheson — proposed creating what he called a permanent "covert political warfare operations directorate within the government."[10] Rather than establishing an additional, separate agency for such "special services" activities, as might have occurred, he helped make the argument that the CIA already provided the legal structure for such unprecedented peacetime work.[11] A month later, there discreetly unfolded a new institution within an institution — to be named, in the blandest spirit of bureaucratic camouflage, the Office of Policy Coordination (OPC). It sat within the CIA, its director nevertheless appointed by the secretary of state. This particular office — its activities conceptualized as a blend of the military and the political-subversive — was kept distinct from the agency's Office of Special Operations, which handled espionage and counterintelligence.

This was a step into new and ill-mapped territory. Pride of place was given to covert action rather than to espionage. The "office," backed by Kennan, would boom from 302 staffers in 1949 to 6,000 in 1952, when it was formally rolled into the CIA, to account for 74 percent of the agency's budget and three-fifths of its personnel — and bringing with this all the disarray that comes from overly rapid growth.[12]

At that point in his life, as the agency was being formed in 1947, the highly emotional Kennan was caught up in a planetary vision of the Great Game. It would be a little later that he came to oppose the creation of NATO, urge the neutralization of Germany, and write off Latin America as a hopeless region placed outside the possibilities of civilization by the "extensive intermarriage" of its people with "Negro slave elements."[13] When not combing his genealogy, he found time to draft a mandate for American operatives to subject the Soviet Union to "political warfare." Stalin being well practiced in political assassinations abroad, America must counter the "vicious covert activities of the USSR, its satellite countries and Communist groups." So Kennan brooded, and soon hatched a peacetime resort to "propaganda, economic warfare, preventive direct action, including sabotage, anti-sabotage, demolition and evacuation measures, subversion against hostile states."[14] Political-warfare operations, which Kennan later admitted "did not work out at all the way I conceived it," included backing the heroic and (short of world war) doomed national resistances behind the Iron Curtain.[15]

Guerrilla tactics and propaganda were to be used not only in Soviet-occupied Eastern Europe but also in the Soviet Union. Once the new National Security Council had endorsed such measures, Kennan and associates cobbled together a variety of catastrophic paramilitary operations. The authorization had been crafted so that "the originating role of the United States government will always be kept concealed."[16] So, too, of course, was the abysmal role of the individuals responsible.

In war after war, there is a temptation — resting on grounds of economy, alleged special knowledge, and usually delusive solidarity —

that compels otherwise practical leaderships to take exiles' claims
seriously. We have just seen it in Iraq. People who would be occupying the presidential palace if what they report about their nations'
public opinion were remotely true find eager ears in which to pour
promises of cheap, easy, popular victory. As natural friends to the
courteous stranger, Americans carry this credulity to a uniquely high
level. In the later 1940s, Washington as well as London was more
than eager to hear from the myriad exiles that entire nations were
poised to be mobilized and armed to tear down Soviet oppression, if
given special outside assistance. But anticipating how a people will
behave is not all that easy.

By 1948, against the background of Stalin's blockade of the Western
zones of Berlin, there converged three unfortunate influences that
pushed Washington to foster resistance within the Soviet Union and
Eastern Europe: guilt over having conceded Eastern Europe and over
having returned millions of innocents, whose many suicides alone
while still being processed through Western hands were a grisly enough
example of the postwar settlement's immorality; eagerness to "do something" in response to Moscow's brutal truculence, over and above
diplomatic measures and expensive enforcement of Western rights in
Berlin via airlift; and the familiar belief that special operations, particularly at the leveraged remove of enabling peasant uprisings,
would be cheap as well as invisible to skittish Western publics hopelessly estranged from geopolitical thinking.

The prospect of giving tangible support to Ukrainian guerrillas
was examined that fall by the U.S. Secretary of Defense, pursued by
Kennan at State, then handed to the CIA and its Policy Coordination
Office, which even more ambitiously intended to disperse some two
thousand exile agents at strategic locations across an apparently
unaware Soviet Union.[17]

Often in league with grievously Soviet-penetrated MI6, from 1949
through 1953 the CIA staged a systematically disastrous strategy of
dropping three- to six-man teams of nationalists into the Ukraine
(still part of the Russian empire) from unmarked planes. It apparently expected handfuls of very brave men equipped with radios and
rifles to bring about in that distant battered land a full-scale revolt
against massive strength that far more encouragement had never

been able to arouse in Occupied France or the Low Countries. Unsurprisingly, the efforts were more often than not manipulated by the Soviet secret police. Captured agents were "turned," spurious radio signals sent, and awaiting executioners on the ground generally urged the agency to "bring 'em on." Reaching out, the Russian operators knocked off Ukrainian nationalist leaders in the West, the most prominent shot in the face as he opened the door to his Munich apartment by a Soviet assassin armed with a pistol firing an ampoule of prussic acid.

Despite a tomblike silence of failure, similar infiltrations were staged into the former Baltic republics by plane and small boat, coordinated right through 1953 by the CIA station in Stockholm. One of that long sequence of reports written over the years by investigators trying to make sense of barely concealable agency screwups did not balk at the conclusion: the exile agents who were still undergoing training had no chance of survival. Not that this would stop the operations for another eighteen months, at the same time that ill-fated successors to World War II's "Dark and Silent" also kept being smuggled into Poland to convey guns and money to a wholly fictitious underground.[18] It was a casual use of lives that would also be seen in the mishandling of patriots and others misled in Korea, China, Tibet, Vietnam, Kurdistan, and Iraq.

As East and West squared off in the late 1940s, the most remarkable assertion of special warfare techniques was not to be found behind the Iron Curtain, nor, at this point, in remote jungles or sierras. It sprang from the most searing tragedy of the cataclysm just passed, to make itself felt in the even more politically complicated milieu of a small, highly accessible coastal country — in the Jews' struggle for a state of their own. Armed terror had been spreading worldwide at least since World War I. Now the fight for a homeland in Palestine awoke both unusual efficiency in execution and a powerful mystique cast by the hideous light of the Holocaust.

The outrages of various factions centering on future prime minister Menachem Begin could be seen in the same gravely determined perspective as had, fifty years earlier, the righteous going up against the czar. Such exalted vision is apparent in Gerold Frank's novelization (in *The Deed*) of the point-blank shooting of the British Minister

Resident and his driver by Begin's Irgun in 1944. Behind this passionate, sacrificial idealism the craving for power burned no less brightly
than it did in the ruthlessness of the imperial state. A pattern of tiny,
ferocious actions by underground militias developed a political weight
beyond all their specific damage: the bombing of an entire hotel with
ninety-three dead by disguised operatives from Irgun (the apex of
terrorist crime for decades); the bombing of the British embassy in
Rome; a daring rescue of compatriots in the Acre fortress prison also
using penetrators in disguise; the unprosecuted assassination of the
UN mediator by future prime minister Yitzhak Shamir's spin-off
Stern Gang. The age of special operations mixing with terror to bring
into existence a modern state was now upon us.[19]

But in a dangerous neighborhood, no state is likely to be able to
build itself on terror and underground resistance alone. When Israel
declared its independence and the Arab League armies struck in May
1948, its people were prepared not only by Wingate's passionate initi-
ation of Night Squad strikes but by the work of a former U.S. Army
Ranger, granted leave from his reserve commitments by the Pentagon. David Daniel Marcus came from the Brooklyn streets to the
West Point Class of 1924, going on to law school and then to serve as a
federal prosecutor. He had returned to uniform a year before Pearl
Harbor, eventually coming to oversee Ranger training and to be
parachuted into Normandy on the eve of D-day. It was a record of
united thought and action that prepared him well for his unprecedented task. Refugee work that brought him into just-liberated death
camps and then ensuing duties as chief of the War Crimes Division at
Nuremberg made him a Zionist and an eager volunteer when, in
1947, David Ben-Gurion (head of the government-in-waiting of the
Jewish state about to be) asked him to recruit an American officer to
serve as military adviser.

Marcus selected himself. The U.S. Army required him not to use
his own name or rank and to conceal his military record when venturing in January 1948 to what was still the British Palestine Mandate. Come war, "Michael Stone" applied the Rangers' hit-and-run
tactics to keep the Egyptian army off balance in the Negev and to
direct the construction of a makeshift winding track that he called
the "Burma Road," which brought in men and equipment through

the mountains to relieve the Arab siege of Jerusalem in June, days before the UN-negotiated ceasefire. In less than a year working with a nation ready for action, Marcus was able to constitute a command structure, write training manuals, and adapt Ranger experience to the Hagana as it evolved under the forced draft of survival from an effective settler paramilitary organization into the nucleus of a regular national army. Ben-Gurion appointed him Israel's first lieutenant general. Six hours before the ceasefire, he was mistakenly shot by a sentry. He is buried at West Point, resting in that citadel of New World warfare after having done so much to fulfill one of the deepest dreams of the Old.

Israel's salvation also rested on the Commando Battalion, led by future defense minister Moshe Dayan, modeled after the Long Range Desert Group. As for the role of terror, it is disturbing to contemplate what might have occurred had the Israelis lost and such accomplished elements as the Stern Gang and the Irgun instead ended up as perforce nihilist refugees scattered through Europe.

The East/West antagonism of which Israel and the Arab states would all the more tragically become a part was, until 1950, confined to that famous line of czarist aspiration from Stettin on the Baltic to Trieste on the Adriatic. NATO had been established in 1949; Moscow had appalled U.S. intelligence and everyone else by proving in September how rapidly it could follow the United States into nuclear standing; and the U.S. Atomic Energy Commission laboratories were making sure that the nation had the wherewithal for deterrence, even if defense spending kept being cut. Kennan may have been the only senior official to speak blithely of his country's readiness for "frontier wars," as he did to the skeptical British Foreign Office mandarins he tried to impress in one of the happily few instances of genuine American imperial initiative.[20] There was otherwise no notion of America entangling itself in such adventures, let alone of crafting the special military capabilities likely to be required.

The Soviet-engineered attack that moved forward that drizzly morning of June 25, 1950, as some 150 North Korean tanks and ninety thousand well-trained soldiers poured into the South, would within four days become America's first "peace-keeping war" when the shaken Truman administration decided that it had no choice but to intervene. "The Korean conflict marked the end . . . of the Fortress America era," wrote paratroop commander Matthew Ridgway, one of the few hero-generals of World War II whose fame would be polished in Korea.[21] From here on, it would no longer be a question of whether to fight limited wars but of how to avoid fighting any other kind — and how many of these new-model conflicts there were to be and with what new kinds of warriors, if any.

Defense spending quickly quadrupled. Although fought in the name of the United Nations, the Korean War drew for its fighting men largely on the United States. At the outset its forces were desperately cornered into the southeastern angle of the Peninsula, only to recoil in triumph almost to the Chinese border, then to be beaten back in the longest retreat ever undergone by American soldiers — until a line roughly at the original divider, the 38th Parallel, was hardened and held.

The CIA's inability to anticipate either the long-prepared June 25 invasion or the well-signaled intervention of some three hundred thousand highly motivated soldiers of the Chinese People's Liberation Army across the Yalu River in November were, as the agency would acknowledge with the gracefulness that comes from only having to concede them a half century later, "two strategic blunders within six months."[22] The amiable admiral at its head was replaced in October by the intimidating General Walter Bedell Smith, Eisenhower's wartime chief of staff, a man with "a cold fish eye and . . . precision-tooled brain," recalled the highest-ranking mole within MI6 about their initial encounter.[23]

Within a week, Smith began trying to bring the eccentric Office of Policy Coordination to heel. He assigned another hardened army general, Lucian Truscott, to examine the activities of these enthusiasts on the front lines of the Cold War. Like Smith, Truscott was neither a West Pointer nor a respecter of elites. Furthermore, he possessed the particular authority for such an assignment of having been a founder of the last war's Rangers and a commander of mountain troops. He wanted to "find out what those weirdos are up to," but the daring amateurs who bubbled through the hands-on side of the agency were not to be restrained for long.[24] The secrecy and minimal accountability that enabled mistakes to be concealed for decade upon decade was already turning the CIA into a hermetic bureaucracy nearly impervious to even the most reform-minded directors, let alone presidents.[25]

Like so much else about this fascinating yet forgotten war, even experts on the subject of U.S. special operations pass over Korea's still-murky record as a cauldron of such activity.[26] Missions were undertaken through a rainbow of outfits, kaleidoscopically turned by a series of organizational changes. The mountainous interior of the five-hundred-mile peninsula and its fifty-four hundred miles of rugged coasts hedged by innumerable small islands is surely a penetrator's paradise, and immediately to the north there beckoned the Manchurian coast. Indeed, by its overnight remobilization of America into a worldwide military power, the Korean War shaped much of the world today. It also revived America's special operations forces.

‡

THERE WERE only two possible outcomes for U.S. special warfare in Korea, given the brawling that promptly erupted between the military's Far East Command and the CIA over which would be responsible for the effort. "Either the two merged to create an incredibly potent special operations force," concludes the definitive study, "or they fell into a counter-productive squabble from which only the Communists could benefit."[27] And so, since the real, enduring institutional enemy is more likely to be found at home, it would unsurprisingly prove to be the latter. The resentments and entrenched suspicions that this destructive wrangle set off resonate to this day.

The ill-will and confusions went deeper than just the pettiness of the "American Caesar," Douglas MacArthur, commander in chief, U.S. Far East Command, and supreme commander, Allied Powers, who had already put the Tokyo police to tailing CIA operatives once the agency got a toehold in Japan during the months before the war. The Pentagon had set itself up for this mess at least since the CIA was born. Having no special units to augment or even reactivate from World War II, the Joint Chiefs of Staff had been exploring possibilities of developing a renewed unconventional capability — perhaps creating a Guerrilla Warfare Corps, perhaps building on precedent and reviving a Ranger Group, perhaps forming an American special forces de facto foreign legion with refugee soldiers from Eastern

Europe, or perhaps just running select officers at various army schools through a course in Ranger tactics.

The Chiefs chose none of these. Manpower and money were scarce; the focus was on airpower and trying to build or at least hold together divisions and fleets. "In essence," explains the army officer whose 2004 obituary would describe him as the father of U.S. Special Forces, "the buck was passed to the CIA."[28] Odd as it may seem today that an ostensibly civilian agency expected itself to dispose of all the nation's special warfare capabilities, the confident, new, well-funded CIA moved fast to fill the void — insouciantly anticipating that its requirements for ships, planes, and uniformed personnel would be met the moment that it got around to asking.

Predictably, once war broke out in Korea, the services themselves squared off over turf. Why shouldn't the air force, asked the equally cocky and newly empowered pilots, be responsible for raiding, parachuting in strike teams behind the lines, conducting guerrilla warfare, even for amphibious assaults from speedy rescue craft that could so readily be transformed with pairs of .50-caliber machine guns into Swift boats? Hadn't the air force been given responsibility for wreaking havoc in the heartlands of America's enemies? The air force's success in taking on much of this role was not due to the logic of its argument nor to the fact that U.S. ground forces were desperately engaged with a formidable but virtually unknown warrior people — and soon with the Chinese, all backed by some seventy thousand Soviet gunners, technicians, and pilots. Instead, to everyone's surprise, including its own, the air force found itself best positioned to wage Ranger-like assaults, guerrilla war, coastal raids, and astounding commando operations because of one unusual player: "Mister Nichols," a hefty, thirty-seven-year-old former motor-pool sergeant from Hackensack, New Jersey, with a sixth-grade education.

Donald Nichols was known in the ghost world where he thrived as "Lawrence of Korea," and his abilities as an intelligence genius, resistance organizer, and combat leader go far beyond those of Lawrence. No other single special operator has had more of an impact on a major war than Nichols nor dealt routinely with its top generals and politicians. This warrior, unknown today, had warned Washington in vain as to the very week in which Pyongyang would strike, and then was the first man to contact MacArthur's Tokyo headquarters to tell them of the horror under way. To the Chinese and North Korean Communists among whom he glided, he was the "Man of Disguises." For good reason, Nichols was the sole participant in this war on whom they placed an enormous bounty (equivalent to $250,000) dead or alive: not General MacArthur or Ridgway, but "Mr. Nichols," as he was addressed by theater commanders, South Korea's president and ministers, British admirals. If there is a pantheon of history's special operators, Nichols is right near the front for his effectiveness. In the years since World War II, no one comes close. And even more than Lawrence and the oftentimes aberrant men of this genre, there were dreadful personal failings.

Nichols arrived in Korea from what had been the China–Burma–India battlefront as an army air corps enlisted man in 1946, just at the moment the United States was drawing down its initial liberating force of fifty thousand soldiers to about five hundred by June 1950.[29] During the years in between, he had made himself fluent in the language and, with a nineteen-year-old Korean wife who would die in childbirth, an expert on the country. He was entrepreneurial enough to springboard an early assignment with a security and intelligence detail guarding a U.S. airbase at Kimpo into an entire network of shadowy contacts throughout the Peninsula, thereby gaining the confidence of South Korean president Syngman Rhee. Dr. Rhee might be a Princeton man, but one may be sure that there was not much daylight between the two when it came to methods of getting their way and unearthing enemies, real or imagined: simulated drownings with a soaking-wet washcloth, cigarette burns on testicles, electricity, as well as the customary mass executions by Rhee's South Korean police state. Soon after the North attacked, which by no means need have been a surprise, Nichols also gained twenty-four-hour-a-day access to the open-minded (and shaken) general commanding what was by then the U.S. Air Force in the Far East. Nichols personally possessed the only intelligence organization in Asia able to provide the specialized insights and methods required.

After mobilizing his network, in the first months of the war he personally conceived, organized, and led a team on an unarmed helicopter one hundred miles into enemy territory (refueling on a west coast island) to strip parts from a downed MiG-15, the most advanced of the Soviet fighter jets, and the most sought-after intelligence prize of the war.[30] Months thereafter, he and another impromptu commando team mounted a further operation to retrieve the complete wreck of another MiG-15 from coastal mud flats, by this time having built a reputation that got him the backup of a combined U.S.–British–South Korean flotilla under a Royal Navy admiral.

Other exploits followed, some still untold: dragging back an abandoned Russian-made T-34 tank (and in those days T-34s were probably the best in the world) under heavy fire, a crucial prize if the air force was to learn how to riddle them; leading a team of twenty South Korean soldiers in night attacks to simply destroy Communist guerrillas plaguing a vital airfield; demolishing a radar station on the Manchurian border; reconnaissance on the coast of China; building in less than a year the air force's Special Activities Unit 1, then its Unit 2, which pioneered the post–World War II evolution of what U.S. Special Operations Command simply calls just that — "special activities," not only including raids, deep reconnaissance, and commando assaults, but assassination and abduction.[31]

As for any Communist agent who tried to penetrate his operations, Mr. Nichols had solutions: "Bail him out in a paper-packed parachute, dump him off the back of a boat at high speed, give him false information plants and let the enemy [execute him] for you."[32] Whatever the means, these were the most impenetrable as well as "the most successful special operations units of the war," concludes a fellow practitioner.[33] Decorations — a Silver Star, a Distinguished Service Cross, a Distinguished Flying Cross, Purple Hearts, for starters — piled up on his jacket. Never wearing insignia and frequently in civilian clothes, Mr. Nichols seems barely to have noticed. By then, the rank of sergeant hardly carried sufficient clout. From his headquarters compound deep in a mountain valley, he pursued his subterranean purposes under the amorphous designation of "representative" of the Special Investigations Unit, U.S. Far East Air Forces.

Nichols, in his old age, took it upon himself to write and publish 250 copies of an autobiography. Under the well-earned title *How Many Times Can I Die,* he claims to have composed this tormented account in "expiation" of the men, women, and children with whose deaths he was all too closely associated.[34] Yet it is left to an air force major who had served as one of his executive officers to sum up the type of people the "Representative" hand-picked, directed, and trained for his missions: "[They] included scholars with advanced degrees, and burly athletic types without higher education, but who could walk all night through enemy forests, paddle canoes, parachute from low altitudes, and kill a man with a single karate blow and able to speak three or four foreign languages." The standard requirements for each were those of "a first place Olympic winner."[35] Before the Green Berets, well before the SEALs, we encounter the prototype of the best of today's U.S. commando outfits — wielded to final effectiveness by that rarest, oddest, and often most troubling form of leadership which seems to spring up from nowhere when desperately needed. One thinks of Robert Rogers on the frontier, of Arnold's march on Quebec, of Andrews' Great Locomotive Raid.

With a rare show of unity, the army and the CIA joined to voice outrage at the very existence of this impudent noncom. The air force was compelled to delete "guerrilla warfare" from Nichols's open-ended remit. But accords between staff officers and spooks made no difference to him. He lived in a world of deadlier, subtler opponents. "Snipers? They were my meat," he notes matter-of-factly. Attempts were made on his life in 1948, 1950, and 1953, and, as he seemed to be bulletproof, in that final year North Korean squads (rapidly identified, captured, and "annihilated," he adds dryly) were sent to kidnap his young half-Korean son, on whom there was also a bounty.[36] Still, he was not about to let others set up as authorities on techniques learned at Harvard or West Point. This was *his* war, as even the North Koreans seemed plainly to concede.

The CIA and the army each believed itself to be responsible for mobilizing partisans, meaning Koreans operating behind Communist lines theoretically as part of UN forces. Thousands of justly embittered refugees were ready to serve as infiltrators to sabotage rail lines and, more valuably, to conduct reconnaissance. Both the agency and the army trained them as parachutists who often went in, until mid-1951, under American team leaders. For the remainder of the war, such deep penetration was deemed too dangerous for U.S. military personnel — but not for Koreans. In fact, the next two years saw a series of U.S.-directed insertions that a postwar report calls "futile and callous," angrily summed up by a smart U.S. operator today as "an unconscionable, two-year-long continuance of suicide missions."[37] For many of these brave people plunging into the below-zero night from U.S. transports, it was the first jump ever; many were young women, wearing tiny cotton shoes and padded cotton jackets, casually remembered as glamorous "starlets" by one of their American handlers.[38]

The Guerrilla Section of the U.S. Far East Command also tried to encourage Korean privateers to seize enemy small craft; to get guerrillas to stage "bank robberies," in hopes of disrupting what it believed there was of a North Korean economy; to liberate POW camps; and to use what it called "terrorist tactics" to assassinate Korean Communist leaders and "selected Soviets."[39] Right after taking over from MacArthur — dismissed by Truman for gross insubordination in April 1951 — General Matthew Ridgway proved unconvinced by the more extreme of these endeavors. He vetoed a well-developed U.S. Army/South Korean plan to abduct and extract by helicopter the senior Soviet adviser to the North Korean People's Army, that general's compound having already been infiltrated by resistance assets. Soviet officers and MiG pilots remained on the hit list, but results were mixed, at best.

No army program existed to select and train partisan advisers. Operations came about more by sudden opportunity than from planning, yet partisan groups raiding from the coastal islands notched up minor victories on both eastern and western flanks. There were not yet any Green Berets to make the leveraging of indigenous guerrillas their life's work. Army Special Forces were just being formed in the drab sandhills of North Carolina at faraway Fort Bragg, but their focus was on Europe: volunteers had to speak at least one European language, to have traveled in the region, and to be ready to blend in behind the lines in Germany or Poland, in civilian clothes.[40] The handful who appeared in Korea, only in the war's last year, found the adjustment tricky.

Seventeen Ranger companies had instead been frantically reconstituted in fall 1950, from the 82nd Airborne Division and from regular army and National Guard units. For the first time, all Rangers were trained as paratroopers, but they still ended up being used for night patrols and to spearhead attacks, not for deep penetration, and only a single time as parachutists — in a joint sabotage team with Korean guerrillas — a poorly planned mission with dreadful casualties. They were high-firepower "gypsy warriors" in soft caps, one of them recalls, who found themselves cooperating with this infantry regiment and then that.[41] Soon after the lines more or less stabilized across the Peninsula, higher command by August 1951 was quick to dismantle the expensively schooled Rangers once again, not to revive them as a battalion of rapidly deployable light infantry until 1974.

Why, it might be asked, did the army — with the rare exception of individual officers able to bond with the island partisans — prove such an ineffective patron of special operations forces? Why was it unable to replicate the considerable successes it had enjoyed with Rangers, Airborne, and even the likes of Merrill's Marauders only half a dozen years before? In part it is because the army of 1950 was in what Joint Chiefs of Staff chairman Omar Bradley called a "deplorable state," reduced to rushing green troops from Japan, then from the United States, into the North Korean meat grinder (and soon against a Chinese People's Liberation Army hardened into iron condition by two decades of war).[42] It seems to have made no practice of recruiting or identifying men with OSS or special warfare experience. And there was one further problem. However much remained to be desired when it came to infiltrating totalitarian regimes, the CIA was operating an effective infiltration program in the army's main transshipment depot in Japan. It was paying several army personnel assignment clerks to examine the records of all troops arriving from the United States for any evidence of guerrilla or irregular experience and then to cut orders for them into various CIA cover outfits. Not until mid-1952 did the army catch on.[43]

Men so recruited were not usefully employed. Neither were the younger CIA officers, fresh out of the best schools, hot for the kind of special service that was already the stuff of OSS reminiscences at so many fashionable weddings. Submariners recall surfacing off the Manchurian coast to put ashore a tall, blond, twenty-two-year-old Princetonian at night, his only apparent qualification for this chilling assignment being that he spoke seemingly fluent Chinese, although the Mandarin form of the language is rare in Manchuria. The valiant amateur was last seen paddling his rubber boat beachward, burying it, and vaulting over the rocks.[44] Perhaps this determined anonym made a vital contribution; more likely he was scooped up to disappear forever into that totalitarian chasm from which no voices are ever heard again, his name listed on the Pentagon rolls as one of that war's 7,330 troops missing in action.

Once MacArthur had been able to retake Seoul for a second time in early 1951, the CIA presence had reached a level of nearly two hundred Americans to run operations behind the lines, abundant quantity being perhaps offset by a question of quality. None spoke Korean. The head of OPC, who was responsible for covert action, had to be removed for trying to pass off on the Pentagon a phony film of a supposedly authentic agency commando mission, the consequent investigation finding his overall résumé to be suspect. An arriving station chief was dismayed to discover that most of the "intelligence" so far collected was equally bogus.[45]

Nonetheless, the agency kept trying to penetrate China itself — not only probing Manchuria but embarking on the miserably unsuccessful project of employing fragments of Chiang Kai-shek's armies to invade Yunan province from Thailand. At least the death toll from the Manchurian adventures only ran into the hundreds rather than that of the thousands of unfortunates who raised their heads in Yunan, where the CIA expected to encourage a million of Mao's new subjects to leap to arms.

Apparently, all 212 Nationalist Chinese agents whom the agency parachuted into Manchuria between 1951 and 1953 were killed or captured on the spot. Giving Yale equal time, two former Eli CIA officers were lured into a trap north of the Yalu when their unmarked transport plane tried to rescue several of these infiltrators. The American judged the more senior, twenty-two-year-old Jack Downey, was imprisoned in China for the next twenty years, his colleague for nineteen, only to be released as part of President Nixon's diplomacy of rapprochement — all this during what some today recall with misty eyes as the golden age of the CIA. And it was just the beginning.

Unlike the army and the air force, the U.S. Navy after 1945 had maintained at least an ongoing acquaintance with special warfare, keeping up four out of World War II's thirty-two Underwater Demolition Teams. This enabled the navy, within two months of the invasion, to assemble a Special Operations Group of frogmen and U.S. Marines for amphibious raids as the North Koreans closed in on the Pusan perimeter. Two modified troop-carrying submarines, highly suitable for silent insertions, had somehow also escaped the frantic postwar economy.

Ultimately, the Marine Corps could find little opportunity in special operations: only one company was trained as Raiders; moreover, every man, specialist or recruit, was needed at the front. It was sixty-seven British Royal Marine Commandos (including the European kayaking champion) that the USS *Perch* slipped ashore on the night of October 1–2, 1950, through a dangerously mined bay on Korea's northwest coast, the destroyer *Maddox* standing by farther out as the *Perch* surfaced. The face-blackened commandos made their way ashore in seven rubber boats, placed pressure charges under the tracks inside a railroad tunnel, witnessed a tremendous explosion, and dashed back to sea amid a hornet's nest of enemy fire.

The war's first successful submarine-launched sabotage mission had gone well, just one man being lost. Other missions ensued, along with equally well-coordinated strikes by carrier-based fighters drawing on real-time intelligence from guerrillas. The following year, for instance, a swarm of P-38s demolished a building far in the north in which senior party officials were meeting. The attack left 144 dead, a truly precise hit resembling today's cruise-missile killings that seemingly come out of nowhere — a staple of the "war on terrorism."

After three years, 36,516 Americans dead, and so many others vanished into unknown fates, the war more or less sputtered out in rabbit-warren entrenchments close to the lines where it had begun. Having, it seemed at the time, gained nothing except getting the aggressor to stop, the country had no stomach for celebrating commando daring or such rather few intelligence coups as the navy's air strike against Kapsan. Just for U.S. infantry to have survived the ghastliness of "frozen Chosin" in the terrible retreat of winter 1950–51 was heroism enough. Americans vowed never again to enter a fight so agonizingly inconclusive, so bereft of allies other than the supposedly "free people" for whom the dying was being done, let alone one on the Asian landmass.

Nichols himself symbolizes the predicament in which the United States found itself in defending such a sordid ally as the likes of Rhee: a brave and noble purpose, yet one that required using the bad against the worse. He was the only foreigner present at one of Rhee's worst massacres (a single atrocity at Suwon against more than 2,000 civilians deemed "Communists," who were shot and bulldozed into pits), staying on afterward as an air force major to train Rhee's spy agency. In 1957, he was hauled back to the United States, to be investigated for vice; then idled, being finally discharged in 1962; thereafter making himself a botanical expert on the mutations and abnormalities of palm trees before descending into homelessness and alcoholism; to die destitute in a veterans' hospital a year after the Cold War ended, ranting that North Korean hit squads were after him. And yet, in a rare example of principled institutional memory, this at times squalid but so often brave and brilliant misfit is one of the heroes in the Air Commando Hall of Fame.

The U.S. rescue of South Korea had been vital to checking Stalin, both in Europe and Asia: Truman understood it to be the defining act of his presidency.[46] Yet it brought two additional unhappy consequences, each highly relevant to our theme. It led to a frustration at home that made itself felt in fears of domestic clandestine penetration. And the actual war pulled America along a path of ever-deeper involvements in the East by directing defense dollars to British Malaya and to French Indochina, each ally insisting within a year of the armistice that it was vital for the United States to intervene in Vietnam in order to stem a Communist tide ready to sweep to Suez.[47]

‡

ALTHOUGH MUCH of Moscow's World War II espionage and technology-theft network had dwindled by 1950, any spy or saboteur with an ordinary grasp of tradecraft could have operated indefinitely in the open American system. Perhaps quite a few did. Traitors such as Alger Hiss, who were dragged before the klieg lights on Capitol Hill, were merely the more expendable because they were so unsubtle. The agents behind some 140 Russian cryptonyms found embedded in

Moscow's broken espionage code have never been identified. Many of them were (are?) likely to be upstanding U.S. citizens, too.

The country also had reason to be alarmed by more shadowy dangers than simply the threat of espionage. The Puerto Rican nationalists who in 1950 had shot their way into Truman's temporary residence at Blair House and in 1954 fired from the press gallery on the House of Representatives had gotten surprisingly far. What if serious operators just as motivated, and trained by a much more sophisticated *apparat,* were able to do more than blast away with revolvers — perhaps, for instance, laying their hands on the deadly new atomic technologies? Barely a decade before, after all, scientists had outlined for FDR the prospect of an atomic weapon, should it ever be developed, being brought into the port of one of America's largest cities aboard a freighter. Who could tell *which* freighter, undoubtedly operating under an arm's-length charter anyway, might vaporize, say, New York, in an early example of what today we call "war without fingerprints"?

An unprecedented sense of vulnerability began to settle over a country so recently remote behind great oceans. Saboteurs might interfere with air force bases or blow up dams in mountain valleys. Russian bombers might appear out of the polar darkness. Perhaps worse was a combination of the two, as we see in a remarkable short story, "Top Secret," which appeared in *Authentic Science Fiction* in 1953, as inquiring minds explored chilling visions of an enemy that could pierce to the heart of the nation from within.

In the story, a hush-hush factory is urgently built outside a typical midwestern small town. All the contractors are paid in cash. (Only one Washington outfit does that.) The townsfolk take it for granted that this is a government plant enshrouded in "national security." It recruits brilliant engineers blacklisted for long-past left-front affiliations. No one asks any questions. The public-spirited local paper runs an editorial entitled, "Don't Stop, Don't Look, Don't Listen!"

In fact, as readers soon see, the Russians have infiltrated respectable-looking businessmen who can faultlessly pass for U.S. defense contractors. The tale ends with the Russians purposefully assembling atomic weapons on American soil. In an early portrayal of nuclear terrorism, the bombs are to be delivered around the country precisely on schedule by the flawless U.S. Mail (a means not then considered science fiction). Might not the hidden enemy find its most effective ally in America's sudden and energetic embrace of security, secrecy, and willed ignorance of the doings of furtive agencies?

It is beginning in the 1950s that we also first see a crop of rogue atomic bomb stories in fiction that have nothing to do with the Russians or any other enemy state such as the movie *Seven Days to Noon,* and the novels *Hostage London,* and *This Town Is Ours,* all featuring a very small number of people working for their own ends who hold in their hands the destiny of a city or nation, and the helplessness of government power. Of course, the practical considerations of loose nukes and embedded infiltrators with weapons of mass destruction would be for a later generation. At least an entity so massive, definable, and familiar as Russia could be understood and hopefully deterred in recognizable ways. Nuclear weapons could even be reassuring. The Strategic Air Command's "hardware," as Omaha headquarters called its scariest bombs, could substitute considerably for expensive conventional forces, perhaps even prevent the next drawn-out agonies of which Korea, many feared, might merely be the first.

When asked by critics how he thought the nation could deal with "little wars" if its defense posture was so largely nuclear, Eisenhower (contemptuous of that horrible term, and never having fought guerrillas), offered an all-too-glib answer: if "the country could win a big one, it could certainly win a small one."[48] His prestige overrode any suspicion of illogic. Another, less-discussed means of defense was to use the agency to snuff out threats below the threshold of visibility before they got out of hand. Stepping forth from the agency's temporary offices on the Mall were self-important internationalist manipulators, global architects with "a sense of excitement, of satisfaction and of jubilation," as a heavily redacted CIA report describes the officers behind one of these operations.[49] They seemed to have been so adept at staging coups in Iran in 1953 as well as in Guatemala in 1954, that the decade was beginning to offer them a ticket to the greatest game of all, with mounting paramilitary clout and soon the roping in of U.S. Special Forces.

In June 1952, the 122 officers and men (including Airborne, former Rangers, and OSS veterans) who had been activated in the initial army Special Forces Group were placed in a unit consciously modeled on the Operational Groups of OSS. The army had dutifully created its own psychological warfare "office," and the Special Forces would be born under its wing — eventually, as their founder predicted, to supersede this strange function. Although treated as a science, "psy war" boiled down in any practical sense to secret operations that boosted the morale of friends or undermined that of enemies. The Psychological Warfare Center at Fort Bragg would in three years accordingly be renamed the Special Warfare Center and School; the ties to the CIA, however, would endure.

Special Forces might offer former Rangers a home but would be altogether distinguished by their mission of fomenting subversion, by their being educated in the language of the people among whom they would work, and by being intellectually and technically equipped to take matters beyond the battlefield — if necessary, right into the enemy homeland. It was no accident that the visionaries included Aaron Bank (the "father of the Green Berets"), who not long before had been designated to lead that strike with German parachutists into the Nazis' National Redoubt, as well as Wendell Fertig of the guerrillas on Mindanao and Russell Volckmann, who had commanded a similarly large and accomplished force on Luzon.

Colonel Bank insisted that his soldiers be "at least on a par with the CIA covert operatives."[50] Of course, all this was getting onto CIA turf. But as the Special Forces were coming into being, it was still believed that the hands-on side of the agency would be responsible for such functions in "peacetime," the army in time of war. Since the record from then through today no longer offered such clear delineations, a far more complicated relationship than was envisioned became inevitable between the CIA and the military's special operations forces.

Vietnam would be where both organizations would find rich opportunities.[51] Eisenhower believed that should France be defeated by the Viet Minh (the Vietnamese Communists) "the gateway to India, Burma, and Thailand [would be] open" to Communism, wrapped in whatever national causes might be convenient. So did Winston Churchill, returned in 1951 as prime minister.[52] Here was a ready role for the CIA: to supply the beleaguered French without advertising direct U.S. involvement. Already in fall 1953, agency contractors were shuttling unmarked C-119 "Flying Boxcars" into Indochina from Japan. The French presented the war as one against insurgent "terrorists."

France possessed its own special forces for work in enemy terrain, including one of the most successful, the secret GCMA (Groupement de Commandos Mixtes Aéroportes, small teams of French airborne advisers leading hill tribesmen) — though not secret enough to avoid a Viet Minh battalion being created solely to hunt them down.[53] French troops also used *dinassauts* (small gunships) on the navigable waterways, a technique the Americans would rediscover with Swift boats. Graham Greene, writing as the most distinguished British journalist in Indochina, accompanied a French amphibious strike team he describes as a "black-clothed Commando of ex–Viet Minh prisoners" led by a curiously named officer (Vandenburg) with "an animal face and dangling hangman's hands."[54] A special force it certainly was, and run by a pro, but within weeks the commandos murdered their officer and deserted, making one wonder how many in this innovative formation had been secretly planted in the first place.

Billions of dollars in U.S. aid were meanwhile welcomed, but without Paris's conceding ultimate independence for Indochina's bedeviled countries or (in the absence of full Anglo-American intervention) permitting U.S. officials any direct contact with anti-Communist Vietnamese patriots opposing Ho Chi Minh. By early 1954, the French command, still fearful of U.S. political "inroads" among its subjects, graciously agreed to accept two U.S. special warfare officers — a grandly named paramilitary Saigon Military Mission — to forge contacts among the Vietnamese.

In the mist-shrouded Dien Bien Phu valley, thirteen thousand hardened Foreign Legionnaires, Berets Rouges paratroopers, and French regulars were cornered and overrun by at least fifty thousand Viet Minh, backed by Chinese artillery and engineers on the surrounding hills. American pilots contracting with the CIA had helped to maintain a tenuous aerial lifeline until the stronghold was finally stormed in May. But this death knell near the Laotian border ensured that agreements were concluded that July at a grand summit in Geneva to stop the fighting in Cambodia, Laos, and Vietnam. The Viet Minh were to withdraw from Laos and Cambodia into a People's Republic controlling northern Vietnam. A non-Communist entity was created in the South, with free elections to follow throughout North and South Vietnam in 1956. Rather than sign the peace accord, the United States merely declared that it generally accepted the terms of the deal. But before Geneva's August 11 deadline, ten more U.S. paramilitary experts arrived to augment the military mission, to conduct last-minute sabotage (such as contaminating gas tanks) in Hanoi, and to cache weapons in Haiphong for stay-behind South Vietnamese agents.[55]

By 1956, Ho Chi Minh's regime was supplementing national spirit with totalitarian ideology, taking more military aid from Moscow and Beijing, forming action committees to organize opposition in the South, and, along the way, imposing agricultural collectivism in the North by grisly "people's tribunals" that executed some fifty thousand farmers.[56] In the South, reactionary oligarchs were creating a nominal republic run by bullies who would make it far easier than it might have been for Communist cadres to infiltrate below the Seventeenth Parallel dividing the two Vietnams. There were no elections nor a North Vietnamese withdrawal from Laos.

By 1957, U.S. Special Forces were beginning what would be a fifteen-year stay, not that they yet possessed any equipment or clothes for jungle action; the army had none to offer.[57] But starting with sixteen soldiers (out of some 1,500 men by now in the overall outfit), the special warriors worked closely with the CIA in its own mission to fulfill a National Security Council mandate "to make more difficult the control by the Viet Minh of North Vietnam."[58] A captain with the Special Forces Mobile Training Team was the first American soldier to fall. The South Vietnamese were meanwhile cobbling their own special unit together at a French-built Commando School reestablished by American friends. And the U.S. Military Assistance Advisory Mission expanded.

It was neighboring Laos, however, on which dollars and weapons were showered — the highest per-capita foreign aid in the world — to build a 25,000-man army amid a desperately poor population of no more than two million. With much of the money stolen by the Vientiane elite, more direct assistance was needed to uphold a Western-leaning monarchy against the better-motivated Pathet Lao. By 1959, one hundred and seven Green Berets on the CIA payroll and in civilian clothes (to avoid violating Laos's ostensible neutrality) arrived to train the lackluster Laotian army. More significantly, they applied their multilingual skills to work with a people who would soon prove to be the only effective anti-Communist fighting force in Laos, a tribe called the Hmong.

Although Stalin had died all too peacefully in bed in 1953 and the Soviet tyranny had abated modestly, authentic Soviet fear of the West, lots of opportunity, and a vision of global transformation kept ensuring an aggressive stance. Plus, to Washington, the sprawling Sino-Soviet axis seemed immutable. Arms and aid were going not only to revolutionaries but to a host of nonaligned countries: Afghanistan, Syria, and Yemen during 1956; Iraq and Indonesia in 1958; Guinea (rich in uranium and copper) in 1959, when Africa was efflorescing into new nationhood and was thought to be the continent of tomorrow. The highest members of the Presidium sweated through their heavy suits in Rangoon and Bandung. At the same time, seemingly potent European allies with all their empires and glories began to shrink before American eyes.

Eisenhower himself flew into Kabul to offer competing aid. It included paving the road to Kandahar (the "Eisenhower Highway"), which promptly fell into decay, was finally ruined by war, and is today being rebuilt with more dollars. A matrix of now-forgotten multilateral alliances (CENTO, SEATO, et al.) and a CIA presence usually accompanied the cash of an ever-wider U.S. world role. At Fort Bragg, it was increasingly clear that the future was more likely to lie somewhere other than behind the European lines of a World War III.

And not just to those at Bragg. In the colony of Malaya throughout the 1950s, the British were facing a campaign of Communist terror, almost entirely rooted among some 15,000 ethnic Chinese guerrillas, on a peninsula four-fifths covered by jungle. A twelve-year contest had begun with the killing of planters and miners in 1948 and the assassination of the British High Commissioner in 1951, forcing a combination of enlightened political compromise and superb special warfare technique. Ad hoc steps such as importing forty-seven Iban jungle trackers from Borneo as a "ferret force" were soon replaced by cool professionalism.

In 1950, Michael "Mad Mike" Calvert, a thirty-five-year-old for-mer British Army welterweight boxing champion and now a colonel who had served both with the SAS and the Chindits (running the Bush Warfare School) during World War II, had embarked on a six-month study of the problem. Traveling alone, on foot, and armed with only a rifle, he accompanied patrols and interviewed villagers, settlers, and administrators. His ensuing plan used "the Emergency" (as the British called the Malaya conflict) to re-create the SAS a year later, overcome growing pains of disorganization, and introduce new methods of counterinsurgency. Small SAS patrols would live in the jungle for months at a time, learning the languages, providing tribes-men with medical care while enrolling them in the sport of man-hunting. In a conflict that drew in Gurkhas and Royal Marine Commandos (working out their mandatory twelve-year enlistments), as well as more traditional line forces, "the task of a special unit," recalls one of Calvert's officers, "was to win the deep jungle while the rest of the Army fought the main battles along the edges."[59] The first battle to win, it had quickly become clear, was that for "hearts and minds"; indeed, this now outworn phrase was coined for the Malaysian struggle.

All depended, of course, on the quality of men; SAS arose practi-cally from scratch. Not only the toughest and smartest of volunteers were required, but ones who could adopt a life of self-discipline and resourcefulness while dealing with exotic allies and subtle enemies. These were soldiers able to criticize superiors knowledgeably, and officers who could calmly appreciate such criticism, all of them men who shared an abhorrence of torture, or at least an understanding that it was operationally stupid. Calvert set the tone by pummeling an Englishman who boasted of having so handled a prisoner.

Jungle warfare was revolutionized with helicopters; Communist political theories of insurrection were studied; everyone assigned to the bush was encouraged to use whatever weapon suited them, whether an M1 carbine, a submachine gun, or a Remington sawed-off pump-action shotgun — the latter a tool much favored for walk-ing point. Training was conducted imaginatively by such methods as sending two men into the jungle to stalk each other with air rifles.

Calvert — yet another strange one right on the edge of conventional civil practices — would end up court-martialed. He had been evacuated home early on with malaria and dysentery, soon to be convicted of "indecency" (a homosexual encounter he blamed on drink) after being given a relatively boring command of regular British troops stationed in Germany. But he became legendary for establishing tactics and standards that proved vital to winning a more or less humane victory in what, by the time the SAS departed in 1958, had become the nation of Malaya. And Malaya offered a model from which U.S. Special Forces were setting out to learn. Quelling "the Emergency" would soon be cited repeatedly as precedent for what the United States hoped to accomplish in Vietnam, although few who made this comparison understood the cultural, ethnic, or geographic differences, let alone bothered with the homework that Calvert had tackled at the start.

While the talents who had created the first modern commandos of 1940 were busy reviving the SAS in a form ever closer to the special operations forces we know today, in the deserts, mountains, and cities of Algeria the French Republic was providing an awful warning of how not to apply such capabilities. During World War II, the *Forces Français d'Interieur* underground army of the Free French had been boldly impressive against a million Wehrmacht occupiers; Eisenhower had compared the value of its sabotage and assassinations to the work of six regular divisions. Now France, the occupier, was again in the 1950s fighting well-concealed, fast-moving guerrillas — but this time not for what it regarded as a colony. Algeria was constitutionally as much a department of France as is, say, the Department of the Seine (albeit, like the American South of the time, with less generous suffrage). Paris was ready to go to the wall to keep it, once rebellion boiled up six months after Dien Bien Phu.

The revolution that ended with Algerian independence in 1962 interests us for three reasons. First, the classic 1964 movie, *The Battle of Algiers,* a chilling re-creation of the urban front of the struggle, was considered important enough by the Pentagon to be screened during 2002–3 as an aid to grasping terrorists' motivations and planning. Second, the willful depravities by which French commandos won that early battle turned the stomachs of their fellow citizens, offering a reminder that elite forces — because they are a particular source of national pride and mystique — have an inordinate potential to pull their society in far more terrible directions than ever that society had intended.[60] Frenchmen learned that the price of final victory would not be worth the torture that the 11ième Battalion Parachutiste de Choc, an Algerian version of the GCMA, and the Commandos de Chasse Gendarmerie, among others, were making routine. Nor would even these brutal practices do much to reduce the open-ended vulnerabilities of new oil and gas pipelines in the desert, which France hoped would transform its energy economy. Finally, Algeria is a warning about the limits of what even battle-hardened armies and special units can accomplish. Smart senior officers in the Algerian war used the lessons of Indochina to achieve a clear military victory — which was turned into a frustrating political defeat by what at the end were no more than six or seven thousand well-armed insurgents.

‡

THE CIA at the time was doing more than just putting on paper its thoughts of how "electrical materials and methods" could be used on presumed evildoers, an approach both to special warfare and counterespionage as foolish as it is reprehensible. (The agency's recent forms of what a recipient may regard as torture, such as "waterboarding" — strapping down a suspect and holding her underwater until she feels herself at the point of drowning — are today euphemized as "elevated measures" and deemed "professional interrogation techniques.")[61]

The role of torture in special operations is significant. Being tempted into its use, as Calvert might have advised, is the mark of the desperate amateur. Even Nichols admitted that "many times false information will be given" to end the agony. Torture is unlikely to work when dealing with true-believing, hard-case opponents, given that martyrs have long been singing while being burned at the stake. Unless one wants to create additional fanatics, its use presumes that flawless intelligence can distinguish one's opponents from the rest of a population. In this type of war, making such distinctions is difficult at best and nearly impossible when an intelligence service is rather short on language skills, regularly performing those interrogations through interpreters.[62]

Whatever its means of persuasion, the agency's paramilitary skills increasingly appeared to offer politicians an easy way to avoid depending on spendthrift generals or wayward allies. Few knew the extent to which certain very early post–World War II triumphs in jiggering elections in France, Italy, and soon the Philippines were to be followed through the 1950s by an uninterrupted series of blunders as the agency passed from wholesale municipal fixing to planetary shadow war. Even use of the U-2, a marvelous hybrid glider/jet created by the CIA and the Lockheed Corporation for high-altitude reconnaissance, kept being bungled. (Eisenhower threatened to impound every cent for overflying the Soviet Union after screwups for which, said the president, he would have shot himself.)[63]

Nor was the quality of analysis, which should have been the CIA's core strength, impressive. Trends and events kept being missed or misread: wild estimates of a "bomber gap" in 1954–55, then yet wilder visions of a "missile gap" four years later, shared only by the self-servingly alarmed air force; surprise as deep as a shaken nation's at the launch of the world's first satellite (despite enormous stacks of illuminating, unclassified, yet untranslated Russian publications); and a final rally to conventional wisdom at decade's end that the Soviet economy was so healthy that it was outstripping America's.[64] Eisenhower compared the CIA's top-secret *Estimate of the World Situation* to the work of a high-school student.

Perhaps this was not an organization to which one should have turned to meet the subtle requirements of special warfare. Just as the agency was acquiring a popular reputation for omniscience, sophisticated veterans such as William F. Buckley Jr. were beginning to mock it. For instance, Indonesia's founding dictator, who had taken the credit for throwing out the Dutch in 1949, was welcoming Soviet aid, moving against newly independent Malaya, and generally making a pest of himself as he dared to ridicule race relations in America. Kennan had shrilly warned that a Communist Indonesia would be "an infection," which "would sweep westward" through South Asia.[65] Agency operatives now went to work, supplying to rebel colonels arms, ammunition, black-painted B-28 bombers flown by American pilots, and an LA-made pornographic propaganda film with a dictator lookalike that was somehow supposed to embarrass rather than flatter this satrap.[66] An assassination attempt had all the earmarks of a CIA operation, Buckley commented in his magazine *National Review* during 1958, because everyone was blown up except the person intended.

More ambitious still for U.S. paramilitary practices was the secret war in Tibet, a mountainously barren and freezing land on the roof of the world. The regime in Beijing had found it convenient to reassert traditional Chinese authority and overrun the country in the first year of the Korean War. By 1957, one of Eisenhower's civilian secret warfare enthusiasts was urging U.S. support for "this Dali Lama fellow."[67] The result was disastrous. "The covert action that George Kennan had levied on the CIA," says one veteran CIA operations officer who saw what unfolded at first hand, turned into an intense agency commitment to already desperate and exhausted rebels.[68] Two hundred and fifty tons of arms, ammunition, and supplies were airdropped at night over the next four years, by air force operators seconded to the CIA's proprietary Air America, including veterans from "special air missions" in Korea — military support to the agency helpfully liaised through the Pentagon's Office of Special Operations.[69] U.S. assistance to Chiang Kai-shek for a 3,000-man special forces group on Taiwan (soon to be four groups totaling 12,000 commandos), meanwhile to be dropped into China from the east, was similarly feckless.

By 1959, the agency was flying Tibetan tribesmen to Colorado for training in weapons, demolition, communications, and guerrilla tactics. (The flatlands outside Washington, D.C., made the first arrivals sick, as might have been guessed.) Not that more than one of the agency's forty-nine instructors spoke their language nor knew much about Tibet's remarkable geography. Once training, of a sort, was completed at an agency camp outside Leadville (including the showing of John Wayne movies at night), the Tibetans were zoomed back halfway around the world to be parachuted onto their country's high-desert plateaus. Early failures should have quenched the enthusiasm, but the agency leadership, recalls the chastened participant quoted above, would have regarded cancellation as a "personal failure."[70] Of course, divisions of China's People's Liberation Army specializing in their own approach to counterinsurgency made short work of the brave, physically tough, but hastily trained guerrillas and their families. Some 10 to 20 percent of the nation would perish.

While eastern Tibet had been seething into rebellion, one of the most successful of all guerrilla efforts won victory on America's very doorstep. Seven days of hunger and sickness at sea had brought eighty-two men to Las Coloradas beach in Cuba's Oriente Province. Three days later, the little emaciated army wandered into a cane field, to be ripped apart by a hurricane of bullets. Twelve would survive, but one was Fidel Castro; another was Che Guevera. Within twenty-five months, an unbeaten band emerged from the Sierra Maestra to take over the capital of one of the most successful third world dictatorships, with unhappy consequences ever since.

For many Americans, this victory also summed up the "decade of inaction," and the negligently insufficient military spending for which Democrats were denouncing the five-star general camping in the Oval Office. Senator John F. Kennedy depicted the entire administration as too weak to deal with a darkening world. "I wasn't the vice president who presided over the communization of Cuba," he sneered at Richard Nixon during the 1960 campaign. Just-retired Army Chief of Staff Maxwell Taylor (soon to be brought back as Kennedy's Chairman of the Joint Chiefs, then to serve as ambassador to South Vietnam) was another powerful critic of supposedly constricted Pentagon spending. He wrote his own denunciation, which proved to be a bestseller among a *Sputnik*-rattled public, calling for "heroic measures" to achieve an adequate level of defense and urging an expansion of U.S. Special Forces as the most effective response to third world subversion.[71] Eisenhower wanted him recalled to duty and court-martialed.

Just ahead lay "a thousand days" of all too readily declared emergencies on some of the world's most morally treacherous terrain, entailing a profligate use of covert and paramilitary action and a ceaseless emphasis on procedures more easily phrased than lived — "nation building," "heroic leadership," "counterinsurgency" — and on the need to find and follow men who were both elite and "tough."[72] This was a stance that boded well for special operations, if not for America.

18

Invasion from the Future
From Both Sides Now, 1961–2010

"They had found nothing more precious than Mind, they
encouraged its dawning everywhere. They became farmers
in the fields of stars; they sowed, and sometimes they
reaped. And sometimes, dispassionately, they had to weed."
ARTHUR C. CLARKE, 2010: ODYSSEY TWO

THREE AND a half hours before he died, President Kennedy roused the Fort Worth Chamber of Commerce with an account of how he had strengthened the country's defense at every level of violence, from skies to ocean depths to jungles: seventeen more Polaris submarines, a doubling of nuclear weapons assigned to Strategic Air Command, 60 percent more tactical nuclear forces in Europe, five more army divisions — and a 600 percent increase in the special warriors fighting in Vietnam. The last was a figure he intended to repeat at lunch to the Dallas Citizens' Council. In what he described at the inauguration as the "hour of maximum danger," Kennedy made it explicit that a "global civil war" was at hand, to be waged throughout the Southern Hemisphere in "a long twilight struggle year in and year out."[1] The men who might best carry out that fight were unlikely to be America's tankers, SAC pilots, submarine drivers, or infantry. Here destiny was shaped in another fashion: the supposedly easy solution with special operations forces led to America's blunder in Vietnam, which still shadows the making of U.S. foreign policies today.

The eagerness heard in the inaugural address to "bear any burden, pay any price" and to welcome the "burden and the glory" would burn itself out within a half-dozen years in the Vietnamese jungles. These enthusiasms were to be replaced in the 1970s, first by President Richard Nixon's self-delusion that he could finesse a political order with Moscow, then by Jimmy Carter's different but equally naive endeavor to re-moralize a foreign policy deformed by Nixon's "realism." In the 1980s, America sustained a stronger and more hopeful approach. Throughout, defense spending reflects each political cycle: way up under Kennedy and Johnson, way down from Nixon until the Carter administration was shocked by the Soviet invasion of Afghanistan in late 1979, then way up again as, along the way, secret warfare played its role in a belatedly developed strategy that finally shut down the Soviet Union. Special operations forces experienced the most disorienting ride on this rollercoaster, to arrive today as the most heavily funded (man for man) military arm of American power.

Ironically, the ongoing Cold War years are about as well understood as the Dark Ages, replete with myths from beginning to end.[2] But much can be explained about how commando forces evolved to become exemplary outfits whose motto to their service brethren might be that of the most time-honored component of U.S. Special Operations Command: "Rangers lead the way." Such units are able to drive an ever-higher sense of possibility into the most hidebound thinking of armies or navies as a whole — whether their own army or navy from which the special force emerges or that of the other side. It is that frame of mind — more so than demonstrations of endurance and superlative skill — that the commando helps disseminate by example among regular fighting men and women.

The very word *commando,* however, is a reminder that it was amateurs, those aggressive bands of South African citizen militia a little more than a hundred years ago, who provided the template for skills and outreach that professionals of the day had not been able to come up with — a vital point when weighing events and vulnerabilities since 2001. "The way to be safe," observed Benjamin Franklin during the birth of the United States, "is never to be secure." There is always one more chink in our defenses, one more inward-pointing cannon among our weapons, another way to use special technique by those who wish us dead. Though self-scrutiny today may be somewhat better than in medieval times, we can hardly envision every truly terrible new possibility. (We probably could not move if we had such an imagination.) Nonetheless, as we will see, the United States has kept undercutting its efforts by ongoing quarrels over which government department is to control secret commando operations.

In a denser, increasingly interconnected world, the talent of the special operator will be matched against the minute, barely palpable, fast-moving, stateless entities likely to be the deadliest of enemies — and the decrease of whose threats against modernity have zero proven correlation with the spread of free elections. They, too, do not need to recruit many thousands: a daring few, formidably armed, may be enough.

We in the democracies may think of special operations forces as playing to our kind of strength, of combining the highest individual initiative with sparkling technologies of intelligence gathering, outreach, and destruction. But the enemies of, say, 2010 are certain to be every bit as dedicated as those now fighting under the green flag of Islam and probably both a lot more difficult to identify and possibly at least as technically sophisticated as ourselves. They may come from the cutting edge of the first world — as was instanced by much of the terrorism of the 1970s and early 1980s and which we now know the U.S. Army helped terminate — and they will assuredly be increasingly able to wage war (biological, fissile, informational) "without fingerprints." America may not even be anticipating many of its worst opponents. Surely, innumerable malcontent forces exist out there that we have yet even to register, let alone to meet in conflict.

‡

MORE THAN most shifts of ambition, the initial burst of enthusiasm for special solutions can be dated almost to the hour when, on Friday, January 20, 1961, the then-oldest president was replaced by the youngest elected one. Youthful and vigorous men who, between 1941 and 1945, had served as junior combat officers or in impressive staff assignments now gripped the levers of government. They had helped change the world once, had no particular regard for the brass, and were as much determined to find their way back to the still-unsullied triumphant ideals of 1945 as they were to carve a path into the future.

"National security" (otherwise known prosaically as defense and world order) became an exciting calling around which to build a career. Many were "action intellectuals," as a reporter described them, or, less flatteringly, "emergency men," who by invoking an endless climate of menace could push their way to the opportunities for power offered by the modern state.[3] It is a type we have seen in public life for many of the years since, and one for which special operations forces can hold a particular allure.

Although there is little similarity between the two, we can detect Kennedy's enthusiasm for these artistic instruments of force in Churchill twenty years before. At presidential order, U.S. superunits boomed, and like the first-act gun in a Chekhov play, it was highly unlikely that they would not be used.[4] Civilians got into the spirit. "They've got the damndest bunch of boy commandos running around . . . you ever saw," remarked UN ambassador Adlai Stevenson to a friend early on after visiting the Kennedy White House.[5]

Over Pentagon objections, Kennedy allowed the expanding Special Forces to wear distinctive headgear to set their mystique apart from the mere ruck of ordinary soldiers. His brother kept such a hat on his desk at the Justice Department. Fit young commandos (the real sort) would regularly be invited to Hyannisport for weekends of games and exercise with the extended family.

The president studied the training manuals and supervised the selection of new equipment. He went to Fort Bragg, and he inspected SEALs at Little Creek, Virginia, pointedly overriding senior officers on matters of discipline. He took to quoting Sun Tzu's 2,400-year-old writings on tactics and strategy. It was the flip side of his administration's overly clever approach to nuclear weapons: aides expounding on the fine-tuning of step-by-step escalation and the percentages of DOE ("death on earth") to follow, as if Red Army marshals, of all people, would even bother thinking about any approach to war that would not go all out from the start.[6] In early 1961, there were four U.S. Special Forces groups, including reserves. Before the decade was out, there would be fourteen.

The equivalent of what today is at least a billion dollars was fast redirected from Kennedy's first defense budget.[7] The navy formed its two initial SEAL teams in January 1962. Air Force Chief of Staff

Curtis LeMay might scoff at all the jungle-warrior snake eating and unhelpfully conclude that the two other services were "simply climb[ing] on the bandwagon" of the latest fad in military spending.[8] But he would not let his service be ignored; the Air Commandos were revived in 1963, with all their former colors and insignia. "I want to tell you one thing," an air force general nonetheless snarled to the Air Commandos' star operator, who had just finished the CIA's Tibet airlift, "you are no different from anybody else in the Air Force, that silly hat and all." (A bush hat was the USAF's version of the Green Beret.) "General," replied the intrepid colonel, "we are a hell of a lot better than the average guy I've seen in the Air Force."[9] Right or not, the exchange exposed a big and familiar problem.

The term *nation building* should have been a reminder that many of the states springing up from the end of Europe's colonial empires were as much nations as a lumberyard is a house. When an actual nation did exist, as in, say, Iran, U.S. purposes were rather far removed from the Green Berets' motto *De Oppresso Liber* (atrocious Latin for "To Free the Oppressed").[10] Aid and training to the shah's SAVAK (secret police) gushed under the Kennedys, as it did to other despots.[11] By 1963, Air Commandos and Green Berets were on the ground to help the shah stomp the rebellious Kurds of the northwest, in what too was deemed "a counterinsurgency mission" for Iran's "armies of freedom."[12] Seeing any friendly dictator as a force of "freedom" was as foolish as believing that Guatemalan colonels — by now conducting a near-genocidal civil war — understood the kind of liberty for which Jefferson had fought.

The CIA kept working away in both nations, although it had bungled — to a nearly inconceivable extent — one of its clueless operations right on America's doorstep three months into the administration, its air-support people even getting Eastern and Central time zones confused at Cuba's Bay of Pigs. Almost none of the intelligence officers involved spoke Spanish. Altogether the performance was "ludicrous or tragic or both," concluded another ensuing investigation, whose report was immediately buried for thirty-six years.[13] No Green Berets or other warriors were involved. The Bay of Pigs venture was a CIA paramilitary special operation and, like nearly all such operations in this era, was "special" only in its ineptness.

Like Eisenhower, Kennedy was at least skeptical about the overall competence of what was becoming euphemized as "Langley," the agency having just relocated to a sprawling 240-acre headquarters in the suburbs. (It would not, for instance, be the organization that detected Russian missiles in Cuba the following year.) But Kennedy was thrilled by the agency-directed Cuban exile teams, which even thereafter were staging hit-and-run amphibious raids. His brother was meanwhile urging CIA "boom and bang" paramilitary operations against industrial targets like the Matahambre copper mine.[14]

And one other old technique of special warfare riveted the president. In those relatively quiet years compared with today, adolescents of various ages were under the spell of Ian Fleming's hypersophisticated Commander James Bond, British intelligence's Agent 007, with "a license to kill."[15] The president read these tales, such as *From Russia with Love,* as did his brother, who was engrossed in Fleming's latest, *Diamonds Are Forever,* while on government business in Jakarta. Fleming himself had been a Kennedy houseguest in spring 1960, had outlined anti-Castro tactics to the senator (proposals similar to those eventually acted on by the CIA), and had kept in constant touch with the CIA's director, who observed to others that he found the novels professionally useful.[16] The Kennedy White House became bizarrely complicit with these techniques as acceptable means of statecraft.

Right from the start, the president's national security adviser, McGeorge Bundy, discussed with the CIA's head of operations the prospect of expanding the agency's killing abilities.[17] Taking the Bond novels a bit too seriously, agency operatives asked British intelligence to become involved in a "hit" on Castro. ("We're not in it anymore," replied a senior officer. "We got out several years ago.")[18] Curious about the man whom insiders hyped as America's answer to the Secret Intelligence Service's fictional superagent, Kennedy asked the CIA to send him over for a look. "So you're the American James Bond?" a bemused president asked the fat, sloppy, pistoleer who shuffled into the Oval Office.[19]

The magic of covert action, counterinsurgency, special warrior units, and global nips and tucks drew together into one vast sticky web around Southeast Asia. There were 692 advisers in South Vietnam at the start of the administration. At his first National Security

Council meeting, within ten days of taking office, Kennedy had urged the CIA to expand its sabotage network in the North, and he authorized the agency to employ Green Berets and navy operators to train South Vietnamese volunteers in order to execute these missions.[20] Within twenty-four hours of shouldering the blame for the Bay of Pigs, he had ordered a review of U.S. options in Vietnam, his first full acknowledgment of this gathering storm. Four hundred Green Berets were to be quietly dispatched. After Soviet premier Nikita Khrushchev shocked him into tears at a summit in Vienna six weeks later, Kennedy's first thought was again to demonstrate toughness in Vietnam.[21] The already boosted number of U.S. advisers was tripled once he returned to Washington. Seven thousand more Americans were sent in November 1961, as the furnace door to a war of tragic naiveté opened wider.

If the United States had to make a stand in Southeast Asia, the president argued privately after a faltering 1962 conference in Geneva to uphold the Royal Laotian government against the Pathet Lao and their North Vietnamese allies, it would be better to do so not in Laos but across the border in South Vietnam.[22] But essentially no one in this administration knew any more about Vietnam than about Laos — certainly not the former Ford Motors executive, Secretary of Defense Robert McNamara, nor McGeorge Bundy, previously the dean of Arts and Sciences at Harvard, who had never so much as been anywhere in Asia. This is significant not only because these men and others less able were to push open that furnace door, but because they also came to shape how the war would be waged — not only to the extent of the White House selecting bombing targets in North Vietnam but, stranger still, directly involving itself in the daily work of the army's Special Forces. For instance, a pivotal, top-secret intelligence-gathering base in Laos, Lima Site 85, would be radio-linked right through to Pennsylvania Avenue — perhaps the last thing any special operator would want in executing his mission. Interference reached into case-by-case clearance for penetrations against North Vietnamese units in Cambodia, secret operations to be suspended when former first lady Jacqueline Kennedy came to visit the temples at Angkor Wat in 1967.[23]

Not for the last time, the U.S. Army, which knew something about fighting wars (and had prevailed in the worst sort of jungle combat just seventeen years earlier) was dubious about a president's facile steps forward. Chief of Staff George Decker, a professionally prudent officer who went so far as to raise an unfounded threat of yellow fever to any Americans deployed in Laos, warned against secretly injecting Green Beret units into Vietnam. There was no such panacea, he said; the U.S. involvement against such an opponent as was coalescing in South Vietnam needed to be looked at as part of a major war, with hundreds of thousands of American troops. As was the fate of another chief before America plunged into Iraq in 2003, he was not reappointed. When journalists and Republican politicians exposed the fact that the U.S. role in Vietnam was becoming much more than "advisory," the embarrassed president insisted that the soldiers and airmen were "not combat troops in the generally accepted sense of the word."[24] True. They were heavily Green Berets and Air Commandos, along with SEALs and a whole penumbra of CIA paramilitary operators and contractors — not that such a distinction was made.

It is worth remembering, as with the Truman Doctrine, that what was being confronted explicitly was "terror" and "terrorist atrocity," though now compounded by "communism." Against a stumbling ally that was a member of the United Nations and the World Bank, little groups of black-pajama-clad executioners loyal to Hanoi had "taken the lives of four thousand civil officers in the last twelve months," the president told Congress. And that was only as early as May 1961.[25] Weakness is not the same as lack of strength, and the Viet Cong were forcing Americans to face an ugly reality, as would the hit-and-run insurgents of our own day: it is impossible to impress people with economic assistance as long as those who accept it court death, or to build any properly functioning grassroots electoral system when hideous reprisals fall on every participating schoolmaster and village elder.

Countering these outrages was regarded — initially — as a role for U.S. special operations forces. And here burst through the infatuation with counterinsurgency and "special warfare." It all became a military (and administration) mantra, conveyed to the rest of the nation by impressionable journalists — not too different from the fawning articles today about "iron majors" in the back of beyond and stories of bright young army officers in Iraq who have just (re)discovered comparisons between 1950s Malaya, 1960s Vietnam, and "pacification" today.[26]

The war arose, reflected the *Washington Post* nearly thirty years later in Bundy's obituary, from "the deepest and most legitimate sources of the American desire to affirm freedom in the world."[27] But Americans would be fighting in a nation about which the civilian leadership knew so little that even the clever Bundy did not understand how South Vietnam had come into being in the first place.[28] "Victory" of a sort was by no means the impossibility that conventional wisdom now has it; yet Washington in its ignorance kept taking steps that assured defeat.[29]

Despite all the evidence of failure arising from sending blind (and doomed) missions into closed Communist societies such as the Ukraine, North Korea, China, and occupied Tibet, the CIA hoped that against North Vietnam — of all places — it could finally perform successful paramilitary operations, just as the OSS had done behind German lines in a welcoming Occupied Europe. And, as in his Cuban involvements, so hoped the president who specifically called for "networks of resistance" to be built right in the North Vietnamese police state.[30]

One means of doing so was to drop into that despotism what would ultimately reach a total of 456 South Vietnamese commandos. Results were identical to the agency's previous adventures: "virtually a 100 percent failure."[31] Hanoi was able to "play back" every captive commando against the Americans — meaning that each became a double agent who lured yet more unfortunates north to their doom. A disappointed president ordered the program, already known by the CIA in 1962 to be worthless, to be transferred to McNamara the following year, to be maintained under Pentagon control as a "magic bullet" for six more years while team after team vanished into the waiting darkness.[32] With "a blatant disregard for the telltale signs of compromise," according to one expert study, the agency also advanced a parallel maritime effort, including "bang and burn operations" by commando frogmen from Taiwan to sabotage North Vietnamese shipping. The level of accomplishment was predictable and a ghastly ongoing example of trying to use special operations forces (hopefully not one's own) in pointless but politically and emotionally seductive circumstances.[33]

In that final autumn of his life, John Kennedy signed off on ousting the arrogant mandarin who had long been upheld as America's strongman in Saigon. Ngo Dinh Diem, an obstacle to "nation building," was using his Green Beret–trained special force (to be named 77 Group in honor of the training teams sent from 77th Special Forces Group at Fort Bragg) against domestic political opponents, and losing the war besides. Yet the alternatives to this garden-variety bully were deplorable. Enabled by the CIA, the murderous November 1, 1963, coup left Washington in what, during the runup to the Iraq War, would be known as the Pottery Barn predicament of foreign policy: you break it, you own it. The United States had openly made a government in Saigon. Unless it decided to "cut and run," in today's parlance, this was now an American war, rather than a war with a stimulating American presence.

Three weeks later, Kennedy was shot. Unnecessarily awed by the stars of Camelot, his successor Lyndon Johnson retained the fallen president's entire national security cohort. Now the self-believed experts were truly in charge.

Johnson, however, had no particular enthusiasm for the dashing elitism of special operations. Like the unglamorous, dutiful Georgian, Dean Rusk, who as secretary of state took on a larger role, LBJ was a reflexively patriotic southern boy who got on well — if warily — with the brass. Among the first of the Kennedy appointees to be let go from his administration was the high-energy West Pointer and veteran of Merrill's Marauders, who, as a senior official at State, had been the greatest publicist of the possibilities of counterinsurgency, the Malaya example, and the winning ways of Green Berets in Vietnam — a "defense intellectual" whose Yale Ph.D. was only one of the credentials that made it increasingly difficult for him to conceal his contempt for the alumnus of Southwest State Teachers College.[34]

Johnson rapidly ordered the end of sabotage and murder plots against Cuba and repeatedly asked Bundy, McNamara, Taylor, and Rusk why fighting for South Vietnam was worth the candle — only to be reassured that Hanoi would fast knuckle under to steadily increasing U.S. pressure. Instead, early 1964 saw the largest clandestine military venture since OSS get under way. The Special Operations Group (SOG; soon redesignated for secrecy's sake as the Studies and Observations Group) began its bold five-year life, jostled between Pentagon, State, and CIA bureaucracies. It was a clandestine joint-services coordinating body with an all-inclusive unconventional warfare mandate covering Laos, Cambodia, Burma, and above the 17th Parallel — everything from reconnaissance to kidnapping missions to conducting long-term South Vietnamese agent penetrations into the North (though no team heading in had ever returned).

At its height some two thousand strong (with 400–500 Americans, choosing their own firearms such as silencer-equipped British Sten guns), SOG included Green Berets, SEALs, Air Commandos, and Vietnamese as well as tribal recruits from such peoples as the Montagnards. "Based upon the military logic that your best men handle the most difficult tasks," recalls a stellar SOG Recon Team leader, "mission success earned you a more dangerous assignment next time."[35] There was no shortage of bravery, but the covert action — especially into Laos to get "eyes on target" of North Vietnamese infiltration via the Ho Chi Minh Trail — became Exhibit A of this war's Pentagon quarrels with the CIA and State Department over who would control these shadow operations.

At least political concerns of plausible deniability, for the moment, precluded using Americans for raids above the 17th Parallel. Nor was the agency allowed to recruit experienced sailors from South Vietnam's budding navy for any cross-beach strikes or offshore bombardments against the North. But no one had said anything against employing PT boat skippers from, say, Norway to lead South Vietnamese frogmen and Sea Commandos in coastal attacks using eighty-eight-foot speedboats acquired from that Nordic ally's Westmoren shipyards.

The CIA had skirted the Pentagon procurement processes in 1962 to buy two of these wooden-hulled "Nasty"-class boats, which were refitted with extra fuel tanks at the naval installation at Little Creek. As in Korea, according to a future CIA director, one agency motivation for this type of attack was to ensure that the Pentagon would not enjoy sole credit for secret operations.[36] Yet these efforts, too, were taken over by the Pentagon (the agency still holding sway in Laos) as more SEAL teams arrived, as did more "Nasty" boats and Norwegian mercenaries. (An attempt to use West Germans flopped after a month in which those other NATO allies, least modest when it comes to practical experience of war, offended American handlers and South Vietnamese trainees alike.)

In July, five boats and their Sea Commando complements hit radar sites near Haiphong, while U.S. officers waited for them back at the pier. Two days later, North Vietnam's own PT boats seemed to have attacked in turn the patrolling destroyer *Maddox*. Under U.S. direction, the Norwegian skippers and Vietnamese commandos struck another coastal radar in the Tonkin Gulf, whereon followed an alleged North Vietnamese attack on another destroyer. While Hanoi's regiments streamed southward along the Ho Chi Minh Trail through Laos, these apparently more clear-cut outrages at sea encouraged Congress to pass a resolution that uncritically authorized the White House to use force as the president saw fit.

As Lawrence Durrell reflects in his memoir of Cyprus, *Bitter Lemons,* there is a kind of war whose objective is to make one's enemy respond devastatingly, thereby ensuring that his actions instill hatred in a population that otherwise might be indifferent.[37] Washington played into Communist hands by selecting that year a U.S. Army general who shoved aside Saigon's inept soldiers in favor of almost indiscriminately deadly big-unit attrition warfare in the twenty-two provinces of South Vietnam. It would be the worst of both worlds: neither overwhelming American force against the North (bombing dams, mining Haiphong harbor, sinking the fishing fleet, etc.) nor well-considered use of commando technique. It was a convulsion of impatience short of all-out war against people too clever to make a practice of frontally attacking U.S. forces. "I *want* them to send more troops," Ho Chi Minh reportedly said to the astonished Soviet premier, knowing that such overextension and additional casualties would cripple the Americans.[38] Send more troops America did, and there would be no further need for the artifice of daring Norwegian seamen.

America's own commandos instead found themselves in the middle of Washington infighting. The 1962 Geneva negotiations had resulted in a lame "accord" that one of the era's supreme diplomats, Averell Harriman, of the railroad fortune, had hammered out and, in his role as ambassador at large, intended to see enforced — at least on the U.S. end. If foreign troops were to be prohibited in Laos (through which ran the Ho Chi Minh Trail), then American-led covert patrols must also be banned. For fifteen crucial months after the CIA transferred secret cross-border missions to the military in early 1964, "SOG was kept out of Laos as the bureaucratic clash continued."[39] So too in Cambodia as Hanoi intensified its use of a trail turned multiexited highway.

‡

AFTER THE last U.S. fighting men departed from South Vietnam in early 1973, and Saigon fell two and a half years later to a straightforward, Soviet-backed conventional armor and infantry offensive against which the United States did nothing, it became too bitter a chore for just about all Americans to ponder, let alone read about the details of the war.[40] Today, following the excitement of Afghanistan and Iraq, a plethora of books, new or reissued, examines just about every aspect of U.S. special operations during the Vietnam War, many written by or with the participants: *Secret Commandos; Charlie Rangers; Navy SEALs: The Early Years; Pathfinder; Stalking the Viet Cong; Recondo; SOG: The Secret Wars of America's Commandos in Vietnam* (describing how ten entire SOG teams disappeared and another fourteen were overrun and annihilated in Cambodia and Laos); and *Marine Sniper,* showing a man turning into a jungle predator, hunting the enemy alone, wary as a serpent, slithering fifty yards a day with a Remington 700 precision rifle as he one by one ended ninety-three lives. Veterans of the Australian and New Zealand SAS who fought alongside the Americans offer their own accounts. "All these guys are good at writing books," snorts a former colonel (unsurprisingly, of armored forces) who had also spent time in the thick of that war's combat.[41]

These memoirs properly convey the heroism that was the entry ticket to such adventures. Bravery and skill, however, were not enough for the tasks being confronted. Despite all the unit citations and Medals of Honor, despite the immense home-front publicity that would place Special Forces Sergeant Barry Sadler's "Ballad of the Green Berets" as the number-one pop hit for five weeks during Beatlemania in 1966, none of the three key purposes assigned the special operations forces could be achieved. They were never able to inflict much inconvenience, let alone pain, within North Vietnam, and the unconventional warfare schemes targeting the North went nowhere — at best; nor could their secret yet terribly exposed camps along the Laotian border do anything serious to impede enemy infiltration; nor, with the exception of one raid that freed some South Vietnamese captives, did they liberate any POWs. Death-defying forays into heavily defended North Vietnamese sanctuaries did in fact succeed in documenting the astonishing scope of the nine-thousand-mile network of jungle roads and paths running through Laos and Cambodia that had become the Ho Chi Minh Trail. Targets were uncovered beneath the foliage for devastating strikes by B-52s, and recon teams sometimes disguised in North Vietnamese uniforms, complete with Chinese weapons, would snatch prisoners for interrogation.[42] Yet U.S. operators were hindered by intense political sensitivities, such as how far and where to venture in, and just about never to step onto the enemy's home ground.

Many of the war's astounding feats — including those by air force rescuers flying World War II–vintage Douglas Skyraiders over jungles stiff with antiaircraft guns — arose from the extreme missions required to save each other's lives. However, the ceaseless flow of singing youthful regiments heading south could only underscore the odds that these operators were up against. It was a war in which Washington's blinkered, great-power strategy of division-sized sweeps to "search and destroy," of sprawling "free-fire zones," and of maximizing "production" of shells fired, bombs dropped, bodies counted (as Robert McNamara calculated) was undone by a movement set obsessively on a single objective, barely reckoning the cost.[43] And it was the antithesis of winning a nation's "hearts and minds," village by village. Special operations forces, including Green Berets with their political-military dexterity, would not only take a backseat but would ride in the trunk.

Consider an example from November 1970 of an admirably conceived operation: a raid by Green Berets backed by Air Force Commandos out of a CIA compound in Thailand to liberate Americans from their North Vietnamese torturers. A core team of fifty-six would-be rescuers appearing by helicopter out of the night performed nearly without a hitch, but months after the target had been identified in the spring. Those in charge first had to compile and rehearse the rescue teams from scratch, painstakingly obtain the necessary diversity of equipment and ammunition for the mission; resolve confusions over helicopters with the CIA; and depend entirely on satellite to collect intelligence because, after nine years of war, no human sources were available on the ground (and North Vietnam's Son Tay prison camp was only twenty-three miles west of Hanoi). More than six months had elapsed between concept and execution, and within five minutes on the ground the rescuers realized that the POWs had been removed from this hell hole. Scores of North Vietnamese soldiers were nonetheless cut down in the closest of close-quarters combat.

By this point in the war, it was too late to build on such daring or even on the successes that had arrived with a new, far subtler commanding general, Creighton Abrams, once his failing predecessor had been kicked upstairs to army chief of staff in 1968. Abrams could emphasize operations by 150 or fewer soldiers, and he could deploy more forces around cities, towns, and villages. Yet public support had long since been squandered against the tenacious North Vietnamese army, which fielded what it called its own "Special Operations Forces" of jungle trackers and counter-reconnaissance units to hunt down not only the American operators but also the CIA-trained indigenous Commando Raiders trying to work against the North from Laos. And as a reminder to us that more recent years are not the first time the U.S. military has encountered such a menace, Hanoi's brand of special warfare also introduced carefully selected "suicide bombers." Brave and selfless men bore satchels and charges against hardened positions and perished, it seems almost gladly, as they breached them.

Against all these mounting odds, there was only so much that could be accomplished by the young commando captains of World War II who, as colonels, had become the Green Berets' top cadre in Vietnam. They were such men as John Singlaub, an OSS veteran of France and China, later an operator for the CIA in Korea as an army major, and then one of the colonels who would lead SOG; "Bull" Simons, who led the Son Tay raid; Donald Blackburn of "Blackburn's Headhunters" on Leyte, fighting the Japanese, and the first SOG commander who, as a brigadier, choreographed that raid from the Pentagon.

And like much of the U.S. Army in this protracted, unfocused war, even the Green Berets by 1969 were falling into visible decline, diluted by inferior officers and inexperienced sergeants after having mushroomed from twenty-three hundred men in early 1962 to nine thousand, though still stretched too thin.[44]

The decay became public when eight Special Forces soldiers were arrested for the dim-witted murder of a pathetic South Vietnamese suspected double agent, in a scheme in which one soldier sought asylum with the CIA from his murderous fellows. ("Most probably," a senior agency officer said helpfully, "Special Forces had already done something stupid.")[45] The dashing hotshot colonel commanding all the Green Berets in Vietnam (fluent in French, M.A. in international relations, a sailboat racer) was imprisoned at the huge Long Binh military base. He had abetted murder and lied directly to Abrams, a brother West Pointer, about his involvement. He had also attempted to press responsibility down on his subordinates. But the colonel got himself released through machinations with the Nixon White House. There would be much to rebuild.

Angry despair over the Vietnam War, as well as a spreading loss of national confidence — while not only Moscow but also Nixon's national security adviser spoke of inevitable U.S. decline — combined with tight budgets to work harshest against the special operations forces.[46] The Special Forces Groups shrank back to three, and the army took the distinctive maroon beret away from its two Airborne divisions; air force special operations forces (no longer called "commandos") were eviscerated; the Department of the Navy considered packing off the SEALs to the Navy Reserves. The marines cut their own famed Force Reconnaissance. These steps were offset only in 1974, less than a year after yet another Arab-Israeli war, when U.S. Army Rangers were reborn in a battalion strength of nine hundred men. (In Vietnam, they had fought just as Long Range Reconnaissance Platoons, and Ranger-qualified soldiers were otherwise sprinkled among conventional formations.) With their Ranger badge, whose design included a tomahawk, a powderhorn, and the Confederate battle flag, they now stepped forth as rapid-deployment light infantry — but on terms that are revealing.

"The Battalion," decreed Abrams, once he was promoted to army chief of staff, "will contain no hoodlums or brigands and if the Battalion is formed of such, it should be disbanded."[47] Special operations forces — even in a form as recognizable as an infantry battalion — were on probation. As for the Green Berets, roles were found during President Carter's administration in jobs much like those of the Depression-era Civilian Conservation Corps: building clinics for Indian tribes in Florida, Arizona, and Montana and providing free medical treatment to impoverished citizens of Hoke and Anson counties in North Carolina. As for those South Vietnamese commandos (*biet kich*) who survived Communist "reeducation" and with whom U.S. operators had worked so intimately, America's immigration authorities stood in their way to freedom; undocumented claims of secret missions were met with disbelief.

‡

BEFORE THE 1970s were out, special warfare was once more coming full circle. Before World War II, as we have seen, it was largely a practice of colonial conflict. Then, between 1939 and 1945, it was brought center stage in the grapple of industrial nations. The 1950s and 1960s saw its procedures return wholeheartedly to far-flung jungles, deserts, and South American mountains: Che Guevara, for instance, was hunted down by the agency in 1967 on the *altiplano,* with Bolivian troops that had been brought up to speed by Green Berets.

Following a quarter century in the bush, we see emerging in the 1970s a breadth of special operations from both ends of the political spectrum back in the developed world: raids against oil terminals, shootouts in the airports and downtowns of big cities and sundry capitals — even French commandos helping rout armed attackers at the Grand Mosque in halfway-developed Saudi Arabia. Britain grappled with the venomous Irish Republican Army, with British diplomats even requiring security details in U.S. cities. Nearly all of this involved a heavy hand by the Soviet KGB (the NKVD having shed its skin for a new name), and it included Moscow's covert backing of European terrorist groups such as Italy's Red Brigades, Germany's Baader-Meinhoff, and Action Directe in France — with U.S. diplomats and soldiers — including the supreme commander in Europe, having barely escaped a bomb — in their sights.

As has not been revealed previously, the U.S. Army had a direct hand in the lethal and rapid evaporation of the three latter gangs. A theater commander in chief (now called a combatant commander) has "force protection assets" such as military police at his disposal to provide physical security to himself, his people, and his facilities. Out of this emerges "intelligence support activities," which can involve so-called human service elements of the Defense Intelligence Agency — and such people have the natural responsibility to know who in that theater might be eager to kill or kidnap U.S. generals. After the 1976 Congressional investigations of the CIA, there was no chance that President Carter would sign off on assassination orders even against leftist gangs on the hunt for American army officers. Nor did the U.S. military or intelligence agencies have any capabilities for the task. Instead, relatively low-ranking military personnel abetted the disposal of European terrorists by sharing critical intelligence insights with counterparts among the domestic security authorities of Italy and France. These allies then handled the special activities, or actual sub-rosa killings.[48]

It was in the enduring cycle of violence between Israelis and Palestinians, however, that state-run special activities reached unprecedented scope, at least when conducted by a democracy. Prime Minister Golda Meir's cabinet authorized the Mossad (the Institute for Intelligence and Special Operations) to extract payback for eleven Israeli athletes slaughtered at the 1972 Munich Olympics by Black September/Palestine Liberation Organization terrorists. In its "Wrath of God" retaliation, the Mossad established tightly compartmentalized hit teams with an interlocking information network backed by its officers in Israeli embassies. Outside experts would be recruited as needed.

Working primarily out of Paris with .22-caliber Berettas and bombs rigged beneath drivers' seats, the operators created terror within the terrorists' cells. Professionally delivered assassination may be the most efficient form of special activities, but only if one is utterly certain of the target. A seemingly compromised operation the following year provides rare insight into Mossad techniques of the time. Behind the Hollywood movie making, it also emphasizes how subject to chance — the Law of Small Numbers — a special operation can be, and the potentially ruinous impact of small mistakes.

An estimated eighteen Israelis were deployed to identify and kill one Ahmed Bouchiki, presumed to be the chief architect of the Munich massacre but perhaps being just what he appeared to be — a twenty-eight-year-old Moroccan immigrant employed as a waiter in the remote Norwegian village of Fargenas who had married a local girl and then moved his way up to a hotel job in the resort town of Lillehammer. Unfortunately for him, he had a resemblance to the man highest on Israel's death list. By summer 1973, Mossad's "Wrath of God" operators, according to one of the six to be captured in Norway, were under intense political pressure to strike fast and hard as over several years they terminated at least eight of the Munich perpetrators and probably others who had been on the sidelines.

Eighteen was considered the best number for tight twenty-four-hour surveillance of Bouchiki and his pregnant wife as, on the final day, they were stalked at the movies and at a local swimming pool. His identity as the mastermind supposedly confirmed, two shooters dispatched Bouchiki with thirteen high-speed, small-caliber bullets as he and his wife got off a bus near their flat. Operational flaws quickly told. Incredibly, Mossad had been using rental cars, and Lillehammer is a steep, curvy, 130-mile drive from Oslo's international airport. Soon after Bouchiki lay dead, a local cop on the main road observed a Peugeot whose passengers simply "didn't look like they were on holiday." Detectives arriving from the capital believed they were investigating a drug hit.

In Oslo, the luck of a license plate number enabled police to intercept two of the agents near the airport. The country's chief homicide inspector, Lief Lier (who has not previously elaborated), focused on "an obvious weak link in what turned out to be a team." In thirty minutes he got the first confession from a "poorly educated" Swedish woman who had been recruited to the enterprise for her languages and Scandinavian appearance. She spilled a safe-house address at which four others could be found, including a security official from the Israeli embassy. Though the house contained cables that turned out to be from Mossad superiors, the various explanations and passports at hand still made the story obscure. Lier admits that one of the men arrested seemed oddly inclined to claustrophobia. He was given a rougher interrogation: locked in a small room, he became the next to crack. Links were made to another safe house in Paris, which inexplicably contained apartment keys and more papers leading to additional staging points.

Sylvia Rafael, a thirty-six-year-old South African who seemed to have had much more practice in these matters than conducting surveillance, maintained her cover story as "Patricia Roxburgh," a Paris-based freelance Canadian journalist. But the bulk of the team had by then escaped, including the two triggermen.

Lier cooperated with France's interior ministry to uncover more details about the network, and prosecution followed in Norway amid global publicity. "You have your job, we have ours," one of the operators said with a shrug before being led to prison. The case would then be reopened in the 1990s to investigate the complicity of any Norwegians. Headed by a new homicide chief who as a teenager had known Bouchiki in the village, it went nowhere, other than this inspector concluding that "the murder was clearly a blunder." But the Lillehammer mission still puzzles Lier for two reasons. "Only later did we learn," he explains, "that a Palestinian living in Switzerland with clear ties to 'Black September' had chosen to vacation some weeks before in Lillehammer. That seems strange to me. Moreover, when people at the level of Mossad are caught with such beautifully dovetailed material, literally letting us open up door after incriminating door, it's too good to be true. So who knows about these wheels within wheels?" Nor was the real Munich mastermind ever caught, Mohammed Daoud Oudeh complaining to the press in 2005 that he was not consulted about the verisimilitude of a forthcoming Spielberg movie based on the operations.[49]

Israel's military commandos were obtaining less ambiguous payment for Munich. In 1973, Beirut was one of the most beautiful cities on the Mediterranean, not yet torn to pieces by civil war and Israel's 1982 invasion, which cost more than seventeen thousand lives. Here occurred a flawlessly coordinated 180-minute night raid, its target including three Munich-connected Palestinians who, in those years, were among the thousands living as unwanted guests in Lebanon. A cross-section of Israeli special force capabilities was brought to bear in a joint operation of naval frogmen-commandos, soldiers of the reconnaissance company of the paratrooper brigade, general staff reconnaissance commandos, and by agents of Mossad.

To be sure, the mission to penetrate to the core of enemy strength was delivered against the clamorously threatening but usually amateurish Palestinian Liberation Organization and one of its bloody, chaotic offshoots, not quite world-class enemies such as, say, the NKVD/KGB or North Vietnam's Special Operations Forces. The four Israeli commando teams (two teams of twelve, two of six), with no hope of backup, by ground or air, or any form of rescue, executed a perfect instance of operational interaction, as well as of turning an opponent's social structure and vulnerabilities completely against him.

Each team had been assigned a specific objective, and each was left to itself after the operators were infiltrated as a group by speedboat from Haifa to a beach south of Beirut. Each of the four teams dispersed into waiting cars, disguising themselves appropriately as rich Arab party-goers, to hit the second, third, and sixth floors of a heavily protected apartment house on the Rue de Verdun; as regular Arab townsfolk, to destroy the seven-story barracks of the Popular Democratic Front for the Liberation of Palestine (PDFL); as PLO fighters, to strike a weapons depot in northern Beirut; and as a PLO security detail, to detonate a bomb factory in the sprawling Sabra refugee camp south of the city. (Ehud Barak, a future prime minister of Israel, was disguised as a woman; only four years before, dressed as a mechanic, he and his team of special operators had stormed a hijacked Belgian airliner.) Since the targets were so far apart, no team could dash to the aid of another. The junior officers in command had full authority to act on their own, to improvise. The killing of the three wanted men, the assault on the PDFL, and the explosions set off by the other two teams were all achieved at a cost of two Israeli lives. But perhaps the greatest and today still-undisclosed prize proved to be the capture in the apartment house of documents that had inestimable value for Mossad's next steps in the ceaseless strike-counterstrike.[50]

Israel's imaginative ruthlessness might set the Pentagon's teeth on edge when Americans found themselves on the receiving end. Six years before, during the 1967 war, an American intelligence vessel, the USS *Liberty,* had been struck after intercepting sensitive Israeli communications. As the captain of the defenseless ship had worked to save his crew after a precise, seventy-five-minute, broad-daylight attack by Israeli fighter jets and torpedo boats (bravery that would earn him the

Medal of Honor), all who had remained alive expected to be finished off by Israeli commandos — though finally and tragically late, the U.S. Mediterranean fleet got word of the slaughter.[51] But what Israel was accomplishing tactically, as in the 1976 rescue of 105 Air France passengers hijacked as hostages to Uganda, riveted the attention of some hard-to-impress people in Washington. So did the excellence of the SAS. Having developed a breadth of skills since Malaya, the SAS was hitting back at the IRA terrorists who were reaching beyond their own bitter ghettoes in Ulster to strike England and, on the coast of the Irish Republic, to kill Lord Mountbatten. Coolly and pleasantly confident as a world statesman, just as he had been when head of Combined Operations, Mountbatten had brushed aside at least one American friend's concern that he would be holidaying at his summer house in Sligo.[52]

‡

Such U.S. Special Forces as remained after Vietnam continued to undergo intensive self-motivated training in the geostrategic skills of desert and jungle warfare. But the urban, airport, and seized-embassy techniques of counterterrorism were another, still little-examined matter. "How come we don't have a unit like the British Special Air Service?" asked the Fort Bragg major general heading what, by 1976, had been given the mild new name of the John F. Kennedy Center for Military Assistance ("Special Warfare" being dropped).[53] The question was posed to Colonel Charles ("Chargin' Charlie") Beckwith, the new commandant of the Special Forces School, an eighteen-year veteran of the discipline who, before having taken a .50-caliber round in the stomach during Vietnam, had trained for a year with the SAS at Herefordshire in an exchange program. He was an incongruous man for this type of work. Warriors who complete Delta Force training pride themselves on a "businesslike" temperament — cool and dispassionately analytical. It is a quality of the best of commandos, as it is among business leaders themselves. Yet Beckwith was a big, blustery fellow prone to yelling matches and happy reconciliations with superiors and subordinates alike. He broke crockery, and that was what the army needed.

With the SAS having developed its antiterrorist Counter Revolutionary Warfare Wing in 1973, the midseventies were an apt time to inquire about U.S. capacities. The interest of U.S. Army planners in its own Special Forces went little further than worrying about what those warriors could provide to support conventional divisions on the battlefield. Air force brass was similarly myopic. But just as the army was activating Beckwith's elite unit of hunters and shooters in fall 1977, an iconoclastic air force captain was forming an equally secret six-man team of combat air controllers called "Brand X," honing itself to provide "special tactics" assistance to the services' commando-raider efforts overall.

As they grew, the Special Tactics units that started as Brand X would work closely with Beckwith's new company, designated "Delta" for no subtler reason than that 1st Special Forces already had detachments A through C. His soldiers were to be relatively older, supremely fit warriors with an additional set of counterterror skills, men who were both smart and informed. "What is your opinion on Truman firing General MacArthur during the Korean War? Was it right or wrong? Why?" Beckwith would grill the very few who made it that far in his grueling Operators Training Course.[54]

If counterinsurgency had been diminished as a worthwhile enterprise after the fall of South Vietnam, perhaps there was at least an opportunity for putting a new edge on army, air force, and navy capabilities in meeting the decade's rising tide of terror right in the developed world. SEAL Team 6 arrived in 1980 to conduct the same sort of direct-action missions carved out by Delta. And in the following year there appeared "Gray Fox," still essentially unknown, and one of the strangest of animals in the U.S. Army's black special operations repertoire. It would focus on gathering human and signals intelligence in the most dangerous of environments. "Terror," it was now recognized, might truly include the prospect of stolen nuclear weapons and questions of how to recover them.[55] Key army officers, including the chief of staff, were coming to see a void in even what the Green Berets could accomplish.[56]

The CIA could not begin to fill it, though responsibility for conducting actual covert or "black" paramilitary operations — as opposed to rescue work — remained at Langley as a jealously guarded function. The agency's analytical side was a mess, certainly in examining the Soviet threat. (The evidence is not only the gross underestimates of Moscow's nuclear capabilities, but utterly ignoring, contrary to all evidence from perceptive insiders, that the KGB was undertaking the largest enemy penetration ever conducted against America — practiced infiltrations of industries and laboratories that remain unrecognized in the history books.)[57] CIA paramilitary officers may account for half of the eighty-three stars chiseled into the wall of the entryway to headquarters, but the agency was blundering as well in its operations even against ragtag Soviet-backed factions in Africa, and by 1976 it was being brought to account before Congress for thirty-one years of schemes, illegal, incompetent, or both — its honorable new director (an OSS Jedburgh veteran) feeling compelled to share most of his agency's worst secrets in open testimony just to save it from further ruin.[58]

The weakening during the 1970s of the military's special operations forces, the newness of the antiterrorist teams, and the painful limitations of the CIA meant that the most ambitious, most complex rescue effort that anyone had ever attempted would again have nearly all odds stacked against it.[59] The seizing of the U.S. Embassy in Tehran during November 1979, and the taking of fifty-three embassy staff by Moslem fundamentalist revolutionaries, was one of those sudden, shocking assaults that can skew the perspective of an entire nation. *America Held Hostage* (the TV show that was the origin of ABC's *Nightline*) became a staple of nightly news. Of course, no one was holding the republic hostage, but after months went by, its means of recovering its people remained embarrassingly few. There were no contingency plans to work up when the decision was made to go in. Quite the contrary. Just three months before the shah's overthrow the preceding January, the CIA had assured President Carter there was not "even a pre-revolutionary situation in Iran."[60]

Ten years had passed between Bull Simons's rescue attempt at Son Tay in 1970 and the one in Tehran during April 1980. The army selected Beckwith to lead his two-and-a-half-year-old Delta Force (still no more than two companies strong) to penetrate a hostile country, infiltrate the faraway enemy capital, storm the twenty-seven-acre embassy compound right in the middle of the city, kill the hostages' guards, simultaneously assault the foreign ministry (where three other hostages were located), then somehow get everyone home. The intervening decade's recoil from special operations thinking had done little to bring together all the pieces, as would have been necessary to pull off a mission of this scope. There was, for starters, no multiservice special-response task force, no interservice coordination for extreme endeavors. It would be like climbing Everest without a base camp.

More than ever, success would have to rest on state-of-the-art intelligence. The raiders had to know the teeming city the way a cop knows his beat, learn the precise whereabouts of all hostages, anticipate the erratic routines of the hothead guards. Beckwith got his first shock when a liaison from the CIA told him literally in a whisper that the agency had no sources of information, nor knew of any, in Iran (a point to be repeated in the run-up to the 2003 Iraq invasion). But they would try to "locate someone in the area." They did: one officer, though unable to speak Farsi, would be recalled from retirement in Italy to help organize on the ground. The agency "made it clear they would not take the risks entailed to get us what we needed," recalls one of Beckwith's people.[61]

Essentially, the military effort that unfolded that spring first had to establish its own on-site intelligence capacity, much as the army is doing today for lack of anything better from Langley. Four operators were sneaked into Tehran on European passports, including Richard Meadows, a legendary Special Forces veteran who had led the team actually into Son Tay prison and who is today remembered as the Green Berets' "Eternal Warrior" by a statue at Fort Bragg — the agency first trying to block his involvement as "an amateur with poor cover . . . and poor training."[62] It was these infiltrators who harvested the vital, last-minute information that one might have expected would be second nature to an intelligence service that had been intertwined with Iran's sordid politics for a generation.

Then came the main event. The operator who headed Air Force Special Tactics/"Brand X" first flew in on a small plane to a desolate spot two hundred miles southeast of Tehran, far from any habitation.[63] It was tersely designated Desert One. He studied soil and rock samples to ensure that the desert floor could sustain the heavy C-130s that would arrive three weeks later; he laid out electronically triggered beacons to create an impromptu three-thousand-foot landing strip; then he slipped back out. On the night of April 24, an air force Special Operations Squadron flew in six mighty C-130s from an island off Oman. Flying nap-of-the-earth, three of the C-130s carried fuel, the others Beckwith's assault party and tons of firepower, as well as a Ranger unit to secure the landing site. Arriving also that night along two different flight paths were eight navy minesweeping helicopters from the carrier USS *Nimitz* cruising in the Indian Ocean. Once refueled by the C-130s, these were to be turned over to Beckwith. He required a minimum of six.

The plan held that the C-130s were then to depart back to safety along with the Rangers. The 132 rescuers would helicopter roughly two and a half hours northwest to a second landing zone some fifty miles outside the capital, on the edge of the salt wastes that surround Garmsar, near the southern foothills of the Elburz Mountains. Arriving before first light, they were to hike some five miles to a wadi where they could hide through the following day; their helicopters were to be flown about fifteen miles farther into the mountains, to be concealed under camouflage nets.

The next night, the rescuers were to be met by six trucks, laid on by Meadows and his original Special Forces infiltrators, who would chauffer them into the city where the force was to split into three teams: thirteen men to blow open the wall of the embassy compound, dash in, eliminate the guards, find and scoop up the prisoners; another to storm the foreign ministry; and the third to secure the nearby soccer stadium, an imaginatively chosen urban staging point for the exit. "The difference between this and the Alamo," said one of the Delta captains designated to hit the embassy, "is that Davy Crockett didn't have to fight his way in." (Should all go haywire, Plan B was to steal cars, dash out north of the city, then try to make it overland so as to surrender in the Soviet Union.)[64]

The whole work of art was to take forty-five minutes. The teams and their liberated countrymen would regroup at the stadium, where the helicopters hidden in the mountains were to swoop in, load, then lift everyone thirty-five miles south of Tehran to the Manzariyeh airfield, which would already be in the hands of a contingent of U.S. Army Rangers from Egypt. Thence all would be spirited away by enormous C-141 StarLifters, the only phase of the operation to be given fighter cover.

Israel's success at Entebbe was in everyone's minds. But this rescue was a bit different from commandos in blackface infiltrating the open runway of an African airport and then having it out with Ugandans and seven terrorist hijackers. "Everything that could go wrong, did," reflects the "Brand X" operator who had personally laid out the refueling site.[65] In that empty wilderness, the tragic mated with the absurd. First, a busload of Iranians on an adjacent road stumbled into the Great Satan's latest enterprise, as did an oil truck, stopped by a light antitank weapon mounted on the handlebars of a Ranger's dirtbike. Fire began soaring some three hundred feet into the sky. Then, of the eight helicopters that were to have arrived at Desert One half an hour after the last C-130 touched down, only six appeared. They arrived separately, between eighty and ninety minutes late, delayed by the common but not reckoned-for chalk-white dust storms of the region (*haboobs*). Of the two other quirky machines, one had been ditched, and the second turned back. A faulty hydraulic pump soon crippled one of the six helicopters. Beckwith showed his command quality and aborted the mission. A gale of sand was being turned up into the night by the screaming engines of all the aircraft, which could not be switched off for fear some might not restart. The demolished truck was blazing in the night in a scene that was a close approximation of hell. One half-blinded helicopter drifted sideways, slamming into a C-130 still carrying crates of ammunition. Three Marine Corps helicopter crewmen and five Air Commandos burned to death before the survivors could evacuate. Delta regrouped at the CIA's Camp Peary in Virginia.

Shaking his head in sorrow, one of the veteran German platoon sergeants from the 1940 glider landing atop Eben Emael would remark to an interviewer that the Americans' mission "wasn't rehearsed enough."[66] More significantly, angry senators on the Armed Services Committee made one point crystal clear to Beckwith and the generals who were soon summoned before them: "We're tired of rescue missions that fail."[67] The committee had at least as much to answer for. "Nothing had been learned from . . . Son Tay," recalled the man from "Brand X," neither at the Pentagon nor on the Hill.[68] A decade largely wasted, and now eight good men as well. No specialized helicopters for commando operations; not enough navy pilots qualified to perform a mission of this length over land, which is why the marines were flying the helicopter/minesweepers; not even a rehearsal to integrate all elements of the intricate, demanding hazard. As for Meadows and his infiltrators in Tehran, CIA handlers had forgotten to let them know that Beckwith would not be arriving; they had to make their own getaway, fast.[69]

Anxious Western European diplomats were quietly saying at the time that nothing comparable to Tehran's outrage would ever have been inflicted on a Soviet embassy. No one would have dared. In Beijing, which for twenty years had been an increasingly frantic enemy of its former blood brother, the highest officials were comparing U.S. policy to that of "Neville Chamberlain" and to "appeasement."[70] By November, a reminder rolled across America that continuing frustration can bring heartfelt reaction. Carter was swept from office in an election that focused more on national strength than any in American history until 2004.

‡

THE FIERCELY armed Soviet giant might not have been long for this world, but the longer it survived in its economically desperate yet predatory condition, the greater the chance that something might go terribly wrong. Time was by no means on the side of the West, as conventional wisdom now has it.

At one level of violence, a whole disturbing range of new Soviet ICBMs had been deployed, despite an arms-control minuet that Moscow blithely ignored at any point it found convenient.[71] At another, the empire's special forces (like KGB intelligence operations) were at their peak. They fit effectively with the rest of Moscow's battery of ambitious outreach as forcefully demonstrated in the sharp, fast, airborne, and armored conquest (as it then seemed) of Afghanistan.

First, in early 1979, the U.S. ambassador had been kidnapped, soon thereafter riddled with bullets in a hotel room by self-declared Russian and Afghan government rescuers, with strong evidence of KGB complicity about which Washington did zilch.[72] Then, on Christmas Eve, well after all American diplomats and aid workers had been recalled from that already leftist make-believe republic, came full-scale invasion: airborne troops landed at Kabul airport, tanks and infantry stormed across the border, and more than seven hundred KGB-directed spetsnaz were at the spearhead. Disguised in Afghan army uniforms, they shot their way into the national palace and summarily liquidated the inconvenient prime minister, his family, and just about all others who happened to be in the building at the time. This was no military coup de main got out of hand. In the words of an Afghan survivor, "The Spetsnaz used weapons equipped with silencers and shot down their adversaries like professional killers."[73]

The Soviet approach to special warfare reflected the old suspicion that any Russian authority always had held of dashing soldierly success. Far from vesting its trust in some unique formidable instrument, Moscow had established a competitive regime of rival elite strike forces in the military and the KGB. This redundancy is not to be confused with disorganization, as some analysts comfortably saw it at the time. Soviet order had always been more about raw power than economic welfare, and where it came to modes of violence and coercion, it knew its business.[74]

The spetsnaz had been revived during the 1950s with a mission of pinpointing and, should war be deemed unavoidable, of destroying the nuclear artillery and short-range missiles that the United States was introducing into Western Europe to bolster NATO's defense. Such operations would also have involved intercepting the U.S. Long Range Reconnaissance Patrols (as they were euphemized): these were the highly focused eight-man teams trained to deploy Special Atomic Demolition Munitions for artillery and missiles right before the outbreak of war. Moreover, no matter what it called itself, the KGB maintained military-terrorist units (*osnaz,* essentially a synonym for spetsnaz) for foreign sabotage, subversion, and assassination.

By the 1980s, Russia had some thirty thousand well-trained and motivated spetsnaz, a number that overshadowed U.S. capacities, in addition to an unknown but assuredly substantial number of osnaz operatives. The Americans probably had an edge in professionalism and equipment, but the spetsnaz also were made up of at least eight companies of some seventy to eighty commandos each, whose wartime mission was specifically and only to seek out and kill enemy military and political leaders. Both the Red Army's spetsnaz and the KGB's operatives could meanwhile participate in subverting the West and, in the "gray terror" that filtered chillingly through the apparatus of its satellite states, covertly train and finance Western European and

Middle Eastern extremists. One sign of how high the Soviet security apparatus felt itself to be riding was in licensing the Bulgarian secret service to murder a dissident national in the heart of London during 1978, with a spring-loaded umbrella that delivered a dose of the poison ricin. It was a statement louder than words, right in the face of the democracies — let them draw their own conclusions.

By this time, spetsnaz were becoming known in the West as the "Soviet SAS," even though their existence was kept as secret as possible for a fighting organization of this size.[75] Spetsnaz had no distinct uniforms, badges, or hats — let alone any PR — but instead a well-prepared offensive role, with weapons caches (including radio transmitters and suitably shabby clothes obtained from railway workers, forest rangers, and other locals) scattered around Western Europe should worse come to worst. Spetsnaz operations would have been able to attain a strategic level of impact inconceivable to the SAS and Green Berets — with a twist of twenty-first-century terror. For example, a pandemic of some suitable disease at seven of NATO's most important naval bases, whose likelihood one Soviet defector all too plausibly outlined, could have halved the combined might of NATO before war broke out.[76] Such a contingency fit well with Moscow's enormous "black biology" program of germ-filled warheads and deadly portable devices, utterly unknown in the West until after the Soviet empire disappeared.

Although few recognized it at the time, the Soviet Union had already shortened its lifespan by encountering the Afghan mujahideen. This was the Soviet empire's most technologically advantaged war, its only failed war, and partly for that reason, its last. After thirty years of exaggerations, misunderstandings, and disappointments in the third world peoples and rebel causes it had chosen to back, the United States now found a truly deadly ally who — once supported by U.S. clandestine warfare — would make an immense contribution to the welcome doom of Marxism-Leninism.

Already in January 1980, President Carter had authorized supplying small arms and artillery to the mujahideen to be shipped through Pakistan, with which the CIA had a working relationship since the early days of the U-2. It would be done with the utmost discretion: money would come from America and Saudi Arabia; the Chinese (eventually Egypt and later on Israel) would provide Soviet-type black-market weaponry. Washington was to be in a position to deny everything; no player wanted to openly poke the Russian bear in the eye. Such diffidence held even under the Reagan administration. Within a year, bipartisan calls in Congress for decisive military assistance launched America on the largest secret operation ever, if measured in money, through which flowed somewhere around $5 billion of weapons, ammunition, sustenance, and bribes before the last Soviet forces withdrew back across the Amu Darya River in early 1989.

Although many spetsnaz were conscripts, they were the cream of the empire's intake. The Soviets may have promised the West that they would stay in Afghanistan as long as it took to subdue resistance, recalling as evidence that it had taken them more than a decade to crush *basmachi* insurgents in Central Asia between the world wars.[77] But their seven spetsnaz units of around 250 men each in Afghanistan had been prepared for war against a Western Europe hugely vulnerable in its complexity. This time in Central Asia, commandos and conventional troops alike found themselves bayoneting smoke. Raids, ambush, reconnaissance, and manhunts for warlords such as Ahmad Shad Massoud (the "Lion of Panjsher") were a different story when the enemy had the disconcerting habit of peering down from steep slopes or of emerging as night stalkers out of the mud-rock alleys of Kandahar, Herat, and Kabul to bomb, assassinate, and abduct.[78]

Looking back, one might think that this first Afghan war for America would have been a natural theater for Special Forces. After all, spetsnaz raiders and KGB terrorist agents dared to venture across the border into Pakistan. So might not their U.S. counterparts have provided a cadre of in-country advisers for the ferocious yet endlessly quarreling guerrillas whose disordered tactics favored noise, excitement, and personal glory?[79] President Ronald Reagan's new CIA director was a cold-eyed New York lawyer-financier of useful ill will, the last OSS veteran to serve in that post. But it would not be the Green Berets he ordered to "go out and kill me 10,000 Russians until they give up."[80] Instead, vengeance for Vietnam would be pursued at one remove.

No U.S. special operations forces of any sort would appear in Afghanistan nor hardly any Americans. The supply pipeline ran through Pakistan, and the powerful Pakistani intelligence agency, Inter-Service Intelligence, controlled it entirely — just as ISI would the CIA's paramilitary hunt for Osama bin Laden twenty years later. The Islamic military regime agreed to help set the bear trap, but it did not want to taunt the bear while doing so. Only the mujahideen leaders of whom it approved were to be supplied. The handful of CIA officers choreographing assistance were even forbidden by Pakistan to distribute money or arms, let alone traverse the barren frontier terrain of mountains and mud to deal directly with the mujahideen (though rare violations of this rule occurred, in no small part because French and British operators were in and out, posing as journalists). Never before had the United States even provided weapons of its own making to anti-Soviet insurgents. With the Soviet Union at the height of its armed strength, with its helicopter-borne spetsnaz growing ever more adept at mountain warfare, the most politically sensitive elements within the CIA's Directorate of Operations (also known as the Clandestine Service) were not about to start violating the "plausible deniability" principle of covert action that might cause serious provocation.[81]

As for the Joint Chiefs of Staff, they no more wanted to touch this tar baby than the CIA wanted them to have any role in Afghanistan whatsoever. The Directorate of Operations was "leading the charge to stop the Stinger idea dead in its tracks" and the Chiefs were loath to release these shoulder-fired surface-to-air heat-seeking missiles to Afghan die-hards.[82] Even much-wanted state-of-the-art .50-caliber sniper rifles (ideal for long-range killing of Soviet officers) were queasily withheld, at least until they were stripped of telescopic sights. Instead, the CIA initially fobbed off on the mujahideen a potpourri of shoddy, expensive, often unsuitable rifles and rockets. This was all the more awkward since few in the CIA hierarchy could sensibly discuss military matters; nearly all were ignorant of military logistics; and few CIA officers connected with the arms-procurement program had ever been soldiers, let alone the type of soldier who could imagine what it was like to fight inside Afghanistan.[83]

Despite prizewinning research, much of the story about how the mujahideen actually received the weapons that enabled them to expel the Soviets remains unknown. The problem besetting U.S. covert operations remained the same as in Korea and Vietnam, as well as in so many of America's subterranean conflicts since 1947. Would it be the Pentagon or the CIA that would control them? With lines of authority over paramilitary operations still disputed — including the secret transfer of weapons as well as delivering the training on how to use them — the situation was muddled, and in Afghanistan it was a stalemate. If the agency channeled the U.S. Army's valuable Stingers to the mujahideen, a grasping Pentagon might then demand a role in the venture. This was a matter of deep concern at Langley.

In 1985, a little-known step occurred that broke the increasingly ugly impasse. For the first time, ten senators proposed legislation to assign command over "special activities" to the defense department, rather than the CIA. Under new management, it was argued, a range of modern weaponry for anticommunist insurgencies could be conveyed directly by the military to the mujahideen who — if properly backed — just might have a truly crippling impact on the Red Army. Several senior Pentagon officials, if not the reluctant brass, were urging this move by Congress, in line with the Reagan administration's directive to undercut Moscow in matters military as well as economic and political. The senators' initiative had its intended and intimidating effect on Langley. Without it, there would have been little chance that better weaponry would ever have been delivered to Afghan guerrillas.[84]

From Congress's list of serious weapons to be passed through to Afghanistan, the CIA yielded to deliver Stingers. But whatever concerned the missiles would have to remain under Langley's authority. Selected Afghan fighters were extracted from the mountains to be trained in giant aircraft hangars built in Pakistan. And the amendment was withdrawn. As soon as the Stingers arrived in summer 1986, the mujahideen used them to shoot three MiG-24 helicopter gunships out of the sky. Victory was possible, at least against Moscow.

Yet the CIA had learned an inside-the-Beltway lesson. From now on it would have a more significant presence on the White House's NSC staff and an expanded lobbying effort on Capitol Hill. The problem of whether the Pentagon or the CIA had ultimate authority over paramilitary operations remained unresolved, to be revisited after 9/11.

The CIA's richest contribution to mujahideen success would turn out to be intelligence photographs, provided by U-2s and other "national technical means" at which it had come to excel. Human intelligence, and possessing the imagination that underlies special warfare, was another story. (The station chief handling these matters in Islamabad in 1986–89 would be promoted to Moscow; the agency was already wide open to devastating KGB penetration.) Meanwhile at Langley, the Directorate of Operations gave itself a champagne party right after the final Soviet columns retreated home; then its own people "got the hell out of there."[85] As for the non-Afghan militants who had joined the mujahideen's jihad, "they're a real disposal problem," remarked one Western diplomat in Peshawar.[86] He had no idea.

Other U.S. paramilitary initiatives were also under way across the more wretched parts of the globe. They composed one pivotal component of a five-part strategy that proved decisive in taking down the Soviet empire.[87] In El Salvador, Guatemala, and Honduras, however, it was most of all a case of backing the bad against the worse, with Special Forces Sergeant Barry Sadler (retired, and to die after being shot in the head during a domestic dispute upon leaving a squalid Guatemala City bar) serving as a sour metaphor for the arc of U.S. third world involvements since the glamorous days of his ballad. Green Beret and Delta commandos were offering counterinsurgency training to regimes unsurpassed in the noncommunist world at slaughtering peasants.

In that terrible morass, it fit right in for Washington, during early 1983, to assign a Delta-led mission to hunt down and erase a particular, newly formed guerrilla unit that had slipped across the Honduran border from Sandinista-dominated Nicaragua. Command Sergeant Major Eric Haney — a warrior as deadly as he was reflective — recalls heading "a mixed unit of Honduran Special Forces, Black Carib trackers, and two teams from [his] Delta Force troop" that trapped the guerrillas atop a jungle mountain. The CIA had pushed hard for the infiltrators to be killed, explicitly the guerrilla leader whom Haney waited to appear on the heights. He dropped him with a rifle bullet through the neck. As the U.S. operators finished off the work and rolled over that still-warm body, they recognized the dead man as Arturo Baez Cruz of United States Special

Forces, Haney's roommate at Delta Force selection only four years earlier. The idiocy remains unexplained, whether it was Staff Sergeant Baez's treason or, as Haney concludes, yet another CIA scheme gone awry.[88]

Most visibly in its own hemisphere, the United States booted out from Grenada thirty Soviet and about fifty Cuban military advisers, as well as several hundred distinctly surprised Cuban combat engineers. But, like Desert One, what came off in October that year was a "foreseeable failure," at least in the eyes of special warfare veterans who discuss their work of a quarter-century ago.[89]

To deal with the aftermath of a murderous intra-Marxist coup, the Pentagon gave its special operators only four short days to get ready to fulfill a detailed mission that the State Department and CIA had drafted more than a week earlier, with little timely input from the commandos. Moreover, no one involved ever had usable maps for this tourist spot. And each segment of America's offensive lineup worked from its own playbook. (A joint task force for special operations had been created after Desert One, but primarily for counterterrorism.) U.S. Atlantic Command, unfamiliar with special operations procedures, scheduled airborne assaults in daylight instead of under cover of darkness. Equally, of course, intelligence was woefully deficient despite the island's foundering in four years of increasingly strange politics — ever since its right-wing dictator had been overthrown by the Mongoose Gang while waiting to harangue the United Nations in New York about UFOs.

It would have been the ultimate triumph of the few against the strong had eight thousand U.S. servicemen not promptly trounced such opponents. And once again, as might be expected, two thousand Rangers, SEALs, Delta Force, helicopter crews, plus marines and the 82nd Airborne paratroopers lived up to their reputations. Yet much else in the chain of command was dreadful: three Rangers killed in the crashes of their Black Hawks (no one having determined beforehand that there were no suitable landing zones alongside certain cliffs); one Delta operator killed when another helicopter was brought down by blistering antiaircraft fire (whereas intelligence had diagnosed only two such guns on the entire island); a lightly armed SEAL team hammered back into the sea (when foolishly sent against an enemy with much stronger firepower); four SEALs of another team drowned when dropped at night in high seas rather than at daybreak. Nine of the seventeen American dead were from special operations. It was an invasion that Colin Powell, after retiring as chairman of the Joint Chiefs, would call "a sloppy success," wrapped up by the army bitterly forwarding an all-too-long list of grievous deficiencies to Langley.[90]

To be sure, the special units had made their own share of mistakes, of kinds unthinkable today: mismatched radio frequencies, ammunition left behind, swamped speedboat motors, a failure to have trained the brave SEALs for night jumps into water, smart operators knuckling under to CIA and army planners who were incredulous that the best pre-invasion reconnaissance (given the usual absence of human sources) might simply be gained by buying one military observer commercial tickets for Barbados and the 150-mile interisland flight to Grenada, making sure he had beach shoes, cab fare, and change for a collect phone call home. All the screwups that occurred in taking an isolated backwater only twice the size of the District of Columbia proved a defining experience. The topmost brass recoiled from their own procedures. "The last thing you want," said no less than the army chief of staff, "is a bunch of dipshits at the Pentagon planning anything."[91]

Waiting to be hanged, it is said, concentrates the mind wonderfully. And on certain points, many could agree. The discipline had never lacked for brave men and extraordinary microskills. Now, the experiences in Iran and Grenada were compelling changes, some that were promising (the vital development of an army Special Operations aviation group) and others that were merely cosmetic (returning Fort Bragg headquarters to its more soldierly name as the John F. Kennedy Center and School for Special Warfare; authorizing a uniform tab to be worn on the left shoulder solely by the Green Berets). Serious efforts on Capitol Hill to give special operators a more autonomous, self-sufficient place in the nation's defense bumped up against a long military history — as we have seen over centuries of Western warfare — of impatience, anger, and even contempt among mainstream officers. To the extent that special operations forces had to collaborate with the CIA, they encountered the casual corruption and lackadaisical standards that characterized the agency's Clandestine Service.[92]

At the level of strategic necessity that America had reached more than a generation after World War II, however, heroic improvisation in special warfare was not remotely enough for pursuing the interests of a world power. The U.S. Special Operations Command (SOCOM) was legislated late in 1985 but required two more statutes, in 1987 and 1988, to surmount what congressional conferees called with public anger "bureaucratic resistance within the Department of Defense."[93] Yet there finally emerged a unified combatant command under which falls the special operations component of every service. With considerable independence from the familiar constraints of each service came the ability to obtain steady promotions for one's people. Men would be able to concentrate on special operations, to build careers in the discipline, and to buy directly the "special operations peculiar" weapons and supplies these warriors require — and in a streamlined acquisitions process not enjoyed by the main branches of the three parent services. Special Operations Command became able to furnish each of the military's five theater combatant commanders worldwide with concert-pitch specialized units while also being able to conduct missions under its own direction.

The accomplishments that have unfolded ever since are well chronicled: Navy SEALs and helicopter pilots from the army's Special Operations Aviation Regiment ensuring the safe passage during 1987–88 of tankers through the Persian Gulf; a 4,400-man joint special operations task force, including the Green Berets' Civil Affairs and Psychological Operations units, to stifle nearly all organized resistance in Manuel Noriega's Panama within twenty-four hours of the December 1989 invasion; and then, in the Gulf War thirteen months later, marvels of deep reconnaissance, of providing the glue among such welcome allies as Syria, of sharing intelligence and preparation with other allies in the Joint Arab Islamic Force; all amid executing feints, psychological warfare, search and rescue, and "keeping Israel out of the war," in the words of the U.S. defense secretary, by going after Iraq's Scud missile terror weapons."[94]

Impressive performance was finally backed by a command structure that special warriors could call their own. But no one in official circles was thinking about the significantly different dangers that were mutating in the dark. During the roaring bull market of the 1980s, for instance, the business press gave much attention to the screen brokerage technologies that had been pioneered by Telerate, a hot young company of the early seventies. A New York financial house had acquired a majority stake in Telerate and was overseeing breakthroughs in the world's first electronic marketplace for government securities. Financial intelligence could now be supplied in real time to a web of corporate clients. Yet technologists remained concerned that perhaps the moneymen did not appreciate fully the value of these complex computer systems. Innovative services were being offered from a London office by 1986, but most reassuring became the fact that it was decided to locate senior technology managers alongside the bankers in the prestigious and supremely secure headquarters of the parent company, Cantor Fitzgerald's suites on the 105th floor of the north tower of the World Trade Center. But a little more attention would have picked up the informed whispers of disquiet from those who recognized that a world changed by IT has to face new weaknesses and new enemies as well as the justly fabulous new opportunities coming more obviously into view.[95]

‡

AMONG ALL the "might have beens" that surrounded the peaceful implosion of the Soviet Union on Christmas Day, 1991, one of the most troubling is the prospect of what might have resulted had the reactionary coup five months earlier been conducted not by using fresh-faced conscripts milling in the Moscow streets but by spetsnaz battalions, say, sent to commandeer even a fraction of the vast Soviet array of bioweapons. At least something claiming to be a Soviet Order — only more fragmented and therefore even less responsible — might well have received a new lease on life amid all the terrifying uncertainty. Instead, 1991 inaugurated a decade of unreflecting prosperity for the United States. With the Red Army out of Eastern Europe and Soviet ICBMs no longer poised for preemptive strikes on U.S. missile fields, there were no particularly convincing reasons for America to maintain big defense budgets or even many of the dubiously valuable bases that previously had been politically immune to closing.

As Wall Street and Silicon Valley boomed, professors debated the "end of history": advancing liberal democracy and market forces seemed to promise a world of near-universal cordial relations against which no transcending ideology could compete. Polls may have shown the military to be the nation's most admired institution among all the New York fortune-making and Washington scandal-mongering, but fighting men were regarded as rather out of tune with a country that had returned to believing that "the business of America is business." Defense secretaries sought advice on the future roles of the special operations forces, always trickiest to place in Pentagon priorities, and all the more so in a world, it seemed, matched so benignly to American dreams. The president might speak of wanting "strong special operations forces to deal with terrorist threats" — "black ninjas," he called them, to a skeptial JCS chairman — but this was said only in passing.[96]

Since 1947, a secret office has existed in the Pentagon under various names. Composed of civilians and military, its purpose has been to advise the defense secretary on covert operations, with the secretary, in turn, then able to share his informed views with the president. Whether known as "the Focal Point" or as the secretary's "Special Activities Staff," it has also provided the legal framework for transferring defense department equipment and personnel to Langley for the CIA's paramilitary ventures. In this administration, such functions for all practical purposes ended. Advice and decisions were kicked upstairs. Perhaps that type of messiness could best be sorted out by the National Security Council, which at this more inclusive level predictably brought inaction just as Al Qaeda was being spawned. Even Delta Force, one of the most secret of the commando units, could be gently mocked in the Internet era: in the movie comedy *Canadian Bacon* (1995), political spin-doctors revive a president's sagging popularity by concocting a war with the brutal neighbor to the north, only to their horror to find him so carried away as to unleash the black-clad commandos of the hush-hush "Omega Force." "But they are not authorized to be used against Caucasians," gasps the defense secretary. As Omega Force storms into action, its warriors are shown to be so tough that when one of them sprains an ankle on the trail, he is casually shot by his comrades as if he were a horse.

To be sure, much was taking place elsewhere than on America's northern border to occupy the real Greek letter unit, as well as the

SEALs, Rangers, and Air Force commandos, besides the largest segment of Special Operations Command, the Green Berets. The Pentagon called such work "Military Operations Other Than War," missions variously described as peace-keeping or humanitarian in places as diversely messy as Somalia, Haiti, Bosnia, and Kosovo. Special Forces Mobile Training Teams were assigned to run counternarcotics missions in Latin America, though prevailing policies forbade them to get involved in shootouts. But the object seemed worthwhile, and the linguistically adept Green Berets were kept busy enough quietly training military units of at least one hundred other countries. At Tampa headquarters, U.S. Special Operations Command was preoccupied with the mechanics of obtaining better noise suppressors for machine guns and a vexing problem of shock absorption on SEAL delivery boats. By 2000, one could detect a certain aimlessness in its annual budget statement to Congress, replete that year with an anodyne subtitle: "Providing Unique Solutions for a Changing World." It could almost have been the Canadian armed forces.

If many of us failed to understand the changes afoot, at least the special operators had the confidence to determinedly keep honing themselves ever sharper. The CIA, however, which might have offered better and more systematic insights on what was brewing, meanwhile fell into even further inadequacy. Why? Not because of budget cuts, since the special operators endured them at least as much as the spies, analysts, and paramilitary types operating out of Langley. The reason is a different way of looking at oneself and one's place in the world.

Special operations forces make exceptionally heavy demands on their people from the outset — sowing, probing, and weeding at the most intense individual levels of performance. Feedback is never-ending; mistakes are scrutinized and to be learned from, with the realization that they are all too likely to become searingly public. Personal accountability at every level of rank is uncompromisingly enforced, just as it is on the captain of a warship whose brilliant career can be ruined should his vessel so much as brush another whether or not he is on the bridge. This is the top athlete's pursuit of constant, excuseless improvement.

The CIA, in contrast, spent the 1991–2001 decade devoting enormous effort not only to rationalizing its final embarrassments in facing the Soviet Union — conceding at most shortcomings in human intelligence — but plastering fig leaves over a whole new generation of operational disasters. These ranged from the lackluster search for what should have been the painfully apparent Russian mole Aldrich Ames once hypersecret "blue border" sources had begun evaporating in the mid-1980s; or the 1996 venture to oust Saddam Hussein that is judged one of the most colossal failures ever in the agency's history — the Kurds (by now friends) set up for rebellion, then abandoned to execution squads when America's operatives withdrew.[97] Pre-9/11 blunders brought everything but dismissals, as warnings were raised with increasing alarm right into 2001 that agency shortcomings were opening the door to catastrophe.

Not long after 9/11, the chairman of the Senate Intelligence Committee would speak of the "Oh my God" factor that set in for anyone seriously examining the CIA: the deeper one looked, the more appalling the bungling that bubbled up. The 9/11 Commission established that the agency lacked "the human capital to do the job," echoing another commission that had tactfully concluded, right before the blow fell, that Langley was suffering "personnel problems."[98] And such insights only repeated, nearly word for word, those of investigations in the early fifties, the early sixties, and the mid-seventies, as well as those escalating alarms after the Soviet Union's collapse. This was an institution whose shortcomings in human intelligence, languages, and information sharing were not inadvertent but ingrained. (Had the Directorate of Operations accomplished marvelous secret successes during the Cold War and the years after to offset its record, such details would have been declassified with lightning speed.) With pockets of exception that harbored the quality of officers who could have excelled in any profession, Langley displayed an ongoing tolerance of mediocrity decade in, decade out. No officials would be reprimanded for poor performance on counterterrorism despite (another) inspector general report.

The CIA nonetheless still retains ownership of America's covert paramilitary operations despite the 9/11 Commission also concluding that the country could "no longer afford two infrastructures" for these activities. The jurisdiction overlap has reasserted itself: the president after 9/11 giving the CIA the lead for disrupting terrorist networks overseas; and a presidential national security directive at the same time ordering the Pentagon to prepare military plans for eliminating terrorist sanctuaries. The muddled system that existed since 1947 had become impervious to change, and one of the few 9/11 Commission recommendations not to be implemented.

Lost opportunities to deal with bin Laden directly had preceded the atrocity, though few would know, including the new president. Days after Al Qaeda had struck New York and Washington, the president had brought to Camp David his "war cabinet," including the secretaries of defense and state, as well as his CIA director. In hours spent examining how America had found itself so exposed, what additional threats it faced, and how to retaliate, the CIA director never saw fit to recount four separate previous occasions at which bin Laden might have been killed or captured — whether in Sudan in 1996 or in 1998 when it might have been possible to snatch him out of Afghanistan with the aid of rented Afghan allies in place.

But there would be no Skorzeny or Delta-type raid: the CIA did not believe it had the capabilities, and Pentagon responses were cautiously perfunctory. Few in U.S. Special Operations Command had examined the matter. As in Afghanistan a dozen years earlier, even the possibility of such paramilitary exploits was a jealously guarded CIA responsibility, not one for military commandos. To the CIA's clandestine service, the Pentagon was a place to turn to for shooting off Tomahawk cruise missiles from a thousand miles away, not for self-directed, covert insertions at the nexus of intelligence and military affairs. The defense secretary would learn about none of these cases for months after Camp David.

The consequences of poor intelligence combined with America's bifurcated approach to covert operations has proved to be an inadequate backing for the U.S. Special Operations Command, whose "number one mission" is to battle terrorism.[99] Tasked with hunting Al Qaeda everywhere, Special Operations Command set about in 2002 to fill the vacuum by adopting tactics that previously had been the domain of the CIA. A task force composed mostly of Delta Force and SEALs was improvised to recruit and maintain spies within enemy networks, to spread disorienting rumors, and to make it profitable to supply (discreetly received) information. Parallel functions have been

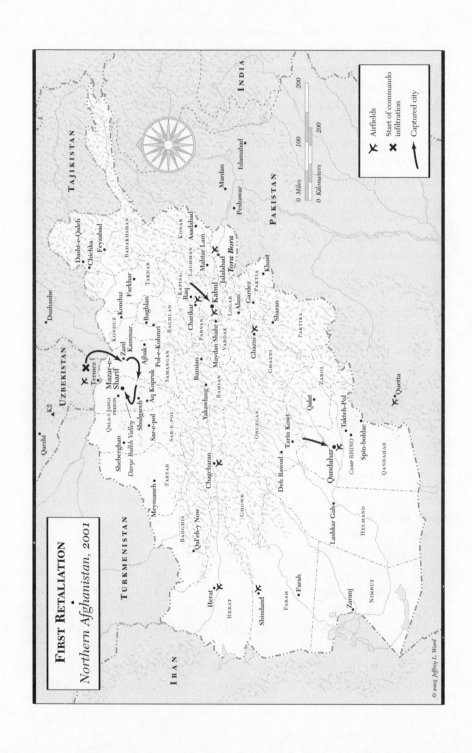

FIRST RETALIATION
Northern Afghanistan, 2001

TAJIKISTAN

INDIA

UZBEKISTAN

TURKMENISTAN

IRAN

PAKISTAN

Islamabad

Mardan

Peshawar

Quetta

Dushanbe

Qarshi

K2

Termez

Mazar-e-Sharif

Qala-i-Jangi PRISON

Darya Balkh Valley

Sheberghan

Meymaneh

Qal'eh-y Now

Chaghcharan

Herat

Shindand

Farah

Zaranj

Lashkar Gah

Qandahar

CAMP RHINO

Spin-boldac

Takteh-Pol

Tarin Kowt

Deh Rawod

Qalat

Ghazni

Gardez

Khost

Sharan

Kabul

Charikar

Maydan Shahr

Bamian

Yakawlang

Sar-e-pol

Shulgareh

Aq Kopruk

Ajbak

Pol-e-Kohmri

Baghlan

Kammar

Zard

Konduz

Farkhar

Chichka

Dasht-e-Qaleh

Feyzabad

Asadabad

Mahtar Lam

Jalalabad

Tora Bora

Runi

Alam

BADAKHSHAN

TAKHAR

KONDUZ

SAMANGAN

BAGHLAN

BAMIAN

SAR-E-POL

FARYAB

BADGHIS

GHOWR

HERAT

FARAH

NIMRUZ

HELMAND

QANDAHAR

ZABOL

ORUZGAN

GHAZNI

VARDAK

LOGAR

PAKTIA

PAKTIKA

KAPISA

LAGHMAN

KONAR

KAPISAY

PARVAN

0 Miles 100 200

0 Kilometers 200

↯ Airfields

✕ Start of commando infiltration

→ Captured city

© 2005 Jeffrey L. Ward

put in place day by day, including by an arm of the Defense Intelligence Agency. Since the CIA itself acknowledges that it will take at least five years (starting from 2004–2005) to revamp its clandestine service, the special operators can count, at least until 2010, on having to fulfill directly many of the responsibilities that, in a nation better prepared, would be the province of civilian intelligence professionals.

Not that top civilians at the Pentagon proved able to meet what lay ahead. After 9/11, the secretary of defense visited Fort Bragg and was impressed by his talks with sergeants who had just pulled down the Taliban. But the ingenuous response, "Let's expand 'em," was akin to a remark by a CEO who has dropped by on some business seminar about corporate culture enthusing afterward, "This stuff is great. I want a culture by Monday."[100] Even with decades of precedent, the insight was lacking that could recognize that commando units cannot be inflated by quick recruiting and overnight training. The startled civil authorities had failed to imagine the necessities of special warfare, as well as its possibilities — a cast of mind that had left America vulnerable in the first place to Al Qaeda and would then open the door to facing a relentlessly bloody insurgency in Iraq.

It took nearly three years after 9/11 — an epoch in the Internet age — for the secretary of defense to come up with a "National Military Strategic Plan for the War on Terrorism," a document that again underscored Special Operations Command as synchronizer of the effort, but one that largely acknowledged the obvious: to resolve turf battles between the services, to ensure that Special Operations Command has a global perspective, even to rely for assistance on major allies and on the governments of the countries where terrorists are present.

Hitting back with special operators at terrorist attackers in Afghanistan and in cells worldwide had been one thing; any president would have been compelled to do so. The historically unprecedented decision to invade a country in order to destroy weapons that did not exist was rather another. The gauzy attempt to remake the Middle East meant throwing the U.S. Army, Navy, Air Force, and Coast Guard into an Iraq utterly unconnected with 9/11. Jets, missiles, submarines, and even tanks had limited use. Among insurgents, the strength of small numbers can contain a peculiar stopping power akin to that accomplished by professional operators: each can stanch the "flow" of even a haphazardly modern nation's infrastructure — its water distribution, electricity grids, oil pipelines — rather than by working "to set things in motion — to throw a rock or wield a club" as in bygone centuries.[101]

"Advice of exiles" had assured the architects of the Iraq war that there would be no resistance once the dictator was toppled. To that end, an inept defense secretary dismissed as "baloney" questions of whether Iraq could reach a price of $300 billion (speaking at the start of the troop commitment lasting "two weeks, two months") and then two years later (at a billion dollars per week), repeating nearly word for word McNamara's business school jargon about reassuring "metrics." ("What you measure improves," the defense secretary stated in 2005. "We have an Iraq Room where we track a whole series of metrics, some are inputs, others are outputs . . . about 60–70 types of metrics.") As the insurgency predicted by more astute observers took hold, the president himself dully invoked John Kennedy's inaugural vow to "bear any burden, pay any price."[102]

It was a closed civilian world of paper and group-think discussion in which the decision-making enthusiasts were rarely burdened by the added authority of military experience (though insisting "we know what we are talking about") while telling a U.S. Army chief of staff that he was ignorant of what would ensue and denouncing another top U.S. general for "dumb clichés."[103] The latest iteration of "emergency men" elbowed themselves forward from among politicians, appointed officials, and eager academics. But all were handicapped further by what intelligence guru Lieutenant General William Odom, director of the National Security Agency in the Reagan administration, noted matter-of-factly was the absence of "humint" in Iraq — or indeed any real understanding of the place. The ignorance reminded him of what had helped bring disaster on the superb force gathering at Desert One to rescue the American hostages in next-door Iran nearly two dozen years before.[104] White House advisers meanwhile offered their loopy opinions — in the Soviet fashion — that "we're an empire now, and when we act, we create our own reality." "History will judge," it was added (as history is doing).[105] Here was a combination of certainty and emotion that was also 180 degrees different from the professional rigor, empirical analyses, and often deep regional expertise of the country's commandos.

There are limits to what the best of militaries can accomplish when larger policy is so much the creature of the moment and is shaped by ill-prepared people so comfortable with loose assumptions. Here the critique is significant for special operators: they will be at the forefront of handling the years of fallout, paying a personal price for bureaucratic confusions and cabinet level incompetence while finding their energies diverted from vital requirements of antiterrorism.

Once again a cadre of civilian policy makers had discovered "small wars" to be not all alike. Though few by this time knew much about him, General George Marshall — "organizer of victory," fine secretary of state, and indispensable defense secretary at the creation of the postwar world — had observed that no democracy is prepared to fight a war for more than seven years (Vietnam clinging just a little longer but in dreadful ways that compromised America's interests for years). Concerning Iraq, the span in Marshall's dictum proved to be much shorter than in the black-and-white, handkerchief-sized TV-screen age. In a world switched on to the digital camera and the Internet, the American public looks for ever more immediate returns on the excitements and alarms from Washington and on the suffering in lives beyond the Beltway.

Smart people in the policy mix had come to know so little of the military — let alone special operators — that startling television prominence and consulting fees could be given for months in Washington to a fat, middle-aged, dishonorably discharged former army private masquerading nationwide on air as a retired Special Forces colonel, replete with silver star and fanciful experience in the 1980 Iran rescue mission, before he was finally exposed by the *New York Times*. His deception was unremarkable at a time when outlandish characters who had been unaware of distinctions between Shi'ites and Sunnis months before or who had previously traveled little in Iraq and Saudi Arabia could pop up as authorities on the Middle East, terror, "national security" itself.[106]

Ultimately, Iraq's occupation was conducted with a belaboring energy that went far beyond ignorance into a truly new form of foolishness. One exhibit is surely the practice of the U.S. Administrator of the Coalition Provisional Authority during 2003–04. He spent much time comparing week-by-week charts of U.S. progress with ones amateurishly created by his enormous staff that showed week-by-week U.S. successes in the 1945–46 occupation of Germany. It was as if Pershing's generals in the Rhineland in 1919 had been sedulously checking the sequence of the U.S. Army's distinctly able occupation of the Confederacy in 1865. The notoriously Teutonic Iraqis continued to disappoint.

Nor will any of this become easier. To confront the invisible, patient, and devastatingly equipped enemies of 2010, new "special operations-peculiar" technologies will be procured (or familiar tools used in new ways). New commando selection courses will be instituted and new relationships eventually built with a credibly professional Clandestine Service. Perhaps even lines of responsibility will at last be drawn between the military and the CIA as to jurisdiction over covert paramilitary action. Amid all the planning, radical approaches could also be taken. For example, select American operators might be embedded for months or years as sleeper cells in environments either hostile or with the likelihood to become so. That would not be in an espionage role (as done by the tiny slice of the agency known as "nonofficial cover officers"), but one of concentrated offense suddenly able to be switched on in crisis, intimately close to the target.

The people most stealthy and skilled for such unprecedented steps might not even come from U.S. Special Operations Command or the CIA: any government department is permitted to run a covert operation under presidential directive — Energy, Agriculture, Labor, or perhaps picked men and women will be drawn on from a New York City Police Department who surpass both the military and the agency in language skills and range of ethnicity. As in the not-so-distant past, citizens who may not have encountered the rigors of Bragg, Coronado, or Camp Peary may possess their own peculiar expertise for focused destruction. It is not too much to expect such departures from familiar ways by the most diverse of nations, with talent banks that no others possess, to be able to scatter and then cut loose not only war-

riors from the military but an additional novel form of select few —
concealing them both just as effectively in overseas daily life as the
9/11 jihadists who went to strip clubs while preparing to fly.

For all the dexterity of special operations forces and the best intentions of policy makers, there nonetheless will be terrible mistakes to
learn from in the years ahead. We live in a world perhaps less
absolutely increasing in disorder than one in which each disorder can
be exploited for planetwide chaos. Whoever those enemies turn out
to be, they will move in ever closer to the pivotal targets, of which
they will have more to hunt because of the splendid complexities of
nations. Moreover, instant communications mean that panic points
can more easily be reached: if we can imagine, for instance, the 9/11
attack as possessing a ground capacity that simply delivered half a
dozen Oklahoma City–sized nitrate-fertilizer explosions in cities
around the United States on that other sunny Tuesday morning.

The more wired a society, the more likely for a single tragedy to
keep multiplying its impact. When a sniper is loose among the shopping centers and gas stations of suburbia, for instance, the effect on
morale is vastly greater than the damage being inflicted. Horrors that
burst upon us can be exaggerated within moments by the human
taste for fabulation, influencing frantic reaction. The shock of an
assault run by U.S. Special Operations Command is that of a civilized
power seeking to confine death and damage to their most relevant
objective. The terrorist, however, rejoices in collateral disaster.
Unlike the state, he does not escalate: he goes all out from the start.
Like those fifteenth-century knights introduced by the historian,
"There [have] to be spectators." His operation must always play to an
audience. He expects it to be remembered for decades — the ghastlier,
the more triumphant.

As we look toward 2010, the advanced industrial democracies are
poised to find themselves more often the targets than the imple-
menters of stealthy small-unit attack. A need will exist to impose ever
more home-front responsibilities on their special warriors beyond, in
America, the SWAT teams of the FBI or those of a constellation of
local SWAT-aspiring police departments possessing mixed shooting
abilities. The more developed a nation, the more industrial ganglia it

contains, like chemical plants — along with many bustling schools and malls — requiring precisely to be *re*taken yet not destroyed once in the wrong hands.

There is a chilling awareness as we think ahead. The harder we work, the more densely intricate the achievements of our societies — and how mountingly vulnerable they must be to the malign, imaginative, proficient few who wish to do us harm. The one consoling fact is that at this feast, amid the wealth of modernity, there are bodyguards with special talents able to match minds and skills with those who beset us. It is a fascinating, terrible, and timeless interplay with which our children, too, will be living. Our story throughout portrays the skeleton at the feast: the grander the feast, the more terrible the skeleton.

CONCLUSION

"We are the Little Folk — we!
Too little to love or to hate.
Leave us alone and you'll see
How we can drag down the State!"
RUDYARD KIPLING, "A PICT SONG"

FOR A lifetime before 9/11, imaginative writers had been working out the number of rakes that were lying around for civilization to step on, not least from enemy operators embedding themselves within a trusting nation sleepily unmindful of how it had generated its own greatest dangers. The wilder spirits of science fiction — Alfred Bester, Theodore Sturgeon, James Blish — would talk together for hours about how the growth of civilization had entailed a reciprocal growth of dreadful exposure. Isaac Asimov was one of the few who did not enjoy such macabre brainstorming (he deeply disliked nuclear power because he believed that its reactors possessed major capacity for going wrong). He felt, as did Poul Anderson, that the proud institutions that grace our lives and the fact that modern liberal democracies require such a high degree of trust to run smoothly made nations that did not fear the "long night" (Anderson's phrase) such sitting ducks that little elaboration would be necessary.[1] Future historians will be perplexed at how late such a stealth attack by a handful of highly motivated killers who hijacked airliners — a vulnerability all too well documented from the 1970s on — could be brought off to such surprised horror on the part of the United States, indeed the citizens of all the democracies.

In fifteen minutes of a sunny late-summer morning, nineteen killers within the gates visited one of the supreme desolations of captive strength (the airliners and America's vibrant acceptance of strangers) on a stunned host country. Nothing short of thermonuclear bombardment could have blasted into overnight orthodoxy the notion that "a different world" had been born on 9/11. But of course the world was not different, altered though it might be by an intensified form of attack from the type of terrorism that had been bleeding the planet for thirty years.[2]

Fundamentally, there was nothing new. We live in an age of instant communication: spectacle was being confused with effective force, as people on television declared that these televised events wrenched our lives poles apart and more precarious than all past time. The intellectual content of the moment became equivalent to the emotional and thereby did a lot of our enemies' work for them. August 6, 1945, had been such a benchmark, when the world indeed had become different. Irrevocably godlike destructive power had then passed into human hands — whose, in the long term, we could not guess. September 11 instead revealed old skills and techniques cunningly applied. Thereafter, technology and science did not cease to work their daily revolutions on industry, medicine, science; the stock market put aside the death of the World Trade Center to bounce back from the dot-com and telecom smashes; and the atrocity made no mark on the coming century's greatest trends, particularly China's compounding growth and commensurate ambition.

For forty years Americans had lived with the fact that most of them could be seared into nuclear ash within hours; they had lost one hundred thousand lives just in seeking to contain Communist power on its peripheries. All the world's terrorists would not be able to do in all their lifetimes what the Soviet empire would have been able to inflict on a single bad day. Yet the sole superpower had invested too much confidence in its mighty external strengths, leaving it obtuse to the world's endless capacity to produce less identifiable enemies. And terrorists, like lawful special operators, excel at grabbing the imagination of whole nations.

The sneak attack was the industrial democracies' first agonized contact with deadly "Little Folk" fighting as shadow countries, not just as nihilist cliques. For too long these people had been beneath the radar screens of constitutional states, and here they deployed techniques of infiltration, stealth, and their own forms of leverage to pierce through our blind spots, with promises of more damage to come. It was also America, the country least constrained in coming to terms with the new, that riposted hard and fast, giving a further deadly twist to approaches and casts of spirit that had been evolving over centuries. These were the relatively small, insightful, supremely focused, pursuing outfits of the sort that had already appeared in the epics and early histories of ages before. By now, a deep pool of talent and character had been forming, with steadily more effective procedures.

‡

WAR HAS transformed itself at least three times in the last five hundred years: by chemistry and metallurgy into gunpowder and firearms; by vast-scale operations (the fruit of democratic and communications revolutions) commensurate with mass production; and by the corrosion of high technology into gas, missiles, and nuclear and germ weaponry. In parallel, the special force has evolved yet further from the pickup raiding and storming party, by way of spearpoint roles in exploration and conquest, to become by the mid-twentieth century a systematic arm of war, arriving today as the preeminent means of dealing with those hidden evil powers of compact destruction.

It has taken war's increasing deadliness — and the increasing divisions of labor within societies hurtling into the future — to bring special operations forces into permanent standing and also to compel constant learning, ever stricter accountability, and ever more focused imagination of tasks and dangers. The passage from the heroism of the unusual moment into a lifelong thoughtful specialty has emerged out of necessity and opportunity alike, intensifying with the subtlety of the commando's targets and the impact of his means. Warriors are more skilled because they must confront more skilled opponents and operate in incredibly more overall skilled societies. A generation ago, only dreamers had even an outline of current possibilities of artificial intelligence, genetics, communications. The year 2010 or earlier will offer equal or greater astonishments, and some of these will be very unpleasant.

For three thousand years the few who dared have been ghosts haunting the complacency of high-walled cities, the blundering of encamped armies, the magnificence of royal courts. We see repeatedly the vulnerability of the unaware mass to the cleverly focused small. The Trojan Horse remains a parable. Achilles and his heroes cannot take Troy by sheer hammering; eventually Odysseus will put Trojan triumphalism to ruin. This is not just a good story but a profound and recurring truth.

The extreme risks and strong rewards of the daring few have shaped our ancestors' lives and now our own. Throughout we see the sheer high spirits of those who set out to do less the impossible than the simply unprecedented. We also can recognize the continuity of task as an enemy's strengths are turned against him, as has occurred since Gideon demonstrated that the more numerous the enemy, the worse he could fall all over himself. But never last and never least comes the presence of imagination, as the commando examines what solid generals may believe unworkable or insignificant and then clears the critical path to a victory that perhaps could not have been achieved (or at least not achieved as fast and efficiently) by an army. As for consistency, the only thing consistent in the special operation is its complete unpredictability — a blade in the grasp of all who use it, the wicked quite as much as the decent.

Units of intense professionalism are at long last in place, yet the vital tasks that may be required of them — and the expertise and resources necessary to accomplishing tomorrow's missions — are ever harder to anticipate. This means that it is no more likely today than on tranquil 9/10 that the ingenious assaults being hatched against us in a dozen covert European laboratories, in several score souks or favelas, can be any better predicted (except in fiction, as virtually all the great disasters have been since at least 1910). What our own special operators may be able to pull off five or ten years ahead will have to depend more than ever on their pivotal talents as improvisers in extremity.

All military establishments, like all other great institutions, are mirrors of their societies. For commandos, that reflection may be through a curved glass — as intensely as a lens, say, used for burning. At their best, special forces focus to maximum efficient deadliness a nation's overall depth of talent, education, and capability to innovate. The more advanced and alert the nation, the more readily it will be able to recruit the tiny fraction of its people who are up to such ventures — and then effectively deploy these men (and surely women) in tandem with less exotic modes of national power.

Special operations enable a nation to make supremely nuanced war, not to be confused with the rear-area doctrines of "controlled escalation" and "flexible response" that contributed so greatly to the disaster in Vietnam, let alone to the kind of vagaries that give rise to chatter about "managing" or "running" the world today, e.g., Iraq. Special operations offer a radically different way to use violence and, beyond a certain point, are not subject to being ratcheted up or extended to a second attempt: they either justify themselves or fail, then to be replaced with other choices. The forces can offer strategic quality without having to call for strategic quantity, which has a way of raising enormous problems when present. (Consider, for instance, the Russian reaction if the thirty thousand U.S. troops that were planned for Afghanistan had actually scrambled into the mountains post-9/11.)

However many centuries away, the warlike originals who lie behind these operations offer us many worthy lessons. At their best, they each possess a temperament that feeds new energies into courage and new dimensions into awareness. That said, the legendary figures of special warfare are often not the sort of people the nation would want to lead a twelve-man Green Beret A-team, let alone to command a Ranger battalion. A special force today, however dashingly it were led by a Pizarro, Drake, or Mosby, or, even more curiously, a Wingate or a Nichols, would create just the sort of disorder that U.S. Special Operations Command — and the schools at Bragg, Coronado, and Hurlburt — iron out as part of the selection. No longer can "Green Beanies," as the rest of the army unlovingly knew them not so long ago, be mocked in the officers' clubs as eccentric cowboys. Like the SEALs and their brothers in the Air Force Special Operations

Wing, U.S. Special Forces soldiers have finally assimilated into their parent service, until soon everyone gets to wear a beret (now the black headgear of the army).

The special operation is above all a powerful exercise of mind; muscle and even disciplined response are essential but secondary. Gideon required the brilliance of perception to see that jugs and lamps may kill more than swords; without his deadly eye for the crack in the seawall, Cochrane's tiny raiding parties along the French coast and his small crew on the *Speedy* would only have been making a fast voyage to the war memorial. Such insight can come from anywhere. We know from the past that men with no military experience (let alone the sort of experience shaped at Fort Bragg) have accomplished many of the most imaginative special operations. If they did have such experience, as in the case of Lord Cochrane, it was often unconnected to the ways of war in which they had made their names.

There are reasons why no commando-personalizing figures have emerged into journalistic or veterans'-reunion legend from the special forces of any nation in recent memory — no tortured Oxonian Lawrence, no gleefully thuggish Skorzeny, no self-bedeviled Nichols. Men like this were more than a bit out of control. In the United States, for instance, an officer on a special operations career path spends more of his life going to school than does a Harvard professor — which is rather likely to be for the best. The more special the force (professionally trained and organized, a familiar presence tied to national policy) the less it and its people are on the margin. Yet the trouble is that the kind of originality that pays off in special warfare at the moment of bloodshed may be functionally related, as they say in the universities, to the presence of those aberrant characters who on the ninety-nine peaceful days out of a hundred properly alarm the armed services — stern institutions whose watchwords in a dangerous world must be predictability and conduct becoming. As a nation's means of waging special warfare become increasingly structured, career-oriented, and seamlessly fitted into its defense establishment, with doctrines hammered out in committee and candidates vetted by psychologists, it is worth asking whether originality may be compromised by pursuing such necessary order and dependability — efforts that can turn into all-too-inevitable bureaucracy.

For instance, consider selection for U.S. special operations forces. Great store is placed in psychological testing to determine "IQ." High scores are required even to be considered for the discipline — despite all the controversies whether central human capacity can be rendered into a supposedly inherent number and how far, even if this could be established at one moment, it remains constant over a lifetime, let alone a day of battle. Such IQ as well as behavioral screening can result in just that kind of assimilation to an established organization that would not work among entrepreneurs or artists. Might this well-meant homogenization obstruct the essential qualities of white-hot, so often frightening improvisation? Might it instead be introducing a more clever level of routine?[3]

Consider, too, the highly classified selection and training regimens for what is commonly known as Delta Force, with a final testing hurdle that long involved a practical puzzle described as "a girl, a bicycle, and a cave." Selection, in fact, is a never-ending process, and everything done depends on individual rather than team effort. The purpose is to discover how one operates alone. And the backgrounds of the men able to pass the ultimate sieving from already rigorously checked ranks are among the most closely held of Pentagon secrets.

As has not been disclosed before, the men able to pass do not come predominantly from initial military occupational specialties in infantry or airborne, as one might expect: they are drawn from earlier service in the army's personnel departments and in its maintenance/mechanics shops.[4] It is an insight that should not surprise us in light of Vladimir Peniakoff's recruitment procedures in the North African deserts of World War II as he constituted the most elite of commandos out of men who "had to have minds like ants, stamp collectors, watchmakers, and accountants" — meaning not only accountant-like in solitary precision but significantly more individualistic than other operators who excel at teamwork. By a truly curious tie, the very first band of elite warriors recorded is that which Achilles, the greatest warrior of the time, brought to Troy, his Myrmidons (Ants), individually heroic but also able to be ferociously coordinated, an echo into the future.

Yet all this may exemplify not only the best but the worst of the sieving processes.

In the current climate of global conflict, all newly appointed U.S.

ambassadors are brought to North Carolina to witness a Delta capabilities exercise, or CAPEX, a display of fast-roping from helicopters and "clearing a room" in a building occupied by mock terrorists. Operators disdainfully call this a dog and pony show, however loved it may be by the brass. If one looks carefully at the dazzling displays, or better yet has the opportunity to spend time with these men, there are no Afro-Americans to be found, an absence even more pronounced than in U.S. special operations overall (relative to enlistment in the respective services). Not long ago — and going by testing at best dubious and by observation that may charitably be styled questionable — one of Delta's top commanders, naturally involved with the selection of his men, saw fit to assert that Afro-Americans are "too eager to please" and "to be in groups."[5] It is a conclusion that might have surprised the Revolution's Rhode Island raider Jack Sisson, or Ben Thompson, the One-Zero (leader) of a famed SOG Recon Team in Laos and Cambodia, and might possibly raise the eyebrows of the current Senior Captain of the Texas Rangers.

For our purposes, the restriction of choice in selecting an elite raises doubts that something may be lacking behind the unquestionable soldierly excellence, a certain lack of creative outreach in forming the very highest performers. Is there enough flexible open-mindedness to stay well ahead of some twenty-year-old thinking strange thoughts in Peshawar or Hamburg?

Like knowing when and when *not* to use a particular type of weapon, it remains important to recognize the limitations of the commando. It is as wise to question whatever role he may have as a fulfiller of policy as it is to be skeptical of the policymakers who frame the objectives. That notion of Washington "managing the world" or of the National Security Council as "the committee that runs the world," let alone the full-throttle perception of the United States as a world empire replete with "imperial grunts," is worse than naive.[6] We are setting ourselves up. The efflorescence of graduate degree programs in "national security" and the plethora of "task forces" at this foreign relations council or that think tank combines with the worst habits of America's last long war against totalitarianism (secrecy imposed, talent misdirected, money stolen, energy diverted from business and science, liberties restricted, confidence in government surely impaired) in a way that only an enemy would wish upon the defenses of a free republic. Tactical incompetences are hidden within an elaborate trellis of "security." The obvious is pursued much more than is the enterprising.

A few overworked, underinformed officials in Washington are not about to "manage" or "run" an ever more complex and not easily transformed world dense with new technologies and six billion people. And including the special operators as one key means of implementing such ambition carries with it the risk of initially small involvements that yet again metastasize into vast, sticky commitments.

Management is a great American contribution to life. It sets out to turn industrial, scientific, and political potential into organized advancement, usually of the citizens of industrial democracies or people who want to be. But it is a much less precise talent than generally believed, as in the breezy business review wisdoms of "managing" a corporation: Peter Drucker made a fine reputation demonstrating the sad realities. It is a term that at a stretch might be applied to the world economy, though the advance of chaos theory teaches us to walk modestly even there. It cannot serve as an organizing principle for the general hope of expanding liberal civil society worldwide or for tasking special operators to handle the levers of a supposed "empire," as has been proclaimed by too many journalists, professors, and excitable White House staffers who themselves have little experience in managing anything.

Lesson one of past decades is that other countries shape their own destinies to a far greater extent than Washington is prepared to believe. We had been spoiled by rebuilding Germany and Japan with their great, disciplined warrior cultures — no likely model for the rest of the world. And President Reagan, for his part, was decisive in pulling down a self-destructive totalitarian order but not in telling the world how to behave.

For the moment, the stature of the commando is high. It rests on soldierly achievement, rather than being regarded, as in the early 1960s, as the point man of a crusade. Today even the motto *De Oppresso Liber* and the pop-tune line "to die to make men free" ring tinnily from another era, as the more astute special operators acknowledge. Instead they regard themselves as superb technical professionals at the fine arts end of the business of war — delivering certain harm to the undeniably guilty who threaten their country and civilization. The nation does not see its special operators as existential wonder workers, as in the 1960s, but rather as something much closer to the American genius, superb problem solvers.

Clandestine forces must be deployed with extreme care, often more judiciously than conventional ones. They are a formless power that can all too easily be squandered.

In other people's countries, all large-scale military presences have a way of looking unpleasantly alike — certainly including American ones in the Middle East. Year by advancing year they fuel antagonism and themselves grow demoralized. The most minimal visible presence, keenly tailored procedures, and concentrated effectiveness combine to meet the requirement for hypereconomical means of violence or intimidation. When it comes to a matter of instilling fear, short of the apocalyptic ravages of nuclear weaponry, the most chilling sensations are best aroused by the blade in the night, rather than by even the most ruthlessly heavy-handed, mightily predictable main battle force. The enemy finds it more unnerving to prepare against the looming unknown of a deadly hand (who can tell where, when, and how it will appear?) than to face a large and anticipated offensive. Far more ancient than any merely human terror are the memories awoken of the tiger just beyond the firelight.

However, it may be trickier for the United States than for other nations to benefit from special operations capabilities, in which it is second to none. Today, all Pentagon war plans are required to have a special operations component. Admirable and sensible. But it remains unclear whether the military men in top command have themselves invested the amount of time, technical study, or attention to foreign peoples as is indispensable in this line of work. We recall the general who possessed a deep special forces background yet yapped about "my God was a real God and his was an idol" in recounting a battle with a Moslem warlord. We see another U.S. Army general, this time one of the most impressive of them commanding conventional forces in Iraq, musing that "Arabs' fear of dogs" might make the participation of such creatures a valuable tool of interrogation. (It is a cliché about people who appear different than oneself that might as well have come out of Selma, Alabama, in 1963.) Nor is it worth being told by the senior U.S. ground commander in Iraq that insurgents can never defeat Americans "on the battlefield": battlefields, as might be known, have nothing to do with it.[7]

Moreover, and perhaps most grave for the country's overall use of power, America may never solve the Achilles' heel of intelligence, meaning that the CIA as the core espionage and analytical organization beneath the National Intelligence Coordinator will take much more than the declared five years, if ever, to rebuild. Some administration officials claim this to be a problem "we [just] recognized after Iraq," which shows the limited curiosity of too many people drawn to careers in "national security."[8]

The country today may have a respectfully cool view of its special operators, in contrast with the excitement of the sixties. But the way they are often discussed in books and magazine cover articles, as well as in policy councils, puts them on a par with Lord-of-the-Rings heroism and magic. Thus it was when Bobby Kennedy treasured the souvenir green beret kept on his desk at the Justice Department. The literally enchanting vision of a national strategy conducted by functionally invisible, comprehensively trained military cadres spreading the American version of democracy might as well have come from Camelot.

Consider, for instance, writings that not only chronicle generally useful military training of what the discipline calls "indigs" (indigenous people) but that also perceive the world-shaping influence of America's special ops in the actions of its "iron majors . . . cementing friendships" in the back of beyond by gestures like handing out foot-long bowie knives to Yemeni tribesmen. Such writings would have made Kipling snort at the lack of sense about the dispassionate hardness of the third world.[9] Romanticizing commandos and what they can accomplish by developing "personal relationships" in, say, Mongolia, keeps confusing touristlike subtactical gestures with warily created — the better to be enduringly respected — overall strength and example. In revivals of America's role as a third world nation-builder, we again hear Kennedy-era rhetoric about special operators in Africa training "the local military to take the law into their own hands" (which hopefully means doing so for the sake of national stability) and being used "to help make a country."[10] Except civil societies do not rotate around their armies; armies are (regrettably) necessary components of many civil societies. And it is anyone's guess, whether the ambitions of these Green Beret– and marine-trained armies will coincide with U.S. interests to come.

Civilian cheerleaders are like a constituency of police buffs. Projecting themselves, such enthusiasts perceive those "iron majors" taking on the role of actual policymakers by default, whether by training foreign armies or by "constantly doing favors" for what are likely at best ephemeral friends whose emotions wax and wane with American power and commitment. Of course the man on the spot needs to make friends, bestow presents, even invite *el general* over for a barbecue. But such relationships need to be as correct as possible, not chummy — and placed in a wide perspective that might be found in the Marshalls and Eisenhowers but probably not in the "iron majors" of journalistic acclaim. One wants shrewd, cold-eyed civilians in air-conditioned offices behind the scenes to override the energies of even the most politically and culturally attuned warriors when it comes to actual policy — and all the more so in a world in which today's antiterrorist chief of police is tomorrow's drug magnate, yesterday's friendly dictator now in the slammer.

The worst danger of misuse comes from the fantasy-realist dream that these forces are the chosen instruments of "American empire," an entity that is not even close to taking material let alone constitutional form outside academic phrasemaking and political conceit.[11] Here too is a superb way for a liberal democracy to set itself up for disaster as policy influentials crow about America's responsibility for "imperial policing." Such noise echoes the self-satisfaction of the strong that opens the door to unhappy surprises from the ostensibly weak, like those little people who are being "policed."[12]

Primacy — which means to have the most powerful voice to assert one's interests, especially when largely defensive — is not empire. There is some final command authority in the term *empire* — "we're here, we're the boss, you can't get rid of us" — which is why it is misleading to style the United States as such. For starters, if a sovereign government cannot run its own finances — and is part of a larger financial system over which it has no veto — it is rather difficult to identify as an empire. Nor does an imperium endure exasperating clients who jerk it around for their own purposes (whether South Vietnamese mandarins, French *enarcs,* or coalition allies pulling out of Iraq). An empire can bring down the governments of its component parts, which is not quite the case in dealing with, say, Spain or Japan (and it is hard to imagine a genuine imperium allowing U.S. industry to learn quality control so painfully from the latter). Today U.S. commandos are deployed in more places than ever before. Yet America is much less "imperial" than at any time in the last half century. Can one imagine operatives now trying to stage poorly reasoned coups in Chile, Indonesia, Guatemala? And the general public's reaction when these facts came out?

The role of the special operations calling is to take steps that *de-*necessitate empire by rolling up a range of dangerous presences without having to deploy capacities of strategic magnitude. (So much of the terrorist's hope lies in the enemy's overreaction and overreach.) Special operators remove from the board certain elements eager to transform the destiny of one or another nation. Ultimately America does not have either the arrogance or the patience to behave imperially, which includes ever deeper involvement with the messy politics of foreigners. It is the pragmatic children of Henry Ford, not the expansive ones of Andrew Jackson, who are instead at work, as they have been since 1945. It is an ongoing attempt to solve a problem by establishing international arrangements (not an empire with its open-ended costs) in which the United States can rally or rent allies to build a greater level of common defense. And then focus on actual business at home and abroad.

To be sure, special operators can add a certain confusion of their own by presenting themselves as "global scouts," serving not only as the ultimate outreach for the highest officers who head America's overseas regional commands but as the invisible helpmates of U.S. ambassadors.[13] It is a posture by no means unqualifiedly endorsed by the dozens of State Department chiefs of mission who find themselves rather nominally heading the "Operational Control Elements" who work from code-accessed rooms within their embassies courtesy of these commands — linguistically adept operators who are responsible for coordinating with headquarters in Stuttgart or Panama such unusual actions as may be required "in-country," including so-called extraordinary rendition.[14]

That Delta Force tattoo in the Carolinas now being presented to U.S. ambassadors is an impressive display, but it does not mirror the even subtler solutions to international difficulties of which the best diplomacy can be capable. The enthusiasms that it reflects can be less than helpful.

As America's prime representatives in foreign countries, for example, ambassadors have always had full responsibility for supervising all U.S. government employees in the nation to which they are accredited, as well as the ultimate decision about who else working for the government can enter the place. One exception now exists: without the ambassador's being informed, special operators may be dispatched by an area combatant commander to neutralize any member of a list of roughly ten top terrorists (like bin Laden). As part of the "global war on terrorism" (briefly rebranded in 2005 as "the struggle against extremism"), however, the Pentagon keeps pushing to get significantly expanded operations into just about any country worthwhile. The argument is that commandos must move fast and stealthily without delay (or interference) brought by any civilian on the ground. Instances of this approach to date have not always been reassuring, the mildest being Green Berets in mufti being detained for illicit border crossings; they cannot be compared to the Pentagon's felt need to create its own intelligence capabilities to compensate for a faltering CIA.[15]

Repeatedly a combatant commander's eagerness to send in his special operators — or of U.S. Special Operations Command desiring to do so on its own sense of urgency — has been cut off by a savvy ambassador's ability to resolve an immediate problem (or eliminate a troubling individual) by working hand in glove with local officials. It is natural that such military officers put forth needle-sharp initiatives that, through no real fault of theirs, appear to reduce otherwise intractable international problems to operational works of art. Yet coming years will see increasing friction between the diplomatic arm and the special operators ready and eager to zoom in to apply their skills to most any problem that can be labeled as incipient terrorism.

There already is a further twist as the more confident of U.S. Foreign Service officers align themselves with the more capable among the CIA operatives attached to their embassies, all in an effort to confine the highly eager commandos to their effective spheres.

‡

IN THE end, it is America's homeland that is the most vulnerable in history. The country's achievements are so many, and so complicatedly woven: complex, liberal, with tremendous opportunities of all sorts to those who move fast, made with a trust in openness and enterprise. That is the secret of its success, but it could equally have been framed by the most likely sort of its early twenty-first-century enemies.

By their very nature, the most advanced nations find themselves doing these enemies' work for them, most directly by developing weapons whose technologies can be bought, stolen, or, eventually, duplicated — what scientists wryly call the "demonstration effect." Let one nation produce an observation balloon or an atomic bomb, and it somehow becomes easier for others also to generate gas or isolate deuterium. Worse because less predictable is the offering up of apparently innocent technologies that can be turned into weapons — airliners last time and who knows what next. The more integrated and rapidly advancing the world, the more often will open societies be creating the means that will be used by the "Little Folk" who hate them.

Many, perhaps most, of the substantial objectives in war are accomplished by great armaments. We have only to think of World War II in Europe (let alone on the Eastern Front) and the Pacific or the recent drive into Iraq. But time and again over the millennia, whole orders have been overturned or reshaped by the impact of special operations, evolving with the march of civilization. To recall merely four instances from so many, 270 men who climbed a harsh, never-before-scaled pinnacle in a storm twenty-four hundred years ago prevented Alexander from being stymied in the middle of nowhere. Much of medieval history would be inconceivable without the resourcefulness that tiny bands brought to taking castles or kings. And if Joan was not imparting the consciousness of a special force to conventional warfare — rather than conveying just another charge of knightly zeal to the French high command — who was? Heaven knows what would have happened in the Americas if the two great civilizations had not been brought down before they could adapt, in much less time than it took to lose in Vietnam. Even World War II would have been rather different without the calculated killing of Yamamoto or the fueling of democratic resistance in Occupied Europe as Communists struggled to wrest control of the underground movements.

To return to our original metaphor, we can consider the special operation as that effort by the small fellow to move the fulcrum of the seesaw on which squats the heavy machine gunner. Such is the general picture. But ultimately — whether it is Odysseus and his twenty-two heroes descending from the belly of the horse or Green Berets, Royal Commandos, and France's 1er RPIMa in Afghanistan — the operation comes down to the individual of heightened awareness, thinking hard as he or she out-tigers the tiger.

The hunt reaches into the beast's own dangerous terrain, into the thickness and gloom of the jungle that was made to hide and feed it. Yet, as when Corbett stalked alone with his spaniel and rifle, it is the target's confident mastery of its dense, well-defended surroundings that makes it vulnerable to the preyer upon predators who has imagined, planned, and willed that one noiseless step further. The tendrils and shadows that otherwise promise the longest of odds are instead made instrumental to the man-eater's downfall. It is a hunt without thrills or chest-beating, as Corbett exemplified — solely a service. Such knots of skill among men so few and daring as he — not simply more shooters thrown in to resolve a challenge so extreme — settled the destiny of villages millennia ago, and sometimes still do. But men and women applying very similar skills and daring in a high-stakes hunt against their own kind have also settled the destiny of nations, and may well keep doing so.

ACKNOWLEDGMENTS

I would like to thank Little, Brown's editor in chief, Geoff Shandler, for helping to guide me along the critical path through three millennia and Timothy Dickinson, unsurpassed bookman, adviser, and friend, for years of fascinating conversations about history, politics, business, and literature. Special gratitude is due to my dear sister Melissa, without whose encouragement, dinners, drinks, and early-morning walks the writing of this book might well have faltered.

There are three institutions with which I work closely: the U.S. Army Historical Foundation, Georgetown University, and Management Assessment Partners (MAP).

At the Army Historical Foundation, much has been learned about U.S. military history since 1945 — and about the army's current concerns — from the senior officers who also serve as directors. I am particularly grateful to the warrior-scholar Lewis Sorley for bringing me into the fold. Georgetown University has provided an academic home for more than fifteen years; President John DeGioia and Government Department chair Robert Lieber have been the most welcoming and stimulating of colleagues, while the university's superb reference librarians have been patient, consistent companions. Research assistant and doctoral candidate Meghan Guilino was a cool customer under the pressure of deadlines.

At MAP, my partners in Europe and the United States have tolerated the time I've chosen to devote to writing about war, conflict, and technology upheavals. Generously, they also understand that such research ultimately provides unique insights on elite leadership and streamlined organizations that are directly applicable to working with the world's most dynamic corporations. Here I'm grateful to Knut A.

Revling, Dr. Susanne Sachtleber, and Robert Coulam, as well as to CFO Anne Bohman.

The solitude of a writer's study is all the more welcome when he can sally out to enjoy the company of friends. I have been blessed with friends who are smart, courageous, and kind: Liaquat Ahamed, Leon Aron, David Braunschvig, David G. Bradley and his entire family, Jim Cravens, technology CEO Donna Farmer, Christopher Grey, Bobby Haft, Sam Holt of the Washington Literary Society, Chip Hunter, John Hauge, Waring Hopkins and Marie-Caroline Decazes van Herpen, historian Charlie McCain, Kerry Moynihan, Michael P. Ryan, Bob Sevigny, literary agent Joe Spieler, Jim Strock, Stacey Wagner, Marc Wall and Eunice Reddick, Jim Wallace, David Webster, Bruce Weinrod, Schuyler White. In one way or another, all have contributed to this book.

Professor Paul Doty, who founded Harvard University's Center for Science and International Affairs, must be acknowledged by a generation of scholars for enabling so many of us so early on to look at the world in new ways.

Finally, a salute to the late William T. Lee, who for decades was the foremost intelligence analyst of Russian military affairs; and also to friend and comrade Giles Whitcomb of the U.S. Navy who, in the long aftermath of Vietnam, finally gave his life for our country.

Derek Leebaert
Prangins, Switzerland
November 2005

NOTES

Chapter 1: Who Dares Wins

1. The conversations involving the secretary of defense were related in a June 2003 interview with Robert Andrews, a veteran Special Forces soldier and CIA officer who had been serving at the time as acting assistant secretary of defense for special operations and low-intensity conflict (SOLIC). He returned to the role of principal deputy assistant secretary, SOLIC, in 2004.

2. The complaints of the former CIA station chief are from his account of these weeks. See Gary C. Schroen, *First In: An Insider's Account of How the CIA Spearheaded the War on Terror in Afghanistan* (New York: Presidio Press, 2005), pp. 33–34, 159, 147–48, 300.

3. CIA was not authorized to conduct laser targeting is from ibid., p. 169. Green Berets were not permitted to dispense "lethal aid," as noted in the definitive account of the Afghan war, Naylor, *Not a Good Day to Die*, p. 72. As for Langley headquarters, a sea of sedans and minivans stretching to the horizon covers the parking lots daily. That only a fraction of them were filled on 9/12 is the angry observation of a senior agency officer (and adviser to CIA Director George Tenet) whom I have interviewed. The agency workforce is not subject to the rules or announcements of OPM, but guidance on liberal leave, as during snowstorms, is taken from it.

4. The maps would eventually be found, their loss to be blamed on the same unresolved agency computer system glitches that four years earlier had lost the names and addresses of hundreds of veteran retirees, many of whom were now asked to return to duty. Gus Weiss, recipient of the CIA's Medal for Merit and former member of the U.S. Intelligence Board, first related the loss to me in December 2001 after he too had returned to service post-9/11. This disclosure has since been cross-referenced.

5. The Republican president had nominated a weak yet politically connected candidate to be SOLIC assistant secretary, but she was vetoed by the chairman of the Senate Armed Services Committee, leaving the post unfilled through 9/11. This Washington consultant and former Hill staffer had been affiliated with a small law and political advocacy firm whose founder had just arrived as undersecretary of defense for policy. John Warner (R., VA) disapproved, though the feelings of her patrons would be salved by appointing her head of national counterintelligence for the U.S. government.

6. "Special Forces," when capitalized, means U.S. Army Special Forces, specifically, the Green Berets. "Special operations forces," often abbreviated as SOF, means all such modern military outfits. In this book we use *special force* and *special forces* (lowercase) as a convenience to describe commando outfits of various sorts, except for the Green Berets. Similarly with *operator* and *operative*. A "special operator" means a hands-on warrior; an "operative" usually means someone functioning at one remove, such as an intelligence officer or his agent. "Delta Force," as insiders remind us, is only a nickname. It is also known by its cover, Combat Applications Group, or, formally, as "JSOC." We use the popular description for convenience.

7. The American steep-skiing pioneer Chris Landry, for instance, has offered the standard definition of extreme skiing: "If you fall you die." See the *New Yorker,* April 18, 2005, p. 105.

8. For Churchill's views, see Cohen, *Commandos and Politicians,* pp. 35–37.

9. "Everyone wants a piece of the pie," explains the official historian of U.S. Army Special Forces at Fort Bragg, a former Green Beret holding a Ph.D. in history. Correspondence with John Briscoe, July 2004.

10. Achilles' warriors at Troy had an identifying name, the *Myrmidons* (Ants), and were commanded by the greatest warrior of the time, which gives them an elite overtone.

11. Peniakoff, *Popski's Private Army,* p. 164.

12. Consider how the outcome of one particular word weaves its way through languages, from being a digging tool (Greek root *spathe*) to a weapon (Spanish *espada,* sword).

13. Lawrence, *Seven Pillars of Wisdom,* p. 184. An excellent essay by Defense Intelligence Agency analyst Jeffrey B. White makes reference to both the bubble charts and to the Druze; see his "A Different Kind of Threat: Some Thoughts on Irregular War," *Studies in Intelligence* 39, no. 5 (1996), CIA Center for Intelligence Studies.

14. The definitive analysis of the workings of a coup are in Luttwak, *Coup d'État;* see pp. 21, 146.

15. W. H. Auden, "The Prince's Dog," in *The Dyer's Hand and Other Essays* (New York: Random House, 1948), p. 202. Interestingly, Arthur Koestler called his novel of the Special Night Squads defending Jewish settlements in Mandate Palestine *Thieves in the Night;* for them, too, the day of the Lord shall come.

Chapter 2: Even Troy Must Fall

1. Evidence for Menelaus's interest in throat-slitting is the *Ilias Mikra* (ca. 600 B.C.), fragment 19, in Davies, *Epicorum Graecorum fragmenta* (1988), Euripides, *Troades* 1054 ff., and the extensive artistic evidence (especially vases) for this part of the tradition.

2. As for conceiving of the Horse, Homer gives no credit to anyone else, while always casting Odysseus as the ultimate cunning figure of the besieging army. The only comparable person is Palamedes, who invented the game of checkers to alleviate the boredom of the siege (and who had tricked Odysseus into coming to Troy). But Odysseus had brought about his death well before the Horse was built.

3. The convenient number twenty-three for an attack party is offered by Tryphiodoros in *Taking of Ilion,* 152–83. Homer says "all the best of the Argives" were in it (*Odyssey* 8.52) but names only five. Virgil mentions only nine, *Aeneid* 2.261–64. Other early writings range from thirty to three thousand.

4. Yadin, *Art of Warfare,* p. 260.

5. Daniel 5:30–31.

6. We perceive such ignorance about chariots because Homer does not describe them as being able to cut through battle lines.

7. Victor Davis Hanson has engagingly explored "the Western way of warfare," as in *Infantry Battles in Classical Greece* (New York: Knopf, 1989), with his insights on free men fighting for what they know, pp. 10–11. For our purposes, however, it is Lendon, *Soldiers & Ghosts,* that is most illuminating. His short essay on guile versus frontal clash in the Greek world, "Bibliographical Notes," pp. 409–12, is indispensable.

8. Peisistratos's first takeover is discussed in Herodotus, *Histories* I.59, and in Plutarch, *Solon* 30.

9. Aristotle, *Athenaion Politeia* 14–15. Peisistratos was a formidable player overall. He seems to have doctored the text even of sacred Homer to endorse Athenian colonial claims. Only an extraordinary operator could have held power as he did, but it took a touch of the criminal mind to obtain it in the first place, let alone to twice restore himself.

10. Re bribes and Sparta, Gylippus himself was convicted of embezzlement and fled into exile.

11. Cartledge, *Spartans,* pp. 5, 7, 49.

12. Kagan, *Peloponnesian War,* p. 1.

13. The relative neglect of examining trickery and other special warfare characteristics in his field is strongly argued by Hellenist John R. Hale; see his "General Phormio's Art of War: A Greek Commentary on a Chinese Classic," in *Polis and Polemos,* ed. Hamilton and Krentz.

14. Henderson, *The Great War between Athens and Sparta,* pp. 134–35.

15. The description is offered by John Arquilla, a professor at the U.S. Naval Postgraduate School, in his anthology *From Troy to Entebbe,* p. 11; Kagan reminds us, however, that in fall 431 B.C. Pericles himself invaded the Megarid with 10,000 hoplites, a morale-boosting step well beyond pinpricks (*Peloponnesian War,* p. 73).

16. Thucydides says of this officer, Hippagretas, that he "lay among the slain for dead," notably not as wounded, which leaves no other explanation than wigging out (Thucydides, *History of the Peloponnesian War,* bk. IV, p. 30).

17. The innovation of flutes and fire must have been all the more surprising to the Athenians because for two thousand years, *Boeotian* meant "oaf." Hanson offers a detailed examination of the battle at Delium and its cultural significance in *Ripples of Battle: How Wars of the Past Still Determine How We Fight, How We Live, and How We Think* (New York: Doubleday, 2003), chap. 3, pp. 171–224. But discussion of the "special" in combat — here meaning the flamethrower — takes up only two sentences. See p. 184.

18. See Pritchett, "Scouts," in *The Greek State at War Part I*, pp. 127–33, and "Surprise Attacks," ibid., *Part II*, pp. 156–63.

19. I am giving a twist to the title of John Osborne's fact-based 1965 play, *A Patriot for Me*, about Austria-Hungary's Colonel Alfred Redl, who treasonously gave the Russians war plans before 1914. In the play, it is the emperor who asks, "Is he a patriot for me?" about his insider/outsider general staff officer, shown to be all homosexual and part Jewish. "Patriot for me" could also be a way that Redl defines himself. Certainly, it is Alcibiades's self-concept.

20. See Appendix B, "Glossary," in *United States Special Operations Posture Statement*, p. 113.

21. As cited in Hanson, *Wars of the Ancient Greeks*, p. 117.

22. Hanson, *Carnage and Culture*, p. 22.

23. Thucydides offers these insights on "the stupid" when he analyzes class warfare and revolution at Korkyra, as Burn observes, *Greece and Rome*, p. 61.

24. For discussion of the sources of creativity in the Greece of fifth century B.C., see Leebaert, "A World to Understand: Technology and the Awakening of Human Possibility," chap. 10 in *Technology 2001*, pp. 293–321.

25. For a general concern about applying the Peloponnesian War to big questions of today, citing such work by Hanson, see Miller, "My Favorite War," particularly her points about "finagling with Thucydides" (p. 23). However, some of the worst uses of history result when trying to discuss special operations today. For instance, Robert D. Kaplan's "Supremacy by Stealth: Ten Rules for Managing the World," *Atlantic Monthly,* July/August 2003, is riddled with mistakes of fact and poor conclusions about U.S. special operators. For starters, it is here that we learn that "Xenophon's Greek army cut through the Persian Empire in 401 B.C. . . . We should be mobile in the same way." In fact, Xenophon's army was retreating for its life. The U.S. Army does not aspire to "be mobile in the same way," losing 40 percent dead in the process. And to believe that "the United States is an international society comparable to Rome in the Second Century" is similarly outlandish. The foreign-born composed most of Rome's army, and these aliens came to Rome to rule.

Chapter 3: Birth of World Power

1. Wheeler, *Stratagem,* pp. xiv, 50–54. Trickery may go back to the start when, during the siege of the Capitol, the starving Romans convinced the Gauls they were well supplied with food by throwing away their last bread; see Frontinus, *The Stratagems*, p. 251.

2. Aristotle's influence on his headstrong young pupil was tremendous not in the professional or technical aspects of philosophy (about which Alexander could care less) but in Alexander's fascination with his tutor's vision of the vastness and variety of the world. Aristotle also poured all too much of his genius into dogmatizing the inferiority of barbarians everywhere, which is played out in Alexander's savagery.

3. Even in fighting Persia the Greeks had deployed brave but small armies, generally innocent of the deeper specialties that can be so valuable in the larger, more versatile forces that build far-reaching empires.

4. Green, *Alexander*, p. 201. This is a trick similar to what had been used when Pelopidas took back Thebes from Spartan authority in 379 B.C.; see Xenophon, *Hellenika*, V. 4.1–5.

5. Green, *Alexander*, re "commando raid," p. 208.

6. Ibid., re "quick commando assault," p. 230.

7. Ezekiel 9:1–8.

8. Victor Davis Hanson estimates that perhaps a quarter-million residents of the cities that opposed Alexander were massacred outright between 334 and 324, as his path drove deeper into Asia.

9. An excellent discussion of the geography, then and now, can be found in Fox, *The Search for Alexander,* pp. 298–302, 317–18.

10. Arrian, *Anabasis,* in *Life of Alexander,* sec. IV.18.4–19.6.

11. Ibid.

12. See Stein, *On Alexander's Track,* concerning the name and location of Aornos, pp. 115–16.

13. *Besieger of Cities* was a bestseller by historical novelist Alfred Duggan (1903–64), whose immensely popular fiction was grounded in meticulous research. Note that Demetrios also relied innovatively on advanced stone-projecting artillery as well as on an enormous siege tower, for example, in besieging Salamis, 307 B.C. Trapped in 285 B.C., he was encouraged to drink himself to death.

14. For those wanting to debate Cicero's originality, see his own admission in *De Officiis,* I, 2. A vain man, he nonetheless admits that it is not his philosophical originality but his eloquence that he brings to his philosophical writings. As for Rome's cannibalizing Greek plays, it is worth remembering that even Plautus had to deal with accusations of "contaminatio."

15. Fuller, *Julius Caesar*, p. 74. "One-armed army" is a description General Fuller uses frequently to describe Rome's shortcomings in cavalry.

16. See Campbell, *Greek and Roman Artillery*, pp. 22–23, on the republic and early empire relying heavily on Greek designs.

17. *The Business of War* is the title of Major General Sir John Kennedy's memoirs (London: Hutchinson, Heinemann, 1957), a phrase deliberately paradoxical given the British approach to war; "to liken war to business competition" was also an insight of Clausewitz's.

18. Lancel, *Hannibal*, p. 81.

19. Bradford, *Hannibal*, p. 61.

20. Lancel, *Hannibal*, p. 86.

21. Each town now has a delightfully colored, tourist-friendly Web site; see www.ossaia.com and www.sanguineto.com.

22. See Goldsworthy, *Cannae*, p. 180, re General Norman Schwarzkopf's inspiration for Desert Storm.

23. Livy, XXII 48, who uses the figure five hundred.

24. Bradford, *Hannibal*, p. 135.

25. However, the sculptures may be ideals, from which others were modeled; as for his height, Suetonius says that he was tall, but apparently, at the end, not sufficiently tall enough to parry the blows.

26. At least one eminent Roman, Calpurnius Piso, went into military command as a calling less exacting than the high-level forensic advocacy that was the main path to civilian fame and office.

27. Suetonius, *Julius Caesar*, LXXV. The defects of Caesar's generalship are impressively argued by Fletcher Pratt, an acute but largely forgotten popular military historian and pioneer of science fiction; see *Hail Caesar!* (New York: Smith and Haas, 1936), chap. 7.

28. Josephus, *Jewish Antiquities*, xix.1, 15 . . . 122.

29. Caesar, *Alexandrian War*, p. 13.

30. Caesar, *History of the Civil War*, II.149–154.

31. Archeologist Peter S. Wells provides the definitive account, explaining the battle's significance as Rome's failure to assimilate Germany to the Mediterranean south, in *The Battle That Stopped Rome*, p. 18; he emphasizes that by *Romans* is meant soldiers in service to the empire, which is the definition we use.

32. Velleius, *Roman History*, II.117ff.

33. Ibid., II, cxviii.2, pp. 298ff.

34. There are estimated to be some seven hundred theories about where the battle, or massacre, occurred. There are also different explanations as to how long it took. I have found Wells's account most convincing. For different versions see, for instance, Czech, "Rome's German Nightmare," pp. 24–31.

35. In turn, Rome could occasionally find itself on the receiving end of astonishing engineering — another Persian emperor, for instance, is said to have impounded a river on the eastern frontier until an immense amount of water had accumulated behind his dam, then released it all at once against the walls of the adjacent city of Nisibis (the modern Nusaybin, still occupying a sensitive frontier spot on the troubled Syrian/Turkish border, just over from Iraq) "like a tremendously powerful battering-ram"; see the Greek historian Theodoret in Dodgeon and Lieu, comps., *The Roman Eastern Frontier*, p. 165.

36. Frontinus, *Stratagems*, "Contaminating waters" is in Book III, stratagem 7, p. 227.

37. Vegetius, *Military Science*, IV.37, pp. 135–36.

38. Goldsworthy, *Roman Warfare*, pp. 182–83; the author also offers a superb explanation of the army's structure and evolution. The *superventores* are noted in Nicolle, *Medieval Warfare Sourcebook*, p. 28.

39. Rome's German-originated horseguards excelled but in smaller numbers; and the Arab long-range conquerors had yet to break out of their peninsula on the wings of Islam.

40. Norman Cantor makes this point about Rome's problem of plague and population in pp. 250–650 in his chilling *In the Wake of the Plague*, a riveting book with its single flaw being a stretch out of his field to offer "a lesson for the American empire today," pp. 190, 214.

Chapter 4: A Terrible Few

1. Jacques Barzun, in *From Dawn to Decadence*, p. 26, is among the historians who caution about using the term *feudalism* when examining medieval times, emphasizing that "vassalage did not necessarily imply a fief, that is, the possessing of land by the vassal." We nonetheless use the term to fit his concise definition of "the idea of loyalty between man and man, the strong feeling backed by an oath that bound a vassal to his lord for military service and other aid."

2. "Britain" means the "land of the painted people": the dying Roman order had a Commissioner of the Saxon Shore, taking his title from the raiders he was confronting, not the people he was defending. As

for Arthur's existence, the best evidence may be that only after 542 was "Arthur" a name given to youths of noble birth, neither it or its Latin version, *Arturus*, previously being known.

3. Eliade, ed., *Encyclopedia of Religion,* "Cattle," vol. 3, pp. 123–27.

4. Some of the vast literature from Greco-Roman antiquity survived to be reproduced frequently in the West, along with additions to military texts that would adapt them to Carolingian warfare. But truly original military treatises, such as quite a few still existing today from Byzantium, are absent. See Timothy Reuter, "Carolingian and Ottoman Warfare," in *Medieval Warfare,* ed. Keen, p. 19. As for technology, there nonetheless are examples of early Carolingian siege machines, as well as the famous attempt by combat engineers to build a Rhine–Main–Danube canal.

5. Bachrach, *Early Carolingian Warfare,* p. x. This is the definitive work on the subject, and chaps. 2 and 3, pp. 51–107, examine military organization and training. However, in R. H. C. Davis, *The Medieval Warhorse* (London: Thames and Hudson, 1989), the author takes issue with Bachrach's description of the use of cavalry in "search and destroy" missions, pp. 12–13.

6. On "covert action," see Bachrach, "Charlemagne," p. 322. In this essay the author explains the biannual meetings, the intelligence evaluation, and the role of senior military planners that he convincingly equates to high-level Pentagon procedures. Given the extent of domestic and political considerations that went into such deliberations, I instead make the comparison to the NSC.

7. Correspondence with Bernard S. Bachrach, August–September 2004.

8. Riley-Smith, *The Crusades,* p. 14.

9. I calculate this by assuming fifty to sixty people per square mile when densely populated; if 300–400 people got off the ships, the defender would have to concentrate 100–150 square miles worth of ill-trained peasants fit to bear arms.

10. Clancy, *Shadow Warriors,* p. 59. Different dates may be given for the first Viking descent. We use that of the assault on the monastery of Lindisfarne in northern England.

11. MacLean, *Kingship and Politics,* p. 17; see also Beeler, *Warfare in Feudal Europe,* p. 20.

12. Oman, *Art of War in the Middle Ages,* p. 53.

13. Had the sequence been different, it probably would have been Harald who won, and England would have been welded to a harsher, bleaker land, less open to what remained of the cultural influences of ancient Rome.

14. The definitive study of the crossbow is Payne-Gallwey, *The Crossbow;* pp. 43–44 discuss its appearance in fourth-century Rome. Payne-Gallwey does not detect a crossbow in the Bayeux Tapestry, though he argues they were used at Hastings. On the presence or not of the crossbow, I am grateful for the advice of Dr. Mathieu Chan Tsin, who has served as a tour guide for the Bayeux Tapestry. As for the role of the lone crossbowman as sniper, how such killers must have hid and shot is shown convincingly by the role of Schwartz Carl, in Howard Pyle's marvelously realistic 1888 children's classic, *Otto of the Silver Hand.*

15. Vegetius, *Military Science,* III, 26, p. 108.

16. Bloch, *Feudal Societies,* p. 83.

17. France, *Western Warfare,* pp. 49, 52.

18. At least three kings of England were liquidated in captivity during this period; more died simply worn out by rebellion. As an example of being "worn out," the extraordinarily capable Henry II gave up the ghost in his mid-fifties, when the very last of his several sons went to war with him.

19. "Strategic tricks" is Thomas Ohlgren's term in the introduction to his *Medieval Outlaws: Ten Tales in Modern English* (Stroud, UK: Sutton Publishing, 1998), p. xxviii; the pioneering work on the subject is Maurice Keen's *The Outlaws of Medieval Legend,* 1963. It is Ohlgren who explains the distinct nature of this literature.

20. Contamine, *War in the Middle Ages,* p. 44.

21. Ibid., p. 101.

22. Ibid., p. 219.

23. Ibid.

24. Norwich, *Normans in the South,* p. 140. Geoffrey of Malaterra offers a somewhat different version than Norwich as to how the Saracens were drawn out. See Hallam, ed., *Chronicles of the Crusades,* p. 49.

25. Riley-Smith, *The Crusades,* offers more detail (pp. 29–30); as for ropes, this is the Arab historian Ibn al-Athir, writing a hundred years later, as included in Hallam, ed., *Chronicles of the Crusades,* p. 81. "Elite force" is the description used in Madden, ed., *Crusades,* p. 42.

26. *Oxford English Dictionary,* "Assassins." English historian John Speed was writing about this "company" in 1611 during an age in which there was a burst of high-profile assassinations (including those of William of Orange and Henri III), as well as numerous attempts on lesser luminaries.

27. Lewis, *The Assassins,* p. xi, emphasizes the significance of virtually no use being made of more certain weapons. It is also significant, when exploring similarities between the twelfth century and today's operations, that Lewis's excellent, recently reprinted book was first published in 1967.

28. Contamine, *War in the Middle Ages,* p. 73.

29. Smail, *Crusading Warfare,* p. 128. However, the exception to such individualism and quests for personal honor can be seen among the Knights Templars and the Hospitalers, living and dying anonymously, without fame to be won. Yet there were never more than five hundred Knights Templars in the Holy Land, and they are remembered for fanatical cavalry charges, not special tactics. A good, well-illustrated overview is Holland, "Firebrands of the Franks," pp. 100–9.

30. Lewis, *The Assassins,* p. 11, notes (and discounts) this allegation. But the prospect of Barbarossa being stalked by assassins underlines the desperation of his siege.

31. Beeler, *Warfare in Feudal Europe,* p. 211.

32. France, *Western Warfare,* pp. 109, 112.

33. The extraordinary men who built and operated machines or dug mines — let alone those who made the final assault — "were rarely provided with the continuity that they needed to become coherent forces"; see ibid., p. 76.

34. Ibid., p. 73.

35. Payne, *The Dream,* p. 182. Payne's convincing argument is that Reynald, more than anyone else, was responsible for the fall of the kingdom; see sec. 4, "The Kings Born in the Holy Land." After generations of settlers held the land, the inevitability of its fall in the face of vastly more numerous and unreconciled Moslems can no more be asserted than, say, the inevitability of the eventual fall of modern Israel.

36. Ibid. Payne provides the figure three hundred (p. 193).

37. The records are ambiguous as to whether it was Saladin or one of his guards who promptly disposed of Reynald. But so concludes Runciman, in *History of the Crusades,* p. 460.

38. The God vs. God opinion is that of Lieutenant General William G. Boykin, a famously courageous soldier who fought in Somalia, delivered during a speech in 2002 while in uniform; see *New York Times,* August 20, 2004, p. A19.

39. Phillips, *The Fourth Crusade,* p. 147.

40. Payne, *The Dream,* quotes Geoffrey de Villehardouin's *Memoirs of the Crusades* to describe the moves of "scouting parties" and the impact of the flames (pp. 275–76). However, it is Phillips's description of Constantinople's penetration that is the most convincing, in *The Fourth Crusade,* pp. 249–57.

41. "Greatest crime" is from Runciman, *History of the Crusades,* vol. 3, p. 130.

42. See the *Cambridge History of Iran,* vol. 5, p. 441, where it is suggested that the practice of wearing mail out of such dread was widespread.

43. Andrew Ayton, "Arms, Armour, and Horses," in Keen, ed., *Medieval Warfare,* p. 196.

44. Cipolla, *Guns and Sails,* p. 17.

45. "the flower-de-luce [symbol of the French royal house]/enters Alagna; in his Vicar, Christ/Himself a captive," Dante, Purg. XX, 87ff.

Chapter 5: The Great Wheel Turns

1. Contamine, *War in the Middle Ages,* p. 214; Procopius, writing in the mid-sixth century A.D., may well be the greatest of the later Greek historians. Significantly for this example, he is one of the best-ever describers of architecture — it being extremely hard to make a structure clearly apparent by words alone. As for when the Renaissance ("rebirth") begins, British historians tend to date it from 1485 with the advent of the Tudors; many others trace its origins to the thirteenth century with advances in schooling, painting, literature, and experimental science. We'll stick with a date somewhere in between.

2. Interview with Wicklund, March 2005. The early hand-held guns, Wicklund explains, came in a number of sizes and required the least training of any kind of firearm. See also Payne-Gallwey, "Development of the Mediaeval Handgun," in *The Crossbow,* pp. 40–42.

3. Hale, *War and Society,* p. 150.

4. Hall, *Weapons and Warfare,* p. 17.

5. Racine, *Les Plaideurs,* act 1, sc. 1.

6. Oman, *War in the Sixteenth Century,* p. 69.

7. We can well conclude that these armies were "polyglot" insofar as Dante observed in his *De Vulgari Eloquentia* that in his time there were a thousand distinct forms of Italian.

8. Murson, *The Scottish Histories,* pp. 102–3.

9. Ibid., p. 104, citing Barbour. However, the Lanercost chronicle of 1201 to 1346 covering the eventful years of the Scottish wars of independence states that the garrison just surrendered after the commander's death.

10. Poul Anderson (1926–2001) was educated as a physicist and worked as a translator of Norse sagas and an author of science fiction. For our purpose of examining special operations thinking, he is to be remembered as the prolific creator of scores of alternative futures.

11. "Shadowing" compelled the invader to concentrate and be ready for battle rather than to wreak havoc through the countryside. On how the French benefited from becoming "strategic defenders," see Clifford Rogers, "The Age of the Hundred Years War," in Keen, ed., *Medieval Warfare*, p. 153.

12. "Escallon" and "Crathor" are not real cities. Jean de Bueil changed the name of all actual places in his text to avoid bringing attention to himself, since he felt that his book was meant to teach knightly values, not to highlight his career. For example, the siege of "Crathor" recalls events from the sieges of Orléans and Lagny-sur-Marne and also stands for the Château de Sablé, where de Bueil was held prisoner. We know this from the Favre/Lecestre edition of *Le Jouvencel* (Geneva: Slatkine, 1996), which contains a commentary by one of his followers, Guillaume Tringant.

13. Special warfare and particular operations by the daring and the few are laced throughout de Bueil's two volumes. See De Bueil, *Le Jouvencel*, vols. 1 and 2. We see early in vol. 1 how he begins to defy regular warfare, with the assaults on "Escallon" and "Crathor," on pp. 74–92. Descriptions of how to take a castle are offered in vol. 2, pp. 42–43, and the role of espionage in this type of conflict on pp. 217–19.

14. DeVries makes this argument in "Use of Gunpowder Weaponry." The chronicles cited are those of testimonies, as from the Duc d'Alençon, during her "retrial," or rehabilitation. Also on Joan, see Kelly DeVries, "Teenagers at War during the Middle Ages," in *The Premodern Teenager: Youth in Society, 1150–1650*, ed. Konrad Eisenbich (Toronto: Centre for Renaissance and Reformation Studies, 2002).

15. The best account has been Runciman, *Fall of Constantinople*. It may just have been replaced by Roger Crowley, *1453* (New York: Hyperion, 2005).

16. Ibid. Runciman explains that specially cast metal wheels were in fact used on the cradles.

17. See the entry for "Dumbarton" in the 1911 edition of the *Encyclopedia Britannica* and the entry on Richard Bannatyne in the *Dictionary of National Biography*, vol. 1 (London: Oxford University Press, 1921), p. 1058, concerning his "Memorials of Transactions in Scotland from 1569 to 1573."

18. Taylor, *Art of War in Italy*, p. 112. This sparkling volume (winner of the 1920 Prince Consort Prize) draws the rough distinction between 1494 and much of what came before, discerning a "desire to win" that exceeded the earlier "desire to fight," including the examples of camouflage and of donning enemy insignia.

19. Featherstone, *Armies and Warfare*, p. 48.

20. Hall, *Weapons and Warfare*, p. 216.

21. Part of Greece is still called the *Agrapha*, "the unenrolled," because for centuries the Turkish authorities rarely got their tax collectors or administrators back in one piece.

Chapter 6: War of the Worlds

1. The judgment of "most militarily successful states," which I used in the Introduction to introduce these societies, is that of historian Felipe Fernandez-Armesto, who also notes the large and successful armies; see his *Civilizations*, p. 395. Montaigne's denunciation of "mechanic victories" is found in his "On Coaches," in *Complete Works*, p. 884.

2. Accounts of the adventure come largely from the Conquistadors themselves, although some reflections have surfaced from the original Nahutatl, as compiled, for instance, in Leon-Portilla, ed., *The Broken Spears*, 1992.

3. Diamond, *Guns, Germs, and Steel*, chap. 3, and specifically pp. 68–74; Hanson offers the strongest argument for technical advantage in a gripping chapter, "Technology and the Wages of Reason," in *Carnage and Culture*, pp. 222–30. In *Warfare*, John Keegan concludes "it was their [the Conquistadors'] horses that gave the invaders the decisive advantage" (p. 339). But I also find this explanation unconvincing in contrast to the true advantages of speed, surprise, improvisation, deadly focus, and supreme confidence. If a few hundred regular European soldiers had had the advantage of a dozen M1 tanks against thousands of Aztec warriors with time to adapt in the mountains, it is still by no means clear that such invaders would have prevailed.

4. Gosse, *The History of Piracy*, p. 27.

5. Hemmings, *Conquest of the Incas,* p. 191; Thomas, *Conquest of Mexico,* pp. 399, 391.

6. Wedgwood, *Thirty Years War,* pp. 21–22.

7. Two gripping, historically sound movies, *Black Robe* (1991), about the Jesuits in Quebec, and *The Mission* (1986), about the Jesuits in Brazil, unconsciously show the classic individual qualities of behind-the-lines operators.

8. As noted by the ship's recorder in his journal on October 11, 1492.

9. Re "slaves," Spain's system of holding Indians in *encomienda,* to skirt laws against slavery, was essentially the same type of forced labor.

10. The number of ships and men that sailed with Cortés is uncertain. For one overview, see Cortés, *Letters from Mexico,* p. 456nn.

11. Thomas, *Conquest of Mexico,* p. 186.

12. For the Aztecs, Prescott tells us, "every war became a crusade"; see *Conquest of Mexico,* chap. 1. The grisly details of plucking out the heart, offering the thigh to the emperor, having the victim's captor eat the remainder, etc., are explained matter-of-factly by George C. Vaillant (father of the psychiatrist-author George E. Vaillant) in "Human Sacrifice," pp. 243–52.

13. Cortés, *Letters from Mexico,* p. 458nn. Pagden reminds us that accounts of the grounding of the ships vary. They may have been burned later.

14. Prescott, *Mexico,* p. 318.

15. Cortés, *Letters from Mexico,* p. 74.

16. Diaz del Castillo, *Discovery and Conquest of Mexico,* pp. 190–91.

17. Ibid.

18. Thomas, *Conquest of Mexico,* p. 435.

19. Gardiner, *Naval Power,* p. 62.

20. Again, accounts vary. Wax may have been used to plug the cannons' touchholes because of the rain. And we know that Cortés had already won over many of his opponents; see Cortés, *Letters from Mexico,* p. 474nn.

21. Prescott, *Mexico,* p. 523.

22. Thomas, *Conquest of Mexico,* pp. 399, 391.

23. This was not necessarily the temple of Huitzilopotchli, as Cortés relates in his Second Letter to the King (Cortés, *Letters from Mexico,* p. 134), since another towering edifice was closer.

24. Ibid., p. 142.

25. The severe fractures down the left side of the skull could be seen in 1946 when Cortés's remains were reburied at the Hospital de Jesus in Mexico City.

26. Cortés, *Letters from Mexico,* p. 145. It is hard to agree that in this battle, or during *la noche triste,* Aztec warriors were preoccupied by any "highly ritualized nature" of combat that might have given the Conquistadors some advantage, as argued by Keegan in *Warfare,* p. 110.

27. Gardiner, *Naval Power,* p. 89.

28. Diamond, *Guns, Germs, and Steel,* neglects to mention the equal impact on the Spaniards' vital Indian allies, p. 210.

29. Prescott, *Mexico,* p. 642; he also reached out to Santo Domingo to secure men and horses, boats, and more ships.

30. Cortés, *Letters from Mexico,* p. 212.

31. Certainly, concludes the historian who best decodes the saga of Cortés's greenwood flotilla, his "employment of combined operations, as he launched coordinated army and navy thrusts against Tenochtitlán, was the first and one of the most prolonged applications of such technique in recorded military history"; see Gardiner, *Naval Power,* p. 195.

32. Thomas, *Conquest of Mexico,* p. 454.

33. Gardiner, *Naval Power,* p. 128.

34. Leo Eaton, producer. "Conquistadors: The Fall of the Aztecs," PBS, May 9, 2001.

35. *The Catholic Encyclopedia* (New York: Robert Appleton Co., 1911), "Pizarro, Francisco."

36. Ian Heath, *Armies of the Aztec and Inca Empires* (London: Foundry Books, 2002).

37. Prescott, *Conquest of Peru,* p. 256.

38. My interview with Wicklund, March 2004. It is important to remember the combat limitations of the firearms of this era: Henry Hudson's explorers, for instance, had been badly mauled on the banks of his newly discovered river because a rainstorm doused their matches, while not affecting the Indians' bowstrings. And De Soto on his march to the Mississippi observed before he died that Indian bowmen could shoot many times faster, and more accurately, than his men with matchlocks.

39. Prescott, *Conquest of Peru,* p. 283. Given Cortés's example and subsequent victories, it is difficult to see this event as "marking the decisive moment in the greatest collision of modern history," as does Diamond, *Guns, Germs, and Steel,* p. 68.

40. Prescott, *Conquest of Peru,* p. 281.

41. This bizarre procedure was the *requerimiento,* or "requirement," compiled by jurists and theologians before any attack might legally be made on Indians. It gave them a (brief) chance to convert, though without benefit of an interpreter. When the document had been hammered out in Spain, one sensible grandee said he did not know whether to weep or to laugh, as cited in Cortés, *Letters from Mexico,* p. 454nn.

42. Hemmings, *Incas,* p. 42.

43. Parker, *Military Revolution,* p. 120.

Chapter 7: No Peace beyond the Line

1. Newer materials also brought improvements in the durability and strength of rope, making sail handling easier and requiring fewer men. Newer, more durable fabrics were developed for sailcloth. Hulls were improved, and the compass came into use.

2. Gosse, *History of Piracy,* p. 2.

3. In fact, the theme of piracy — including the activities of Drake, Morgan, Kidd, and others — has been used creatively to examine the governance of modern electronic communications; see the book on technology and rules by Harvard Business School professor (and fellow disciple of Ray Vernon's) Spar, *Ruling the Waves,* pp. 38–60.

4. Thomas, *Conquest of Mexico,* p. 146.

5. The British naval historian N. A. M. Rodger valuably reminds us that the quasi-independent states of Tunis, Tripoli, and Algiers were not truly *pirates* in legal status, and also that *reprisals* and *privateering* are not synonymous, each having distinct legal status. Even Drake was not a pirate to Spaniards but a *corsair,* given that they saw him as always working for the state. For the sake of clarity, as does historian Harry Kelsey, we nonetheless adhere to familiar usage. See N. A. M. Rodger, "The New Atlantic: Naval Warfare in the Sixteenth Century," in *War at Sea,* ed. Hattendorf and Ungar, pp. 240–47.

6. See Kelsey, *Sir John Hawkins,* pp. 18, 69.

7. Milton, *White Gold,* p. 6.

8. In his latest authoritative book, Rodger again explains that these raids were not piracy but "publicly declared war waged largely by private interests," and he even mentions a need for English "moderation." Given the recurring coastal invasions of England and the ceaseless slaving it is hard to see the case for moderation — or, really, the distinctions between *pirate* and *corsair.* See Rodger, *Command of the Ocean,* p. 22.

9. Milton, *White Gold,* pp. 13–15. Murad's name would be adopted by two subsequent and particularly infamous Barbary captains, one in the early seventeenth century, the other in the early nineteenth. Both were European converts to Islam.

10. Gosse, *History of Piracy,* p. 60.

11. As used in W. H. Fitchett, "Fights for the Flag," *Cornhill* magazine, February 1898, p. 148.

12. Gosse, *History of Piracy,* p. 115.

13. Kelsey, *Sir Francis Drake,* pp. 11, 32–33.

14. So much is vague about Drake's exploits in the Americas, starting here. While I have found Kelsey's biography to be the most convincing, another superb source on which I rely does not mention such a bluff during the entry into San Juan de Ulua. See Bawlf, *Secret Voyage,* pp. 36–37.

15. Bawlf, ibid., pp. 31–32, offers the other version of the story at Nombre de Dios, telling of a real treasure that Drake's party was unable to remove.

16. Although if he did not get as far north as British Columbia, as has been strongly argued, he likely then would have cut across to stop at Mindanao, the southernmost of the Philippine Islands. Bawlf, ibid., pp. 267–327, makes a powerful case for a very far "Northern Voyage."

17. See Keynes, *A Treatise on Money,* vol. 2, p. 157.

18. In her superb portrait of Drake, Lucy Hughes-Hallet writes of his "sense of humour" and jocular nature. But, as she additionally notes, and to me seems predominant, it was the humor of "the cat who suddenly lifts its paw and lets the mouse run"; see her *Heroes,* pp. 229, 274.

19. Kelsey, *Queen's Pirate,* p. 259.

20. Thomson, *Sir Francis Drake,* p. 185, notes the part of the allies.

21. Kelsey, *Queen's Pirate,* p. 265.

22. Arquilla, *From Troy to Entebbe,* pp. 12–21.

23. Hughes-Hallet, *Heroes,* p. 296, citing a Spanish customs officer.

24. Quoted in Fuller, *Military History,* vol. 2, p. 29.

25. This is how a penniless English squire longingly, if obliquely, puts his ambitions in what sounds like a euphemism for piracy; see Hugh Trevor-Roper, *Men and Events* (New York: Harper and Bros., 1957), p. 200, quoting Sir John Oglander's entry in his *Commonplace Book.*

26. Alexander Exquemelin (pen name of Dutch barber/surgeon/adventurer Henry Smeeks), *Bucaniers of America,* vol. 1, pp. 53–54. The book contains previously published writings of the late seventeenth century by several participants, including "Exquemelin."

27. Ibid., p. 52.

28. A wooden ship, after all, lies lower in the water and may offer gun or galley ports to climb through. Once ships have engines and turrets, they are more difficult to attack — the difference being that between breaking into, say, a house and a pillbox.

29. Exquemelin, *Bucaniers of America,* vol. 2, p. 11.

30. Earle, *Spanish Main,* p. 41.

31. Exquemelin, *Bucaniers of America,* vol. 1, p. 75.

32. "Whoever heard of a flagship," marvels one fine historian, "being sacrificed as a fireship?" See Earle, *Spanish Main,* p. 126.

33. Lane, *Pillaging the Empire,* pp. 114–19.

34. Gosse, *History of Piracy,* p. 162.

35. Exquemelin, *Bucaniers of America,* vol. 2, p. 9.

36. Gosse, *History of Piracy,* p. 170.

37. Detailed yet ultimately unconvincing arguments to the contrary have been advanced, notably by Rediker in *Deep Blue Sea,* chap. 6.

38. Convoy-keeping was one of the great institutional skills to come into being during these years, another example of the deepening of talents and transactions at the civil base of war.

Chapter 8: A Hazard of New Fortunes

1. Amerigo Vespucci, working for the Medici, and a German banking rival of the Medici, the Walsers, for a while laid hands on Venezuela — their principal operative got lost for seven years in the jungle and emerged only to be beheaded by Spanish authorities.

2. In the 1530s it was a capital offense in France to purchase the vernacular Bible.

3. Arnold, *The Renaissance at War,* p. 95.

4. "I consider the great loss which all chivalry doth suffer this day," said one of the Spanish captains as he pitched a pavilion over Bayard and brought the dying man a priest. See de Mailles, *History of Bayard the Good,* pp. 418–20.

5. Except, perhaps, in faraway Russia, which was evolving in its own way. See Brian L. Davies, "The Development of Russian Military Power, 1453–1815," in *European Warfare,* ed. Black, pp. 177–79.

6. For an American having a reciprocal club membership with the Cavalry and Guards in London, this observation can still be made on every twenty-first-century visit.

7. Parker, *Military Revolution,* in which he addresses such vulnerabilities, pp. 13–16.

8. Although still pretty inaccurate — and not improving significantly for many years — the musket's raw stopping power was able to rip through armor at two hundred yards, *if* it registered. An unsighted smoothbore at that range was probably as accurate with the eyes closed as open.

9. These sniping towers were used, for instance, during the 1573 attack on Haarlem.

10. Arnold, *The Renaissance at War,* p. 50.

11. Oman, *Sixteenth Century,* p. 385.

12. Ibid., p. 343.

13. Philip II refrained from a truly unique means of war — simply washing away the Dutch. Since most of the areas of rebellion lay below sea level, his field commanders suggested just breaking the dikes "to flood this country." Even he found that too extreme. See Parker, "The Etiquette of Atrocity," p. 19.

14. Motley, *Dutch Republic,* chap. 8.

15. More, *Utopia,* p. 90. The alternative, "chosen and picked young men," is from the Bedford series translation (Boston: Bedford/St. Martin's, 1999), p. 183.

16. Arnold, *The Renaissance at War,* p. 50, describes the boats differently.

17. Oman, *Sixteenth Century,* p. 545.

18. Montluc's book is *Commentaires,* ed. Paul Courteault (Paris: Gallimard, 1964); the High Court was known as the *Parlement.*

19. Mattingly, in *Defeat of the Spanish Armada*, pp. 215–24, shows us the extent to which the secret Committee of Sixteen rallied each of Paris's sixteen *quartiers* and was backed in turn by four hundred men with armor under their blouses and pistols in their sleeves.

20. The extent of Pentagon buzz over military "transformation" and its results under the defense secretary of the time are examined in "How Tech Failed," in *Technology Review* (MIT), November 2004. On earlier "transformation," see, for example, Wheeler, *Making of a World Power*. The designated years come from Black's conclusive definitions in *European Warfare, 1660–1815,* p. 32; Francis Bacon (1620), Selection, 373–74 (*Novum Organum,* aphorism 129).

21. Previously, medals would be given to everyone in a particular campaign, such as those Englishmen who fought the Spanish Armada. Charles I instead singled out men of both forlorn hopes and of those outfits that managed to destroy fireships. See the entry under "Medals," in *Encyclopedia Britannica* (1911), vol. 18, pp. 3–5.

22. Note the use of forlorn hopes during the Mexican War, as discussed in chap. 11. As applied today, although without the formal name, Maureen Dowd of the *New York Times* describes a highly similar team of firemen who prayed before heading up the stairs of the doomed south tower of the World Trade Center on 9/11.

23. General Smith's obituary, in the *New York Times,* January 13, 1967.

24. See Taylor, *War in Italy,* chap. 4, "Cavalry," in which he emphasizes that "specialization is indeed the word which best describes the development of the art of war at this period," p. 76, noting the example of the Venetian *stradiots.* Light cavalry in the early sixteenth century had an auxiliary character, hardly able to decide the course of a campaign.

25. Re shooting from hedges, see *Oxford English Dictionary,* "Dragoon."

26. That sweeping yet apt designation of "general war" is Munck's, in his *Seventeenth Century Europe,* p. 94.

27. Defoe, *Memoirs of a Cavalier,* p. 103.

28. There were ten soldiers of fortune altogether in the impromptu hit team, including a Scot, a Spaniard, and an Italian. Only swords could be used; firearms would have sounded the alarm.

29. *Low-intensity warfare,* usually so described by those not participating, is a modern military term for *guerrilla war.* The tie between Werwolf resistance during the Thirty Years' War and the brief Nazi experience after the 1945 surrender is made by Fritz, *Endkampf,* pp. 195–96.

30. See Trevor-Roper, *Plunder of the Arts,* particularly pp. 16, 40, 44.

31. Parker, *Revolution,* p. 41. In Roots, *Great Rebellion,* p. 127, we read, moreover, of "royalist groups appearing from nowhere" that took important garrisoned towns almost overnight: Carlisle, Scarborough, Pontefract, and (with some Scots who had their own agenda) Berwick.

32. Thomas Babington Macaulay, *History of England* (Philadelphia: Porter and Coates, 1885), vol. 1, p. 112. Loyalist fighters, Macaulay adds, were accustomed to "manly and perilous sport," an observation that underscores ties between extreme activities.

33. Defoe, *Memoirs of a Cavalier,* p. 226.

34. Cromwell may be remembered, wrote Macaulay, as "the greatest prince who has ever ruled England." See John Raymond, *The Doge of Dover and Other Essays* (London: MacGibbon and Kee, 1960), p. 56. In his Oxford tutorials, historian A. J. P. Taylor would add "far and away" to Macaulay's description of Cromwell as "greatest prince," Dickinson interview, June 2005.

35. The quotations are from Carlyle's *Letters and Speeches of Oliver Cromwell* and can be found in the *Oxford Dictionary of Quotations,* 2nd ed. (London: Oxford University Press, 1966), p. 167.

36. Boswell's father, Lord Auchinleck, to Dr. Johnson in *Boswell's Journal of a Tour to the Hebrides with Samuel Johnson* (New York: McGraw Hill, 1961), p. 376, although he used the Scots word *lith.*

37. Pepys, *Diary,* vol. 4, pp. 373–74.

Chapter 9: The Old World and the New

1. Brumwell, *Redcoats,* p. 25.

2. Ellis, *George Washington,* citing Washington in 1755.

3. "The cry for war was raised by the city of London," explains Thomas Babington Macaulay, "and echoed and re-echoed from every corner of the realm," in "War of the Spanish Succession," *The Edinburgh Review,* January 1833, printed in *Critical and Historical Essays* (New York: Dutton, 1927), p. 507. He also reminds Englishmen of the time how in awe their ancestors had been of the Spaniards (p. 491).

4. A good comparison between marines of the different nations, with reference to the "special force," can be found in the 1911 edition of the *Encyclopedia Britannica,* "Marine."

5. Brooks, *The Royal Marines,* pp. 1, 3.

6. Glete, *Warfare at Sea,* p. 55.

7. Churchill, *Marlborough,* vol. 1, pp. 105–6.

8. Cyril Field, *Britain's Sea-Soldiers: A History of the Royal Marines* (London: Lyceum Press, 1924), p. 49.

9. Marlborough had seen his share of sieges. M. d'Artagnan, the real-life hero fictionalized in the Musketeer novels, was killed a few yards away from him at Maastricht. See Churchill, *Marlborough,* vol. 1, p. 97.

10. Churchill, *Marlborough,* vol. 5, p. 432, as after the Battle of Oudenarde.

11. Black, *Eighteenth-Century Europe,* pp. 321–26.

12. For that most money-minded of great generals, as we know from his private affairs, it was a sum, says Macaulay gleefully, "which he doubtly never ceased to regret to the last moment of his long career." *History of England,* vol. 4, p. 70.

13. In his writings and lectures on seventeenth- and eighteenth-century warfare, Jeremy Black has addressed the problem of today's writers making twenty-first-century comparisons with naval "reach" of the time and other facile conclusions about empire. Yet R. Kaplan, in "Supremacy by Stealth," p. 78, again misuses history to argue that Venice "creat[ed] conditions for its own demise," whereas its empire fell because the Turks conquered its eastern Mediterranean holdings in a garden-variety clash of imperialisms — the Greeks hardly rose to apply Venetian values to local conditions.

14. Black, *European Warfare,* p. 110.

15. Brooks, *Royal Marines,* p. 51; John P. Roche, *Shadow and Substance: Essays on the Theory and Structure of Politics* (New York: Macmillan, 1964), p. 370, notes "mutinous crews" to argue for abolishing the USMC.

16. Harding, *Amphibious Warfare,* p. 169. Moreover, the lightest cannon that could profitably be used against stone fortifications of this era had barrels weighing 1.75 tons; the most effective piece, a naval gun straight off the fleet, weighed between 2.5 and 3 tons, not including all the paraphernalia of powder and gunners' tools.

17. Anson, *A Voyage round the World,* pp. 23–24. The authorship of these bestselling memoirs has been debated since Anson, like recent U.S. generals who have published celebrated memoirs, had a known aversion to writing.

18. Ibid., p. 25.

19. Shankland, *Byron of the Wager,* p. 241, this volume being one of the finest books on the history of the sea.

20. Anson, *A Voyage round the World,* p. 253.

21. *Dictionary of National Biography,* "Anson, George"; the prize from his circumnavigation consisted of thirty-two wagons laden with 298 chests of silver, 18 of gold, and 20 barrels of gold dust, amounting to about £500,000.

22. See *Dictionnaire de biographie française* (Paris: Librarie Letouzey, 1994), "Kerguélen de Trémarc."

23. Foster, trans., *Military Instructions,* Article I.

24. See Koch, "The Prussian Guards," pp. 110–11. Frederick's officer corps was more open to talent from below than the presence of semifeudal squireens in nearly all the top slots might indicate, and not all his troops were itching to desert, as shown by their holding together in night attacks.

25. Foster, trans., *Military Instructions,* Article XXI, "Of the Surprise of Towns," and Article XI, "Of the Tricks and Stratagems of War." One scheme was to dress a local big shot as a pauper, send him into the enemy camp, and, if he did not return on his own initiative with enough information, then to kill his family.

26. Duffy, *Military Experience,* p. 53.

27. Ibid., pp. 273–77.

28. Re "chess-like," the most eminent being Maurice de Saxe, *Mes rêveries,* written in 1732, but posthumously published in 1757. Re "messier," Parker, *Military Revolution,* p. 150, citing La Croix's "Treatise on Small Wars" of 1754.

29. Pierre-Joseph Bourcet, *Dictionnaire de biographie française,* vol. 6, p. 1422.

30. P. J. Thomas, *Mercantilism and the East India Trade* (London: Frank Cass, 1963), p. 10.

31. The Portuguese already had endured a similarly tricky time in Africa, being stalemated for generations on the Angola and Mozambique frontiers, despite adopting dispersed African tactics and recruiting African fighters. Worn out by fever and far from home, they were defeated on the Zambezi by natives armed with spears.

32. Lawrence James, *The Rise and Fall of the British Empire* (New York: St. Martin's Press, 1994), p. 125, citing Robert Orme's *A History of the Military Transactions of the British Nation in Indostan.*

33. Boxer, *Seaborne Empire*, p. 235. The intensity of struggle on even large islands is true of zoology as it is of politics and history. A species confined to an island will be wiped out unless it radically adapts. There is little room for retreat, and conflict is a fight to the finish. In human affairs, intruders have already made much effort to get to the island and will not easily depart. Their scope of offensive operations may also be greater than on a land mass because they can use seaborne power to strike from various directions.

34. Brumwell, *White Devil*, p. 100. In chap. 3, Brumwell offers an excellent analysis, "The Ranging Way of War," pp. 97–131.

35. Haefeli and Sweeney, *Captors and Captives*, p. 52. I am grateful to Professor Sweeney for personally explaining the significance of the *troupes*.

36. The ten officers and cadets and perhaps a half-dozen enlisted men were Canadian-born members of the *troupes;* the other French raiders were probably militiamen with experience as trappers. My correspondence and conversations with Professor Sweeney, History Department, Amherst College, September–November 2003.

37. See Church, *The History of the Eastern Expeditions.* Church was a copious note-taker. The most dramatic description of the Deerfield raid, as well as the most authoritative discussion of its context, is in Haefeli and Sweeney, *Captors and Captives,* Part III.

38. Ward, *Breaking the Backcountry*, pp. 32–43.

39. Once William Pitt took charge as a secretary of state in 1757, he became a singular driving force, able to focus and energize British policies toward victory.

40. The defeat is often explained incorrectly as an ambush; see a contemporary account in E. B. O'Callaghan, "Braddock's Defeat," *Documents Relative to the Colonial History of the State of New York* 10: 303–4.

41. The column's vulnerability to the Indians while on the march is convincingly demonstrated by Ward, *Breaking the Backcountry*, pp. 41–43. Brumwell, however, sees the march differently in his equally thorough study, p. 15.

42. See the excellent discussion of Indian raiders in Ward, *Breaking the Backcountry*, pp. 46–52.

43. Ellis, *George Washington*, pp. 25–26.

44. Loescher, *Rogers' Rangers.*

45. Hubbard, "Americans," p. 81.

46. Brumwell, *White Devil*, p. 11. The epic is known as the St. Francis raid — and Rogers thereafter was called "White Devil" by the Indians. The raid is the focus of Brumwell's stirringly written account.

47. Brumwell, *Redcoats*, cover material. He also describes the woodland raiding of rogue whites, pp. 171–79.

48. Duffy, *Age of Reason*, p. 281, citing William Smith, who had campaigned against Pontiac, and wrote, in 1766, *An Historical Account of the Expedition against the Ohio Indians.*

49. An excellent overview of Rangers' preparation and capabilities, including living off the land, can be found in McLynn, *1759,* chap. 10. A comprehensive biography on the life and times of Robert Rogers, the first since 1959, is forthcoming from John Ross, the noted writer on the considerations of risk. On speed skating, see Augustus Mason, *The Romance and Tragedy of Pioneer Life* (Chicago: Jones Bros., 1883), p. 193. The book draws on journals of those who had been present.

50. "Plan of Discipline," in *Journals of Major Robert Rodgers,* Dublin, 1769.

51. "Miscellaneous Notes on Rangers," compiled by Rene Chartrand, this document being the commissioning order from the Commander in Chief of H. M. Forces in North America to Rogers, in Boston, March 24, 1756, www.militaryheritage.com.

52. Brisson interview, March 2005.

53. Reilly, *Wolfe of Quebec*, pp. 223, 253.

54. Brumwell, *White Devil*, p. 184, citing the papers of one of Wolfe's brigadiers.

55. Among the many narratives of what has been described as the most dramatic event of the eighteenth century, the best remains Hibbert, *Wolfe at Quebec.* It is he who documents the one-woman-per-company order (p. 79) and the evidence of treachery (pp. 123–24).

56. Re "picked men," see Hibbert, *Wolfe at Quebec*, p. 126.

57. McLynn, *1759,* p. 302.

58. De Crèvecoeur, *Letters,* p. 46. I speculate that De Crèvecoeur was a sleeper agent because of the distinct peculiarity of a former French army officer farming — at this juncture — in upstate New York. However, an eminent student of Europe's eighteenth-century intelligence services, Jeremy Black, disagrees, as we discussed in February 2004.

Chapter 10: To Try Men's Souls

1. Ellis, *George Washington,* p. 111.
2. Randall, *George Washington,* p. 397. However, the French historian's priorities, as Randall does not mention, may have been skewed by lingering French fury over Washington's role in the spring 1754 expedition in which the French commander was killed in circumstances charged to be "assassination."
3. Smith, p. 24.
4. Randall, *Benedict Arnold,* p. 150.
5. Princeton University was then still called the College of New Jersey, the name being changed in 1896. A fine synopsis of Burr's role as a raider in 1777 can be found in the novel *Burr,* by Gore Vidal (New York: Random House, 1973), pp. 106–7.
6. Randall, *Arnold,* p. 152, notes the practice of distortion by British army clerks; Leebaert, *Fifty-Year Wound,* p. 222 re the U.S. distortion of modern maps.
7. Black, *European Warfare,* p. 43; Roberts, ed., *March to Quebec* (memoirs of John Joseph Hewnrym), p. 301.
8. Randall, *Arnold,* p. 164, re the biographer quotation.
9. Martin, *Benedict Arnold,* p. 138.
10. See Roberts, ed., *March to Quebec;* literate because mostly New Englanders and Bible readers, as in memoirs by common soldiers.
11. Martin, *Benedict Arnold,* pp. 160, 163. However, a smallpox epidemic that claimed about 100,000 lives was ravaging the continent. The British may have had no need to send any of the afflicted Arnold's way.
12. Ibid., p. 170.
13. Mahan, *War of American Independence,* p. 25.
14. Rogers, ed., *Hadden's Journal,* pp. 25, 29; James Hadden was a lieutenant of the Royal Artillery.
15. Ibid., p. 44.
16. Kirby, re "terror," p. 358.
17. Citing General Burgoyne in Black, *Eighteenth Century Europe,* p. 118.
18. One of the best books on the battle is Ketchum, *Saratoga.* In dispensing credit, Ketchum first notes Arnold, then the riflemen and light infantrymen (p. 404). His analysis of the horrific role and fighting style of the Indians whom the British unleashed is chilling (pp. 265–84).
19. Washington never appears to have submitted a strategic plan to Congress (nor did it ask for one), and he kept few records that might illuminate. Nor did he have true confidants, in contrast to the young men on his staff. On "predatory war," see McCullough, *1776,* p. 249.
20. Washington summarily hanged deserters and in New Jersey during 1780 quickly surrounded two hundred mutineers with a "special force" ready for that purpose, arresting the ringleaders and then marching them off to be shot by their comrades. Pancake, *Destructive War,* p. 155.
21. Ketchum, *Victory at Yorktown,* p. 75, quoting Washington's order to "Light Horse Harry" Lee, who organized the plot.
22. Ewald, *Diary of the American War,* p. 108.
23. Americans who engaged in rangerlike duties with Loyalist forces as "volunteer jaegers" risked being killed when captured, as we see in Dohla, *Hessian Diary,* p. 46.
24. Billias, *General John Glover,* records this appellation throughout a book that is notable for its use of Marblehead Town Records, orderly books, and the contemporary press.
25. Ibid., p. 104.
26. Benson J. Lossing, *Pictorial Field Book of the Revolution* (New York: Harper and Brothers, 1859), vol. 2, chap. 28.
27. *Providence Gazette,* November 3, 1821. Prescott would later be exchanged for General Charles Lee, abducted by Banastre Tarleton's raiding party.
28. On the Vietnam comparison, see Wiencek, *An Imperfect God,* who also discusses Washington's reservations about arming black soldiers and the general's belated acceptance of the fact, pp. 200–8.
29. "Market stoppers" were light troops used to prevent the smuggling of provisions into the city by Loyalists. See "Allan McLane," *Dictionary of American Biography* (New York: Scribner's, 1961), vol. 6, p. 113.
30. Dohla, *Hessian Diary,* p. 143, on "combed and powdered hair." Details of this kidnapping plot are unclear and obliquely recorded. Ketchum, in *Victory at Yorktown,* p. 87, cites the journal of Baron Ludwig von Closen but concludes that the mission was never implemented. However, that is open to debate given the sudden response.

31. In Vietnam, for instance, it was the revolutionaries' ability to overrun main battle units that dragged France to the table in 1954; twenty-one years later, it was not the Viet Cong who inflicted Communism on the South but superbly professional North Vietnamese armor and infantry divisions.

32. Ellis, *George Washington,* p. 129.

33. Pancake, *Destructive War,* p. 122.

34. Although vital, only two hundred of the "Over Mountain Men" were at this decisive battle, thereafter, as often happens with special outfits, entering legend as being the bulk of the force (interview, May 2005, with Robert M. Dunkerly, PIO, Kings Mountain National Military Park).

35. A highly creative warrior, Ferguson is also remembered for inventing a futuristic breech-loading rifle that enabled a man to shoot fast and reload while lying down. Only some one to two hundred of these fine rifles, perfect for woodland fighting, were used during the war and none at Kings Mountain; see Peterson, *A History of Firearms,* pp. 37–39. The illustrations, as of Ferguson's breech-loading rifle, are particularly helpful.

36. Potter, *Autobiography,* p. 54.

37. See the first-hand account in Roberts, as editor of *March to Quebec,* p. 56. Tarleton's Legion also had artillery and two battalions of British regulars to back up his cavalry and foot.

38. As for the "grotesque," consider John Hanson in Maryland sending "traitors" to be drawn and quartered and "lynch" deriving from Colonel Lynch putting down the Tories in the lead-mining area of western Virginia; the letter concerning arson was not sent, as explained in Thomas, *John Paul Jones,* p. 172.

39. Pancake, *Destructive War,* p. 203.

40. The death threats and a likely attempt are noted in Bass, *Green Dragoon,* p. 4. It is Bass who invented the nickname "Green Dragoon" and not the Patriots as commonly believed.

41. The real American presence at sea was that of the roughly 2,500 duly commissioned privateering vessels, carrying over these years perhaps 80,000 men (many times the size of the Continental Army), which by war's end had captured some 2,300 prizes. See Smith, *Marines in the Revolution,* p. 265.

42. Bremen, which had been eager to take advantage of Hamburg's dependence on British trade, received the first U.S. consul after the Revolution.

43. Smith, *Marines in the Revolution,* p. 139; Thomas, *Jones,* p. 158, quoting Lafayette on "terror"; Thomas, pp. 113–31, offers a far less laudatory description of the cruise of the *Ranger* than does the official history. Explanations of the Whitehaven raid vary in their details, but they are similar. My narrative uses the report from the *Cumberland Packet,* Whitehaven, April 23, as printed in the *London Chronicle,* April 28, 1778, p. 406 (Library of Congress microfiche).

44. Ibid., *London Chronicle.* The American traitor at Whitehaven had disclosed to British magistrates all specifications of the *Ranger* and the names of its officers.

45. See original documents of the mission in *Barbary Wars, Operations,* vol. 3, "Philadelphia, Destruction and Burning of." Nelson's tribute is featured most recently in "The Making of an American Hero," Stephen Decatur House Museum, exhibit, 2004.

46. The best analysis of the theories remains Allen, *Our Navy,* pp. 207–10; the heroic explanation of throwing the lantern, alas, is the least likely according to Allen.

47. For this special force within a special force, see Samuel Edwards, *Barbary General: The Life of William Eaton* (Englewood Cliffs, NJ: Prentice Hall, 1968), p. 189. However, the definitive work on the subject is Zacks's marvelously researched and written *Pirate Coast;* pp. 168–74 discuss the composition of Eaton's force.

48. See *Barbary Wars, Operations,* vol. 4 re Somers, p. 306; the best narrative of Eaton's battle is Zacks, *Pirate Coast,* chaps. 18–19.

49. Vidal, *Burr,* p. 107, re "fighting Indian-style"; Jefferson's belief is known from the records surrounding the trail and the intensity of his personally supervised prosecution.

50. Melton, *Aaron Burr,* p. 132.

51. Robertson, ed., *Reports of the Trials,* I:205–6.

Chapter 11: The Fate of Glory

1. Black, ed., cautions that we must remember the extent to which the Revolutionary Army's effectiveness was also a product of prerevolutionary change, a convincing argument he makes frequently and which is best distilled in his concluding chapter to *European Warfare, 1453–1815.* As for the immensity of the Revolutionary Army, it had grown to 983,000 men by 1793.

2. As in the American Revolution, few of the technological breakthroughs were applied to battle. Balloons, like rockets, and the submarine that Robert Fulton introduced to Bonaparte, required a deeper level of development before they would make themselves felt. The little-known role of aerial bombardment after the rebellious citizens of Venice tossed out their occupiers to restore a republic is discussed in *Scientific American,* March 1849, in the article "More about Balloons," p. 205. At the initiative of an Austrian lieutenant, hot-air balloons, each carrying thirty-three pounds of explosives, were launched with half-hour fuses over the very difficult-to-attack City in the Sea.

3. Pierre Chaunu, in Reynald Secher, *Le genocide franco-français: La Vendée-Vengée* (Paris: Presses universitaires de France, 1988), p. 24.

4. Joes, *Guerrilla Conflict,* p. 67, a superb book extending from the American Revolution to the Civil War.

5. The exile guerrilla camp, redolent of post–World War II U.S. operations, as against Cuba or China, is noted in Pocock, *Terror before Trafalgar,* p. 130.

6. Barnett, *Bonaparte,* introductory material.

7. Ibid., pp. 5–16.

8. Rodger, *Command of the Oceans,* on poisoning "his own wounded," p. 464.

9. Ibid., p. 464. Smith seems to have been working under orders from the Foreign Office, though Rodger does not speculate.

10. The best study of Smith's exploits and of the era's covert operations is Sparrow, *Secret Service;* on "Chouan practices," mercenaries, and infiltration, see pp. 181, 186, 190.

11. Johnston, ed., *In the Words of Napoleon,* pp. 324, 325.

12. De Marbot, *The Exploits of Baron de Marbot,* p. 13.

13. *The Annual Register* (London: Harding and Wright, 1807), p. 25, explained that their "business is to hover around the enemy and annoy him . . . like a vulture watches his prey."

14. Horne, *How Far to Austerlitz?* p. 101. Horne explains that this was before 1807.

15. Sparrow, *Secret Service,* makes these points about the Scarlet Pimpernel, pp. 22, 174–85, and names several of the operators on whom Baroness Orczy likely drew.

16. The science fiction story is "He Walked around the Horses," Piper, pp. 502–23.

17. Sparrow, *Secret Service,* p. 336.

18. The best analysis in English of d'Antraigues's mischief is Duckworth's marvelously researched *The D'Antraigues Phenomenon;* for Tilsit and for d'Antraigues's demise, see pp. 292 and 301–8. Re "papers," see Peter Dixon, *George Canning: Politician and Statesman* (New York: Mason Carter, 1976), p. 173. In *The Changing Anatomy of Britain* (New York: Random House, 1982), p. 240, Anthony Sampson convincingly alludes to the existence of such classified documents. Had they been released since, many would know.

19. Wellington's decision not to allow his artillery to shoot down Bonaparte is in Sir Edward S. Creasy's *The Fifteen Decisive Battles of the World* (New York: E. P. Dutton, 1937), p. 397, n 1. However, Bonaparte himself had no such inhibitions about killing commanders in the field, boasting, accurately or not, that he had laid the battery that cut down his mortal rival General Moreau, who had gone over to the Allies.

20. Churchill, *The World Crisis,* where he recounts conferring with Lieutenant General Lord Dundonald, Cochrane's grandson, to explore using "noxious though not necessarily deadly fumes," vol. 2, p. 72; Cochrane had recommended sulfur.

21. Most of the other thirty-eight men had left the *Speedy* for various reasons, not as casualties.

22. Cochrane, *Autobiography of a Seaman,* vol. 1, p. 365.

23. Ibid., p. 369.

24. Ian Grimble, *The Sea Wolf: The Life of Admiral Cochrane* (London: Blond & Briggs, 1978), p. 80.

25. Cochrane, *Autobiography of a Seaman,* vol. 1, p. 304, re "wooden case."

26. In Marryat, *Frank Mildmay,* p. 90. The factually accurate defense of the fortress of Rosas is explained thrillingly in chap. 7. Elsewhere in his writing, Marryat is able to describe convincingly how the murderous cunning of an everyman can thwart the vicious arbitrariness of the state, another point germane to special operations; see "The Story of the Greek Slave," in *The Pacha of Many Tales.*

27. The scale of the detonation, however, proved disappointing, probably again due to the difficulties of setting off a powder train in the absence of a modern fuse.

28. Grimble, *Sea Wolf,* p. 91.

29. This aphorism is attributed to Wellington; it isn't specifically documented but is believable because so perfectly in character.

30. Bryant, *Jackets of Green,* pp. 13, 32.

31. Carl von Clausewitz, *On War* (Princeton: Princeton University Press, 1976), p. 220; for staff college, see Huber, "Napoleon in Spain," pp. 91–92. Afghan experience is invoked in Chandler, *Napoleonic Wars,* p. 172.

32. Chandler, *Napoleonic Wars,* p. 172.

33. De Marbot, *Baron de Marbot,* p. 106.

34. G. H. Lovett, *Napoleon and the Birth of Modern Spain* (New York: New York University Press, 1965), p. 675.

35. Also, as in Vietnam, there was no overall command in Spain responsible for counterinsurgency or much else.

36. On the different identities, see Tone, *Fatal Knot;* on the extent of commitment, see Charles Esdaile, "Popular Mobilisation in Spain, 1808–1810: A Reassessment," in Rowe, ed., *Collaboration and Resistance,* p. 102; Esdaile, *Peninsular War,* re smugglers, p. 252.

37. The roughly 600,000 men were from every corner of his empire.

38. The description of Bonaparte re "advice" is from Kipling's "St. Helena Lullaby"; estimates of how many men went into Russia and came out vary widely. A concise comparison is in Joes, *Guerrilla Conflict,* pp. 122–23; Cossacks are described as "special operations forces" by Michael Dirda, a descendant, in *Book World,* March 2, 2003, p. 15.

39. An excellent chronology, as well as an understanding of the consequences, is found in Dague, "Henri Clarke"; see also Schom, chap. 14, "Malet's Malaise," in *Napoleon Bonaparte,* pp. 617–27.

40. Lefebvre, *Napoleon from Tilsit to Waterloo,* p. 363.

41. Some U.S. privateers, however, more than paid their way, one ship alone carrying off $5 million of English property; see Thomson, *Mercenaries, Pirates, and Sovereigns,* p. 10.

42. This has long been a description of the slave revolution that began in 1791 in what was then Saint-Dominique, and the phrase is used in Dubois, *Avengers of the New World,* p. 129. It hardly took British intervention in 1793 to incite mutual massacres in a war in which black revolutionaries, as Dubois explains, consistently used "ruse and ingenuity" against the weight of France (p. 295).

43. A "measure of war" because Britain, of course, was a great slaveholding empire; there was a confused and inaccurate notion that merely entering the home country and vessels of the empire freed any slave who set foot there. Not quite.

44. John McNish Weiss, "The Corps of Colonial Marines: Black Freedom Fighters of the War of 1812," paper delivered at the University of the West Indies, St. Augustine, Trinidad and Tobago, January 4, 2001.

45. Cochrane, *Autobiography of a Seaman,* vol. 2, p. 342.

46. Government securities became "consols," annuities from a Consolidated Fund.

47. House of Commons, June 2, 1818.

48. Grimble, *Sea Wolf,* p. 191.

49. Pocock, *Terror before Trafalgar,* p. 226. The rumor that Cochrane might rescue Bonaparte arose from Cochrane's proposal that the ex-dictator, who lived until 1821, would make a dandy Emperor of Brazil.

50. Wendy Hinde, *George Canning* (London: Collins, 1973), p. 385.

51. Barzun, *Dawn to Decadence,* offers a wider span of years "when Romanticism was the spirit of the age," roughly from the last decade of the eighteenth century through the first half of the nineteenth. In his incisive treatment of the phenomenon, "The Work of Mind and Heart," and subsequent chapters in pt. 3, he also notes the range of insurrections during 1830: Spain, Portugal, Naples, the Papal States, Poland, Belgium, etc. (see pp. 469 and 497).

52. Dumas' fictional operation figures the taking of a Dutch fortress in the sixth and final tale of the Musketeer series, *The Son of Porthos.* One could argue, however, that the first depictions might be those of Jean de Bueil long before.

Chapter 12: New Frontiers

1. Dawson, *Doniphan's Epic March,* is the definitive account of what was closer to a 5,000-mile trek led by Alexander W. Doniphan, a natural leader who, while in Santa Fe, was also the first administrator of a U.S. military government in conquered enemy lands.

2. Frazier, ed., *The United States and Mexico at War,* p. 419.

3. Wilson, *Colt,* p. 18.

4. Reid, *Scouting Expeditions,* p. 38.

5. Percival was at the time captain of the USS *Constitution* during its round-the-world flag-showing cruise. DaNang was where the USMC would come ashore in 1965. Percival took the city when he got wind that

the Minh Ming emperor of Vietnam was about to impale a French bishop; Percival is portrayed as the quasi-fictional hero of the first chronicle of the Corps, in Wise, *Tales for the Marines,* a book by a naval officer.

6. David Nevin, *The Mexican War* (Alexandria, VA: Time-Life Books, 1978), offers a detailed discussion of Major Sam Ringgold's "flying artillery," pp. 13, 26–27.

7. Reid, *Scouting Expeditions,* p. 53; the disdain for taking prisoners, in this case that of the celebrated Ranger Captain Samuel H. Walker, is also recorded in Oswandel, *Notes of the Mexican War, 1846–47–48,* p. 192.

8. Crawford et al., *Encyclopedia of the Mexican-American War,* p. 288.

9. Hitchcock, *Diary,* pp. 338, 343; Smith and Judah, *Chronicles of the Gringos,* pp. 229–30.

10. See U.S. Senate Doc. 7, 30th Congress, 1st Session, "Notes of a Military Reconnaissance," reprinted in Ross Calvin, ed., *Lieutenant Emory Reports* (Albuquerque: University of New Mexico Press, 1951).

11. Smith and Judah, *Chronicles of the Gringos,* from the journal of Daniel Harvey Hill, p. 257, his spelling.

12. Ibid., p. 262.

13. Ibid., pp. 496–97.

14. Mexico's guerrilla war is little known in the United States, but Irving Levinson breaks new ground in *Wars within War* (Fort Worth: Texas Christian University Press, 2005).

15. American dead, according to the U.S. Defense Department, were 13,283, most from disease and exposure, out of the 116,000 who served, an unusually steep fatality ratio, especially for a war of less than two years' duration.

16. Bernard DeVoto, *The Year of Decision: 1846* (Boston: Little, Brown, 1943), p. 15.

17. Lawrence, *Lawrence,* p. 142. The book is written by Lawrence's great-grandson, based on India Office records and on family papers that the author compiled during World War II. My description of Rasul Khan leading the Guides at Gorindghar builds on Younghusband, *Guides,* a history written by one of the Corps' commanders.

18. *Dictionary of National Biography,* "Hodson, William."

19. It was Michael Faraday, perhaps the most eminent experimental physicist in history, who offered the Admiralty's conclusion. See *Dictionary of National Biography,* "Cochrane."

20. Cochrane, *Autobiography of a Seaman,* vol. 1, p. 334.

21. The notion of the special force in the Crimea did not transcend the almost archeological form of the forlorn hope. We see thirty "Borderers," for instance, charging straight into the center of a Russian battalion to undo an assault of 6,000, as described in Warner, *Crimean War,* pp. 77–78.

22. Codman, *Crimean War,* pp. 84–85.

23. Crichton's *The Great Train Robbery* is riveting narrative fiction that uses the event's court records and that also cites the headlines. Though he makes these operatives considerably more interesting than they actually were, his understanding of life and criminal technique in Victorian England should satisfy any historian.

24. Hughes-Hallet, *Heroes,* p. 449.

25. Trevelyan, *Garibaldi,* p. 200.

26. Hughes-Hallet, *Heroes,* p. 484.

27. Dennis Mack Smith, *Garibaldi* (Westport, CT: Greenwood Press, 1956), p. 98.

28. See Alfred Vagts, *The Military Attaché* (Princeton, NJ: Princeton University Press, 1967) for the best discussion of how such activities evolved.

Chapter 13: Strange Fulfillments

1. The Tennessee campaign was considered vital because it could rally a sympathetic population in that region and drive a wedge between Georgia and the Carolinas.

2. References for quotations and narrative of the raid draw on the original accounts in "The Locomotive Chase in Georgia" by the Rev. William Pittenger, a participant from the 2nd Ohio, in *Battles and Leaders of the Civil War* (New York: T. Yoseloff, 1956), pp. 709–16; see also his book *Capturing a Locomotive;* note also "Marion Ross and the Great Locomotive Chase" by Scott Sanders, Antioch University archivist, privately printed.

3. Canada was only united in 1867, under the shock of the Union victory. That it called itself a Dominion when it did so was a scared concession to U.S. republican sensibilities.

4. Brandt, *Burn New York,* p. 71; on yellow fever, see Ann Larabee, *The Dynamite Fiend: The Chilling Tale of a Confederate Spy* (London: Palgrave Macmillan, 2005), p. 49.

5. *New York Times,* November 27, 1864.

6. Brandt, *Burn New York,* p. 32 re West Point; *New York Times,* March 26, 1865; *Brooklyn Daily Eagle,* March 25, 1865.

7. Mosby's unsettling presence may best be reflected on the monstrously misrepresenting cover of a dime novel that came out in the moment of Union victory — dousing his bed at the Astor House with "Greek fire." Ramage records this woodcut from *Jack Mosby, the Guerrilla* in his definitive biography, *Gray Ghost,* p. 5.

8. General Order 100, also known as the Lieber Code after a law professor at Columbia, was adopted by the War Department in 1863. There had been substantial codification of the laws of war over the centuries, but this was the first pertaining to armies in the field and would be emulated in Europe.

9. Ramage, *Gray Ghost,* p. 19.

10. Mosby, from his *Reminiscences* and *Memoirs,* as collected in Connelly, *On War and Leadership,* p. 53.

11. Ibid., p. 54.

12. Ibid., p. 56.

13. Mosby, *Mosby's War Reminiscences,* p. 145; to understand how the Mosby legend has developed, see Ashdown and Caudill, *The Mosby Myth.*

14. Connelly, *On War and Leadership,* p. 63.

15. Ramage, *Gray Ghost,* p. 194, quoting General Sheridan; Custer was a colonel until October 1864.

16. See Tidwell, *Come Retribution,* pp. 3–29. Although much of Tidwell's evidence is circumstantial, as would be expected when researching an enterprise for which records were unlikely to be kept, this book by former U.S. intelligence analysts makes a powerful argument for such a plot. As another provocative and seriously researched volume on the assassination reveals (in accord with Professor William C. Cooper, dean of Jefferson Davis biographers), Davis knew of Booth's "kidnap" plot and at least did nothing to stop it. See Higham, *Murdering Mr. Lincoln,* p. 112.

17. Garibaldi's Army of the Vosges is described as being composed of 10,000 *francs-tireurs* in Ridley, *Garibaldi,* p. 604.

18. Studies for an outlandish German joint naval-military occupation of the U.S. east coast circa 1889 are in H. H. Herwig and D. F. Trask, "Naval Operations Plans between Germany and the USA, 1898–1913. A Study of Strategic Planning in the Age of Imperialism," in Paul Kennedy, ed., *The War Plans of the Great Powers, 1880–1914* (London: Allen and Unwin, 1979). See pp. 42–43.

19. Russian plans to cut British communications are in Paul Kennedy, "Imperial Cable Communications and Strategy, 1870–1914," in Kennedy, ed., *The War Plans of the Great Powers,* p. 78.

20. In the Manitoba rebellion, the *Métis,* a classic marginalized frontier people (offspring of French trappers and local Indians), clashed with authority now imposed by Canada's new national government.

21. On page one, "race" is the explanation given for Boer tenacity in Doyle, *The Great Boer War.* Doyle formed this judgment while serving as a doctor in the war. His book collects many of his writings from the field.

22. Major General J. F. C. Fuller so titled his book. See Fuller, *Gentlemen's Wars.* Like Doyle, Fuller served in the war. An example of this gentlemanly behavior is the Boers' handing back a badly wounded British general and expressing concern to his wife.

23. *Reader's Encyclopedia of American Literature,* 2nd ed. (New York: Harper Collins, 2002), "A Message to Garcia." By comparison, the sales of that worldwide modern publishing phenomenon, *The Da Vinci Code,* are a measly 25–30 million copies.

24. Ralph Waldo Emerson had delivered inspirational lectures about the subject of enterprise, but he was not addressing a business audience. His line about "a better mousetrap," for instance, was apparently extracted from lectures to women.

Chapter 14: From Spark to Flame

1. The exhortation was used by future prime minister Ramsay MacDonald, after World War I, on the triumph of socialism.

2. In fact, the much-misunderstood Pax Britannica was an epoch of peace that happened to occur over the years when Britain's was the most pervasive presence in the world. Its power was significant, but the Pax was not shaping the world system nor did it hold up the peace, let alone put an end to slavery, however hard it fought the slave trade. The last slave to be returned to his owner by a British court, however briefly, was in 1927. That is why popular comparisons of this sentimental illusion to a supposed "Pax Americana" are so bizarre now; for instance, journalist Max Boot argues that troubled lands today

"truly cry out for the sort of enlightened foreign administration once provided by self-confident English-men in jodhpurs and pith helmets." See Emily Eakin, *New York Times,* March 31, 2002. Lest one think he is joking, the notion of Britain as having been "the world's policeman" is repeated in his *Savage Wars of Peace: Small Wars and the Rise of American Power* (New York: Basic Books, 2002), p. xviiff.

3. Good numbers can be found in Fischer, *Germany's Aims,* pp. 35–36; and in Ferguson, *The Pity of War,* pp. 90–95.

4. Kaplan, "Supremacy," has asserted, "A hundred years ago the British Navy looked fairly invincible for all time," p. 68. In no part of the nineteenth century would a British naval officer have agreed. A hundred and five years before Kaplan's revelation, for instance, there had been hysterics at the Foreign Office when it was thought a French invasion fleet was already at sea. Lord Salisbury went so far as to mock the navy's reluctance to contemplate taking on the Dardanelles forts in 1890 by saying he had not realized British warships were made of porcelain. See Taylor, *Struggle for Mastery,* p. 361, n2.

5. Fischer, *Germany's Aims,* p. 126, quoting von Moltke, nephew of the chief of the general staff in the Franco-Prussian War.

6. What we know today as Britain's storied police unit, the Special Branch, originated as the Special *Irish* Branch in 1883 against Fenian terrorism (my italics).

7. See Churchill, *World Crisis,* vol. 1, pp. 47–49.

8. See Dupuy and Baumer, *Little Wars of the United States* (New York: Hawthorne Books, 1968). Max Boot's *Savage Wars* is very similar in its case studies, arguments, and conclusions about "little" or "small" wars, terms soldiers abhor.

9. About the Philippines, 1899–1902, Boot, *Savage Wars,* p. 128, concludes it to be "one of the most suc-cessful counterinsurgencies waged by a Western army in modern times," as if such "modern times" has relevance to, say, 2002, and then he wraps up with lessons for U.S. policies today — again aping nine-teenth-century British practices "to defend and to expand the empire." "If Americans cannot adopt a similarly bloody-minded attitude, then they have no business undertaking imperial policing today," p. 347, a view dated no sooner than it was written.

10. Not that the science of Indian fighting had actually been studied in the service schools, its brutal practices being unknown to Clausewitz or Jomini, whose texts were the wisdom of these years. What was known of it came from the different personal experiences of certain senior officers.

11. Farrow, *Mountain Scouting;* Gates, "Indians and Insurrectos," pp. 59–68; Linn, *Philippine War.* "Very recent experience" included the twenty-five-man reconnaissance unit known as "Young's Scouts," ten of whom received the Medal of Honor for rushing a bridge that had been set afire by some six hundred *Insurrectos* over an unfordable river at San Isidro. However, these heroes were not special operators as we now think of them. They were from the 1st North Dakota and 2nd Oregon Volunteer Infantry regiments.

12. Dupuy and Baumer, *Little Wars of the United States,* pp. 91–92, denounce "do-gooder backfire" in the United States against "essential 'third degree' methods"; Max Boot, "Torture at Gitmo? Ask the Mau Mau," *Los Angeles Times,* Latimes.com, June 30, 2005, again echoes Dupuy and Baumer but gets British military history wrong in the process. In chap. 17, we will see how torture has been anathema to the SAS from the start.

13. An excellent study of Aguinaldo's capture is offered by the superb Research Historian of the Army Historical Foundation, Sellinger, "Desperate Undertaking."

14. One of the best analyses of Saudi Arabia remains Robert Lacey's *The Kingdom* (London: Hutchin-son, 1981). The raid and the assessment compose chap. 3, pp. 39–52.

15. Ibid., plus personal discussions; during my first visit to Riyadh, in 1970, I was taken by several of Abdul Aziz's many grandsons to Mismak's nail-studded door. Tellings of the Great Adventure were arranged, offered in intricate detail by children of the original forty.

16. Letter from Vice President Theodore Roosevelt to Frederick Funston, March 30, 1901, Research Archives, Home and Museum of Major General Frederick Funston, Iola, Kansas.

17. Re Foch's reputation for immediately massing 100,000 men on a 120-by-100-meter rectangle, see Liddell Hart, *Foch: Man of Orleans* (Boston: Little, Brown, 1932), p. 22.

18. Italy may have suffered the most devastating defeat in colonial history when an entire army was wiped out by the Ethiopians at Adowa in 1896.

19. A. J. P. Taylor to his student, Timothy Dickinson. From Dickinson interview, 2005.

20. America's Civil War had been studied in Europe, but the two sides once divided were not regarded as great powers. There might be some useful cavalry insights from the Shenandoah Valley or lessons from Lee's offensives, yet surely the American experience did not apply to truly scientific twentieth-century possibilities.

21. Liddell Hart, *Foch*, p. 44.

22. Major General Sir Edward Spears, *The Picnic Basket* (London: Secker and Warburg, 1967), p. 32.

23. This was an immense national rumor, really a mass hallucination, starting in California, of strange flying machines descending on the United States. See Daniel Cohen, *The Great Airship Mystery: A UFO of the 1890s* (New York: Dodd Mead, 1981).

24. As one brave British Guards officer remembered of his years at the front, officers of elite units could issue the most inane orders in the exhaustion of combat and have their stupidest of utterances be regarded as profound. See Chandos, *Memoirs,* pp. 85–90.

25. Glorney Bolton, *Pétain* (London: Allen and Unwin, 1957), p. 93.

26. The spider at the center of this particular web, known as "Apis" (Dragutin Dimitrijevic), apparently had planned an outrage in Sarajevo to embarrass his own government. As we think about a limited special operations alternative to Austria's ultimatum, however, David Fromkin observes that Vienna had in any event started drafting its plan "to crush Serbia two weeks *before* Sarajevo." Fromkin makes this point in his definitive *Europe's Last Summer,* p. 160.

27. The cableship was the *Telconia;* see Spar, *Ruling the Waves,* p. 143.

28. Roskill, *Hankey,* vol. 1, pp. 96, 146–51.

29. See Churchill, *World Crisis,* vol. 2, pp. 81–83, re misapplication of the tank as seen by its senior patron.

30. Hopkirk, *Like Hidden Fire,* p. 58.

31. Fischer, *Germany's Aims,* pp. 143–44. The committee was led by a sociologist and approved by the Zionist League in Berlin but turned out to be more concerned with securing Jewish rights within the Central Powers. Others in the German government also did not want to anticipate postwar territorial adjustments.

32. Hopkirk, *Like Hidden Fire,* p. 103.

33. Sykes, *Wassmuss,* p. 44.

34. Ibid., see chap. 11. Sykes interviewed several of the Persian and German combatants, though Wassmuss died in 1931. There is also an excellent review by W. Adolphe Roberts in *New York Herald Tribune Books,* August 16, 1936.

35. See Fromkin, "T. E. Lawrence," for the most insightful interpretation of Lawrence's significance.

36. Liddell Hart, *T. E. Lawrence,* p. 208.

37. Lawrence, *Seven Pillars of Wisdom,* p. 215.

38. Max Boot, "What Makes Some Soldiers 'Special?'" *Washington Post,* op-ed, November 6, 2002, imagines Lawrence dressed so as to avoid being an easy target in a British uniform, except that Lawrence's flowing native garb itself stood out from his advisees.

39. Connelly, *On War and Leadership,* p. 87.

40. Tormenting the Turks in the desert may have done little more to win the war than did duels of special operators in Iran and Afghanistan. However, the British command fighting in Palestine — the capture of Jerusalem, the three battles of Gaza — was glad to have a mobile flying arm on its flank. See Robert Blake, *The Decline of Power: 1915–1964* (New York: Oxford University Press, 1985), p. 50.

41. For my reference to "comprehend," see Drury, *German Stormtrooper,* p. 4. Drury's excellent analysis also examines the stormtroopers' weapons, tactics, and role within the German army.

42. Ibid., p. 6. Drury notes that these other two titles were considered but not why they were rejected.

43. See the poignantly illustrated Frantzen, *Bloody Good,* for how states portrayed the ideals of knighthood, although the author stops short of addressing himself in detail to the stormtroopers.

44. Rommel, *Attacks,* p. 126. This is the unabridged translation of Rommel's *Infanterie Greift An,* first published in 1937.

45. In 2003, during a seminar at Georgetown University, I explored the tie between Rommel's World War I innovations and the next war's commando action with one of my former thesis advisers, the military historian Sir Michael Howard. He also discerned the influence.

46. Erich Ludendorff, *Ludendorff's Own Story* (New York: Harper and Brothers, 1920), vol. 2, p. 326.

47. Chatterton, *Q-Ships and Their Story,* p. 3. In the next war, Germany would use nine heavily armed raiders (flying neutral or Allied flags), disguised so as to strike unsuspecting tankers or freighters. This was indeed surprise and deception, but the victims were hardly "the strong."

48. Q-ships accounted for just 10 percent of U-boat sinkings but had a larger impact on their performance. That Germany was able to maintain the numbers of her undersea fleet to the end only shows its ever-decreasing effectiveness; the same number of submarines simply could no longer choke the seaways.

49. Arquilla, *From Troy to Entebbe,* p. 171.
50. Stock, *Zeebrugge,* p. 6.

Chapter 15: Sinister Twilight
1. Fromkin, p. 6.
2. Churchill, *The World Crisis: The Aftermath,* p. 241.
3. Dunsterville, *The Adventures of Dunsterforce,* p. 9.
4. Lucas, *Kommando,* p. 11.
5. Among these Soviet operatives, for instance, was Mikhail Borodin, to be known in the West as "Stalin's man in China," instructing Ho Chi Minh, as well as Chiang Kai-shek, just before Chiang found anti-Communism more profitable.
6. Likely after pressure from the White House, the State Department's entire Division of Eastern European Affairs was abolished in 1937 and its library dismantled. "Here, if ever," says Kennan, "was a point at which there was indeed the smell of Soviet influence, or strongly pro-Soviet influence, somewhere in the higher reaches of government" George Kennan, *Memoirs 1925–1950* (Boston: Little, Brown, 1967), p. 85.
7. Fuller, *Military History,* vol. 3, p. 380.
8. Significant pieces of Maginot's creation, not least some impressive fortress guns, were judged worthy of maintaining against the Red Army right through the late 1960s, with U.S. support.
9. The most exciting book on Italian seaborne special operations draws on Italian, German, British, and U.S. archives. It is Greene and Massignani, *The Black Prince and the Sea Devils.* The clandestine accomplishments of World War I are described on pp. 1–8.
10. Ibid., p. 11.
11. William H. Burgess, "Assessing Spetsnaz," in *Inside Spetsnaz,* ed. Burgess, p. 4.
12. Owen A. Lock, "The Spanish Civil War," ibid., p. 47.
13. One of the best descriptions of this combat is Byron Farwell, *The Great War in Africa, 1914–1918* (New York: Norton, 1986). The Germans did not surrender until three days after the armistice.
14. Lucas, *Kommando,* p. 25.
15. Kurowski, *Brandenburgers,* p. 10. This is a translation of a superbly detailed and somewhat troubling book, based on interviews with surviving commandos and members of the Nazi foreign intelligence service. The author states his purpose to be "to establish the good name" of the Brandenburgers and to "prove that the accusations made against them are groundless," p. viii.
16. The tie between Alvin York and Gideon is interesting. York may have been the best shot in Fentress County, but he was close to being a conscientious objector, only persuaded to fight by a commander who spoke gently with him about the Bible and the great Judge. See Roosevelt Jr., "The Sword of the Lord and of Gideon," in *Rank and File.*
17. The twist of "Dalyrimple" is that the young man's boss is so impressed by his having stuck it out dutifully in the stockroom for a year that the political machine backs this hero/clerk secretly turned burglar for the State Senate, with higher office certain to follow.
18. Holt, "Joint Plan Red," pp. 48–56; see also Holt, *Naval Warfare,* pp. 169–70. Alternatively, there were experts who concluded it to be "about as unthinkable that we should enter armed conflict with our nearest neighbors across the Pacific [Japan] as it is that we should go to war with our nearest neighbors across the Atlantic [Britain]." So said Thomas W. Lamont, the banker who served as director of the Japan Society (*New York Times,* January 6, 1928).
19. Robert Sherrod, *History of Marine Corps Aviation in World War II* (Baltimore: Nautical and Aviation Publishing, 1987), p. 3.
20. To discerning analysts, however, Gallipoli was not a definitive refutation of amphibious warfare, only an encyclopedia of how not to do it.
21. Moskin, *The U.S. Marine Corps Story,* p. 221.
22. After World War II, U.S. investigators heard that, once in the Palau Islands, Ellis was nonetheless able to move in with a native girl, apparently drank heavily, and spent his time prowling around Japanese installations. One morning he was said to have gotten "crazy drunk" and then to have died by 5 P.M. on May 12, 1923, on Koror. The USN suspicion was poison. The insane pharmacist's mate was killed later that year "in the Tokyo earthquake." A good overview of the case can be found in Moskin, ibid., pp. 219–23.
23. Calvacante interview, March 2005. Millett, *Semper Fidelis,* pp. 325–26, on Ellis's influence on USMC practices.

24. "Mars," of course, is the 1938 Orson Welles broadcast of "War of the Worlds"; Mons and the hoax of the German projectionists are discussed in Melvin Harris, *Investigating the Unexplained* (Amherst, N.Y.: Prometheus Books, 2003), p. 221n; Fussell explains the British origins of the canard about the angels in his classic *The Great War,* pp. 115–16.

Chapter 16: So Far, the Main Event

1. The point about guerrillas in World War II being able to be handled like "regular units" is made in Heilbrunn's classic *Warfare in the Enemy's Rear,* p. 204.
2. Interview with Robert Andrews, previously and currently Principal Deputy Assistant Secretary of Defense, SOLIC, 2003.
3. This segment of BBC history was explained to me by historian Alan Bullock (Lord Bullock), initially a member of the BBC's wartime European Service. St. Catherine's College, Oxford, 1980.
4. Kurowski, *Brandenburgers,* pp. 69–71. In the invasion of Norway, a unit of the Brandenburg battalion had infiltrated a week before the invasion using commercial airliners, merchant ships, and ferries, disguised as tourists, seamen, and diplomats. The Brandenburgers reconnoitered and, at the moment of invasion, were in place to seize buildings and create chaos.
5. My explanation of the Eben Emael assault builds on Part II, Selected Evidence, of the 1992 report for the Office of the Secretary of Defense, "A Systematic Review of 'Commando' (Special) Operations, 1939–1980," pp. 1–34, by C&L Associates. In addition to Eben Emael, units in disguise penetrated to the bridges at Nieuport to secure sluice gates to prevent flooding; other units disguised as refugees (their weapons hidden in prams and trucks) mingled with fleeing civilians to seize bridges and create chaos.
6. Mosier, *Blitzkrieg Myth,* p. 128.
7. The two German construction companies that had helped build Eben Emael, the firms Hochtief and Dycherhoff & Widmann, are today thriving multinational corporations.
8. McRaven, *Spec Ops,* pp. 57, 39.
9. Ibid., p. 55.
10. Maass, *Netherlands at War,* p. 35; Heilbrunn, *Warfare,* p. 60.
11. "The Breakthrough in the West," in B. H. Liddell Hart, ed., *The Rommel Papers* (New York: Harcourt, Brace, 1953), p. 20.
12. The Paris raid is from Kurowski, *Brandenburgers,* using original interviews, p. 51. The number of French casualties that follows is from May, *Strange Victory,* p. 7.
13. Churchill, *The Second World War,* vol. 2, p. 217.
14. Stafford, *Secret Agent,* p. 10.
15. One creative example of Nazi propaganda exploiting collateral damage is a poster of Joan of Arc burning at the stake, the apelike English dancing around her. In the background is seen Rouen in flames as bombers with the Allied roundels soar overhead: *Les meurtriers retournent toujours aux leurs crimes* ("Murderers always return to the scene of their crimes") the caption cries.
16. Parker, *Commandos,* p. 33.
17. After the war, Americans wanted those deer rifles returned, which was one of the early controversies surrounding the ongoing Combined Chiefs of Staff.
18. To state — in the Washington think-tank world's effort to use history for making policy recommendations — that Marshall "ruthlessly discarded the old for the new" by firing dozens of army generals and scores of colonels after becoming chief of staff in September 1939, is wrong. The myth was repeated by Colonel Douglas MacGregor, USA, at a Security Policy Working Group conference concerning "The Effect of Recent Military Operations on America's Armed Forces," October 19, 2004. During the five months of severest pruning in 1941, only thirty-one colonels were dropped; generals tended to be reassigned. I am grateful to Larry I. Bland, editor of the George C. Marshall Papers, for this observation.
19. Young, *Commando,* p. 145. The author is a British Army brigadier who was a founder of the commandos.
20. Parker, *Commandos,* p. 115.
21. Ibid., p. 37.
22. Special Service Companies were formed first in 1940, soon redesignated "Independent Companies," then formed into Special Service Battalions under HQ Special Service Brigade, reporting to Combined Operations HQ: the battalions were named commandos in 1941 and, by 1944, had been constituted as commando brigades.
23. Stephen Dorril, *MI6: Inside the Covert World of Her Majesty's Secret Intelligence Service* (New York: Free Press, 2000), p. 20.

24. Millar, *Waiting in the Night*. First published in London the year before, this is a classic account by an SOE operative of his wartime work in France. The Germans always referred to the men and women of the Maquis as "terrorists." Had the French and Polish resistance been able to strike at their enemy's civilian targets such as restaurants or apartment houses — as do real terrorists today — there is no doubt they would have done so. But neither had such reach into Germany.

25. Stafford, *Secret Agent*, p. 60.

26. Despite the importance of the Suez Canal, Britain's generals were instructed in 1940–41 that, if the choice had to be made, it would have to be sacrificed to save Iraq's oilfields. At least until 1948, the priority to defend Suez and the Gulf — rather than Europe — as the core of British defense strategy can be seen in records of the Chiefs of Staff and in discussions with their U.S. counterparts. Examples in the U.S. National Archives include November 4, 1948, JP (48) 130, "Meeting of U.S. and British Planners, Washington, 18–26 October 1948," and, in Britain's Public Records Office, COS (48) 130, Defe 4/16, September 17, 1948.

27. The pivotal role of New Zealanders is noted by the most discerning of critics. See Peniakoff, *Popski's Private Army*, p. 12.

28. Ibid., p. 64.

29. Clark, in *The Fall of Crete*, p. 54, reprints the "Ten Commandments of the Parachutist," Commandment Eight being to "grasp the full purpose of every enterprise, so that if your leader be killed you can yourself fulfill it." Being the "German warrior incarnate" are the final three words of Commandment Ten.

30. On trucks, see Lucas, *Kommando*, p. 86. For further details of the invasion, including Germany's failed plans for naval reinforcement, see the definitive study, Beevor, *Crete*.

31. Alanbrooke, *War Diaries*, p. 169.

32. In March 1945, during the tactically successful yet high-casualty Operation Varsity, the U.S. used gliders and paratroopers to smash German defenses from the rear on the east bank of the Rhine in the war's last airborne deployment. See historian Matthew J. Seelinger's excellent article in *On Point*, Fall/Winter 2005, pp. 9–17. But the Germans were the only ones to bring off strategic airborne missions: it was the same combination of big ideas and incisive analysis that gave them primacy in the missile and the armored assault.

33. Moss, *Ill Met by Moonlight*, pp. 22–23, 101.

34. Ibid., p. 174.

35. The unlikely alternative of kidnapping Rommel à la Kreipe was also a possibility. Major General J. F. C. Fuller, perhaps the most profound British military thinker in uniform, all along protested bitterly at the prospect of assassinating enemy commanders. But an unfortunate October 1939 article in the British fascist newspaper had compromised his authority. His argument linking the moral decay of concentration camps with that of commando raids against generals can be seen in Fuller, *The Second World War, 1939–1945* (Margate, UK: Eyre, 1948), p. 407.

36. Parker, *Commandos*, p. 68.

37. Ibid., p. 90. St. Nazaire was the raid about which Mountbatten was most proud, recalling that it could "only be attempted because it . . . appear[ed] to the enemy to be absolutely impossible to undertake."

38. The Americans and Canadians collaborated to create a joint 1st Special Service Force ready to operate as small raiding groups in snow-covered regions. As for the attack by canoes (or kayaks) on Bordeaux, it was led by C. E. Lucas Phillips. His book, *Cockleshell Heroes* (London: Heinemann, 1956), is a classic of commando literature.

39. King, "Rangers," p. 21.

40. The term is taken from the title of Ross's definitive and marvelously illustrated *Supercommandos*.

41. The raid on Makin Island by the USMC's Second Raider Battalion was led by Lieutenant Colonel (later Brigadier General) Evans Carlson. He had been one of FDR's "favored agents" as the president's personal correspondent with Mao Tse-tung's Communist guerrillas in China during 1938. Another was William Donovan, who would lead the OSS.

42. Christopher Bayly and Tim Harper, *Forgotten Armies: The Fall of British Asia, 1941–1945* (Cambridge, MA: Harvard University Press, 2005), pp. 134–35. What followed the fall of British colonial Malaya and Singapore, notes Benjamin Schwartz, was yet again the vastly worse "medieval sadism of the Japanese." See his review of *Forgotten Armies* in the *New York Times Book Review*, April 17, 2005.

43. See Powell, *The Third Force: ANGUA's New Guinea War, 1942–46*, p. vii.

44. Fiction may best reflect Fertig's special accomplishments. See Baldwin, *The Fighting Agents*.

45. Hogan, *U.S. Army Special Operations*, chap. 4, p. 5.

46. PBS, "The American Experience," Edwin Ramsey interview, re MacArthur acknowledgment in Tokyo, 1947; on the private army of Donald Kennedy in South Georgia, see Walter Lord, *Lonely Vigil* (New York: Viking, 1977), pp. 168–91.

47. Davis, *Lightning Strike*, p. 253. Davis explains how the after-action reports of the American as well as Japanese pilots conflict about what precisely occurred during these ferocious ten minutes.

48. This quotation is offered in Samuel Eliot Morison, *The Two Ocean War: A Short History of the United States Navy in the Second World War* (Boston: Little, Brown, 1963), p. 274.

49. Two fine books document what Hitler expected to be a two-year sabotage campaign: Dobbs, *Saboteurs*, pp. 32–33; Abella and Gordon, *Shadow Enemies*, which also uses FBI archives.

50. Smith, *OSS*, p. 2.

51. Ibid., p. 33. The importance of British assistance was Donovan's conclusion. In *The Jedburghs: France, 1944, and the Secret Untold History of the First Special Forces* (New York: Public Affairs, 2005), Will Irwin describes OSS training in the Catoctin mountains near what is now Camp David, pp. 46–52.

52. Ibid., p. 7.

53. Ibid., p. 57. Forgoing assassinations, OSS provided other crucial assistance to the landings, known as Operation Torch.

54. A good collection of recent oral histories can be found in O'Donnell, *OSS*. However, the book needs to be used with caution, as explained by the CIA History Staff's Clayton D. Laurie in *Studies in Intelligence*, CIA Center for the Study of Intelligence, vol. 49, no. 1, 2005, pp. 67–70.

55. Padfield, *Doenitz*, p. 412, citing SS-Sturmbannführer Macher (my italics).

56. MacDonald, *Heydrich*, pp. vii, 182.

57. The German numbers are from Bartov, *Hitler's Army*, pp. 364–65; Soviet dead are from Stephan, *Stalin's Secret War*, pp. 41–42; the 228 number includes German allies by June–July 1944, compared to much fewer in the area of Normandy after D-day. Also see Richard Overy, *Russia's War: Blood upon the Snow* (New York: TV Books, 1991), p. 289. The book is based on the BBC documentary of the same name.

58. On the obscure and otherwise poorly studied special operations force Kampfgeschwader 200, see Thomas and Ketley, *KG 200*. KG 200's ground/air operations in France are examined on pp. 100–09.

59. Ibid., on NKVD paratroopers, see pp. 79–80; on operations, see pp. 135, 180. On the rail-line attacks, see also Kurowski, *Brandenburgers*, pp. 87–97.

60. Shepherd, *War in the Wild East*. Shepherd focuses on the Wehrmacht's 221st Security Division, one of five operating in the Army Group Center Rear Area. His definitive work examines sinking training levels and morale and notes on p. 170, for instance, how Soviet mine-layers with machine pistols kept outgunning German riflemen in close combat.

61. My explanation of Maikop builds on work for the Office of the Secretary of Defense, C&L Associates, pp. 147–68.

62. *Kommandobefehl*, October 18, 1942, circulated by General Alfred Jodl the following day. He also swung at Nuremberg for promulgating the Commissar Order to execute Soviet apparatchiks, amid other crimes.

63. Skorzeny, *Secret Missions*, p. 11.

64. Ibid., pp. 19, 141, 146.

65. McRaven, *Spec Ops*, p. 180.

66. An apt description of Skorzeny as a "terrorist" is offered by Hugh Trevor-Roper, *The Last Days of Hitler* (New York: Macmillan, 1946), p. 87. That General Student was most responsible for the rescue of Mussolini is shown in Lucas, *Eagles*, chap. 10.

67. Skorzeny, *Secret Missions*, p. 144.

68. Macksey, *The Searchers*, pp. 237–239.

69. Hoffmann, *Hitler's Personal Security*, p. 248.

70. It is inscribed in Latin: *Nos a Gulielmo victi victoris patriam liberavimus*. Literally, the translation would be "We, having been conquered by William, freed the land of the conqueror." Only one of the SAS dead is over thirty.

71. Skorzeny, *Secret Missions*, p. 222.

72. Part of the order is reprinted in Lucas, *Kommando*, p. 128.

73. For the special force command structure and the fit with partisans, see Heilbrunn, *Warfare*, p. 97. Significantly, Eisenhower approved the use of SAS teams in France in the manner they thought best, overcoming objections of conventional commanders who hoped to throw them into the front lines. On Skorzeny and the National Redoubt, see Thomas and Ketley, *KG 200*, p. 165.

74. On "witless comparisons," see Daniel Benjamin, "Condi's Phony History," *Slate*, August 29, 2003. Following the U.S. invasion of Iraq, comparisons were made by National Security Assistant Rice and

Defense Secretary Rumsfeld between alleged mere "pockets of resistance" and Nazi "werewolves," as in these officials' August 2003 speeches to the VFW. However, the three to five thousand deaths experienced in Germany during 1945–47 were from essentially no organized emanations of *Werwolf* activities but rather from small-scale acts of local intimidation and violence, including those so justifiably exacted by Jews. See Fritz, *Endkampf*, pp. 197–207. Had *Werwolfs* appeared, there would be a shelf of books on how the U.S. Army put them down.

75. The postwar "prosperity" of the SS is underscored by the fact that 85 percent of the SS members who served even at Auschwitz got away scot-free. New light is thrown on this place of horror but also on the unaccountability of the perpetrators, in Rees, *Auschwitz*. Note Rees's chronicle of the contented career of one Rottenführer (corporal) Oskar Groening and also his observations on the absence of retribution, pp. 274–78. On "rumors" of Skorzeny, see Joachim Fest, *Speer: The Final Verdict* (London: Weidenfeld and Nicolson, 2001), p. 314.

76. Hogan, *U.S. Army Special Operations,* chap. 5, p. 2.

77. Ibid., chap. 4, p. 10.

78. *Paris Match,* May 26, 2004, *Debarouement la Merre des batailles,* p. 68.

79. Hogan, *U.S. Army Special Operations,* chap. 3, p. 3.

80. Webster, *Burma Road,* p. 238, quoting Stilwell.

81. Alanbrooke, *Diaries,* p. 436.

82. Tulloch, *Wingate in Peace and War,* p. 24.

83. Rooney, *Wingate and the Chindits,* p. 30.

84. Ibid., p. 56, citing the Wingate Papers.

85. Alanbrooke, *Diaries,* p. 436.

86. James R. W. Titus, "The Air Expeditionary Force in Perspective," Airpower Research Institute, ARR Occasional Paper No. 1, January 15, 1999.

87. Rooney, *Wingate and the Chindits,* p. 112, from the Wingate Papers.

88. Ogburn, *The Marauders,* p. 7.

89. Ibid., p. 275.

90. Hogan, *U.S. Army Special Operations,* chap. 5, p. 15, concludes there was such a major role for special operations; Heilbrunn, *Warfare,* p. 97, discerns the "grotesque situations"; Ogden, *The Marauders,* p. 139, personally attests to the "independent wars"; Smith, *OSS,* p. 348, observes OSS's "typical" inefficiency.

Chapter 17: Dawn Like Thunder

1. Gregory Fossedal, *Our Finest Hour: Will Clayton, the Marshall Plan and the Triumph of Democracy* (Stanford, CA: Hoover Institution Press, 1993), p. 169.

2. PRO, FO 371/60996 AN193 160, January 27, 1947.

3. See the argument in William T. R. Fox, *The Super-Powers: The United States, Britain, and the Soviet Union* (New York: Harcourt Brace, 1944), to indicate why the definition best suits the global presence of the British Empire and Commonwealth.

4. The declining size of the U.S. Army underscores the evaporation of Americans in uniform: 8,133,000 officers and men in September 1945; 1,891,011 in January 1946; and 991,285 a year after that. Figures are supplied by the U.S. Army Historical Foundation.

5. Military budgets hit their Cold War low in FY 1948. By 1949, for example, the single undermanned U.S. division in Europe operated just twelve tanks in Germany capable of combat. See Sorley, *Thunderbolt,* p. 109.

6. The seminal influence of Britain's Labour government and particularly of Foreign Secretary Ernest Bevin is documented in Leebaert, *The Fifty-Year Wound,* chap. 2.

7. The initiatives laid out in the president's speech of March 17, 1947, became known as the Truman Doctrine.

8. It was, indeed, Communist "terror," extending to the *pedomasoma,* the kidnapping of some twenty-eight thousand village children between the ages of three and fourteen, only a third ever to reappear.

9. *New York Times,* September 25, 1947.

10. The put-down is that of former Secretary of State Dean Acheson, in Douglas Brinkley, *Dean Acheson: The Cold War Years, 1953–1971* (New Haven, CT: Yale University Press, 1992), p. 92. Creation of what would become OPC is well discussed in Kennan's obituary, *New York Times,* March 18, 2005, p. 1.

11. Admiral Sidney Souers, former chief of Naval Intelligence, who was the first Director of Central Intelligence, pressed the legal argument. See Establishment of a Special Services Unit in CIA, June 2, 1948, Memorandum to the National Security Council, IP00004, National Security Archives.

12. The "disarray" from this expansion has been recalled in my interviews with men then serving in a cross-section of CIA/OPC responsibilities, including William Lee, Charles Liechtenstein, and Carleton Swift.

13. Kennan is described as "emotional" because (among many other examples) of his request for cyanide pills when posted to Moscow as ambassador in 1952, bizarrely fearing he would "break under torture." See Walter Hixson, *George F. Kennan: Cold War Iconoclast* (New York: Columbia University Press, 1989), p. 125, citing the CIA's Peter de Silva. Kennan's too-little-known views on "intermarriage," and indeed on the deficiencies caused by impure (i.e., Negro) "human blood," are from *FRUS* 1948/1, GFK to Secretary of State, February 24, 1948, p. 509, and from *FRUS* 1950/2 "Memorandum" by the Counselor to the Secretary of State, pp. 601, 607.

14. *FRUS* 1945–1950, "Emergence of the Intelligence Establishment," Document 292, NSC 10/2, June 18, 1948, p. 714.

15. Grose, *Operation Rollback,* p. 96.

16. Ibid., p. 172.

17. Carleton Swift interview, 2003.

18. Grose, *Operation Rollback,* p. 19. The investigator was General Lucian Truscott.

19. On Jewish terror and the atrocities of Messrs. Begin and Shamir, see the evidence in Bell, *Terror.* To excuse the bombing of the King David Hotel, with its many civilian dead, by saying it housed British headquarters, is like Timothy McVeigh's argument that the Murrah building was bombed because it housed offices of the FBI.

20. Kennan's penchant for "frontier wars" and "police action" came from a near-frantic belief that Communism would push forth in Southeast Asia, Latin America, and perhaps Japan. Foreign Office mandarins, such as Gladwyn Jebb, British ambassador to the UN, were skeptical of most of his conclusions, doubting that his "competence matches his learning." See PRO, Record of Conversation, FO 371/76383, September 20, 1949.

21. Matthew Ridgway, *Soldier: The Memoirs of Matthew B. Ridgway* (New York: Harper Brothers, 1956), p. 5.

22. P. K. Rose, "Two Strategic Intelligence Mistakes in Korea, 1950," Directorate of Operations, CIA, *Studies in Intelligence,* Fall–Winter 2001. The CIA also believed North Korea's army to be a third of its actual size.

23. Philby, *My Silent War,* p. 250.

24. Evan Thomas, *The Very Best Men: Four Who Dared; The Early Years of the CIA* (New York: Simon and Schuster, 1995), p. 65.

25. Reporter Steve Coll describes the CIA of 1969 and after as "an agency full of people who had problems with authority." This is a dreadful mischaracterization, since already by then (with only a few exceptions) CIA officers both at headquarters and those who worked out of U.S. embassies had a remarkably pliant fit with bureaucracy, as those who have dealt with such officers at home and in the field can attest. See Coll's otherwise thorough *Ghost Wars,* p. 22.

26. Susan Marquis, *Unconventional Warfare: Rebuilding U.S. Special Operations Forces* (Washington, D.C.: Brookings Institution, 1997), p. 11, mistakenly concludes that such operations were "largely ignored in the Korean theater." As far as the war record being obscured, the war simply did not start in the way that prevailing academic treatments insist; see the Russian sources in Leebaert, *The Fifty-Year Wound,* p. 90, and William T. Lee, "The Korean War Was Stalin's Show," Occasional Paper 99–1, Center for National Security Law, University of Virginia, 1999.

27. Haas, *Devil's Shadow,* p. 211. The author of this superb study has spent his career in the army and navy, as well as in USAF special operations.

28. *Los Angeles Times,* obituary, April 2, 2004; Bank, *From OSS to Green Berets,* p. 146.

29. The 50,000 figure is provided by the U.S. Army Historical Foundation. It includes the first arriving elements from the 7th Infantry Division, followed by the army's 24th Corps, comprising the 6th, 7th, and 40th infantry divisions.

30. As if to underscore the contradictions in post-WWII security policies among the democracies, the state-of-the-art Merlin engines of the MiG-15s being used so effectively to kill American pilots had been sold to the Russians by the British in 1947.

31. Nichols, *How Many Times,* p. 130. Significantly, this strange and obscure little memoir has a foreword contributed by one of the top four-star generals of the Korean War era, E. E. Partridge, USAF.

32. Ibid., p. 135.

33. Haas, *Devil's Shadow,* p. 78.

34. Nichols, *How Many Times,* pp. 1, 111.

35. Ibid., p. 148.

36. Ibid., p. 191.

37. Haas, *Devil's Shadow,* p. 60.

38. Schemmer, ed., *U.S. Special Operations Forces,* p. 93, uncritically quoting Harry Aderholt, then a USAF captain, who (for better reasons than this ongoing disaster) would become a legendary figure in U.S. special operations.

39. Headquarters Far East Command Liaison Detachment, 8240th Army Unit, April 11, 1952, National Archives.

40. Bank, *From OSS to Green Berets,* pp. 168–69; see also Malcom, *My Secret War in North Korea,* for one of the few firsthand accounts of special operations in Korea. The introduction is by Major General John Singlaub, USA (ret.) another legendary operator in World War II, Korea, and Vietnam.

41. Black, "Behind the Lines," p. 20. The author was with the 8th Airborne Ranger Company in Korea.

42. Omar N. Bradley and Clay Blair, *A General's Life* (New York: Simon and Schuster, 1983), p. 474.

43. Haas, *Devil's Shadow,* p. 62.

44. Ibid., p. 111.

45. The original OPC chief in Korea was the mysterious Hans Tofte, born in Denmark, who lived in Manchuria for eight years, worked for OSS, then managed a family business in Iowa from 1947 to 1950, before arriving at the CIA, to be fired in 1966 for squirreling away classified CIA materials in his mother's house. On bogus intelligence and a successor to Tofte, see Andrew, *For the President's Eyes Only,* p. 193.

46. Leebaert, *The Fifty-Year Wound,* pp. 130, 137.

47. British alarm, its urging of Washington to agree on joint intervention in Vietnam, and the extent to which France was echoing British arguments are consistent from 1952 until London's sudden reversal at the beginning of the Geneva conference in April 1954. See "Defence of South East Asia in Global Strategy," 1953, PRO, FO 371/101276 FZ1195/2, and further documentation in Leebaert, *The Fifty-Year Wound,* chaps. 3 and 4.

48. For discussion of Eisenhower's "New Look," see Leebaert, *The Fifty-Year Wound,* p. 149.

49. In the CIA's history of Operation Ajax, "Overthrow of Premier Mossadeq of Iran, November 1952– August 1953," March 1954, CIA Clandestine Services History.

50. Bank, *OSS to Green Berets,* p. 172.

51. The exercise of this "license" was ideally to be done in concert with "designated representatives of the Secretary of State and the Secretary of Defense"; see James S. Lay Jr., "National Security Council Directive on Covert Operations," March 15, 1954, note by the executive secretary to the National Security Council, IP00651, National Security Archives.

52. *FRUS* 1952–1954, vol. XII, pt. 1, Indochina, Eisenhower at 141st NSC meeting, April 28, 1953.

53. A solid analysis that uses the best sources to explain the composition and deployments of France's special forces is Montbrun, *Les chemins sans croix.*

54. Greene, *Reflections,* p. 179; the story is told in his essay "Catholics at War," written in early 1954.

55. The best book on this aspect of U.S. involvement is Conboy and Andrade, *Spies and Commandos;* on early "sabotage," see p. 9.

56. The number killed in this savage collectivism — and the terribly remembered arrival of the apparatchiks with their black leather shoes and attaché cases — is from Stephane Courtois et al., *The Black Book of Communism* (Cambridge, MA: Harvard University Press, 1999), p. 569.

57. Appropriate tropical gear would not arrive until 1959, according to Brigadier General William Yarborough, quoted in Clancy, *Shadow Warriors,* p. 95.

58. *United States–Vietnamese Relations, 1945–1967,* study prepared for the Department of Defense, vol. 10 (Washington, DC: GPO, 1971), p. 737.

59. Allen, *Savage Wars of Peace,* p. 51.

60. Even disclosures today about what occurred nearly forty years ago create outrage, as in the reaction to General Paul Aussaresses's confession, *Services Speciaux.* A less-controversial book that explains much of France's special forces experience after the 1957 Battle of Algiers is Alles, *Commandos de Chasse Gendarmerie.* The emphasis on FLN capture, psychological operations, and the scope of the "hunt" is laid out on pp. 14–18.

61. Tim Weiner, "The Spy Agency's Many Mean Ways," *New York Times,* February 9, 1997, p. 7. On near-drowning (which leaves no inconvenient marks), the process is known as "waterboarding." Its use was deemed acceptable among CIA "professional . . . techniques" by then-director Porter Gosse; see the *New York Times,* March 18, 2005, p. 1.

62. CIA torture of the innocent has a rich Cold War precedent, as shown by the case of KGB defector Yuri Orlov. It is hard to believe that CIA abilities to separate the good from the bad have improved sufficiently since.

63. Curtis Peebles, *Shadow Flights: America's Secret Air War against the Soviet Union* (Novato, CA: Presidio Press, 2000), p. 213, re "shot himself." Eisenhower was fed up with both the CIA and the USAF, which repeatedly and falsely assured him that reconnaissance at 70,000 feet would never be detected. See Leebaert, *The Fifty-Year Wound,* pp. 216–17.

64. Re the "missile gap," see Central Intelligence Agency, NIE 11–8–1969, August 1, 1960; note chart 29157 7–60.

65. Noam Chomsky, *Year 501: The Conquest Continues* (Boston: South End Press, 1993), p. 121.

66. George McGhee, *On the Front Line in the Cold War* (Westport, CT: Praeger, 1997), p. 145, on pornography, for which the CIA tried to blame the Soviets. As is known from other sources, the CIA used Bing Crosby to help produce the film.

67. Knaus, *Orphans of the Cold,* p. 212.

68. Ibid., p. 157.

69. Haas, *Apollo's Warriors,* p. 141.

70. Knaus, *Orphans of the Cold,* p. 217.

71. Maxwell Taylor, *The Uncertain Trumpet* (New York: Harper, 1960), p. 100.

72. It might be guessed who Arthur Schlesinger Jr. has in mind in his "On Heroic Leadership"; "tough" and "toughness" were words repeated incessantly by John Kennedy, even in his admiration for poet Robert Frost. See Kazin, *Contemporaries,* p. 373.

Chapter 18: Invasion from the Future

1. *Public Papers,* Kennedy, Item 1: "Inaugural Address," January 20, 1961, p. 2.

2. The myths include everything from the role of Mr. Kennan at the beginning to the origins of the Korean War, to the events of the Cuban Missile Crisis, to the causes of the war in Vietnam and that war's supposed hopelessness, to intelligence estimates and arms control dealings with the USSR in the 1960s and 1970s, and finally to the way it all ended. Despite countless books, articles, and even a (misleading) CNN documentary series, surprisingly little is known about the Cold War because its leading students have limited their work to a narrow slice of history (1945–91), leaving little room to draw comparisons with rich precedent. Moreover, they frequently concentrate on relatively easy-to-examine politico-military issues in U.S. state papers, less often availing themselves of the extensive Russian-language sources, and just about never deploying those Russian sources such as memoirs or regimental histories coming after 1991. Should such sources be used and that mixture be attained, their writings are unlikely to include the necessary additional insights drawn from business history, imaginative literature, and the evolution of transformative technologies during these kaleidoscopic decades. Not to mention the neglect of framing all this by a comprehensive inside/outside scrutiny of U.S. intelligence operations and analyses.

3. "A new priesthood of action intellectuals" was Theodore White's widely echoed phrase before he went on to write a paean to John Kennedy as president. It is quoted, for instance, in James W. Hilty, *Robert Kennedy: Brother Protector* (Philadelphia: Temple University Press, 1997), p. 258. *Emergency men* is a term used long before by historian Jacob Burckhardt to describe the kind of people he predicted would afflict the coming age.

4. National Security Memorandum 56, signed by President Kennedy in June 1961, tasked all military services except the USMC to form their own counterinsurgency forces.

5. Michael Isenberg, *Shield of the Republic: The United States Navy in an Era of Cold War and Violent Peace* (New York: St. Martin's, 1993), p. 298.

6. Theodore White, *The Making of the President, 1960* (New York: Atheneum, 1961), p. 406.

7. A hundred million dollars was designated in the Pentagon, and I reach the approximately $1 billion figure by calculating both inflation and purchasing power within the U.S. economy of 1961. In the absence of easily accessible sources, confusion can exist over the numbers and dates of the Special Forces Groups (SFG). Active have been: 1st SFG 1957–74 (reactivated later); 3rd SFG 1963–69 (reactivated later); 5th SFG 1964–present; 6th SFG 1963–71; 77th SFG becomes 7th SFG June 1960–; 8th SFG 1963–72; 10th SFG 1953–present; USAR 9th SFG 1960–66; 11th SFG 1960–94; 12th SFG 1960–94; 13th SFG 1960–66; 17th SFG 1960–66; 24th SFG 1960–66; Army National Guard 19th SFG & 20th SFG 1960–present. Bear in mind that some of the U.S. Army Reserve SFGs have been essentially headquarter staffs.

8. Curtis LeMay, *America Is in Danger* (New York: Funk and Wagnalls, 1968), p. 123.

9. Haas, *Apollo's Warriors,* p. 191. The insults were exchanged between the general then heading USAF Tactical Air Command and Colonel Harry C. Aderholt.

10. In Georgetown University's Classics Department, Professor Charles McNelis concludes "atrocious." It should read either *"liberare vexatos"* or *"liberare oppressos."*

11. As part of what he described as "the global civil war," President Kennedy's administration created the Office of Public Safety within the equally new Agency for International Development. It began distributing an unprecedented amount of police assistance to some of the grossest violators of human rights outside the Communist world. Training was provided to the police forces of the likes of Nicaragua's Somoza and Paraguay's Stroessner, as well as to Iran, the Philippines, Guatemala, etc. By Executive Order, he also created the International Police Academy in Washington to assist. For instance, see National Security Archive, Foreign Police Training file, HQ 62-107929, 1962–1963, and "Police Aid and Political Will," Washington Office on Latin America, 1987.

12. Haas, *Apollo's Warriors,* p. 235; Maxwell Taylor on "armies of freedom," quoted in Jack Raymond, *Power at the Pentagon* (New York: Harper & Row, 1964), pp. 112–13, n. 92.

13. See Lyman Kirkpatrick, "The Inspector General's Survey of the Cuban Operation," CIA, 1962, National Security Archive.

14. Seymour Hersh, *The Dark Side of Camelot* (Boston: Little, Brown, 1997), p. 380, quoting JFK's excitement about the raids into Cuba. On "boom and bang," see Shackley, *Spymaster,* p. 53.

15. This era of the Cold War, 1960–63, has been described as "the crisis years." Many of these crises, however, were largely self-inflicted — as in the 1962 Cuban Missile Crisis that followed eighteen months of anti-Castro commando raids and assassination attempts. Dangers, too, may be exaggerated. For instance, note the reflections of A. Dokuchchaev, the KGB colonel in charge of Soviet warheads in Cuba, in "100-Dnevng Ydarnyy Kruz." I have particularly found research by many writers on the Missile Crisis, such as various edited materials by Philip Zelikow, to be surprisingly incomplete.

16. Gus Russo, *Live by the Sword* (Baltimore: Bancroft Press, 1998), pp. 45–46; Allen Dulles, oral history, Kennedy Presidential Library; "The Spy Boss Who Loved Bond," in Sheldon Lane, ed., *For Bond Lovers Only* (New York: Panther Books, 1965), pp. 155–56; on RFK, the source is Evan Thomas, *Robert Kennedy: His Life* (New York: Simon and Schuster, 2000), p. 166. Arthur Schlesinger Jr.'s arguments, as in a letter to the editor (*New York Times Book Review,* February 4, 2001), that JFK's being a fan of Bond was a PR "gag," can easily be dismissed.

17. Hersh, *The Dark Side,* p. 190. Hersh is documenting a 1961 conversation about "executive action" between Bundy and Richard Bissell, then head of CIA operations.

18. Quoted in Wright, *Spycatcher,* p. 160.

19. Quoted in Lawrence Freedman, *Kennedy's Wars: Berlin, Cuba, Laos, Vietnam* (New York: Oxford University Press, 2000), p. 151, discusses William Harvey, who had established the Executive Action Capability at White House urging. Former Kennedy administration officials at Freedman's book presentation (Woodrow Wilson International Center for Scholars, February 8, 2001) recalled the president's acute disappointment in meeting Harvey.

20. National Security Action Memorandum 52, "Vietnam," May 11, 1961.

21. Hersh, *The Dark Side,* re "tears," pp. 252–53; James Reston, *Deadline: A Memoir* (New York: Random House, 1991), p. 288, re "first thought."

22. Richard Reeves, *President Kennedy: Profile of Power* (New York: Simon and Schuster, 1993), p. 75.

23. Plaster, *SOG,* p. 111.

24. Quoted in Freedman, *Kennedy's Wars,* p. 360.

25. Kennedy, *Public Papers,* Item 205: "Special Message to Congress on Urgent National Needs," May 25, 1961.

26. "Iron majors" is from Robert D. Kaplan's "Supremacy by Stealth" in which additional silliness includes advice to bring back the "pre-Vietnam" rules in U.S. foreign policy (i.e., the "covert means" that got the country into Guatemala, Indonesia, and Vietnam itself). His advice, like that of journalist Max Boot, is to "Speak Victorian" in foreign policy, but he mishmashes the history of Palmerston, Gladstone, Disraeli, and Salisbury, pp. 73 etc. Another recent article addressing the subject of counterinsurgency as if it were brand-new — to journalist and subject alike — is a wide-eyed profile of an army major in Iraq who has written a thesis comparing Malaya with Vietnam. See Peter Maass, "The Counterinsurgent," *New York Times Magazine,* January 11, 2004.

27. *Washington Post,* September 17, 1996.

28. Robert McNamara et al., *Argument without End: In Search of Answers to the Vietnam Tragedy* (New York: Public Affairs, 1999), p. 61.

29. Strong arguments can be made that the United States had won the war by 1971, meaning that the relative security of South Vietnam and its impressive ability to defend itself — at least to the extent that any European NATO member would have been able to defend itself against such conventional might — had been achieved. Evidence of such ability is how the following year's massive Easter invasion by the North was repulsed without U.S. support on the ground. See Sorley's superbly argued *A Better War.*

30. *Pentagon Papers,* as cited in Conboy and Andrate, *Spies and Commandos,* p. 75.

31. Haas, *Apollo's Warriors,* p. 297 re "failure"; Plaster, *SOG,* disagrees, p. 73. Both authors are renowned special operators. For insights by a shrewd civilian analyst, see Shultz, *The Secret War against Hanoi.*

32. Tourison, *Secret Army, Secret War,* p. 109.

33. Conboy and Andrade, *Spies and Commandos,* p. 65.

34. The official, and former commando, mentioned is Roger Hilsman, who went on to be a respected professor at Columbia University. I was struck during his graduate-student seminars years later by the contempt he harbored for LBJ. While in office, he had pressed for the "strategic hamlet" tactic that had worked in Malaya, although he acknowledged that it might take some twenty years to work in South Vietnam.

35. Plaster, *SOG,* p. 145.

36. Conboy and Andrade, *Spies and Commandos,* p. 70, citing William Colby, who at the time was head of CIA Far East operations.

37. Durrell's *Bitter Lemons* recounts his life on Cyprus during 1953–56, including the last two as press officer to the blundering colonial authorities as Royal Marine Commandos and parachutists confronted the Greek EOKA insurgency. The book contains seminal insights on terrorism and counterinsurgency, notably pp. 215–18.

38. Heikal, *The Sphinx and the Commissar,* p. 164.

39. Prime Minister Kosygin relaying this to Egypt's President Nasser. Shultz, *The Secret War,* p. 212.

40. Note that merely one article concerning the Vietnam War was published in *International Security* between 1976 and 1981 amid dozens on SALT, NATO, regional power balances, nuclear proliferation, military history, and other concerns.

41. Lewis Sorley interview, June 2004.

42. See photograph of a SOG team so disguised.

43. See Leebaert, *The Fifty-Year Wound,* pp. 349–50. McNamara was lulled by the industrial doctrine that the bigger the investment, the larger the return — an old-fashioned business concept even by 1967. It is also a belief utterly contrary to the workings of SOF.

44. The decline of the army in Vietnam is shown by the likes of Lieutenant William Calley receiving a commission, let alone commanding troops. As for the Special Forces, the judgments of "inferior" and "decline" are those of Special Forces captain Budge E. Williams, from comparing his two tours of 1967 and 1969, and his own indictment in 1969 may underscore the point. See Stein, *A Murder in Wartime,* p. 60. One of the era's most renowned operators noted Special Forces laxity already in 1965; see Beckwith, *Delta Force,* pp. 57–59.

45. Re "stupid," see Shackley, *Spymaster,* p. 251; the arrest and prosecutions were not, as apologists have argued, an attempt by top army command to "get" the Green Berets for their insouciance or for their annoying ties to the CIA. Rather, Colonel Robert Rheault had proved himself a liar and an accessory to what looks like murder. The military historian and West Pointer Lewis Sorley, who interviewed Rheault, provides further evidence of the lies in *Thunderbolt;* see chap. 20, "Murder and the Green Berets." Contrary to popular belief, the inane euphemism to "terminate with extreme prejudice" did not come out of Langley. It was coined by the press and parroted by Rheault's men.

46. Moscow's crowing in the 1970s about U.S. decline went beyond propaganda. See Richard E. Day, *Cold War Capital: The View from Moscow,* 1945–1975 (New York: Oxford University Press, 1995). Talks with Soviet officials in the 1970s made it clear to me that such open writings on U.S. inflation, productivity, and fiscal policies were convincing to them. In *On Watch: A Memoir* (New York: Times Books, 1976), p. 319, Admiral Elmo Zumwalt convincingly describes Henry Kissinger's 1973 ruminations that America "has passed its high point like so many other civilizations." Kissinger's many denials of what he said to Zumwalt are harder to believe because of their contradictions.

47. This is a sentence from what is known as "Abrams' Charter," the instructions from the chief of staff who revived the Rangers.

48. The role of the U.S. Army in eliminating European terrorists was explained to me by Major General Robert H. Scales, USA (ret.), former commandant of the U.S. Army War College, who served in West Germany after Vietnam. He is also coauthor of the excellent *The Iraq War: A Military History* (Cambridge, MA: Harvard University Press, 2003). Scales interview, January 2005. The details of how this was worked through DIA and SACEUR "force protection elements" come from an off-the-record 2005 interview with another source. U.S. Army involvement would have encountered the 1976 Executive Order banning assassination (renewed in 1981 and moribund today). However, that order was never enforceable by criminal law, and it could have been revoked or suspended by any president at any time.

49. Interviews during May and June 2005 with retired Norwegian chief investigators Lier and Thune. The unapprehended Daoud was aggrieved at being ignored by Steven Spielberg. Reuters, September 6, 2005.

50. My account of the 1973 Israeli operation in Beirut builds on work conducted for OSD by C&L Associates. The number of 17,000 killed, most of them Palestinian and Lebanese, is from a *New York Times* editorial, August 31, 2005.

51. The belief of the USS *Liberty*'s surviving crew that they would be finished off by Israeli commandos is in Ennes, *Assault on the* Liberty, chap. 6, in addition to my interviews with survivors. The evidence that the attack was deliberate becomes ever more overwhelming, as understood by the CIA director of the time, the director of the National Security Agency and his deputy, the secretary of state, former CNO and then Chairman of the Joint Chiefs Admiral Thomas Moorer, among many others with a direct vantage point who have all gone on the record. Contrary to the writings of one of the deniers of such intent, Judge A. Jay Cristol, there have never been any congressional investigations into the killing of these thirty-four sailors and intelligence specialists. A good overview is David C. Walsh, "Friendless Fire," Naval Institute *Proceedings,* June 2003, and the analysis by James Bamford in *Body of Secrets: Anatomy of the Ultra-Secret National Security Agency, From the Cold War through the Dawn of the New Century* (New York: Doubleday, 2001), pp. 185–239.

52. I worked closely with Mountbatten during that final summer of 1979 and, in July, expressed my concern about his spending any time in Sligo.

53. Beckwith, *Delta Force,* p. 103.

54. Ibid., p. 136. One of Beckwith's many valuable insights was his requirement that officers who presumed to lead unconventional units better have led conventional ones first.

55. The prospect of nuclear-armed terrorists and assaults on reactors and conveyances was a fad (and a surprisingly imaginative one) popular among academics of defense studies in the mid-1970s. Serious treatment of the subject then yielded to endless seminars and grants on U.S.-Soviet arms control. See the one contemporary article in *International Security* on the subject, "Nuclear Terror," David M. Rosenbaum, 1, no. 3 (1977).

56. Among the far-sighted senior army officers was one of Creighton Abrams's successors as army chief of staff, General Edward "Shy" Meyer, who, by 1979, was speaking of the overall "hollowness" of the U.S. Army. I discussed these issues with him that year during his visit to Harvard.

57. For a taste of CIA analytical failings, see n. 71 below. The penetration of the United States by Line X of the KGB during the 1970s, the obtuseness of the CIA and the FBI, as well as the ways in which the essentially privately organized American Trade Craft Society confronted such penetration constitute one of the Cold War's most dramatic of espionage sagas. I have disclosed it in *Fifty-Year Wound,* pp. 397–400, 461–63.

58. It has long been wondered why CIA director William Colby volunteered so much information to the Senate investigative committee headed by Frank Church. The answer, as he told me two years later, is that he was maneuvering to save the CIA from further ruin by making the nation's political leaders complicit in what they had long enabled. No need to put their names and particular decisions in the material. He believed he was cautioning the former Minority Leader in the House, President Gerald Ford, as well as specific senators and congressmen still on Capitol Hill, that they too were involved, given that they had signed off on much that had occurred.

59. The popular belief is incorrect that the CIA was made any weaker by the Church committee hearings. The argument that President Carter's CIA director, warrior/scholar Admiral Stansfield Turner, "decimated the Agency's HUMINT ranks," or as described by Coll, *Ghost Wars,* p. 360, was a "failed CIA director," is preposterous. I judge this from my encounters with those ranks in the U.S. and Soviet Union before and after. The Clandestine Service was larger and (relative to previous performance) probably stronger when Turner left than when he arrived.

60. Jimmy Carter, *Keeping Faith: Memoirs of a President* (New York: Bantam Books, 1992), p. 438.

61. Beckwith, *Delta Force,* pp. 218, 222; Haney, *Inside Delta,* p. 232. CSM Haney was a founding member of Delta. David Mamet has compared this warrant officer's memoirs to those of Grant and to the great military novels of Burns, Crane, and Pressfield.

62. See Martin, "Major Richard Meadows (ret.)." Written by historian David Martin, the essay is published on the excellent veteran-maintained Global Special Operations Web site.

63. The daring flight into Iran was courtesy of CIA pilots and an agency Twin Otter. But the CIA landed on the wrong side of the road along which the airstrip was to be mapped, thereby skewing the original design.

64. Beckwith, *Delta Force,* p. 222; on "surrender," see Haney, *Inside Delta,* p. 234.

65. Carney and Schemmer, *No Room for Error,* p. 86.

66. McRaven, *Spec Ops,* p. 40. The observation is from McRaven's interview with Rudolph Witzig, Granite Force commander. I've added the head shaking, which can be surmised.

67. Beckwith, *Delta Force,* p. 325.

68. Carney and Schemmer, *No Room for Error,* p. 86.

69. Martin, "Major Richard Meadows," Global Special Operations Web site essay.

70. William Burr, ed., *The Kissinger Transcripts: The Top Secret Talks with Beijing and Moscow* (New York: Norton, 1999), pp. 373, 385, 389, 405.

71. It has become an urban myth to note, as does journalist Fareed Zakaria in "Exaggerating the Threats," *Newsweek,* June 16, 2003, that the Team B analysis by expert outsiders, which in 1976 eviscerated years of CIA National Intelligence Estimates of Soviet capabilities, was "wildly off the mark," a mistake also made repeatedly by Bill Keller of the *New York Times.* Russian sources now show that the critics were fundamentally correct on the pivotal issues: the accuracy of MIRV-equipped Soviet missiles, the scope of Soviet civil defense, the chronic ABM treaty violations. Much was underestimated, such as the number of Soviet warheads, and some of the worst (i.e., bioweapons) undetected even by the critics of the CIA Estimates. Russian-language sources — particularly memoirs and unit histories published after 1991 — clarify the extent to which Soviet ICBMs posed a first-strike threat to their U.S. counterparts — in accord with the Soviet doctrine of preemption. For starters, see Karpenko, ed., *Raketnyye Komompleksy,* or Pervov, *Oborony Strany.* See Leebaert, *Fifty-Year Wound,* chaps. 7 and 8, for comparisons of such sources and additional evidence with the faulty CIA NIEs of those years. Conclusive support for Team B–related conclusions and the "mess" of CIA analyses can be found in Harvard's *Journal of Cold War Studies* (Spring–Summer 2005); see the two-part article by William T. Lee, "Counterforce Capabilities of Soviet ICBMs during the Cold War."

72. The strong evidence comes from AID contractor Flemming Heegard, who was with Ambassador Dubbs that final day, and whom I interviewed in 2001.

73. *Figaro,* September 6, 1984.

74. For a discussion of Soviet military doctrine and organization at the time, see my opening chapter in Leebaert, ed., *Soviet Military Thinking,* pp. 3–28. Chap. 3, by Sovietologist Fritz Ermarth, offers contrasts between U.S. and Soviet thought.

75. Viktor Suvorov, *Spetsnaz: The Story behind the Soviet SAS* (London: Hamish Hamilton, 1987). This is the title of the British edition of Suvorov's book. "Suvorov" is the pseudonym of a defector from Soviet military intelligence (GRU). His personal accounts of spetsnaz units were, in the West, considered exaggerated if not paranoid at the time.

76. Ibid. "Suvorov" explains this scenario in chap. 15. His depiction of special warfare as it would have been waged by Soviet spetsnaz has many similarities with the threats now posed by nonstate opponents.

77. Comparisons of Afghanistan to combat against the *basmachi* were common among Soviet officials in 1981. I heard them in Moscow that spring from senior officials in the Ministry of Foreign Affairs. Jack Matlock, who was in charge of the U.S. embassy for most of 1981, also cites them in *Reagan and Gorbachev: How the Cold War Ended* (New York: Random House, 2004), p. 29.

78. See the collection of interviews with mujahideen guerrillas by two analysts from Fort Leavenworth's Foreign Military Studies Office: Jalali and Grau, eds., *The Other Side of the Mountain.* See also the excellent review by William C. Green in *Naval War College Review* (Summer 2003).

79. Coll, *Ghost Wars,* p. 131, notes that Special Forces offered their teaching in new weapons and techniques within Pakistan. However, it is in his discussion of putative 1980s "right wingers" who made this possible that Coll loses his reportorial objectivity. See, for starters, p. 168.

80. Milton Bearden, *Washington Post,* December 12, 1998.

81. Stinger missiles were being provided to Joseph Savimbi's American-backed UNITA rebels in Angola, but such assistance in faraway Southern Africa was believed in Washington to be much less provocative.

82. "Politics of Covert Action: The U.S., the Mujahideen, and the Stinger Missiles," Kennedy School of Government Case C15-99-15446.0, Harvard University, 1999, re "tracks."

83. Yousaf and Adkin, *Afghanistan the Bear Trap,* pp. 83–84. Among the many books published on the U.S. role in Afghanistan during the 1980s, this one by the infantry general who headed Pakistan's ISI is the most revealing on logistical and institutional problems; his observations cited here are cross-referenced with Saudi participants.

84. The author was encountering these issues in consulting work for the Department of Defense.

85. Milton Bearden is quoted in "One Man and a Global Web of Violence," *New York Times,* January 14, 2001, p. A16.

86. The unnamed diplomat is quoted in Mary Anne Weaver, "Letter from Pakistan," *New Yorker,* June 12, 1995, p. 44. Morrice, Lord St. Brides, previously high commissioner in Pakistan and in India, expressed the same concerns to me at the time.

87. See my review essay of Jack Matlock's *Reagan and Gorbachev* for the *Claremont Review of Books,* Summer 2005, Web site. An expanded argument is in Leebaert, *The Fifty-Year Wound,* chap. 10.

88. Haney, *Inside Delta Force,* pp. 339–92; Juan Tamayo, "Green Beret's Sandanista," *Miami Herald,* September 3, 2003.

89. Schemmer, ed., *U.S. Special Operations Forces,* p. 134. This is a unique, large-sized, well-illustrated, riveting volume edited and written by half a dozen veteran U.S. authorities on the profession.

90. Colin Powell, *My American Journey* (New York: Random House, 1995), p. 292.

91. General Edward Meyer, Oral History Transcript, U.S. Army Military History Institute, October 10, 2001.

92. Lackadaisical standards in CIA operations — except in some extraordinary technical accomplishments such as the 1974 *Glomar Explorer* — can be demonstrated by much additional evidence, such as Moscow's anxiety in the 1980s that Washington was no longer taking the formidable East Germans seriously because the CIA officers it placed were so bumbling, as noted by spymaster Marcus Wolf in *Man without a Face* (New York: Public Affairs, 1997, p. 316). The more serious charge of "casual corruption" comes from 1980s practices at Camp Peary where CIA career trainees prepare for clandestine service. They would frequently hear from CIA veteran instructors about the additional benefits that could accrue from pocketing money officially disbursed for their agents. It is significant that the unimpressively credentialed traitor Harold Nicholson was considered a valued instructor there into the 1990s.

93. Schemmer, ed., *U.S. Special Operations Forces,* p. 140.

94. Carney and Schemmer, *No Room for Error,* p. 234.

95. Anxiety about airliners being crashed into the Twin Towers was one of the scenarios discussed among the New York–based science fiction writers noted in the conclusion, their brain-storming sessions including Timothy Dickinson of *Harper's* and the *Paris Review.*

96. Quoted in Coll, *Ghost Wars,* pp. 241, 503.

97. For readers interested in the CIA 1991–2001 rationalizations, largely through courtesy of university conferences, see Leebaert, *The Fifty-Year Wound,* chap. 12; *blue border* was the term for information derived from U.S. agents in the Soviet Union, so described because of the color of the file folders at Langley; on Iraq "judgment," see Cockburn and Cockburn, *Out of the Ashes,* pp. 174, 197, 229, 230.

98. Senator Roberts; Thomas Keen testimony; James Schlesinger, Hart-Rudman Commission.

99. *United States Special Operations Posture Statement 2003–2004: Transforming the Force at the Forefront of the War on Terrorism,* Washington, DC: GPO, 2003, p. 3.

100. "Expand 'em" is from an off-the-record interview with a senior Department of Defense official.

101. The disruption of a society's dependence on "flow technology" was an insight of historian Daniel Boorstin. George Will has revived it in discussing the leverage of insurgents in Iraq. See George F. Will, "In Iraq, an Echo of Algiers," *Washington Post,* April 28, 2005.

102. "Advice of exiles" was the reason given by General de Jong, USMC, for no postinvasion planning. *Lehrer News Hour,* December 9, 2004; Secretary of Defense Rumsfeld's initial scoffing was rebroadcast on NPR's *Morning Edition,* December 16, 2004. From 2001 even into 2003, he was more extolled in the U.S. press than anyone in that office since McNamara during 1961–63. Historian John Keegan's gushing *Vanity Fair* profile (February 2003) about "the right man at the right time," schooled "at the most military of the great Ivy League colleges" (Princeton, of all places), is one such embarrassment. Secretary Rumsfeld's remarks about metrics are from an interview on NPR's *Morning Edition,* March 30, 2005. The president's quotation is from the *New York Times,* October 26, 2004, p. 1.

103. Secretary Rumsfeld re "know what we are talking about" is from an interview on NPR, March 30, 2005. The charges of "cliché" and "hopelessly confused thinking" were shot at General Wesley Clark,

USA (ret.) by Richard Perle, chairman of the Defense Policy Board (and previously a valued player in ending the Cold War), before the House Armed Services Committee in September 2002, as revisited in a joint appearance before the same committee in 2005. See the *Washington Post,* April 7, 2005, p. A10. The limited business and financial experience of the vice president and the defense secretary also told, as the president's chief economic adviser was dismissed for supposedly wayward cost estimates. (Such experience as Messrs. Cheney and Rumsfeld possessed had been obtained from cashing in previous government service for CEO administrative slots.)

104. CSPAN, *Washington Journal,* July 11, 2004. My own skepticism about invading Iraq was based on minimal faith in CIA estimates, especially CIA conclusions about WMD, as conveyed in my discussion with former Deputy Assistant Secretary of Defense Kathleen Troia on January 30, 2003.

105. "Faith, Certainty, and the Presidency of George W. Bush," Ron Suskind, *New York Times Magazine,* October 17, 2004, p. 51. It was a view common within the NSC of the time.

106. The fraudulent Special Forces colonel was one Joe A. Cafasso, who worked as an expert consultant for Fox News for four months in 2002 and as a commentator on WABC radio. I encountered him at the height of his prominence and was incredulous that anyone could believe him ever to have been a Special Forces officer, and so cautioned the veteran journalist and MGM executive Janet Janjigian. Eventually he was exposed by the *Times*'s Jim Rutenberg, "At Fox News, the Colonel Who Wasn't," April 29, 2003. Among the others discredited can be included a former *San Francisco Chronicle* obituary writer turned expert on "Islamic pluralism"; the "neocon" columnists who chomped unreservedly for the Iraq war; and a frequently published retired lieutenant colonel braying that "our responses to terrorist acts should make the world gasp" — precisely what not to do in an effective antiterrorist policy. See "The Road to Mecca Part II," Clifford Geertz, *New York Review of Books,* July 3, 2003, and Ralph Peters cited in *The Hunt for Bin Laden,* Robin Moore (New York: Ballantine, 2003), p. xxi.

Conclusion

1. Specific expectations of disaster were percolating in genres besides science fiction, as in techno-thriller novelist Tom Clancy's attention to jets as missiles. The Sunday before 9/11, the *New York Times Book Review* praised Ed McBain's *Money, Money, Money,* a novel of the 87th Precinct. McBain describes a specifically Al Qaeda bombing of what is obviously Carnegie Hall.

2. The president of the United States proclaimed that we had passed into "a different world" — a phrase less understandably repeated by more reflective people, including John Lewis Gaddis, historian of the Cold War, indicating a view of the world conceived in rather narrow terms of the primacy of state power. See John Lewis Gaddis, author of *Surprise, Security and the American Experience,* on C-SPAN, "Book Notes," May 16, 2004.

3. The authenticating scores that one may be able to notch up in IQ and behavioral testing may be predictive of utility in many other circumstances, but perhaps not in the ones most applicable here. Better approaches exist, as originally demonstrated by the U.S. Air Force, in "multiple intelligence" assessments. For instance, see explanations of a cognitive model as applied to select fighter pilots known for "wearing" their jets (i.e., for being "naturals" who perform significantly above even other top airmen). The model is explained in Robert J. Sternberg, *Encyclopedia of Human Intelligence* (New York: Macmillan, 1994), pp. 1049–51.

4. Sources for my discussion of Delta come from off-the-record interviews with U.S. Army officers having direct experience.

5. Off-the-record interview with a U.S. Army general who shared this discussion.

6. "Inside the Committee That Runs the World" was the title of a much-discussed article (and of a subsequent book) by David J. Rothkopf in the March/April issue of *Foreign Policy* magazine. It reviewed the history of the National Security Council, but, like so many solipsistic foreign policy writings, the article and book were oblivious as to the clout of business, finance, science, and technology on shaping events. NSC staffers, who are academics and bureaucrats serving for months or a few years at most, run nothing. And one may ask what influence their principals — including the president — have on this larger world beyond "national security."

7. The quotation about "Arabs' fear of dogs" by General Ricardo Sanchez could have come right out of Selma 1963 if we recall the cliché of "Negroes being afraid of dogs" and Romain Gary's novel *White Dog,* about a sad creature being trained to exploit that fear. On Sanchez, see the *New York Times,* March 30, 2005. Re "battlefield," this is General John Abizaid before the Senate Armed Services Committee, September 29, 2005.

8. John Bolton, confirmation hearings, Senate Foreign Relations Committee, April 11, 2005.

9. Previous chapters have criticized a cover article in the July/August issue of *The Atlantic*, "Supremacy by Stealth: Ten Rules for Managing the World," by Robert D. Kaplan, expanded in his book *Imperial Grunts: The American Military on the Ground* (New York: Random House, 2005). Many of the examples from history that underlie these "rules" are wrong: presenting "Xenophon's army," retreating for its life, for how "we should be mobile in the same way" (almost certainly abandoning or killing its many wounded); facile comparisons of imperial Rome and the United States, of insurgency in El Salvador and in South Vietnam; the stance of the late-nineteenth-century Royal Navy; and so forth. The point is less to argue history than to show how weak can be the evidence for envisioning a strategy based on commando stealth for U.S. "managing" of the twenty-first-century world.

10. Robert Kaplan, C-SPAN "Book TV," interview, April 3, 2005. In another vividly written article laden with mistakes ("America's African Rifles," *The Atlantic Monthly,* April 2005), Kaplan celebrates troop training missions to Niger and Chad without noting that the U.S. trainers do not speak the common colonial language, French. All is translated for these "imperial grunts," the U.S. Marines.

11. History is put to surprisingly bad uses in the comparison of America to empire by a range of other writers. Even as interesting a historian as Paul Kennedy falls prey to such generalization. He provides, for instance, a wrong impression of U.S. similarities to Rome's "worldwide imperial ambitions" in *The Australian,* August 4, 2004, by comparing U.S. forces to Roman legions — but the legions inevitably put down very long-term roots wherever they were deployed, roots of twenty to several hundred years. Caesar had new elite legions that followed him around, but this was hardly standard: a rather big difference. As for Professor Kennedy's details, the Cardwell system was brought into force in the early 1870s, well after the Khyber Pass disaster, his essay thereby confusing Sir Louis Cavagnari's unhappy undertakings of 1879 with the 1840s. Americans today feel nothing akin to the ambitions of an army for whom conquest was a way of life, as in Rome, and they hardly share the national enthusiasms that backed the armies of Queen Victoria or King George.

12. See, for instance, the July 28, 2001, op-ed essay by Michael Ignatieff in the *Washington Post* that matter-of-factly uses this term. After Afghanistan and Iraq, such faux descriptions of the republic as "empire" became even more frequent.

13. The role as "global scouts" is proclaimed in Schemmer, ed., *U.S. Special Operations Forces,* p. 12, a useful but often politically obtuse book, as in its belief that SOF "liberated Haiti from decades of dictatorship in 1995," p. 11.

14. The eager backup to ambassadors is stated in the "USSOCOM Mission" on page 1 of the *United States Special Operations Forces Posture Statement 2003–2004.* One problem of the linguistically adept OCEs is that, unlike the Foreign Service officers, the language in which these operators have been trained is often not the one of the country in which they are stationed. The OCEs were removed from Chad in 2005, for example, in part because they spoke competent Russian but not French.

15. An overview of the controversy and several examples of where such dispatching of special operations forces have caused turmoil is in Ann Scott Tyson and Dana Priest, "Pentagon Seeking Leeway," *Washington Post,* February 24, 2005. I have interviewed U.S. ambassadors, in particular of North African countries, who offer further examples of how such covert operations have been worryingly counterproductive.

SELECTED BIBLIOGRAPHY

Nonfiction

Abella, Alex, and Scott Gordon. *Shadow Enemies: Hitler's Secret Terror Plot against the United States.* Guilford, CT: Lyons Press, 2002.

Alanbrooke, Field Marshal Lord. *War Diaries, 1939–1945.* Edited by Alex Danchev. London: Weidenfeld and Nicholson, 2001.

Allen, Charles. *The Savage Wars of Peace.* London: Michael Joseph, 1990.

Allen, Gardner W. *Our Navy and the Barbary Corsairs* (1905). Reprint. Hamden, CT: Archon Books, 1965.

Alles, Jean-François. *Commandos de Chasse Gendarmerie, Algérie, 1959–1962, récit et témoignages.* Paris: Atlante Editions, 2000.

Andrew, Christopher. *For the President's Eyes Only: Secret Intelligence and the American Presidency, from Washington to Bush.* New York: HarperCollins, 1995.

Anson, George. *A Voyage round the World in the Years MDCCXL, I, II, III, IV.* Compiled by Richard Walter and Benjamin Robins (London, 1748). Reprint. New York: Oxford University Press, 1974.

Arnold, Thomas. *The Renaissance at War.* London: Cassell and Co., 2001.

Arquilla, John. *From Troy to Entebbe: Special Operations in Ancient and Modern Times.* Lanham, MD: University Press of America, 1996.

Arrian. *The Life of Alexander the Great.* Translated by Aubrey de Selincourt. London: Folio Society, 1970.

Ashdown, Paul, and Edward Caudill. *The Mosby Myth: A Confederate Hero in Life and Legend.* Wilmington, DE: Scholarly Resources, 2002.

Aussaresses, General Paul. *Services Speciaux: Algérie, 1955–1957.* Paris: Perrin, 2001.

Bachrach, Bernard S. "Charlemagne and the Carolingian General Staff." *Journal of Military History* (April 2002).

———. *Early Carolingian Warfare: Prelude to Empire.* Philadelphia: University of Pennsylvania Press, 2001.

Bank, Aaron. *From OSS to Green Berets: The Birth of Special Forces.* Novato, CA: Presidio, 1986.

Barnett, Correlli. *Bonaparte.* London: Allen and Unwin, 1978.

Barter, Lieutenant General Richard. *The Siege of Delhi: Mutiny Memoirs of an Old Officer.* London: Folio Society, 1984.

Bartov, Omer. *Hitler's Army: Soldiers, Nazis, and War in the Third Reich.* Oxford: Oxford University Press, 1991.

Barzun, Jacques. *From Dawn to Decadence: 500 Years of Western Cultural Life, 1500 to the Present.* New York: HarperCollins, 2000.

Bass, Robert D. *The Green Dragoon: The Lives of Banastre Tarleton and Mary Robinson.* New York: Henry Holt, 1957.

Bawlf, Samuel. *The Secret Voyage of Sir Francis Drake, 1577–1580.* New York: Walker and Company, 2003.

Beckwith, Colonel Charles. *Delta Force: The Army's Elite Counterterrorist Unit.* New York: HarperCollins, 1983.

Beeler, John. *Warfare in Feudal Europe, 730–1200.* Ithaca: Cornell University Press, 1971.

Beevor, Antony. *Crete: The Battle and the Resistance.* Boulder, CO: Westview Press, 1994.

Bell, J. Bowyer. *Terror out of Zion: Irgun Zvai, Leumi LEHI, and the Palestine Underground, 1929–1949.* New York: St. Martin's Press, 1977.

Billias, George Athan. *General John Glover and His Marblehead Mariners.* New York: Henry Holt, 1960.

Black, Jeremy. *Eighteenth Century Europe, 1700–1789.* New York: St. Martin's Press, 1990.

———. *European Warfare, 1660–1815.* New Haven: Yale University Press, 1994.

———, ed. *European Warfare, 1453–1815.* New York: St. Martin's Press, 1999.

Black, Robert. "Behind the Lines: The Rangers' Lonely War in Korea." *Military History Quarterly,* Summer 2000.

Blake, Robert. *The Decline of Power, 1915–1964.* New York: Oxford University Press, 1985.

Bloch, Marc. *Feudal Society.* Translated by L. A. Manyon. Chicago: University of Chicago Press, 1964.

Bobbitt, Philip. *The Shield of Achilles: War, Peace, and the Course of History.* New York: Knopf, 2002.

Boxer, C. R. *The Dutch Seaborne Empire.* London: Hutchinson, 1977.

Bradford, Ernle. *Hannibal.* Ware, UK: Wordsworth Editions, 2000.

Brandt, Nat. *The Man Who Tried to Burn New York.* Syracuse, NY: Syracuse University Press, 1986.

Brooks, Richard. *The Royal Marines: 1664 to the Present.* Annapolis, MD: Naval Institute Press, 2002.

Brumwell, Stephen. *Redcoats: The British Soldier and War in the Americas, 1755–1763.* Cambridge: Cambridge University Press, 2003.

———. *White Devil: A True Story of War, Savagery, and Vengeance in Colonial America.* Cambridge, MA: Da Capo Press, 2004.

Bryant, Arthur. *Jackets of Green: A Study of the History, Philosophy, and Character of the Rifle Brigade.* London: Collins, 1972.

Burgess, William H., ed. *Inside Spetsnaz: Soviet Special Operations, A Critical Analysis.* Novato, CA: Presidio Press, 1990.

Burn, A. R. *Greece and Rome: 750 B.C.–565 A.D.* Glenview, IL: Scott, Foresman, 1970.

Caesar, Julius. *Alexandrian, African, and Spanish Wars.* Translated by A. G. Way. Cambridge, MA: Harvard University Press, 1955.

———. *War Commentaries.* Translated by John Warrington. New York: Dutton, 1958.

Campbell, Duncan B. *Greek and Roman Artillery 399 B.C.–A.D. 363.* Oxford: Osprey Publishing, 2003.

Cantor, Norman F. *In the Wake of the Plague: The Black Death and the World It Made.* New York: Free Press, 2001.

Carney, Colonel John T., and Benjamin F. Schemmer. *No Room for Error: The Covert Operations of America's Special Tactics Units from Iran to Afghanistan.* New York: Random House, 2002.

Cartledge, Paul. *The Spartans: An Epic History.* London: Pan Macmillan, 2002.

Chandler, David G. *On the Napoleonic Wars.* London: Greenhill, 1994.

Chandos (Oliver Lyttelton, 1st Viscount). *The Memoirs of Lord Chandos.* London: Bodley Head, 1962.

Chatterton, Lieutenant Commander E. Keble. *Q-Ships and Their Story.* Boston: Charles E. Lauriat Co., 1923.

Church, Benjamin. *The History of the Eastern Expeditions of 1689, 1690, 1692, 1696 and 1704 against the Indians and the French.* Boston: Wiggin and W. P. Lunt, 1867.

Churchill, Winston S. *Marlborough: His Life and Times.* Vols. 1–6. New York: Scribner's and Sons, 1933–38.

———. *The Second World War.* Vol. 2. Boston: Houghton Mifflin, 1949.

———. *The World Crisis.* Vols. 1–4. New York: Scribner's, 1923–29.

Cipolla, Carlo. *Guns and Sails in the Early Phase of European Expansion, 1400–1700.* London: Collins, 1965.

Clancy, Tom, with General Carl Stiner (ret.). *Shadow Warriors: Inside the Special Forces.* New York: G. P. Putnam, 2002.

Clark, Alan. *The Fall of Crete.* London: Anthony Blond Ltd., 1962.

Cochrane, Thomas, Tenth Earl of Dundonald. *Autobiography of a Seaman.* London: Richard Bentley, 1860.

Cockburn, Christopher, and Patrick Cockburn. *Out of the Ashes: The Resurrection of Saddam Hussein.* New York: HarperPerennial, 2000.

Codman, John. *An American Transport in the Crimean War.* New York: Bonner, Silver and Co., 1896.

Cohen, Elliott. *Commandos and Politicians: Elite Military Units in Modern Democracies.* Cambridge, MA: Harvard Center of International Affairs, 1978.

Coll, Steve. *Ghost Wars: The Secret History of the CIA, Afghanistan and Bin Laden, from the Soviet Invasion to September 10, 2001.* New York: Penguin, 2004.

Conboy, Kenneth, and Dale Andrade. *Spies and Commandos: How America Lost the Secret War in North Vietnam.* Lawrence: University of Kansas Press, 2000.

Connelly, Owen. *On War and Leadership.* Princeton: Princeton University Press, 2002.

Contamine, Philippe. *War in the Middle Ages.* Oxford: Basil Blackwell, 1984.

Corneille, Major John. *Journal of My Service in India.* London: Folio Society, 1966.

Cortés, Hernan. *Letters from Mexico.* Translated and edited by Anthony Pagden. New Haven: Yale University Press, 1971.

Crawford, Mark et al. *Encyclopedia of the Mexican-American War.* Santa Barbara: ABC-CLIO, 1999.

Czech, Kenneth P. "Rome's German Nightmare." *MHQ: Quarterly Journal of Military History* (Autumn 1992).

Da Cunha, Euclides. *Rebellion in the Backlands.* Chicago: University of Chicago Press, 1957.

Dague, Everett. "Henri Clarke, Minister of War, and the Malet Conspiracy." *Napoleon Scholarship: Journal of the International Napoleonic Society* 1, no. 2 (December 1998).

Davis, Donald A. *Lightning Strike: The Secret Mission to Kill Admiral Yamamoto and Avenge Pearl Harbor.* New York: St. Martin's Press, 2005.

Davis, R. H. C. *The Medieval Warhorse.* London: Thames and Hudson, 1989.

Dawson, Joseph G. *Doniphan's Epic March: The First Missouri Volunteers in the Mexican War.* Lawrence: University of Kansas Press, 1999.

De Bueil, Jean. *Le Jouvencel, Volumes I and II.* Paris: Librairie Renouard, 1888, 1889.

De Crèvecoeur, M. G. J. *Letters from an American Farmer.* Philadelphia: Matthew Carey, 1793.

De Mailles, Jacques. *History of Bayard the Good, Chevalier sans peur et sans reproche, compiled by the Loyal Serviteur.* Translated from the French. London: Chapman and Hall, 1883.

De Marbot, Jean Baptiste. *The Exploits of Baron de Marbot.* Edited by Christopher Summerville. London: Constable, 2000.

DeVries, Kelly. "Teenagers at War during the Middle Ages," in *The Premodern Teenager: Youth in Society, 1150–1650.* Edited by Konrad Eisenbich. Toronto: Centre for Renaissance and Reformation Studies, 2002.

———. "The Use of Gunpowder Weaponry by and against Joan of Arc during the Hundred Years' War," *Guns and Men in Medieval Europe, 1200–1500.* Aldershot, UK: Ashgate Publishing, 2002.

Diamond, Jared. *Guns, Germs, and Steel: The Fates of Human Societies.* New York: Norton, 1997.

Diaz del Castillo, Bernal. *The Discovery and Conquest of Mexico, 1517–1521.* Translated by A. P. Maudslay. New York: Farrar, Straus, 1956.

Dobbs, Michael. *Saboteurs: The Nazi Raid on America.* New York: Knopf, 2004.

Dodgeon, M. H., and Samuel Lieu, comps. *The Roman Eastern Frontier and the Persian Wars (A.D. 226–363): A Documentary History.* London: Routledge, 1991.

Dohla, Johann Conrad. *A Hessian Diary of the American Revolution.* Translated by Bruce Burgoyne. Norman: University of Oklahoma Press, 1990.

Dokuchchaev, Colonel A. "100-Dnevng Ydarnyy Kruz." *Krasnaya Zvezda* (November 6, 1992).

Doyle, Arthur Conan. *The Great Boer War.* New York: McClure Phillips and Co., 1902.

Drury, Ian. *German Stormtrooper, 1914–1918.* Oxford, UK: Osprey Publishing, 1995.

Dubois, Laurent. *Avengers of the New World: The Story of the Haitian Revolution.* Cambridge, MA: Harvard University Press, 2004.

Duckworth, Colin. *The D'Antraigues Phenomenon.* Newcastle, UK: Avero, 1986.

Duffy, Christopher. *The Military Experience in the Age of Reason.* London: Routledge, 1987.

Dunsterville, Major General L. C. *The Adventures of Dunsterforce.* London: Edward Arnold, 1920.

Dupuy, R. Ernest, and William H. Baumer. *The Little Wars of the United States.* New York: Hawthorne Books, 1968.

Durrell, Lawrence. *Bitter Lemons.* London: Faber and Faber, 1957.

Earle, Peter. *The Sack of Panama: Sir Henry Morgan's Adventures on the Spanish Main.* New York: Viking, 1981.

Eliade, Mircea, ed. *The Encyclopedia of Religion.* New York: Macmillan, 1987.

Ellis, Joseph J. *His Excellency George Washington.* New York: Knopf, 2004.

Ennes, James M. Jr. *Assault on the* Liberty: *The Untold Story of the Israeli Attack on an American Intelligence Ship.* New York: Random House, 1979.

Esdaile, Charles. *The Peninsular War.* New York: Palgrave, 2003.

Ewald, Captain Johann. *Diary of the American War: A Hessian Journal by Captain Johann Ewald.* New Haven: Yale University Press, 1979.

Exquemelin, Alexander. *The History of the Bucaniers of America.* Vols. I and II. London: T. Evans, 1777.

Farrow, Edward S. *Mountain Scouting: A Handbook for Officers and Soldiers on the Frontiers.* Norman: University of Oklahoma Press, 2000.

Featherstone, Donald. *Armies and Warfare in the Pike-and-Shot Era.* London: Constable and Co., 1998.

Ferguson, Niall. *The Pity of War: Explaining World War I.* New York: Basic Books, 1999.

Fernandez-Armesto, Felipe. *Civilizations: Culture, Ambition, and the Transformations of Nature.* New York: Simon and Schuster, 2001.

Fischer, Fritz. *Germany's Aims in the First World War.* New York: Norton, 1968.

Foster, T. E., trans. *Military Instructions from the Late King of Prussia to His Generals.* 5th ed. London: Crutwell, 1818.

Fox, Robin Lane. *The Search for Alexander.* Boston: Little, Brown, 1980.

France, John. *Western Warfare in the Age of the Crusades, 1000–1300.* Ithaca: Cornell University Press, 1999.

Frantzen, Allen J. *Bloody Good: Chivalry, Sacrifice, and the Great War.* Chicago: University of Chicago Press, 2003.

Frazier, Donald S., ed. *The United States and Mexico at War: Nineteenth-Century Expansionism and Conflict.* New York: Simon and Schuster, 1998.

Fritz, Stephen G. *Endkampf: Soldiers, Civilians, and the Death of the Third Reich.* Lexington: University of Kentucky Press, 2004.

Fromkin, David. *Europe's Last Summer: Who Started the Great War in 1914?* New York: Knopf, 2004.

———. "The Importance of T. E. Lawrence." *New Criterion* 10, no. 1 (September 1991).

Frontinus, Sextus Julius. *Stratagems. Aqueducts of Rome.* Translated by Charles E. Bennett. Cambridge, MA: Harvard University Press, 1980.

Fuller, Major General J. F. C. *Julius Caesar: Man, Soldier, and Tyrant.* New Brunswick, NJ: Rutgers University Press, 1965.

———. *The Last of the Gentlemen's Wars, a Subaltern's Journal.* London: Faber and Faber, 1937.

———. *Military History of the Western World,* Vols. I–III. New York: Funk and Wagnalls, 1954–56.

Fussell, Paul. *The Great War and Modern Memory.* New York: Oxford University Press, 1975.

Gardiner, C. Harvey. *Naval Power in the Conquest of Mexico.* New York: Greenwood Press, 1956.

Gates, John M. "Indians and Insurrectos: The U.S. Army's Experience with Insurgency." *Parameters* 13, no. 1 (March 1983): 59–68.

Glete, Jan. *Warfare at Sea, 1500–1650: Maritime Conflicts and the Transformation of Europe.* London: Routledge, 2000.

Goldsworthy, Adrian. *Cannae.* London: Cassell, 2001.

———. *Roman Warfare.* London: Cassell, 2000.

Gosse, Philip. *The History of Piracy.* New York: Burt Franklin, 1932.

Green, Peter. *Alexander of Macedon, 356–323 B.C.: A Historical Biography.* Los Angeles: University of California Press, 1991.

Greene, Graham. *Reflections*. London: Viking Penguin, 1990.

Greene, Jack, and Alessandro Massignani. *The Black Prince and the Sea Devils: The Story of Valerio Borghese and the Elite Units of the Decima MAS*. Cambridge, MA: Da Capo Press, 2004.

Grose, Peter. *Operation Rollback: America's Secret War behind the Iron Curtain*. Boston: Houghton Mifflin, 2000.

Haas, Michael E. *In the Devil's Shadow: UN Special Operations during the Korean War*. Annapolis, MD: Naval Institute Press, 2000.

Haefeli, Evan, and Kevin Sweeney. *Captors and Captives: The 1704 French and Indian Raid on Deerfield*. Amherst: University of Massachusetts Press, 2003.

Hale, J. R. *War and Society in Renaissance Europe, 1450–1620*. New York: St. Martin's Press, 1985.

Hall, Bert S. *Weapons and Warfare in Renaissance Europe: Gunpowder, Technology and Tactics*. Baltimore: Johns Hopkins University Press, 1997.

Hallam, Elizabeth, ed. *Chronicles of the Crusades: Eye-Witness Accounts of the Wars between Christianity and Islam*. London: Weidenfeld and Nicolson, 1989.

Hamilton, Charles D., and Peter Krentz, eds. *Polis and Polemos: Essays on Politics, War, and History in Ancient Greece in Honor of Donald Kagan*. Claremont, CA: Regina Books, 1997.

Haney, Eric L. *Inside Delta Force*. New York: Dell, 2002.

Hanson, Victor Davis. *Carnage and Culture: Landmark Battles in the Rise of Western Power*. New York: Doubleday, 2001.

———. *The Wars of the Ancient Greeks and Their Innovation of Modern Military Culture*. London: Cassell, 1999.

Harding, Richard. *Amphibious Warfare in the Eighteenth Century: The British Expedition to the West Indies, 1740–1742*. London: Royal Historical Society, 1991.

Hattendorf, John B., and Richard W. Ungar, eds. *War at Sea in the Middle Ages and the Renaissance*. Suffolk, UK: Boydell Press, 2003.

Heikal, Mohammed. *The Sphinx and the Commissar: The Rise and Fall of Soviet Influence in the Middle East*. New York: Harper and Row, 1978.

Heilbrunn, Otto. *Warfare in the Enemy's Rear*. London: George Allen and Unwin, 1965.

Hemmings, John. *The Conquest of the Incas*. New York: Harcourt Brace, 1970.

Henderson, Bernard W. *The Great War between Athens and Sparta*. London: Macmillan, 1927.

Herold, Christopher, ed. *The Mind of Napoleon: A Selection from His Written and Spoken Words*. New York: Columbia University Press, 1955.

Hersh, Seymour. *Chain of Command: The Road from 9/11 to Abu Ghraib*. New York: HarperCollins, 2004.

———. *The Dark Side of Camelot*. Boston: Little, Brown, 1997.

Hibbert, Christopher. *Wolfe at Quebec*. London: Longmans, 1959.

Higham, Charles. *Murdering Mr. Lincoln: A New Detection of the 19th Century's Most Famous Crime*. Beverly Hills, CA: New Millennium, 2004.

Hitchcock, Ethan Allen. *Fifty Years in Camp and Field: Diary of Major-General Ethan Allen Hitchcock, USA*. Edited by W. A. Croffut. New York: Putnam, 1909.

Hoffmann, Peter. *Hitler's Personal Security*. Cambridge, MA: MIT Press, 1979.

Holland, Cecelia. "Firebrands of the Franks." *MHQ: Quarterly Journal of Military History* (Autumn 1992).

Holt, Thaddeus. "Joint Plan Red." *Quarterly Journal of Military History*. Autumn 1988.

———. *Naval Warfare in the Twentieth Century*. London: Croom Helm, 1977.

Homer. *Iliad*. Translated by Robert Fitzgerald. New York: Farrar, Straus and Giroux, 2004.

Hopkirk, Peter. *Like Hidden Fire: The Plot to Bring Down the British Empire*. New York: Kodansha America, 1994.

Horne, Alistair. *How Far to Austerlitz? Napoleon, 1805–1815*. New York: St. Martin's Press, 1996.

Hubbard, Jake T. "Americans as Guerrilla Fighters: Robert Rogers and His Rangers," *American Heritage,* August 1971.

Hughes-Hallet, Lucy. *Heroes*. London: Fourth Estate, 2004.

Joes, Anthony James. *Guerrilla Conflict before the Cold War*. Westport, CT: Praeger, 1996.

Johnson, Dominic. *Overconfidence and War*. Cambridge, MA: Harvard University Press, 2004.

Johnston, R. M., ed. *In the Words of Napoleon: The Emperor Day by Day,* with new material added to the 1910 edition by Philip Haythornthwaite. London: Greenhill Books, 2002.

Josephus, Flavius. *Complete Works*. Grand Rapids, MI: Kregel Publishers, 1960.

Kagan, Donald. *The Peloponnesian War*. New York: Viking, 2003.

Karpenko, A. V., ed. *Otechestveniye Strategicheskiye Raketniye Komompleksy*. St. Petersburg: Nevkiy Bastion, 1999.

Kazin, Alfred. *Contemporaries from the 19th Century to the Present*. New York: Horizon Press, 1982.

Keegan, John. *A History of Warfare*. New York: Knopf, 1993.

Keen, Maurice, ed. *Medieval Warfare*. New York: Oxford University Press, 1999.

Kelsey, Harry. *Sir Francis Drake: The Queen's Pirate*. New Haven: Yale University Press, 1998.

———. *Sir John Hawkins: Queen Elizabeth's Slave Trader*. New Haven: Yale University Press, 2003.

Kemp, Peter, ed. *Oxford Companion to Ships and the Sea*. London: Oxford University Press, 1976.

Kennedy, Paul. *The War Plans of the Great Powers, 1880–1914*. Winchester, MA: Allen and Unwin, 1979.

Ketchum, Richard M. *Saratoga: Turning Point of America's Revolutionary War*. New York: Henry Holt, 1997.

———. *Victory at Yorktown: The Campaign That Won the Revolution*. New York: Henry Holt, 2004.

Keynes, John Maynard. *A Treatise on Money*. London: Macmillan, 1930.

Knaus, John Kenneth. *Orphans of the Cold: America and the Tibetan Struggle for Survival*. New York: Public Affairs, 1999.

Koch, Hans W. "The Prussian Guards in the Eighteenth Century." Hamish Ion and Keith Neilson, eds. *Elite Formations in War and Peace*. Westport, CT: Praeger, 1996.

Kurowski, Franz. *The Brandenburgers: Global Mission*. Translated by David Johnston. Winnipeg: Federowicz, 1997.

Lancel, Serge. *Hannibal*. Paris: Librairie Athène Fayard, 1995.

Lane, Kris E. *Pillaging the Empire: Piracy in the Americas, 1500–1750*. Armonk, NY: M. E. Sharpe, 1998.

Laqueur, Walter. *A History of Terrorism*. Boston: Little, Brown, 1977.

Lawrence, John. *Lawrence of Lucknow*. London: Hodder and Stoughton, 1990.

Lawrence, T. E. *Seven Pillars of Wisdom*. Hertfordshire, U.K.: Wordsworth, 1997.

Leebaert, Derek. *The Fifty-Year Wound: How America's Cold War Victory Shapes Our World*. Boston: Little, Brown, 2003.

———. *Technology 2001: The Future of Computing and Communications*. Cambridge, MA: MIT Press, 1991.

Leebaert, Derek, ed. *Soviet Military Thinking*. Boston: Allen and Unwin, 1981.

Lefebvre, Georges. *Napoleon from Tilsit to Waterloo*. Princeton: Princeton University Press, 1947.

Lendon, J. E. *Soldiers and Ghosts: A History of Battle in Classical Antiquity*. New Haven: Yale University Press, 2005.

Leon-Portilla, Miguel, ed. *The Broken Spears: The Aztec Account of the Conquest of Mexico*. Boston: Beacon Press, 1992.

Lewis, Bernard. *The Assassins: A Radical Sect in Islam*. New York: Basic Books, 2003.

Liddell Hart, Basil. *Foch: The Man of Orleans*. Boston: Little, Brown, 1932.

———. *"T. E. Lawrence" in Arabia and After*. London: Jonathan Cape, 1934.

Liddell Hart, Basil, ed. *The Rommel Papers*. New York: Harcourt Brace, 1953.

Linn, Brian. *The Philippine War, 1899–1902*. Lawrence: University Press of Kansas, 2000.

Livy. *Stories of Rome*. Translated by Roger Nichols. New York: Cambridge University Press, 1982.

Loescher, Burt Garfield. *Rogers' Rangers: The First Green Berets*. San Mateo, CA: printed privately, 1969.

Lucas, James. *Kommando: German Special Forces of World War Two*. London: Orion Publishing, 1985.

———. *Storming Eagles: German Airborne Forces in World War II*. London: Arms and Armour, 1988.

Ludendorff, Erich. *Ludendorff's Own Story*. New York: Harper and Bros., 1920.

Luttwak, Edward. *Coup d'Etat: A Practical Handbook.* Cambridge, MA: Harvard University Press, 1979.

———. *The Grand Strategy of the Roman Empire.* Baltimore: Johns Hopkins University Press, 1976.

Maass, Walter B. *The Netherlands at War, 1940–1945.* London: Abelard-Schuman, 1970.

MacDonald, Callum. *The Killing of SS-Obergruppenführer Reinhard Heydrich.* New York: Free Press, 1989.

Mack Smith, Dennis. *Garibaldi.* Westport, CT: Greenwood Press, 1956.

Macksey, Kenneth. *The Searchers: Radio Intercept in Two World Wars.* London: Cassell, 2003.

MacLean, Simon. *Kingship and Politics in the Late Ninth Century: Charles the Fat and the End of the Carolingian Empire.* Cambridge: Cambridge University Press, 2003.

Madden, Thomas, F., ed. *Crusades.* Ann Arbor: University of Michigan Press, 2003.

Mahan, Alfred Thayer. *The Major Operations of the Navies in the War of American Independence.* New York: Greenwood Press, 1969.

Malcom, Ben S. *White Tigers: My Secret War in North Korea.* Washington, D.C.: Brassey's, 1996.

Martin, James Kirby. *Benedict Arnold: An American Warrior Reconsidered.* New York: New York University Press, 1997.

Mattingly, Garret. *The Defeat of the Spanish Armada.* Boston: Houghton Mifflin, 1959.

May, Ernest. *Strange Victory: Hitler's Conquest of France.* New York: Farrar, Straus and Giroux, 2000.

McCullough, David. *1776.* New York: Simon and Schuster, 2005.

McLynn, Frank. *1759: The Year Britain Became Master of the World.* New York: Atlantic Monthly Press, 2004.

McRaven, William H. *Spec Ops: Case Studies in Special Operations Warfare.* Novato, CA: Presidio, 1995.

Melton, Buckner F. *Aaron Burr: Conspiracy to Treason.* New York: Wiley, 2002.

Millar, George. *Waiting in the Night: A Story of the Maquis.* Garden City, NY: Doubleday, 1946.

Miller, Laura. "My Favorite War." *New York Review of Books* (March 21, 2004).

Millett, Allan R. *Semper Fidelis: The History of the United States Marine Corps.* New York: Macmillan, 1980.

Milton, Giles. *White Gold: The Extraordinary Story of Thomas Pellow and North Africa's One Million European Slaves.* London: Hodder and Stoughton, 2004.

Montaigne, Michel de. *Complete Works: Essays, Travel Journal, Letters.* Translated by Donald M. Frame. New York: Knopf, 2003.

Montbrun, Deodat Puy. *Les chemins sans croix: Commandos spéciaux en Indochine.* Paris: Presses de la Cité, 1964.

Morgenthau, Henry. *Secrets of the Bosphorus: Constantinople, 1913–1916.* London: Hutchinson, 1918.

Morison, Samuel Eliot. *The Two Ocean War: A Short History of the United States Navy in the Second World War.* Boston: Little, Brown, 1963.

Mosby, John S. *Mosby's War Reminiscences and Stuart's Cavalry Campaigns.* 1887. Reprint. New York: Pageant Book Co., 1958.

Mosier, John. *The Blitzkrieg Myth: How Hitler and the Allies Misread the Strategic Realities of World War II.* New York: HarperCollins, 2003.

———. *Myth of the Great War.* New York: HarperCollins, 2001.

Moskin, J. Robert. *The U.S. Marine Corps Story.* Boston: Little, Brown, 1977.

Moss, W. Stanley. *Ill Met by Moonlight.* New York: Macmillan, 1950.

Motley, John Lothrop. *Rise of the Dutch Republic.* New York: Harper and Bros., 1900.

Munck, Thomas. *Seventeenth Century Europe, 1596–1700.* New York: St. Martin's Press, 1990.

Murson, A. F. *The Scottish Histories: King Robert the Bruce.* Adapted. New Lanark, Scotland: Geddes and Grosset, 2000.

Naylor, Sean. *Not a Good Day to Die: The Untold Story of Operation Anaconda.* New York: Berkley Publishing Group, 2005.

Nichols, Donald. *How Many Times Must I Die?* Brooksville, FL: Brooksville Printing, 1981.

Nicolle, David. *Medieval Warfare Sourcebook. Volume I: Warfare in Western Christendom.* London: Arms and Armour Press, 1995.

Norwich, John Julius. *The Normans in the South, 1016–1130.* London: Longmans, Green, 1967.

O'Callaghan, E. B. *Documents Relative to the Colonial History of the State of New York.* Albany: Weed, Parsons and Co., 1855, Vol. X.

O'Donnell, Patrick K. *OSS: Operatives, Spies, Saboteurs: The Unknown Story of the Men and Women of World War II's OSS.* New York: Free Press, 2000.

Ogburn, Charleton. *The Marauders.* New York: Harper, 1959.

Oman, C. W. *The Art of War in the Middle Ages, A.D. 378–1515.* Revised and edited by John H. Beeler. Ithaca: Cornell University Press, 1968.

———. *A History of the Art of War in the Middle Ages.* London: Methuen, 1978.

———. *A History of the Art of War in the Sixteenth Century.* New York: Dutton, 1937.

Oswandel, J. J. *Notes of the Mexican War, 1846–47–48.* Philadelphia: n.p., 1885.

Overy, Richard. *Russia's War: Blood upon the Snow.* New York: TV Books, 1991.

Padfield, Peter. *Doenitz: The Last Führer.* New York: Harper and Row, 1984.

Pakenham, Thomas. *The Boer War.* London: Weidenfeld and Nicholson, 1979.

Pancake, John S. *This Destructive War: The British Campaign in the Carolinas, 1780–1782.* University, AL: University of Alabama Press, 1985.

Parker, Geoffrey. "The Etiquette of Atrocity." *MHQ: Quarterly Journal of Military History* (Summer 1993).

———. *The Military Revolution: Military Innovation and the Rise of the West, 1500–1800.* Cambridge: Cambridge University Press, 1988.

Parker, John. *Commandos: The Inside Story of Britain's Most Elite Fighting Force.* London: Headline, 2000.

Payne, Robert. *The Dream and the Tomb.* New York: Stein and Day, 1984.

Payne-Gallwey, Sir Ralph. *The Crossbow: Mediaeval and Modern Military and Sporting, Its Construction History & Management.* New York: Holland Press, 1958.

Peniakoff, Lieutenant Colonel Vladimir. *Popski's Private Army.* New York: Doubleday, 1950.

Pepys, Samuel. *The Diary of Samuel Pepys.* Vols. 3–4. Edited by Robert Latham and William Matthews. Berkeley, CA: University of California Press, 1974.

Pervov, M. *Zentinoye Raketnoye Oruzhiye Protivovozdushnoy Oborony Strany.* Moscow: ZAO PFG, 2001.

Peskin, Allan. *Winfield Scott and the Profession of Arms.* Kent, OH: Kent State University Press, 2004.

Peterson, Harold L. *A History of Firearms.* New York: Charles Scribner's Sons, 1961.

Philby, Kim. *My Silent War.* New York: Grove Press, 1968.

Phillips, Jonathan. *The Fourth Crusade and the Sack of Constantinople.* New York: Viking, 2004.

Pittenger, Reverend William. *Capturing a Locomotive.* 1881. Available through Digital Scanning, Inc.

Plaster, John L. *SOG: The Secret Wars of America's Commandos in Vietnam.* New York: Simon and Schuster, 1997.

Pocock, Tom. *The Terror before Trafalgar: Nelson, Napoleon and the Secret War.* New York: Norton, 2002.

Potter, James. *Autobiography of a Revolutionary Soldier.* 1859. Revised by John Roberts. Reprint. New York: Arno Press, 1979.

Powell, Alan. *The Third Force: ANGUA's New Guinea War, 1942–46.* Melbourne: Oxford University Press, 2003.

Pratt, Fletcher. *Hail Caesar!* New York: Smith and Haas, 1936.

Prescott, William H. *History of the Conquest of Mexico.* New York: Modern Library, 1998.

———. *History of the Conquest of Peru.* New York: Modern Library, 1998.

Pritchett, Kendrick W. *The Greek State at War.* Parts 1 and 2. Berkeley: University of California Press, 1971–74.

Ramage, James A. *Gray Ghost: The Life of Col. John Singleton Mosby.* Lexington: University of Kentucky Press, 1999.

Randall, Willard S. *Benedict Arnold: Patriot and Traitor.* New York: Morrow, 1990.

———. *George Washington: A Life.* New York: Henry Holt, 1997.

Rediker, Marcus. *Between the Devil and the Deep Blue Sea: Merchant Seamen, Pirates, and the Anglo-American Maritime World, 1700–1750.* Cambridge: Cambridge University Press, 1987.

Rees, Laurence. *How Mankind Committed the Ultimate Infamy at Auschwitz: A New History*. New York: Public Affairs, 2005.

Reid, Samuel C. *Scouting Expeditions of McCulloch's Texas Rangers*. Philadelphia: n.p., 1847.

Reilly, Robin. *Wolfe of Quebec*. London: Cassell, 1960.

Reitz, Denys. *Commando: A Boer Journal of the Boer War*. London: Faber and Faber, 1929.

Ridley, Jasper. *Garibaldi*. London: Constable, 1974.

Riley-Smith, Jonathan. *The Crusades*. New Haven: Yale University Press, 1987.

Roberts, Kenneth, ed. *March to Quebec: Journals of the Members of Arnold's Expedition*. New York: Doubleday, 1938.

Robertson, David, ed. *Reports of the Trials of Colonel Aaron Burr in the Circuit Court of the United States*. Vol. 1. New York: Da Capo Press, 1969.

Rodger, N. A. M. *Command of the Ocean: A Naval History of Britain, 1649–1815*. New York: Norton, 2004.

Rogers, Horatio, ed. *Hadden's Journal and Orderly Books: A Journal Kept in Canada and Upon Burgoyne's Campaign in 1776 and 1777*. Albany, N.Y.: Joel Munsell's Sons, 1884.

Rogers, Robert. *Journals of Major Robert Rogers*. New Canaan, CT: Readex Microprint, 1966.

Rommel, Erwin. *Attacks*. Provo, UT: Athena Press, 1979.

Rooney, David. *Wingate and the Chindits: Redressing the Balance*. London: Cassell, 1994.

Roosevelt, Theodore Jr. *Rank and File: True Stories of the Great War*. New York: Scribner's, 1928.

Roots, Ivan. *The Great Rebellion, 1642–1660*. London: B. T. Batsford Ltd., 1966.

Rosenbaum, David M. "Nuclear Terror." *International Security*, 1, no. 3 (1977).

Roskill, Stephen. *Hankey, Man of Secrets, Vol. I*. New York: St. Martin's Press, 1970.

Ross, Robert Todd. *The Supercommandos: First Special Service Force, 1942–1944*. Atglen, PA: Schiffer Military History, 2000.

Rowe, Michael, ed. *Collaboration and Resistance in Napoleonic Europe: State Formation in an Age of Upheaval, c. 1800–1815*. New York: Palgrave, 2003.

Runciman, Steven. *The Fall of Constantinople, 1453*. Cambridge: Cambridge University Press, 1965.

———. *A History of the Crusades, Vols. 1–3*. Cambridge: Cambridge University Press, 1951–54.

Schama, Simon. *Citizens: A Chronicle of the French Revolution*. New York: Random House, 1989.

Schemmer, Benjamin F., ed. *U.S. Special Operations Forces*. Tampa, FL: Special Operations Warrior Foundation, 2003.

Schlesinger, Arthur Jr. "On Heroic Leadership and the Dilemma of Strong Men and Weak Peoples." *Encounter* (December 1960).

Schom, Alan. *Napoleon Bonaparte*. New York: HarperCollins, 1997.

Sellinger, Matthew. "A Desperate Undertaking." *On Point,* Summer 1999 (vol. 5, no. 2).

Shackley, Theodore. *Spymaster: My Life in the CIA*. Potomac, MD: Potomac Books, 2005.

Shankland, Peter. *Byron of the Wager*. New York: Coward, McCann, 1975.

Shepherd, Ben. *War in the Wild East: The German Army and Soviet Partisans*. Cambridge, MA: Harvard University Press, 2004.

Shultz, Richard H. *The Secret War against Hanoi*. New York: HarperCollins, 1999.

Skorzeny, Otto. *Secret Missions*. Translated by Jacques LeClercq. New York: Dutton, 1950.

Smail, R. C. *Crusading Warfare, 1097–1193*. Cambridge: Cambridge University Press, 1995.

Smith, George Winston, and Charles Judah. *Chronicles of the Gringos: The U.S. Army in the Mexican War, 1846–1848, Accounts of Eyewitnesses and Combatants*. Albuquerque: University of New Mexico Press, 1968.

Smith, R. Harris. *OSS: The Secret History of America's First Central Intelligence Agency*. Berkeley: University of California Press, 1972.

Sorley, Lewis. *A Better War: The Unexamined Victories and Final Tragedy of America's Last Years in Vietnam*. New York: Harcourt Brace, 1999.

———. *Thunderbolt: General Creighton Abrams and the Army of His Times*. New York: Simon and Schuster, 1992.

Spar, Deborah L. *Ruling the Waves: Cycles of Discovery, Chaos, and Wealth from the Compass to the Internet.* New York: Harcourt, 2001.

Sparrow, Elizabeth. *Secret Service: British Agents in France, 1792–1815.* Woodbridge, UK: Boydell Press, 1999.

Stafford, David. *Secret Agent: The True Story of the Covert War against Hitler.* New York: Overlook Press, 2000.

Stein, Jeff. *A Murder in Wartime: The Untold Spy Story That Changed the Course of the Vietnam War.* New York: St. Martin's Press, 1992.

Stein, Marc Aurel. *On Alexander's Track to the Indus: Personal Narrative of Explorations on the North-West Frontier of India.* London: Macmillan, 1929.

Stephan, Robert W. *Stalin's Secret War: Soviet Counterintelligence against the Nazis, 1941–1945.* Lawrence: University of Kansas Press, 2004.

Stock, James W. *Zeebrugge, 23 April 1918.* New York: Random House, 1974.

Suetonius. *Lives of the Twelve Caesars.* Translated by Robert Graves. New York: Welcome Rain Publishing, 2001.

Sykes, Christopher. *Wassmuss, the German Lawrence.* New York: Longmans, 1936.

Taylor, A. J. P. *The Struggle for Mastery in Europe.* London: Oxford University Press, 1957.

Taylor, F. L. *The Art of War in Italy, 1494–1529.* Cambridge: Cambridge University Press, 1921.

Thomas, Evan. *John Paul Jones: Sailor, Hero, Father of the American Navy.* New York: Simon and Schuster, 2003.

Thomas, Geoffrey J., and Barry Ketley. *KG 200: The Luftwaffe's Most Secret Unit.* Sussex, UK: Hikoki Publications, 2003.

Thomas, Hugh. *The Conquest of Mexico.* London: Hutchinson, 1993.

Thomson, Janice E. *Mercenaries, Pirates, and Sovereigns: State Building and Extraterritorial Violence in Early Modern Europe.* Princeton: Princeton University Press, 1994.

Thucydides. *History of the Peloponnesian War.* Translated by Benjamin Jowett. New York: Prometheus Books, 1998.

Tidwell, William A., with James O. Hall and David Winfred Gaddy. *Come Retribution: The Confederate Secret Service and the Assassination of Lincoln.* Oxford, MS: University of Mississippi Press, 1988.

Tone, John. *The Fatal Knot: The Guerrilla War in Navarre and the Defeat of Napoleon in Spain.* Chapel Hill: University of North Carolina Press, 1994.

Tourison, Sedgwick. *Secret Army, Secret War: Washington's Tragic Spy Operations in North Vietnam.* Annapolis: Naval Institute Press, 1995.

Trevelyan, George Macaulay. *Garibaldi and the Thousand.* New York: Longmans, Green, 1933.

Treverton, Gregory F. *Covert Action: The Limits of Intervention in the Postwar World.* New York: Basic Books, 1987.

Trevor-Roper, Hugh. *The Plunder of the Arts in the Seventeenth Century.* London: Thames and Hudson, 1970.

Tulloch, Major General Derek. *Wingate in Peace and War.* Edited by Arthur Swinson. London: History Book Club, 1972.

Vaillant, George C. "Human Sacrifice in Ancient Mexico." *Natural History* 33 (1931), pp. 243–52.

Vegetius, Renatus. *Epitome of Military Science.* Translated by N. P. Milnar. Liverpool: Liverpool University Press, 1993.

Velleius Paterculus. *Compendium of Roman History.* Translated by F. W. Shipley. Loeb Classical Library. Cambridge, MA: Harvard University Press, 1924.

Ward, Matthew. *Breaking the Backcountry: The Seven Years' War in Virginia and Pennsylvania, 1754–1765.* Pittsburgh: University of Pittsburgh Press, 2003.

Warner, Philip. *The Crimean War: A Reappraisal.* New York: Taplinger, 1973.

Webster, Donovan. *The Burma Road: The Epic Story of the China–Burma–India Theater in World War II.* New York: Farrar, Straus and Giroux, 2003.

Wedgwood, C. V. *The Thirty Years' War.* London: Jonathan Cape, 1964.

Weiss, John McNish. "The Corps of Colonial Marines: Black Freedom Fighters of the War of 1812." Paper delivered at the University of the West Indies, St. Augustine, Trinidad and Tobago, January 4, 2001.

Wells, Peter. *The Battle That Stopped Rome: Emperor Augustus, Arminius, and the Slaughter of the Legions in the Teutoburg Forest.* New York: Norton, 2003.

Wheeler, Everett. *Stratagem and the Vocabulary of Military Trickery.* Leiden: E. J. Brill, 1998.

Wheeler, James Scott. *The Making of a World Power: War and the Military Revolution in Seventeenth Century England.* Stroud, UK: Sutton Publishing, 1999.

Wiencek, Henry. *An Imperfect God: George Washington, His Slaves and the Creation of America.* New York: Farrar, Straus and Giroux, 2003.

Wilson, R. L. *Colt: An American Legend: The Official History of Colt Firearms from 1836 to the Present.* New York: Abbeville Publishing, 1985.

Wright, Peter. *Spycatcher: The Candid Autobiography of a Senior Intelligence Officer.* New York: Viking, 1987.

Yadin, Yigael. *The Art of Warfare in Biblical Lands in the Light of Archaeological Study.* Vol. Two. New York: McGraw-Hill, 1963.

Young, Peter. *Commando.* New York: Ballantine, 1969.

Younghusband, Colonel G. J. *The Story of the Guides.* London: Macmillan, 1908.

Yousaf, Mohammed, and Adkin, Mark. *Afghanistan the Bear Trap: The Defeat of a Superpower.* Havertown, PA: Casemate, 1992.

Zacks, Richard. *The Pirate Coast: Thomas Jefferson, the First Marines, and the Secret Missions of 1805.* New York: Hyperion, 2005.

Fiction

Anderson, Poul. *The High Crusade.* New York: MacFadden Books, 1968.

Baldwin, Alex (W. E. B. Griffith). *The Fighting Agents.* New York: G. P. Putnam, 1987.

Balzac, Honoré. *Les Chouans.* Paris: Presses de la Renaissance, 1976.

Buchan, John. *The Courts of the Morning.* London: T. Nelson, 1932.

———. *Greenmantle.* London: Penguin Books, 1956.

———. *The Power-House.* London: William Blackwood, 1916.

———. *The Thirty-Nine Steps.* New York: Oxford University Press, 1993.

Cervantes, Miguel. *Don Quixote.* Philadelphia: Chelsea House Publishers, 2001.

Chesterton, G. K. *The Napoleon of Notting Hill.* Mineola, NY: Dover Publications, 1991.

Crichton, Michael. *The Great Train Robbery.* New York: Knopf, 1975.

Cooper, James Fenimore. *The Last of the Mohicans.* New York: Penguin, 1986.

Defoe, Daniel. *Memoirs of a Cavalier.* Oxford: Oxford University Press, 1991.

Duggan, Alfred. *Besieger of Cities.* New York: Pantheon, 1963.

Dumas, Alexandre. *Son of Porthos.* New York: F. M. Lupton, 1892.

Faulkner, William. "Turnabout." *Collected Stories of William Faulkner.* New York: Random House, 1950.

Fitzgerald, F. Scott. "Dalyrimple Goes Wrong." *Flappers and Philosophers.* New York: Washington Square Press, 1996.

———. *Tender Is the Night.* New York: Charles Scribner, 1962.

Garrett, Randall. "Despoilers of the Golden Empire." *Astounding* (March 1959).

Grahame, Kenneth. *The Wind in the Willows.* New York: Heritage Press, 1940.

Heaney, Seamus, trans. *Beowulf.* New York: Norton, 2000.

Household, Geoffrey. *Rogue Male.* London: Chatto and Windus, 1939.

———. *Thing to Love.* London: White Lion Publishers, 1972.

Marryat, Frederick. *Frank Mildmay, or the Naval Officer.* Ithaca: McBooks Press (Classics of Naval Literature), 1997.

———. "The Story of the Greek Slave." *The Pacha of Many Tales.* London: George Routledge, 1880.

Maugham, W. Somerset, ed. *Maugham's Choice of Kipling's Best.* Garden City, NY: Doubleday, 1953.

More, Thomas. *Utopia*. Cambridge: Cambridge University Press, 1988.

Ohlgren, Thomas. *Medieval Outlaws: Ten Tales in Modern English*. Stroud, UK: Sutton Publishing, 1998.

Parkinson, C. Northcote. *Dead Reckoning*. Ithaca: McBooks Press (Classics of Naval Literature), 2003.

———. *The Fireship*. Ithaca: McBooks Press (Classics of Naval Literature), 2002.

Piper, H. Beam. "He Walked around the Horses." 1948. Anthologized in *A Science Fiction Argosy*. Edited by Damon Knight. New York: Simon and Schuster, 1972.

Pyle, Howard. *Otto of the Silver Hand*. New York: Looking Glass Library, 1888.

Russell, Eric Frank. "Top Secret." *Astounding,* August 1956.

Thomason, Major John W. *Fix Bayonets!* New York: Scribner's, 1934.

———. *Salt Winds and Gobi Dust*. Annapolis: Naval Institute Press, 1994.

Tolstoy, Leo. *The Raid*. New York: New American Library, 1981.

———. *War and Peace*. New York: Simon and Schuster, 1942.

Vidal, Gore. *Burr*. New York: Random House, 1973.

Wise, Henry Augustus. *Tales for the Marines*. New York: J. C. Derby, 1855.

U.S. Government Publications

Barbary Wars, Operations. Vols. I–VI, Office of Naval Records. Washington, DC: GPO, 1942.

Barnett, Frank et al., eds. *Special Operations in U.S. Strategy*. Washington, DC: National Defense University Press, 1984.

Briscoe, Charles H. et al. *Weapon of Choice: U.S. Army Special Operations Forces in Afghanistan*. Fort Leavenworth, KS: Combat Studies Institute Press, 2004.

Haas, Michael E. *Apollo's Warriors: U.S. Air Force Special Operations during the Cold War*. Maxwell AFB, AL: Air University Press, 1997.

Hartzog, General William W. *American Military Heritage*. Washington, DC: Center of Military History, United States Army, 2001.

Hogan, David W. Jr. *U.S. Army Special Operations in World War II*. Washington, DC: U.S. Army Center of Military History, 1992.

Huber, Thomas M. "Napoleon in Spain and Naples: Fortified Compound Warfare." Fort Leavenworth: Combat Studies Institute, Command and General Staff College, 2002.

Jalali, Ali A., and Lester W. Grau, eds. *The Other Side of the Mountain: Mujahideen Tactics in the Soviet-Afghan War*. Quantico, VA: U.S. Marine Corps Studies and Analysis Division, 1998.

King, Michael J. "Rangers: Selected Combat Operations in World War II." *Leavenworth Papers*. Fort Leavenworth: U.S. Army Command and General Staff College, June 1985.

Smith, Charles R. *Marines in the Revolution: A History of the Continental Marines in the American Revolution*. Washington, DC: History Division, USMC, 1975.

United States Special Operations Posture Statement, 2003–2004: Transforming the Force at the Forefront of the War on Terrorism. Washington, DC: GPO, 2003.

White, Jeffrey B. "A Different Kind of Threat: Some Thoughts on Irregular War." CIA Center for Intelligence Studies. *Studies in Intelligence* 39, no. 5 (1996).

Correspondence and On-the-Record Interviews

Robert Andrews, U.S. Department of Defense
Bernard S. Bachrach, University of Minnesota
Dennis A. Barrow, Fairfield Historical Society
Jeremy Black, University of Essex
Lawrence I. Bland, George C. Marshall Papers
John Briscoe, U.S. Army Special Forces
Stephen Brisson, Mackinac State Historical Park
Bernard Calvalcante, U.S. Naval Historical Center

Elaine Davis, Alamo Library
Timothy Dickinson, *Paris Review*
Robert Dunkerly, Kings Mountain National Military Park
Christopher Fox, Ticonderoga National Historic Landmark
General William Hartzog, USA ret.
Jon T. Hoffman, Marine Corps History and Museums Division
Campbell James, OSS
Admiral Jerome Johnson, USN ret.
Joanne Knight, Combat Studies Institute, Fort Leavenworth
Lief Lier, KRIPOS, Ministry of Justice, Norway
Bert Lippincott III, Newport Historical Society
Colonel Paul Ostrowski, U.S. Army Special Forces
John L. Plaster, UltimateSniper
Captain John Park, USN ret.
Michael Pillsbury, U.S. Department of Defense
Ronn Richard, Cleveland Foundation
Major General Robert Scales, USA ret.
Matthew Seelinger, Army Historical Foundation
Judith Shofner, Texas Ranger Research Center
Lewis Sorley, U.S. Army Historical Foundation
Jeff Stein, *Roll Call*
Kevin Sweeney, Amherst College
Carleton Swift, OSS, CIA ret.
Ola Thune, KRIPOS, Ministry of Justice, Norway
Amy Weinstein, New-York Historical Society
Gus Weiss, American Trade Craft Society
Douglas Wicklund, National Firearms Museum
James Woolsey, former director, CIA

INDEX

Vietnam, 252, 387; Percival's seizure of Tourane in, 345, 617–18n.5. *See also* Indochina

Vietnam War, 389, 391, 496, 527, 532–33, 537–48, 577, 585, 615n.31, 631nn. 29, 34, 44, 45; aftermath of, 544; coup against Diem and, 541; interagency rivalries and, 542, 543–44; "Nasty"-class boats in, 542–43; SOG and, 541–42; U.S. entry into, 522–24, 628n.47; U.S. special operations in North Vietnam in, 524, 538, 540, 544–46

Vikings, 98, 104–5, 106–7, 605nn. 10, 13

Visigoths, 99

Volckmann, Russell, 522

Völkerwanderung, 99

Voltaire (François-Marie Arouet), 253

voltigeurs, 315–16, 329

V-1 rockets, 484

Waffen-SS, 274, 473, 476

Wahhabism, 392–93, 426

Wales, 109, 312

Wallenstein, Albrecht von, 228, 611n.28

Waman Poma, 175

War of 1812, 333–35, 345, 346

War Office (Britain), 245, 247

War of the Rails (1943–44), 476

War of the Spanish Succession (1701–14), 237, 240–42, 244, 249, 611n.3

Wars of Religion (France), 222–23

Washington, D.C., British attack on (1814), 334

Washington, George, 300, 315, 614n.2; in American Revolution, 275, 278–79, 280, 287, 288–89, 290–91, 292, 293, 297, 614nn. 19, 20, 28; in French and Indian War, 259, 261, 262

Wasmuss, Wilhelm, 402, 403, 405

"waterboarding," 528, 628n.61

water supply, attacks on, 94, 169

Waugh, Evelyn, 461

Wayne, "Mad" Anthony, 305

Wehrmacht, 445, 447, 456, 466, 476, 480, 485, 486, 527

Weizmann, Chaim, 491

Wellington, Arthur Wellesley, Duke of, 315, 328–29, 347, 350

Wells, H. G., 8, 438

Werwolf resistance: after World War II, 7, 487, 611n.29, 625–26n.74; in Thirty Years' War, 228, 611n.29

Western Desert Force, 457

West Point (military academy), 348, 436

West Point, battle of (1780), 287

Wheat, Chatham, 360

Whitehaven raid (1778), 298, 615nn. 43, 44

Wilhelm II, Kaiser of Germany, 387, 401–2, 403, 420

William Penn, 354

William the Conqueror, 107, 239

William the Silent, Prince of Orange, 221

Wilson, Edmund, 370

Wind in the Willows, The (Grahame), 464

Wingate, Orde, 34, 46, 490–94, 507

winter warfare, 263, 265

Wolfe, James, 266–69, 284, 285

Wolseley, Garnet, 378

World War I, 8, 322, 396–416, 419–21, 434, 436, 437, 440, 449, 454; aftermath of, 419–25; Arab insurgency and, 405–8; arms buildup before, 386; attitude toward casualties in, 416; Austria's response to assassination and, 398–99, 621n.26; civilized aspect of warfare in, 399, 411; in East Africa, 434; in Eastern Europe, 400; European dynasties ended by, 420; French paratroopers in, 410; German efforts to stoke militant Islam in, 401–5; German mountain troops in, 409–10; German storm troopers in, 408–9, 410; intellectual climate during run-up to, 385–87, 396–98; monuments to, 419–20; naming of, 420–21; Ottomans and, 400–403, 406–8; roots of World War II in, 420; submarine warfare in, 411–15, 454, 621n.48; technological advances in, 397–98, 408; Western Front in, 399–400, 405, 408–11

World War II, 4, 10, 22, 30–31, 35, 36, 55, 168, 257, 317, 347, 408, 431, 440, 442–97, 499, 596, 621n.47; abductions and assassinations in, 374, 456, 462–64, 469–70, 472, 473, 474, 476, 485, 527, 596, 624n.35; British special operations in occupied Europe in, 37, 452–57, 464–66, 474, 480, 481, 484; China–Burma–India theater in, 447, 455, 467–68, 489–90, 492–96; competition among participants in, 472, 496, 497; in Crete, 460–62; decentralization of authority in, 445; demobilization after, 501–2, 510–11, 626n.4; in Denmark and Norway, 446–47, 452, 465, 487, 623n.4; Eastern Front in, 332, 474–80, 484, 485; European theater in, 445–57, 464–66, 473–87, 488; fall of Reich in, 485–87; France's fall in, 451–52; geographical vastness and variety in, 444; indigenous resistance in, 444, 447, 452–53, 456, 462, 468–69, 490, 491–92, 495, 527, 596, 624n.24; intellectual climate during run-up to, 419–41; in Low Countries, 448–51, 456, 473, 487, 623n.5; in Middle East, 457–60, 481, 624n.26; in North Africa, 457–60, 462–64, 466, 472, 491–92; Pacific theater in, 467–70, 472, 487–88, 489–90; Poland's fall in, 445, 446, 473; roots in World War I of, 420; sabotage fears in U.S. during, 470–71; start of, 445–46; strategic importance of special operations in, 443–45, 496–97; technological advances and, 442, 444; U.S. special operations

ABOUT THE AUTHOR

Derek Leebaert is a professor at Georgetown University, a director of the U.S. Army Historical Foundation, and a consultant to U.S. government agencies. He is a founding editor of *International Security,* and his last book was the bestselling *The Fifty-Year Wound: How America's Cold War Victory Shapes Our World.* He is a former captain of the Harvard University Pistol Team, and he served in the U.S. Marine Corps. He lives in Washington, D.C., and in Geneva, Switzerland, where he is an adviser with Management Assessment Partners.